Stefanie Armbruster
Watching Nostalgia

Stefanie Armbruster (Dr.) lives in Munich, Germany, and works in the television sector. Her research interests include cultural and media studies with a focus on innovation and nostalgia.

STEFANIE ARMBRUSTER

Watching Nostalgia

An analysis of nostalgic television fiction and its reception

[transcript]

Written with the support of the Universitat Autònoma de Barcelona

Bibliographic information published by the Deutsche Nationalbibliothek
The Deutsche Nationalbibliothek lists this publication in the Deutsche Natio-
nalbibliografie; detailed bibliographic data are available in the Internet at
http://dnb.d-nb.de

Cover layout: Kordula Röckenhaus, Bielefeld
Cover illustration: Siberica / fotolia.com
Proofread by Johanna Ellsworth, Brendon Hooper
Typeset by Stefanie Armbruster
Printed in Germany
Print-ISBN 978-3-8376-3509-6
PDF-ISBN 978-3-8394-3509-0

Content

PART II – TEXT

5. The 'genres' of nostalgic fiction | 83

6. Case studies on nostalgia on the textual level | 95

PART III – RECEPTION

7. The reception of nostalgia | 199

Participant:

Was ich total interessant finde, weil eigentlich sind ja alle Ausschnitte, die wir gesehn haben, ham 'nen nostalgischen Hintergrund. [...] Also *Knight Rider* war ja wirklich original. Und da ham wir ja nostalgische Empfindungen, und zum Beispiel *Mad Men* ist ja neu, is ja aber [in] 'ne andere Zeit versetzt. Is ja aber auch nostalgisch. Aber nur, halt wieder anders...

[What I find totally interesting, well, is that all the excerpts we saw have a nostalgic background. Well, *Knight Rider* was really original. And there we have nostalgic feelings. And, for example, *Mad Men* is new but set in another time. And it's also nostalgic. But again in a different way ....]

Interviewer:

Und würdest du sagen, du bist nostalgisch?
[And would you say that you are nostalgic?]

Participant:

Ja. auf jeden Fall.
[Yes. For sure.]

Acknowledgements

This publication is based on my doctoral thesis, which I defended at the *Department of Audiovisual Communication and Advertising* at *Autonomous University of Barcelona (UAB)* in 2013, and which was given an *Extraordinary Doctorate Award* in 2015. The investigation would not have been possible without the support of many people and institutions to whom I want to express my warmest thanks and gratitude. In particular, I would like to thank my supervisors, Emili Prado Picó and Matilde Delgado Reina, from the *Department of Audiovisual Communication and Advertising* at *Autonomous University of Barcelona* and Lothar Mikos from the *Department of Media Studies* at *Film University Babelsberg "Konrad Wolf"* in Potsdam-Babelsberg. It was their thoughtful advice, scholarly experience, encouragement and patience that allowed me to write this thesis.

I also want to thank my friends and colleagues at the *Autonomous University of Barcelona*. Throughout the years of my doctoral studies I was happy to be surrounded by a group of friendly, inspiring and cooperative people to whom I owe thanks. First of all, I shall mention all those who went through the same trajectory of writing their thesis. My special thanks go to Helena Puertas Grau and Maria Fernanda Luna Rassa, who assisted in the conduction of my Spanish focus group discussions. Also "Thank you", Maria, for always having an open ear and offering me a helping hand when I needed one.

Furthermore, I would like to thank the professors at the *Department of Audiovisual Communication and Advertising*, who in the yearly *Pruebas de Seguimiento* commented on my work and encouraged me to continue. I am especially grateful to Ernest Verdura and Candi Casademont for their help and advice whenever I entered the administrative office of our department. I would also like to thank the staff members of the UAB communication library. Further thanks go to the *Department of Audiovisual Communication and Advertising*, which supported my research financially in providing me with the *PIF Fellowship*, and to the *Autonomous University* for giving me a short-term research travel grant. In this course, I would like to thank again Lothar Mikos and the *Department of Media Studies* at the *Film*

University Babelsberg "Konrad Wolf". Apart from that, this thesis would not be complete without the focus group discussions. My special thanks go to the anonymous participants who dedicated their time and shared their experiences with me. I am also indebted to friends and family for their essential support throughout the years and to Brendon Hooper, who revised the English text throughout this study. Furthermore, I would like to thank the staff members of *transcript* for their supervision and Johanna Ellsworth for giving the English text a second revision. I am particularly grateful to Rainer Winter, *Alpen-Adria-Universität Klagenfurt*, who supported the publication in his *Cultural Studies* book series.

Finally, my sincere thanks go to my parents, Lore und Paul, who have supported me ever since I can remember, encouraging me in whatever I am doing. Most of all, I would like to thank Tilman. Thank you all!

Stefanie Armbruster
Munich, Mai 2016

1. Introduction

"Wer hat an der Uhr gedreht?" [Who reset the clock?] was the title of an article in the German magazine *Focus* with reference to the Oscar nominations of *Hugo Cabret* (Scorsese, 2011), *Midnight in Paris* (Allen, 2011) or *The Artist* (Hazanavicius, 2011) in 2012 (Brand and Pauli, 2012, p. 83 [o.t.][1]). Nostalgic, say the authors, are the times in which we live. And indeed: nostalgia is everywhere! Films appeal to nostalgia, music appeals to nostalgia, and advertisements call upon the nostalgic feeling.[2] Also, in German and Spanish television the nostalgic look back is ever present. Just as Kompare (2005, p. 221) states, "[t]he 'old,' 'new,' and the 'newly old,' continue to merge on the TV-time machine". Even if you just focus on international programmes broadcasted in both countries between 2009 and 2011, with reruns such as *Knight Rider* (NBC, 1982), *The A-Team* (NBC, 1983), *Alf* (NBC, 1986) or *The Avengers* (ITV, 1961), remakes like *90210* (The CW, 2008), *Burn Notice* (USA Network, 2007), and *Hawaii Five-0* (CBS, 2010) or period dramas, such as *Downtown Abbey* (ITV, 2010), *Borgia* (Sky Italia, 2011), *The Tudors* (BBC2 et al., 2007) or *Mad Men* (AMC, 2007), you will come up with a list of programmes that take their inspiration from the past on a wide range.

Even though you may certainly state that not every one of these formats is *per se* nostalgic and provokes nostalgia in its audiences, the previously quoted interview section (see Page 8) exemplifies that the different programme categories are classified as nostalgia texts by audiences. At the same time, they are associated with

---

1   On the following pages, my own translations of non-English quotes are marked with the abbreviation "o.t.".

2   This shall not mean that our times are marked by a higher degree of nostalgia than others. Wilson (1998, as cited in Storey, 2001, p. 244) highlights, for example, that the "'evidence [especially Hollywood films from the 1920s onwards] from the past that pastiche and nostalgia have been pervasive in popular culture throughout the twentieth century and indeed earlier appears to contradict Jameson's belief that 'nostalgia mode' is peculiarly a feature of his postmodern era'".

the feeling of nostalgia. We can state that across the boundaries of genres, nostalgia is a decisive characteristic of contemporary television fiction and its reception is "not only", as Feyerabend emphasises in a more general context of contemporary nostalgia, "on a national level but indeed on a more global or transnational scope" (Feyerabend, 2009, p. 5). However, the phenomenon, as far as the interrelation between text and reception is concerned, is only minimally investigated by media and television studies, not to mention the lack of country comparative studies.

Although, so it can be argued, an interdisciplinary approach is needed in order to investigate nostalgia in television adequately, the different disciplines, which meet on the subject of nostalgia, only barely enrich each other. This study wants to contribute its part to such a synthesis of the disciplines and collaborate in the process of filling the gap regarding the lack of investigation into the interrelation of text and reception. The questions whether nostalgia is reactionary or progressive and if it impedes innovation or not will be set aside (for further reading see e.g. Keightley and Pickering, 2012, pp. 133 ff.). It is rather about grasping the characteristics of 'nostalgic objects' and their reception in the field of television. The main questions are: What is nostalgia in television? And: How can the phenomenon be grasped theoretically? Further sub-questions already reflect the later composition of the work. The following questions will be posed: What are the 'genres' of nostalgia? What textual characteristics does it have? How far does a nostalgic text prefigure nostalgic emotions? And finally: How are the nostalgic texts received from within the frames of different groups of audiences and against the background of different lifeworlds? In the end, against the backdrop of a specific sample of nostalgia texts and a specific group of recipients, a first picture of nostalgic television fiction and its reception in Germany and Spain will be drawn.

The overall frame of the investigation is inevitably enhanced by the researcher's own disciplinary background in media and communication studies. An important influence is 'reception aesthetics', which sees the investigation of the interrelation of text and reception and its respective socio-cultural contexts as inevitable (see e.g. Mikos, 2001; Chandler and Munday, 2011, p. 358).

In order to investigate the questions mentioned above, the study consists of three main parts: Part I provides the theoretical background for the investigation; Part II is dedicated to the television analysis of a total of six examples from different nostalgia 'genres'; and Part III investigates the reception, conducting focus group discussions with two different age groups from both Germany and Spain.

First some basic definitions of nostalgia are provided. Here, the study highlights the origins of the term and major connotative changes it went through. Specific meanings in the German and Spanish cultures are also considered. Already at this point, bridging the gap between text and reception appears to be necessary. The questions of how we can explain nostalgia concretely and which approaches in order to explain the phenomenon exist are focused on in the following section, the review of literature. By means of using the discourse, many aspects can be clarified. First characteristics of nostalgia can be explained. At the same time, however, an analysis model that enables us to investigate the interrelation of nostalgia on the level of the text and nostalgia on the level of reception is not provided. Due to that fact, two additional chapters, titled *Two 'archives' – nostalgia's relationship to the past* and *Aesthetic emotions – on nostalgia's relationship to the present*, which deal with memory studies and the study of aesthetic emotions, supplement the existing investigations on nostalgia.

The understanding of nostalgia as an emotion is central. The study here departs from such authors as Jameson (e.g. 1991), who describe postmodern nostalgia as being explicitly affectless. Correspondingly, the subject is approached. Inspired by investigations of suspense and television (see e.g. Mikos, 1996; Haible, 2003) in the context of which it is assumed that suspense is a "complex network of spectator's cognitive and emotional activities that might have been stimulated by various textual characteristics" (Mikos, 1996, p. 37), this investigation of nostalgia also considers both cognitive and emotional aspects. Text, reception and the interrelation between the two will be investigated, just as Eder (2005) argued in the context of the investigation of emotions and media in general (Bartsch et al., 2007a, p. 10). In the interdisciplinary working method, cognitive psychology and its investigation of aesthetic emotions will also be central.

The integration of theories on aesthetic emotions into the investigation of nostalgia has not been entirely neglected in media studies. Cardwell (2002), for example, considers the emotive characteristics of nostalgia. Her work is an important point of reference for this study as well. But if we want to bridge the gap between the nostalgic text and the nostalgic emotion, we need to go further.

In the focus is Tan's (1996) approach on aesthetic emotions, which, although not developed for television, has proven to be transferable. Depending on the respective object of appraisal, the author basically distinguishes between two different forms of emotions: First, the so-called "fiction emotions" or "F emotions" that find their stimulus on the fictional level of the text, and secondly, so-called "artefact emotions" or "A emotions" that are provoked by the artefact level. The categories will serve to combine the different approaches to nostalgia. On the one hand, on the basis of Tan's 'radical object-centrism', the discourse is taken into a new 'order'. The different studies on nostalgia are, so to say, unravelled and combined. On the other hand, the theory of aesthetic emotions works as a bridge in whose context the existing studies may be made applicable to an investigation of both the cognitive and emotional components in nostalgia. In doing so, the first section of the work generates the framework for the further investigation of nostalgia in different 'genres'. First 'modules' of analysis for nostalgia are generated. Basically, and in using and 'continuing' Tan's terminology, 'F nostalgia' and 'A nostalgia' and further empathetic and non-empathetic sub-groups are assumed.

In the second and third part of the study, the framework is applied, and assumptions are investigated. The main aim here is to identify nostalgia in television fiction, more precisely in television series in the form of reruns, remakes and period dramas, and its reception by German and Spanish audiences from two age groups. The focus has mainly been set for practical reasons and in order to limit the empirical domain. Regarding the 'genre' selection, it can also be stated that other programme forms in television are marked by the 'look back'.[3] However, we can assume that television series in their different occurrences play a special role as potential triggers of nostalgia. It was and is not only one of the main "pillars" of European television (Prado and Delgado, 2010 [o.t.]), according to García-Muñoz et al. (2012, p. 349), television fiction in general is also "one of the most highly appreciated genres amongst audiences". As Smith highlights, television series in particular "may engross millions [of audiences] for years or even decades, forming a vital part of the affective and everyday life of a nation" (Smith, 2006, p. 1) and beyond, as the study will show. With, as Moragas and Prado (2000, p. 185) state, American fiction being a "common denominator", especially the television series is a programme form that has long since been traded worldwide. This makes it again appropriate for country-comparative (reception) research.

At the same time the study focuses on two different age groups from Germany and Spain. By doing that, "culturally specific meanings" (Pickering and Keightley, 2006, p. 934) of nostalgia and differences against the background of different memories can be taken into consideration. With a view on the media memories, mainly 'overlaps' between the age groups are expected (see also Volkmer, 2006c, pp. 256 ff. on generational entelechies in the global public space). By selecting these two countries, two 'memory communities' were chosen in which the experience of fascism, respectively its memory, can be considered to have left its mark on possible nostalgias.[4] Due to the focus on international broadcasts, questions of representation

---

3   With regards to German television, we may, for example, refer to so-called *historytainment* formats, such as *Die Burg* [The Castle] (ProSieben, 2005), *Schwarzwaldhaus 1902* [The Black Forest House 1902] (Das Erste, 2002) or shows such as *Die DDR-Show* [The GDR Show] (RTL, 2003), as they have been named by Bleicher (2007) in the broader context of self-references in media. Similar formats can be identified on Spanish television, such as the living-history format *Curso del 63* (Antena 3, 2009) or its new *Curso del 73* (Antena 3, 2011) edition, the Spanish adaptations of the British format *That'll teach , 'Em* (Channel 4, 2003) or the television show *Los mejores años de nuestra vida* [The best years of our lives] (TV1, 2009).

4   As Schlipphacke (2010, p.14) states with a view on Germany and Austria, "nostalgia after Nazism is fraught with the burdens of history" (2010, p. 15), even though the "taboo on

do not have to be posed in the light of this – it is the reception study where the different contexts are taken into account. Different connotations of nostalgia among different groups of recipients, as they can be identified on the basis of the questionnaire, are set into interrelation to provoked nostalgias or non-nostalgia. The focuses will enable us to study the range of possible triggers of nostalgia and different influential factors for their reception on a broad level.

In Part II, first of all the broader category of 'nostalgia film', respectively 'nostalgia television', is described and fragmented into sub-categories. It can be said that Tan's 'radical object-centrism' is decisive here as well. Thus, based on the existing writings, the 'fragmentation' concentrates primarily on the different objects on the macro-level. Different 'genres' of nostalgia – more precisely: reruns, remakes and period dramas – are separated and described more closely against the special German and Spanish backdrops, too. The 'modules' as distinguished on the basis of Tan's theory are then re-combined with a view on the characteristics of each 'genre'. In doing this, each sub-chapter contains an introduction, which reflects upon potential nostalgia objects within the respective 'genres'.

The 'modules' are then applied in the television analysis of two 'genre' examples each. In order to be able to compare possible similarities and differences between Germany and Spain, it has been focused on those television series that were broadcasted in both countries, among them the German and Spanish reruns of *Knight Rider* (NBC, 1982) and *The Avengers* (ITV, 1961) and their respective remakes as well as the two period dramas *Mad Men* (AMC, 2007) and *Borgia* (Sky Italia, 2011). Those series have been chosen that can be seen as exemplary for their category. Apart from that, the respective first-runs, and respectively "premakes"[5], of the selected reruns and remakes fall into the so-called "reminiscence bump" (Eysenck and Keane, 2005, p. 266), and in the "formative" years of each age group, namely those years that, with reference to the literature, can be assumed to be best remembered, respectively to be especially decisive in the formation of a generation (Volkmer, 2005, p. 236; Volkmer, 2006a, p. 6). In the light of this, differences in the reception of the two different age groups are already assumed. Further clues on potential differences between the countries can be found when making a contextualisation of

---

nostalgia" "does not foreclose nostalgic longing" (Schlipphacke, 2010, p. 31). Schlipphacke investigates this on the example of contemporary literature and film. Regarding the Spanish context, with Morgan-Tamosunas (2000, p. 116) it can be stated that "the historical associations of Francoist period cinema with perceptions of manipulation, misinterpretation and the privileging of a highly prescribed socio-cultural and ideological discourse, have [...] produced critical wariness of the [costume drama] genre".

5   This term has been proposed by Oltmann (2008) in order to point to the source of inspiration of a remake. It shall also be applied in this study.

the respective series into the respective German and Spanish backgrounds in the course of the television analyses. In part, a consideration of the public discourse in the form of newspaper articles in both countries allows further assumptions. The question if the nostalgia on offer in the text does indeed provoke nostalgia in its audiences is scrutinised in Part III.

Based on questionnaires and focus group interviews with two different age groups from both Germany and Spain, it is here where the results of the television analysis are set in relation to the reception and where further characteristics of nostalgia in television are scrutinised inductively. Again, Tan's 'object-centrism' will lead this. In particular this means that the potential triggers and objects of appraisal in the context of which nostalgia is developed are now in the focus. A final conclusion will shortly reflect on the applicability of the theoretical framework and further need of research.

If we want to investigate nostalgia in television comprehensively, many aspects from the general characteristics of nostalgia and its dependence on different memory communities, aspects of archive and genre, textual aspects, emotive aspects to the concrete process of reception have to be recognised. Only an interdisciplinary, multi-method approach can cope with that task. This study wants to collaborate in the process of filling this gap. It summarises, combines, modifies and explores. Against this "explorative" backdrop it cannot be excluded that limitations may arise. This is taken into account by a systematic exposure of working steps in the course of the study and an explicit reflection of possible shortcomings in its end. In any case, in the following chapters the work will provide first responses that help to better understand the interrelation between 'nostalgic texts' and the nostalgic reception, on the basis of which further studies may follow.

Part I – Theoretical background and methodological design

2. Nostalgia

Before the theoretical discourse of nostalgia shall be presented, the following chapter takes a first look at the general definition of the term 'nostalgia', its origins and the connotative changes it went through.

2.1 A FIRST DEFINITION – THE ORIGINS OF THE TERM AND ITS DEVELOPMENT

The term 'nostalgia', as it is used in English, German or several Romance languages, such as Spanish, was coined by the Swiss physician Johannes Hofer, who used it in his dissertation titled *De Nostalgia, Heimwehe oder Heimsehnsucht* (1678) (see e.g. Pfannkuche, 1978). The word is derived from the Greek *nóstos*, which means 'return (to the homeland)' and *álgos*, which signifies 'pain' or 'grief' (Pfannkuche, 1978, p. 7; Hart, 1973, p. 398; Corominas, 1981, p. 240). While with Boym (2001, p. 12) it can be stated that the term would later replace both the German *Heimweh* and the Spanish *mal de corazón*, the term also went through major connotative changes from its "migration" "into new social contexts and discourses" (Sprengler, 2011, p. 11).

In the past, *nostalgia* signified a pathological phenomenon. Swiss soldiers and students who, far away from their usual surroundings, would develop symptoms such as insomnia, anorexia, melancholic madness or abjectness, were commonly diagnosed with the condition (Pfannkuche, 1978, pp. 124 f.; Davis, 1979, pp. 1 f.). These "symptoms of nostalgia were understood to be triggered in its victims through sights, sounds, smells, tastes – any of a number of associations that might influence them to recall the homes and environments they had unwillingly left behind" (Hirsch and Spitzer, 2002, p. 258). In the second half of the eighteenth century, the phenomenon – still part of the medical discourse – underwent first changes. By this time, according to Fischer (1980, p. 12 [o.t.]), the physician J. G. Zimmermann (1764) had already accentuated the importance of a certain "symbolical link to reality". When the phenomenon began to interest psychiatrists, it "went from being a *curable* medical illness to an *incurable* (indeed unassuageable) condition of the spirit or psyche" (Hutcheon, 2000, p. 194 [italic emphasis in the original]). This "demise as a medical condition can", according to Sprengler (2011, p. 14), "[...] also be explained by a growing interest in mental afflictions in the late eighteenth century". Rousseau (1764), as referred to by Fischer (1980, p. 12 [o.t.]), finally sets the "symbolical mediation" of the nostalgic yearning in the centre of the definition. Now nostalgia does not only signify the yearning for a location but also a longing for the way of living linked to this location, for instance the "simple and un-decayed customs" of rural areas in times of industrialization (Brockhaus, 1991, p. 6 [o.t.]). As Sprengler (2011, p. 16) highlights with reference to Casey (1987), "[o]ther changes happening within modernity [...] [such as] the privatization of the family" (Sprengler, 2011, p. 16) led to a further "shift in responsibility from the community to the family as the source of the longing sentiment". Around 1828, a description in the German *Allgemeine Enzyklopädie* reflects the expansion of the use of the word nostalgia from the fixation on "geographical locations" towards "'locations'" in time, such as the personal past in the form of childhood or adolescence (Fischer, 1980, p. 13 [o.t.]). From then on, it did not take long for nostalgia to stop being tagged a medical disease.

"In 1899, The Lancet published an opinion piece defending the Royal College of Physicians' decision to exclude it from its 'Nomenclature of Diseases', arguing that it was 'a purely selfish disorder' and unworthy of medical classification." (Sullivan, 2010, p. 585)

However, regarding the public discourse, the term seems to have had less significance for a long time: While in both medicine and psychology nostalgia was used up to the end of the nineteenth century (Pfannkuche, 1978, pp. 8) – Grainge (2002, p. 19) states that it "retained a medical resonance as late as 1946" – the term homesickness was used more commonly (Brockhaus, 1931, pp. 511, 329). According to Fischer (1980, p. 15), in the 1950s, nostalgia even seems to have vanished from 'social consciousness'. The case seems to have been slightly different in Spain. Here a search for the term in the online database of the daily newspaper *La Vanguardia* (2011) shows that 'nostalgia' was – if only rarely (one to 20 times per year) – already used in the public discourse between 1881-1940 and that its usage increased from 1941 on. Thus, it is not surprising when Fischer (1980, p. 15) highlights that it was the Spanish encyclopaedia *Enciclopedia Universal Ilustrada* (1959) that can be deemed responsible for re-launching the term in Germany by the end of the 1950s. Nevertheless, the medical connotation, in combination with the idea of homeland, dominates here (Enciclopedia Universal Ilustrada, 1958, p. 1193), whereas the public discourse presented by newspaper articles already reflects a wider application.[1] In the 1970s, mainly influenced by the so-called 'wave of nostalgia', and in terms of the booming interest in "pre-industrial" life and societies from the mass media and cultural criticism, nostalgia finally became a cultural term and firmly rooted in everyday language (Brockhaus, 1991, p. 6; Kremkau, 2003, p. 11). The temporal dimension is now a dominant part of its definition (Fischer, 1980, p. 16). As Fischer (1980, p. 16 [o.t.]) highlights, nostalgia signifies a person's "feeling of loss" that finds its object not only in the absence of the home country but also in cultural artefacts. "Thus what is meant is a specific connection to tradition, to a thing, not the object itself" (Fischer, 1980, p. 16 [o.t.]). In this context Fischer (1980) already emphasises the strong relevance of reception in the definition of nostalgia. Thus, the "'nostalgic object'", he states, contains "structural elements", which "allow" for nostalgia; however, it is "not nostalgic *per se*" (Fischer, 1980, p. 269 [footnote 68] [o.t.]). This is more explicit in this following quotation where Fischer also refers to Sontag's (1968) work on camp:

"In current language to behave nostalgic towards an object means to relate biographical-intimate emotions to it that are fed by the past; it further means to maintain the realization of the nostalgic satisfaction on a symbolic level since the historical context of the object is not perceived at the same time. On the other hand, it allows the nostalgia infected 'to enjoy the failed attempt rather than to be disappointed about it'." (Fischer, 1980, p. 16 [o.t.])

For Cook (2005, p. 2 [my italics]), today's nostalgia "can be defined as a state of longing for *something* that is known to be irretrievable".

2.2 Literature Review – Discourses of Nostalgia

As the definition and the use of the term show, *nostalgia* has long been part of the medical and psychological discourse. Mainly due to the so-called 'wave of nostalgia' in the 1970s it also became of greater interest for other disciplines. Judging from the number of publications on the topic, the theoretical discourse of nostalgia as a media and cultural phenomenon got its major impulses in that time. This paragraph will give a review of these works. Due to the fact that authors with different backgrounds deal with nostalgia and since, as Sprengler (2011, p. 33) puts it, "[t]here is a fair degree of cross-fertilization between disciplines", a relatively wide range of

---

1   Next to "nostalgia de la patria" [nostalgia for the homeland] (Montsant, 1946 [o.t.]) or "nostalgia a los viejos cafés" [nostalgia for the old cafés] (Clarasó, 1956 [o.t.]), which indeed is directed toward a lost physical space, authors here refer, for instance, to "la nostalgia por la aventura" [nostalgia for adventure] (Gutiérrez Gili, 1936 [o.t.]).

approaches from critical theory, anthropology, history, sociology, film and television studies up to media and cultural studies has been considered. In most cases it cannot be directly called a discussion – as authors mostly only partly relate to each other – which is why the paragraph highlights similar argumentation lines that emerge across the boundaries of the disciplines. A sub-chapter will give insights into the discourse in Germany and Spain. Even though parts of the discourse will be set aside in the course of the work, only this broad look at the subject will give a comprehensive introduction and make it possible to draw on relevant links regarding the representation and reception of nostalgia in television and to reflect on further need of research. Since the purpose of this work is not to conduct experimental studies, it will exclude an intensive review of nostalgia in consumer studies (see e.g. Holak and Havlena, 1998) or psychology (see e.g. Sedikides et al., 2004). However, some references on these works will be made in a subsequent chapter that creates the link from nostalgia to theories on aesthetic emotions in film and television studies.

2.2.1 Nostalgia as a contemporary malaise

During the heyday of the so-called 'wave of nostalgia' many works were published that first of all tried to find an explanation for the appearance of the phenomenon (see also Kremkau, 2003, pp. 16 f.). Using the example of the U.S.A., Lasch (1984) gives an overview of these first assessments. The author explains that, on the part of many intellectuals, nostalgia was rejected for being regressive, conservative or restorative, and shows that it was mostly described as a symptom or disease resulting from social changes at the time. According to Lasch, three main theses are dominant: (1) the thesis that "nostalgia expresses a legitimate revulsion against decadence" (Lasch, 1984, p. 68); (2) the shock thesis claiming that "'[c]aught in the transition from the industrial to postindustrial society, Americans in large numbers felt themselves losing their psychological, social and moral bearings'" (Clecak, 1983, cited in Lasch, 1984, p. 69); and (3) the thesis of "identity repair", proclaiming that the "'nostalgia wave of the seventies' […] was a response to the 'massive identity dislocations' of the sixties" (Lasch, 1984, p. 69), held, for instance, by Fred Davis, who is cited only partially here (1979). It will be shown that similar assessments of nostalgia appear in discourses in other countries, such as Germany; however, it has to be said that Lasch's presentation is characterised by a certain polemic aspect. At least, it can be argued, the additional value of, for example, Davis' work, for the nostalgia discourse is not sufficiently recognised by subsuming it under the label 'trauma of rapid change'. Thus the field of 'identity' has become one of the major ones within the nostalgia discourse. This will now be explored in more detail.

2.2.2 Nostalgia and identity

Davis was not the first author outside the field of psychology who investigated nostalgia in the context of identity. As Kremkau (2003, p. 19) notes, in the 1960s, the theologian and philosopher Ralph Harper (1966) ascribed nostalgia to processes of identity formation. Kant, as referred to by Boym (2001, p. 13), already "saw in the combination of melancholy, nostalgia and self-awareness a unique aesthetic sense that did not objectify the past but rather heightened one's sensitivity to the dilemmas of life and moral freedom". Apart from that, the link between nostalgia and identity has to be seen in the wider context of memory studies (see e.g. Assmann, 2006; Lowenthal, 1986), where memory and identity has been investigated intensively over the past years (Kremkau, 2003, p. 6). Nevertheless, Davis is certainly one of the most cited scholars within the nostalgia discourse. He is also representative of authors who have been subsumed under the label 'mood agents' by Grainge (2002) – those who emphasise that nostalgia is a "feeling determined by a concept of longing and loss" (Grainge, 2002, p. 11) and triggered "in the context of present fears" (Grainge, 2002, p. 24).

According to Davis (1979, p. 31), nostalgia is one of the mechanisms we employ to (re)construct our identities, above all "in the context of present fears, discontents, anxieties or uncertainties" (Davis, 1977, p. 420). As examples, Davis (1979, p. 49) names transition phases, such as the change "from childhood to pubescence", or historical changes in general. Regarding the individual level, the author assumes that since nostalgia generates continuity, it helps people to defend and maintain an awareness of their identity and to cultivate an appreciation of a former self in those phases (Davis, 1979, pp. 35 f.).

This also applies to a collective level[2], where Davis (1979, p. 111) sees nostalgia as a mediator for the creation of, for instance, generational identity. In any case, nostalgia is not reduced to being regressive, conservative or restorative but is understood to appear in different shades. Davis (1979) distinguishes three forms of nostalgia, namely simple, reflexive and interpreted nostalgia:

---

2 "Collective nostalgia, however, refers to that condition in which the symbolic objects are of a highly public, widely shared, and familiar character, those symbolic resources from the past that under proper conditions can trigger wave upon wave of nostalgic feeling in millions of persons at the same time. [...] By contrast, private nostalgia refers to those symbolic images and allusions from the past that by virtue of their source in a particular person's biography tend to be more idiosyncratic, individuated, and particularistic in their reference, e.g., the memory of a parent's smile, the garden view from a certain window of a house once lived in, for Proust the little cakes from his childhood at Combray." (Davis, 1979, pp. 122 f.)

(1) "'Simple nostalgia' is that subjective state which harbors the largely unexamined belief that THINGS WERE BETTER [...] *THEN* THAN *NOW*." (Davis, 1979, p. 18 [emphasis in the original])

(2) "*Second order* or *Reflexive Nostalgia*: Here the person does more than sentimentalize some past and censure, if only implicitly, some present. In perhaps an inchoate though nevertheless psychologically active fashion he or she summons to feeling and thought certain empirically oriented questions concerning the truth, accuracy, completeness, or representativeness of the nostalgic claim." (Davis, 1979, p. 21 [emphasis in the original])

(3) "*Third Order* or *Interpreted Nostalgia* [...] moves beyond issues of the historical accuracy or felicity of the nostalgic claim on the past and, even as the reaction unfolds, questions and, potentially at least, renders problematic the very reaction itself". (Davis, 1979, p. 24 [emphasis in the original])

Aside from this, Davis classifies nostalgia as both "emotion" (Davis, 1979, pp. 47 f.) and *"form of consciousness"*[3] (Davis, 1979, p. 78 [italic emphasis in the original]) and differentiates it from other states related to the past such as "[h]istory, remembrance, recollection, reminiscence, revivification, and recall" (Davis, 1979, p. 13). "[T]he nostalgic feeling", explains Davis, "is infused with imputations of past beauty, pleasure, joy, satisfaction, goodness, happiness, love, and the like, in sum, any or several of the *positive* affects of being" (Davis, 1979, p. 14 [italic emphasis in the original]).

While the author makes the emotional side of nostalgia more tangible, its material basis is only cursorily studied. Thus Davis refers to nostalgia in arts and other media (see e.g. Davis, 1979, pp. 129 ff.); however, detailed analyses are not provided. Furthermore, the author sees a kind of automatic relationship between the nostalgic object and nostalgia as an emotion at work[4], which earns him criticism from scholars associated with cultural studies, such as Pickering and Keightley (2006, p. 929).

---

3   Thereby, Davis refers to the concept of "multiple realities" developed by Alfred Schutz (Davis, 1979, pp. 74 ff.). "To sum up, nostalgia as a form of consciousness can be characterized in Schutzian terms as: a heightened focus on things past (time perspective) along with an enhanced credence in them (epoché), accompanied by considerable musing (form of spontaneity), mild detachment of that sense of we-ness strains our conduct." (Davis, 1979, p. 81)

4   The artist, so Davis, "'knows' by training, intuition, and prior exercise what configuration of lines, pigments, sounds, movements, or words will touch nostalgic 'chords' in the audience. The audience, too, without necessarily having any immediate or 'real' reason for feeling nostalgic, will upon seeing or hearing the material respond nostalgically" (Davis, 1979, p. 82).

Somehow prefigured by and in some respect comparable to Davis is the work of Boym (2001), one of the few American authors who dedicated a whole monograph to the topic of nostalgia (see also Legg, 2004, pp. 100 ff.). Boym investigates nostalgia in the context of the transition processes after the end of the Cold War with an emphasis on post-communist communities. Nostalgia is likewise understood as a mediator between individual and collective identities. As Boym (2001, p. xvi) argues, "nostalgia is about the relationship between individual biography and the biography of groups and nations, between personal and collective memory". Comparable to Davis, Boym (2001) sees nostalgia as a symptom of the present global age – a "defense mechanism in a time of accelerated rhythms of life and historical upheavals" (Boym, 2001, p. xiv). Like Davis, she puts the emphasis less on the analysis of nostalgic objects but on the nostalgic person or collective. Also, the categorisation she proposes is comparable to her predecessor, even though it stresses more on the dependence of different kinds of memory. Boym (2001) distinguishes between two categories of nostalgia, namely "restorative" and "reflective" nostalgia. Restorative nostalgia, characteristic for national movements and more about 'national' memory than individual memory, "stresses *nostos* and attempts a transhistorical reconstruction of the lost home" (Boym, 2001, p. xviii [italic emphasis in the original]). It is a kind of nostalgia that does not reflect upon itself and locates the "absolute truth" in the past (Boym, 2001, p. xviii). Reflective nostalgia, "thrives in *algia*, the longing itself, and delays the homecoming – wistfully, ironically, desperately. [...] [It] dwells on the ambivalences of human longing and belonging and does not shy away from the contradictions of modernity." (Boym, 2001, p. xviii) This kind of nostalgia, says Boym (2001, p. 49), calls the absolute truth into doubt and does not want to rebuild the past. It is "more about individual and cultural memory" (Boym, 2001, p. 49).

Next to Boym and Davis, the philosopher and scholar of religious studies Hart (1973) also relates nostalgia to matters of identity, and this mainly on the level of the individual. By referring both to the concept of the "life-project" and to the discussion on the "constitution of the I" of the German sociologist and philosopher Scheler (1966), nostalgia is understood as "an instance of one of these unique moments of 'gathering'" (Hart, 1973, p. 405) – an experience which may make us feel sure of ourselves. It is mainly studied by taking the work of Marcel Proust as an example.

2.2.3 Nostalgia: death of historicity or paradigm shift

The spectrum of postmodern theory is another major field in which nostalgia is discussed. As Chase and Shaw (1989, p. 15) highlight, "some cultural critiques have identified the whole experience of postmodernity as a kind of macro-nostalgia". "History", according to Lipsitz (1994, p. 28), has been rejected altogether. A comprehensive look on the discussion cannot be provided in this review. Nevertheless, within the discursive field, two positions on nostalgia can perhaps be seen as paradigmatic; namely one position from the Marxist cultural critic Fredric Jameson on the one hand, and one position from the literary scientist Linda Hutcheon on the other hand. On the basis of their work, other similar argumentation lines in the context of *nostalgia as death of historicity or paradigm shift* can be pointed out.

Jameson, like Baudrillard, whose concepts decisively influenced his theory (Winter, 2010, p. 59; Felluga, 2011), describes postmodernism as a-historic. Instead of historicity it is dominated by "'historicism'", "the random cannibalization of all the styles of the past" (Jameson, 1991, p. 18). The presented past is seen as nothing but depthless and affectless "'pastness'". Since, according to the author, it has nothing to do either with the past or with the present but rather is, as Radstone and Hodgkin (2003, p. 22) put it, a "substitute for a truly historic consciousness" – a representative of "our ideas and cultural stereotypes about [...] [the] past" (Jameson, 1998, p. 10) – nostalgia is described as quasi paradigmatic for this matter of fact. In order to back his thesis, Jameson draws on examples from architecture, literature, video-art, television or film – the latter being one of his main objects. Above all the 'ordinary' nostalgia film, also termed "nostalgia-deco" or "pastiche" (Jameson, 1991), perfectly illustrates the postmodern condition, namely the exposition of historicism "in a bad sense of an omnipresent and indiscriminate appetite for dead styles" (Jameson, 1991, p. 286). Using, as Jameson (1991, p. 20) argues, "a whole battery of aesthetic signs" in order to 'program' the spectators in the nostalgia mode, these films expose nostalgia in a pure superficial, respectively stylistic, manner – "the past as fashion plate and glossy image" (Jameson, 1991, p. 118).

Jameson not only denies that the audiences have any ability for an active reception of the 'nostalgia films' – a fact that made him a target of criticism by scholars associated with cultural studies (see e.g. Pickering and Keightley, 2006, p. 923; 929) – as opposed to other authors (see e.g. Schweinitz, 2006[5]; Hutcheon, 1984; 2000) he also intermingles the different ways of referring to the past by subsuming every kind of intertextuality under the title of "'nostalgia' art language" (Jameson, 1991, pp. 19 f.), so that it even seems as if he mainly uses the term in order to moan about the postmodern condition as such. And indeed, retrospectively Jameson wants 'nostalgia film' to be understood as

"in no way [...] as passionate expressions of that older longing once called nostalgia but rather quite the opposite; they are a depersonalized visual curiosity [...] 'without affect' [...]. But one can no more alter a term like this retroactively than substitute some altogether different word for postmodernism itself." (Jameson, 1991, p. xvii)

---

9   Under the label of the postmodern dealing with stereotypes, Schweinitz (2006, p. 290) distinguishes between nostalgia and, for instance, fascination, irony, and mockery.

In contrast to the mood-agent Davis, Jameson, so Grainge (2002, pp. 36 f.) denies nostalgia any affective relation to the past but rather describes it as a pure style or surface phenomenon, which is why Grainge also subsumes him under the so-called 'mode' agents. Similar argumentation lines can be found in the works of authors such as Graham (1984) or Lasch (1984).[6]

The elaboration of nostalgia made by Hutcheon (1984; 2000) is the opposite. Mainly concentrating on architecture and literature – here, mostly on the so-called "historiographic metafiction" – Hutcheon (1984, p. 4) defends the works of postmodernism. Instead of proclaiming the death of history, she rather observes a paradigm shift, highlighting that "[d]espite its detractors, the postmodern is not ahistorical or dehistoricized, though it does question our (perhaps unacknowledged) assumptions about what constitutes historical knowledge" (Hutcheon, 1984, p. xii). Thus, what, according to Hutcheon (1984), vanished with the rise of the postmodern is not history at all but rather the light-heartedness that dominated dealing with history until then. Hutcheon's work on nostalgia must be seen against this backdrop even though her first examination of the phenomenon within the concept of postmodernism is rather nihilistic. Arguing that the "'postmodern' has little to do with nostalgia and much to do with irony" (Hutcheon, 2000, p. 190), nostalgia, when it was mentioned, is likewise negatively connoted. The simplifications, nevertheless, seem to result from a polemical extinction in service of the positive definition of postmodernism.[7] In her more recent work, Hutcheon (2000) refuses first rough assessments of the phenomenon and studies nostalgia more closely. Even though not to the same degree as irony, she now ascribes a certain role to increase the awareness of the textuality of the past to it, which is typical for her understanding of postmodernism. First of all, nostalgia is no longer only seen as a conservative

---

6   Graham (1984, p. 350 [italic emphasis in the original]) describes the "apparent obsession with recent history [around 1984]" as an "obsession with *pseudo*history" to be equated with amnesia. The commercialization of nostalgia is seen as the expression of this tendency (Graham, 1984, p. 348). As Jameson does, the author thereby describes nostalgia as an a-historic phenomenon of "pure form" (Graham, 1984, pp. 360 ff.) and likewise equalises it with the intertextuality of postmodern culture in general (Graham, 1984, pp. 350, 354). In contemporary film, she argues, "the world of film becomes the *only* world" (Graham, 1984, p. 360 [italic emphasis in the original]). This similarly applies to Lasch (1984). Under the subtitle of "losing history", he describes the widespread nostalgia of the 1980s as a conglomeration of dead styles (Lasch, 1984, p. 70). The "'nostalgia boom'", respectively 'cultural fashion' nostalgia, is described as a hype created by the media (Lasch, 1984, p. 70).

7   In a later article she writes that she'll "try to understand why [...] [she] had earlier chosen to all but ignore the nostalgic dimension of the postmodern in favour of the ironic" (Hutcheon, 2000, p. 190).

revisionist but "conservative in its praxis" yet "transideological" since utilised by the left and the right (Hutcheon, 2000, p. 199)[8]. Secondly, nostalgia is distinguished from other forms relating to the past. As she says, "There are, of course, many ways to look backward. You can look and reject. Or you can look and linger longingly." (Hutcheon, 2000, p. 196)

Hutcheon's work mainly focuses on literature. However, similar approaches that open up different perspectives on postmodern engagement with history can also be observed within the film studies discourse of nostalgia. Dika (2003, p. 9), for instance, following Jameson, describes and uses nostalgia film as a general subcategory to indicate the "tendency to return to past film images", namely to use pictures of other pictures or to return to old genres (see e.g. Dika, 2003, p. 55). However, within this frame the author elaborates on forms of resistance – "film and art that use past images and genres in oppositional ways" (Dika, 2003, p. 20) – which is where her perspective most evidently diverges from Jameson's. Similar to Schweinitz (2006), who mentions nostalgia as one possible way postmodern culture deals with stereotypes, nostalgia becomes one of many potential characteristics of the postmodern text (see e.g. Dika, 2003, pp. 58, 89). In detailed analysis and by a method that considers "textuality, temporality and the relationship of the image to the natural real" (Dika, 2003, p. 224), the postmodern aesthetic could be said to be 'broken open'.[9]

To identify the critical potential of nostalgia films is also the purpose of a more recent work written by Sprengler (2011). In contrast to Dika, the author exclusively concentrates on the level of the artefact, stating "we need to consider how the visual dimensions of the cinema might be the source of both its nostalgic label *and* its critical consciousness when bolstered or even impeded by narrative and thematic content" (Sprengler, 2011, p. 90 [italic emphasis in the original]).

---

8   Nonetheless, when Hutcheon later comes to the conclusion that postmodern nostalgia is always accompanied by a certain ironic distance, it almost seems as if she suddenly decided to refuse the positive definition of the phenomenon. "[M]ay be", so she says "one way the postmodern has of taking responsibility for such responses by creating a small part of the distance necessary for reflective thought" (Hutcheon, 2000, p. 207), almost as if the viewers otherwise wouldn't reflect on what they receive.

9   For instance, regarding 'new genre films', "disjunctions" between the new film and the classical genre are analysed (Dika, 2003, p. 216). In the case of genre films, such as Bertolucci's *The Conformist* (1970), it is analysed how "arguably 'nostalgic' surface[s] […] [are] set against the historical events represented by those images" (Dika, 2003, p. 98) and the knowledge of the respective audiences (Dika, 2003, p. 98).

2.2.4 Nostalgia and the (re)construction of 'history'

Comparable to the position of Hutcheon is the line of argument, which, put simply, investigates nostalgia in the context of the (re)construction of history and tradition – a line of argument that can predominantly be observed in the British scientific reflection on nostalgia, which, according to Kremkau (2003, pp. 21 f. [o.t.]), started around the mid-1980s mainly in the field of historical studies and often led to the "typical British" context of cultural heritage. One study that in a major section pays attention to nostalgia is *The Past is a Foreign Country* (1986) by Lowenthal. In seven chapters the author presents a broad examination of the role and characteristics of 'history' from different perspectives, such as art and architectural history, psychology or archaeology (Lowenthal, 1986, p. xxv). The title of the book can be understood as being antithetical to the author's conclusions on the characteristics of memory, history and relics, because all three categories are described as appropriation rather than truthful reflection of the past. Thus, even though Lowenthal does not explicitly consider historicity from a poststructuralist standpoint, the notion of poststructuralism surrounds the statements, above all, the definition of history as "by its nature consensual" (Lowenthal, 1986, p. 214). Corresponding is the author's attitude towards nostalgia – according to Lowenthal (1986, p. 4), the 1980s' "universal catchword for looking back". Its manifestations are located but only superficially investigated on a broad sample of disciplines from arts, architecture, furniture and autobiographies, film and advertisements to the history of ideas and restoration (Lowenthal, 1986, pp. 4 f.; Kremkau, 2003, p. 21). In contrast to other critics (see e.g. Jameson 1991; Lasch, 1984) who mostly mock nostalgia for its lacking seriousness regarding historicity, the function of the "'ghost features kept in existence by nostalgia'" is mainly seen in the context of a sense-making process regarding the present and a justification of present attitudes both used in the service of the left and the right (Lowenthal, 1986, p. 40).

Further essays on nostalgia have been collected in *The Imagined Past* in the context of a conference on the uses of history, hosted by the University of Leeds in 1985 (see also Kremkaus, 2003, p. 22). The publication encompasses a wide range of disciplines from history and literary studies, politics and philosophy to art history (Chase and Shaw, 1989a). Already the introduction of the collection characterises the phenomenon as being manifold, both regarding its connotation and the circle of people it concerns (from the individual to classes to the 'collective') (Chase and Shaw, 1989). Correspondingly, the articles presented hold a wide range of perspectives on the topic. Lowenthal, deepening his earlier studies on nostalgia, this time explicitly distinguishes himself from other British (and American) scholars who denounce nostalgia as being "reactionary, regressive, [and] ridiculous" (Lowenthal, 1989, p. 20 [addition by the author]).

"[I]t is wrong to imagine that there exists some non-nostalgic reading of the past that is by contrast 'honest' or authentically 'true'. Nostalgia shares its presentist bias, if not its anodyne aims, with many other historical perspectives." (Lowenthal, 1989, p. 30)

Nearly without exception, the contributors to the publication do not criticise the nostalgic return to the past in general (see Kremkau, 2003, p. 22), but rather analyse it critically in the context of the present and use it in order to highlight the constructedness of many historical perspectives and its blurred boundaries to "invented traditions" (Chase and Shaw, 1989, pp. 11 ff.) or myths (Stafford, 1989, pp. 33 ff.). The authors are thereby well aware of the 'dangers' of nostalgia. Thus, Chase and Shaw (1989, p. 14) highlight, "[w]e should look carefully at the process of cultural construction to see how, when, and by whom they become articulated, and look equally carefully at their intentions and effects". Exemplary, the "self-serving" nostalgia of President Ronald Reagan in the U.S. or the (re)construction of British 'heritage' during Thatcherism in the 1980s (Lowenthal, 1989, pp. 25 f.; see also Croft, 1989, p. 168) are named by authors of the collection.

The heritage context is also what film-related discourses of nostalgia are linked to, namely in discussions on so-called English heritage films. Authors writing about the subject (Higson, 1993; 2006; Wollen, 1991), for example, focus on costume dramas, such as *Brideshead Revisited* (ITV, 1981), *Chariots of Fire* (Hudson, 1981), *Another Country* (Kanievska, 1984) or *A Room with a View* (Ivory, 1986). The question of a (re)construction of the national past and national tradition is important here as well. Thus, for Higson (2006, p. 93), heritage films "[by] turning their backs on the industrialised, chaotic present [...] nostalgically re-construct an imperialist and upper-class Britain (or its other side, the picturesque poverty of *Little Dorrit*)". The author then makes a detailed analysis of the textual characteristics of heritage films by stating that:

"Even those films that develop an ironic narrative of the past end up celebrating and legitimating the spectacle of one class and one cultural tradition and identity at the expense of others through the discourse of authenticity, and the obsession with the visual splendours of period details." (Higson, 2006, p. 100)

While the earlier work of Higson (1993) was very much alike to Jameson's description of the films as an emotionless spectacle of the surface (Higson, 1993, p. 119), in later texts he opens the view towards a more reflective treatment of nostalgia and he, as he states himself, "adopted a perspective much closer to reception studies", trying to likewise consider the "range of readings and audience responses these films have generated" (Higson, 2006, p. 109). In any case, the analysis of the nostalgia 'mode' dominates the investigation.

This similarly applies to Wollen (1991), who, however, does not endeavour to investigate the textual characteristics in detail. Wollen (1991, p. 179) also puts the question of how nostalgic screen fictions reconstruct the "national identity" via the reconstruction of the national heritage in the centre of her work. As from the perspective of other authors highlighted in this section on "Nostalgia and the (re)construction of 'history'", from Wollen's point of view, "nostalgic screen fiction", even though its spectrum may sometimes limit the perspective, rather retrieves the past back for the "investigation" of the audiences (Wollen, 1991, p. 180).

Lastly, the work of Cardwell (2002) is referred to, even though it could be said that it almost exceeds the limits of this section. In integrating Smith's (1999) concept of filmic moods, her work, which is dedicated to adaptations within the heritage genre, takes a decisive step towards an analysis of the interrelations between 'mood' and 'mode' (Cardwell, 2002, pp. 144 ff.). This is also why it can be seen as a lead-over to the subsequent section of this literature review titled *Nostalgia and cultural style*, which will argue for that combination.

2.2.5 Nostalgia and cultural style

This section of the literature review unifies those works that may be placed inside or at least tend towards the fluid "set of formation" (Hall, 1992, p. 278) of *Cultural Studies,* insofar as their authors are less concerned with the reasons and consequences of nostalgia and more concerned with questions about its characteristics. The authors who are subsumed under this section first of all deplore the lack of research that surrounds the aesthetic and reception of nostalgia and engage a multi-perspective view of the phenomenon.

One of the first scholars to be commented here is the film scientist Grainge. Based on the nostalgia discourse, it has already been mentioned that Grainge (2002, pp. 35 ff.) distinguishes between nostalgia as a structure of feeling and nostalgia as a style, respectively between nostalgia mood and nostalgia mode. According to Grainge (2002, p. 36), a model that is able to grasp nostalgia must be able to "mediate" between these "poles". Grainge's (2002) own study focuses on black and white aesthetics. With the focus on a black and white aesthetic employed in advertising and in Hollywood film and print media, Grainge concentrates his work on visual aspects, referred to as the 'nostalgia mode'. This is not only a calculated disregard of the side of reception – by shifting the centre of the investigation towards monochrome, nostalgia, the point of origin is also put into a secondary position.

In reference to black and white, indeed the different possible meanings of the stylistic code, such as "intellectual abstraction, artistic integrity, documentary realism, archival evidence, fashion chic, and film classicism, depending on the nature of a text's production and reception" (Grainge, 2002, p. 69), are highlighted, but the possible meanings of nostalgia as a style are scrutinised less thoroughly. Referring to *Schindler's List*, he postulates:

"To think of the Holocaust in terms of nostalgia is clearly perverse. However, if one concentrates more on the (monochrome) mode of *Schindler's List* than on its actual subject matter, there is perhaps a character of nostalgia for a previous cinematic moment." (Grainge, 2002, p. 131)

Criticising Grainge, Pickering and Keightley (Pickering and Keightley, 2006, p. 932) state that "[a]lthough not claiming a complete loss of meaning, Grainge asserts that, as an aesthetic style of memory, monochrome representation defers a text's content to its evocation of a generalised feeling of pastness". And indeed, by doing so, it may be argued that he declares black and white to be intertextual per se and intertextuality to be nostalgic – arguing with a similar logic to Jameson. In this sense, all contemporaneous black and white films could be called nostalgic. However, later it will be shown to what extent the work is productive for the analysis of nostalgia also in the context of the present investigation.

Equally important in this context is the work of the social scientist Stuart Tannock who, like Davis, relates nostalgia to both certain discontentedness and the search for a stable identity on the side of the nostalgic subject (Tannock, 1995, p. 454). Tannock criticises the general negative connotation of nostalgia, which he believes is located in a narrow perspective analysis. According to him (1995, p. 456) the critique of "content, author, and audience" has to be separated from the general nostalgia critique.

"The 'positively evaluated' past is approached as a source for something now perceived to be missing; but it need not be thought of as a time of general happiness, peacefulness, stability, or freedom. Invoking the past, the nostalgic subject may be involved in escaping or evading, in critiquing, or in mobilizing to overcome the present experience of loss of identity, lack of agency, or absence of community." (Tannock, 1995, p. 454)

In any case, nostalgia's modalities are multiple and surely not only reactionary (Tannock 1995, p. 454). In his article, Tannock refers both to the "nostalgic text" (Tannock, 1995, p. 461) and the nostalgic "structure of feeling" (Tannock, 1995, p. 453) or "emotion" (Tannock, 1995, p. 456). Even though the interrelation of both is not further scrutinised, the author aspires to grasp the characteristics more closely. Central to this is the "rhetoric of nostalgia", which consists of: (1) the "prelapsarian world", with the source of nostalgia as being free from any negative components (2) the "'lapse'" and (3) the present, respectively "postlapsarian world" (with lacks and deficits) (Tannock, 1995, pp. 456 f.). "A critical reading of the nostalgic structure of rhetoric should focus, then," says Tannock (1995, p. 457), "on the construction of a prelapsarian world, but also on the continuity asserted, and the discontinuity posited, between a prelapsarian past and a postlapsarian present".

Lastly, a discourse contribution of the British media scientists Pickering and Keightley (2006) shall be considered. The authors – who in many areas refer to the concepts of Grainge (2002) and Tannock (1995) – put in a nutshell what could be summarised under the title 'Towards a cultural studies perspective on nostalgia'. Thus, they reject critique of media nostalgia, for example the postmodern theory of mistakenly homogenising the audiences, stripping them of active participation, and for seeing nostalgic thinking and nostalgic texts as interchangeable (Pickering and Keightley, 2006, pp. 924, 929). Instead, they stress that "nostalgia is a way of thinking and feeling rather than being directly produced or constituted by consuming nostalgic media texts, but there are nevertheless cultural artefacts that facilitate nostalgia as a way of feeling and thinking" (Pickering and Keighley, 2006, p. 930). This consequently leads to the statement that on the side of the text "the modes of representation and operation involved in the communication of nostalgia" (Pickering and Keightley, 2006, p. 930) have to be worked out. On the side of the viewers, "different sites of meaning-making" (Pickering and Keightley, 2006, p. 929) have to be taken into account – always keeping in mind that nostalgia "is subject to circumstance, motivation, and interests, and over both time and space, to degree, variation and change" (Pickering and Keightley, 2006, p. 929). This is a statement that will also be relevant in the course of this work.

2.2.6 Nostalgia in Germany and Spain

As the following sub-chapters show, similar strands of argumentation can be exemplarily identified on the Spanish and German discourse of nostalgia.

2.2.6.1 Germany: from *Nostalgie* to *Ostalgie*

As in other countries, in the German-speaking countries the discussion was stimulated by the so-called 'nostalgia wave', which found its expression in different cultural fields, such as film and television, music, fashion, advertising, design, or architecture. And in terms of disciplines that consider the topic, the academic discourse is just as broad. Alongside a revived interest in nostalgia on the part of medicine history –, Kremkau (2003, p. 16) refers to the two dissertations of Brunnert (1984) and Pfannkuche (1978) – nostalgia is discussed by sociologists, historians, educationalists or anthropologists (see also Kremkau 2003, pp. 15 f.). Their first assessments can be subsumed under what has previously been referred to as 'nostalgia as a contemporary malaise'. Thus the intellectuals address nostalgia less as a textual but rather as a social phenomenon. Without exceptions, the authors have "cultural critical intentions" (Kremkau, 2003, p. 15 [o.t.]). Be it that nostalgia is seen as escapism or regression towards pre-industrial circumstances (see Schivelbusch, 1973; Gehlen, 1976), that it is equalised with a new conservatism or related to a certain ignorance for history (see Baacke, 1976), the contributors to the discourse, whether from the left or from the right political spectrum, are all quite sceptical towards the phenomenon. Baacke (1976), educationalist and member of the Frankfurt School, does not only describe nostalgia as a-historical, uncritical, un-political, and flat, he also sees it as a "symptom of a certain intellectual, artistic and mental immatureness" (Baacke, 1976, p. 444 [o.t.]), which is the reflection of a collective alienation in the course of modernisation (Baacke, 1976, pp. 450 ff.). Furthermore, Gehlen (1973) – an anthropologist and antagonist of the Frankfurt School – claims that the accelerated modern era, which is dominated by terrorism, unemployment and the loss of values, is responsible for nostalgia (Gehlen 1973, p. 439). The only author who is less fatalistic towards the phenomenon is Schivelbusch (1973), a member of the German school of cultural studies. Like his contemporaries, he sees nostalgia as a collective regression in the course of the hectic industrialised world (Schivelbusch, 1973, pp. 275 f.). Nevertheless, his explanatory model is not based upon the assumption of a regressive mind, but relates to Barthes' work on the libidinal relationship of consumers towards commodities (Schivelbusch, 1973, p. 274). Because, he assumes, in the industrialised world consumer products are constantly replaced by new ones, human beings escape into nostalgia (Schivelbusch, 1973, pp. 274 f.). All in all, even though different lines of argument can be shown, the scholars agree that nostalgia is a reaction on modern times. However, detailed analyses of nostalgic objects are not provided, not to mention a consideration of the side of reception.

An exception can be found in the dissertation of the design and architecture critique Fischer (1980). The author pursues a more holistic view of the subject. Although he confirms the conservative, escapist or regressive tendencies of nostalgia (see e.g. Fischer, 1980, pp. 52 f., 182) – which is very similar to what has been subsumed under the label *nostalgia and (re)construction of 'history'* – he also underpins its capacity of making history accessible (Fischer, 1980, p. 55), its potential innovative power in contrasting with the contemporary or in meeting the actual *zeitgeist* (Fischer, 1980, pp. 45, 179), and its critical potential concerning the present (Fischer, 1980, p. 246). His assumptions are based on concrete investigations – even though thematically broadly applied. Fischer (1980) does not only give an overview on nostalgia in fields such as design, television or architecture, he also centres on nostalgia's semantic fields from kitsch to the 'fantastic' and its forms of representation. Already in the introductory section, Fischer (1980) points out the importance of a differentiation between object level and reception: "The term 'nostalgic object' [...] signifies that it is about an object which inherits structural elements that allow the submission, respectively the development of nostalgic sentiments of identification." (Fischer, 1980, p. 269 [footnote 68] [o.t.]) Even though in this widely applied investigation many aspects – for instance this latter one – are only touched upon, one can say that Fischer extends the discourse towards describing nostalgia as a multiple phenomenon – an approach that also has been formulated by scholars of *Cultural Studies*.

More recently, the discourse has flared up again in the context of the Ostalgie/Westalgie[10] discussion (see e.g. Ludewig 2006; Blum 2000), which, although not restricted to German speaking regions (for further reading see Cooke, 2003; Allan, 2006; Enns, 2007), are also linked to the existing, general nostalgia discourse.

2.2.6.2 Nostalgia in Spain

In Spain, the nostalgia discourse was also inspired by a so-called 'wave of nostalgia' in the 1970s. Only a brief look at non-academic publications, such as the daily newspaper *La Vanguardia,* shows a relative accumulation of nostalgia-related articles between 1969 and 1974 (*La Vanguardia,* 2011). As the ongoing reinforcement of nostalgia in the United States is occurring[11], similar tendencies in Spanish society are discovered (see e.g. *La Vanguardia Española,* 1974). Generally, the public discourse seems less emotionalised. The phenomenon is rather perceived as a self-evident component of society with critical potential rather than as a reactionary bone of contention.

In regards to academic publications, many monograph titles refer to "nostalgia", whereupon the term only contains a kind of an eye-catcher rather than an indication of the topic. In any case the term is used in a very general manner, signifying a longing for material as well as immaterial objects.[12] Apart from that, recent publications in the field of audiovisual culture can be found that are dedicated solely to nostalgia. The Spanish series *Cuéntame Cómo Pasó* (TVE, 2001) is often at the centre of investigation. Referring particularly to Boym's (2011) concept of reflexive

---

10 'Ostalgie' is a term derived from a combination of *nostalgie,* the German word for nostalgia, and *Osten,* the German word for East, which in this case stands for the former German Democratic Republic (GDR). 'Westalgie' is the West-German counterpart to 'Ostalgie', namely nostalgia for the West, respectively *Westen* as it is in German.

11 "Never a country which bases upon the myth of being young on the one hand and the figure of the old Uncle Sam on the other, has been so nostalgic for yesterday." (A.Z., 1974 [o.t.]); Original quotation: "Nunca un país con el mito de ser joven contrapuesto a la figura del Viejo Tio Sam, se había sentido tan nostalgico de ayer." (A.Z., 1974)

12 See e.g. *Nostalgia. La cultura del exilio vasco* (Amezaga Aresti, 1993), *Nostalgia de la aventura* (Filmoteca Valencia, 1989), *La nostalgia de los libros perdidos* (Amat Noguera, 1998), and *Religiosidad popular. Nostalgia de lo mágico* (Maldonado, 1975).

nostalgia and to Fiske's (1987) concept of television realism, the Spanish scholar Corbalán (2009, pp. 345 f.) explains how the series confronts the personal historical reconstruction of the viewers with the personal historical reconstruction, which is presented by the narrator of the series. In making a text analysis and preparing qualitative questionnaires, Corbalán is one of the few authors who realises what has been demanded by scholars, here subsumed under the label 'nostalgia and cultural style' (for more details see Chapter 7.1).

In a more detailed textual analysis, Laffond and Gómez (2009), when making a comparative analysis between *Cuéntame Cómo Pasó* (TVE, 2001) and the American series *The Wonder Years* (ABC, 1988), explain how nostalgia is evoked on different levels of the text, such as typology of the protagonists, representation of family, presentation of values or dominant characteristics of the formal level. Here – similar to the monograph titles mentioned previously – they distinguish between different directions of nostalgia, such as "nostalgia for the neighbourhood" (Laffond and Gómez, 2009, p. 398 [o.t.]) or "nostalgia for the epoch" (Laffond and Gómez, 2009, p. 401 [o.t.]). As a matter of course, the 'banal' nostalgia is distinguished from "reflexive and moderately critical" nostalgia (Laffond and Gómez, 2009, p. 399 [o.t.]). Additionally, Laffond and Gómez perform a comparison between the nostalgic narration and 'actual' historical events in a similar fashion to what has been claimed by authors such as Pickering and Keightley (2006). Nevertheless, Laffond and Gómez underpin their analysis with works on history and television. The nostalgia discourse stays rather excluded.

Beyond that, further essays on television's engagement with history have been collected under the title *Historias de la Pequeña Pantalla*[13] (López et. al., 2009), among which an article written by Teresa Herrera-De La Muela is dedicated to nostalgia. The author draws on modern myth theory in order to explain textual characteristics that make reruns of the television series *Verano Azul* (TVE, 1981) capable for nostalgic reception. Her work may be allocated to what has previously been referred to as 'nostalgia and the (re)construction of history'.

---

13 Whole title *Historias de la Pequeña Pantalla: Representaciones históricas en la televisión de la España democrática* (López et al., 2009), translatable as: 'Histories of the Small Screen: The representation of history in the television of the democratic Spain' (2009).

2.3 CONCLUSION ON THE DISCOURSE AND TRANSITION TO FOLLOWING RESEARCH STEPS

"Despite the word's changing connotations since the seventeenth century, there remains one indisputable, albeit banal, feature of nostalgia upon which all agree, from those who have reflected only casually on the phenomenon to those who have studied it closely: This is that the material of nostalgic experience is the past." (Davis, 1977, p. 415)

The above passage is quoted from an article by the sociologist Fred Davis in 1977. By this time, the so-called 'nostalgia wave' had inspired a huge amount of academic investigation on the topic of nostalgia. In the beginning this was an emotional discourse with, as Sprengler (2011, p. 31) put it, "most heated debates [...] on positive or negative effect[s]". Later a change of trend led the discussion towards more dimensional definitions. Today – several decades later – the quotation is apt to introduce this conclusive chapter on the current state of nostalgia discourse. Also in the present day, the theoretical grasping of nostalgia is difficult. Perhaps the only common denominator is that nostalgia somehow refers to the past. In this chosen form of presentation it also becomes apparent that a dispersion of the discourse has occurred[14] – a dispersion insofar as there is no consistent research tradition in the sense of Rogers' description as "a series of investigations on a similar topic in which successive studies are influenced by preceding inquiries" (Rogers, 2003, p. 39). "Deployment of the category in such different academic domains as psychology, history and cultural studies creates difficulties of application and reference within a coherent explanatory framework." (Pickering and Keightley, 2006, p. 922)

Only a few authors, such as Davis (1977; 1979) and Jameson (1991), are regularly cited and 'processed'. In many cases, instead of harnessing a predecessor's investigations, the discourse is still caught up in a struggle to position the phenomenon. This

---

14 Here, the fact that the dominant lines of argument have been considered shall be pointed out. The boundaries between these strands are not always clear-cut. Thus Lowenthal, who has been subsumed under the title of *Nostalgia and the (re)construction of 'history'* here, likewise links nostalgia to the construction of identity (Lowenthal, 1986, pp. 193 ff.), Jameson (1989) as cited in Hutcheon (2000, p. 202) "feels that the postmodern taste for [nostalgia] films corresponds to certain needs in what he calls 'our present economic-psychic constitution'", the film scholar Sprengler, subsumed under the label *Nostalgia: death of historicity or paradigm shift* in this context, also links to cultural studies with her investigation; the sociologist Davis, here referred to under the label *Nostalgia and Identity*, likewise draws on nostalgia as a cultural style, and Boym's concept of restorative nostalgia, subsumed under the label of *Nostalgia and identity*, is at the same time linked to what here has been called *Nostalgia and the (re)construction of 'history'*.

is not only reflected by a broad range of assessments of nostalgia from different perspectives – explanations range from *Nostalgia as a contemporary malaise*, *Nostalgia and Identity*, *Nostalgia: death of historicity or paradigm shift*, *Nostalgia and the (re)construction of 'history'* to *Nostalgia and cultural style* – but also by the definition of nostalgia as such. A previous definition of the term is not always a self-evident component of the works, which makes a discussion on a common basis more difficult. Some authors clearly distinguish nostalgia from other forms of referring to the past (see e.g. Hart, 1973; Davis, 1979), while others, such as Jameson (1991), use it "in no way [...] as passionate expressions of that older longing once called nostalgia" (Jameson, 1991, p. xvii) and draw the frame so wide that any intertextual reference could be called nostalgic. The dispersion is equally observable among works that approach nostalgia from a film and television studies perspective. Apart from the fact that they, as the rest of the discourse, approach nostalgia in film and television from different standpoints as have been explained, they also focus, I would argue, on different levels of the text, respectively on different objects of nostalgia, which is what makes their application additionally difficult.

At the same time the dispersion of the discourse can be described in a more positive way, namely as a multi-layered quality. It could be shown that nostalgia is not un-investigated, and the phenomenon has been studied from different perspectives, which in combination could be applicable for further investigation. Authors such as Grainge (2002) and Pickering and Keightley (2006) have already highlighted the importance of a perspective on nostalgia, which combines both the 'mood' and the 'mode' perspective. Here one can argue that huge parts of, as Pickering and Keightley (2006, pp. 929 f.) call it, "the modes of representation and operation involved in the communication of nostalgia" and "different sites of meaning-making", are already in part investigated within the different strands.[15] But they have to be made applicable. They have to be 'ordered' to make them usable in combination. One must think about elements that may work as a bridge between text and reception.

Three following sub-chapters of this conclusion will briefly reflect upon aspects that can already be useful for the analysis of nostalgia on these two levels and others that are not clear in the discourse but that can be clarified by further theory from outside the nostalgia discourse. Three points shall be highlighted: (1) *Nostalgia as a 'mood'*, (2) *From the cognitive-emotional to the textual part of nostalgia* and (3) *The bandwidth of nostalgia*. They will lead over to the following chapters.

---

15 Thus Davis makes no in-depth analysis of concrete examples or of the complex interrelation of text and reception, but his differentiation of nostalgia may teach us a lot about the general characteristics of nostalgia.

2.3.1 Nostalgia 'mood'

Firstly, mostly in the spectrum of authors who Grainge (2002) also calls the "mood agents", nostalgia is frequently described as a past-related affect. According to Davis, "the nostalgic feeling is infused with imputations of past beauty, pleasure, joy, satisfaction, goodness, happiness, love, and the like, in sum, any or several of the *positive* affects of being" (Davis, 1979, p. 14 [italic emphasis in the original]). At another place the author highlights that it is "more likely to be classed with such familiar emotions as love, jealousy, and fear" and set against "such 'conditions' as melancholia, obsessive compulsion, or claustrophobia" (Davis, 1979, p. 5). Thus Davis talks about the "nostalgic feeling" (Davis, 1979, p. 14) but later calls it an "emotion" (Davis, 1979, p. 82). Grainge (2002, p. 11), however, subsumes this idea under the so-called 'mood agents'. Furthermore, Cardwell, who investigates the subject more closely, also states that it "is difficult to determine […] whether nostalgia is better understood as a feeling or an emotion" (Cardwell, 2002, p. 144).

However, if nostalgia, apart from being a 'mode', can be called an emotion and is an emotion that television can elicit in its viewers, studying emotions in relation to film and television will be highly relevant for its analysis. Cardwell (2002), as previously mentioned, already makes a step into this direction. This investigation will look at further studies on emotions and aesthetic emotions from outside the nostalgia discourse.

2.3.2 From the cognitive-emotional to the textual part of nostalgia

Secondly, and without falling prey to a simple cause-and-effect way of thinking, the nostalgia discourse from outside film and television theory already characterises the phenomenon closely. The aspects outlined here can again be made useful for the investigation of nostalgia in television, both regarding the textual level and the reception. Thus Davis (1979, p. 13) describes nostalgia as being different from remembrance, reminiscence, or recall. At the same time, nostalgia can be linked to a certain bittersweet sadness, which has its origin in the irretrievability of the past the 'nostalgist' longs for (Hart, 1973, p. 399). This may also be the reason why nostalgia is often brought together with what has been named "aura" by Walter Benjamin (see e.g. Boym, 2001, p. 45), "the unique apparition of a distance, however near it may be" (Benjamin, 1936 [2008], p. 23).

Nostalgia includes the present by embracing circumstances and conditions, which are seen as being worse in comparison to the past (Davis, 1979, p. 15). This is also where another constitutive factor of the "rhetoric of nostalgia" is linked, that is its trisection in prelapsarian, 'lapse', and postlapsarian world (Tannock, 1995) and its composition of "loss, lack and longing" (Pickering and Keightley, 2006, p. 921). As

Pickering and Keightley (2006) highlight with reference to Smith (1998) and Lowenthal (1989), "a desire to imaginatively return to earlier times is then felt to correlate with an acute dissatisfaction with the present and to involve an attempt to recapture a putative continuity and coherence unavailable in the fragmented modern or late modern environment" (Pickering and Keightley, 2006, p. 923).

In contrast to memory, where the past present and the actual present are different, in the case of nostalgia "the past present coincides with the actual present by including it 'in some way'" (Hart, 1973, p. 404). According to Davis (1977, p. 416), this is reflected in the fact that the "knowledge" that something is past is an experience that is made in the present. Furthermore, closing the circle, it can be explained by the fact that emotions are always an issue of the present (see Bennett, 2003, p. 27). Further, this study will here review the categories which have been described by Davis and Boym, according to which nostalgia can adopt various stances – from simple to reflexive to interpreted nostalgia (Davis, 1979, pp. 18 ff.) or from restorative to reflective nostalgia (Boym, 2001). Apart from that, within film and television studies, concrete textual characteristics of nostalgia are explained.

2.3.3 The bandwidth of nostalgia

Thirdly, many scholars agree that the reference of modern nostalgia somehow is the past. "Modern societies", according to Chase and Shaw (1989, p. 2), "share a view of time as linear with an undetermined future. If either of these requirements is not met, then nostalgia seems very unlikely". Nevertheless, it is not always clear which bandwidth (both regarding the human memory and the physical archive) nostalgic material may refer to. From this, the following questions occur: What are the minimum and maximum time spans of nostalgia? Is nostalgia a matter of personal past and therefore comprises only the time span that refers to personal experience, or will objects that are outside the lifespan of a person also trigger it?

Regarding the question of the minimum time span an object has to go through in order to serve as a trigger for nostalgia, we can refer to Davis (1977; 1979) and Lowenthal (1986; 1989). Both authors highlight the necessity of a certain contrast to present times. Lowenthal refers to "revolutionary change" that "rapidly distanced all known pasts" and may therefore create sources for nostalgia (Lowenthal, 1986, p. 49). Furthermore, Davis (1977, p. 417) argues that there should be "some necessary passage of time before the events of our lives come to serve as fit objects of nostalgia". According to him, this 'necessary' depends on the way the nostalgic person "make[s]" events "contrast" with the present (Davis, 1977, p. 417; Davis, 1979, p. 12). From Davis's perspective, a 'contrast-generator' could be, for instance, the beginning of another life passage or changes rendered by history (Davis, 1979, p. 49). This is also in line with what Böhn (2007, p. 146) highlights with reference to

Friedl (1990), namely that "situations of abrupt political change, combined with the destruction of former social structures and hierarchies, have always favoured nostalgia and musealization". With Davis (1979) it can be stated that relating to private experiences, such as a "parent's smile [or] the garden view from a certain window of a house once lived in", changes are likely to occur within very a short time span, so that an object or experience of the latest past could become an object of nostalgia as well (Davis, 1979, pp. 122 f.).

In general, authors (see e.g. Fischer 1980, p. 196) observe an overall reduction of the time spans of nostalgia. This is explained with reference to the accelerated circulation of goods, the "increasing pressure to innovate", and the faster storage of documents in modern times (see e.g. Fischer, 1980, p. 196 [o.t.]). As Huyssen (1995) states, "'The more memory we store on data banks, the more the past is sucked into the orbit of the present, ready to be called up on the screen'." (Huyssen, 1995 cited in Hutcheon, 2000, p. 197)

The definition of the maximum time span mostly depends on whether an author considers personal memories as a basis for nostalgia, if personal memories are considered as an only basis for nostalgia or if the frame is drawn wider than that. Describing "the repulsive effect of current conditions" (Gehlen, 1976, p. 438 [o.t.]) as a main source of nostalgia in the 1970s, Gehlen (1976, p. 438) generally settles the time of reference from 1850 up to pre-World War I times. With nostalgia placed in a fixed time span, the author has an outsider status. More common is a consideration of the time spans of nostalgia that start from personal experiences. Only Hart (1973, p. 412) argues that nostalgia "occurs essentially for the individual in the privacy of his memory and in the exclusiveness of his own personal history". Most other authors consider the possibility of a kind of 'transferability' of memories. According to Fischer (1980, p. 16), next to personal memories, biographical links can also be generated artificially. In this context he describes the possibility of the symbolical appropriation of biographies by the consumption of media that extend the time span of personal experiences (Fischer, 1980, p. 41). Fischer (1980, p. 16 [o.t.]) describes this as "pseudo- or cryptobiographical" memory. According to Lowenthal (1986, p. 6), nostalgia encompasses a range of past that becomes broader each time. He claims "the past we depend on to make sense of the present [...] stems mainly from our own few years of experience" (Lowenthal, 1986, p. 40), but, at the same time, "we conceive of things not only as seen, but also as heard and read about before" (Lowenthal, 1986, p. 40). With reference to Tyler (1977), Lowenthal (1986, p. 197) draws on the possibility of the formation of 'second-hand memories' by the adaptation of family memories. Furthermore, he states, "people are so eager to be part of 'history' that they falsely 'remember' their responses to, or even having been present at, some momentous event" (Lowenthal, 1986, p. 197).

Davis (1977; 1979) makes a similar argument. On the one hand the author states that the material of nostalgia is "personally experienced past rather than one drawn solely from, for example, chronicles, almanacs, history books, memorial tablets or, for that matter, legend" (Davis, 1977, p. 416).[16] On the other hand, he opens up the spectrum by arguing that "when today's adolescents reach middle age it is probable that their nostalgic revivals will include symbolic fragments and residues of what had been the nostalgia of their parents" (Davis, 1979, pp. 61 f.). This means that nostalgia actually does not *solely* relate to personally experienced past but that this past can also be 'transmitted'. In this case it could at least embrace more than one generation. But Davis does not leave it at that. In the context of media nostalgia, he amplifies the 'transmittability' of memories by the use of media (Davis, 1979, pp. 119 ff.). Thus, Davis argues, "media products may now serve memory where once houses, streets and persons did" (Davis, 1979, p. 129) and as personal experiences, this adopted memory or, as Davis (1979, p. 121) describes it, "created, secondhand reality", may again work as a basis for nostalgia.

Boym (2001) has also considered that media somehow has the power to generate second-hand memories. As she states, "[i]t seems that 1990s nostalgia for the Brezhnev era was partially based on the old Soviet movies that reappeared on Russian TV at that time" (Boym, 2001, p. 61). Additionally, she refers to evoked involuntary memories and the difficulty to distinguish whether these memories belong to personal experiences or to a once-seen television commercial (Boym, 2001, p. 352). It's a nostalgia, as Boym states elsewhere in her study, which Appadurai (1996) also defines "as 'ersatz nostalgia' or armchair nostalgia, 'nostalgia without lived experience or collective historical memory'" (Appadurai, 1996 cited in Boym 2001, p. 38). Since this point will be crucial not only for the general framing of nostalgia's material basis (be it memory or archive), but also for considering its reception later, it shall be explained in a further chapter, which integrates studies on memory and archives that have their origin outside the nostalgia discourse.

---

16 Since personal experiences strongly relate to life passages, "nostalgia acquires considerable sociological significance" (Davis, 1979, p. 12). Additionally, the life passages and events are to a high degree collective; it is here where Davis draws the line to nostalgia as a collective experience. Nostalgia, so Davis, thus "mediates the selection, distillation, refinement, and integration of those scenes, events, personalities, attitudes, and practices from the past that make an identifiable *generation* of what would otherwise remain a featureless demographic cohort" (Davis, 1979, p. 111 [italic emphasis in the original]).

3. Two 'archives' – nostalgia's relationship to the past

As Chase and Shaw (1989, p. 4) state, one of the "requirement[s] for nostalgia is that objects, buildings and images from the past should be available". This means, a description of nostalgia regarding text and reception should include the fact that the phenomenon which always appears with a reference to 'the past' has to be considered in its relation regarding two 'archives': On the one hand, the human memory with, as Landsberg (1997, p. 85) calls it, "one's intellectual and emotional archive", and on the other hand, physical and digital archives, such as television archives or libraries. We have already seen first clues of this in the nostalgia discourse; however, it has been shown that answers are diverse and sometimes divergent. This study will therefore combine studies on nostalgia with those on memory and archives that have their origin outside the nostalgia discourse. To further clarify the nostalgia discourse, the study will draw on both personal and 'collective' memories. Two sub-chapters highlight the characteristics of "prosthetic memories" and media recollections. Finally, a section on physical/digital archives draws a picture of the changing notion of archives in the course of the time referring both to Germany and Spain, because only what has been stored can be made productive again for the uses of nostalgia.

3.1 MEMORY

As highlighted by Schmidt (1991, p. 9), despite its almost century-long history, there does not exist any consistent theory of memory at all. Nevertheless, inside the philosophical-cultural-historical and the biologic-physiologic discourses of memory, some concepts seem to build some kind of denominators. As Schmidt (1991, p. 26) and Parkin (1993, p. 2) note, in experimental psychology William James' (1890) concept of the memory became generally accepted. James (1890), as referred to by Parkin (1993, p. 2), basically distinguishes short-term and long-term memory as primary and secondary memory. According to Eysenck and Keane (2005, p. 191), primary memory or short-term memory is built up by information that remains in the consciousness after its perception and that belongs to the "psychological present". Secondary or long-term memory "contains information about events that have left consciousness and are therefore part of the psychological past" (Eysenck and Keane, 2005, p. 191), such as our last vacation or how to drive a car (Eysenck and Keane, 2005, p. 229). Hereby, following the literature (Schmidt, 1991, p. 11; see also Eysenck and Keane, 2005, p. 261 on every day memory), store-house concepts of the memory are mostly rejected. Instead, memory is conceptualised as being under permanent construction (see e.g. Schmidt, 1991, p. 11).[1]

3.1.1 Personal memory

Except for Gehlen (1976, p. 438), who puts the reference time of nostalgia between 1850 and the pre-First World War era and in so doing declares personal experience to be an unnecessary condition, the scholars of nostalgia discourse (see e.g. Hart, 1973; Davis, 1979; Fischer, 1980; Lowenthal, 1986) agree that nostalgia somehow refers to personal memory or individual memory, which in cognitive psychology (Robinson, 1992; Eysenck and Keane, 2005, pp. 263 ff.) is also called "autobiographical memory".

"'[A]utobiographical memory is memory of events of one's own life'" (Conway and Rubin, 1993 cited in Eysenck and Keane, 2005, p. 263). According to Howe and Courage (1997), as referred to by Eysenck and Keane (2005, p. 264), it emerges with "'the development of the cognitive self late in the second year of life'" and, as investigations from cognitive psychology show, it is most active "between 10 and 30, and especially between 15 and 25" (Eysenck and Keane, 2005, p. 263) – a phenomenon that is also called a "reminiscence bump" (Eysenck and Keane, 2005, p. 266). Autobiographical memory, according to Robinson (1992, p. 244), as a kind of long-term memory, "can be distinguished from knowledge of other people's experiences or public events, and from general knowledge and skills" (Robinson, 1992, p. 223). As Ebbrecht highlights with reference to Welzer (2005), "next to a cognitive-reflexive dimension the memories always also have an 'emotional tone'" (Ebbrecht, 2008, p. 88 [o.t.]).

Investigating autobiographical memory is to a large degree related to the way we "organize" and "retrieve" information of our personal past (Parkin, 1993, p. 5 [o.t.]). Therefore, what we remember is seen as "influenced by various motivational factors" and contextual factors, such as the occasion of the recall (Eysenck and Keane, 2005, p. 262), "the location of remembering as well as the location of the event

---

1 Schmidt (1991, p. 11 [o.t.]) here refers to Müller's (1911-1917) concept of the "creative role of memory" and Bartlett's (1932) work on the "dynamic character" of retention and recall.

remembered" (Kumar et al., 2006, p. 211). Additionally, Barclay and Hodges (1988) as referred to by Robinson (1992, p. 237), argue that "memories are regularly reconfigured as we revise our self-perceptions and personal histories". Furthermore, state Eysenck and Keane (2005, pp. 263, 269), what is stored in the autobiographical memory is influenced by the goals of the working-self, such as life goals, emotions and personal meaning. Mills and Coleman (1994), as cited in Wilson (1999), explicitly call nostalgia a "'type of autobiographical memory'".

Similarly, it is also formulated by the philosophical-cultural-historical discourse of personal memory. Despite the fact that memory is grasped as an "active process" of permanent reworking (Popular Memory Group, 1982, p. 243), following Halbwachs, authors such as Assmann (2006, p. 25) note that individual memory is also socially determined by its dependence on oral exchange. For this reason, Assmann (2006, p. 25 [o.t.]) also calls individual memory "communicative memory". "By telling, listening, questioning and retelling", she stresses, "the radius of the individual memories expands" (Assmann, 2006, pp. 25 f. [o.t.]) to the extent that it comprises various generations (Assmann, 2006, p. 26). This means that the boundaries between personal memories and, for instance, family memories become blurred (Assmann, 2006, p. 206). Since human beings are integrated into different so-called "Wir-Gruppen" [we-groups], they share memories on different levels (Assmann, 2006, p. 22 [o.t.]). Family is only one of them. According to Assmann (2006, p. 22), others may be, for example, peer groups or generations. Regarding the latter, each person is influenced by certain "key experiences" of his or her peers and shares "cultural interpretative patterns", worldviews or values with the group (Assmann, 2006, p. 26 [o.t.]). As Assmann (2006, p. 26) notes, Karl Mannheim called this "Generationengedächtnis" [generational memory]. In this context he introduced the term "'entelechies'" (Mannheim, 1951 cited in Volkmer, 2006a, p. 7) which, according to Volkmer (2006a, p. 7), refers to the "underlying structure of common experiences of each generation". This development from the individual to the social memory becomes especially apparent in the case of media memories (see 3.1.4).

3.1.2 'Collective' memory

As previously shown, the nostalgia discourse does not solely relate to nostalgias that arise in the private but also to those that arise in broader contexts. Davis (1979), for instance, refers to "collective nostalgia" which, one can assume, is based on collective memories. Collective memory is also a topic of the memory discourse. According to Schmidt (1991, p. 39 [o.t.]) who here refers to Heijl (1987), "cognitive parallelism and homogeneity" generated via, for example, common socialisation or the use of mass media, "inter-subjectively allow the complex construction of 'narrative families', which can also be seen as an equivalent of the term 'collective memory'".

Nevertheless, the distinction between individual and collective memory is something that has been applied in everyday use but that has often been questioned critically by scientists (see e.g. Assmann, 2006, pp. 29 ff.). According to Assmann (2006, p. 35), the term collective memory is much too "vague". It is rather that both the intergenerational social memory, which has its basis in different social groups, and the trans-generational cultural memory, which is based on symbolical storage media, such as photographs and films, contain collective elements (Assmann, 2006, pp. 35 f., 54, 60). From individual to collective, Assmann notes (2006, p. 59), memory passes through various "we-groups". "Only those memory formations, which, together with strong bonds of loyalty, also produce strongly standardized we-identities, can be called 'collective' in a narrow sense" (Assmann, 2006, p. 36 [o.t.]). The author (2006, p. 36) here refers exemplary to 'national' memory.

3.1.2.1 Excursus: retrieval of memories

In regards to autobiographical memories within cognitive psychology (see e.g. Eysenck and Keane 2005), two forms of retrieval are distinguished – generative retrieval and direct retrieval. Generative retrieval, according to Conway et al. (2001), as cited in Eysenck and Keane (2005, p. 269), signifies the way in which "'memories are actively and intentionally constructed through an interaction between the working self goal structure and the autobiographical memory knowledge base'". It is a form of voluntary memory (Eysenck and Keane, 2005, pp. 269 ff.). Direct retrieval, involving involuntary memories, "occurs when someone encounters a specific cue that causes activation to spread from the relevant specific autobiographical memory to more general associated memories" (Eysenck and Keane, 2005, p. 269). In this context, Teer-Tomaselli also talks about so-called "triggers" – "stimuli that recall particular memories" (Teer-Tomaselli, 2006, p. 242).[2] Sutton (2010) suggests that these processes may both work on a conscious and on an unconscious level:

"He [the person who remembers] may simply find himself tearful, the music making him sad because of its previous coupling with affliction in his experience, although he remains unaware of this association. Alternatively, he may be well aware of the specific and tragic past occasions on which he has heard the galliard, perhaps being able to give detailed affective, temporal, and contextual information about those past experiences, and perhaps even to use this knowledge to work through the revived emotions." (Sutton, 2010)

---

2   See also Hoskin (2004, p. 110) on "iconic events" in television which work as triggers in order to release specific memories.

Referring to the results of his own research on the subject, Berntsen (1998), as cited in Eysenck and Keane (2005, p. 271), highlights that "'we maintain a considerable amount of specific episodes in memory which may often be inaccessible for voluntary [generative] retrieval but highly accessible for involuntary [direct] retrieval'". This point is especially interesting since the philosophical-cultural-historical discourse often relates nostalgia to involuntary memories. Some authors even go so far as to restrict nostalgia to this kind of retention. One example to which several authors refer is Marcel Proust's description of the so-called "mémoire involontaire" in *In Search of Lost Time*, suggesting that "'[t]he past is hidden somewhere [...] beyond the reach of the intellect, in some material object [...] which we do not suspect'" (Kern citing Proust, cited in Klippel, 1997, p. 15). According to Hart (1973, p. 397), the works of Proust have "given expression to the basic elements of the experience" of nostalgia. The author thus restricts the nostalgic longing to its involuntary aspects and stresses, "a nostalgic past, unlike a memory of the past [...] cannot be recalled at will" (Hart, 1973, p. 397). Schivelbusch (1973, p. 275 [o.t.]) draws a similar picture, describing the Bergson-Proustian *mémoire involontaire* as the "personal-private variant" of nostalgia.

The retrieval of emotions is a different case. According to Claparède (1911), as cited in Bennett (2003, p. 27), "'[i]t is impossible to feel emotions as past. One cannot be a spectator of one's own feelings; one feels them, or one does not feel them; one cannot imagine them without stripping them of their affective essence'". From this, Bennett states that "[e]motions are felt only as they are experienced in the present; in memory they become ideas, representations, and representation inherently implies distance, perspective" (Bennett, 2003, p. 27). Nevertheless, this does not mean that emotions stay irretrievable. As previously mentioned, memory is always infused with an "'emotional tone'" (Welzer, 2005 cited in Ebbrecht, 2008, p. 88 [o.t.]). In this case cues or triggers may serve to reactivate the previously felt emotion. Therefore, Bennett (2003, p. 27) states, referring to James, "if emotions are not retrievable from memory, they are *revivable;* hence, we don't remember grief or ecstasy, but by recalling a situation that produces those sensations we can produce a new bout of emotion".

3.1.3 Postmemory and prosthetic memory

As previously discussed, various authors from within the nostalgia discourse draw on the possibility of 'transmitted' memories as a basis for nostalgia. Nevertheless, relating these questions, the lines of argument are diverse, and the theoretical foundation is unclear. With Assmann (2006) we have seen that the individual memory is always interrelated with the memories of other "we-groups". Assmann already comes to talk about the subject of (media-) 'transmitted' memories (see e.g.

Assmann, 2006, pp. 59 ff.; 133). The philosophical-cultural-historical discourse of memory offers two further useful concepts here: first Alison Landsberg's concept of the "prosthetic memory" (Landsberg, 1995; 1997), and secondly, Marianne Hirsch's work on postmemory (see e.g. Hirsch, 2001). Both authors somehow break with the distinction of 'real' and 'unreal' memories. Both authors somehow let the "boundaries between individuals", as Radstone and Hodgkin (2003, p. 2) describe it, melt and at the same time make the melting of the boundaries between the memories of the different "we-groups" (Assmann, 2006) more tangible.

With the term "prosthetic", Landsberg signifies memories that, in contrast to autobiographic memories, "do not come from a person's lived experience in a strict sense" (Landsberg, 1995, p. 175). Nevertheless, as she suggests, they cannot be distinguished from these 'real' memories, as they have been "experienced with one's own body" (Landsberg, 1997, p. 66). Mass media, such as theme parks, interactive museums such as the *United States Holocaust Memorial Museum*, film, and television build the centre of her argument. This is because, according to Landsberg (1995, p. 179), what individuals see and explore via mass media "might affect them so significantly" that it "actually become[s] part of their own personal archive of experience". This potential of the media, above all the transgenerational 'transmission' of knowledge, becomes especially important against the backdrop of eye-witnesses of the Holocaust, who are dying out – a point that is outlined in a later article by Landsberg (1997). Her main argument is that despite the always claimed danger of "historical revisionism", mass media with its potential for stimulating prosthetic memory also "provide individuals with a public opportunity to have an experiential relationship to a collective or cultural past" (Landsberg, 1997, p. 74).

Furthermore, Hirsch's concept of so-called postmemories describes the possibility of a kind of 'transmission' or adoption of memories. She developed her theory originally in the context of Holocaust memories (see e.g. Hirsch, 2001).

"Postmemory most specifically describes the relationship of children of survivors of cultural or collective trauma to the experiences of their parents, experiences that they 'remember' only as the narratives and images with which they grew up, but that are so powerful, so monumental, as to construct memories in their own right". (Hirsch, 2001, p. 9)

It is *"retrospective witnessing by adoption"* (Hirsch, 2001, p. 10 [italic emphasis in the original]). Nevertheless, this is the first strict sense of the term presented by Hirsch. Firstly, in a wider sense, postmemory is not restricted to families (Hirsch, 2001, p. 9). Therefore, the author (2001, pp. 9 f. [my comment]) states, "through particular forms of identification, adoption, and projection, it can be more broadly [transgenerationally] available". Secondly, as Hirsch and Spitzer (2002, p. 257) explain in a later work, it is not exclusively linked to cultural or collective trauma but can also be applied to the adoption of positive nostalgic memories. The nostalgia 'transmitted' to the next generation expresses itself again in a "rootless" nostalgia, according to Hirsch and Spitzer (2002, p. 263) – "a longing driven by the layered postmemories". In this point, Hirsch and Spitzer differ from Landsberg, who seems to break with the distinction of 'real' and 'unreal' memories. Nevertheless, both concepts make nostalgia on the basis of adopted memories probable and allow this study to widen the reference-time of nostalgia, regarding both the level of the text and the level of reception.

3.1.4 Media memories

Media memories can somehow be located on each of the previously mentioned levels – individual, 'collective', and prosthetic. With the increase of leisure time in the modern era, "[t]he prominence of mass media cultural products in our lives has [...] been greatly accelerated" (Davis, 1979, p. 127). Furthermore, states Böhn (2007, p. 146), "they are also the object of our personal memory" and biography.

Hackl (2001, p. 88) shows, with reference to Du Bois (1993), that we remember media contents, such as television programmes, often better and recall them easier than, for example, personal family experiences. What is remembered, Hoffmann and Kutscha state (2010, p. 226) in the context of films, may have once caused intensive emotions. Aside from this, media memories may work as cues or anchors by which recipients recall emotions that were, for instance, related to the reception (Hoffmann and Kutscha, 2010, p. 226) or whole reception situations (Böhn, 2007). As Böhn (2007, p. 145) argues, "the circumstances of the moment of our first hearing [of a special song] will often be remembered when we here the same music again". The same applies to television programmes. Perhaps every reader of this book has a personal experience with this kind of remembrance. Thus, as O'Sullivan (1991, p. 163) shows, early television memory "tends to function as a point of symbolic, biographical reference". The media memories are entwined with our personal life stories. Apart from memories of specific programmes, the author shows that "[m]any of the recollections of TV in the period appear to function as 'markers' for remembered domestic situations or celebrations involving particular relatives or friendships" (O'Sullivan, 1991, p. 170) but also for "historical events and process" (O'Sullivan, 1991, p. 172).

Later, in a further step, media memories become one crucial factor that generates the previously mentioned fluidity between the memories of different "we-groups". As Kompare notes in the national context of the U.S.A., "some of [...][the] country's most prominent collective memories of the last 50 years have centered on television" (Kompare, 2005, p. 106). Therefore to continue without the disputed term 'collective', it can be assumed that media memories reinforce so-called 'we-identities' by, as it can be said with Palacio (2008, p. 11 [o.t.]), "unifying" recipients against those who do not know the programmes.

"Past television clearly functions in this manner today, as a cultural and historical resource for all generations. It is widely used as a cultural touchstone, instantly signifying particular times." (Kompare, 2005, p. 103)

This point does not only apply to the national level. As shown by several studies in the context of The Global Media Project (Volkmer, 2006), media experiences differ between different age groups. According to Volkmer (2006a, p. 6), "media has shaped generational-specific worldviews and very particular notions of the global public space". Media events, such as royal weddings or football World Cups, "are often of considerable interest to many populations" and become integrated in the memories of a 'global' audience (Moran, 2010, p. 14).[3] Not to mention that formats today, more than ever, are traded worldwide (Moran, 2010, p. 15). With Moragas and Prado (2000), it can be assumed that in a European, respectively Spanish/German, context this applies particularly to American fiction – the "common denominator of European taste" (Moragas and Prado, 2000, p. 230 [o.t.]). Additionally, the internet shares content throughout the world, so that "generations growing up worldwide dispose of media-shaped 'experiential contexts'" (Volkmer, 2005, p. 235 [o.t.]).

Finally, media memories are strongly linked to the mediation of memories – the bridge to what has been previously described under the terms prosthetic or postmemory (see Chapter 3.1.3). Also, in this case, the process cannot be restricted to the national level. As Lipsitz (1994, p. 5) puts it, "consumers of electronic mass media can experience a common heritage with people they have never seen, they can acquire memories of a past to which they have no geographic or biological connection".

3.2 PHYSICAL AND DIGITAL ARCHIVES

It has been shown that memory – from individual and social to cultural memory – relies on the interchange of narratives between different individuals and "we-groups". As Klippel and Winkler (1994, pp. 125 f.) stress, in non-literate societies this interchange has been organised via oral transmission of repeated texts. "Literate

---

3   The term 'global' as it is used by Volkmer should here not be interpreted in a very strict sense. Maybe 'widely shared' would also be suitable. Moran argues for instance that "[w]hile the collective audience for such events fall into the billions, nevertheless there are viewers and even nations bypassed by such coverage. Global television seems as much a phantom as local television." (Moran, 2010, p. 14)

societies additionally build up storages or archives, in which media documents are collected and are made available again for the individual production of sense" (Schmidt, 1991, p. 46 [o.t.]). As various authors (see e.g. Assmann and Assmann, 1990 cited in Schmidt, 1991, p. 46; Innis, 1972, p. 10) highlight, consequently the range of the individual memory is extended, and it becomes "verifiable" (Innis, 1972, p. 10).

Nevertheless, as states Wirth (2005, pp. 17 f.), the pure existence of archives does not mean that everything is collected and that everything is accessible to everybody. First, only the things that are seen as valuable from the perspective of the specific culture at a certain time are stored (Wirth, 2005, pp. 17 f.; Groys, 2004, p. 56). Secondly, regarding access, "public, private, and secret archives" have to be distinguished (Wirth, 2005, p. 18 [o.t.]). Furthermore, authors (Wirth, 2005, pp. 25 f.; Edmondson, 1997) refer to further difficulties of the restricted physical durability and format obsolescence. It is for that reason that many scholars note that archives today are rather "'dynamic systems of self-organized liquid data'" (Assmann, 2001 cited in Wirth, 2005, p. 25 [o.t.]) with the internet as the epitome of this development (Wirth, 2005, p. 25).

3.2.1 Television archives in Germany and Spain

In regards to television, the previously outlined scenario is indeed quite fitting. As Nelson and Cooke (2010, p. xviii) highlight, "[m]any archives remain patchy in their coverage and difficult to access, and some material is, of course, irretrievably lost because transmitted live prior to recording technologies". On the example of archive access to German *Fernsehspiele* (television plays), Anderson (2010, p. 101) points out "numerous dilemmas for the prospective researcher" to access archive material. In general, states Anderson (2010, p. 94 [italic emphasis in the original]), three categories of difficulties appear – "*incompleteness, insularity, regionalisation*". Only the first is important for the research presented here.

Aside from the fact that early television was a live-medium and only partly recorded on film (Ernst, 2007, pp. 168 f.), throughout television history and particularly in the period between 1950 and 1960, both in East and in West Germany preservation was not always a priority (Anderson, 2010, p. 93). With reference to Pollert (1996), Anderson (2010) notes that private broadcasters, permitted in Germany since the early 1980s, "have long refused to commit themselves to archive their own materials for reasons other than their own commercial interests" (Anderson, 2010, p. 93). In other cases "some records have been deleted, destroyed, or lost" (Anderson, 2010, p. 95). A legal depository as it exists for the publication of books does not exist for film (see Orbanz, 2007, p. 83; Lersch, 2008). However, in 2006, a German Television Museum was founded (Stiftung Deutsche Kinemathek,

2012). Although the museum also has to do without several documents and struggles with licences, copyrights and a lack of financing (Niggemeier, 2006), the institution nevertheless has contributed to the legitimacy of television as a cultural value. At least public service broadcasters have been more ambitious regarding the online availability of current programmes. However, the so-called *Telemedienkonzept* "requires that ARD and ZDF remove certain videos from their web portals after a period of time" (Berthold et al., 2010, p. 14).

The state of television archives in Spain is not very different. Despite the fact that regular transmissions of Spanish television have officially existed since 1956 (Palacio, 2001, p. 31) – the same year that magnetic recording has been made possible by Ampex[4] (see also Fernández-Quijada and Fortino, 2009, p. 546) – in 2008 the archive situation was far from being perfect, and access to historical programme sources was extremely difficult (Palacio, 2008, p. 12). As described by Palacio (2008, p. 12), as well as the access to the archives of the public broadcaster *Radiotelevisión Española* (RTVE) being restricted, its first Documentation Centre was not launched until 1982. "[A] huge amount of previous material has not been catalogued or is missing" (Palacio, 2008, p. 12 [o.t.]). This was a similar situation with private television channels, which were launched in 1990 (Palacio, 2008, p. 12). Today, the state of affairs is only slightly different. There are few regulations that obligate the channels to store their programmes – not to mention the non-existence of a legal deposit (Fernández-Quijada and Fortino, 2009, p. 546). A public television archive still does not exist, nor does a public television museum.

Nevertheless, television did arrive in the museum. For example the exhibitions *TV World. Television Culture* (*Món TV. La cultura de la televisió*) launched in 1999 in the *Centre de Cultura Contemporània de Barcelona* (CCCB) and *Are You Ready For TV?* (*¿Estáis listos para la televisión?*) launched in 2010 in the *Museum of Contemporary Art of Barcelona* (MACBA) can be named here.[5] As Fernández-

---

4   Palacio hints to the fact that Spanish television was live until around the mid-1960s (Palacio, 2008, p. 145).

5   While the first exhibition dealt with the representation of reality in television and its social impact and contained everything from television series, documentaries and newsreels to game shows (Balló, 1999), the latter approaches television from a rather highbrow perspective, which is mainly reflected in its selection. The exposition, as Martínez highlights, has "no museological strategy" (Martínez, 2010a, p. 8) nor does it want to gather the popular Spanish television heritage. Instead it presents a choice of worldwide works of artists and philosophers, such as Jean-Luc Godard, Guy Debord, Richard Serra, Carlota Fay Schoolman, or Andy Warhol, who, as the curator suggests, "were, or are, outside of their time" (Martínez, 2010) and only "pretending to be television" (Martínez, 2010a, p. 7). This is surely far from the "validation of the popular" as it is, for instance, described by Kompare (2005, p. 102) in the US-American context.

Quijada and Fortino (2009, p. 545) explain, the private channels still show little ambition in preserving and making the heritage of television available. However, since 2006 the legal obligations for the public service broadcasters have become stricter, obligating RTVE to "digitise, conserve and preserve" the archive and to facilitate its availability (Ministerio de la Presidencia, 2006 [o.t.]; Fernández-Quijada and Fortino, 2009, p. 546). This also applies to the accessibility of current content via the internet. While public broadcasters grant access to an orderly collection of complete versions of their contents in part up to the 1980s[6], on the internet only some of the private channels' more recent programmes can be accessed (see e.g. Antena 3, 2012; Telecinco, 2012). Apart from that, internet portals such as YouTube or storage media such as DVDs have at least supported a selective and partly fragmented access to the television archives both in Germany and in Spain.

3.3 CONCLUSION

As shown previously regarding the memory discourse, memory is not an archive but instead is conceptualised as something that undergoes permanent reconstruction. Built up around the second year of an individual and especially active between the age of 10 and 30 (Eysenck and Keane, 2005, p. 263), its structuring and recall is influenced by aspects such as personal goals and social expectations (Eysenck and Keane, 2005, pp. 269, 263). With Assmann (2006) it can be stated that there are no clear distinguishable boundaries between, for instance, individual memory and the memory of one's family. Thus, as Assmann highlights, "[a]lready the memory of individual experience is underlined and interwoven with the experiences of others, since it is based on the communicative exchange and therefore depends on inter-linkage and confirmation" (Assmann, 2006, p. 59 [o.t.]). Scholars from the *Popular Memory Group* highlight that "[p]rivate memories cannot [...] be readily unscrambled from the effects of dominant historical discourses" (Popular Memory Group, 1982, p. 211).

The membership and participation in different "we-groups" (Assmann, 2006, p. 59) is of particular relevance. Non-existent personal experiences may be replaced by "secondary experience" (Assmann, 2006, pp. 59 f. [o.t.]). Furthermore, there is evidence that memories may also be subsequently 'created' by using mass media. Therefore, media contents are not only part of personal memories as they are part of the viewers' personal lives or of the memory of different "we-groups" and work as

---

6   See e.g. the coverage of *Cuéntame cómo pasó* on *RTVE A la carta* which goes back to 2002 (RTVE a la carta, 2011). In 2011, the collection of TVE's daily news *Telediario* reaches back to 14 April.2008 and offers complete versions (RTVE a la carta, 2011a). Apart from that, an archive with 'historical' pieces is accessible (RTVE a la carta, 2011b).

triggers and anchors for personally made experiences or group experiences; they may also serve in order to 'transmit' memories of actions and events that have not been personally experienced by an individual. In order to explain this, this study draws on two theoretical approaches; Hirsch's (2001) concept of "postmemories" and Landsberg's (1995) concept of the so-called "prosthetic memories". They describe the possibility of a trans-generational and even a trans-cultural adoption of memories. Finally, it can be stated what Ebbrecht (2008), with reference to Welzer (2005), highlights:

"Memory traces of personal experiences which have taken place in a different space-time context, the revival of personal emotions or emotions conveyed by the media, such as the import of 'foreign' memories merge into the memory experience (see Welzer 2005, 40)." (Ebbrecht, 2008, p. 90 [o.t.])

Using this background, several assumptions and conclusions concerning nostalgia can be made both regarding the textual part of nostalgia and the part of reception. First, considering that autobiographical memory is especially active during the so-called "reminiscence bump" (Eysenck and Keane, 2005, pp. 263 ff.), we may suggest that nostalgia towards that time span is likewise explicitly active. This also coincides with the work of the sociologist Davis (1979, p. 60) who notes that late teenager-years are often an object of nostalgia. Additionally, Kumar et al. (2006, p. 219) observed in the context of *The Global Media Project* that the nostalgic colouring of memory may increase with the temporal distance. Both points have to be kept in mind with regard to the reception study. Secondly, the notion of multiple nostalgias has an additional meaning. It cannot only refer to the reflective meta-levels, such as the question of whether a text explores or a viewer experiences a simple, a reflexive or an interpreted kind of nostalgia (Davis, 1979, pp. 18 ff.) but also refers to the question of whether nostalgia is personal or 'shared', and whether it is based on 'real' or 'prosthetic' memories.[7] Therefore, this section on memory could help to underpin and examine major aspects and help to clarify some discrepancies and uncertainties.

Firstly, since the boundaries between the different memories are vague, it is difficult, if not impossible, to distinguish whether nostalgia is individual or 'shared'. Secondly, even though they are shared, only a few memories, such as 'national' memory, are 'collective' in the strict sense (Assmann, 2006, p. 36). This is also congruent with works on transcultural media research (Hepp, 2009). As Hepp (2009) states, it is on the level of "nation" and "association of nations" where "territorial

---

7   In consumer studies Havlena and Holak "discuss nostalgia imagery, using a four-way typology - personal, interpersonal, cultural, and virtual - based on two dimensions related to: (1) whether the nostalgia is personal or collective in nature and (2) whether it results from direct or indirect experience" (Holak and Havlena, 1998, p. 224).

cultural thickenings" appear. Therefore, what Davis (1979, p. 122) calls "collective nostalgia" shall in the course of the study rather be broken down into several 'we'-nostalgias. Only Boym's "restorative nostalgia", which "evokes national past and future" (Boym, 2001, p. 49), will be seen as collective in a strict sense.

Since Europe, which will be important regarding the country-comparison in this study, can apparently only be partly seen as a memory-based cultural community (Assmann, 2006, pp. 250 ff.), it can be assumed that on this level there will be less 'shared' nostalgia. On the other hand, with the rise of the 'global' audience and the rise of trans-border media memories[8], trans-border or global nostalgias can be expected (see Feyerabend 2009, p. 5). As Feyerabend (2009, p. 5) states, a "general cultural nostalgia, which functions not only on a national level but indeed on a more global or trans-national scope" becomes possible. According to Hepp (2009), next to "diaspora", "social movements" and "religious communities", it is "popular cultural communities" where "deterritorial cultural thickening" (Hepp, 2009) appears.

The term *prosthetic memory* or *postmemory* is also relevant here. In order to be able to define some possible time spans of nostalgia texts and target groups of nostalgia, the question was whether nostalgia only refers to first-hand experiences, or if they may also be based on a kind of adopted memory. With the theories on prosthetic memory and postmemory, the possibility of nostalgia on the basis of a 'transmitted' memory has been supported. Apart from that, the 'transmission' of nostalgia (see Hirsch and Spitzer, 2002, p. 257) has been shown to be possible as well. In this context, both those series temporarily located in the distant past and those located in a more recent past could work as a basis for memory-related nostalgia.

Media contents play a crucial role here. They are not only the provider of a basis of 'shared' experiences. Feyerabend highlights:

"[A] member of the so-called 'Generation X' can watch the same film and – in spite of not having shared the filmed experience (which, in this case, takes place before the viewer is born) – relate to the content and harbor a nostalgic notion for one or several aspects for what is seen: for example, a fondness for Marilyn Monroe, interest in the filmic genre, an adoration of 1950s culture, music, architecture, and so on, all of which will, at least through the 'mediating' experience of the mass media and postmemory, have entered his/her mnemonic archive." (Feyerabend, 2009, pp. 46 f.)

They are part of the viewers' personal lives or of the memory of different "we-groups" and may thus be the object of nostalgia, they may work as triggers for personally made experiences or group experiences, but they may also serve in order

---

8　Apart from that Higson also refers to the fact that "cross-cultural intertextuality [...] is such a strong feature of contemporary aesthetics" (Higson, 2003, p. 6).

to 'transmit' memories of actions and events that have not been personally experienced by the subject and provoke nostalgia on that level.

A viewer may be nostalgic towards aspects of a series or experiences made with it, he/she may be nostalgic towards an experience or situation whereby the series works as a cue or anchor to recall that[9], and it may help provoking nostalgia towards, for example, the 1960s as something that has been experienced in the course of the reception of a film about the 1960s.

Finally, the section contained a sub-chapter about physical/digital archives. They are important for nostalgia in two respects: on the one hand they make the contents of the past available for the (nostalgic) reuse in the present (see e.g. Fischer, 1980, p. 196; Huyssen, 1995 cited in Hutcheon, 2000, p. 197). On the other hand, they play a part in the valorisation of the past (see e.g. Kompare, 2005, pp. 101 ff.), a matter that will be relevant in the context of nostalgia and reruns and remakes. Not only regarding the reception, but also regarding the text, it will have to be clarified in which way the different nostalgia 'genres' relate to the archive, respectively to memory. In this respect we may also talk about multiple nostalgias, and this chapter will be of importance to the later analysis.

---

9   Davis explains this in the context of the interrelations between personal and 'collective' memory: "[A] nostalgic summoning of 'everybody's favorite song from 1943' (essentially a collectively oriented symbol) may inwardly shade off into some very private reminiscences of a particular romance in a particular place on a particular day, replete with special fragrances, sounds, and visual traces" (Davis, 1979, p. 124).

4. Aesthetic emotions – on nostalgia's relationship to the present

As a last step towards the analysis of nostalgia in television, this section draws on emotions as part of the film and television studies' discourse. After briefly drawing on the history of the discipline in general, it shall first be shown in which way nostalgia fits the definition of emotions, and then the different ways of the audiovisual text to provoke emotive reactions in its viewers shall be studied. Tan's categorisation of (sub-) types of emotions experienced by the film viewer will serve as a basis for the description. As Tan (1996, pp. 1 ff.) explains, in comparison to scholars who predominantly studied emotions in relation to single film genres, his approach attempts to give a more general, exemplary insight into the "emotional potential" of film, which is what makes it also transferable to television. According to Tan (1996, p. 81), "[t]he first classification of film emotions is related to the aspect of the stimulus on which the situational meaning is based, namely, either the fictional action or the film as artefact". In a second classification the emotions are "characterized according to the criterion of empathy" (Tan, 1996, p. 82).

4.1 THE DISCOURSE OF EMOTIONS IN FILM AND TELEVISION STUDIES

While psychology has dealt with emotions since its beginnings, the investigation of emotions in film, television, and media studies is relatively young (Tröhler and Hediger, 2005, pp. 7 ff.). Thus, in early film studies up to the 1950s the legitimisation of "film as art" was central (Tröhler and Hediger, 2005, p. 7 [o.t.]). Also in later strands within film theory, Tröhler and Hediger (2005, p. 10) refer, for instance, to Bordwell's (1989) cognitive approach; the study of emotions was less important. Today, many scholars focus their study on the emotive reactions on film. In one group, Tröhler and Hediger (2005) refer to Serge Daney, Pascal Bonitzer, Raymond Bellour, Jacques Aumont, Nicole Brenez, Laura Marks or Giuliana Bruno, and in a separate group they refer to authors such as Noël Carroll, Murray Smith, Ed Tan, Peter Wuss, Torben Grodal, Linda Williams, Christine Noll Brinckmann, and Hans Jürgen Wulff. Following the authors' approach (Tröhler and Hediger, 2005, pp. 10 ff.), the first group can be seen as the 'philosophical-aesthetic' strand of study, while the latter belongs to the 'psychological-cognitivist' one, which will be predominantly applied in this section. It may be assumed that most of the assessments made in the context of film are likewise transferable to television (see e.g. Tan, 1996, p. 37).

Besides, these works have also influenced the study about emotions in media and television studies. As shown by Krotz (1993, pp. 91 f.), in media and television studies, emotional affects are investigated as a significant aspect of the reception of television. In the early 1990s, Krotz (1993, p. 94) referred to a range of scholars who deal with the subject of emotions in the context of television, among them Herta Sturm, Herta Herzog, Jan-Uwe Rogge, Dolf Zillmann or Saxer and Märki-Koepp. In describing television as a "flow of feeling", Krotz (1992, p. 115) himself declares the emotive aspect of television as a defining factor of the medium. A broad range of writings from articles to chapters to complete monographs (see e.g. Prado, 1999; Mikos, 2001, pp. 110 ff.; Döveling, 2005; Bartsch et al., 2007; Döveling et al., 2011) shows that also in more recent times, the interest in emotions and television is just as significant.

4.2 CHARACTERISTICS OF EMOTIONS

A lot of literature (see Zillmann, 2004, pp. 102 ff.; Barlett and Gentile, 2011, p. 60) usually distinguishes between affect, emotions and moods. According to Barlett and Gentile (2011, p. 60), Larson (2000) "defines affect as a feeling tone that is evaluative, and can be either positive or negative, and comprises both mood and emotions". It is therefore a sort of overall category. Moods are not directed towards an object (Tan, 1996, p. 204; Zillmann, 2004, p. 108); they are characterised by a long duration and are also often described as having low affect intensity (Zillmann, 2004, p. 108). Emotions, on the other hand, are characterised by high affect intensity, shorter duration, and a higher directedness towards an object or a certain circumstance (Zillmann, 2004, p. 102, p. 108; Eder, 2005, pp. 227 ff.).

Frijda (1986, pp. 453 ff.), who represents the so-called appraisal theory, now assumes that objects or circumstances acquire the characteristics of a stimulus because they are respectively 'appraised' on the side of the subject. Tan (1996, p. 44), notes that the "emotional system is geared toward establishing the relevance of certain situations for the concerns of the individual and, if such relevance exists, to enforce the priority of cognition and action in accordance with those concerns". According to the "patterns of appraisal" (Mangold et al., 2001, p. 167 [o.t.]), different emotions emerge. From this, we can state that (1) any "emotion signals a concern" (Tan, 2002, p. 32), and (2) any emotion may be defined by either "the consciousness of a change in action readiness[1], which is experienced as motivated or caused by situations that have been appraised in a specific manner" (Tan, 1996, p. 47 with reference to Frijda (1986)) or by "the nature of the emotional object" (Frijda, 1986, p. 73). As Mikos (2001, p. 111) notes, the social component of emotions also has to be taken into consideration. According to the author, emotions are always related to the "social reality of the individuals" since they arise in "situational contexts of social interactions" (Mikos, 2001, p. 111 [o.t.]).

As Zillmann (2004, p. 104) describes it in regards to single emotions among scholars, there is only consensus about the so-called basic emotions of fear and anger. While Plutchik (1962, 1980), as cited in Zillmann (2004, p. 104), additionally identifies joy, trust, surprise, sadness, disgust and anticipation, Ekman (1982, 1984) – referring to facial expressions – names six basic states of emotions, which are, apart from fear and anger, happiness and sadness, surprise and disgust (Zillmann, 2004, p. 105). Emotions that are not considered to be basic are often described as specialisations of the latter (Tan, 2005, p. 267), or as "mixtures or blends" (Frijda, 1986, p. 72). Nevertheless, not all theorists agree on this point. According to Frijda (1986, p. 72) "most important nonbasic emotions cannot be so defined". The scholar (1986, p. 73) rather stays with his twofold model of definition, consisting of the factors 'action-readiness' and 'emotional object'. This model shall also be referred to in order to further scrutinise nostalgia as an emotion.

4.2.1 Nostalgia as an emotion

Nostalgia is mentioned as an emotion by various authors: While Furno-Lamude and Anderson (1999, p. 371), with reference to Starobinski (1966), describe nostalgia as "an emotional upheaval, related to the workings of memory", Johnson and Multhaup (1992, p. 39) list it among other "[e]motions or affective responses", and Stearns (2008, p. 21) discusses nostalgia in the context of historical research on emotions. Referring to Gardner (1985), Holak and Havlena (1998, p. 218) describe that "nostalgia may be experienced as an intense emotion, it is also likely to take the form of a weaker mood that colors the individual's experience".

In general, also from the perspective of a personal experience, it may be argued that nostalgia fits the criteria of the definition of emotions. Like other emotive reactions, nostalgia, which is provoked, for example, during the course of watching a television series, may be temporarily limited and directed towards an object or circumstance. You are nostalgic because of something. As argued by Frijda (1986,

---

1   "Emotional action tendencies [...] are states of readiness to achieve or maintain a given kind of relationship with the environment." (Frijda, 1986, p. 75)

p. 73), nostalgia, as other emotions like jealousy or shame, is even primarily defined by its object, which, according to the author (1986, p. 76), can be loosely described as 'something past'. Therefore, it cannot be "recognized from expression alone" and its categorisation is "highly dependent upon which objects – sort of events – are being distinguished and considered important by the environment providing the categorization" (Frija, 1986, pp. 73 f.). In this context, Frijda (1986, p. 74) highlights the importance of a consideration of "cultural differences" regarding the object-defined emotions. The "action tendency" is here locatable on the "mental plane" (Frijda, 1986, p. 76).

"Nostalgia is awareness that something past, while desired, cannot be regained, except by maintaining proximity in thought. If search tendency nevertheless gets the upper hand, it turns into recurring grief; if impotence with respect to desire is added, it turns into belated painful suffering." (Frijda, 1986, p. 76)

Regarding this background, a study of nostalgia in the context of aesthetic emotions is important and makes sense. However, when, as Holak and Havlena (1998) suggest, nostalgia may likewise appear in form of a mood, concepts on film and television and mood have at least to be kept in mind in the course of the film and television analysis and the reception study.

4.3 AESTHETIC EMOTIONS

Referring to the "appraised object" (Visch et al., 2010, p. 1440), Tan (1996) draws the basic distinction between "fiction emotions" or "fictional world emotions"; the so–called "F emotions", respectively "FW emotions", and "artefact emotions", also called "A emotions". While the stimulus in the first case is "rooted in the fictional world and the concerns addressed by that world" (Tan, 1996, p. 65), in the latter case it is connected to a concentration on the film as an artefact (Tan, 1996, pp. 64 f.).

4.3.1 Fiction emotions

Regarding Tan (1996), one can state that F emotions dominantly arise in the reception of the traditional feature film or fiction television programmes. Here the so-called diegetic effect – "the illusion of being present in the fictional world" (Tan, 1996, p. 52) – states that the viewers first of all concentrate on what occurs in the fictional world of the film (Tan, 1996, p. 81). "[R]ealistic effects", notes Bruun Vaage (2007, p. 190), ensure that the viewers "may become immersed in the fictional world". At the same time, the text conceals its constructedness (Tan, 1996, p. 53, p. 81; see also Ang, 1986, p. 50).

F emotions are generally described as so-called "witness emotions" (see e.g. Tan, 1996, p. 82; Schneider, 2005, p. 145; Bruun Vaage, 2007, p. 189). When the emotion is rooted in an 'empathetic understanding' of a protagonist, it is related to so-called 'empathetic F emotions' (Tan 1996, p. 82). In the case that "the focus of the situational meaning is limited to the event itself, as a scene" (Tan, 1996, p. 175), the F emotions are non-empathetic. According to the literature (Tan, 1996; Schneider, 2005), they may be provoked by 'spectacles' such as the look of a character (Schneider, 2005, p. 145), a "breathtaking landscape" or "indoor spaces that most people have never been privileged to enter" (Tan, 1996, p. 83) as they occur, for instance, in costume dramas or historical dramas (Tan, 1996, p. 175). As examples for emotions that may appear as non-empathetic F emotions, Tan (1996, p. 175) lists enjoyment, excitement or horror. Furthermore, according to the author, "fear of witnessing certain fictional events or a desire to watch other events" (Tan, 1996, pp. 82 f.) is non-empathetic. Here it also becomes apparent that the emotions may be strongly related to genres (Tan, 1996, pp. 175 f.), as it is also mentioned by other authors (Carroll, 1999, pp. 34 ff.; Wuss, 2005, pp. 219 ff.; Mikos, 2008, p. 33). Therefore, the versed viewer of horror films, for instance, knows that the murderer, who has been overpowered at the end of the film, will probably get up again to raise his axe against the hero. In this case, the viewer may feel fear without being empathetically involved. Thus, genres are not only connected to certain emotions – "comedies are funny, dramas are sad, horror films are frightening" (Bartsch, 2007, p. 124), they also "generate[...] narrative expectations (Grodal, 1997) and emotional moods (Tan, 1996)" (Visch et al. 2010, p. 1440).

4.3.1.1 Empathy

Since, as Tan notes (1996, p. 82), "the action in the traditional feature film narration is realized by protagonists who display human traits and whose goals and fate are of interest to the film viewer", F emotions are mostly empathetic. Above all, this relates to film genres such as the melodrama or the psychological drama where "the explication of the meaning of events for the characters enjoy primacy" (Tan, 1996, p. 176) and there is no room for "intellectual distancing" (Ang, 1985, p. 62).

However, a consistent definition of the phenomenon does not exist. According to Wuss (2005, p. 217 [o.t.]), theoretical attempts reach from "'Fremdverstehen'" [understanding others] to "'Teilhabe an den Emotionen anderer'" [sharing the emotions of others]. Wuss himself is of the opinion that an understanding of "empathy as 'empathetic understanding' seems to be most productive" (Wuss, 2005, p. 218 [o.t.]). Similarly, Tan defines empathy as "all the cognitive operations on the part of the viewer that lead to a more complete understanding of the situational meaning for the character" (Tan, 1996, p. 172). The empathetic emotion, he argues, "is characterized by the fact that the situational meaning structure of the situation for a character is part of the meaning for the viewer" (Tan, 1996, p. 174). In doing this, the author draws a line of questioning that would be disputed by others, which is that this either signifies that the viewers share the same feelings with the character or not. While Neill argues, "if he [the protagonist] is in an emotional state, to empathize with him is to experience the emotion(s) that he experiences" (Neill, 1996, p. 176), other authors (see e.g. Bruun Vaage, 2007; Tan, 1996) open up various possibilities. Tan becomes more explicit, stating that

"a situation evoked in a character does not necessarily coincide with the empathetic emotion of the viewer. [...] And yet these emotions may be seen as empathetic, because their quality is determined by the viewer's understanding of the situational meaning for the character." (Tan, 1996, p. 174)

In any case, as Brinckmann (2005, p. 335) argues, the empathetic emotion normally embraces a lesser extent and is imbued with personal emotions of the viewers. While the viewer is normally immersed into the fictional world here, Bruun Vaage (2007, p. 195) shows with recourse on the literature that "[e]pisodes where personal memories and personal relevance are triggered may indeed often trigger self-reflection". In this case, explains Bruun Vaage (2007, p. 196), the fictional world is left.

According to Tan (1996, p. 82, p. 179), empathy embraces emotions such as hope, fear, admiration, shame, anger or sympathy. Tan (1996, p. 178) suggests the latter is a "precondition for empathetic enjoyment". Other authors (Brinckmann, 2005, p. 339; Eder, 2005, p. 237) argue that it is neither a necessary nor a sufficient condition for the empathetic emotion, even though a sympathetic disposition with a character facilitates empathy. This similarly applies to identification (see e.g. Brinckmann, 2005, p. 339), which is often mistakenly equalled with empathy.

Furthermore, the literature (see e.g. Brinckmann, 2005; Eder, 2005; Bruun Vaage 2008; Mikos, 2008) distinguishes narrative, dramaturgical and aesthetic devices that may reinforce the empathetic understanding both in film and on television. As Eder (2005, p. 237) highlights, audiovisual texts facilitate empathy, for instance, by impeding the tempo or with specific music. 'Subjectivation' via body language, voice or explicit expression of the emotions by gesture and mimic are named (Brinckmann, 2005, pp. 336 f.). Brinckmann (2005, p. 340) argues that close-ups of the character's face are specially important. Other devices that increase the 'subjectivation' are point-of-view structures, perception shots, "mind screen" or "stream-of-consciousness structures" (Brinckmann, 2005, p. 343; Bruun Vaage, 2008, p. 36; Mikos, 2008, pp. 227 f.).

In general, many scholars assume that it is not one factor alone that influences empathy, but rather the interplay of different aspects of the text: Wulff (2002), as cited in Mikos (2008, p. 32 [o.t.]), uses the so-called "'empathic field'" term. Here, he moves away from the character-centrism that is usually implied in the term empathy and rather points to the significance of the "symbolical contexts," inside which a character is integrated in a film and regarding to which empathy is developed (Wulff, 2002 referred to in Mikos, 2008, p. 32 [o.t.]). According to Brinckmann (2005, p. 341), the whole mise-en-scène may help the development of empathetic emotions. Català (2009, pp. 36 ff.) here also refers to a 'visualization of the inner world', respectively a 'visualization of emotions'. Morari (2007) describes a similar circumstance by using the term "'emotional objectivation'". According to the author (2007, p. 93), this kind of visual manifestation of emotions "represents the functional basis of visual metaphors, as well as non-narrative film structures". Again, these processes are thought to be especially dominant in the genre of melodramas (see e.g. Kappelhoff, 2005; Català, 2009).

4.3.1.1.1 Somatic empathy

Next to the empathy that is related to imagination, the literature (see e.g. Brinckmann, 2005, p. 335; Eder 2005, p. 237) distinguishes a more body-related type which has been called somatic empathy, motor mimicry or, when referring to facial reactions, facial feedback. This kind of empathy is less dependent on how we understand a situation, but is rather a kind of automatic reproduction of expressions related to the body (Eder, 2005, pp. 236 f.; Bruun Vaage, 2008, p. 29). Brinckmann (2005, p. 335 [o.t.]) refers to "'somatic empathy'" or "'motor mimicry'" "when we innervate muscular effort of another person in our own body". As well as film genres such as thriller, horror or action films (see e.g. Mikos, 2008, pp. 179 f.), which can also potentially provoke bodily reactions, some art forms put an emphasis on this kind of empathy. Elsaesser (2005, p. 426 [o.t.]) highlights so-called "body-centred performance art", such as the works of the Viennese actionist Vallie Export. Bennett (2003, pp. 29 ff.) refers to the "art of sense memory" of artists such as Dennis Del Favero.

4.3.2 Artefact emotions

The traditional feature film tends to hide its formal level. Nevertheless, as suggested by Tan (1996, p. 65), unexpected changes in the plot or incongruences in the presentation can "cause the viewer[s] to become aware of the telling of the story". Furthermore, according to Tan (2002, p. 38), "intense feelings caused by fictional representations" may provoke the viewers' awareness of the artefact level. In these cases, so-called A emotions or artefact emotions – "emotions that arise from concerns related to the artefact" (Tan, 1996, p. 65) – may be elicited. As typical artefact emotions, authors (Tan, 1996, p. 82; Visch et al., 2010, p. 1442) name admiration, astonishment, desire (for example for the return of a certain element) or enjoyment, focused, for instance, on "spectacular special effects, a sample of superb acting talent, and/or impressive photography or staging" (Tan, 1996, p. 65). When it comes from a focus on the film as an artefact, fascination may also appear as an A emotion (Visch et al., 2010, p. 1439). Since they are led by an enjoyment of the formal aspects of the text, Tan (1996 pp. 34 f., 65) supposes that A emotions most probably appear in recipients who are characterised by a certain "cinephilia" or film fandom.

4.3.2.1 Internal and external empathetic artefact emotions
Similar to the fiction emotions, which may arise as empathetic F emotions as well, A emotions have empathetic counterparts (Tan, 1996, p. 82). The first kind of this empathetic engagement relates to empathetic artefact emotions as an "external" aesthetic experience. According to Tan, it has "to do with synthetic proprioceptive activity, such as mirroring a certain type of movement on the screen" (Tan, 1996, p. 82). As an example, he refers to "the viewer's delight at a whirling camera movement in combination with a lyrical sound track" (Tan, 1996, p. 82).

Nevertheless, as stated by Bruun Vaage (2007, p. 193), "aesthetic engagement need not be external, it can also be internal to the fictional world". For this reason, the author (2007, p. 193) distinguishes a second kind of empathetic artefact emotions, which is also called "internal aesthetic engagement". In a first step, she refers to observations made by Grodal (2000), who had described that moments of narrative stagnancy can give way to "unfocused subjective associations" (Bruun Vaage, 2007, p. 193) on the side of the viewers. Apart from that, this kind of empathy may be evoked when "sensuous experience[s]", be it of characters or of events, are specially emphasised (Bruun Vaage, 2007, p. 193). While, Bruun Vaage states (2007, p. 193), "in fictional engagement the imagination is used in narrative playfulness, [...] in aesthetic experiences the imagination engages the spectator in sensuous playfulness". This means that upon seeing a cake, viewers may imagine the taste of it. Following the camera through an old attic, they could imagine how old things 'surrounding them' might smell.

4.4 MAKING THE TRANSFER TO NOSTALGIA IN TELEVISION: CONCLUSIONS, HYPOTHESES, AND TRANSITION TO THE ANALYTICAL PARTS

With regards to theories of emotions it was shown that nostalgia may be conceptualised as an emotion. It is also likely to appear as a mood. To further study the question of the cognitive and emotional components of nostalgia, this last section, on the way to the analytical part, presented the theoretical basis of aesthetic emotions in order to combine it with nostalgia. We have seen that in the course of watching a film or a television programme various different emotions, so-called aesthetic emotions, may be provoked. Depending on the object of appraisal (Visch et al., 2010, p. 1440), these emotions may be classified as so-called fiction emotions or fictional world emotions, which are empathetic F emotions and somatic-empathetic F emotions on the one hand, and artefact emotions, including internal and external artefact emotions on the other hand. Moods are also relevant to the investigation of film since (1) the aspiration of a mood may be a motive to watch a film or a television programme (Tan, 1996, p. 204) – key word mood management (Zillmann, 1988) – (2) the genres generate moods (Tan, 1996), and (3) moods may lay the ground for some emotions and inhibit others (Tan, 1996, p. 204).

If we transfer this to nostalgia, we can make the following conclusions and assumptions. Regarding mood characteristics – generally since genres generate emotional moods (Tan, 1996) – it has to be seen if nostalgia 'genres' exist. Since "[m]ood is a disposition that encourages certain emotions" (Tan, 1996, p. 204), they can be expected to influence nostalgia in the course of the reception. In the context of period dramas, Cardwell (2002) has already taken important steps in this direction, as will be further explained in the following sub-chapter (4.4.1).

Later, regarding the emotive characteristics of nostalgia, first assumptions can be made, which later have to be compared with the existing nostalgia discourse. It can be assumed that depending on the respective object that is in the centre of the (nostalgic) appraisal, different nostalgias can be distinguished. First, on a non-empathetic fictional level it can be assumed that nostalgia may for instance be provoked by a nostalgic fictional world – a fictional world that enables its viewers to immerse into past beauty, highlighted against an unsatisfactory present, and so every level of the audiovisual text may contribute to the narration. Secondly, we can assume that nostalgia may arise as an empathetic F emotion – what with reference to Tan (1996) may be called 'empathetic F nostalgia'. According to Tan's (1996, p. 174) understanding of empathy, the empathetic emotion can, but does not have to, be concordant with the character's emotion. However, we may assume that an 'empathetic understanding' of a character may favour nostalgia in both cases. Viewers may, for example, 'share' nostalgic feelings with a nostalgic character or feel nostalgia due to an empathetic understanding of a protagonist who is not explicitly nostalgic.[2] Referring to concepts such as "emotional objectivation" and "visual narration", it is possible that nostalgia expresses itself on every level of the

---

2   See also Mikos (2008, p. 178 [o.t.]), who states: "It does not matter whether the actor feels the represented emotions or not, but it is the complex interplay of narrative, dramaturgy, aesthetic and design that creates the opportunity for the audience to feel empathy."

audiovisual text. From the mise-en-scène up to single formal devices, everything may be imbued with nostalgia. As many scholars refer to the fact that empathy normally ties in with analogue experiences from the spectator's own life and often leads to the uncoupling of similar personal emotions (Brinckmann, 2005) or provokes self-reflection (Bruun Vaage, 2007), a very personal nostalgia may presumably be related to empathy, which may also leave the fictional world, just as Bruun Vaage (2007, p. 196) describes it in the context of empathy and self-reflection in general. Since, as Frijda (1986, p. 73) argues, nostalgia belongs to a type of emotions that "have no characteristic facial expression and their presence cannot be recognized by means of expressive behaviour alone", the possibility of something like a 'somatic empathetic nostalgia' can probably be excluded.

Furthermore, many studies distinguish so-called artefact emotions. Here, a consideration in the context of nostalgia seems appropriate. We may assume that 'artefact nostalgia' may be triggered by increased attention on certain stylistic elements that have already lost their dominance – maybe the longing desire for the return of a certain artefact or an experience (another A emotion) that was related to it. As Tan (1996, pp. 34 f.) argues, artefact emotions probably arise in people who have a special affection for the medium. Therefore, in case of nostalgia and television, a target group of very 'telephile' viewers could be imagined. However, it can at least be assumed that in regards to television, everybody who was a child of his/her time could be an 'expert'. This will undergo further scrutiny in the reception section of this study.

Lastly, the literature distinguishes between external and internal empathetic artefact emotions. According to Tan (1996, p. 82), external empathetic artefact emotions arise, for example, in the course of "synthetic proprioceptive activity". Nostalgia as an emotion, which is primarily defined by its object (Frijda, 1986, p. 73), can thus be assumed not to be relevant in this context. The case is different regarding the internal empathetic artefact emotions. As Bruun Vaage (2007, p. 193) argues, the internal aesthetic engagement is a "sensuous playfulness". Therefore "unfocussed subjective associations" (Bruun Vaage, 2007, p. 193) may come from this. Consequently, most probably nostalgic sentiments may arise in this context. It is additionally important that on every one of these levels personal memories and emotions are interwoven. As Mikos notes, "emotions as situational quality of experience and sensual experience" always rely "on earlier experiences, which have been important for the life story of the audiences" (Mikos, 2008, p. 32 [o.t.]). In case that they prevail, we can assume that what I would call viewers' 'own' nostalgia may be most dominant.

Regarding empathetic F emotions, respectively 'empathetic F nostalgia', and also regarding internal aesthetic engagement, this has already been established. According to Mikos, "visual correspondence" between the "scenic arrangement of an audiovisual text or situation" and the memory of a bygone experience can elicit the reawakening of emotions that have been related to this memory (Mikos, 2001, p. 114 [o.t.]). Certain affects could be reactivated with "corresponding situations in the film and television texts" (Mikos, 2008, p. 33 [o.t.]). In the broader context of 'prosthetic memories', Ebbrecht (2008, p. 93 [o.t.]) describes a similar process that mainly concerns the fictional world and where viewers "synchronise" autobiographical experiences with the audiovisual texts. The development of nostalgia is also possible here.

The question now is: Where do we locate the 'object' of the nostalgic longing? When it is part of the fictional world, such as a positively viewed past that is put in contrast with a negative present, the gap between the prelapsarian and the postlapsarian world, which according to Tannock (1995) is so essential for nostalgia, is situated inside the text and the nostalgia, so we can assume, may be elicited in every viewer who gives the text this connotative meaning and who is capable of feeling this nostalgia.[3] In other cases, such as 'F nostalgia' as a longing towards a lost emotion, or nostalgia directed towards a memory that has been triggered by the text, the nostalgia can be assumed to arise individually, respectively in different "we-groups". Referring to the background of memory studies, here we can ask to what extent the respective object of nostalgia is 'shared'. When it is about media memories, for example, a 'shared' nostalgia between Germany and Spain would be very likely.

Nevertheless, when we look at the emotive aspects of nostalgia, differences between Spain and Germany can be expected. Although the basic emotions seem to be similar in different cultures (Krotz, 1993, p. 104; Smith, 2005, p. 303; Ekman, 1982 cited in Tan, 2005, p. 266), this seems not always to be the case regarding the more specific emotions. As Krotz argues, "feeling depends [...] on cultural, social and personality-related determinants" (Krotz, 1993, p. 98 [o.t.]). Furthermore Mikos (2001, p. 111) as previously mentioned, highlights the respective social realities of the recipients as determinative factors for the development of emotions. Therefore the meaning of the word nostalgia is the same both in Germany and in Spain. The question whether this also applies to the cognitive and emotional aspects of nostalgia will have to be examined.

In this context, the statement that nostalgia is multiple gains another element of significance: the term relates neither only to the meta level, i.e. whether nostalgia is simple, reflexive or interpreted (Davis, 1979, pp. 18 ff.), nor to the question of whether the nostalgia is personal or "we-group" related, 'real' or "prosthetic" or if it is based upon an object represented in the viewer's memory or physically visible, but

---

3   As Tan (1996, p. 66) writes, "With respect to the fictional world, the cognitive coding of the stimulus requires little more than a knowledge of the world, which almost everyone who is part of Western society has at his or her disposal."

also points to the fact that nostalgia may arise in the context of the fictional world or may be artefact based. The theory of aesthetic emotions provides a basis to the question of how the television text may elicit these nostalgias. However, even though they appear with other labels, the developed categories are not all new. As will be shown in a further sub-chapter to this conclusion, they are in part congruent with the nostalgia discourse and may be complemented by the latter. On the other side, the identified categories will help to structure the discourse and fill some gaps where the discourse left questions open. Following this last revision and another short methodological reflection, the work will lead over to Part II, where the categories will be applied.

4.4.1 A combination of the approaches – towards the 'modules' of analysis

Apart from a few studies, such as from the film and television scholar Cardwell (2002) – which will be commented in more detail in this section – film and television studies do not consider the interrelation of textual and emotive aspects of nostalgia as being central to the investigation of the topic. Apart from Jameson (1991), who denies contemporary nostalgia any affective component, other authors, such as Sprengler (2011), investigate the topic in the context of "visual triggers" which, says Sprengler (2011, p. 33), "are often mobilized in a self-conscious way that signifies the idea of nostalgia without necessarily evoking an emotional response". Even though the side of reception is included in the conceptualisation and analysis of nostalgia – if not, it would make no sense when Sprengler talks of "visual triggers"; the evocation of nostalgia is mentioned throughout the work of Sprengler (2011), and also Dika refers in the context of *American Graffiti* to the fact that "the major question is one of reception" (Dika, 2003, p. 94) – the focus, however, stays on textual nostalgia.

Nevertheless, the consideration of previous studies is one major part in the context of this investigation. In the case that the affective side is not already part of the theoretical concepts, the outlined transfer of studies on aesthetic emotions to nostalgia can work as a bridge in whose context the existing studies may be made useful for an investigation of both 'mood' and mode, to consider both the cognitive and emotional components in nostalgia, and thus to provide a first step regarding the claim of scholars from the spectrum of cultural studies (see Grainge, 2002; Pickering and Keightley, 2006) for a combination of 'mood' and mode, in order to deal adequately with nostalgia.

An incorporation of these studies in the categories deduced from Tan and others is possible.[4] First, the identified categories are not all new for the nostalgia discourse where similar concepts can be observed, even though they have not been deduced from the theory of aesthetic emotions and even though they do not appear with the same labels. There are indeed many points of accordance, which makes this chapter in part a reconstruction of the existing discourse. At the same time this verifies the applicability of the categories. Secondly, together with other studies from the nostalgia discourse, the combination of the approaches will 'fill' the categories with the necessary content in order to make them useful for the analysis. Further refinements can be made with a view on the question of how the texts may work as triggers for nostalgia. Thirdly, the combination of the approaches facilitates the systematisation of the dispersed nostalgia discourse. It will help to refine the 'list' of possible nostalgia triggers, respectively help the 'search for the gap'.

Before the single categories shall be studied, Cardwell's (2002) notion of nostalgia as a mood will be considered. As previously mentioned, Cardwell (2002) is one of a few scholars within the film and television studies discourse of nostalgia who takes account of the emotive characteristics of nostalgia. In the context of heritage films, she emphasises that "the relationship and differences between textual style and mood (i.e. the style and mood that can be 'found' within a text) and extra-textual 'nostalgia' (broadly the audience's feeling or emotional response) remain unexplored" (Cardwell, 2002, p. 143). She further examines nostalgia under Smith's (1999) concept of moods, according to which "'the primary emotive effect of film is to create mood'" (Smith, 1999 cited in Cardwell, 2002, p. 145). From this, the author assumes that the nostalgic texts contain so-called "emotion markers" (Cardwell, 2002, p. 147) that reinforce the nostalgic mood again and again. For Cardwell (2002, p. 147), this supports the definition of the heritage genre as a nostalgia genre. This fact is also relevant in the course of this study, since genres affect moods and expectations of the viewers. Even though Cardwell only roughly refers to Tan's study (see Cardwell, 2002, p. 107) in order to identify the "emotion markers", and the categories introduced by the author are not as fully explored as in this study, her study interlocks with the present approach and can also be seen as one of its starting points.

---

4   Even though huge parts refer to Tan, his theory, it should be recalled, is utilised inside the framework of an approach oriented on 'reception aesthetics'. The television text is not seen as an 'emotion machine' in any case but rather as prefigurative for, as Prommer et al. (2003, p. 60 [o.t.]) put it in the context of a reception analysis on humour, "the cognitive and emotional engagement of the audiences". Apart from that, from Hediger (2002) it can be highlighted that "Tan described the film as an emotion machine, but this does not alter the fact that also he in the end treated the film as a programme that must be processed by the spectator: the emotions that are produced by the film remain attached to the cognitive processes of the viewers" (Hediger, 2002, p. 49 [footnote 16] [o.t.]).

In general, it may be stated that the basis for a potential 'F nostalgia' is frequently described in the discourse both in its empathetic or non-empathetic form. Scholars studying heritage films most often refer to a fictional world dominated by the nostalgic look at a better past which, it shall be argued in the light of aesthetic emotions, lays the ground for 'F nostalgia'. Wollen (1991), for instance, demonstrates a general nostalgia in heritage culture in the television series *Brideshead Revisited* (ITV, 1981) or films such as *A Passage to India* (Lean, 1984) or *A Room with a View* (Ivory, 1986). They "are all nostalgic in that pasts were represented as entirely better places" (Wollen, 1991, p. 186). This similarly applies to Higson (see e.g. 2006). As he notes, "[b]y turning their backs on the industrialized, chaotic present, they [the heritage films] nostalgically reconstruct an imperialist and upper-class Britain (or its other side, the picturesque poverty of *Little Dorrit*)" (Higson, 2006, p. 93). That also reruns may cause nostalgia on the F level if they import a 'whitewashed' perspective into the present is shown by Herrera-De La Muela (2009). This is similarly shown by Fischer (1980, p. 45) on the example of returning film genres.

Furthermore, characteristics of the texts – the "iconography of the genre" (Higson, 2006, p. 97) – are identified, showing that nostalgia may be supported by every single level of the text. They are identified as "both a bid for historical realism (and visual pleasure) and a function of the nostalgic mode (seeking an imaginary historical plenitude)" (Higson, 2006, p. 97). Higson refers to the selection of places and settings, such as country houses and picturesque, verdant landscapes, the mise-en-scène – a "spectacle of authentic objects" (Higson, 2006, p. 105), which makes the past desirable, actors (intertextual references to other heritage films), narration (intertextual references to an 'original', slow narration) or a "pictorialist" camera style (Higson, 2006, pp. 97 ff.).

Also with reference to other authors, formal devices that evoke nostalgia related to the fictional world can be highlighted. Various authors (see Dyer, 2005; Sprengler, 2011) emphasise the specific function music may have in evoking nostalgia. As Sprengler stresses, "[a]ccording to recent film scholarship, music can be nostalgic as a trigger evoking nostalgic longing in its listener and in its structure" (Sprengler, 2011, p. 76). In the first case, music may work as a "mnemonic prompt by calling to mind experiences from the time it was first heard or the time during which it was most often listened to" (Sprengler, 2011, p. 76).[5] In the second case, Sprengler (2011, p. 77) refers to a study conducted by Flinn (1992). The scholar describes the ability of some film music scores "to connote an '[...] nostalgic condition'" (Flinn, 1992 cited in Sprengler, 2011, p. 77), pointing to the fact that the "scores are structured around a musical desire to return to an earlier moment through a series of melodic forays that stray from the original key only to return to it in the end" (Sprengler,

---

5   It has to be seen if other levels of the text may not work as "mnemonic prompt[s]" as well.

2011, p. 77). Dyer notes that the instrumentation of *The Godfather* (Coppola, 1972) consisting of "restrained trumpets or mandolins" (Dyer, 2005, p. 133 [o.t.]) seems nostalgic. Other scholars highlight formal devices that may evoke nostalgia. With reference to Konigsberg (1997), Brockmann notes that slow motion "'is particularly effective in evoking a mood of nostalgia'" (Konigsberg, 1997 cited in Brockmann, 2005, p. 155).

Finally, what shall be called 'fiction nostalgia' is demonstrated on contemporary films set in contemporary times. Fischer (1980, p. 18), for instance, names Segal's *Love Story* (1969) as an example for nostalgia in cinema, not because of its recreation of a certain period or the adoption of a bygone style, but because the film staged a longing for the "American way of life" during the Vietnam war. Furthermore, the television scholar Smith (2009a) shows that the Spanish drama series *Pelotas* (TVE, 2009-2010) displays a certain nostalgia for past types of urban cohabitation (Smith, 2009a, p. 79), which, we can argue, is an 'F nostalgia', too.

Various authors have noted the general possibility of what has previously been referred to as 'empathetic fiction nostalgia'. Cardwell (2002) refers to nostalgia inherent in the diegesis of *Brideshead Revisited* (ITV, 1981), where "nostalgia is encouraged in the viewer through eliciting his or her sympathy for the characters" (Cardwell, 2002, p. 123). She illuminates several "focal-points" of the protagonist's nostalgia (Cardwell, 2002, pp. 125 ff.). Here, the flashback narrative plays a central part (Cardwell, 2002, p. 123). This similarly applies to Higson (2003), who argues that "[i]n some films, the nostalgic perspective is built into the narrative itself, since the films purport to present us the reminiscences of one of the protagonists as an older man or woman" (Higson, 2003, p. 83). He also refers to "flashback narratives" in films such as *Mrs Dalloway* (Gorris, 1997) or *Chariots of Fire* (Hudson, 1981) (Higson, 2003, p. 83).

The source of 'empathetic F nostalgia' is mentioned but not further investigated by Sprengler (see e.g. Sprengler, 2011, pp. 25, 74 ff.), who highlights the general possibility of nostalgia "enabled by identifying with characters who wistfully long for past times, childhood or home" (Sprengler, 2011, p. 25). Holdsworth (2011) describes the protagonists' longing in *Life on Mars*, which makes the narrative nostalgic (Holdsworth, 2011, p. 107). Furthermore, Feyerabend refers to the possibility of 'empathetic fiction nostalgia', stating that "the reader/viewer can participate in a protagonist's nostalgia" (Feyerabend, 2009, p. 55). She later notes that "[t]he viewers can share this [nostalgic] sentiment, as probably everyone likewise has recollections that instantaneously come to mind" (Feyerabend, 2009, p. 66).

With a reference to the theory of aesthetic emotions (Brinckmann, 2005, p. 339; Eder, 2005, pp. 236f.), we can suppose that identification is not essential for the development of 'empathetic F nostalgia'. This similarly applies to personal memories that may be triggered in the course of reception (Bruun Vaage, 2007, p. 195). Apart from that, from the perspective of a broader understanding of empathy (see e.g. Tan, 1996) it can be supposed that 'empathetic F nostalgia' would not explicitly rely on a nostalgia felt by a character. However, it can also be stated that the category is underpinned by the discourse.

Aside from this, the discourse shows that nostalgia in the course of "emotional objectivation" and "visual narration" expresses itself on every level of the audiovisual text. The film theorist Català refers to this circumstance in the context of the postmodern "giro intimista" [intimistic turn] (Català, 2009, p. 32 [o.t.]), which he considers to be related to a postmodern 'melodramatic aesthetic' in whose course nostalgia infuses everything including material forms (Català, 2009, p. 15).

Also 'artefact nostalgia' – a nostalgia stemming from a concentration on the artefact level of a film or television programme, rather than from an immersion into the fictional world – is implicit to the film and television discourse of nostalgia. Kompare (2005) mentions nostalgia directed at the artefact in the broad context of the rerun as an artefact as a whole. The author describes how "reruns played a key role in the new nostalgia of the seventies" (Kompare, 2005, p. 103). He already makes clear that on this level "retrospective classifications" (Kompare, 2005, p. 105, 139) are important in preparing the ground for the possible nostalgic reception, respectively in the creation of the 'gap' between a better then and the worse now, which is so important for nostalgia.

Regarding single levels of the text, intertextual references are often called nostalgic. First, we must refer to Jameson (1991). Within the frame of aesthetic emotions, his work can again be explored for 'real' nostalgia when situated within the category of 'artefact nostalgia'. Therefore, Jameson's main criteria for calling a film 'nostalgic', as previously mentioned, is the 'intertextual' character – the effect of the "connotation of 'pastness'" (Jameson, 1991, p. 20), which is significant for postmodernism as a "cultural dominant" (Jameson, 1991, p. 4) in general. According to Jameson, on different levels, such as actors, mise-en-scène, setting, plot up to the design of credits, 'nostalgia' is exhibited in anachronistic "aesthetic signs". For instance, intertextual references to an 'original' in the case of a remake, references to an 'outdated' "styles of acting" or the type of actors cast for a role or the 'intertextual' references of period dramas to a former representation of the period are named here (Jameson, 1991, pp. 20 ff., 281 f.; 1998, p. 8). As previously mentioned, and as Jameson notes, nostalgia in a strict sense is not the topic of his work. "'Nostalgia film'," says Jameson, should rather be understood as being representative for any kind of postmodern artefact (Jameson, 1991, p. xvii). Thus the scholar denies the nostalgia film every relation to affect.

Nevertheless, this is not where Jameson's engagement with nostalgia ends. First, Jameson himself is somehow nostalgic towards a loss of the 'real' (see also Storey,

2001, p. 245, 249). His work reminds you of what Stauth and Turner (1988, pp. 512 f.) call "[t]he elitist critique of mass culture", which, the authors say, "nostalgically presupposes a world in which there was a unity of art, feeling and communal relation". Storey (2001) also explicitly points out that fact. As the author states:

"There may therefore be a certain (postmodern) irony in Jameson's complaint about nostalgia effacing history, given that his own critique is structured by a profound nostalgia for modernist 'certainty', promoted, as it is, at the expense of detailed historical understanding of the traditions of popular entertainment." (Storey, 2001, p. 245)

Secondly, as a result, we may state that Jameson's descriptions fit what Tan expresses by calling it "awareness of the artefact" (Tan, 1996, p. 65). In this respect the intertextual references Jameson highlights may be described as originating in the reading of a cineaste, who, against the backdrop of his knowledge of the medium, concentrates on the level of the artefact.[6] And thirdly, Jameson's descriptions of nostalgia film are not emotionless. For example, Jameson writes about the science fiction series *Star Wars*, another example of 'nostalgia film'. Jameson puts the series in the context of the "Saturday afternoon serial of the Buck Rogers type", "one", as he stresses, "of the most important cultural experiences of the generations that grew up from the 1930s to the 1950s" (Jameson, 1998, p. 8).[7] He then revives some of the most important characteristics connected to this genre, or, as it could also be argued, some of his most present memories:

"*Star Wars* reinvents this experience in form of a pastiche. [...] Far from being a pointless satire of such dead forms, *Star Wars* satisfies a deep (might I even say repressed?) longing to experience them again: it is a complex object in which on some first level children and adolescents can take the adventure straight, while the adult public is able to gratify a deeper and more properly nostalgic desire to return to that old period and to live its strange old aesthetic artefacts through once again." (Jameson, 1998, p. 8)

---

6   In this context it is worth considering what Dika (2003) writes about Carroll's (1982) work on the 'new condition' of culture: "Using the term 'allusionism' rather than Jameson's 'pastiche,' Carroll discusses the rising presence of recent films that recycle such elements as plots, themes, lines of dialogues, lighting, styles, and gestures from the history of film into new works. Unlike Jameson (whose essay was published a year later), Carroll does not see this style as being caused by postmodern cultural condition, but rather he sees it as a result of the rise of film literacy among an educated group of moviegoers and moviemakers." (Dika, 2003, p. 14)

7   Jameson (* 1934) himself grew up in this era.

Besides the fact that Jameson relates different receptions of the 'nostalgia film' to the memory of different "we-groups", he also describes the cognitive and emotional components of what shall be called 'artefact nostalgia', respectively the viewers' 'own artefact nostalgia' here. With Mikos it can be stated "that intertextuality does not only activate the knowledge of the audiences, but also modes of experiences which, among others, are emotionally bounded" (Mikos 2008, p. 278 [o.t.]). Depending on the "retrospective classification", obviously nostalgia may be one of them. The understanding of intertextuality as a potential trigger for viewers' 'own artefact nostalgia' is further supported by studies from the spectrum of memory studies. Furthermore, O'Sullivan describes how television memories may work as reference point to remember "aspects of the difference perceived between identity or circumstance 'then' and 'now'" (O'Sullivan, 1991, p. 163). Therefore, we may also locate a further gap here.

Intertextuality as a potential trigger for 'artefact nostalgia' is further supported by other scholars within the nostalgia discourse. In the course of her investigation on the oeuvre of Woody Allen, Feyerabend states that in order to provoke nostalgia in the viewers, Allen uses a lot of "references" to "literature, philosophy, psychoanalysis, theatre, film, music, art, or celebrities" (Feyerabend, 2009, p. 242). Looking at adaptations among heritage films, Powrie states that "[c]learly, all of these films are nostalgic in the sense that they are literary adaptations, and therefore play upon the replay of real or imagined pleasures connected with the act of reading (or viewing in the case of theatre)" (Powrie, 1997, p. 14). Böhn (2007) refers to quotations, for instance, of formal elements, suggesting that they "can be used to play with the emotions associated with these forms or to create a historical distance from them which may cause a nostalgic longing for their restoration" (Böhn, 2007, p. 150).

If we understand intertextuality as "[t]he various links in form and content which bind any text to other texts" (Chandler and Munday, 2011, p. 224), here is also where Grainge's work on 'monochrome memories' can be placed. In the context of the film *Schindler's List* (Spielberg, 1993), the author states that "if one concentrates more on the (monochrome) mode [...] there is perhaps a character of nostalgia for a previous cinematic moment" (Grainge, 2002, p. 131). The author has been criticised for this classification of black-and-white aesthetic as the "evocation of a generalized feeling of pastness" (Pickering and Keightley, 2006, p. 932). However, if we understand the statement as one that has been made by a cineaste who concentrates on the artefact level of the film, just as Tan (1996) describes it in the context of 'artefact emotions', monochrome aesthetic becomes understandable as a possible trigger for 'A nostalgia'. In any case, an analysis that also considers intertextuality as a potential trigger for nostalgia can never be conclusive, just as intertextuality can never be analysed conclusively, since it is defined by all texts with which viewers approach a current text, is socially determined, and dynamic (Mikos, 2008, pp. 272 ff.). Indeed, whether the artefact is integrated in a nostalgic rhetoric at a later point has to be scrutinised. With Hutcheon (2000, p. 196) we may assume that there are various "ways to look backward".[8]

Here, and this is where the study will follow the work of Dika (2003) and Sprengler (2011), the study will comment on the authors who explain forms of resistance of the 'nostalgic' text and who will allow this study to explain different degrees of reflexivity of nostalgias, similar to those that have been described by Davis as simple, reflexive or interpreted nostalgia (Davis, 1979, pp. 18 ff.).[9] According to Dika, the 'nostalgia films' can take a "variety of positions regarding their replication of old images, and in so doing [...] raise new questions" (Dika, 2003, p. 197). The intertextual references described by Jameson are again explored for multiple 'ways of looking back' and among them multiple nostalgias, both critical and uncritical. Since the intertextual character is understood to import a critical potential into the narration of the past, the analysis is relevant for what has been called 'fiction nostalgia' here.

An explanation of the critical potential of nostalgia films is also the purpose of a more recent work by Sprengler (2011). Her main thesis is that "props [and costumes] might initiate oppositional and critical readings" (Sprengler, 2011, p. 4) and display their critical potential by bringing in "their own histories into a film" (Sprengler, 2011, p. 4). Backed by prop theory, the objects' "own histories" (Sprengler, 2011, p. 4) are described as the "'cultural baggage'" (Lord, cited in Sprengler, 2011, p. 94) an object has accommodated in the context of its production and in the contexts of its use within the course of time. Her analysis concentrates on films that "mobilize props, costumes and 'deliberate archaism'" (Sprengler, 2011, p. 3). As Sprengler explains with reference to Le Sueur (1977), the latter signifies films that "strive to recreate not only the look and feel of the period in question but also the appearance of art from that distant time" (Sprengler, 2011, p. 86). They are distinguished from films that employ what Le Sueur (1977) calls "'surface realism'" (see Sprengler 2011, pp. 144, 163). "Surface realism is produced through the use of period markers such as dress, cars and setting and is indicative of the obsession with period details characteristic of all nostalgic art." (Sprengler, 2011, p. 85) Much like Dika (2003),

---

8   As Storey (2001, p. 244) highlights, "The intertextual, understood as a form of borrowing from what already exists, is always also (at least potentially) a making new from combinations of what is old. In this way, popular culture is and has always been more than a pastiche or a nostalgic recycling of what has been before."

9   This shall not mean that other authors don't refer to modes of resistance within the texts as well. Wollen (1991), for instance, highlights "occasional hints of something rotten" (Wollen, 1991, p. 182) in the fictional world her nostalgia films encompass, which also means that certain gradations of nostalgia are made here.

Sprengler lets you look at different dimensions of 'A nostalgia' on the level of intertextual references and 'F nostalgia' directed at the fictional world.

The possibility of 'internal empathetic artefact nostalgia' is not discussed in the nostalgia discourse. However, this is perhaps where you could put the famous 'Madeleine' example of Marcel Proust – an example where the sensuous experience of the protagonist steps into the foreground and "internal aesthetic engagement" may arise.

In conclusion, we may say that film and television studies only scarcely consider the emotive aspects of nostalgia or the interrelation of text and reception. Not without a reason Grainge (2002) introduced the 'mood'[10]/mode dichotomy. However, it has been shown that those studies which mainly focus on nostalgia as a style can be explored for an investigation which aims to combine 'mood' and mode. The theory of aesthetic emotions may work as a bridge here. It tells us *where* to search and what possible categories could be like. The broader nostalgia discourse gives us indicators of the characteristics of nostalgia or the existence of different degrees of reflexivity (Davis, 1979) and therefore informs us about *what* to search. It could be shown that a combination of theories on aesthetic emotions and the nostalgia discourse of film and television studies allows us to 'fill' the categories with the necessary contents, and at the same time to supplement and further refine the existing discussion. A one-on-one ratio transition is not always possible. With reference to the literature it cannot always be said whether an artefact works as a "mnemonic prompt", stemming from an immersion into the fictional world or due to a concentration on the film as an artefact. When we assume that nostalgia may be directed towards emotions that were once related to a television programme, we cannot always say whether this is related to the F or the A level of the text. In any case, here the 'object of appraisal' must be closely considered whenever possible.

Aside from this, one can argue, it is the combination on the basis of the theory of aesthetic emotions that makes an eclectic use of the discourse actually possible. With its radical 'object-centrism' the theory of aesthetic emotions allows us to understand the differences between the studies and to give them a 'new order' to make them usable in combination. One can say that it allows for a restructure of the discourse and gives the different objects the scholars deal with a name. Against the backdrop of aesthetic emotions, discrepancies within the nostalgia discourse become explainable. Thus, for example, it has been shown that when Grainge (2002) describes black-and-white aesthetic as nostalgic, it is not about nostalgia *per se* but about 'artefact nostalgia'. Or when Higson (2006) states that the heritage genre is a

---

10 Mood is set in simple quotation marks here since, as has been shown, nostalgia contains both characteristics of a mood and an emotion.

nostalgia genre, it is mostly about 'fiction nostalgia'.[11] We should keep these differences in mind. Alternatively, in order to apply the existing theories and to understand and compare them, the basis of discussion – the object – has to be made clear.

With a focus on the two questions (1) Where are potential nostalgia objects? and (2) Where are potential gaps?, the 'fragmented' discourse, respectively the 'modules' of analysis, can now be merged systematically in the course of the case studies of different nostalgia 'genres'. If we refer to the memory discourse, we may assume that these objects may again be widely 'shared' or not. The 'genres' shall be explained in a subsequent chapter (see Part II). Before this, a chapter on methodology will explain the following steps of research.[12]

4.4.2 Methodology

In order to investigate nostalgia both as a textual mode and emotional state, an interdisciplinary approach is necessary, which can integrate existing studies from within the nostalgia discourse, studies from the perspective of memory studies, and studies from the spectrum of aesthetic emotions. First steps towards the combination of the approaches have been made. However, since "[a]ny attempt to understand the relationship between the media and emotions on a wide basis must consider at least three aspects: the structure of the media offer, the emotion of the audience and the systematic interrelations between the two (see Eder 2005)" (Bartsch et al., 2007a, p. 10 [o.t.]), reception studies should be additionally conducted.

The frame for the combination, and therefore the overall frame for this study, is reception theory, more precisely 'reception aesthetics', as deduced from the German *Rezeptionsästhetik* (Chandler and Munday, 2011, p. 358). The study will draw on what has been proposed in the context of the so-called *Babelsberg Approach*, which, inspired by the method of triangulation, argues for the combination of different qualitative methods, such as film and television analysis and reception studies (Mikos

---

11 Probably this is also the reason why *American Graffiti* (Lucas, 1973) is assigned to the nostalgia films in some cases and is not assigned to them in other cases. As Grainge (2002, p. 25) highlights, Davis sees the 'hyperrealism' of Coppola's *American Graffiti* as "artistic failures as nostalgia films" (Davis, 1979, p. 89), while for Jameson (1991) this is an example for the typical nostalgia film. Grainge explains this by subsuming Davis under the mood agents and Jameson under the mode agents. At the same time, however, it could be argued that while Davis searches for the narration of the better past as an attribute for nostalgia, the intertextuality stands in the foreground for Jameson.

12 An earlier draft of this combination of approaches has been presented at the conference *Discourse, Communication, Conversation Conference*, Loughborough University, 21-23 March 2012 (see Armbruster, 2012).

and Prommer, 2005, pp. 162 ff.). Using this perspective, the study will be able to consider the properties of nostalgia. Inside this frame, existing studies from different disciplines can be used without falling prey to total relativism. Presumed differences between Spain and Germany will also be considered. Therefore, the work contains two further sections, one dedicated to the film and television analysis of presumed triggers for nostalgia and one dedicated to the investigation of the reception.

4.4.2.1 Film and television analysis

Following Prommer et al. (2003, p. 60 [o.t.]), the investigation assumes the television programmes to be "communication media" which "communicate with the audiences" and which, on the textual level, "prefigure the cognitive and emotional activity of the spectators" (Prommer et al., 2003, p. 60 [o.t]). Correspondingly, not only will each level of the text from narration, aesthetics and design to characters be analysed systematically, but contextual factors will also be considered (Mikos, 2008). The interdisciplinarity of film and television analysis, which obliges the researcher to integrate theories depending on the respective research interest (Mikos, 2008, p. 41), make the method especially appropriate for this study. In combination of the theories on nostalgia, memory and aesthetic emotions, it will explain potential triggers for nostalgia on the textual level. For this purpose, the 'modules', as they will be called, in which the discourses have been fragmented, will be recombined depending on the respective nostalgia 'genre'. Each sub-chapter of analysis will then be advanced by this respective theoretical reflection (see Chapter 6 for more details).

4.4.2.2 Reception study

The question if a potential trigger for nostalgia is 'decoded'[13] as such by the audiences will be scrutinised in a reception study, one of the "standard instruments" of qualitative media studies (Prommer and Mikos, 2005, p. 193 [o.t.]). The focus group discussion, which will be applied in this research, is a widely used method.

"'The focus group is a special type of groups in terms of purpose, size, composition, and procedures [...]. In summary, a focus group is a carefully planned discussion designed to obtain perceptions on a defined area of interest in a permissive, non-threatening environment'." (Krueger, 1994 cited in Lamnek, 2005, p. 26 [omission in the original])

Liebes and Katz (1990, p. 7) name the "discussion group as a simulation of the social mechanisms which contribute to the viewers' understandings, interpretations, and evaluations". Focus groups allow the disclosure of "emotional backgrounds" of statements (Lamnek, 2005, p. 84 [o.t.]). They provide insights into the "structure and processes" of both individual and collective views (Lamnek, 2005, p. 84 [o.t.]; see

---

13   Here, the study refers to Hall (1973 [2000]).

also Paus-Haase et al., 1999, p. 43), and will allow this study to explain the actual reception of the nostalgia that is on offer in the texts and the transitions between personal nostalgias and those which are 'shared' among larger "we-groups" (see Part III for more details). Using the qualitative method, no representativeness will be gained or aspired to. Instead and with focus on the specific sample of the study, it will be possible to obtain in-depth information about nostalgia, its backgrounds and sufficient conditions, as may not be possible with quantitative research.

Part II – Text

5. The 'genres' of nostalgic fiction

In order to lead over to the film and television analysis of presumed nostalgia on offer in the text, this paragraph will contain a revision of different 'genres' of nostalgia. The chapter will mainly draw on categorisations of nostalgia as made in film studies. Although many authors also explore nostalgia television under the label of nostalgia film, in order not to lose sight of the specific characteristics of television by mainly using this film-centred theory, the study will also consult studies from within television studies and other academic disciplines that contribute to the investigation of nostalgia in television. Since nostalgia, comparable to suspense (Carroll, 1999, p. 42), can be assumed to be possibly provoked by a range of different texts, in most cases it is not referred to as a genre in the strict sense of the word. For this reason, the term is mostly put into single quotation marks. Nevertheless, nostalgia film or nostalgia television may be discussed as groups of films and television programmes that are widely considered under the label of nostalgia.

The term 'nostalgia film' has different meanings, which is why it shall be defined in a first step. Also here, as can be argued, the differences may be explained with different foci on different objects.[1] While one author uses 'nostalgia film' in order to refer to the intertextual character of postmodern cinema (see e.g. Jameson, 1991), another foregrounds the representation of past beauty (see e.g. Higson, 2006) in its definition, no matter if there is an intertextual relation to past representations or not. Correspondingly, depending on the perspective of the author, 'nostalgia film' comprises a wider or smaller range of 'genres'.

---

[1] Böhn (2007) partly describes the different foci the descriptions of nostalgia genres may have. The author names period pictures – they refer "to a bygone world at the level of representation" (Böhn, 2007, p. 145) – and remakes, which refer "to a previous movie and implicitly or explicitly to a past of the mediating film" (Böhn, 2007, p. 145); quotations of, for instance, formal elements (Böhn, 2007, p. 150), and "re-adoptions of seemingly outdated film-genres" (Böhn, 2007, pp. 144 f.) are also named.

Perhaps the widest frame can be seen from Jameson (1991)[2] and Grainge (2002). Jameson divides nostalgia films into "postnostalgia" films, such as *Blue Velvet* (Lynch, 1986) or *Something Wild* (Demme, 1986), and 'ordinary' nostalgia films, also named "nostalgia-deco" or "pastiche", for example presented by films such as *American Graffiti* (Lucas, 1973) or *Body Heat* (Kasdan, 1981) (Jameson, 1991, pp. 279-296). Already these examples show that nostalgia films are not restricted to one specific genre. They rather encompass everything from period dramas or coming-of-age films (e.g. *American Graffiti*), thriller remakes (e.g. *Body Heat*) with "a contemporary setting" (Jameson, 1998, p. 9) up to science fiction remakes (e.g. *Star Wars*). The main criterion is their intertextual character – the effect of the "connotation of 'pastness'" (Jameson, 1991, p. 20). With *American Graffiti* (Lucas, 1973), this is expressed by the "stylistic recuperation" of the 1950s, which, according to Jameson (1991, p. 281), instead of basing upon the reality of the 1950s, exclusively refers to other representations of the time – something that Le Sueur (1977 cited in Sprengler, 2011, p. 86) also calls "'deliberate archaism'". In the case of *Body Heat* (1981) – Kasdan's remake of the film noir *Double Indemnity* (Wilder, 1944) – nostalgia is expressed in the intertextual references to further versions of the text (Jameson, 1991, p. 20). If, with Grainge (2002), we understand the black-and-white aesthetic as one possible (intertextual) mode of nostalgia, the frame of 'nostalgia films' can even be drawn wider towards all genres and generic categories that employ the 'nostalgia style'.

Furthermore, Dika (2003), following Jameson, describes and uses nostalgia film as a general subcategory to indicate the "tendency to return to past film images" (Dika, 2003, p. 9). Apart from remakes such as Gus van Sant's *Psycho* (1998) and period recreations based upon past images, such as *American Graffiti* (Lucas, 1973), the category nostalgia film here encompasses also "new"[3] "genre films", such as *Badlands* (1973) or nostalgic returns[4] of classic film genres, such as the western or the gangster film (Dika, 2003, pp. 3, 90, 205 ff.). Only the latter again builds a wider

---

2   Even though Fredric Jameson was not the first to apply the term *nostalgia film* (Jameson, 1991, p. xvii) – Sprengler indicates that the term goes back to the text *Theory Number Five: Anatomy of Nostalgia Film: Heritage and Methods* by Marc Le Sueur in 1977 – Jameson's work builds the centre of the discussion (Sprengler, 2011, p. 83).

3   'New' here refers to the fact that while "[t]he recycling of past conventions into new works has once been the very definition of genre production, [...] the more recent films can be distinguished by their discontinuous movement, one that *skips a generation* (significantly, that of the 1960s) in its evocation of previous forms. This type of discontinuity imparts an indelible connotation of pastness onto the works, and it does so in a way that distinguishes them from earlier genre films." (Dika, 2003, pp. 55 f. [italic emphasis in the original])

4   "Unlike the genres of an earlier period [...] these forms display a second-hand quality, a feeling of being copies of the original." (Dika, 2003, p. 207)

category, ranging from the "inclusion of old film clips into new works" (Dika, 2003, p. 220) to the return of classic titles or the return of classic elements on the level of character, image and story (Dika, 2003, pp. 78, 220).

Focused differently, but still broad, is the 'nostalgia film' according to Cook (2005, p. 14). In her definition the intertextual character of the images is less important. Central is rather that the films "reconstruct[...] an idealised past as a site of pleasurable contemplation and yearning" (Cook, 2005, p. 3). Coming from here, 'nostalgia film' or "nostalgic memory film", as Cook mostly calls it, incorporates "heritage cinema, period melodramas and westerns, as well as remakes and pastiches" (Cook, 2005, p. 3). All these genres, says Cook,

"conjure[...] up a golden age, which is both celebrated and mourned, providing an opportunity to reflect upon and interrogate the present. Past and present are conflated, as contemporary concerns are superimposed on earlier historical periods in the process of reconstruction. Despite all their claims to authenticity, nostalgic fictions depend upon a slippage between current styles and period fashion in order to draw audiences in to the experience." (Cook, 2005, p. 10)

Finally, Powrie (1997) concentrates his examination of nostalgia films on works that aspire "to recreate specific historical periods" (Powrie, 1997, p. 13) and locates nostalgia film within the frame of so-called "quality costume drama, labelled heritage film by Andrew Higson" (Powrie, 1997, p. 13). As this quotation indicates, the link of costume drama, respectively heritage cinema, to nostalgia film does not have its origin in Powrie's work. In general, the literature relates the heritage genre to nostalgia. Thus, even though Higson, one of the most quoted experts of the genre, does not use the term 'nostalgia film', he ascribes nostalgia to the heritage films (Higson, 2006, p. 93).

If we look at television, it can be stated that even though the term 'nostalgia television' seems to be less common than 'nostalgia film', television is not outside the considerations of nostalgia. Firstly, works on nostalgia film to a certain extent also include television. In his broadly conceived investigation of intertextuality, Jameson (1991, pp. 280 f.) for instance also refers to self-referential period representations in television. Examples from within the spectrum of film, such as the period drama *American Graffiti* (Lucas, 1973) or the thriller remake *Body Heat* (Kasdan, 1981), have their 'genre' equivalents in television. Also Grainge's (2002) investigation on the black-and-white aesthetic can be equally applied to other media. Furthermore, Cook's and Dika's nostalgia genres, namely remakes, period melodramas, heritage dramas or westerns, have an equivalent in television. Above all, the heritage genre or the wider category of the quality costume drama self-evidently includes television series such as *Brideshead Revisited* (ITV, 1981) or *The Jewel in the Crown* (ITV, 1983) (see e.g. Higson, 1993; 2006).

Secondly, authors explicitly focus on nostalgia and television. In her book *Television, Memory and Nostalgia* Holdsworth (2011) investigates the hybrid period drama *Life on Mars* (BBC One, 2006) under the label of nostalgia. In an earlier section of this study, it has been shown that researchers in the Spanish context refer to the period drama *Cuéntame Cómo Pasó* (TVE) as an example of nostalgia in television (see e.g. Corbalán, 2009; Laffond and Gómez, 2009). Another reference that has been named was Herrera-De La Muela's study (2009) on possible nostalgic readings of reruns. This context is also one of the most common fields in which nostalgia in television is mentioned (see e.g. Davis, 1979, pp. 130 ff. on 'old TV shows' and their replays; Fischer, 1980, pp. 18 f., who refers to reruns of the so-called *Heimatfilm* on German television; Williams, 1994, pp. 173 f.; Spigel, 1995; Grainge, 2002, pp. 47 f.; Kompare, 2005). The category may encompass nearly every television genre from drama series to game shows (see Chapter 5.1). Lastly, nostalgia in television is discussed in the context of contemporary drama series set in contemporary times, such as the Spanish drama series *Pelotas* (TVE, 2009) (Smith, 2009a, p. 79).

Since it is not the purpose of this study to explain the whole range of nostalgia 'genres' but to investigate the variety of nostalgia on the level of the text and its reception in different contexts, a clearly restricted quantity of examples is necessary. The study will therefore focus on television fiction, more precisely on reruns, remakes and period dramas. In the following section the characteristics of these 'genres' shall be outlined in more detail. They will give a first survey of the main fields, inside which nostalgia in television fiction can be expected. It is not the purpose of the section to claim that every example inside the categories is *per se* nostalgic. Whether a single programme can finally be named nostalgic has to be scrutinised in in-depth case studies, which will be the purpose of a subsequent section. Perhaps this will not always be the case. From the previous chapters we already know that a mere reference to the past is not enough. As Hutcheon (2000, p. 196) expresses, there are surely "many ways to look backward" and not everyone has to be nostalgic.

5.1 TELEVISION RERUNS

In its broadest sense *rerun* means everything that is not first-run, therefore repetition, reissues, or retransmissions are used as synonyms (William, 1994, p. 162; Kompare, 2005, pp. xi, 170). Furthermore, according to Contreras and Palacio (2003), other more "euphemistic formulas" can be named, such as "multidifusiones" [multidiffusions] or "segundo pases" [second passes] (Contreras and Palacio, 2003, pp. 215 f. [o.t.]). All these terms signify the practice of broadcasting a programme more than once, with purposes such as the amortisation of production costs, the adaptation on the advertisement market, or the addressing of different audiences at different times (Contreras and Palacio, 2003, p. 215; Schümchen, 2006, pp. 172 f.).

Two main kinds of reruns can be distinguished, namely "short-term repetitions" (Schümchen, 2006, p. 146 [o.t.]) and 'long-term' repetitions. Schümchen (2006, p. 146 [o.t.]) uses the term "short-term repetitions" in order to describe repetitions in the context of early retransmission of programmes, as they can mostly be found in full programme channels. As an example of this kind of reruns, the author refers to fictional programmes in particular, such as TV films, feature films, daily soaps or series (Schümchen, 2006, pp. 146, 170 ff.). Some first-runs, daily soaps for instance, are repeated in the morning slots of the following day (Schümchen, 2006, p. 146).

The second type of rerun, a rather 'long-term' type of repetitions, draws back on what Kompare (2006) names "television heritage". For example, the author refers to reruns of 1950s television series in the 1970s (Kompare, 2006, pp. 101 ff.). Also these repetitions seem to be mostly concentrated on fictional series. However, they may also encompass a bigger range of genres than the short-term reruns. Kompare (2005, pp. 110 f.), for example, refers to reruns of shows and game shows, but also to news retrospectives, such as *NBC: The First Fifty Years* (NBC 1976) or *CBS: On the Air* (CBS 1978), which include rerun pieces.

In general, reruns have not always been part of television schedules. As Williams (1994, p. 162) shows, until the Second World War in the U.S., reuses of television programmes were uncommon. "Repeat audience attendance was desirable, but maintaining a constant flow of individual patrons week after week remained a greater priority." (Williams, 1994, p. 162) It was not until the 1950s, when it became apparent that "repeats were successful in attracting not only the rapidly growing 'new' television audience, but also viewers who had already seen the original broadcasts" (Kompare, 2005, p. xvi), that it became a frequent practice (Williams, 1994, p. 163; Kompare, 2005, p. 131).

This is in line with what Schümchen (2006, p. 170) notes regarding Germany, where repetitions have long been seen as an indicator of the lesser quality of the television programme. However, according to Hickethier (1998, pp. 130 f.), already with the early expansions of ARD[5] in the late 1950s, repetitions were broadcasted during the non-primetime in order to fill the programme schedules. After the approval of private broadcasters in 1986 (Hickethier, 1998, p. 417), the number of reruns on German television further increased (Schümchen, 2006, p. 170). Many series that

---

5   The acronym ARD stands for *Arbeitsgemeinschaft der öffentlich-rechtlichen Rundfunkanstalten der Bundesrepublik Deutschland* [Consortium of public-law broadcasting institutions of the Federal Republic of Germany].

have been launched by private broadcasters had already been aired on public service channels (Hickethier, 1998, p. 436; see also Klippel and Winkler, 1994, p. 123). A quotation from *Der Spiegel* (1998), one of Germany's most widely read weekly magazines, documents this development:

"'Experts have calculated that in the seventies, one out of ten, and today [1998] every third broadcasting minute includes a dacapo. Furthermore, the intervals between first and second broadcast have become shorter. And, unlike before, hardly any viewer complains about it. On the contrary, protest letters reach the stations if digestible mixes will not be served again'."
(Der Spiegel, 1998 cited in Schümchen, 2006, p. 170 [o.t.])[6]

The quotation not only underlines the increase of reruns on German television, it also indicates the changing connotation of reruns from a disruptive element towards a broadly accepted service (Schümchen, 2006, pp. 170 f.) – a development that, according to Schümchen (2006, p. 171) must be seen in the context of the increasing extension of the television programme, which made it more difficult for the viewers to follow the first-run programme. With reference to Furno-Lamude and Anderson (1992), it can be stated that within the course of time, watching reruns also became related to other "gratifications" than first-run watching, with nostalgia as one of them. Accordingly, some (pay-)TV channels have (nostalgic) rerun programmes as their main selling point. The most explicit is perhaps the special-interest channel *Sky Nostalgia.* Apart from that, *MGM Channel, kabel eins classics, Das Vierte* (2008-2012) and *Heimatkanal* (on the German *Heimatfilm* and nostalgia see also Ludewig, 2011) can be named. While *Sky Nostalgia, kabel eins classics,* and *Das Vierte* (2008-2012) point to its programme mix of 'classic' movies and cult series (Sky, 2011), *MGM Channel* and *Heimatkanal* have their main focus on film reruns. We can also assume that other channels may focus on cheaper rerun programmes, an assumption that cannot be investigated further in this study.

Also in Spain, the use of reruns has increased over the past decades (Contreras and Palacio, 2003, p. 215). Contreras and Palacio (2003, p. 216) refer here to both short-term repetitions (e.g. *Ally McBeal* on Telecinco) and long-term repetitions (see e.g. *Los vigilantes de la playa [Baywatch]* on Antena 3). Apart from the financial crisis of the television channels that has more recently increased reruns from the 1970s and 1980s (Bernal, 2012), a major factor was also the new multi-channel

---

6   Original quotation: "'Fachleute haben ausgerechnet, dass in den siebziger Jahren jede zehnte, heute aber jede dritte Sendeminute ein Dakapo beinhaltet. Außerdem sind die Zeitabstände zwischen Erst- und Zweitausstrahlung deutlich kürzer geworden. Und anders als früher ärgert sich heute kaum ein Seher darüber. Im Gegenteil: Protestbriefe erreichen jetzt die Sender, wenn sattsam Verwurstetes nicht noch einmal serviert wird'." *(Der Spiegel,* 1998 cited in Schümchen, 2006, p. 170)

landscape, which has grown since the admittance of private television channels at the end of the 1980s (Moragas and Prado, 2000, p. 212; Contreras and Palacio, 2003, pp. 215 f.). In this context, Contreras and Palacio (2003, pp. 215 ff.) describe a development regarding the audience's acceptance similar to that in Germany. While, as the authors note (2003, p. 215), the reruns often provoke critique, "the audiences will demand these broadcasts since every time it will be more difficult to concentrate big audiences with a single run" (Contreras and Palacio, 2003, p. 216 [o.t.]). Here we may also assume that apart from the demand of reruns from audiences who haven't seen the first-run, new 'gratifications', such as nostalgia, play a major role. Thus in Spain, *LaSexta3*, which focuses on classical and modern films, may be seen as in parts a rerun dedicated channel. As Contreras and Palacio (2003, p. 216) indicate, also for the pay-TV channel Canal+, reruns are one of the most important components. The institutionalisation of the nostalgia rerun is seen with the Spanish *Canal Nostalgia*. First broadcasted in 1996 on satellite television and later, from 2005 to 2007, under the title *TVE-50* in DVB-T, the channel was exclusively dedicated to show the archive material of TVE (see e.g. EvaSF, 2005; Sanchéz, 2010; Tele Digital, 2010). Since 2010 it has been transmitted via IPTV (see e.g. Tele Digital, 2010).

Canal Nostalgia also reflects another development in the 'nostalgia industry', namely the growing importance of digital contents, also distributed via the internet in general. According to Prado (2010 [o.t.]) "online television consumption is an activity to that internet users dedicate each time more hours and videographic contents occupy more space than any other type of data". Since, as Kompare (2005, p. 222) argues, "'new' media have a[...] historic tendency to repackage 'old' media", reruns are among their prior contents. Whether via legal (see e.g. Livestream, 2012; RTVE a la Carta, 2011b) or illegal internet sites – as Kompare (2005, p. 223) indicates, "[i]n an ongoing age of hacking, poaching, dubbing and 'ripping', the activities of [...] [the] users alter the rules of repetition" – the audience's access to rerun programme has increased. Furthermore, says Kompare (2005), recording methods, such as VCRs, are "explicitly designed upon the premise of mediated repetition, and have thus added a significant new dimension to the concept of the rerun, and to the very concept of the media text" (Kompare, 2005, p. 199). The "ultimate bearers of televisual repetition" (Kompare, 2005, p. 200) are DVD box sets. Kompare (2005, p. 208 [italic emphasis in the original]) calls this the *"acquisitive repetition"*.

5.2 TELEVISION REMAKES

According to the Oxford English Dictionary (2012), a remake is "a film or piece of music that has been filmed or recorded again and rereleased". As Oltmann (2008, p. 12) notes, it "adapts a story [...] to changing historical and cultural conditions and contexts" (Oltmann, 2008, p. 11 [o.t.]). According to the literature (Horton and McDougal, 1998; Oltmann, 2008) this again has consequences for the source text. Thus, in so doing, as Horton and McDougal (1998, p. 3) state, "a new text (the hypertext) [also] transforms a hypotext". According to Oltmann (2008, p. 27) it is the remake that gives the "premake"[7] the status of the 'original'. The reception of the remake, says Oltmann (2008, pp. 31 ff. [italic emphasis in the original]), may be understood as a kind of *"rewriting"* of the premake and as continuation of its discourses.

Generally, remakes are not always easy to differentiate from, for instance, sequels and prequels, spin-offs or parodies (Oltmann, 2008, p. 24). This is also the reason why Dika (2003, p. 205) talks of a general "crisis [...] of the 'remake' as a descriptive category". With Oltmann (2008, p. 11) two main types of remakes can be distinguished, namely remakes that realise the adaptation on a local level – the author names for example Hollywood remakes of French comedies – or those that realise the adaptation on a temporal level, such as remakes of early Hollywood films in the 1990s. These categories are sufficient in the context of this work.[8] They may also be transferred to television.

Regarding television, adaptations on the local level also encompass examples in the context of the trans-border format trade like the German and Spanish adaptations of the British format *Who Wants to Be a Millionaire*. According to Moran (2009, p. 115), "[t]he TV program format is a kind of template or recipe whereby particular industry knowledges are packaged to facilitate this process of remaking". The format 'remakes' may further be divided into "'close' and 'open' adaptations" (Moran, 2009, pp. 118 f.). These are not relevant in the context of this work.

In this context, television remakes that may be located on a temporal level are more important. Exemplary it may be referred to contemporary U.S. remakes of early U.S. television programmes as they have been broadcasted both in Germany and Spain: among them *Knight Rider* (NBC, 2008) and *Knight Rider* (NBC, 1982); *90210* (The CW, 2008) and *Beverly Hills, 90210* (FOX, 1990); *Hawaii Five-0* (CBS, 2010)

---

7 Following Oltmann (2008), this term shall also be used in this work in case that it is referred to the first film. When it is called 'original', the term is at least put into simple quotation marks.

8 For a deeper categorisation see e.g. Eberwein (1998, pp. 28 ff.) who, in the context of film, distinguishes between a total of fifteen categories of remakes with different subcategories each.

and *Hawaii Five-0* (CBS, 1968); or *V* (ABC, 2009) and *V - The Final Battle* (NBC, 1983). Other examples show that overlaps between the temporal and local level are not unusual. Thus *The Golden Girls* (NBC, 1985), for instance, which was originally broadcasted in the U.S. and, since 1986 has been broadcasted in a synchronised version in Spain, was adapted both on a temporal and on a local level when the Spanish remake version *Las chicas de oro* (TVE, 2010) was produced.

The strategy of remaking 'old' texts into new ones is not restricted to one medium. It also happens from one medium to another. There is also a lot of exchange from film to television and vice versa. Here, Eberwein (1998, p. 29) refers to three different possibilities: "a) A film remade as [a] television film [...]; b) a film remade as a television miniseries [...]; c) a television series remade as a film". Regarding the latter, which is furthermore relevant in the context of this work, Black (2004, p. 99) even talks about a "recent vogue" in 2004. Here he refers to *Star Trek* (e.g. Wise, 1979; Abrams, 2009), *The Flintstones* (Levant, 1994), *The Addams Family* (Sonnenfeld, 1991), or *Wild Wild West* (Sonnenfeld, 1999) among others – all in all examples that "draw on a variety of television genres" (Black, 2004, p. 100) from science fiction to western.[9] With Black (2004, p. 101), the remakes of television programmes may be further categorised according to their relation to the sources: "they update the time frame (or not), alter the characters and/or the casting (or not), change from animation to live-action, renarrate familiar events, narrate new events, and so forth". Here, we may also apply Oltmann's (2008) distinction in local and temporal adaptations, whereby the latter is again most relevant in the context of this work.

As in the case of reruns, remakes are often made for economic reasons (see also e.g. Frutkin, 2008, p. 8) – "the remake as 'presold' property", as Braudy (1998, p. 328) puts it. "But", Braudy continues, "to conclude that remakes happen primarily for financial reasons obscures the way in which the remaker must also believe that this particular story still inspires what Ira Konigsberg here calls 'another attempt to get it right'" (Braudy, 1998, p. 328) and, most important in the context of this work, that it might be related to added 'gratifications', such as nostalgia.

---

9 Further examples are *Mission Impossible* (De Palma, USA, 1996), a film remake of the television series *Mission: Impossible* (ABC, 1988), *Wickie und die starken Männer* [Vicky the Viking] (Herbig, D, 2009), a live-action remake of the German/Japanese/Austrian animation series broadcasted in the 1970s (J/D 1972-1974), *The A-Team* (Carnahan, 2010), a regarding the time frame updated film remake of the 1980s television series *The A-Team* (NBC, 1983), *Miami Vice* (Mann, 2006), a temporally updated film remake of *Miami Vice* (NBC, 1984) or *Águila Roja* (Écija, 2011), a film remake of the Spanish television series with the same title.

5.3 PERIOD DRAMAS

The group of films that shall be commented in this section have many labels. Apart from period drama, a label that shall be used in this work, authors refer to them as costume dramas, heritage films, period films or also period pieces (Higson, 2003, p. 9; Neely, 2005, pp. 241 f.; Smith, 2006, p. 31; Voigts-Virchow, 2007, p. 123). In general, clear boundaries are hard to find. According to Çelik Norman (2009):

"Defining the parameters of the genre is problematic. The commercial labels 'period drama' and 'costume drama' may be attached by promoters and reviewers to any work with historical setting. No distinction is made between films based on literary classics, original film scripts and modern novels. There is no agreement as to when a historical moment becomes a 'period' and no effort to determine the significance of the historical context in the narrative of the film." (Çelik Norman, 2009, p. 56)

However, with a view on the literature, some lines may be drawn. A narrow definition is made in Glen Creeber's *Television Genre Book* (2008), where the costume drama indeed appears as a single television genre (Nelson, 2008). With television series such as *The Jewel in the Crown* or *Brideshead Revisited*, Nelson (2008, p. 49) describes the category as "big-budged, sumptuous" adaptations of English novels, both classic and modern (Nelson, 2008, p. 50). A broader definition is given by Higson (2003), who focuses on film but likewise refers to examples from television. The author describes the genre as follows:

"These are films set in the past, telling stories of the manners and proprieties, but also the often transgressive romantic entanglements of the upper and upper middle-class English, in carefully detailed and visually splendid period reconstructions." (Higson, 2003, p. 1)

Higson (2003, p. 12) takes the stance that "the costume drama label covers all period films, whether they depict actual historical figures or clearly fictional figures". Therefore, they may encompass historical events or be literature adaptations (Higson, 2003, p. 12) and include both those films set in the distant and those set in the more recent past (Higson, 2003, p. 34). Even though his investigation focuses on the English costume drama since 1980, he uses the label in a broader sense and highlights its fluidity regarding other genres (Higson, 2003, p. 12). This makes Higson's definition transferable to other national context. Powrie (2003) for example, applies the work of Higson in a French context. Also in other countries period dramas belong to the self-evident components of the television landscape.

As Smith (2006, p. 31) highlights, "[f]rom Francoism, through the transition, to the consolidation of Socialist dominance, period drama held a major place on Spanish television". It seems that the 'legacy' of Franco's regime can be seen as one of the main reasons for that (see e.g. Morgan-Tamosunas, 2000, p. 113). Thus, as Morgan-Tamosunas (2000, p. 113) stresses with respect to film, under Franco the tone and content of any representations of history was strictly determined, always in line with the regime.

"It was [thus] hardly surprising [...] that one of the first cultural projects of the transition – in cinema and other forms of cultural production – was one of historical retrieval, with the purpose of rewriting recent Spanish history from the previously disfranchised perspective of the losing side of the civil war." (Morgan-Tamosunas, 2000, p. 113)

This goes hand in hand with what Palacio (2008) notes regarding television. As he states, "[t]he basic operation of the huge TVE productions [during the transition] consisted in contributing to change the collective imagination of the Spaniards" (Palacio, 2008, p. 153 [o.t.]). For example, Palacio (2008, pp. 153 f.) refers to period series such as *Curro Jiménez* (1976), *Cervantes* (1980), *Fortunata y Jacinta* (1980), or *Los gozos y las sombras* (1982).

As Smith (2006, p. 31) highlights with reference to Palacio (2001), today "in-house 'fiction' remains the key element in lending legitimacy to a single channel or an entire TV system". More recent examples are *Águila Roja* (TVE1, 2009), an adventure series set in the Spain of the seventeenth century, or *Bandolera* (Antena 3, 2011) set in the Andalusia of the late nineteenth century. Clear period pieces, even though about the more recent past, are *La chica de ayer* (Antena 3, 2009), the Spanish adaptation of the British television series *Life on Mars* (BBC, 2006), or the long-running period drama *Cuéntame cómo pasó* (La 1, 2001), which in 2011 reached its thirteenth season. Other Spanish period dramas deal with the time of the Second Spanish Republic (1931-1936/39) with series such as *El Grand Hotel* (Antena 3, 2011), *La Señora* (La 1, 2009), or *Amar en tiempos revueltos* (La 1, 2002).[10] Apart from that, period dramas broadcasted in Spain in the time span 2009 to 2011 embrace international productions such as *Borgia – Una familia consagrada al vicio* (Cosmopolitan TV, 2011; original title: *Borgia*), *Los Borgia* (Cuatro, 2011; original

---

10 In contrast to the 1970s and 1980s period pieces that have been named by Palacio (2008), these examples are neither literature adaptations nor biopics; they rather take historical facts as their starting point or background in order to narrate a hybrid of romantic dramas, melodramas, crime and/or adventure stories. While the period telenovela *Amar en tiempos revueltos* (La 1, 2002) foregrounds history – as Smith shows, "the pure romantic elements [...] are constantly embedded in historical or political commentary or vice versa] (Smith, 2009, p. 128 [o.t.]) – in other examples, such as *El Grand Hotel* (Antena 3, 2011), the historical background plays a rather secondary role even though issues of class and gender are consequently broached here as well.

title: *The Borgias*), or *Los Tudor* (Canal+, 2007; La1, 2010; original title: *The Tudors*), which retell European heritage in the form of, as Higson (2003, p. 4) puts it, "old stories about its monarchs" or popes. Other productions on Spanish television that show pieces of the American past are *Aquellos Maravillosos 70* (Antena3 Neox; original title: *That 70s Show*), or *Mad Men* (Cuatro, 2009; AMC, 2007).

It is a different case regarding the German television landscape. Apart from few local in-house productions, such as *Weißensee* (ARD, 2010) – a family drama series set in the German Democratic Republic of the 1980s, between 2009 and 2011 period television series mainly encompassed those U.S. or European productions that already have been mentioned in the Spanish context. *Borgia* (Sky Italia, 2011; ZDF, 2011), *The Borgias* (Showtime, 2011; ProSieben, 2011), or *The Tudors* (Showtime 2007; ProSieben, 2008) have likewise been broadcasted on German television. In-house period drama productions that retell German history encompass, above all, TV movies such as *Go West – Freiheit um jeden Preis* (ProSieben, 2011), *Hindenburg* (RTL, 2011), *Laconia* (Das Erste, 2011), or *Der Baader Meinhof Komplex* (Das Erste, 2009).

6. Case studies on nostalgia on the textual level

This section is dedicated to the qualitative television analysis of nostalgia on offer in the text. It will provide an in-depth analysis of two examples of nostalgia 'genres' as previously outlined. In order to compare possible similarities and differences between Germany and Spain, an emphasis has been put on those television series which were broadcasted in both countries. The series have been extracted from a sample of three years (2009-2011) of Spanish and German television fiction, choosing the best examples of their category. Since some of the outlined nostalgias are dependent on memory and since several investigations into the side of cognitive psychology could show that memory is most active "between 10 and 30" (Eysenck and Keane, 2005, p. 263), five examples have been further chosen according to the "reminiscence bump" of two different age groups. At the same time two, respectively three, fall into the "formative" years, namely those years of childhood and early adulthood which according to Mannheim are especially decisive in the formation of a generation (Volkmer, 2005, p. 236; Volkmer, 2006a, p. 6), of each age group. In order to cross-check possible nostalgias against the backdrop of a purely media-transmitted, "prosthetic" memory, one example is situated outside the life-span of both age groups. The following series are part of the sample:

- The first season of the rerun *Knight Rider* (NBC, 1982) (*Knight Rider* (RTLplus, 1985); *El coche fantástico* (TVE, 1985)) and the fifth season of the rerun *The Avengers* (ITV, 1961) (*Mit Schirm, Charme und Melone* (ZDF, 1966); *Los Vengadores* (TVE, 1966)).
- The first season of the remake *Knight Rider* (NBC, 2008) (*Knight Rider* (RTL, 2009); *El coche fantástico* (La1, 2008)) and the film remake *The Avengers* (Chechik, 1998).
- The first season each of the period dramas *Mad Men* (AMC, 2007) (Fox, 2009; Cuatro, 2009) and *Borgia* (Sky Italia, 2011) (*Borgia* (ZDF, 2011); *Borgia – Una familia consagrada al vicio* (Cosmopolitan TV, 2011)).

In each case, the analysis focuses on the levels of context, narration, aesthetic and design and characters (Mikos, 2008). Following the premises of the television analysis (Mikos, 2008) as they have also been stressed in the methodological part, it will integrate aspects from the nostalgia discourse, memory discourse and studies on aesthetic emotions as they have been outlined and combined in the theoretical section.It has been shown that concerning nostalgia, context and living environment are especially important, because in relation to different memories, personal or "we-group" related, 'real' or "prosthetic", it may or may not elicit nostalgias in different "we-groups". Here, the study must contain an ethnographic component. The Spanish and German audiences and possible smaller "we-groups", their "specific cultural contexts" and the "backgrounds of lifeworlds" (Mikos and Prommer, 2005, p. 163 [o.t.]) will be considered, insofar that each analysis is accompanied by a short review of the respective temporal contexts and programme contexts. Thereby, it should be noted here, no claims of completeness or depth can be made.

Later, every level of the texts will be examined regarding in which way it may "prefigure the cognitive and emotional activities of the spectators" (Prommer et al., 2003, p. 60 [o.t]) in order to work as a trigger for nostalgia and where the possible nostalgia triggers may be located, be it on the level of the fictional world or on the level of the artefact. Where it is suitable, the public discourse in newspaper articles will be considered – as Higson (2003, p. 2) says, the "very specific audience of professional cultural commentators" and "film critics". In the German context, mainly articles in *Süddeutsche Zeitung* (SDZ), *Frankfurter Allgemeine Zeitung* (FAZ) and the *Frankfurter Allgemeine Sonntagszeitung* (FAS) will be examined. Regarding the Spanish context, articles in *La Vanguardia, El País, ABC*, and *El Mundo* will be consulted. A complete discourse analysis will not be done here. The discourse fragments (this could be whole newspaper articles or text passages) will be scrutinised regarding the question if the observations, arguments and comments made correspond with what has been explained on the textual level as a potential trigger for nostalgia. Some first conclusions regarding eventually shared nostalgias in different "we-groups" can be drawn here. Both the cross-checking and contextualisation will give some first indicators of possible different readings. In some aspects it will further allow the analysis to integrate the perspective of "different cultural mappings" (Hepp, 2009), just as Hepp (2009) notes in the context of transcultural studies in general. However, in this step of the analysis the complex memory circumstances can only be considered in a very simplified form. If a reading is actually made, it will be scrutinised in the reception study in the last part of this work.

Next to the general genre contextualisation that has been previously mentioned, each sub-chapter is preceded by a short revision of the theoretical part in which the 'modules' that have been gained from the combination of the approaches shall be re-combined with a view on the analysis of the single genres. In the case of the remakes, the dominant relation to the past is the 'reference' to the premake, regarding reruns, it is both the 'reference' to the first-run and the relation to the 'original' temporal context, and in the case of period dramas, it is the narration of the better past. Coming from here, it will have to be seen if in each nostalgia 'genre', as they have been described previously, different nostalgias and nostalgia triggers are dominant. While 'artefact nostalgia' is expected to be dominant in remakes, period dramas are thought to offer above all potential triggers of what is called 'F nostalgia', and reruns are assumed to contain a mix of 'F and A nostalgia'.

6.1 RERUNS AND NOSTALGIA

Aside from the general lack of research regarding nostalgia and television and the fact that a similar lack of research concerning television reruns has been highlighted by several authors (Furno-Lamude and Anderson, 1992, p. 362; Spigel, 1995, p. 18; Kompare, 2005), television reruns are named frequently when it comes to nostalgia and television, both in the scientific (Furno-Lamude and Anderson, 1992; Williams, 1994, pp. 173 f.; Spigel, 1995; Grainge, 2002; Kompare, 2005; Dika, 2003, pp. 22 f.) and the public discourse[1]. With reference to the literature, the introductory chapter on television reruns already stated that over time a shift of connotation of the programme form has taken place, whereby nostalgia can be seen as one possible added meaning. This chapter will now look at reruns as possible triggers for nostalgia. The author is conscious of the fact that different readings of the reruns are possible – some of them may be explicitly not nostalgic. Nevertheless, the purpose of this analysis is to identify those levels of the text which, according to the theoretical section, may possibly provoke nostalgia and favour the nostalgic emotion. The question if the nostalgia on offer is finally 'decoded' will be scrutinised in the reception analysis in Part III of this study. Since some authors have already named reruns in the context of the nostalgic feeling, here we can draw on some previous studies. Further refinements will be made by means of application of the 'modules' as they have been worked out in the theoretical part of the work.

In contrast to other forms of nostalgia-fiction which will also be considered, reruns are the television programmes that have been seen as worth preserving and

1 Starting from U.S. cable channels such as *Nostalgia Network* (later *Nostalgia Good-TV*) launched in 1984 (Grainge, 2002, pp. 48 f.), the Spanish *Canal Nostalgia* (1996-2005) respectively *TVE 50 Años* (2005-2007) featuring TVE's (Televisión Española's) archive programme, or the German pay-TV channel *Sky Nostalgie,* all specialize in television reruns – not to mention the high number of rerun-related content one finds by conducting a simple search for "nostalgia and television" via Google.

that have been taken from the archives as they are. It can be assumed that they have not been subject to "erosion or accretion" (Lowenthal, 1986, p. 125) on the material layer; they did not undergo any changes, neither regarding their formal structure nor regarding their content. When they haven't been nostalgic before, for example reruns of nostalgic period dramas, as first-runs they probably did not work as triggers for nostalgia.[2] The only thing that has changed is the context: the programme context, the political context, the historical, or cultural context, and their reception, or as Bennett and Woollacott (1987) would say, the "'reading formation'", "those specific determinations which bear in upon, mould and configure the relations between texts and readers in determinant conditions of reading" (Bennett and Woollacott, 1987, p. 64). Mikos (2008, p. 285 [o.t.]) suggests in this context that, for example, the repetition of *Dallas* is perceived in different ways than the first-run, since it is decoded on the basis of different "discursive practices". Due to the 'displacement', a whole range of references and 'gaps' between past and present arise, some of which depend upon the knowledge of the first-run and the knowledge of the 'original' programme context (e.g. one that sets the first-run reception against the rerun-reception); others are also recognisable without the knowledge of the first-run (e.g. clashes with the new programme context). They will be explored in more detail. The main questions are: What are the potential objects of nostalgia and which aspects provoke the fact that the new reading is nostalgic?

First and foremost, when reruns may be called nostalgia 'genre' as it is supported both by the academic and the public discourse, then we may assume that nostalgia is one mood audiences may expect when they watch a rerun. Later, the text and its context have to be further analysed. Regarding the macro level, more precisely: the level of the rerun as a whole, a reference to Kompare's (2005) study is suitable. As Kompare argues, "[c]hanging perceptions, more than anything else, have had the most significant effects on the cultural status of television. The past itself cannot change, but its meanings and uses for the present can." (Kompare, 2005, p. 107) In the U.S. context Kompare explains how different 'reading formations' contributed to a revaluation of reruns in the 1970s (Kompare, 2005, p. 103). The author concentrates on the localisation of the cultural creation of possible gaps between 'now' and 'then' on a macro-level (Kompare, 2005, p. 107). Here, Kompare refers to a whole range of factors for changing connotation, highlighting "retrospective classifications of television museums and archives, journalistic commentary, academic inquiry, and nascent fan cultures" (Kompare, 2005, p. 105). All together they contributed to a "growing legitimation of past television" (Kompare, 2005, p. 120) and to the construction of a "television heritage" in the U.S. – serving parts of the necessary basis for the narration of the better (television) past (Kompare, 2005, p. 139).[2] By

---

2   For example the study shall refer to some aspects the author highlights. A key factor is the
    myth of the 'Golden Age of Television' in America (Kompare, 2005, p. 107). "While",

attaching to these narratives, one may suppose that even recipients who do not know the first-run can acquire knowledge upon which the narration of a better past, respectively nostalgia, may be enabled.

Kompare (2005) refers only to a collective scope here. From the theoretical part, above all from the study of Davis (1977) to which Kompare (2005, p. 114) also refers, it can be deduced that equal processes of "retrospective classification" arise on the individual level. In this context it must be considered what O'Sullivan (1991, p. 163) points out regarding early television memories and how they work as reference points that make us aware of changes between our past and present identity. This is probably where another 'gap' may be located, which makes the rerun a potential trigger for nostalgia at least for those who remember the first-run. As we can assume that the rerun as a whole may already work as a "mnemonic prompt" (see Sprengler, 2011, p. 76 in the context of music and nostalgia), the analysis will take possible reference points into account by considering aspects of genres, the rerun/first-run in its 'original' cultural context, and the rerun/first-run in its 'original' programme context both in Germany and Spain. Additionally, the public discourse will be considered. The reception study in Part III of this book will facilitate more concrete observations.

Taking the theoretical background of aesthetic emotions into consideration, it is suggested that the nostalgic reading may concern every single level of the text. Also at this point the existence or creation of a gap in relation to present modes can be expected to be essential. Be it on the textual level or regarding the reception, nostalgia contains references to the prelapsarian, lapse and postlapsarian circumstances (Tannock, 1995), whereby the present is shown as worse in comparison to the past

says Kompare (2005, p. 111), "the Golden Age was most heavily promoted by television itself, it could only achieve long-term legitimation" by entering the museum and archives. Apart from that, Kompare highlights that scholars began to investigate television and its cultural value. "Through such designations [namely the concern with social and cultural relevance of television], the lines of an academic television heritage were drawn." (Kompare, 2005, p. 123) Lastly, argues Kompare (2005, pp. 114 ff.), the broad perception of change regarding the living circumstances in the 1970s and before contributed to the valorization of the past. In this context the author refers explicitly to the work of Davis (1974) and his approach to nostalgia as dependent on "'the way we *make* [...] [the past] contrast'" with the present (Davis, 1974 cited in Kompare, 2005, p. 114 [italic emphasis in the original]) – an assessment which is often shared by whole generations and especially present among "adolescents and young adults" (Davis, 1974 cited in Kompare, 2005, p. 115). On this level, Kompare shows how journalistic articles, books and others create 'we-identities' around television programmes, such as the one for the so-called 'Baby Boomers' (Kompare, 2005, pp. 115 f.). In the context of this work we may also suggest that processes of remaking contribute to the valorisation of the premake, for instance, by giving it the status of an 'original' (Oltmann, 2008, p. 27), as mentioned.

(Davis, 1979, p. 15), whether, as it has been noted with reference to Davis (1979, pp. 18 ff.), in the form of simple, reflexive, or interpreted nostalgia.

Assuming that 'artefact nostalgia' is important when it comes to television reruns, the first question must be how the audiences become aware of an artefact (see also Tan, 1996, p. 65). Tan (1996, pp. 34 f.) supposes that artefact emotions are more likely to arise in people who have a special affection for the medium. In the context of television reruns, these are probably the viewers who know the first-run. For them, we can suppose, any artefact of the rerun may evoke memories, or, as Sprengler (2011, p. 76) highlights in the context of music and nostalgia, may work as a "mnemonic prompt" and, depending on the "retrospective classification", as a potential trigger for nostalgia. Further, as Tan (1996, p. 65) highlights, "[s]udden twists in the plot" or very intensive F emotions can effect that the viewers become aware of the artefact level (Tan, 1996, p. 65; Visch et al., 2010, p. 1440). This may also apply to television reruns. However, one can argue here, there is one factor that mainly assures that a rerun or a single artefact of that rerun catches the attention of both the audiences who know and those who don't know the first-run, which is its "differential quality". The term "differential quality" was coined by Christiansen (1909) and has later been used by the Russian Formalists (Striedter, 1989). It points to the novelty a device can contain by contrasting with others. Novelty in turn is again a major source of attention (see e.g. Werber, 1998; Eder 2002, pp. 42 f.). Christiansen explicitly refers to the fact that in the course of time, forms can go through a 'growth' "caused by enstrangement; new differences arise and qualities of mood often associate refreshingly into the aesthetic objects" (Christiansen, 1909, p. 124 [o.t.]). A first question may then be in which way the television rerun or a single aspect of it contrasts with the *new* context. In this context, Lowenthal (1986) is worth mentioning. As the author notes, "[t]he awareness of things past derives from two distinct but often conjoined traits: antiquity and decay. Antiquity involves cognizance of historical change, decay of biological or material change." (Lowenthal, 1986, p. 125) Since "erosion or accretion" (Lowenthal, 1986, p. 125) are not normally observable in the reruns that the study shall refer to here[3], antiquity is what is interesting in this context. According to Lowenthal (1986, p. 125) its "marks" are "anachronistic styles or historical associations". This is in line with Tashiro, who notes that "[o]bjects selected for their transparent resonance become opaque; those included as neutral filler[s] find unexpected prominence within the obsessions of a new setting" (Tashiro, 1998, p. 8).

It is here where nostalgia may enter the single levels of the rerun both for those who know and those who don't know the first-run. By using the term "historical associations", Lowenthal (1986, p. 125) hints at a first point. Thus, over the course

---

3 This does not mean that video material does not run the risk of eroding (for more on that, see e.g. Ernst 2007, pp. 153 ff.).

of time, single artefacts may gain (new) referential character, such as a general indexical relationship to (cultural) products of the era, which is also recognisable for those who do not know the first-run.[4] Also on this level artefacts may work as a "mnemonic prompt" and, depending on the respective "retrospective classification", provoke nostalgia. As Sprengler (2011, p. 94) shows with reference to Lord, props may have a "'cultural baggage'" that may impede or support nostalgia.

Apart from that, the single levels may contain further characteristics that may favour a nostalgic reading or not. It can be assumed that also artefacts exposed by reruns may make the past desirable, just as Higson (2003) describes it in the context of the heritage film. Here, it is surely relevant what Sprengler (2011), in the contexts of the 1950s, calls the "self-mythologizing efforts" of an era, and that makes the objects it produced good objects of nostalgia from a present position (Sprengler, 2011, p. 47).

This similar applies to the level of the fictional world. Thus reruns, it has been mentioned previously, when they are not reruns of, for example, nostalgic period dramas or already as first-runs enabled 'empathetic F nostalgia', most probably do not expose nostalgia. However, it may be expected that examples can be found that favour a nostalgic reading. In this context Herrera-De La Muela's (2009) work on the Spanish teen-series *Verano Azul* (1982) can be considered. With reference to the terminology of White and Schwoch (1997), the television scholar shows how the rerun of the 1980s series favours nostalgia since its first-run already worked as an "agente historiador" [agent of history] (2009, p. 158 [o.t.]) that naturalises the conflicts of the transition era (Herrera-De La Muela, 2009). Similar observations have been made by Dika (2003) regarding the function of the television reruns in the "flow of television programming" (Dika, 2003, p. 203). The 1960s shows she refers to

"reflected little [...] historical upheaval; instead they presented viewers with linear narratives, stable time and space, and integrated characters and images. The return of these products in our contemporary era still carries the connotation of order within a context of historical disruption and hence serves as a form of denial." (Dika, 2003, p. 203)

---

4   In the course of their investigation on "popular music and photography as technologies of memory", Keightley and Pickering (2006, p. 152) describe a shift towards the mere "historical representation". "Where these [may have] had little, if any, significance in the past [...], they become considerably more salient as a result of the passage of time." (Keightley and Pickering, 2006, p. 152) The reruns, we can say, become icons of their time. In the context of photography, the same mechanism is described by Fischer (1981, p. 126).

These observations are in line with Bennett (1996) who, in the context of the reproduction of the "'classic text of the European imperial archive'" (Bennett, 1996 cited in Hutcheon, 2000, p. 201), refers to a similar mechanism. It is, says Bennett,

> "'always to risk its willing and wistfully nostalgic assent to (re)claim its own authority. Those texts are simply so heavily overcoded, value laden, that the production and reception of the 'new' text necessarily becomes bound to the tradition that encompasses and promotes the old 'authentic' version'." (Bennett, 1996 cited in Hutcheon, 2000, p. 201)

Consequently, in this context it is inevitable to hold the picture of the time that is painted against 'real history'. Apart from that, regarding the rerun, we must consider if the text enables 'empathetic F nostalgia' or if it exposes nostalgic music. If, as Böhn (2007, p. 150) suggested, quotations may lead to "nostalgic longing" towards the "restoration" of past emotions, we can at least assume that any F or A emotion that is remembered in the context of the first-run and that is lacking from a present position can be the object of nostalgia.

Accordingly, the analysis will contain the following research steps. A general description of the format will be followed by a brief contextualisation of the rerun against the socio-political and programme background of the time of its 'original' broadcast both in Germany and Spain. In a second step, "retrospective classifications" in both countries will be discussed. The following analysis will look at the micro-level. Here, it can already partly be considered which "we-group" the respective potential trigger for nostalgia is targeted at. References to the public discourse, in form of press articles, provide further evidence. In the centre of the analysis there are two examples, *Knight Rider* (NBC, 1982), respectively *Knight Rider* (RTLplus, 1985) and *El coche fantástico* (TVE, 1985) and *The Avengers* (ITV, 1961), respectively *Mit Schirm, Charme und Melone* (ZDF, 1966) and *Los Vengadores* (TVE, 1966). Both were broadcasted as first-runs on German and Spanish television and could be viewed as reruns between 2009 and 2011.

6.1.1 Analysis of nostalgia in *Knight Rider*

Knight Rider is an American action series released in the U.S. by Universal Television in 1982 (Moody, 2001, p. 69; Niggemeier and Reufsteck, 2005, p. 664). The series ran for four seasons. Apart from the remake *Knight Rider* (NBC, 2008), which will be considered in a further section of this work, several spin-offs of the series were produced, such as *Team Knight Rider* (NBC, 1997) and the TV movie *Knight Rider 2000* (1991). As Moody (2001, p. 69) argues, children have been "wooed partly by the range of toys and merchandise marketed in conjunction with the series". Today the complete seasons are available on DVD.

Knight Rider is centred on Michael Knight (David Hasselhoff), a Vietnam veteran and ex-policeman who changes his identity after nearly dying from a gunshot wound. As we learn, the rich and terminally ill businessman Wilton Knight chose him to fight against crime for his Foundation for Law and Government (FLAG). On his quest, Michael is supported by KITT (Knight Industries Two Thousand), a talking super-computer-car in the form of a black Pontiac Trans-Am. KITT is equipped with diverse features, such as rockets, smoke bombs, a surveillance mode, a turbo boost, and beyond that, a know-it-all personality. Michael also relies on a support-team, consisting of Devon Miles (Edward Mulhare), the leader of the foundation after Wilton Knight's death, and the mechanic Bonnie Barstow (Patricia McPherson), and their mobile home headquarters in the form of a truck.

Apart from certain science fiction elements, the series could be assigned to the action adventure genre (Moody, 2001, p. 69) – later represented by series such as *The A-Team* (NBC, 1983) or *Airwolf* (CBS, 1984). As Miller states in the context of American television in 2001 and 2008, the genre, despite "[c]heap or rerun action series [which] survived on cable networks and satellite services" (Miller, 2001, p. 17; 2008, p. 24), is "largely over as far as broadcast TV is concerned" (Miller, 2008, p. 24). Creeber (2008) shows that the genre relived a certain renaissance in the form of the high-quality blockbuster series *24* (Fox, 2001), both broadcasted on German (RTL II, 2003) and on Spanish television (Antena 3, 2003). However, argues Creeber (2008, p. 27) "*24* was distinctly different in form and style to the action series of the past". For example, the author (2008, p. 27) here refers to an increased realism, higher levels of suspense and stylistic novelties, such as its specific use of the split-screen.[5]

6.1.1.1 *El coche fantástico* in Spain

Knight Rider, or *El coche fantástico* as is its Spanish title, was first broadcasted in Spain on the public-service broadcasting channel TVE in 1985 (Capilla and Solé, 1999, p. 58). According to *El Mundo*, it was one of the most popular series of the 1980s (Cuartango, 2008; see also *La Vanguardia*, 1985). Antena 3 bought the series in 1990 (*La Vanguardia*, 1990) and broadcasted it from 1991 to 1998 (*La Vanguardia*, 2006). Further reruns of the series were broadcasted on Antena 3 between 2005 and 2008 (Aniorte, 2008) and on Cuatro from 2007 to 2009 (Manuls, 2007). In 2010, the digital channel Antena Neox showed various seasons in random order (Neox, 2011). In 2011, the series could be viewed on Telecinco (*La Vanguardia*, 2011a).

---

5   Correspondingly it is not further astonishing that *Frankfurter Allgemeine Sonntagszeitung* discussed *Knight Rider* as come back of the "guten, alten und einfach gestrickten Action-Epen der achtziger Jahre" [good, old, simply structured action-epics of the eighties] (*Frankfurter Allgemeine Sonntagszeitung*, 1996 [o.t.]) already in 1996.

6.1.1.1.1 Some contextual notes – 1980s Spain

In order to give a brief idea of the socio-political context, and if we apply the term *Transición* [transition] – the change from the dictatorial regime of Franco to a democratic society (Palacio, 2011, p. 201) – in its broadest sense, mid-1980s Spain was at the end phase of this era. In its widest definition, stresses Palacio (2011, p. 201), the *Transición* has been described as encompassing the years of late Francoism until 1986, when Spain became a member of the European Union.

By that time, the strongest political party was the *Spanish Socialist Party* (PSOE) (Juliá, 1999, p. 111), and Spain, "[h]itherto separated [...] from the welfare states that existed in Europe" (Juliá, 1999, pp. 115 f.), went through a time of economic growth (see also Palacio, 2008, p. 94). According to Juliá (1999, p. 116), a sensation of "tranquillity and security" started to accompany the spirit of optimism that had already marked the early years of *Transición* (Juliá, 1999, p. 116). In this respect it is not surprising that *El coche fantástico* is described in *El Mundo* as representative of "'this epoch of the first times during which not everything was possible, but it seemed that way'." (Garcia Ruipérez, 2011 [o.t.])[6].

In the mid-1980s, Spanish television audiences lived through the last years before the introduction of commercial television with "no fewer than twenty home-grown prime-time fiction serials, of which the great majority were period pieces" (Smith, 2006, p. 31). As Palacio (2008, p. 159) notes, Spanish series, such as *Anillos de oro* (TVE, 1983), *Segunda enseñanza* (TVE, 1986), or *Tristeza de amor* (TVE, 1986), very much reflected the social climate. International series from *Alf* (TVE, 1988; NBC, 1986), *Las Chicas de Oro* (TVE, 1986) [The Golden Girls, NBC, 1985], *Dinastía* (TVE, 1983) [Dynasty, ABC, 1981], *MASH* (TVE, 1983; CBS, 1972), *Corrupción en Miami* (TVE, 1986) [Miami Vice, NBC 1984] or *El Equipo A* (TVE, 1985) [The A-Team, NBC, 1983] to *Heimat* (autonomous channels, 1985; ARD, 1982), *MacGyver* (TVE, 1987; ABC, 1985), or *Magnum* (autonomous channels, 1985) were also shown.

6.1.1.1.2 Discourses on *El coche fantástico*

As Kompare (2005, p. 105) states, regarding the creation of a gap between 'then' and 'now', "retrospective classifications" of institutions such as television museums and others are relevant. In the theoretical part of this study it already has been shown that the television museum in Spain is less important than in the US, where Kompare's study is situated. Among the two temporal exhibitions that have been named, only *TV World. Television Culture (Món TV. La cultura de la televisió)* could support the

---

6 Original quotation: *"Teatro Nuevo Alcalá se embarque en un viaje a los 80, 'aquella época de las primeras veces en que no todo era posible pero, eso sí, lo parecía'."* (Garcia Ruipérez, 2011)

construction of a television heritage.[7] However, *Knight Rider* was not included in the quality fiction on which the exposition focused on. In general, the specific Spanish context is rather marginally discussed. The second exposition, titled *Are You Ready For TV? (¿Estáis listos para la televisión?)*, did not consider popular television fiction.

Regarding the academic discourse with reference to Jordan and Morgan-Tamosunas (2000), it can be stated that those designations, which, according to Kompare (2005), are concerned with social and cultural relevance of television and draw "the lines of an academic television heritage" (Kompare, 2005, p. 123), are "establishing" themselves (Jordan and Morgan-Tamosunas, 2000, p. 1). However, it seems that *Knight Rider* has not been considered in a Spanish context up to now. 'Golden age myths', as they have been created around certain epochs of Spanish television (Smith, 2006, p. 12; Ministerio de Educación y Ciencia, 2007; Palacio, 2008, p. 51), also do not include *El coche fantástico*.

Nevertheless, apart from that, other institutions had their part in creating an aura of television heritage around the series and providing the ground for possible nostalgic readings. Alongside television channels and single programmes – the period show *Peta Zeta* (Antena 3, 2008), for example, presented *Knight Rider* as one of the period's icons (Quilez, 2008), also Cuatro highlights the rerun as "classic" (Cuatro, 2006) – non-academic television compendiums in Spain include *El coche fantástico*. For example the compendiums *Telemanía. Las 500 mejores series de TV de nuestra vida* [Telemania. The top 500 Television Series of Our Lives] (Capilla and Solé, 1999) and *Televisión de Culto. 100 series míticas* [Cult Television. 100 Mythical Series] (Blanco, 1996) show a clear valorisation of the series they contain.

Furthermore, the public discourse promotes the series as part of television heritage. Here, *El coche fantástico* is named a "título de culto" [cult title] (Broc, 2009 [o.t.]), "ícono de la televisión de los ochenta" [icon of 1980s television] (*La Vanguardia*, 2009 [o.t.]), "mito[...] televisivo[...]" [television myth] (Cornejo, 2008 [o.t.]), "verdadero mito de los adolescentes que hoy transitan la cuarentena" [true myth of the adolescents who are now (2009) in their 40s] (Carol, 2009 [o.t.]), or just "emblemática[...]" [emblematic] series (Cuervo, 2004 [o.t.]).

Lastly, *El coche fantástico* has a Spanish-speaking fan club (Club de Fans, 2011). Websites such as elcochefantastico.net (2011) give Spanish-speaking *aficionados* a discussion forum. Furthermore, the remake *Knight Rider* (NBC, 2008) and the discourses that surround it hold a part in the transformation and valorisation of the premake. TVE, for instance, remembers the original in the context of the remake as "la mítica serie" [the mythical series] of the 1980s (RTVE, 2011[o.t.]). Further

---

7 As Ramoneda, the director of CCCB, puts it: "And whether we like it or not, television is a phenomenon which has played a central role in shaping the mind-set of our society" (Ramoneda, 1999).

discourses that establish the premake as a potential trigger for nostalgia will be noted in the context of the remake-analysis (see Chapter 6.2.1.1).

6.1.1.2 *Knight Rider* in Germany

As of 2012, apart from brief interruptions, the synchronised German version of *Knight Rider* was broadcasted nearly continuously on German television. The first broadcast of the series can be dated back to 1985 (Niggemeier and Reufsteck, 2005, p. 665) – at that time, as Moorstedt states (2009), Michael Knight and KITT were distinct heroes for German children. It was the first success of the private channel RTLplus (Niggemeier and Reufsteck, 2005, p. 665). Later, *Knight Rider* could also be watched on the public service channel Das Erste (1991), the private channels RTL (1993-1994; 1996; 2002-2003), RTL II (1996-1997) and various other private channels throughout the years. Since 2005, reruns of the series have been shown on the private channel *Das Vierte*[8] and, since 2009, on the pay-TV channel *AXN* (2009-2011) (Imfernsehen, 2011). Since 2011, the series has also been transmitted in HD on the pay-TV channel TNT.

6.1.1.2.1 Some contextual notes – 1980s Germany

When *Knight Rider* was first broadcasted, West Germany was undergoing major changes on the political level. After more than a decade, the government changed from the Social Democrat Party (SPD) and Free Democratic Party (FDP) coalition to a coalition of the Christian Democratic Union (CDU) and the Free Democratic Party (FDP). With this change the *Ära Kohl* [era Kohl] (Schildt, 2002) began, named after the then CDU chancellor Helmut Kohl. Germany in the 1980s was also shaped by a mobilisation of the peace and environmentalist movement, the fall of the Berlin Wall (1989), and the German Reunification (1990), but it also faced major political scandals, such as the so-called *Flick-Affäre* [Flick affair] or the *Barschel-Affäre* [Barschel affair] in 1987 (Schildt, 2002). As Heidemann (2002) notes, the national debt of the German Democratic Republic (GDR) increasingly affected the living circumstances of its citizens. Apart from that, the author (2002) names two factors which finally led to the downfall of the state: firstly, the lack of democratic legitimacy, and secondly, Gorbachev's reform politics, which accentuated the inability of the government to implement reforms. Increasing demonstrations for political changes and liberalisation and mass flights finally brought the end of the German Democratic Republic in 1989 (Heidemann, 2002; Pulzer, 1999, p. 40).

Regarding television, the mid-1980s reflected the beginning of the so-called dual system in West Germany. As Hickethier (1998, pp. 450 ff.) shows, programmes included mini-series focusing on German and European history or literary films.

---

8   In 2006, *Knight Rider* reached a 1.4% market share in the 14-49 age group on *Das Vierte* (ots, 2006).

Apart from that, television series such as *Liebling Kreuzberg* [Darling Kreuzberg] (SFB and others, 1986), *Die Schwarzwaldklinik* [The Black Forest Clinic] (ZDF, 1985) or *Die Lindenstraße* (ARD, 1985) could be viewed (Hickethier, 1998, pp. 460 ff.). While according to Hickethier (1998, p. 462) both private and public service channels broadcasted American series and serials such as *Dallas* (ARD, 1981), *Der Denver-Clan* (ABC, 1981; ZDF, 1983) [*Dynasty*], *Magnum* (ARD, 1984), *Miami Vice* (ARD, 1986), *The A-Team* (Das Erste, 1987), or *Bonanza* (ARD 1962-1965; Sat.1, 1987), programmes with more violent content, such as *Airwolf* (Sat.1, 1986), were shown on private channels (Hickethier, 1998, pp. 446 f.). In the GDR, the reception of West German television was widespread (Linke, 1987, p. 48; see also Meyer, 2010).

6.1.1.2.2 Discourses on *Knight Rider* today

Also in the German case "retrospective classifications" of *Knight Rider* may be observed. Regarding television museums and archives, *Knight Rider* was not included in the collection of the *Deutsche Kinemathek – Museum für Film und Fernsehen* at least until 2006. However, as stated by its curator in *Frankfurter Allgemeine Sonntagszeitung*, its integration indeed had been aspired (Niggemeier, 2006). Alone this discussion, we can argue, exposes *Knight Rider* as part of the (German) television heritage. Apart from that, in general, the museum understands television as part of everyday culture (Niggemeier, 2006) and also includes it in its valorisation process.

It is a similar case regarding the academic discourse. Apart from two studies that focus on *Knight Rider* from a media pedagogical perspective (Schmidbauer and Löhr, 1992; Anfang and Schorb, 1998), in general the rising "concern with social and cultural 'relevance'" (Kompare, 2005, p. 122) of television, which Kompare sees as fundamental for the drawing of the "lines of an academic television heritage" and for an eventual subsequent nostalgic reading, can be observed in Germany as well. Referring to Goldbeck (2004, pp. 58 ff.), the reception of *Cultural Studies* approaches, whose start may be located in the 1990s, increased over the last decades. A growing scientific interest in popular culture on the side of media and communication studies was observed (Goldbeck, 2004, p. 16).

Aside from this, the series is contained in non-academic compendiums on television such as *Kultserien und ihre Stars – Das Pflichtprogramm* [cult series and their stars – the compulsory programme] (Keller, 1998 [o.t.]) or *Kultserien im Fernsehen* [cult series on television] (Haderer and Bachschwöll, 1996 [o.t.]). Television channels promote *Knight Rider* as part of television's heritage. According to Weichert (2002 [o.t.]) RTL calls it a "Manifest der 80er" [manifest of the 1980s]. *Das Vierte* refers to *Knight Rider* as a "Serienklassiker" [classic series] (see Das Vierte, 2007 [o.t.]) and to KITT as "legendär[...]" [legendary] (ots, 2006 [o.t.]).

The public discourse in the form of newspaper articles also holds its part in the "retrospective classification" of *Knight Rider*. Authors name the series "ein Kulterlebnis" [a cult experience] (Weichert, 2002 [o.t.]), "Achziger-Kultserie" [Nineteen-eighties cult series] (Sauerbrey, 2009 [o.t.]), "Kultserie aus America" [cult series from America] (Bäumer, 2003 [o.t.]), "eine Attraktion aus dem TV-Museum, die heute noch Programme füllt" [an attraction from the TV-museum that still fills the programme] (Feldmer, 2006 [o.t.]), the "unschlagbar kultige Serie" [unbeatable cult series] (cepes, 2002 [o.t.]), "die legendäre[...] TV-Serie" [the legendary TV-series] (Zirnstein, 2011 [o.t.]), or "Kultserie der 80er" [cult series of the 1980s] (Dinauer, 1999, [o.t.]). Finally, *Knight Rider* is part of a fan culture reflected on fan websites (Schulte, 2011) or in fan literature (Schulte, 2009). Furthermore, as will be shown in the context of the remake-analysis, the discourse about the remake *Knight Rider* (NBC, 2008) establishes the premake as a potential trigger for nostalgia in Germany as well.

6.1.1.3 Nostalgia on the single levels of the text

6.1.1.3.1 Narration

With the exception of Episode Number 19, in which Michael meets his fiancée from his former life[9], the narration of *Knight Rider* is not nostalgic in the sense that it is narrated from the perspective of a protagonist who longs for a better past, as Higson (2003) has for instance described it in the context of the heritage film. Apart from the pilot, which contextualises the series and tells the history of Michael Long's metamorphosis to Michael Knight, each episode follows a similar scheme. An exposition that usually introduces the new case is followed by Michael Knight and

---

9   This episode with the title *White Bird* is the only one in which Michael Knight is directly confronted with his past identity, Michael Long. The episode starts when a newspaper article on his former fiancée, Stephanie Mason, catches Michael's attention. Stephanie has been arrested for collaborating in an illegal money transaction, which Michael is unwilling to accept. He thus starts investigating into the case in the course of which it turns out that the woman is innocent. Due to his investigations Michael starts to fall prey to nostalgia. Most evidently this is articulated in a flashback (min. 00:06:00) in form of a montage sequence of sepia-tinted photographs of his former fiancée, underlined with Stephanie's declaration of love and romantic rock music (the song *White Bird Must Fly* by the band *It's A Beautiful Day* (1969)). Subsequently Michael reveals his feelings and his simple intentions to retrieve this part of his past back into a presence that lacks any comparable relationships. Miles instead brings him back to reality and provides the interpretative layer hinting at the negative side of his former identity as a cop with enemies who are out to kill him. His conclusion "You can't go back. You can't even afford to look back" lets us correctly anticipate the end of this episode.

KITT's coming into action. In their fight against injustice – often cases of corruption or sabotage – they usually get the attention of their opponents, who then in turn do their best to obstruct the mission. Action scenes, in the form of chases and fights in which KITT demonstrates its skills, then follow. In the last minutes, the duo prevents the worst-case scenario from happening, so at the end of the episode 'order' is restored. A sub-plot usually integrates Michael's romantic interests with one of the central, innocent female characters. A certain sense of humour is found in the conversations between Michael and KITT, usually when KITT's computer-brain is unable to understand human behaviour and Michael's explanations lead to an even greater lack of understanding. Due to its simplicity the series clearly contrasts with today's quality television and insofar exposes a clear gap between 'then' and 'now'.

Apart from that, in a dominant strand, the series may be read as simplifying Cold War politics by turning them into a simple good-bad dichotomy in favour of the West. It presents the 1980s as somehow less complex, as if it was easier to tell right from wrong. In this respect, the 'return' of the series may, just as Dika puts it in the context of reruns in general, hold "the connotation of order within a context of historical disruption and hence serves as a form of denial" (Dika, 2003, p. 203). In doing so, the rerun of the series enables 'F nostalgia' or serves the pattern for individual nostalgia directed towards the 'original' temporal context. At the same time, other readings are possible. According to Moody (2001, p. 71), regarding other aspects, *Knight Rider* presents a "much more complex and ambiguous vision". A dominant factor, the television scholar argues (2001, p. 74), is that the series frequently highlights small communities or private persons that are "threatened by high-level corruption and the machinations of big business", often on a state governmental level. The series often comes to ambiguous conclusions in relation to the state authorities itself.[10] From this perspective, it may be argued, the nostalgic narration is rather undermined.

6.1.1.3.2 Aesthetic and design

The aesthetic and design of *Knight Rider* is instantly recognisable as being part of the 1980s. Already the credits relate to past television. The use of technicolour aesthetics makes the series look anachronistic to the viewers who are used to contemporary television.

Camera, montage and lighting

Camera, montage and lighting of *Knight Rider* are conventional and simple. Dominant camera views are long shots that establish new settings or expose the

---

10 See, for example, the first episode on *Deadly Maneuvers* on arms running in the U.S. Army. The "go army!" sticker on KITT can only be understood as ironic comment; or *Just My Bill* which portrays a corrupt political system.

velocity and skilfulness of KITT, the major prop of the series. The human body is rather shown in longer shots, such as medium close-ups, while nearer close-ups focus on the exposition of objects, above all the aspects of KITT. Camera movements are mostly restricted to panoramas and optical zooms, travelling shots are exceptional (see e.g. Season 1, Episode 3). Regarding the lighting, the dominant style is normal-key. Editing follows the principals of continuity editing. All in all, and not without reason, Caldwell (1995, p. 57) compared the series with "proficient, but very neutral, B-film style from the lot". *Knight Rider* clearly differs from the "cinematic style" (Caldwell, 1995) exposed by contemporary series. This may create "historical associations" in contemporary viewers and, depending on respective "retrospective classification", trigger 'artefact nostalgia'.

For example, we can refer to the utilisation of the split-screen technique. From the third episode on, creators of the series introduced this feature whenever important plot points appear. The camera zooms in on a face or object and the frame freezes. The size of the freeze frame is now reduced towards the right side of a black background on whose left side an oval still frame of KITT is situated.[11] The utilisation of split-screen is indeed not historical. Often neglected in the television past, lately its use in the action series *24* (Fox, 2001; RTL2, 2003; Antena 3, 2003) led to a certain 'renaissance' of the device (see e.g. Talen, 2002). However, apart from that, the 1980s series in its simplicity, relative slowness and stylistic reservation may not be compared to the "'feature-style cinematography'" (Caldwell, 1995 cited in Shimpach, 2010, p. 131) of *24*. While the latter employs the split-screen as a mode of transition or in order to express simultaneity (Shimpach, 2010, pp. 130 ff.), *Knight Rider* exposes it rather for its own sake, displays it, or, utilising Sontag's words on camp, emphasises "texture, sensuous surface, and style at the expense of content" (Sontag, 1964). It gains certain "campiness", at least when regarded with the temporal distance of today's rerun viewers, which makes it differ from current uses.[12]

The same applies to the use of zoom in *Knight Rider*. As Hickethier (2001, p. 70) states, zoom is today a broadly used stylistic device. However, while today's television series are characterised by a moderate utilisation of the feature, the sometimes repetitive use of abrupt zooms in *Knight Rider* (see e.g. Season 1, Episode

---

11 See here for instance Season Number 1, Episode Number 3 *Slammin' Sammy's Stunt Show Spectacular*, min. 00:43:30. See also similar freeze-screen-shot-combinations in the 1980s, such as in the video clip *Billy Jean* by Michael Jackson (1983).

12 As Sontag (1964) shows, "[c]amp is art that proposes itself seriously, but cannot be taken altogether seriously because it is 'too much'". Apart from that, the temporal aspect is an important component in Sontag's definition of camp. "Thus, things are campy, not when they become old – but when we become less involved in them, and can enjoy, instead of be frustrated by, the failure of the attempt." (Sontag, 1964)

19, min. 00:06:00) seems anachronistic from today's perspective.[13] Here is also where a further 'gap' may be located. Thus what may have been fascinating in a 1980s context, be it inside the fictional world of *Knight Rider* or be it as an artefact, is rather old-fashioned from today's perspective.

Settings

Knight Rider is set in an everyday American location. Dominant features are small town backgrounds, American highways, and desert-like landscapes, as they could exist in a contemporary series and with little narrative relevance. In this respect the series does not seem anachronistic. It contains little of what Straubhaar (1991) called "cultural proximity" both to a Spanish and a German cultural context. Not to mention the fact that "sensuous experience" is only scarcely found in the foreground. The arousal of 'internal empathetic artefact nostalgia' is not favoured here.

Props and costumes

Knight Rider uses a lot of props – internationally traded consumer goods such as MS DOS video games, bulky car phones, or drainpipe jeans – that may work as period markers beyond national borders and provoke 'artefact nostalgia' in both the viewers who know and those who don't know the first-run.[14] They may provoke the viewers' 'own artefact nostalgia' in the case that they function as "mnemonic prompt[s]" by reminding recipients of a moment of earlier reception.

The main prop of the series is KITT, a black Pontiac Trans Am, equipped with a range of technical finesses and a computer brain that establishes it as one of the leading 'characters'. The car's position as main prop already becomes obvious in the introductory sequence of the series where a clear majority of the shots is dedicated to the car. While longer shots show its speed and manoeuvrability, a range of close ups highlight technical features. According to Moody (2001, p. 72), "KITT was a computerized car – an everyday artefact in which the new 'futuristic' technologies had been successfully incorporated".

Despite the fact that the prop is directly recognisable as belonging to the 1980s and, depending on the subject position, may thus provoke 'A nostalgia' or the viewers' 'own A nostalgia', this is also where a further 'gap' between the

---

13   Spanish audiences who have been socialised with 1970s' television may be reminded of the television programmes by Valerio Lazarov who not seldom has been called "'Rey del Zoom'" [King of Zoom] (I.G., 2009 [o.t.]) or "Mister Zoom" (EFE, 2009) in the public discourse.

14   See, for example, Weichert, who states that "Musik, Klamotten, ja sogar die Frisuren machen aus der TV-Serie ein 'Manifest der 80er Jahre', so RTL zur Wiederholung aller 88 Folgen" ["according to RTL about the repetition of 88 episodes, music, dresses, and even hairstyles make the TV series a 'manifest of the 1980s'" (Weichert, 2002 [o.t.]).

prelapsarian and postlapsarian world in the series rerun may be located, for those who know the first-run. What may have been 'futuristic' in the 1980s and/or inside the fictional world of the 'original' *Knight Rider* is less probable or even outdated from today's point of view. Fascination, joy, whatever A or F emotion may have been provoked from a past point of view is probably gone from a present point of view. It must be seen in the reception study if this lack can be a potential trigger for the viewers' 'own nostalgia' directed towards the former (A or F) emotion.

A corresponding assumption is at least supported by the public discourse. Apart from the fact that the car as the main prop of the series was and has kept on being one of the central topics of the Spanish public discourse on *Knight Rider* (see e.g. Jimenez, 1987; *La Vanguardia*, 1990; Carol, 2009), the discourse well reflects the 'gap' between the once-fascinating car and its lost impact from today's perspective. While earlier discourse fragments mention the fantastic abilities of the vehicle (see e.g. *La Vanguardia*, 1990)[15], current articles rather compare present automobiles with "*el coche fantástico*" (see e.g. *ABC*, 2004; Cuartango, 2008; Sevillano, 2009). In some articles, the lost fascination is explicitly stated. According to Carol in *La Vanguardia*, "*Knight Rider* was [...] a celebration of technology as a weapon to dominate the earth, today it seems normal to us that a car talks, even though it is the GPS" (Carol, 2009 [o.t.]).[16] "That a car moves without conductor stopped being a topic reserved to science fiction films" (Prat, 2005 [o.t.])[17] Prat states in his article titled *El coche fantástico* [The Fantastic Car].

The same applies to the German public discourse. In the context of the remake of *Knight Rider*, Moorstedt hints to the fact that "the utopia of someday has become obsolete. Cars have been able to speak ('turn left') and have contained powerful computer processors for several years now." (Moorstedt, 2009 [o.t.])[18] In *Süddeutsche Zeitung*, Georgescu puts it as follows: "While in the 1980s only experts of the US-series *Knight Rider* knew that cars can talk and simultaneously deal with a difficult situation, technicians have now constructed an intelligent vehicle ready to

---

15 The author describes the main prop as: "ese coche tan especial, un vehículo indestructible y con un cerebro propio" [this so very special car, an indestructible vehicle with a brain of its own] (*La Vanguardia*, 1990 [o.t.]).

16 Original quotation: "*El coche fantástico* resultaba, además, un canto a la tecnología como arma para dominar la Tierra, por más que hoy nos parece normal que nos hable el auto, aunque sea mediante el GPS." (Carol, 2009)

17 Original quotation: "Que un automóvil se desplace sin que haya un conductor al volante ha dejado ya de ser un asunto reservado a las películas de ciencia ficción." (Prat, 2005)

18 Original quotation: "[D]ie Utopie von einst ist überholt. Längst können Autos sprechen ('vorne links abbiegen') und besitzen kraftvolle Computerprozessoren." (Moorstedt, 2009)

go into production." (Georgescu, 1998 [o.t.])[19] Also, Dinauer highlights that today's technical possibilities would turn the 1980s oldie green with envy (Dinauer, 1999 [o.t.])[20]. Finally, Boie stresses: "'Knight Rider' seemed to come from the future." (Boie, 2009 [o.t.])[21] The simple past he uses indicates that these times have long since been over.

Apart from these aspects, the car's "cultural baggage" itself contains 'gaps' between different worlds, which today, depending on the subject position, make it considerable as a possible trigger for 'A nostalgia'. Its "implicit meaning", to use a term applied by Tashiro (1998, p. 12), changed in the course of time. Firstly, *Pontiac* as one of the oldest brands of General Motors stands for the rise and fall of the American car industry (see e.g. Hodgson, 2006). Above all in the 1960s, a time when mineral resources seemed to last forever and emissions were no topic at all, the Pontiac Firebird gained mythical status as a sports car (Listri, 2009). Today it is more a relic than a sign of these 'golden' times. Secondly, *Pontiac* has travelled through popular culture. A change of connotation can be observed here, which provides a clear gap between 'then' and 'now' and, depending on the subject position, may serve the necessary basis for 'artefact nostalgia'. While the car's representational construction in a film such as *Smokey and the Bandit* (Needham, 1977) supports a masculinity of the hero that is built upon physical strength and a patriarchal habit, twenty years later in *American Beauty* (Mendes, 1999) it symbolised a decaying image of white masculinity mourned after by a man in his mid-40s and in a midlife crisis.

The public discourse in both Germany and Spain above all reflects the loss of the 'mythical' status of the car. Under the title *"El final de una leyenda"* [The end of a legend] and with a clear nostalgic stance, the Spanish newspaper *La Vanguardia* discusses "[t]he definite retirement of Pontiac [as] the allegory for a not so far time in which racing along the motorway was a sign of power, the cars burned cheap gasoline and Detroit was the industrial capital of the country" (Carol, 2009 [o.t.])[22].

---

19 Original quotation: "Während in den 80er Jahren höchstens Kenner der US-Serie Knight Rider wußten, daß Autos sprechen und dabei auch noch Gefahren meistern können, haben die Techniker nun das intelligente Fahrzeug fast bis zur Serienreife konstruiert." (Georgescu, 1998)

20 Original quotation: "[D]ie[...] Spielereien auf der damaligen 'Wissensbasis' würden den Achziger-Oldie heutzutage recht peinlich wirken lassen." (Dinauer, 1999)

21 Original quotation: "'Knight Rider' schien aus der Zukunft zu kommen" (Boie, 2009).

22 Original quotation: "La jubilación definitiva del Pontiac es la alegoría de un tiempo no tan lejano en el que correr en la carretera era signo de poder, los coches quemaban gasolina barata y Detroit era la capital industrial del país. Los ochenta fueron la decada de Ronald Reagan, cuando el mundo percibía lo americano como la iglesia verdadera y su fe alcanzaba al mundo comunista [...]." (Carol, 2009)

In an article titled *"La última batalla de Pontiac"* [The Last Battle of Pontiac] *El País* writes that *"Knight Rider* exists. The mythical brand struggles with vending or closure because of the crisis." (Listri, 2009 [o.t.])[23] Additionally, the article hints at the cultural impact KITT had in the Spain of the 1980s, where imitations of the 'fantastic car' appeared on motorways (Listri, 2009).

This similarly applies to the German discourse. Here, Dinauer of the German newspaper *Süddeutsche Zeitung* highlights KITT as being representative of a time "when cars still used to guzzle a lot of gasoline and the Russians were always bad" (Dinauer, 1999 [o.t.])[24]. With the Pontiac, says Boie, "dies a symbol of American pop-culture. Because between 1982 to 1986 the Pontiac Trans AM was the car of Michael Knight, the casual hero of the television series *'Knight Rider'* interpreted by David Hasselhoff" (Boie, 2009a [o.t.])[25].

Music

Each episode starts with a keyboard score – a driving melody that builds the *leitmotiv* linked to KITT and Michael throughout the series. Since, as Sprengler (2011, p. 76) highlights, a "song can function as a mnemonic prompt", it is likely that the *Knight Rider* opening credits may provoke (nostalgic) associations in those viewers who have a memory of it. Apart from that, the synthesised sounds are clearly recognisable as belonging to the 1980s also for those who do not know the first-run.

This similarly applies to the further score. Even though *Knight Rider* exposes here almost no original songs but mainly newly composed instrumental music with less recognition value, from a present point of view the reference to the 1980s is always apparent. Furthermore, the music has a dramatic function, mainly to support suspense and action or to create a romantic atmosphere. The generation of a "'nostalgic condition'", as Flinn (1992, cited in Sprengler, 2011, p. 77) calls it, is no dominant function of the music.[26]

---

23 Original quotation: "El coche fantástico sí existe; La mítica marca se debate entre su venta o cierre por la crisis." (Listri, 2009)

24 Original quotation: "als die Autos noch mächtig Benzin schluckten und die Russen immer böse waren" (Dinauer, 1999).

25 Original quotation: "Mit [...][Pontiac] stirbt ein amerikanisches Popkultur-Symbol. Denn der Pontiac Trans AM war von 1982 bis 1986 das Auto von Michael Knight, dem von David Hasselhoff gespielten, lässigen Helden der Fernsehserie 'Knight Rider'." (Boie, 2009a)

26 An exception is Episode Number 19 where Michael is confronted with his past identity. The episode exposes original songs. Thus in various sequences the 1960s romantic rock song *White Bird Must Fly* is central. It not only reflects the nostalgic condition of the protagonist and invites the audiences' empathy, it also creates time references to the 1960s, which may trigger the viewers' own associations.

6.1.1.3.3 Characters

Next to KITT, who, we can argue, is depicted as the second leading figure, Michael Knight is the main character of the series. This paragraph concentrates on him. Other characters are mainly relevant in case they interact with Michael or KITT or to legitimise the heroes' actions.

Michael Knight

Except from the previously mentioned Episode Number 19, which exposes the nostalgia of Knight towards his former identity and indeed may provoke an 'empathetic F nostalgia' in the spectator who feels with the protagonist, the character Michael Knight as such is not nostalgic. In general, the viewers get to know little about his past, and when they do get information (from an ex-cop or ex-Vietnam soldier), it is not presented as being worth longing for – on the contrary. Independent of the question whether the protagonist himself feels nostalgia or not, the action series with its general focuses "on action rather than character" (Miller, 2001, p. 17) does not favour empathy on the level of the fictional world. 'Empathetic F nostalgia' is thus probably not a form of nostalgia that may be dominantly provoked by the rerun.

According to critics, such as Caldwell (1995) as referred to by Moody (2001, p. 70), the character "appears to derive from a dated and simplistic formula of TV crime-fighting in which a hard-boiled detective fights for justice on behalf of the wider community". He contrasts with tendencies in contemporary television, where the psychological profiles of the protagonists are more complex each time (see e.g. Vilches et al., 2009, p. 119 on *House* (Fox, 2004)). Here, there is also a clear gap between 'then' and 'now', which, depending on the subject position and at least favoured by the "retrospective classifications" of the series, may provoke 'A nostalgia'.

Depending on the reading, a further potential trigger for nostalgia can be presumed with regard to the image of masculinity Michael Knight represents. The "lone crusader in a dangerous world" represents typical characteristics of the (American) masculine hero who used to "flee[...] from the home" while "the women are the stable forces" (Gabbard, 2008, pp. 61 f. [o.t.])[27]. He is exposed as containing character traits that are consistent with dominant ideas of masculinity of the 1980s ("'self-assured, unafraid, in control and autonomous'" (Hite, 1981 cited in Fiske, 1987, p. 200)). Inside the closed and linear narration, this masculinity is positively connoted since it helps the protagonist reach his goals. From a present point of view and depending on the position of the reading subject, the idealised narration of the past may enable 'F nostalgia'.

---

27 Original quotation: "En la cultura de Estados Unidos el héroe huye del hogar – las mujeres son las fuerzas estabilizadoras." (Gabbard, 2008, pp. 61 f.)

At the same time, the characterisation of Michael Knight also relates to an ambivalent concept of white masculinity.[28] As Moody shows, "Michael Knight has a distinctly unspectacularized – even 'feminised' – masculine persona, allowing him to respond sensitively to the human dilemmas that are the narrative focus for many of the crimes he encounters" (Moody, 2001, p. 78). It is often his emotional rather than physical competence that makes the protagonist succeed (see e.g. Season 1, Episode 18). Consequently, argues Moody (2001, p. 78), the character Michael Knight can also be described as a "manifestation of the 1980s New Man", which "eschewed traditional, 'armour-plated' machismo in favour of a more emotionally literate masculine ideal" and rather refers to the present. Following this reading, nostalgia is less the issue.

David Hasselhoff – the rise and fall of a person(a)

Firstly, the actor David Hasselhoff contains intertextual references. Besides his television roles as Michael Knight in *Knight Rider* and Mitch Buchannon in *Baywatch* (NBC, 1989; Antena 3, 1991; Das Erste, 1990), both in Germany and Spain Hasselhoff's past image is shaped by his singing career and other activities. In the Spain of the 1980s Hasselhoff presented his first album in *Sábado Noche* (TVE, 1987-1989) (Jimenez, 1987) – one of Spain's most popular prime-time shows at that time – performed in one of Spain's famous New Year's Eve programmes (see Reyes, 2006), and was known for his charity activities (ABC, 1987).

It is a similar case with Germany, which, was probably the country where Hasselhoff became most successful. The culmination of Hasselhoff's triumph in Germany was surely his performance during the ceremony of the German reunification in 1989 (Löbert, 2006). As Fromme (2010) states in *Süddeutsche Zeitung*, "I've Been Looking for Freedom", the song he interpreted, was the Number One hit for eight months in the German charts. Already on this level and always depending upon the respective "retrospective classification" of the reference, Hasselhoff may work as potential trigger for 'A nostalgia' or a viewer's 'own A nostalgia' in both those viewers who know and those who don't know *Knight Rider*.

Secondly, despite the character Michael Knight, the private person and the star persona[29] of David Hasselhoff provide a clear gap between a 'then' and 'now' or a pre- and postlapsarian world that also makes him a possible trigger for 'artefact nostalgia'. The star image clashes here with an actual image that is rather dominated by the private person Hasselhoff, by alcoholism and personal failure. This is also reflected by the public discourses both in Germany and Spain. When his past

---

28 "The action hero on screen in the twentieth century [in general] has been an important site of interrogating, rearticulating, and reasserting masculinity as cultural conditions have transformed the meanings of its performance." (Shimpach, 2010, p. 38)

29 Thumin (1986, p. 71) defines persona as "a public image which derives from the performance and the utterances of the person".

activities are in the centre of attention, David Hasselhoff is – as Belinchón (2011 [o.t.]) puts it in *El País* – the "mito" [myth] or "leyenda de las tardes de la televisión" [legend of the TV night]. Other authors call him "uno de los personajes televisivos más conocidos" [one of the best-known television personalities] (Cuna, 1999 [o.t.]), "[e]l mítico [...] conductor del coche fantástico" [the mythical [...] driver of the fantastic car] (*El Mundo*, 2010 [o.t.])[30], or the "Actionheld der 80er" [action hero of the 1980s] (Bäumer, 2003 [o.t.]). Articles that focus instead on his current career paint a rather sad picture. They centre on his alcoholism and other unpleasant details from his private life (*ABC*, 2004a; *El País*, 2007; Cuervo, 2004; Reyes, 2006; Löbert, 2006; *ABC*, 2009).

Some of them explicitly contrast the past and present image of the actor. "Formerly", writes Selleras in *La Vanguardia,* "he was a statuesque life-guard, a proud driver of the fantastic car. Now he has become a sad and old imitation of the characters he once interpreted." (Salleras, 2010 [o.t.])[31] This similarly applies to the German public discourse. In *Süddeutsche Zeitung*:

"David Hasselhoff has become famous for his roles in the TV series '*Knight Rider*' and '*Baywatch*', also as a singer he enjoyed success with hits like 'Looking for Freedom'. In recent years, however, he only made headlines because of his alcohol addiction." (Süddeutsche Zeitung, 2009 [o.t.])[32]

Pollmer describes him as someone "who flew so much higher than others, but who also fell so much deeper" (Pollmer, 2011 [o.t.])[33]. And in a swansong on the good old days of television, Schader (2006) moans the fall of David Hasselhoff next to the end of other television icons, such as Rudi Carrell, a famous German TV show host.[34]

---

30 A clear distinction between his television character and the private person is not always made (see e.g. Jimenez, 1987; Belmonte, 2006; Bosch, 2011).

31 Original quotation: "Antaño fue un escultural vigilante de la playa y un orgulloso conductor de un coche fantástico. Ahora se ha convertido en una triste y anciana imitación de los personajes que protagonizó." (Salleras, 2010)

32 Original quotation: "Berühmt geworden ist David Hasselhoff durch seine Rollen in den TV-Serien 'Knight Rider' und 'Baywatch', auch als Sänger feiert er mit Hits wie 'Looking for Freedom' Erfolge. In den letzten Jahren machte er indes nur noch mit Schlagzeilen über seine Alkoholsucht von sich Reden." (Süddeutsche Zeitung, 2009)

33 Original quotation: Hasselhoff, "der so viel höher flog als andere, aber auch so viel tiefer fiel" (Pollmer, 2011).

34 A resumed part of this analysis has been presented at the *4th European Communication Conference* Bilgi University Istanbul, 24-27 October 2012 (Armbruster, 2012b).

6.1.2 Analysis of nostalgia in *The Avengers*

The Avengers is a British crime series originally produced and broadcasted on British television between 1961 and 1969 (Niggemeier and Reufsteck, 2005, p. 807). The series contains a total of six seasons, from which the first four seasons were in black-and- white. Season five, on which this analysis will mainly focus, and six were colour episodes.

In the centre of these episodes is John Steed (Patrick Macnee), a special agent in the service of the British queen, who investigates difficult cases: mysterious deaths, the disappearance of dubious businessmen, attacks of hostile agents or cases of hypnosis. Dressed in a tailor-made suit and equipped with a steel-filled bowler hat and an umbrella, which, with its dagger inside, often serves in order to knock out his opponents, Steed is the British gentleman *par excellence*. He is supported by Emma Peel (Diana Rigg) – called into action by Steed's ritual "Mrs Peel – we're needed". Intelligent, attractive, always perfectly styled and, apart from that, with karate skills, she is the ideal partner.[35] Following Miller (2008, p. 25), the series may be described as a hybrid of the spy genre, a subcategory of the action series and the thriller genre (see also O'Day, 2001, p. 221). Apart from that, as highlighted by Niggemeier and Reufsteck (2005, p. 808), it contains parodic elements.

6.1.2.1 *Los Vengadores* in Spain

The Avengers, or better, *Los Vengadores*, the Spanish title of the series, was first broadcasted in Spain on TVE in 1966, starting with the third season on (Capilla and Solé, 1999, p. 231). The fourth and fifth seasons of the series could be watched in 1967 (*ABC*, 1967; *ABC*, 1967a)[36]. Later, in 1970, the episodes featuring Linda Thorson were broadcasted (*La Vanguardia Española*, 1970). In 1990, *Los Nuevos Vengadores* could be watched on Canal 9, the same year that La2 showed several reruns of the series (Berciano, 1990; Herms, 1990). In 1991, the fifth season of *Los Vengadores* was broadcasted on La 1 (see e.g. *La Vanguardia*, 1991; *La Vanguardia*, 1991a). Further reruns of the series have been shown in 1994 on Canal Clásico (De la Calle, 1994) in 1997, on the satellite channel Canal Digital (*La Vanguardia*, 1997) in 1997, on Cultura TV (*El País*, 1997) or on Canal+ (*La Vanguardia*, 1999) in 1999.

---

35 In later episodes, Peel is substituted by Tara King (Linda Thorson). In *The New Avengers* (1976-1977), which revived the series seven years after its last broadcast, followed Purdey (Joanna Lumley) and Mike Gambit (Gareth Hunt) as Steed's assistants (Niggemeier and Reufsteck, 2005, p. 808).

36 According to the newspaper *ABC*, *Escape in Time* (Season 5, Episode 3) was broadcasted on 8.10.1967 (ABC, 1967b) and *The Bird Who Knew Too Much* (Season 5, Episode 5) on 15.10.1967.

Between 2009 and 2011, the episodes with Diana Rigg as Emma Peel, which also stand in the centre of this analysis, were re-broadcasted on Calle13.

6.1.2.1.1 Some contextual notes – 1960s Spain

In the 1960s, when *Los Vengadores* was first broadcasted in Spain, the country went through the so-called "'Spanish miracle'" – a rapid period of economic growth that "transformed Spain's agrarian economy into an industrial one" (Boyd, 1999, p. 99). This significant change started with the increase in power of some technocrats with a close relationship to Opus Dei (Boyd, 1999, p. 99).

"Fearing that rising social conflict might destroy the dictatorship and the traditional Catholic culture it guaranteed, the Opus ministers advocated controlled economic modernization that would raise living standards without raising expectations for political change." (Boyd, 1999, p. 99)

For the first time, Spaniards had access to a broader range of consumer goods and a rising mass consumer culture (Palacio, 2008, p. 73; Boyd, 1999, p. 100). Additionally, the country increasingly opened up for international tourism (Alcojar et al., 2006, pp. 15 ff.). However, these factors could not distract from the absence of political self-determination and liberty under Franco's regime. Rather the contrary was the case. As Boyd (1999, p. 100) describes, the "rising material well-being subverted the Francoist 'peace' by exposing the political and cultural gulf that still separated Spain from her European neighbors". Increasing opposition of the working class and "student unrest" followed (Boyd, 1999, p. 100). While, argues Boyd (1999, p. 101), new laws seemed to respond to this movement and to extend freedom slightly, by the end of the 1960s, with the "political ascendancy of Carrero" a "return to a hard-line policy on labor and student unrest, press censorship, and Basque terrorism" (Body, 1999, p. 101) is highlighted.

Almost parallel to the rapid economic growth, more precisely between 1964 and 1969, Spanish television went through the so-called Golden Age – a heyday of TVE's live dramas, such as *Estudio 1* or *Novela*, but also through a climax of political repression and censorship (Smith, 2006, p. 12; Ministerio de Educación y Ciencia, 2007; Palacio, 2008, p. 51). While Spaniards in the late 1950s/early 1960s could already watch many international programmes, such as *Te quiero, Lucy* (TVE, 1958) [I Love Lucy, CBS, 1951], *Cisco Kid* (TVE, 1959) [The Cisco Kid, Syndication, 1950], *Bonanza* (TVE, 1963) [Bonanza, NBC, 1959], *Furia* (TVE, 1961) [Fury, NBC, 1955], or *Doctor Kildare* (TVE, 1964) [Dr Kildare, NBC 1961], now, as Deacon highlights (1999, p. 313), "[p]rograms were purchased from abroad on a large scale, especially light entertainment series". Apart from *Los Vengadores* (TVE, 1966) [The Avengers, ITC 1961], the list includes *La Familia Munster* (TVE, 1965)

[The Munsters, CBS 1964], *El Superagente 86* (TVE, 1968) [Get Smart, NBC, 1965], *Misión Imposible* (TVE, 1968) [Mission Impossible, CBS, 1966], *Sam Sade* (TVE, 1972) [CBS, 1971], or *Colombo* (TVE, 1972) [NBC, 1971].

According to Palacio (2008, p. 148), Spanish productions were also characterised by an international scope. Valerio Lazarov produced formally innovative fiction, such as *El irreal Madrid* (TVE, 1969) [The unreal Madrid], *Osaka Show* (1970), or *360 grados alrededor de...* (Palacio, 2008, p. 150). The second channel TVE2, launched in 1966, had a more cultural orientation (Palacio, 2008, p. 73), and more innovative and experimental formats (Palacio, 2008, p. 128).

Nevertheless, the public discourse suggests that the hybrid mix of *Los Vengadores* clearly clashed with the existing programme. Still, more recent articles recall the fascination about the novelty of the series. "*Los Vengadores*", said *La Vanguardia* in 1990, "offered an ironic alternative for the spy series and films that augmented in the decade of the Sixties" (Herms, 1990 [o.t.])[37]. It was, says another author of the same newspaper, "en la línea de otras series de la época, aunque en tono paródico" [in line with other series of the epoch, even though with a parodic tone] (*La Vanguadia*, 1990a [o.t.]). Pérez also highlights that the series implemented a new topic to the genre, namely "el espionaje como juego" [espionage as game] (Pérez, 2010 [o.t.]). It has to be seen in the reception study if nostalgia towards a former fascination (A emotion) may be observed among those who know the first-run.

6.1.2.1.2 Discourses on *Los Vengadores* today

Considering "retrospective classifications of television museums and archives, journalistic commentary, academic inquiry, and nascent fan culture" (Kompare, 2005, p. 105), *Los Vengadores* has been restructured as belonging to (Spain's) television heritage. In contrast to *Knight Rider*, *Los Vengadores* is included inside the collection of *TV World. Television Culture (Món TV. La cultura de la televisió)*. Asked for the "best fiction series", two television experts who express their views in the exhibition catalogue, highlight the series explicitly (Savall cited in Balló et al., 1999, p. 165; Trashorras in Balló et al., 1999, p. 165).

Apart from a general valorisation of popular culture in those parts of the academic discourse that are increasingly influenced by cultural studies (see e.g. Jordan and Morgan-Tamosunas, 2000), in Spain the series falls into the epoch which, according to Palacio (2008, p. 48 [o.t.]), has also been called the 'Golden Age' by some authors – "the time of the star directors" (Palacio, 2008, p. 86 [o.t.]). That the valorisation of that epoch also concerns the imported format is, above all, shown by a publication of the film scientist Xavier Pérez (1998), exclusively dedicated to the series. In his book with the emblematic title *El Universo de los Vengadores*, the author calls the series

---

37 Original quotation: "'Los Vengadores' ofrecía una alternativa irónica a las series y películas de agentes secretos que proliferaron en la década de los sesenta." (Herms, 1990)

"[...] mythical [and] the most unpredictable [...] of all those that have been realised in the television studios all around the world during this prodigious decade of the 60s" (Pérez, 1998, p. 12 [o.t.]). However, the work is less written with analytical purposes but rather as a collection of background information – very similar to the fan books on the series. An investigation of the series in the explicit Spanish context is not provided.

The non-academic discourse in form of television compendiums includes *Los Vengadores* among *Televisión de Culto. 100 series míticas* [Cult Television. 100 Mythical Series] (Blanco, 1996 [o.t.]), *Los Mejores series de la historia de la televisión* [The Best Series of Television History] (González-Fierro Santos and Mena, 2008 [o.t.]) or as "serie de culto" [cult series] (Capilla and Solé, 1999, p. 232 [o.t.]) among *Las 500 mejores series de TV de nuestra vida* [The 500 Best Television Series of Our Lives] (Capilla and Solé, 1999 [o.t.]).

A valorisation of the series as part of the Spanish television heritage can also be observed in the public discourse. *La Vanguardia* highlights *Los Vengadores* as "más popular de todos los tiempos" [most popular of all times] (Ramos, 1995 [o.t.]), or "serie de culto" [cult series] (Battle Caminal, 1995; Herms, 1990 [o.t.]). In the same newspaper, Pérez calls *Los Vengadores* "la serie más descreída y placentera de la década" [the most incredible and enjoyable series of all decades] (Pérez, 2010 [o.t.]) and part of "la primera edad de oro de las series" [the first golden age of television series] (Pérez, 2010 [o.t.]). In the context of the remake it is called "legendaria" [legendary] (Parrondo, 1998 [o.t.]), "mítica" [mythical] (*La Vanguardia*, 1990a [o.t.]), "un símbolo imprescindible de los 'sixties'" [an indispensable symbol of the sixties] (Parrondo, 1998a [o.t.]) or just one of the "clásicos" "que han hecho historia" [classics that made history] (*La Vanguardia*, 1999 [o.t.]). The case regarding *El País* is no different. Here, in the context of the remake, *Los Vengadores* is described as "mítica serie televisiva" [mythical television series] (Jose and Moreno, 2003 [o.t.]), "la más popular serie británica de televisión de los años sesenta" [the most popular British television series of the sixties] (Gómez, 1997 [o.t.]) or "la pareja de espías [...] más famosa del mundo" [the most famous spy couple of the world] (L.G., 1997 [o.t.]).

While a similar valorisation on the side of the television channels could not be noticed, *Los Vengadores* is indeed highlighted in fan circles and publications. In 1999, Blanco refers to "fan clubs, postcards, toys and all types of merchandising" (Blanco, 1999, p. 37 [o.t.]) around the cult title. A broad circle of fan-pages, as can be found, for example in the United Kingdom or the United States (theavengers.tv, 2008), however, cannot be attested. A DVD collection with the synchronised Spanish version as it exists, for example, on the German or American market, has also not been published within the timeframe of this study. That the remake *The Avengers*

(Chechik, 1998) and its discourses are part of the valorisation of the premake will be shown in the context of the remake-analysis.

6.1.2.2 *Mit Schirm, Charme und Melone* in Germany

The first-run of *The Avengers*, respectively *Mit Schirm, Charme und Melone*, was broadcasted between 1966 and 1970 on the public service channel ZDF (Niggemeier and Reufsteck, 2005, p. 808). In the beginning, the 36 episodes with Diana Rigg could be viewed (Niggemeier and Reufsteck, 2005, pp. 808). Later, 10 further episodes with the actress Linda Thorson were broadcasted (Niggemeier and Reufsteck, 2005, pp. 808). Following an article in the German newspaper *Stuttgarter Zeitung*, the first 13 episodes *Mit Schirm, Charme und Melone* alone reached an average market-share of 67 per cent (*Stuttgarter Zeitung*, 1967 cited in Baumgart, 2002, p. 89). Between 1985 and 1988, Sat.1 aired further first-run episodes which had not been aired before by the public service channels, due to violent or sexually 'provocative' contents (Niggemeier and Reufsteck, 2005, p. 808).

Later, in 1995, reruns of the series could be watched on RTL2 (*Frankfurter Allgemeine Sonntagszeitung*, 1995), in 2007 on kabel eins or the pay-TV channel Premiere Nostalgie (2006-2007 and 2008). Between 2009 and 2011 the cultural channel Arte broadcasted episodes of all seasons, and some of them (Seasons Number 1-3) had never been broadcasted in Germany before (Imfernsehen, 2011a; Imfernsehen, 2011b). Here, the colour episodes with Diana Rigg playing the part of Emma Peel, which are in the focus of this work, could also be watched again.

6.1.2.2.1 Some contextual notes – 1960s Germany

In Germany, *Mit Schirm, Charme und Melone* was broadcasted at a time that was marked by decisive social changes and generational conflicts. Firstly, in 1961, the Berlin Wall was built, which dramatically influenced private and political life in both parts of Germany (Schiele, 1999, p. 9) and would later lead to significant changes of East/West politics (Schiele, 1999, p. 7). Secondly, mainly influenced by the student movement, the whole system of values – above all of West German society – underwent significant changes.

As the so-called "68er", a significant group of the younger generation attempted to break the silence surrounding the crimes committed under the Nazi dictatorship (Golz, 2003, p. 2) and to break with the "mugginess and petit bourgeois narrow-mindedness of the Adenauer-era" (Hickethier, 1991, p. 192 [o.t.]). The movement found its expression, for instance, in the opposition against the Vietnam war, 'sexual liberation', the demand for better qualifications and equal rights in education and in the so-called Extraparliamentary Opposition (APO) (Hickethier, 1991, p. 192). As Semler shows, it felt "in line with the cultural avant-garde in the USA" (Semler,

2003, p. 4 [o.t.])[38]. Britain, where youth culture could develop more easily, was one of the major examples (Siegfried, 2003, p. 25). It was a different case in the German Democratic Republic (GDR). As Kirchenwitz shows, the 1960s were marked by a tougher ideological line than the time of relative liberalisation in the 1970s, especially the late 1960s (Kirchenwitz, 2003, p. 8).

Regarding television, the time was marked by relative programme extension in West Germany due to the launch of ZDF (since 1963), which, according to Hickethier (1998, pp. 236 f.), led to an increase of serialised forms often realised by programme buying from abroad. Next to *Mit Schirm, Charme und Melone* [The Avengers] (ITV, 1961; ZDF, 1966), the author (Hickethier, 1998, pp. 236 f.) highlights programmes such as *Bonanza* (NBC, 1959; ARD, 1962), *Perry Mason* (CBS, 1957; ARD, 1959), or *Kobra, übernehmen Sie* (ARD, 1967) [Mission: Impossible (CBS, 1966)]. Due to the development of new aesthetic concepts and a quantitative increase, the 1960s have often been called the "Blütezeit" [heydays] of the television play (Hickethier, 1998, pp. 242 ff. [o.t.]) As Meyer (2010, p. 29) shows with reference to inquiries made by *Deutsche Fernsehfunk* in the mid-1960s, 85 per cent of GDR citizens had access to West German television.

Similar to Spain, following Hickethier (1998, p. 237), it can be stated that also in Germany the ironic tone of *Mit Schirm, Charme und Melone* contrasted with the yet existing programme. Apart from that, the series was among the first selected popular entertainment formats to be transmitted in colour (*Der Spiegel*, 1967 cited in Hickethier, 1998, p. 213). Thus, it can be expected to have left its traces on cultural memory.

This assumption also corresponds with the public discourse, where the sense of humour of *Mit Schirm, Charme und Melone* still shows today. Clearly aiming at the ironic stance of the series, Malt (1998) argues in *Süddeutsche Zeitung*: "What distinguished *The Avengers* from other spy series at that time was this belief that nothing, absolutely nothing would be reason enough not to keep the good form." (Malt, 1998 [o.t.])[39] This similarly applies to Martenstein from *Der Tagesspiegel* who also highlights that the series favoured jokes over action when he states: "Sometimes it is better to spend your money on a successful punch line than on an exploding car." (Martenstein, 1998 [o.t.])[40]

---

38 Original quotation: Man fühlte sich "im Einklang mit der kulturellen Avantgarde in den USA" (Semler, 2003, p. 4).

39 Original quotation: "Was die Avengers von anderen Agentenserien jener Zeit unterschied, war diese Überzeugung, daß nichts, aber wirklich gar nichts, Anlaß genug wäre, nicht die gute Form zu wahren." (Malt, 1998)

40 Original quotation: "Gelegentlich ist es besser, sein Geld für eine gelungene Pointe auszugeben als für ein explodierendes Auto." (Martenstein, 1998)

6.1.2.2.2 Discourses on *Mit Schirm, Charme und Melone* today

As in Spain, the German version *Mit Schirm, Charme und Melone* is subject to broad "retrospective classifications". Firstly, the series has been retrospectively valorised due to its integration into the museum. In 2002, *Mit Schirm, Charme und Melone* was launched by the exhibition *Fernsehen macht glücklich* [television makes happy] of the *Deutsche Kinemathek – Museum für Film und Fernsehen* (Raulff, 2002; Kilb, 2002). In 2004, the museum also launched the series as part of the retrospective *Die Kommissarinnen* [the commissioners] (Stiftung Deutsche Kinemathek, 2005, p. 53).

Apart from a general valorisation of popular culture in those parts of the academic discourse that are increasingly influenced by cultural studies, in Germany, as in Spain, the first-run of the series occurs in a time span that television scholars (Hickethier, 1998, p. 242) describe not only as "Blütezeit" [heydays] of the television play but also as a time of increasing experimentations (Hickethier, 1998, p. 135), which are also contrasted with later decades of German television, such as the time before and during its privatisation (Hickethier, 1998, pp. 314 ff.). Furthermore, single academic works highlight the series explicitly. A monograph with the title *Das Konzept Emma Peel. Der unerwartete Charme der Emanzipation: 'The Avengers' und das Publikum* [The concept Emma Peel. The unexpected charm of emancipation: 'The Avengers' and the audiences] (Baumgart, 2002 [o.t.]) investigates and valorises the series regarding its still observable modernity and the positive impacts it had on the representation of women on television. In non-academic publications the series is valorised due to its inclusion in *Kultserien im Fernsehen* [cult series on television] (Haderer and Bachschwöll, 1996 [o.t.]) or CD compilations, such as *Die größten TV Hits aller Zeiten – die besten Kultserien* [The greatest TV hits of all times – the best cult series] (2004, Universal [o.t.]).

Newspaper articles call *Mit Schirm, Charme und Melone* "Kult" [cult] (Malt, 1998 [o.t.]), "Klassiker" [a classic] (Pavlovic, 2007 [o.t.]) or "Kultserie" [cult series] (Martenstein, 1998 [o.t.]). Emma Peel appears here as the "'Queen of Kult-TV'" [queen of cult-TV] (her, 2003 [o.t.]). Apart from that, the channels that broadcasted the reruns also hold their part in the retrospective construction. Arte highlights *Mit Schirm, Charme und Melone* as "Kultserie aus den 60er Jahren" [cult series from the 1960s] (Arte, 2011 [o.t.]). Kabel eins broadcasted the series under the umbrella "Die Originale!" [The Originals!].

Finally, *Mit Schirm, Charme und Melone* is surrounded by a (German) fan-community represented by fan-pages on the internet (see e.g. Spillmann, 2011; Collector's Homepage, 2011; D'Heil, 2011; Kucinski, 2012). Furthermore, merchandising articles, DVD compilations or music CDs of the series are available (see e.g. Kucinski, 2012). The series has been included in retrospectives of local cinemas, for instance in Bavaria (Malt, 1998; her, 2003). Non-academic publications, such as *Mrs. Peel, wir werden gebraucht!* [Mrs. Peel, we're needed!] (Fischer, 2009) supply fans and non-fans with background information about the series. As it will be further outlined in chapter 6.2.2.1, also in Germany the remake *The Avenger* (Chechik, 1998) and the discourses that surround it hold their part in the "retrospective classification" of the series.

6.1.2.3 Nostalgia on the single levels of the text

6.1.2.3.1 Narration

The Avengers represents the typical series with closed episodes but continuity regarding basic settings or leading characters. Each episode follows the same basic scheme: first, an exposition introduces a case, frequently starting with either the murder of a British agent (see e.g. *Escape in Time*, *The Bird Who Knew Too Much*, *A Funny Thing Happened on the Way* or *Something Nasty in the Nursery*), or the murder of a civilian, which later turns out to be related to a mad scientist or power-thirsty individuals (see e.g. *The Hidden Tiger*, *The Fear Merchants*, *The Living Dead* or *Never, Never Say Die*) (see also Baumgart, 2002, pp. 17 f.).

The next scene, in most cases situated in Emma Peel's flat, presents Steed's ritual "Mrs Peel – we're needed" in an always different variation. In the following, the couple starts to investigate the case and to fight for the restoration of 'order'. Here, the same scheme is repeated with new differences and all in all "'widely absurd plots'" (*Daily Telegraph*, 1964 cited in Baumgart, 2002, p. 16) that position the series inside pop entertainment (Baumgart, 2002, p. 16) and make it clash with today's dominant series culture. After a first joint examination of the crime scene, Steed and Peel begin to investigate independently from each other in order to come to the same solution. As a rule, in the course of their investigation more and more victims appear as Steed and Peel are always just too late to avoid that – which, also as a rule, never leads to any compassion on their side. In a last show-down, they are finally able to overcome the perpetrators. The closing "tag scene" with a final punch line (Baumgart, 2002, p. 19) mostly takes place in the flat of Emma Peel (see e.g. *From Venus with Love*, *The Fear Merchants* or *The Winged Avenger*) – at least in the colour episodes of the series. These scenes often lead to a final scene where the couple leaves the setting in peculiar antique vehicles (see e.g. *Escape in Time*, *The See-through Man* or *The Bird Who Knew Too Much*), as it was also dominant in the black-and-white episodes of the series.

We can state that the narration of *The Avengers* is not nostalgic in the sense that it exposes the longing toward a better past in contrast to a lacking present or that it is narrated from the perspective of a longing character. The series rather pleads for a rational combination of both tradition and progress – something, which is above all reflected by its leading characters, Emma Peel and John Steed (see also the further analysis). Those episodes that explicitly deal with history avoid the nostalgic viewpoint.[41]

The same applies when we describe the rerun of the series from today's perspective. In terms of Herrera-De La Muela (2009), who highlights the question of whether a rerun works as an idealising "agente historiador" [historical agent] (Herrera-De La Muela, 2009, p. 158) or not, *The Avengers* cannot be seen as favouring a nostalgic reception of its 1960s context. Apart from the fact that the series with its absurd plots and settings mostly avoids "the 'yardstick of social reality'" (Buxton, 1990, p. 101), the series' ambiguous sense of humour questions the constituents of the stability its protagonists restore – from 'Britishness' as such up to the political system. Above all the patriarchal structure of the 1960s is both exposed and undermined. Miller (2004, p. 188) argues that the series "materializes a transcendent new world, one after patriarchy (or at least on the way to 'after patriarchy' via an utopian alternative universe) and after empire". Accordingly, it is less a glorification of the 1960s but rather an optimistic gaze towards the future.

At the same time, the pop series exposes a range of intertextual references, which, depending on the subject position and respective "retrospective classifications", may elicit 'artefact nostalgia', respectively viewers' 'own artefact nostalgia'. As Baumgart (2002, pp. 120 f.) shows, several episode titles relate to films or novels[42], single episodes contain explicit references to film history (see *Epic,* Season 5, Episode11) or other popular culture products, such as comics (see *Winged Avengers*, Season 5, Episode 6). In other episodes, such as *The Correct Way to Kill* (Season 5, Episode 9) or *The Superlative Seven* (Season 5, Episode 12), the series remakes itself (Pérez, 1998, p. 38).

---

41 See e.g. *Escape in Time* (Season 5, Episode 3), where the attempt to hide in the past becomes the undoing of several highly decorated villains. In the course of the episode Peel and Steed make their own reflections about the (British) past that are far from approaching "the past as a stable source of value and meaning" (Tannock, 1995, p. 455). While Peel reviews women's lack of independence throughout history (see 2:12:48 ff.), Steed, who comments his following 'time travel' to 1790 with the words "I always had a hankering for the eighteenth century", directly undermines this statement with his characteristic humour by adding, "where will I be? Waterloo?" (see min. 2:03:08 ff.). Also in other episodes, the longing look towards the past becomes the fatal doom for its subject. In *The Fear Merchants* (Season 5, Episode 2) the past in the form of returned traumas and phobias makes a couple of businessmen go mad. In *Something Nasty in the Nursery* (Season 5, Episode 14) the evocation of the past makes some government officials unknowing traitors of official secrets.

42 See e.g. *Room Without a View* (Season 4, Episode 15), which refers to the Forster novel and James Ivory's film *A Room with a View. The Bird Who Knew Too Much* (Season 5, Episode 5) refers to the Hitchcock film *The Man Who Knew Too Much* (1956).

6.1.2.3.2 Aesthetic and design

The Avengers is characterised by a clear emphasise on style. While the narration is schematic, aesthetic and design step more into the foreground. Not without reason Buxton classifies *The Avengers* as a so-called "'pop' series" – a genre that "rejects 'depth'" on the level of narration but promotes "the idea that the true meaning is hidden behind the surface appearance" (Buxton, 1990, p. 97). Already the colour spectrum of the series leads the viewers to the 1960s. Following the pop tradition, the colour episodes of the series fall back on an almost "psychedelic chromatology", as Pérez (1998, p. 45 [o.t.]) calls it, and exposes extensive colour planes with maximum contrast and intensiveness.

Camera, montage, and lighting

In general, camera, montage, and lighting of *The Avengers* are conventional. As its narration relies on causal relations and avoids unusual temporal leaps, the editing assures narrative continuity. The lighting is dominantly in normal-key style without claiming significant narrative importance. Since most of the action takes place in the interior and is shot in the television studio, the camera mainly moves in a close-up range.

However, with this simplicity of the early television drama, the series obviously contrasts with the "cinematic style" of contemporary television. Furthermore, the series presents stylistic differences that stick out and that approximate it to the pop tradition. Often the decoupage of dialogue scenes in a conventional shot-reverse scheme is avoided. The camera is then allowed to move freely in the space covering a range of movements – from rapid zooms to longer travelling shots (see e.g. Season 5, Episode 3, min. 1:43:46-1:43:56). Added to this are small-scale formal experiments, such as distorted or reversed cameras (see e.g. *The House that Jack Build* (Season 4, Episode 23)), which reflect, for example, the mental state of a protagonist (Baumgart, 2002, p. 41). As Baumgart (2002, p. 16) highlights with reference to Hickethier (1998), in so doing the series has very much in common with the aesthetic innovations of pop entertainment, as was present in German television of the 1960s in the form of music shows. Regarding Spain, here the television experiments of Valerio Lazarov can be named, in whose comparison *The Avengers* is, however, a rather moderate form of unconventionality. A creation of "historical associations" and 'artefact nostalgia' in viewers from both countries is imaginable.

Setting

The Avengers is mainly set in interior spaces clearly identifiable as décor and very stylised. As Buxton (1990, p. 101) highlights, "[f]antastic plots are juxtaposed with banal, ordinary locations". Its dominant setting is a 1960s fantasy London, a city which in the series is mostly empty and where "[n]othing is what it seems. A luxury hotel contains a concentration camp... a marriage bureau hides an assassination agency." (Buxton, 1990, p. 101) The series differs here clearly from today's television and reminds you of teleplays from the 1960s. Depending on the subject position and respective "retrospective classifications", this may indeed provoke 'artefact nostalgia', respectively viewers' 'own artefact nostalgia'. Due to the low degree of "cultural proximity" and the fact that the series does not favour empathetic F emotions (see also 6.1.2.3.3), the evocation of 'internal empathetic artefact nostalgia' is rather improbable. If we exclude media memories or media-transmitted memories, it can also be assumed that there is little correspondence to audiences' 'scenic memories' of the 1960s, which makes the evocation of respective reminiscences and nostalgia rather less probable.

Décor, props and costumes

It is décor, props and costumes that are most significant in *The Avengers,* which have the largest part in making it a "pop" example (Buxton, 1990, p. 96) and which mark the 'antiquity' of the series. From today's perspective these elements seem "anachronistic" and certainly may provoke "historical associations". The series has a referential character to other stylistic experiments as made in 1960s pop television, both in Germany and in Spain, which makes it a potential trigger for 'A nostalgia' or 'own A nostalgia' for those who draw this connection and retrospectively classify it correspondingly.

The same applies to the single props and costumes. They are also decisive period markers, which already makes them potential triggers for 'A nostalgia' or the viewers' 'own A nostalgia' for both who know and who do not know the first-run, and in case they work as "mnemonic prompt[s]".

Later, the "surfaces [...] are themselves rich in meaning" (Buxton, 1990, p. 97), especially regarding the characterisation of their protagonists. While Steed, beginning with his tailor-made suit and bowler hat and his vintage car up to the Edwardian décor of his flat, is characterised by a rather conservative look – which was already anachronistic even from a 1960s perspective – everything that surrounds Emma Peel was highly modern and stylish from a 1960s point of view. As Miller (1997) highlights, already Cathy Gale, Emma's predecessor, "'wore knee-high boots, tailored leather suits and trench coat at a time when such outfits were only seen in porn magazines and fetishist outlets'" (Miller, 1997 cited in Baumgart, 2002, p. 56). This tradition has been continued in the Emma Peel character. In the black-and-white episodes she was also equipped with leather suits with an S&M connotation (Baumgart, 2002, p. 55). In the colour episodes with Alan Hughes as designer in charge, she mainly wore extravagant one-piece suits – later known as "'Emmapeeler'" (Baumgart, 2002, p. 56).

Even though the pop style had been introduced both in Germany and Spain, in the late 1960s, when trousers only started to become part of women's wardrobes (Nuys-Henkelmann, 1987, p. 46), this was a clear extension of boundaries and a provider of attention. Today's public discourse still reflects this former fascination. As Llopart notes in *La Vanguardia*, the costumes "hicieron historia en la pequeña pantalla" [made history on the small screen] (Llopart, 2010 [o.t.]) in Spain. In an ironic tone Jimenez writes in *El Mundo*: "[I]f we had not seen Diana Rigg dressed and combed as Emma Peel, we wouldn't have known what a designer beret is until [...] the 90s" (Jimenez, 1996 [o.t.])[43]. The same applies to Germany, where, up to more recent examples, Emma Peel's extravagant style and the design objects that surrounded her are at the centre of newspaper articles (Bartetzko, 1998; Güntzel, 2000; malt, 2008; Schinhofen, 2009). According to Niggemeier and Reufsteck (2005, p. 808), Peel's style influenced a lacquer and leather fashion in the 1960s.

From today's perspective, the style is part of a succession in which the space-age style, Op Art or hippie fashion has long since supplanted each other (see e.g. Loschke, 2005, p. 81). Thus what may have been 'futuristic' in the 1960s and may have caused (F and A) emotions, such as adoration, fascination or joy, is less so from a present perspective.[44] Here, we can speculate, is also where a further 'gap' between prelapsarian and postlapsarian world in the series rerun may be located, at least for those who know the first-run. Nostalgia towards this lost fascination, be it in form of an A or F emotion, is thus probable and will be further scrutinised in Part III.

Music

The Avengers uses almost no original songs but mainly originally composed instrumental music. Each (colour) episode starts with a jazz-influenced big band score – a driving melody that is also taken up as credits music and as a *leitmotiv* related to Peel and Steed. In case that it works as a "mnemonic prompt", it is likely that the music may trigger memories and, depending on the respective "retrospective classification", nostalgia in those viewers who know the first-run. Apart from that, the big band music is directly identifiable as belonging to the 1950s/1960s, which may also work as a memory point for those who do not know the series. It can be supposed that other instrumental music has a rather low recall value. Its function is dramatic, mainly supporting the suspense. The generation of a "'nostalgic condition'" is not a function of the music.

---

43 Original quotation: "[S]i no hubieramos visto a Diana Rigg vestida y peinada de Emma Peel, no sabríamos lo que es una boina de diseño hasta [...] los 90." (Jimenez, 1996)

44 As Hart puts it in the general context of nostalgia, "'[t]hen', e.g. in the present of the memory world, [the] [...] future was not yet determined" (Hart, 1973, p. 403). In contrast with today "from the standpoint of the remembering I future given in memory appears determined up to the very moment to the present remembering" (Hart, 1973, p. 404).

6.1.2.3.3 Characters

Central to *The Avengers* episodes on which this analysis focuses are John Steed (Patrick Macnee) and Emma Peel (Diana Rigg). Following the pop tradition, they are types, or, as Buxton (1990, p. 100) puts it, "ideological machines rather than 'real' characters". Neither a deeper psychologising (Baumgart, 2002, p. 23) nor character development can be observed. Design objects that surround them also define their characterisation (Buxton, 1990, pp. 97 ff.). On this general basis we can already state that Peel and Steed decisively contrast with characters that are dominant in today's television and that show a much higher degree of psychologising. Depending on the subject position, this makes the characters potential triggers for 'A nostalgia'. At the same time, the detachment exposed by the characters rather impedes the development of empathy, which makes 'empathetic F nostalgia' unlikely.

John Steed

As Miller (2004, p. 187) highlights, John Steed embodies "both a foppish style harking back to the Regency and modish 1960s chic". In so doing, from a present point of view he is directly readable as a character from the past. For 1960s audiences he already seemed anachronistic. With his preference for a past style within a narration that is situated in the 1960s, the character could even be described as nostalgic. However, his dealing with the past is far from simple longing. It rather contains a reflexive layer, often filled with irony.

Following the pop-series tradition, props, décor and costumes that surround him mainly show this reflexivity. Here, 'lacks' of the past are compensated with 'achievements' of the present. Steed may indeed prefer Edwardian clothing; however, his bowler hat is filled with steel. On the one hand, he drinks his afternoon tea from a nineteenth-century porcelain pot, which, on the other hand, is electrically heated.

Apart from that, the character is exposed as being fully conscious of the shortcomings of his antique companions and exposes that in an ironic manner (see e.g. *The Bird Who Knew Too Much* (Season 5, Episode 5); min. 1:07:00). Furthermore, the final punch line that shows Steed and Peel vanishing in an antique vehicle that is always a different one with different defects – one time it runs backwards, another time it does not run at all – highlights this ironic refraction of the glorification of the old.

The characterisation of Steed as reflexive nostalgic contrasts with other (secondary) characters exposed throughout the series, characters that are nearly obsessed with the past – unable to cope with the present. Without exception these characters are negatively connoted. While the old railway-station maniac in *A Funny Thing Happened On The Way To...* (Season 5, Episode 13) or the combat-nostalgic general in *From Venus with Love* (Season 5, Episode 1) are simply painted as cranky mavericks, in other episodes, such as *Epic* (Episode 5, Episode 11) or *Death at Bargain Prices* (Season 4, Episode 4), the longing towards the past even becomes a danger for others. In any case, the provocation of an 'empathetic F nostalgia' is less probable. As previously referred to, the "ideological machines" (Buxton, 1990, p. 100) do not favour empathy.

Additionally, regarding his further character traits, Steed can rather be described as combining both tradition and modernity. As Miller (2004, p. 188) highlights, he is "a playboy who destabilizes conventional masculinity [of the 1960s] and signifies both a disappearing genteel world and a new, brash one". Steed thus extended images of masculinity as they were dominant both in Germany and Spain in the 1960s. As Baumgart shows, Steed is "beyond domineering phrases or imperious gestures" (Baumgart, 2002, p. 22 [o.t.]). Regarding these characteristics, he rather fits into the present.

Emma Peel

Emma Peel (Diana Rigg) and her predecessor, "personified", as Miller (2004, p. 187) states, "modernity *tout court*: hip, leggy, sexy, brilliant, physically competent women who took nonsense from no man and were Steed's superiors intellectually and his equal in combat". The series is full of "explicit hints at [Peel's] intelligence and independence" (Baumgart, 2002, p. 20 [o.t.]). Patriarchal attitude is directly debilitated both in form of verbal (see also Baumgart, 2002), p. 54) and mimic commentary (see e.g. *Escape in Time* (Season 5, Episode 3), *A Funny Thing Happened on the Way* (Season 5, Episode 13)). At the same time, the character contains, as Baumgart (2002, p. 27 [o.t.]) calls it, an accentuated "feminine-erotic" component, which makes her come close to conventional conceptions of women in the 1960s (Baumgart, 2002, p. 55).

In any case, leading feminine characters like her contrasted with dominant images of femininity in the 1960s, both in Germany and in Spain. According to Baumgart (2002, pp. 88, 91), German television of the 1960s was dominated by a traditional image of femininity that denied women's independence and mainly put them into secondary positions. The author (Baumgart, 2002, pp. 91 ff.) refers here also to international series, such as *Hawaii Five-O* (CBS, 1968) [*Hawaii 5-0* (ARD, 1971)], *I Spy* (NBC, 1965) [*Tennisschläger und Kanonen* (ZDF, 1968)], *Mission: Impossible* (CBS, 1966) [*Kobra, übernehmen Sie* (ARD, 1967)], *Time Tunnel* (ABC, 1966) [ARD, 1971] or *Bonanza* (NBC, 1959) [ARD, 1962], which were also broadcasted on Spanish television at that time (see *Hawai 5-0* (TVE, 1973), *Yo soy Espía* (TVE, 1979), *Misión Imposible* (TVE, 1968), *El Túnel de tiempo* (TVE, 1966), *Bonanza* (TVE, 1963)).

Regarding social reality, the case is not much different. West Germany indeed went through significant social and cultural changes in the course of the '68 movement; however, as Helwig (1997; 1997a) shows, even feminine members of the movement saw themselves confronted with patriarchal structures. In East Germany, the case was only slightly different. On the one hand, says Helwig (1997b), the integration of women into the world of work was highly supported. On the other hand, there was a clear adherence to traditional role models. Under Franco's regime in Spain, where it was the Catholic Church that determined values (Boyd, 1999, p. 93), women, argues Sotelo (2006, p. 4), "were robbed of their integration into society and their international networks, and restricted to their biological functions".

Consequently, it can be stated, in both countries the series clashed with dominant social and political norms. The public discourse in the form of newspaper articles and commentary from the 1990s up to today reflects that the series still conjures up the memory of this extension of the boundaries. As a rule, Emma Peel is in the centre of the discourse. In Spain, several authors of *La Vanguardia* highlight the amplification of feminine roles by the series. Llopart (2010) stresses here that Emma Peel opened a new way for feminine characters in the action and crime genre. So does Herms (1990). For the author, the series was an "inversión de los roles, todavía infrecuente en los años sesenta" [inversion of roles which were still infrequent in the Sixties] (Herms, 1990 [o.t.]). According to Ramos (1995 [o.t.]) *Los Vengadores* contained "ideas y actitudes avanzadas para la época" [ideas and attitudes advanced for that epoch]. "Thirty years ago," notes the author, it "[...] was the bible of television feminism" (Ramos, 1995 [o.t.])[45]. This is also in line with what Gómez writes in *El País*: "Unusual for the epoch," says the author, "Peel did not depend on her companion John Steed, but both were partners with equal responsibilities" (Gómez, 1997 [o.t.])[46]. The same applies to the discourse in Germany. Bartetzko of the *Frankfurter Allgemeine Zeitung* describes Peel as "everything between emancipation and the hippie lifestyle, lady and dominatrix that characterised the fantasies of femininity of the Sixties" (Bartetzko, 1998 [o.t.])[47]. Her appearance in television is described as the "endgültige Demontage" [final dismantling] (Bartetzko, 1998 [o.t.]) of the dominant femininity at that time. A similar view is held by Sterneborg (2008) of *Süddeutsche Zeitung*. "[S]he has", says the author, "influenced the image of femininity of a whole generation and beyond. At a time, when frightened horror queens were still popular in the movies, she took her fate and that of the world

---

45 Original quotation: "'Los Vengadores' fue hace treinta años la biblia del feminismo televisivo [...] ." (Ramos, 1995)

46 Original quotation: "Inusual para la época, Peel no depende de su compañero, John Steed, sino que ambos son socios con iguales responsabilidades." (Gómez, 1997)

47 Original quotation: "alles, was zwischen Emanzipation und Hippietum, Dame und Domina die Weiblichkeitsphantasien der sechziger Jahre ausmachte" (Bartetzko, 1998).

into her own hands." (Sterneborg, 2008 [o.t.])[48] Furthermore, Hermanski (1998) states: "[d]ie Agentin ist eine der stärksten Frauengestalten" [the agent is one of the strongest feminine characters] (Hermanski, 1998 [o.t.]). Martenstein (1998 [o.t.]) calls her "eine Amazone und ein Geschöpf der Beatles-Ära" [an Amazon and a creature from the Beatles era]. In *Frankfurter Allgemeine Zeitung*, Rathgeb (1999) describes Peel as the German's essential preparation for the "Geschlechterkampf" [battle of the sexes]. The author with the abbreviation apl ponders: "How she, dressed in tight lacquer, competed a fencing duel for training purposes against Steed as early as in the first episode of October 1965, was breathtaking for that time and still is, from today's perspective, in the light of Miss Peel's fetishisation with a twinkle." (apl, 2007 [o.t.])[49] In the light of this it can be stated that in both countries and among those who know the first-run a nostalgia directed towards this past fascination, be it located on the A or on the F level of the text, may be presumed.

If this is indeed the case, it does not only depend upon the position of the (nostalgic) subject but also only applies in the case that a distinct 'gap' can be described. Already some of the above quotations confirm that the fascination with Emma Peel still exists from today's perspective. Similarly, we could deduce this with a view on today's television landscape. Thus, on the one hand, it can be stated that within both German and Spanish television, representations of women who do not conform to traditional gender stereotypes are, as Baumgart (2002, p. 7 [o.t.] puts it, "no exception any more" (see also García de Castro, 2002, p. 239). Emma Peel indeed found its continuation in today's television.[50] On the other hand, forms of stereotyped femininity and unequal gender representations are still found on today's television.[51] While Peel, following Baumgart (2002, pp. 109 f.), implicated – almost in a Brechtian manner – the will to change, contemporary emancipated characters rather support a consolidation of the actual conditions in representing emancipation

---

48 Original quotation: "[S]ie hat das Frauenbild einer ganzen Generation und weit darüber hinaus geprägt. Als im Kino noch die verschreckten Horror-Queens populär waren, nahm sie ihr Schicksal und das der Welt selbst in die Hand." (Sterneborg, 2008)

49 Original quotation: "Wie sie schon in ihrer ersten Folge vom Oktober 1965 in engem Lack gegen Steed ein Fechtduell zu Trainingszwecken austrug, das war für die Zeit atemraubend und ist es in der augenzwinkernden Fetischisierung von Miss Peel immer noch." (apl, 2007)

50 As Engell and Kissel (1994) highlight in *Frankfurter Allgemeine Zeitung*, Peel was a source of inspiration for similar characters on early German television at that time. She was, says Sternborg (2008 [o.t.]), a "Wegbereiterin für die moderne Action-Amazonen" [forerunner for modern action Amazons], and "abrió el camino" [opened up the way], Lloprat notes (2010 [o.t.]).

51 See e.g. Creeber, 2008, p. 28, on feminine stereotypes in *24*; García-Muñoz et al., 2012, on gender representation in television fiction.

as already realised and broadly attainable. Considered from this position, both F or A emotions, such as fascination or admiration, are more imaginable than nostalgia.

In contrast to *Knight Rider*, which, on the level of the leading star, David Hasselhoff, also offers a clear gap between the pre- and the postlapsarian world, similar observations regarding *The Avengers* cannot be made. Even though, according to Black (2004, p. 106 [italic emphasis in the original]), Emma Peel (Diana Rigg) may also be described as a *"charactor*, a character that is particularly resistant to abstraction from a given actor", a view at the public discourse suggests that the actress lost none of her high persona and star persona status after she left the series.[52] Both actors have references to other films, however, certainly none as dominant as *The Avengers*.

6.1.3 A first conclusion on reruns as potential triggers for nostalgia

On the background of the theoretical part, it has been assumed that television reruns offer a mix of 'F and A nostalgia'. This has been verified in the course of the television analysis. On both the level of the rerun as a whole and single levels of the texts from (1) narration to (2) aesthetic and design and (3) characters, the two examples contain possible triggers for nostalgia as they have been described in the theoretical part on nostalgia in television reruns. A consideration of the public discourse served first indicators as to whether a contrast between 'then' and 'now' is generated and whether the past is constructed as 'golden' or not. That *The Avengers* and *Knight Rider* as part of the nostalgia 'genre' of the reruns create the expectation of nostalgia could not be considered in the course of the television analysis but has to be kept in mind with a view on the later reception study.

The first 'gap'-localisation concentrates on the respective rerun as a whole. Of course, the study can here only consider broader socio-cultural contexts, such as the genre context, cultural context, and the programme context in which the respective first-runs have been broadcasted. The description of the temporal background has been restricted to the time span of the first-run. In the case of *Knight Rider*, this is the 1980s, in the case of *The Avengers* it is the 1960s. It must be kept in mind that, throughout the years, not only in the time span 2009-2011 that is relevant here, both

---

52 Articles that focus on the actress highlight Diana Rigg as an important person of the British society (*La Vanguardia*, 2000) or as a still successful theatrical actress (Ramos, 1996; Ramos, 1998; Bartetzko, 1998). In 1999, the society section in *Süddeutsche Zeitung* hinted at the fact that the 61-year-old actress had been voted the "'Fernsehstar mit dem größten Sexappeal aller Zeiten'" [television star with the greatest sex appeal of all times] (*Süddeutsche Zeitung*, 1999 [o.t.]). Also in 2008, Diana Rigg was still the "Queen of Cool" due to her television past as Emma Peel (Sterneborg, 2008).

series have been shown as reruns. It is thus likely that memory anchors were set at points of time that are different from the time of the first broadcast – an aspect which has to be worked out more closely in the reception study.

Regarding the socio-political context, two very different frames in Germany and Spain have been described. In the 1960s, the time when *Los Vengadores* was broadcasted, Spain lived through a time of economic growth – the so-called "'Spanish miracle'" (Boyd, 1999, p. 99) – but was still under the Franco dictatorship. The public discourse on the rerun does not support nostalgia towards the temporal context. However, since nostalgia depends upon the subject position and how the single viewer "makes" the time contrast with the present, it is also not impossible and has to be further investigated in the reception study. Here, we shall also refer to the work of Tannock, who argues that "[t]he 'positively evaluated' past is approached as a source for something now perceived to be missing; but it need not be thought of as a time of general happiness, peacefulness, stability, or freedom" (Tannock, 1995, p. 454). In Germany, the 1960s were a time of social change and changes in values. Here a possible nostalgic reading also has to be further scrutinised in the reception study. It is surely favoured by the fact that Britain was one of the major examples of the youth movement at that time (Siegfried, 2003, p. 25).

Both in Germany and in Spain, the first-run of the series falls into a time span of television which often has been described as 'golden' with respect to its rich production of TV plays. In both countries the hybrid mix of the series contrasted with the present programme. The fascination about this past extension of creative boundaries still finds its reflection in the public discourse and provides the basis for a possible later integration of the series into a nostalgic line of argument created by the audiences.

When *El coche fantástico* was broadcasted in Spain in the 1980s, half a decade after the fall of Franco's regime, Spain still experienced a spirit of optimism and economic growth (Juliá, 1999). Here, one discourse fragment describes the rerun as a representative of "'aquella época'" [this epoch] (see García Ruipérez, 2011 [o.t.]) and thus installs it as a possible trigger for nostalgia. In the German context – the context chapter refers to the beginnings of the so-called 'Kohl-era', political scandals, anti-nuclear movement, growing discontentment in the East but also the opening of the Berlin Wall – no such 'valorising' articles could be found. Since nostalgia may also be related to rather personal contexts, any further conclusions cannot be made before the reception study in Part III.

Regarding the programme context in which the first-run of *Knight Rider*, respectively *El coche fantástico*, was broadcasted, the analysis shows that in Germany the series falls into the first years of the dual television system, which was accompanied by controversial discussions about the decrease in quality. It is a similar case in Spain. Although here private channels were not introduced before the 1990s, the series can be situated within the transition process towards the new period that was later characterised by hard competition between private and public broadcasters and accusations of the "new private stations [...] lowering the quality of scheduling" (Smith, 2006, p. 3). It is unsurprising that Cuervo (2004) describes *El coche fantástico* as "serie[...] emblemática[...] de la tele más commercial de los 80 y 90" [an emblematic series of the more commercial television of the 1980s and 1990s] (Cuervo, 2004 [o.t.]). In both countries the series cannot be supposed to have elicited a fascination of novelty. It was rather surrounded by very similar programmes, such as *The A-Team* or other action-driven series from the Reagan era. A nostalgia that may be located on this general level is thus rather improbable.

The discourses that surround *Mit Schirm, Charme und Melone* and *Los Vengadores* hold their part in the "retrospective classification" of the series as potential trigger for nostalgia both in Germany and Spain. While, generally speaking, in the German case a more explicit legitimisation of past television can be observed, those contributions that probably have most influence on and/or reflect the public opinion best, such as the public discourse in the form of newspaper articles, are equally distributed. It is a similar case regarding *Knight Rider*, respectively *El coche fantástico*. Apart from differences regarding the valorisations on the side of museums and academic publications, both in Germany and Spain, television channels, non-academic publications, journalistic articles and fan culture show a clear "retrospective classification" of the series which serves parts of the necessary basis for the narration of the better (television) past. It has to be seen in the reception analysis if nostalgia on the basis of these 'acquired' "retrospective classifications" is possible.

Later, following the premises of film and television analysis (see Mikos 2008), both series, *The Avengers* and *Knight Rider*, have been analysed regarding possible triggers for nostalgia on the level of (1) narration, (2) aesthetic and design (including camera, montage, lighting, location, props, décor, costume, and music), and (3) characters. In general, it can be presumed that each of these levels can work as a "mnemonic prompt" for those who have memories of the first-run which, depending on the respective "retrospective classification", may lead to nostalgia. This similarly applies to the general referential character the reruns have from today's perspective. Both recognizable for those who know and for those who don't know the first-run, single levels of the text become, as said by Keightley and Pickering (2006, p. 152) in the context of music and photography, "historical representations" for their time. Diverse stylistic devices of the texts explicitly promote nostalgia, others don't.

On the level of its narration *The Avengers* is rather unlikely to provoke 'F nostalgia'. Its narration is not nostalgic, empathy is not favoured, nor is it narrated from the perspective of a nostalgic character. Rather the contrary is the case. Some episodes even explicitly connote the longing towards the past negatively. Regarding the series position towards its own temporal background, *The Avengers* can also not be described as a trigger for nostalgia. The series does not work as a mystifying "agente historiador" but instead it is critical towards the dominant system. However, also with reference to the literature on the series (see Baumgart 2002; Pérez 1998), it has further been shown that *The Avengers* exposes many intertextual references. Based on the theoretical section, it can be presumed that on this level the series possibly provokes 'A nostalgia' in those viewers who realise the references and retrospectively classify them or their context as being worth longing for. Furthermore, the release of viewers' 'own artefact nostalgia' on the basis of the references is possible. The public discourse does not provide indicators regarding this aspect. It has to be seen again in the reception study if this is the case.

Regarding *Knight Rider*, it is slightly different. With respect to the temporal background of the series and depending on the reading, the series indeed can be seen as a mystifying "agente historiador" in so far that it simplifies Cold-War politics on a simple good-bad dichotomy. From today's perspective, the evocation of 'F nostalgia' may be possible.

With respect to aesthetic and design, the analysis identifies "marks", such as "anachronistic styles or historical associations" (Lowenthal, 1986, p. 125), mostly by relating the original text to its *new* context. On this level, both series are instantly recognisable as belonging to another era. Already the artificial colours that the opening credits of *Knight Rider* expose contrast with contemporary television aesthetics. With its simplicity of camera, montage, and lighting, *Knight Rider* refers to other "zero-degree" style exemplars from the 1980s and collides with contemporary television. "Differential quality" is also provided by its anachronistic use of split-screen and zoom. 'A nostalgia' is possible, especially in the context of the "retrospective classifications" of the series it is not improbable.

The same applies to the colour spectrum of *The Avengers* with a, "psychedelic chromatology", as Pérez (1998, p. 45 [o.t.]) puts it. Regarding camera, montage and lighting, the rerun contrasts clearly with contemporary television. Small-scale experiments relate the series to aesthetic innovations as they could be observed in 1960s pop TV, both in Germany and in Spain.

In both series, the setting is probably not important as a potential trigger for nostalgia. Both reruns have no "cultural proximity" to a German or Spanish context. Moreover, empathy is not favoured, neither by the first nor by the latter. In both cases the evocation of 'empathetic artefact nostalgia' is thus rather improbable.

The level of décor, props and costumes is more important. As shown by Sprengler (2011), artefacts are central to the period recreations in film. Also with respect to the reruns, we may assume that they are the most important period markers. Thus, even though inside the "zero-degree" style of *Knight Rider* the mise-en-scène has less relevance, what Tashiro (1998) states in the context of shifting "cultural environment[s]" in general counts here: "[T]hose [objects once] included as neutral filler[s] find unexpected prominence within the obsessions of a new setting" (Tashiro, 1998, p. 8). The analysis highlights that not only the car but also other props of the series are clearly anachronistic from today's perspective and likely to evoke 'A nostalgia' or the viewers' 'own A nostalgia' in both those viewers who know and those who do not know the first-run. The car is also where another major gap between 'then' and 'now' could be located: while KITT in the 1980s evoked a fascination – be it on the level of the artefact or on the level of the fictional world – in its (infantile) audiences, today such visions have already been realised or have become obsolete. 'F' or 'A nostalgia', which is directed towards this lost utopia, is probable. The existence of the gap is also supported by the public discourse in the form of newspaper articles. Further gaps could be found with respect to the "cultural baggage" (Sprengler, 2011, p. 99) of the main prop. Thus, the car is not only a symbol of the rise and fall of the American car industry, its "implicit meaning" (Tashiro, 1998, p. 12) has also changed from a symbol of masculinity, which is built on physical strength, towards symbolising an image of masculinity in decline.

With respect to *The Avengers*, the main gap can be found in the sole difference between décor, props and costumes 'then' and 'now'. The décor stands in direct contrast to what we are used to from contemporary television and reminds you of early television dramas. Apart from that, props and costumes are also decisive period markers in *The Avengers* – clearly identifiable as belonging to the 1960s and likely to provoke 'A nostalgia' or the viewers' 'own A nostalgia'. As reflected by the public discourse, mainly the props and costumes that characterise Emma Peel expanded the boundaries valid then and attracted the attention of the audiences. However, and here is where another main gap has been found, what was futuristic and fascinating 'then' – be it in the context of the artefact level or in the context of the fictional world – may, depending on the reading, be less so from today's perspective. Here, referencing the public discourse provides first indicators of the existence of the 'gap'; however, it has to be seen in the reception study if a 'F' or 'A nostalgia' can be found here.

Regarding the music, it can be stated that both *Knight Rider* and *The Avengers* are clearly anachronistic from today's perspective and provide the gap between 'then' and 'now', which is so decisive for nostalgia. Furthermore, in the context of the "retrospective classifications" an 'A nostalgia' triggered on this level is thus not improbable. Since the music can work as a "mnemonic prompt", the repeating motives that are exposed by both series are likely to provoke the viewer's own nostalgia in those who know the first-run. In both cases, the generation of a "'nostalgic condition'" (Flinn, 1992 cited in Sprengler, 2011, p. 77) is not a dominant function of the music.

Finally, the study takes a close look at possible triggers for nostalgia on the level of the characters. Regarding *Knight Rider*, the analysis focuses on the lead character,

Michael Knight, played by David Hasselhoff. With one exception where the character longs for his past identity, no access to "the past as a stable source of value and meaning" (Tannock, 1995, p. 455) can be observed on the side of the character. Also independent of the question whether the series exposes a nostalgic character or not, it does not favour empathy. 'Empathetic F nostalgia' is thus rather improbable. Clear 'gaps' between 'then' and 'now' could rather be identified regarding other aspects of the character, which at least provide the disposition for nostalgia. Here it has been highlighted that his simplicity contrasts with today's dominant trend towards psychologising and, depending on "respective classifications", makes him a possible trigger for 'A nostalgia'. Also on the level of David Hasselhoff as a person(a), a clear gap could be found, which may be described as a history of rise and fall, both reflected in the German and Spanish public discourse. An 'A nostalgia' located here is thus possible as well. Moreover, the star persona of David Hasselhoff contains intertextual references not only to other 1980s' series but also to public events in the 1980s. It has to be seen in the reception study if the viewers also generate these references and if, depending on respective "retrospective classifications", they lead to nostalgia.

In contrast to that, none of the main actors of *The Avengers* – neither Diana Rigg nor Patrick Macnee – provides such a gap with respect to persona or person. Also their intertextual referential character is rather less important. Empathy is not favoured by the text. However, Emma Peel (Diana Rigg) and John Steed (Patrick Macnee), who are both pop characters without deeper psychologising (Baumgart, 2002, p. 23), contrast with characters as they are dominant in today's television and refer to similar examples from the era. Depending on respective "retrospective classifications", this can lead to nostalgia. A further 'gap' could be located with reference to Peel (Diana Rigg). The character contrasted both with the social reality and with feminine leading characters as they were dominant both in German and Spanish television in the 1960s. The analysis shows that, depending on the perspective, this is less so from today's perspective. In case that the 'utopia' of once is seen as lost from today's perspective, a nostalgia directed towards the lost fascination is probable for those who know the first-run. As the public discourse has shown, a reading that is still dominated by the fascination of extended boundaries is more likely. In this case nostalgia can be excluded.

In summary, it can be stated that both *The Avengers* and *Knight Rider* prefigure nostalgia on various levels. It has to be seen in the reception analysis in Part III of this book if the nostalgia on offer in the reruns is actually decoded as such. Of course different readings are always possible; not all of them are going to be nostalgic. Here, decisive differences can be expected regarding the different audience groups. Alongside the differences between Germany and Spain it must be considered that different age groups can have different relationships to the respective temporal contexts. While both the 55 to 65-year-olds and the 25 to 35-year-olds have their own (and probably differently coloured) memories of the 1980s, the 25 to 35-year-olds have "prosthetic memories" of the 1960s at the most. Apart from that, the first-runs were broadcasted in different life spans of the age groups, which again can be supposed to have left different marks on their memories[53] – this will be looked at in the last part of the study. Furthermore, and independent of the age of the viewers, it must be distinguished between those who have seen the first-run and those who have not. For instance, only those who have seen the first-run can be supposed to remember the rerun in its 'original' programme context. Due to the referential character of the rerun, the socio-political, cultural or genre context instead is likely also relevant for those who did not see the first-run, but have a general knowledge of the context. [54]

6.2 REMAKES AND NOSTALGIA

Remakes are included within the broad category of nostalgia film and nostalgia television (Jameson, 1998; Dika, 2003; pp. 202 ff. on film remakes of television series; Cook, 2005). The same applies to the non-academic discourse where nostalgia and remakes are frequently mentioned together (Steinberg 2010, p. 8; Rehfeld, 2011). On a first and general layer, we may therefore call remakes nostalgia 'genres' and may assume that nostalgia is one mood audiences expect when they decide to watch a remake.

Without exception, remakes that relate to a temporally distant 'original' and not to a locally distant one are in the centre of the discussion. Exceptions include traded formats or canned programmes, which are imported from one country to another and which, depending on the constitution of the television memory of the import country, may rather be seen as novelties (see e.g. Armbruster and Mikos, 2009, on the German version of *Who Wants to Be a Millionaire?*) than as potential triggers for nostalgia.

From this we may further expect that the main 'gap' between past and present, which the remake exposes, is the intertextual reference to the premake. As Horton and McDougal (1998, p. 3 [italic emphasis in the original]) show, "[i]n terms of intertextuality [...] remakes – films that to one degree or another *announce* to us that

---

53 In particular, significant differences between childhood and adulthood memories may be expected.

54 A summary of the rerun analysis (Chapter 6.1 and Chapter 8.1) and its discussion was first published as the article *Transnational Nostalgia in Europe. Television Reruns in the Reception of Two Generations in Germany and Spain*, by Stefanie Armbruster, in: Eichner, S. and Prommer, E., eds. *Fernsehen: Europäische Perspektiven. Festschrift Prof. Dr. Lothar Mikos*. Konstanz/München: UVK, pp. 121-135.

they embrace one or more previous movies – are clearly something of a special case, or at least a more intense one". There is no reason why this should not also apply to television remakes. Therefore, against the backdrop of the theoretical part on aesthetic emotions and nostalgia, it is assumed that on a first and dominant layer[55] the remake provokes 'artefact nostalgia'. Since, as Hutcheon has mentioned it in the context of nostalgia in general, there are probably "many ways to look backward" (Hutcheon, 2000, p. 196), whereby nostalgia is just one of them, as in the case of the reruns, the main question must be what factors influence the fact that the "look backward" is nostalgic?

It may be assumed that already the remake as a whole, thus, the remake as an artefact, is related to the premake. In case that the title has not been changed or still refers to the premake title, according to Leitch (1990, p. 142), memories can be expected to be evoked already on that level. Later, the public discourse, producers, advertisements, television channels and others may be supposed to create the relation. Apart from the remake's position toward its reference, which probably is less relevant on this general layer, here we can ask to what extent the premake and its contexts are presented as a potential object of nostalgia. We can assume that the "changing perceptions" (Kompare, 2005, p. 107) in the form of "retrospective classifications" (Kompare, 2005, p. 105) Kompare highlights in the context of the television reruns are also important in the context of remake and premake. Later, the discourse of the producers as it is often integrated in the DVD versions of the remake has to be taken into consideration – a factor that in the context of the reruns had less relevance or none at all. Presumably, "retrospective classifications" may also be noticeable here.

In line with the view presented by Oltmann (2008, p. 42), who calls the premake "unfinished business" and hints at the fact that only the remake gives the premake the status of the 'original' and continues its discourses (Oltmann, 2008, pp. 27 ff.), we may assume that already the remake as such and the discourses that surround it are a kind of "retrospective classifications". Since television memories may also function as very personal memory points (O'Sullivan, 1991, p. 163), a nostalgia related to the personal past of the viewers is also imaginable. Here, the rather private "retrospective classifications" of the viewers have to be taken into account, which will be investigated in Part III. It has to be kept in mind that the 'then' in this case does not have to be the time span of the first broadcast of the premake. The previous

---

55 As Leitch shows, the remake aims at different audiences, "the audience that has never heard of the original film it is based on, the audience that has heard of the film but not seen it, the audience that has seen it but does not remember it, the audience that has seen it but liked it little enough to hope for an improvement, and the audience that has seen it and enjoyed it" (Leitch, 1990, p. 140). They "ideally [...] provide additional enjoyment to audiences who recognize their borrowings from their sources" (Leitch, 1990, p. 140).

chapter already showed that television series are often re-broadcasted, which widens the temporal background of potential memory points.

Later, on a micro level, we may suppose that every single artefact of the remake that contains intertextual references to the premake may work as a "mnemonic prompt" for those who know the premake and, depending on the respective "retrospective classification" of the reference, generate nostalgia. As in the context of the reruns, here we can assume that audiences not only become aware of the artefact via, for instance, "[s]udden twists in the plot" as they have been highlighted by Tan (1996, p. 65) in the general context of artefact emotions, but that – depending on its usage – it is rather the mere repetition or non-repetition which exposes the borrowing and let the 'knowing' spectator become aware of it.[56] Consequently, every level of the text needs to be examined regarding intertextual references to the premake.

Depending on whether it is a modern translation or the past temporal context is maintained, the "awareness of things past", as Lowenthal (1986, p. 125) says, may derive from different sources. While, we can assume, in the first case – the modern translation – it is the comparison and the difference or non-difference to the 'original', a comparison which again can only be made by the 'knowing' spectator, in the second case it is also the difference between the represented past and the remake viewer's own present. As Dika highlights with reference to Jameson (1991), a remake that updates the temporal context of the premake, may also "create the 'look and feel' of pastness" by manipulating "the lighting, the choice of colors, and the grain of the film, as well as its composition and framing [...] [in order] to refer to past images" (Dika, 2003, p. 10).

Since, in contrast to the television reruns, it is not 'just' the "reading formation" which has changed, but the remake itself is a reconsideration of a past text, it may adopt different attitudes towards the premake or its temporal context, which again may be articulated on every single level of the text. This must also be considered in the analysis. In case that the remake maintains the temporal context of the premake, it may, also depending on the characteristics of the premake, take a nostalgic or non-nostalgic position towards the respective temporal background (see Cook, 2005 on *Far from Heaven* (Haynes, 2002)). Here, an important question is also if the viewers recognise the borrowings or not – either against a 'real' or a "prosthetic memory". The same applies to the case that the remake transfers the temporal context of the premake into the contemporary – the "conventional" sort of remakes, as Cook (2005, p. 11) notes. So the initial questions are: Which position holds the premake towards its temporal background? Which position holds the remake towards the premake?

---

56 In the context of remakes, Horton and McDougal (1998, p. 6) refer to the Russian Formalist Sklovsky and his concept of defamiliarisation, highlighting that "[o]ne way of achieving this, he noted, was repetition with a difference".

Does the remake, for instance, reproduce an eventually mystifying perspective or, as Sprengler (2011) puts it in the context of reruns, "self-mythologizing efforts" of the 'original' on its temporal context, does it thus create a 'gap' between a positive 'then' and a 'now' and therefore favour 'F nostalgia', or does it rather continue open discourses of the premake in a way that such a reading is hampered?

The importance of an analysis of these different positions is particularly emphasised by Dika (2003), Cook (2005), and Sprengler (2011). On the example of *Psycho* (Van Sant, 1998) Dika (2003, pp. 212 ff.) shows how a remake may support a critical look at the new temporal background by creating moments of friction, disruption and the revelation of the image surface. The relation between premake and remake and between the image of the past and the actual past is in the centre of Cook's analysis of Hayne's *Far From Heaven* – a remake which maintains the temporal context of its 1950s' source (Cook, 2005, pp. 10 ff.). Cook shows that the film on the one hand reproduces the 1950s "projected by those melodramas" it refers to. However,

"[w]here many remakes mimic the original, *Far From Heaven* mirrors its source material (appropriately enough, given Sirk's predilection for mirror shots). [...] The mirror image, like the cinematic image, inevitably reflects a distorted view of its subject, and Haynes' retrospective lens produces a reverse likeness in which aspects of the original films – in particular, themes they were unable to address openly – are made explicit." (Cook, 2005, pp. 10 f.)

Both authors thus compare both premake/remake and image/"natural real" (Dika, 2003, p. 224) and ask for the continuation or critical review the premake once established, in order to locate different kinds of nostalgias or to show that nostalgia is not a topic at all. Here it is central that the interaction of all levels of text and their contribution to the narration are considered. Furthermore, Sprengler (2011) highlights in her study about populuxe props that the remake may gain a reflexive layer by the props it exposes and "their own histories" (Sprengler, 2011, p. 4) that are imported. If we assume with reference to Mikos (2008, p. 278) that intertextual references may also activate experiences and related emotional contents, there is another source where the remake may contain possible 'gaps' for those who know the premake. The same may be assumed with reference to Böhn (2007, p. 150), who suggests that quotations may lead to the "nostalgic longing" towards the "restoration" of emotions once felt in the context of the references.

Lastly and independent of the intertextual references to the premake, it must be considered if the remake adopts other nostalgic strategies. Independent of the premake, a remake may also present the past from the perspective of a nostalgic protagonist, just as Higson (2003, p. 83) described it in the context of the period pictures, and/or favour empathy that may lead to 'empathetic F nostalgia'. Furthermore, a remake may expose nostalgic music or be the object of 'empathetic artefact nostalgia'.

Accordingly, the following analysis asks how and against which background the two remakes of *Knight Rider* and *The Avengers* may work as triggers for nostalgia. The analysis will contain the following research steps. Firstly, a general description of the remakes will be presented. Later, the temporal context and "retrospective classifications" of the respective premakes as they have already been worked out in the context of *Knight Rider* (NBC, 1982) and *The Avengers* (ITV, 1961) in both countries will be considered shortly. The following analysis of the micro-level will examine every level of the audiovisual text according to the previously mentioned assumptions. In order to gain a general view, which can also be compared to the analysis of the reruns and period dramas, a mere comparison between premake and remake shall be avoided. The study will also ask if the remake, independent of its source of inspiration, may be described as a trigger for nostalgia. In order to cross-check the analysis and to identify first possible "cultural mappings" (Hepp, 2009), both German and Spanish newspaper articles shall be consulted.

6.2.1 Analysis of nostalgia in *Knight Rider* (NBC, 2008)

Knight Rider (NBC, 2008), the television remake of the 1980s series *Knight Rider* (NBC, 1982), is an American action series produced by Universal Media Studios and originally broadcasted by NBC. The series contains one season. It is available on DVD both in German and in Spanish synchronisation. *Knight Rider* (NBC, 2008) was broadcasted both on German and Spanish television. In Germany, the pilot of the remake could be viewed on the private channel RTL, which also broadcasted the following episodes, in 2010 (Moorstedt, 2009). With the first episode the series reached a market share of 22.8 per cent among the 14 to 49-year-olds; later episodes went down to 20.7 per cent within the same target group (Krei, 2009). In 2011, the series was also broadcasted on the private channel SuperRTL. In Spain the pilot of the remake could be viewed on the public channel La 1 in 2008, where it reached a share of 24 per cent (Formula TV, 2009). Further episodes have been broadcasted on the same channel in 2009. They reached an average market share of 17.6 per cent (Formula TV, 2011). In 2009 and 2010, repetitions of the first season could be watched on La1 and Calle 13.

The pilot episode narrates the background story of the series, introducing Mike Tracer (Justin Bruening), a former soldier of the U.S. Army who will soon adopt the name of his father, Michael Knight (David Hasselhoff). Mike is called into action by his former girlfriend Sarah Graiman (Deanna Russo), whose father, Charles (Bruce Davison), the creator of the original KITT and member of a secret Pentagon project team, has been kidnapped by terrorists. Accompanied by KITT (Knight Industries *Three* Thousand), now a Ford Mustang Shelby, and supported by the FBI agent Carrie (Sydney Tamiia Poitier) and *Knight Industries*, Sarah and Mike start to search for Charles. The 'new' Michael Knight, who works for *Knight Industries* and the government and later for the independent and re-founded *Foundation for Law and Order* (FLAG), is the central character featured in the series. In his fight against 'evil in a dangerous world' he is supported and directed by an expert team. The home base has changed to a modern hangar, and KITT is often transported via airplane. As in the premake, the fabulous car is equipped with diverse features yet now assigned to the modern world.

Despite the fact that the pilot episode, as Leitch would say, is "teasing knowing audiences [...][and] bring[s] new audiences up" (Leitch, 1990, p. 140) by creating continuance by establishing Michael Knight (David Hasselhoff) as Mike's father, it also gives the remake spin-off elements. The rest of the series is a clear remake, or, as Cook puts it in the context of remakes in general, a "modern translation" (Cook, 2005, p. 11) – transferred into the new millennium. As the premake, the remake may be assigned to the action adventure genre.

6.2.1.1 A short contextualisation

Knight Rider (NBC, 2008) is clearly contextualised within the frame of the 1980s premake. Already the title of the remake evokes the predecessor and its 1980s context. Later, the television channels both in Germany and in Spain presented the remake within the context of *Knight Rider* (NBC, 1982) (RTL, 2011a; RTVE, 2011). The DVD version of the remake explicitly promotes DVD collections of the 'original' series. The same applies to the public discourse in both countries (see e.g. *El País*, 2009a; *La Vanguardia*, 2009; *La Vanguardia*, 2009a; Mateos and Campelo, 2009; Moorstedt, 2009; Bracero, 2011). One can state that it is almost appealing to the memory of the predecessor and, it may be argued, it even promotes the retrospective construction of this memory.

Consequently, on a first and general layer, the premake context is relevant for the analysis of potential nostalgias. This has been outlined in Chapter 6.1 and shall not be repeated here. Since the series has been re-broadcasted at various times both in Germany and in Spain, memory anchors may have been set throughout the series' 'biography' – something which has to be kept in mind with a view on the reception analysis. Later, it must be considered in which way the premake as an artefact as a whole is installed as a potential object of nostalgia.

In the context of the television reruns of *Knight Rider* (NBC, 1982) it has been stressed that "retrospective classifications" favour a nostalgic reading of the 'original' television series. Valorisations by television channels, non-academic and academic publications, fans or newspaper articles, which serve the necessary basis for the narration of the better (television) past, have been dealt with in Sections 6.1.1.1.2 and 6.1.1.2.2.

Furthermore, in both countries the discourse about the remake explicitly generates the link to the premake and the valorising discourses that surround it. It also holds its part in the valorisation of the latter. In Germany, RTL highlights *Knight Rider* (NBC, 2008) combined with the premake, describing it as a "Kultserie aus den 80ern" [cult series from the 1980s] (RTL, 2011 [o.t.]). TVE calls it the "remake de la mítica serie" [remake of the mythical series] (RTVE, 2011 [o.t.]). The producer of the remake contextualises *Knight Rider* (NBC, 2008) as "one of those iconic shows" (RTVE, 2011a; *El coche fantástico*, DVD Extras).

The public discourse in both countries explicitly valorises the premake in the context of the remake. The Spanish *El País* stresses that "la popular serie de los años ochenta regresa" [the popular series of the 1980s comes back] (*El País*, 2009a [o.t.]). *La Vanguardia* highlights "NBC [...] ha recuperado *El coche fantástico*, icono de la televisión de los ochenta" [NBC has retrieved *El coche fantástico*, icon of the television of the Eighties] (*La Vanguardia*, 2009 [o.t.]); Broc (2009) talks about the "relectura de un título de culto" [reinterpretation of a cult title] (Broc, 2009 [o.t.]), and another author calls the remake "la nueva versión de [...] la mítica serie de los años ochenta" [the new version of the mythical series of the Eighties] (*ABC*, 2008 [o.t.]). This similarly applies to the German discourse. *Der Tagesspiegel* notes that "RTL setzt die Achtziger-Jahre-Kultserie [...] fort" [RTL continues the 1980s cult series] (Sauerbrey, 2009 [o.t.]). In other cases, the valorisation of the premake goes hand in hand with a de-valorisation of the remake. According to Moorstedt, "RTL shows the new edition of '*Knight Rider*' – but the old times are not reproducible." (Moorstedt, 2009 [o.t.])[57]. Denk notes more critically: "The new edition is so unnecessary that it was cancelled after one season – and we prefer to show the 1980s original again" (Denk, 2009 [o.t.])[58]. As a result, it can be stated that *Knight Rider* (NBC, 1982) is not only inevitably related to the remake, gaining the status of the 'original', just as Oltmann (2008) describes it in the context of remakes in general, but the discourse also constructs a 'gap' between the better 'original' and worse remake, which establishes the premake as a potential object of nostalgia.

---

57 Original quotation: "RTL zeigt die Neuauflage von 'Knight Rider' – doch die alten Zeiten sind nicht reproduzierbar." (Moorstedt, 2009)

58 Original quotation: "Diese Neuauflage ist so überflüssig, dass sie schon nach einer Staffel abgesetzt wurde – und wir lieber nochmal das 80er Original zeigen." (Denk, 2009)

6.2.1.2 Nostalgia on the single levels of the text

6.2.1.2.1 Narration

Knight Rider (NBC, 2008), set in the United States around the turn of the last millennium, updates the time frame of the premake. The remake may not be described as accessing a past nostalgically, nor is it narrated from the perspective of a nostalgic character. Yet the present that is represented contains the 'feel of pastness'. Where the premake exposes different visions on its 1980s present, one that simplifies Cold War politics to simple good-bad dichotomies and one that paints an "ambiguous" picture of the time (Moody, 2001, p. 71), *Knight Rider* (NBC, 2008) opts for the reactionary half. Mainly in the first eleven episodes, where Michael Knight has strong ties to state authorities, the ancient good-bad dichotomies are simply 'modernised' and find their continuation in equal poles – such as scrupulous, good (U.S.) versus unscrupulous, bad (Chinese) capitalism (see e.g. Season 1, Episode 2), or the good U.S. versus the bad Islamist or power-hungry terrorists. The fact that moments of reflection, which seem to break these simplicities, are only supported by KITT, the artificial intelligence (see e.g. Season 1, Episode 1), only further supports the dominant reading. It can be stated that the present of the series is infused with a past "connotation of order" of the premake, which indeed may be understood as the nostalgic wish to return to a past simplicity. Critical frictions between premake and remake cannot be observed.

This interpretation is in part supported by the public discourse, where some authors explicitly highlight that the remake still wears the "espíritu de los 80" [spirit of the 1980s] (*La Vanguardia*, 2009b [o.t.]) and "mantiene el mismo sabor que en los 80 en su lucha contra el crimen organizado" [maintains this same flavour in its fight against organised crime] (*La Vanguardia*, 2009b [o.t.]). Moorstedt of the German *Süddeutsche Zeitung* notes that "von Drehbuchseite her [gibt es] keine Neuerungen" [regarding the script, there are no novelties] (Moorstedt, 2009 [o.t.]).

Regarding other aspects of the narration, *Knight Rider* (NBC, 2008) indeed transports its predecessor into the present. Even though the remake follows a linear scheme, which always stays the same and is similar to the 1980s premake, the cases to be solved now afford the scientific knowledge of the team, which brings further suspense-loaded narrative stands into the series (see e.g. Season 1, Episode 4). Shorter suspense curves are provided by smaller obstacles that have to be solved in the course of the action and are always done so at the last minute (see e.g. Season 1, Episode 2; min. 0:08:35 – 0:15:30). Here, the remake contains similarities to contemporary series, such as *24* where time is also "always about urgency" (Shimpach, 2010, p. 131). Other plot lines narrate the romantic interests between Michael and Sarah or the revelation of Michael's traumatic past. While the main narrative strands are closed within one episode, the latter two spread over several episodes. By doing that, the series not only increases the suspense and multiplies the narrative strands in comparison to the premake but also gains elements of the "continuous narrative" of the serial that were less well developed in the premake. You could say that it has shifted towards the trend of contemporary action/melo-drama hybrids (Williams, 1994, referred to in Shimpach, 2010, p. 36) and therefore contrasts with the simple narrative model of the 'original'. In this sense, it cannot be discussed as a nostalgic handling of the source; rather the contrary is the case. Nevertheless, in doing so, and always in case that the reference to the premake is generated by the audiences, a clear 'gap' between 'then' and 'now' has been constructed which, depending on the subject position and respective "retrospective classifications", supports nostalgia towards the 'original'.

Furthermore, the remake narrative employs various intertextual references to its 1980s predecessor. It makes use of dramatic fragments, themes and situations of the premake and combines them in a new way. Once implicit aspects, such as the romantic interests between the premake characters Michael and Bonny, are now highlighted as individual narrative strands; a strategy that Black (2004, p. 102) calls "in-filling". Against the backdrop of the theoretical section we may assume, that, at least for the more detached audiences, the intertextual references may work as "mnemonic prompt[s]" and, depending on the "retrospective classification" of the predecessor, lead to 'artefact nostalgia', respectively the viewers' 'own artefact nostalgia'.

6.2.1.2.2 Aesthetic and design

Regarding its aesthetic and design, *Knight Rider* (NBC, 2008) is a modernised version of the premake. At the same time borrowings from the 'original' provide it with the "awareness of things past".

Camera, montage and lighting

Knight Rider (NBC, 2008) employs a mobile camera with a wide range of shots from close-ups to long shots. While the premake seems anachronistic, if not campy, due to the sometime repetitive, abrupt utilisation of zooms, in *Knight Rider* (NBC, 2008) the device is applied self-evidently and without exposing it. Lavish crane shots, panoramas, and travelling shots are constantly used. This gives the series a dynamic, cinematic look. The same applies to lighting and editing. Where the premake with its "zero-degree" style (Caldwell, 1995, pp. 55 ff.) utilises a constant normal key lighting, *Knight Rider* (NBC, 2008) employs an illumination that is dependent upon location and dramaturgy. The editing is decisively accelerated. Additionally, the remake exposes computer-generated effects. Animated travelling shots move through the interior of the car. Further animated sequences appear throughout the series (see e.g. Season 1, Episode 11, min. 0:28:21).

Here, the remake exposes analogies to the "videographic look" that has been described by Shimpach (2010, p. 132) in the context of contemporary action series, such as *24*. Consequently, it can be stated that camera, montage and lighting are less reminiscent of the premake; they rather correspond to contemporary televisuality. The remake here becomes a representative of the television 'now' that, depending on the subject position, may be set against the television 'then' represented by the premake. For those who generate the reference to the predecessor, a clear 'gap' arises. That this may lead to 'artefact nostalgia' directed towards the 'original' on the part of the German and Spanish viewers is supported by the intensive "retrospective classification" of the premake but has to be further scrutinised in the reception study. A critical stance or reflexivity due to frictions between past and present representation cannot be observed.

Setting

This similarly applies to the settings *Knight Rider* (NBC, 2008) exposes. On the one hand, the remake here refers to the 1980s premake. As in the predecessor, main spaces are the interior of the car and the home base of the foundation, which is clearly reminiscent of the 'original' and makes the remake a possible "mnemonic prompt" for those who know the premake. On the other hand, *Knight Rider* (NBC, 2008) transports its predecessor into the present. Here, the remake refers to trends in contemporary television. Already the hangar headquarters simulate "the control room of a live television production, [or] the control center of a video surveillance operation" (Shimpach, 2010, p. 132) just as Shimpach observes it in the context of *24* (Fox, 2001). Again the remake may here be described as representative of television 'now' that, depending on the subject position, may be set against television 'then' represented by the premake.

With its hangar home base, highways, desert-like landscapes, and 'typical' American cities, *Knight Rider* (NBC, 2008) contains little "cultural proximity" to a German or Spanish background – not to mention the fact that there is hardly any sensuous exploration of settings in the the action series. The arousal of 'internal empathetic artefact nostalgia' is not favoured.

Décor, props and costumes

In *Knight Rider* (NBC, 2008), décor, props and costumes are no signifiers of pastness in the sense that they belong to another era. The remake has been modernised and transported to the present. The objects it exposes are contemporary and unlikely to provoke 'artefact nostalgia'. The "awareness of things past" arises here only from the intertextual references to the premake, which first and foremost may be located on the level of the series' main prop. As its predecessor, *Knight Rider* (NBC, 2008) features a car named KITT, this time a Ford Mustang Shelby. With its red front laser and enigmatic sound it is clearly reminiscent of the 'original' and may work as a potential "mnemonic prompt" for those audiences who know the premake.

In the context of *Knight Rider* (NBC, 1982) it has been shown that from today's perspective the rerun-car provides a gap between 'then' and 'now' concerning the fascination it once released and the loss of the latter from today's perspective (see 6.1.1.3.2). It has been assumed that this characteristic makes it a potential trigger for nostalgia for the 'knowing audiences'. This similarly applies to the remake car, even though other readings are favoured as well. On the one hand, the remake is conscious of discourses regarding the lack, takes them up explicitly[59] and tries to undermine them. Consequently, KITT is equipped with new features – the 'new' car transforms via 3D-animation into a race-car version, the once bullet-proof lining now restores automatically – features that obviously try to still make the car appear to be futuristic and to provoke similar fascinations to those its 1980s predecessor provoked. If this strategy is successful, nostalgia can rather be excluded. On the other hand, if this is not the case, we may indeed assume that the arousal of a nostalgic longing for the "restoration" of the past emotion is possible, just as Böhn (2007, p. 150) described it in the context of quotations in general. Again the remake is conscious of this possible reading and exposes this knowledge in various episodes that explicitly highlight the motive of childhood/boyhood fascination (see e.g. Season 1, Episode 3; Episode 15). In this respect, the remake almost appeals to childhood memories and to a possible nostalgia on this level. Apart from that, intertextual references to the 1980s series *The Transformers* (Sky One, 1984) appeal to the childhood/boyhood memories of a broader audience.

The public discourse in the form of newspaper articles gives evidence of both readings. As reflected by Forn (2009), the remake may indeed maintain the fascination of its predecessor. The author notes in *La Vanguardia* "[e]l nuevo KITT es aún más fantástico" [the new KITT is even more fantastic] (Forn, 2009 [o.t.]). The fascination is shared by another author in *La Vanguardia* who is of the opinion that "the new technologies and special computer effects make sure that the pirouettes of the blabbermouth super car are even more impossible, if procurable, than its predecessor" (*La Vanguardia*, 2009 [o.t.])[60]. This similarly applies to Broc (2009), who also highlights the *Transformers* references of the series. The author states that "the effects are of quality and the new car, a Ford Mustang, which seems like a demonic Transformer, lets the finesses of the legendary Pontiac Firebird resemble those of a *Supermirafiori* [a standard medium-sized car of the 1970s to 1980s]"

---

59 See e.g. Season 1, Episode 1, min. 0:03:09, where one of the characters says, "My car talks to me... It's called GPS".

60 Original quotation: "sin embargo las nuevas tecnologías y los efectos especiales por ordenador sí aseguran que las piruetas del supercoche parlanchín vayan a ser todavía más imposibles, si cabe, que las de su antecesor" (*La Vanguardia*, 2009).

(Broc, 2009 [o.t.])[61]. However, he clearly indicates that the remake is not "tan fantástico..." [as fantastic] (Broc, 2009 [o.t.]) as its predecessor. This is also in line with what is predominantly reflected by the German discourse. While Sauerbrey (2009) simply stresses the modernisation of the car, Moorstedt in *Süddeutsche Zeitung* dismantles the remake strategies and mocks the lost fascination. As the author highlights, "the utopia of once is obsolete [...] Therefore one adorns the new car with science fiction accessories [...]. While the original K.I.T.T still looked like an artefact from a not-too-distant future, it seems as if his successor comes from the MTV workshop *Pimp My Ride*" (Moorstedt, 2009 [o.t.])[62]. A similar stance is taken by Rehfeld in *Der Spiegel*. "'*Knight Rider*'", he notes, "failed [...] because there was nothing to add to the high-tech charm of the original. Today we associate annoying navigation systems, seat belt and distance alerts with 'intelligent' cars." (Rehfeld, 2011 [o.t.])[63] Also here the public discourse gives first evidence of a possible reception. The question whether the triggers for nostalgia are actually decoded by the audiences will have to be further scrutinised in the reception study.

Music
Knight Rider (NBC, 2008) exposes both pre-existing and newly composed contemporary music without the 'connotation of pastness'. It has a dramatic function when it supports suspense, action, or romantic moments. The generation of a "'nostalgic condition'" is no function of the music. However, also on this level the remake contains intertextual references. It takes over the original theme song and remixes it as a techno-rock version, also utilised as *leitmotiv* throughout the episodes. Independent of the modernisation, the music is clearly reminiscent of the past and likely to work as a "mnemonic prompt" and, depending on the respective "retrospective classification", to trigger 'artefact nostalgia' respectively viewers' 'own artefact nostalgia' in those who have memories of the premake. A critical or self-reflexive stance of the music cannot be observed.

---

61 Original quotation: "[L]os efectos son de calidad y el nuevo coche, un Ford Mustang que parece un Transformer demoníaco, hace que las prestaciones del legendario Pontiac Firebird parezcan las de un Supermirafiori" (Broc, 2009).

62 Original quotation: "[D]ie Utopie von einst ist überholt [...]. Also schmückt man das neue Serienauto mit Science-Fiction-Accessoires [...]. Sah das Original K.I.T.T mit seinen aggressiv geschwungenen Linien noch aus wie ein Artefakt aus einer nicht allzu weit entfernten Zukunft, meint man, sein Nachfolger entstamme aus der MTV-Werkstatt Pimp my Ride." (Moorstedt, 2009)

63 Original quotation: "'Knight Rider' scheiterte [...] weil der Hightech-Faszination des Originals nichts hinzuzufügen war. Heute assoziiert man mit 'intelligenten' Autos nervtötende Navigationssysteme, Gurt- und Entfernungswarner." (Rehfeld, 2011)

6.2.1.2.3 Characters

Although the remake maintains the basic constellation of 'the man and his car', it clearly transports its predecessor into the present. First and foremost, the narration is less focused on the duo. While Bonnie and Devon of the premake move towards the centre of interest only in exceptional episodes, the support team of the remake, consisting of a core constellation of three members and an additional secondary row, has more narrative importance. It is the team that provides the last-minute rescue. Furthermore, shorter narrative strands focus on the characters. Here, in contrast to the premake, "the explication of the meaning of events for the characters enjoys primacy" (Tan, 1996, p. 176), just as Tan describes it in the context of empathy in general. In doing this, the remake refers to contemporary series, such as *CSI* (see *C.S.I.– Crime Scene Investigation* (CBS, 2000) with its spin-offs *CSI: Miami* (CBS, 2002) or *CSI: New York* (CBS, 2004)) or also *24* (Fox, 2001), reflecting the contemporary trend towards ensemble casts (Mittell, 2006) and highlighting the gap between action series 'today' and 'then'.

Also on the level of the characters, *Knight Rider* (NBC, 2008) exposes intertextual references to the premake. Next to a clear continuity regarding the main characters, Michael Knight (Justin Bruening) and KITT, basic characteristics of Bonny – the highly educated car mechanic – and Devon – the distinguished gentleman – continue in the remake-characters Sarah and Charles as well. With the appearance of David Hasselhoff (as Michael Knight Senior) in the pilot episode, also a case of personnel continuity between remake and premake may be described. Since, as Sprengler highlights, actors may "echo" past roles (Sprengler, 2010, p. 81), his quality as former leading character of the premake can be assumed to pop up in the audiences, triggering memories of the premake character or (media) memories related to him. Apart from that, a clear 'gap' between the star persona's past and present identity could be noticed in Section 6.1.1.3.3, which again serves the basis for potential 'artefact nostalgia'. Period casting, the "practice of selecting actors based on their resemblance to film stars of times past" (Sprengler, 2011, p. 80) or, in this case, based on their resemblance to former *Knight Rider* actors, cannot be observed.

Michael Knight

As in the 'original' series, Michael Knight (Justin Bruening) is the leading character of *Knight Rider* (NBC, 2008). The clothes he wears and his styling paint him as a modern character without anachronisms. However, here the remake character also contains explicit intertextual references to the premake that not only make it a potential "mnemonic prompt" and, depending on the respective "retrospective classification", a potential trigger for nostalgia but also support nostalgia on the fictional level.

With his name, the remake-character clearly evokes the premake and provides a taste of 'pastness' for those audiences who recognise the reference. Further aspects of the character's features – white, heterosexual, male, around 30, a former soldier with a traumatic past – are reminiscent of the predecessor. A reflective layer is not provided. At the same time the remake picks up and continues discourses of the premake. In contrast to the predecessor, the 'new' Michael is no "lone crusader in a dangerous world". He hands over a lot of responsibility to the other team members, and the narration focuses less on him. However, this fact is not presented as self-evident or as a necessary development. The troubled, traditional masculinity is rather staged as being problematic for the new American hero. While the predecessor Michael with his character traits of the emotional mediator first develops strategies to meet the requirements of the modern world, the remake character rejects the continuation of this line but moans about his lost privileges. One can even argue that the remake is "'shot through with nostalgia, with an obsession with images and definitions of masculinity and masculine codes of behaviour, and with images of male narcissism and the threats posed to it by women, society and the law'" (Neale, 1993 cited in Shimpach, 2010, p. 46), just as Neale once described it in the context of the late-era western. This fact becomes not only apparent in situations where Michael's displeasure of the cutting of his privileges is explicitly articulated, or in those scenes where he contrasts his traditional white masculinity to the female characters (see the pilot episode, min. 0:37:09), it is also exposed by the remake, for instance, in conversations about the topic (see Season 1, Episode 2).[64] Independently of whether the viewers recognise the intertextual references to the premake or not, in doing so, *Knight Rider* (NBC, 2008) becomes not only a potential trigger for 'empathetic F nostalgia' – whether or not the protagonist himself is nostalgic – but also supports 'non-empathetic F nostalgia' for a moment before once dominant images of masculinity are disrupted.

The public discourse gives few but first evidences of respective observations of the anachronistic character similarities between the premake- and the remake-Michael. Here the Spanish *La Vanguardia* simply calls the remake character the "nuevo" [new] Michael Knight (*La Vanguardia*, 2009 [o.t.]). In the German

---

64 Examples include a conversation between Michael and KITT (min. 0:26:54 ff.). KITT: "I am researching the delineation of gender roles in the classic western. Men appeared to be limited to fighting, playing cards and consuming prodigious amounts of whiskey." Mike: "Yeah, the good old days." Mike now changes the topic, emphasising his responsibility for Sarah. His statement is undermined and exposed as outdated 'macho' behaviour by a western film scene simultaneously screened on the video display of the computer-car. Since this oppositional reading is, however, implemented by the artificial intelligence, you could argue that it leaves the reactionary and anachronistic version as the 'natural' version of the 'truth' and as dominant reading.

Tagesspiegel, Sauerbrey describes the similarities and changes more closely, finding a conclusion that, it may be argued, almost nostalgically moans the losses regarding the protagonist's masculinity: "Alas, you think when you see the new *Knight Rider*. How times have changed, and with them the cars and men." (Sauerbrey, 2009 [o.t.])[65]

6.2.2 Analysis of nostalgia in *The Avengers* (Chechik, 1998)

The Avengers (Chechik, 1998) is a film remake of the previously analysed television series with the same title (ITV, 1961). In 1998, the film was released in German and Spanish cinemas. Since then it was broadcasted on both German and Spanish television. Between 2009 and 2011, it could be watched on several channels, including the private German television channels Sat.1 and kabel eins (see e.g. Weis, 2009). In Spain it was broadcasted on the private channel LaSexta in 2009. *The Avengers* also contains aspects of the temporally less distant rerun, which at least has to be kept in mind during the analysis. A synchronised DVD version of the film is available in both countries.

The film focuses on the British agent John Steed, played by Ralph Fiennes. The character is called into action when inexplicable climate changes begin to threaten the peace of the British capital, London. His bosses – "Mother" (Jim Broadbent) and "Father" (Fiona Shaw) – assign the climate expert Dr Emma Peel (Uma Thurman) to assist him. She is meant to investigate the case but at the same time she is one of the major suspects, since it was her or her look-alike who initialised the sabotage against Prospero – the governmental weather project. Soon, however, the duo picks up the trail of a mad scientist, Sir August de Wynter (Sean Connery). The ex-member of the ministry not only abuses an investigation he once conducted on cloning – with Emma Peel as his very victim – but also uses an advanced version of the governmental weather programme for his own purposes, which is to blackmail worldwide governments with ice age scenarios. While de Wynter is about to prepare the last step of his diabolic plan, Emma and Steed enter his power station. At the last minute they stop the worst-case scenario from happening.

As the television series, *The Avengers* (Chechik, 1998) is a hybrid of spy genre, action film, and thriller with an emphasis on the latter two. And as the series, the film contains elements of parody.

6.2.2.1 A short contextualisation

The Avengers (Chechik, 1998) – *Mit Schirm, Charme und Melone* in German and *Los Vengadores* in Spanish – is clearly contextualised within the frame of the premake. Alone the title evokes memories of the 'original' television series.

---

65 Original quotation: "Hach, denkt man, wenn man den neuen Knight Rider sieht, wie haben sich die Zeiten geändert. Und mit ihnen die Autos und die Männer." (Sauerbrey, 2009)

Furthermore, the discourses that surround the remake periodically refer to the 1960s predecessor. When both German and Spanish newspaper articles discuss the *The Avengers* remake, they always do so in the context of the 'original'.[66] Both the production company Warner Brothers Productions and its producer Jerry Weintraub highlight that the film is based upon the series (Weintraub in Pérez, 1998, p. 169; Warner Brothers, 2011). Already on this general layer we may assume that the premake and its context are important memory points.

Consequently, as in the case of the *Knight Rider* remake, on a first and general layer, the premake context as it has been outlined in Chapter 6.1 is relevant for the analysis of potential nostalgias. With a view on the later reception analysis, it should be kept in mind that the 'original' series has been re-broadcasted in the past few decades. Secondly, it must be considered in which way the premake as an artefact as a whole is installed as a potential object of nostalgia. Here, the context chapter on the rerun already shows that the 'original' television series of *The Avengers* was subject to broad "retrospective classifications" (Kompare, 2005, p. 105). Despite some minor country-specific differences (see 6.1.3)[67], this favours nostalgia directed towards the 'original' television series both in Germany and Spain.

Apart from the fact that in the public discourse *The Avengers* (Chechik, 1998) is always put in the context of the television series – which means that the valorising discourse about the 'original' is linked to the remake – the remake-discourse itself is also part of the valorisation of the premake. Several discourse fragments in Spanish newspapers valorise the premake in the context of the remake (see e.g. Gómez, 1997; Gómez, 1997a; Cavestany, 1998; Parrondo, 1998a). Here, authors describe the 'original' as a "mítica serie británica" [mythical British series] (Jose and Moreno, 2003 [o.t.]), "legendaria serie británica de aventuras" [legendary British adventure series] (Parrondo, 1998 [o.t.]) or "la serie […] más popular de todos los tiempos" [the most popular series of all times] (Ramos, 1995 [o.t.]). Some articles explicitly devalue the remake in this context. Jose and Moreno state in *El País* (2003 [o.t.]), for example, that "la altura del listón impuesto por su predecesora resulta insuperable" [the height of the bar which has been set by his predecessor is unattainable].

---

66 Regarding Spain, see Ramos, 1995; L.G., 1997; Gómez, 1997; Gómez, 1997a; Cavestany, 1998; Llopart, 1998; Parrondo, 1998; Parrondo, 1998a; Jose and Moreno, 2003. Regarding Germany, see Seidel, 1998; Hermanski, 1998; malt, 1998; Gärtner, 1998; Martenstein, 1998; Zylka, 1998.

67 In Spain, in contrast to Germany, those valorisations on the side of museums and academic publications mostly go without the specific Spanish perspective. Also regarding the fan culture the cases diverge slightly, since in Germany a livelier fan community could be observed. In contrast to Spain (2009-2011) the premake is here also available as DVD collection, which all the more highlights the greater appreciation and suggests that the series may have been kept better in memory.

Cavestany emphasises in the same newspaper that "en el caso de *Los vengadores como en muchos otros, las comparaciones suelen ser favorables al producto original*" [in the case of *Los Vengadore*, as in many others, the comparisons are usually in favour of the original] (Cavestany, 1998 [o.t.]). The same applies to the German discourse. "Now, thirty years later in the movies," says Seidel in *Frankfurter Allgemeine Zeitung*, "'*The Avengers*' are nothing but a monstrous misunderstanding." (Seidel, 1998 [o.t.])[68]. According to the author Malt, "the screen was too large for the recent launch of *The Avengers*." (Malt, 1998 [o.t.])[69]. Hermanski describes how bland the remake is in comparison to the "Markenzeichen der Originalserie" [brand of the original series] (Hermanski, 1998 [o.t]).

As in the context of the *Knight Rider* remake, it may be stated that the remake is not only contextualised with the premake and gives the premake the status of the 'original', just as it was observed by Oltmann (2008, pp. 14 ff.) in the context of remakes in general, but also becomes part of the narration of the better 'then' in comparison to the lacking 'now', making the premake a potential nostalgia object. In contrast to *Knight Rider* (NBC, 2008), a less intensive retrospective valorisation on the side of the television channels can be observed. However, here the producer also valorises the series as a childhood icon and creates a 'we-identity' around the series when he explains his motivation to produce the remake: "'I was one of those millions of young people who were in love with Emma Peel'." (Weintraub cited in Pérez, 1998, p. 169 [o.t.])[70]

6.2.2.2 Nostalgia on the single levels of the text

6.2.2.2.1 Narration

The narration of *The Avengers* (1998) can be described as being classical, according to Bordwell (1985, p. 157): It is linearly developed, causal- and stereotype-dominated. While a first plot line focuses on a clear-cut problem with the two main characters coming into action, entering into conflict with others, solving the problem, and finally restoring order, a second line involves the romantic interests between the agent couple. In general, the narration, set around the turn of the millennium, cannot be called nostalgic. Neither is it presented from the perspective of a nostalgic character. However, what makes the remake a potential trigger for nostalgia are the intertextual references it exposes. *The Avengers* (Chechik, 1998) retells dramatic

---

68 Original quotation: "'The Avengers' nun dreißig Jahre später im Kino sind nichts als ein monströses Mißverständnis" (Seidel, 1998).

69 Original quotation: "Die Leinwand war eine Nummer zu groß, als die *Avengers* unlängst ins Kino kamen." (Malt, 1998)

70 Original quotation: "'Yo era uno de aquellos milliones de jóvenes que estaban enamorados de Emma Peel'." (Weintraub cited in Pérez, 1998, p. 169)

elements from the original television series and combines them in a new way. It inserts events "where the film presumes to tell us things that the show left implied or entirely mysterious" (Black, 2004, p. 102).

With its character selection of Emma Peel and John Steed, the remake basically refers to the fourth and fifth season of the premake. Regarding the general theme, its main reference is *A Surfeit of H2O* (Season 4, Episode 8)[71] – an episode of the original series in which Steed and Peel investigate mysterious cases of death in the periphery of a factory that manipulates the weather in its surroundings. Other reference episodes are *The House That Jack Built* (Season 4, Episode 23) or *The Joker* (Season 5, Episode 15). Apart from that, the remake relates to *Doppelgänger* (see e.g. Season 5, Episode 10, and Season 5, Episode 16), amnesia motifs (see e.g. Season 6, Episode 1) or "various invisible man episodes" (Black, 2004, p. 114, n10) (see e.g. Season 5, Episode 4). Other aspects of the remake, for instance the integration of the characters "Mother" (not introduced until the last Peel episode) and "Father" (see also 6.2.2.2.3) or the kiss between Steed and Peel, depart from the Peel/Steed-episodes but employ references to other *The Avengers* seasons (see e.g. Season 3, Episode 16). Even though modernised, through these intertextual references, the remake may create an "awareness of things past" in those viewers who associate it with the premake, may work as a "mnemonic prompt" and, depending on the respective "retrospective classification", provoke nostalgia.

Later, the remake also links to the media memory of a broader audience of those who never saw the 'original' series. Already in the exposition of the remake – a training session for John Steed (Ralph Fiennes), where the committed viewer who saw the 'original' series may find reminiscences to various *Avengers* episodes (see e.g. Season 5, Episode 3, or Season 5, Episode 14) – a situation is exposed that also reminds you of typical James Bond-opening scenes. However, a critical layer, for instance released by frictions between the premake and the remake, or between the remake and its further sources, or characteristics of self-reflexivity cannot be found. By integrating the references into its closed narrative, the remake does not tend to explicitly disclose its sources of influence.

6.2.2.2.2 Aesthetic and design

The aspiration to appeal to a broad audience of both those who have seen and those who have not seen the premake can also be observed on other levels of the text. On the one hand, *The Avengers* (Chechik, 1998) is a modernised version of the 'original' series. On the other hand, the level of aesthetic and design contains various elements, which are clearly reminiscent of the predecessor or of other past media forms. Apart

---

71 While the episode was broadcasted on Spanish Television (TVE1) in 1967 (ABC, 1967c), German television (TV Berlin) did not release it before 1998 (Imfernsehen, 2011a) – which should be considered with a view on the reception study.

from the title that refers to the 1960s premake, already the title sequence evokes the predecessor series, exposing *The Avengers'* icons (umbrella, bowler hat and Emma Peel's silhouette). At the same time, it reminds you of psychedelic record sleeves and posters of the 1960s, a reference that is also recognisable for those audiences who do not know the television series.

Camera, montage, and lighting

Where the 'original' series has the character of an intimate play, the remake exposes lavish crane shots up to aerial shots and lighting, depending on the dramatic situation. The action scenes are accompanied by a cinematic, accelerated editing. Where the 'original' disposes of limited resources, the remake falls back on large-scale 3D-animation and computer-generated effects. All in all, regarding camera, montage and lighting, the remake is not nostalgic. With its feature film cinematography it is neither reminiscent of the television series nor of other media 'pasts', but rather presents a clear gap between 'then' and 'now' for those who see it in the context of the premake.

Setting

On the level of its settings, *The Avengers* (1998) clearly refers to the television series. Even though the remake exposes its large budget in opulent settings, which make it differ from the series, the intertextual references to its source of inspiration are always present. Also, in the remake "nothing is what it seems", just as Buxton (1990, p. 101) highlighted it in the context of the premake. An underground car park holds the control centre of the British Secret Service, a baroque palace contains a labyrinth, and a telephone booth hides a lift[72]. Furthermore, references relate to single episodes of the series. With the labyrinthine mansion alone the film refers to episodes of the predecessor (see e.g. Season 4, Episode 23; Season 5, Episode 15). In the case that the references are recognised by the audiences and that they are respectively retrospectively classified, they may lead to 'artefact nostalgia' or audience's 'own artefact nostalgia'. A sensuous exploration of the setting, for instance from the perspective of a protagonist, is rather unimportant in the film. Similar to the 'original' series, the film exposes typified characters that do not favour empathy. It is therefore unlikely to trigger 'internal aesthetic artefact nostalgia'.

Decór, props and costumes

It has been shown that décor, props and costumes are decisive period markers in the 'original' series. They give *The Avengers* (ITV, 1961) the look and feel of the 1960s. Furthermore, the series' décor is directly identifiable as such; it reminds you of the early teleplays as they have been realised both in Germany and in Spain during the

---

72 The remake here refers clearly to the credits of the 1960s television series *Get Smart* (NBC, 1965), which was broadcasted both on German and Spanish television.

1960s. This does not apply to the remake. The expensive sets and décor rather keep up the tradition of the contemporary big-budget blockbuster. Later, *The Avengers* (Chechik, 1998) exposes a variety of styles from throughout the centuries, which makes a temporal categorisation more difficult. In doing so, the remake may perhaps have some punctual effects of "historical associations"; however, due to the excessive period mix a clear (nostalgic) strategy cannot be observed.

It is a different case regarding the intertextual references to the premake that the remake exposes on the level of décor, props and costumes. Here, the "awareness of things past" may arise in those viewers who recognise the reference. Décor, props, and costumes clearly underline the film's fidelity regarding its role model and refer to the pop style of the 'original'.

As in the 'original', décor, props and costumes are used in order to characterise the protagonists (see also 6.2.2.2.3). While Steed's flat is furnished in an antique style, full of accessories from past times, Peel's apartment contains a mix of pop art and contemporary design elements. Already here, the remake is reminiscent of *The Avengers* (ITV, 1961) and likely to trigger respective memories and 'artefact nostalgia' in viewers who know the premake.

Steed's (Ralph Fiennes) costumes have an Edwardian style. Like his predecessor, he is equipped with tailor-made suits, bowler hat, umbrella, and a vintage vehicle – objects which were already anachronistic in the 1960s and which from today's perspective gained the intertextual reference to the premake. As in the series, 'lacks' of the past are compensated with 'achievements' of the – now modernised – present. Thus, also the 'new' Steed wears a bowler hat filled with steel, his suit hides a flak jacket, and his pocket-watch holds a high-tech tracking mechanism. Yet the precondition for a reflexive nostalgia of the remake-Steed (Ralph Fiennes) fizzles out, since it stays far less exposed than in the predecessor format. The reflexivity, it may be argued, is undermined by further elements, such as dialogues and comportment of the character that paint him as being rather reactionary (see 6.2.2.2.3).

Similarly, this applies to Emma Peel (Uma Thurman). The props that surround her and costumes she wears are clearly reminiscent of the 'original'. As in the case of the predecessor, her wardrobe ranges from black leather suits, ladies' costumes and miniskirts to the so-called 'Emmapeeler'. In both cases it is likely that props and costumes trigger memories of the 'original' and, depending on respective "retrospective classifications", 'artefact nostalgia' or a viewer's 'own artefact nostalgia' in those audiences who know the series.

The public discourse provides evidence that the references are also made by the audiences. Gómez notes in *El País* that "the costumes are a fundamental element in the visual style of the film. [...] Anthony Powell [...] opted for the retention of three symbols of masculinity of the series: the three-piece suit [...], the bowler hat and the umbrella." (Gómez, 1997a [o.t.])[73] Also Hermanski, a writer of the German newspaper *Süddeutsche Zeitung*, emphasises that "[t]he look of the new *Avengers* adheres to the hallmarks of the original series" (Hermanski, 1998 [o.t.])[74].

However, what was fascinating and extended the boundaries both in Germany and Spain in the 1960s is reminiscent from today's perspective. Against the contemporary backdrop "'Uma Peel'"[75] is no provocation any more – one could even argue that she is reactionary since the "feminine-erotic" (Baumgart, 2002, p. 27 [o.t.]) component that has been integrated via the costumes and which already made the predecessor Emma approach conventional conceptions of femininity in the 1960s (Baumgart, 2002, p. 55), stays in the foreground. No 'adjustments' of further character traits can be found (see 6.2.2.2.3). Regarding the lost fascination and lack of overstepping of boundaries, a clear gap between the *The Avengers* experience 'then' and 'now' may be located, which may also be a source of 'A nostalgia'.

Music

The music in *The Avengers* (1998) has a dramatic function when it supports suspense, mystery, or action, or a narrative function ironically commenting a situation (see e.g. min. 0:25:09). The remake employs mostly original non-diegetic instrumental music that is unlikely to provoke 'artefact nostalgia' or to support a nostalgic narration. The creation of a "'nostalgic condition'" is also not one of its functions. While the 'original' series employed a rather intimate Big Band score, the remake uses a huge orchestra – less reminiscent of the predecessor and more reminiscent of major feature film productions, such as the contemporary *James Bond* series.

At the same time, the remake refers to its source of inspiration, employing a modernised version of the original *Avengers* title theme. In case the audiences perceive the reference, the *The Avengers* (Chechik, 1998) soundtrack may indeed provoke an "awareness of things past". In those viewers who recognise the reference it may function as a "mnemonic prompt" and, depending on the respective "retrospective classification", work as a potential trigger for nostalgia.

---

73 Original quotation: "El vestuario es un elemento fundamental en el estilo visual de la película. [...] Anthony Powell [...] ha obtado por mantener tres símbolos masculinos de la serie original: el traje de tres piezas [...], el bombín y el paraguas." (Gómez, 1997a)

74 Original quotation: "Der Look der neuen Avengers hält sich an die Markenzeichen der Originalserie." (Hermanski, 1998)

75 According to Black (2004, pp. 99 f.), the discourse on the remake created the "witticism 'Uma Peel,' a name designed to refer exclusively to Uma-as-Emma and to protect both Emma Peel and Diana Rigg from sacrilege".

6.2.2.2.3 Characters

Furthermore, on the level of the characters, it is the intertextual reference to the premake that is most dominant. Apart from one case of personnel continuity between premake and remake – Patrick Macnee, the former Steed actor, here acts as the speaking part of the invisible Jones[76] – and the continuity regarding the main characters, Steed and Peel, diverse secondary characters refer to the 'original' as well. "Mother" (Jim Broadbent), for example, is a character that was introduced in the last Peel episode (see Season 6, Episode 1). Here, the remake uses not only the so-called "period casting" – Broadbent has been obviously selected due to his resemblance to the series character – but the character is oriented on the premake, too.

As suggested by Pérez (1998, p. 174), De Wynter (Sean Connery) may be described as a combination of different antagonists as they appeared throughout the 'original' series. The continuity between premake and remake regarding the main characters is most obvious. Apart from the fact that *The Avengers* (Chechik, 1998), as Dika notes in the context of remakes in general, "feature[s] big-name movie stars" (Dika, 2003, p. 203), who import their own past roles and also attract the attention of those audiences who do not know the 'original' series[77], both are clearly reminiscent of the 'original'. Starting with the name or his function within the narration but also regarding the objects that surround and characterise him, there are many parallels between the remake and the premake Steeds. With her name, costumes, objects that surround her or other details that determine the character – presumed widow, highly educated with karate skills – the remake Peel (Uma Thurman) is also clearly reminiscent of the 'original' character. In case that they are recognised by the viewers, these intertextual references alone may already trigger memories of the television series and, depending on the respective "retrospective classification", lead to 'artefact nostalgia' respectively viewers' 'own artefact nostalgia'.

Later, additional possible triggers for nostalgia may be found on the level of the characters. While already in the 1960s the 'original' Steed extended the then dominant image of masculinity, the 'new' Steed reintroduces obsolete patriarchal manners. Always eager to gain the upper hand in his relationship to Peel, he tries to impose his will – "Play according to the rules!", "Do not eat macaroons!", "Tea, please!" – and finally succeeds. Where the premake character extended boundaries and was likely to provoke fascination, joy, or admiration in its audiences, the remake falls back on obsolete gender roles. In doing this, the remake establishes itself as a

---

76 The effect has neither been continued in the synchronised German version (see Zylka, 1998) nor in the Spanish one (El Doblaje, 2010; 2011).

77 With films such as *The English Patient* (Minghella, 1997), *Wuthering Heights* (Kosminsky, 1992) or *Oscar and Lucinda* (Armstrong, 1997), Ralph Fiennes clearly refers to the heritage genre (Higson, 2003, p. 32). Uma Thurman echoes (past) roles in films such as *Kill Bill: Vol.1* (Tarantino, 2003) or *Kill Bill: Vol.2* (Tarantino, 2004).

potential trigger for nostalgia toward the lost positive emotion (be it on the F or A level of the text) and for those audiences who see the remake in the context of their experiences with the premake. Apart from that and independent of the premake, due to its narration of a present infused with traditional role models painted in a positive way, the character contributes to a "reassertion of patriarchy", as Dika calls it in the context of remakes of old television series (Dika, 2003, p. 204), which makes it a possible trigger for 'F nostalgia'.

This similarly applies to Peel's character. Even though discourses on the emancipated role model are explicitly picked up, the remake Emma is not able to extend established boundaries, as her predecessor did. Already the first meeting between the characters makes that clear, where Peel (Uma Thurman) barges into an all-male club (see min. 0:06:49 ff.). Firstly, in line with Baumgart (2002, p. 138) it may be stated that the staged crossing of boundaries is far from the naturalness with which the 'original' Emma acted and with which she emphasised traditional gender distributions as being obsolete. Secondly, while the 'original' Emma fought against obsolete patriarchal structures in her 1960s reality, the rules that are disrespected by Uma Peel were made in 1762, which seems almost like a parody. Thirdly, the friendship between Steed and Peel is far from materialising a world "after patriarchy", as it was described by Miller (2004, p. 188) in the context of *The Avengers* (ITV, 1961). Rather the contrary is the case. Steed's attempt to 'domesticate' Emma ("Play by the rules!") finally succeeds. Leaving aside the fact that the remake states an obsolete opposition of traditional masculine and feminine traits, every fascination (be it in the form of an A or F emotion) that may have been provoked in the context of the 'original' is lost. The optimistic gaze towards the future has been substituted by a reactionary re-installation of traditional boundaries. Thus, a clear gap between 'then' and 'now' may be located, which may be the potential source of nostalgia directed towards the premake.

The public discourse provides evidence for various readings. Without exception the remake Peel is related to her predecessor here. While on the one hand the continuity regarding the premake is highlighted, on the other hand the gap between the two versions is emphasised. The loss of the fascination with Peel's ability to extend the boundaries is mainly reflected by the German public discourse. While, according to Hermanski, the 'original' Peel was "eine der stärksten Frauengestalten" [one of the strongest female characters], in the remake "Steed and the Amazon kiss each other, and he puts the tailor-made black boots on her feet" (Hermanski, 1998 [o.t.])[78]. Also, Seidel takes the stance that "Uma Thurman may be as slim and long-legged as Mrs Peel, but the sophistication and sex appeal of the latter gave way to a

---

78 Original quotation: "Hier küssen sich Steed und die Amazone, und er zieht ihr die maßgeschneiderten schwarzen Stiefel an." (Hermanski, 1998)

coquetry with female charm, which only seems importunate" (Seidel, 1998 [o.t.])[79]. Disappointed, Martenstein notes that "Thurman seems more American and un-intellectual than ever" (Martenstein, 1998 [o.t.])[80]. Zykla asks almost nostalgically, "So this is supposed to be Emma Peel? [...] The Amazon for whom I have firmly attended two years of fencing and karate classes." (Zylka, 1998 [o.t.])[81] It is a different case regarding the Spanish newspapers. They rather highlight the similarities between the premake and the remake character. However, the comparison between the remake character and its 'original', as it can be observed in some appraisals, also gives evidence of a certain de-valorisation of the remake here. While Gomez stresses that "[e]l guión [...] intenta capturar el espíritu de los personajes originales" [the script intends to capture the spirit of the original characters] (Gómez, 1997), according to Parrondo "Uma Thurman recreates the pop style, which had been made popular by Mrs Diana Rigg, in '*Los Vengadores*'" (Parrondo, 1998a [o.t.])[82]. As argued by Llopart, "martial arts, the bossiness and the sinuous leather suits are presented by Uma Thurman, maintaining the spirit of the 'Sixties' of the original in the film" (Llopart, 1998 [o.t.])[83]. Gómez (1997) also agrees with this view. The author states in *El País* "[a]s the original Emma Peel, the actress [...] dressed in black leather, with a jump suit that marks her silhouette, practices self-defence and professes absolute independence" (Gómez, 1997 [o.t.])[84]. The author known as L.G. even describes the "modelitos eróticos y provocadores" [erotic and provocative models] as being "acordes con una imagen actualizada de la espía Peel" [conform to an updated image of Peel, the spy] (L.G., 1997 [o.t.]) who unintentionally once more highlights the 'loss' from an emancipated, feminine perspective.

As the premake, *The Avengers* (1998) does not favour an empathetic understanding of its typified characters. 'Empathetic F nostalgia' can rather be

---

79 Original quotation: "Uma Thurman mag so schlank und langbeinig sein, wie Mrs. Peel das will, doch deren Raffinement und sex appeal sind einem Kokettieren mit weiblichen Reizen gewichen, das nur aufdringlich wirkt" (Seidel, 1998).

80 Original quotation: "Thurman wirkt amerikanischer und unintellektueller denn je." (Martenstein, 1998)

81 Original quotation: "Das soll Emma Peel sein? [...] Die Amazone, wegen der ich zwei entschlossene Jahre lang Fecht- und Karatekurse belegt habe." (Zylka, 1998)

82 Original quotation: "Uma Thurman recrea en 'Los Vengadores' el estilo pop que popularizó Diana Rigg como la señora Emma Peel." (Parrondo, 1998a)

83 Original quotation: "[...] [L]as artes marciales, la decisión y los sinuosos trajes de cuero los pone la norteamericana Uma Thurman, manteniendo en el filme el espiritu 'sixties' de la original señora Peel [...]." (Llopart, 1998)

84 Original quotation: "Como la original Emma Peel, la actriz [...] viste en cuero negro, con un buzo ajustado que marca su silueta, practica la autodefensa y profesa una independencia absoluta." (Gómez, 1997)

excluded. In general, there can be no talk of "confounding the past and the present in a way that addresses our current historical period" (Dika, 2003, p. 211), such as Dika notes in the context of her analysis of *Psycho* (Van Sant, 1998). The remake lacks any critical perspective. Where the 'original' is anything but an 'agent' of the 1960s, the remake tries hard to ignore the critical potential of its source of inspiration.

6.2.4 First conclusion on the remakes as potential triggers for nostalgia

The analysis focused on two examples of remakes which in the time span of 2009-2011 were broadcasted both on German and Spanish television, namely *Knight Rider* (NBC, 2008) and *The Avengers* (Chechik, 1998). While the first is a representative of television series remakes of television series, the latter represents the species of film remake of a television series. Apart from the fact that the *The Avengers* (Chechik, 1998) adaptation also took place on a local level, both mainly refer to the temporal level since they are adaptations of a temporally distant premake. Both remakes update their predecessors. *Knight Rider* (NBC, 2008), situated shortly after the turn of the millennium, refers to the 1980s television series *Knight Rider* (NBC, 1982; TVE, 1985, RTLplus, 1985), which was set in a 1980s present, while *The Avengers* (Chechik, 1998), situated in a not clearly definable time around the turn of the millennium, is reminiscent of the 1960s series with the same title (ITV, 1961; TVE, 1966; ZDF, 1966), which was set in the 1960s.

First and foremost, it has been shown with reference to both the academic and non-academic discourse that remakes can be subsumed under the category of nostalgia 'genres'. They can be expected to create the expectation of nostalgia. However, in the television analysis this point could not be investigated further. It is important with a view on the later reception analysis.

In the television analysis, the disposition of the remake as a potential trigger for nostalgia was investigated. With reference to the theoretical part, it has been assumed that 'A nostalgia' is the dominant form of nostalgia prefigured by the remake. This has been verified in the course of the analysis even though other forms of nostalgia could also be highlighted as being possible. On both the level of the remake as a whole and the single levels of the remakes – from (1) narration to (2) aesthetic and design to (3) characters – possible 'gaps' between a pre-and postlapsarian world (see Tannock, 1995, pp. 456 f.) could be described. The 'modules' that were filtered out in the theoretical section proved to be an applicable and reasonable analysis scheme. The public discourse served first indicators of the reception of a gap; however, whether the triggers for nostalgia are finally perceived as such will be further scrutinised in Part III.

The major 'gap' in the case of the remakes was expected to be located around the intertextual reference to the premake. On a first and general layer, both remakes are contextualised with their respective premakes. In both cases, already the title clearly evokes memories of the premake. The same applies to other discourses around the remakes, such as the public discourse in the form of newspaper articles or the discourse of the producers. As a result, the analysis first studies the respective contexts. A review of "retrospective classifications" of the premakes provides evidence of whether or not they are likely to be the object of a nostalgia triggered on this general layer.

Regarding the evocation of the temporal contexts of the premakes, profound differences between German and Spanish recipients and different age groups may be expected. Firstly, it has to be taken into consideration that while both age groups may remember the 1980s, only the age group of the 55 to 65-year-olds disposes of personal memories of the 1960s. Secondly, regarding the socio-political context of the 1960s but also regarding the 1980s-context, Germany and Spain diverge tremendously. Apart from that, both reference-premakes have been broadcasted as reruns throughout the years, which means that audiences may have contextualised them in points of time that may be different from the date of the original broadcast.

In both cases, *Knight Rider* (NBC, 2008) and *The Avengers* (Chechik, 1998) nostalgia for the premake is favoured by "retrospective classifications" of the 'original' in general and of the 'original' in the context of the remake in both the German and the Spanish public discourse. Regarding both *Knight Rider* (2008) and *The Avengers* (Chechik, 1998), but most evident in the latter case, it is the German discourse that tends to devalue the remake on the back of a valorisation of the predecessor.

Further on in the study, every single level of the remakes was analysed. Since both remakes "update the time frame" (Black, 2004, p. 101) of their predecessors the "awareness of things past", as Lowenthal would put it, derives not from a contrast to the present but from the intertextual references to the temporally distant premake. Also on the single levels of the text, it is mainly the intertextual reference to the premake that makes both remakes potential triggers for nostalgia. Here, two main triggers for nostalgia may be distinguished: One that finds its source in the referential character to the premake and evoked memories, and another one that surges more directly from the 'gap' between remake and premake.

With respect to the first point, it is shown that *Knight Rider* (NBC, 2008), apart from the title sequence, contains intertextual references to the premake on nearly every level of the text: On the level of (1) narration where it integrates dramatic fragments and situations from various 'original' episodes, (2) settings, (3) props, above all regarding the car, (4) music where the remake uses the 'original' *Knight Rider* theme, and, (5) characters. In the case of *The Avengers* (Chechik, 1998), apart from the title and title sequence, intertextual references to the 'original' series may above all be located on the levels of (1) narration, where *The Avengers* (Chechik, 1998) retells parts of 'original' episodes, (2) setting, (3) décor, props, and costumes, (4) music, with its references to the 'original' title theme, and (5) characters. On every level that is reminiscent of the premake, both remakes may evoke 'artefact nostalgia' directed towards the premake or viewers' 'own artefact nostalgia' in the case that the triggered media memory "function[s] as a point of symbolic, biographical reference" (O'Sullivan, 1991, p. 163). It has been shown that in both cases nostalgia towards the premake is favoured by respective "retrospective classifications" on a general layer. Frictions between remake and premake, which may hamper the nostalgic look on the premake or lead into a critical dialogue with the present, could not be observed in either case. Roughly speaking, major differences in the reception may therefore be assumed between those who know the first-run and those who do not know it. Only for those who know it or who have a "prosthetic memory" of it, memories may arise. Since it is about popular cultural products that were broadcasted both on German and Spanish television, an area that according to Hepp (2009) is characterised by "deterritorial cultural thickenings", minor differences between the countries and more pronounced differences between different age groups may be expected. While both the 25 to 35-year-olds and the 55 to 65-year-olds may know the series *Knight Rider* (NBC, 1982), in the case of *The Avengers* (Chechik, 1998), the 25 to 35-year-olds have probably not seen the 'original' series. Since in both cases the title already evokes the premake, it can be assumed that at least for the 'knowing' audiences the premake as subtext is always present. In case that every aspect of the remake is seen against the backdrop of the predecessor, it cannot be excluded that levels that do not directly refer to the 'original' may also trigger memories. Differences may also draw attention – this, however, has to be crosschecked in the reception study of the work.

Apart from that, both remakes contain other potential nostalgia triggers that work only in the context of the premake. Next to the intertextual references, *Knight Rider* (NBC, 2008) generates a clear gap between 'then' and 'now' when its "cinematic style" is contrasted with the "zero-degree" predecessor. On the level of the characters the contemporary ensemble-cast ('now') contrasts with the one-man show of the 'original' ('then'). Apart from the "retrospective classifications", the text itself favours a nostalgia directed towards the 'original' in highlighting the protagonists longing for the "good old days" of masculine privileges. Lastly, the *Knight Rider* remake serves and also refers explicitly to possible discourses of the lost fascination (be it in the form of an F or A emotion) through its main prop – a further potential gap between 'then' and 'now' and a potential trigger for 'A or F nostalgia'. It is a similar case for *The Avengers* (Chechik, 1998). Here, next to the intertextual references, the remake creates a clear gap between 'then' and 'now', contrasting the low-budget style of its predecessor ('then') with its "cinematic style" and score ('now'). On the level of décor, props and costumes, a clear gap between the once 'boundary-breaking' qualities of Peel's wardrobe ('then') and the lost provocation ('now') from today's perspective could be noted, which can also be seen as a potential trigger for nostalgia for the 'knowing' audiences. The same applies to the characters of Steed and Peel. Also on this level, a clear gap between the 'boundary-breaking' characteristics of the premake characters ('then') and the loss of these qualities ('now') has been highlighted. In most cases the public discourse gives evidence of respective readings. However, whether these potential triggers for nostalgia are indeed perceived as such has to be scrutinised in the reception study.

In a last step, both remakes have been analysed regarding further potential triggers for nostalgia that also work independently of the premake, respectively without the knowledge of the premake. On the level of narration, *Knight Rider* (NBC, 2008) promotes (fiction) nostalgia when it opts for the simplifying components of the 'original', presenting a present that is infused with Cold War good-bad dichotomies. Later, the 'new' Knight character incarnates nostalgia towards an obsolete model of masculinity of the 'good old days' as it is also presented by the reactionary reading of the predecessor, enabling both 'F nostalgia' and 'empathetic F nostalgia'. This similarly applies to *The Avengers* (Chechik, 1998). The remake exposes potential triggers for 'F nostalgia' on the levels of narration and character favouring traditional gender roles presented in a positive way from today's point of view. While the *Knight Rider* remake opted for the reactionary half of the predecessor format here, *The Avengers* (Chechik, 1998) ignores the progressive character of its premake. Emerging frictions between the premake and remake that could add value to the new version or reflect about its source, were not noted. Rather the contrary is the case. The remake character is rather used as an excuse in order to transport un-reflected, old-fashioned values into the present. Here, nostalgia shows itself from the reactionary side.

Further there are also examples of intertextual references that work without the knowledge of the 'original' and where the remakes almost aspire to appeal to the (childhood) memories of the not-knowing audiences. Both remakes contain references to other media texts, some of them from the time span of their reference-series. Insofar it is likely that the remake may also evoke (media) memories of the time span of the respective premake in those audiences who do not know the predecessor series but who recognise other references. However, since both texts, with their closed form, do not favour the recognition of the reference and frictions between premake and remake are avoided, a dynamic relation between the past and present can also not be found here.

Concluding, it can be stated that both remakes prefigure nostalgia on various levels. Whether the nostalgia on offer in the text is actually decoded as such by the viewers will be seen in Part III of the book.

6.3 PERIOD DRAMAS AND NOSTALGIA

Period dramas are frequently referred to when it comes to nostalgia and television. Nearly all the authors listed in Section 4.4.1 on *The combination of approaches* and Section 5 on *The 'genres' of nostalgic fiction* focus on period dramas as one or as their main example (Davis, 1979; Jameson, 1991; Powrie, 1997; Cardwell, 2002; Higson, 2003; 2006; Dika, 2003; Cook, 2005; Sprengler, 2011; Holdsworth, 2011). In this context, Cardwell (2002) already establishes the relation between the heritage genre and the nostalgic mood. Here we can assume that nostalgia is the mood audiences expect when they watch examples of the 'genre'. In Chapter 4.4.1, other works from the discourse were combined with the theory of aesthetic emotions. They shall be used in the course of the following analysis and only briefly recapped in this section. Some aspects, which concern the heritage genre more specifically, shall be drawn out in greater detail.

As Cook states, "[t]he nostalgic memory film [such as the period melodrama *Far from Heaven*] conjures up a golden age, which is both celebrated and mourned, providing an opportunity to reflect upon and interrogate the present" (Cook, 2005, p. 10). They may do so on several levels of the text. On a rather general one, Jameson (1991) highlights the nostalgic character of the period recreations with a focus on their intertextuality, thus with a focus on the merely 'nostalgic' preference of past elements over contemporary ones – be it on the level of interpretation, mise-en-scène, setting, plot, and others. In Section 4.4.1 and with regard to Jameson's own (emotional) argument, intertextuality has already been supposed as a potential trigger for 'artefact nostalgia' or a viewer's 'own artefact nostalgia'. However, apart from the fact that not every period drama foregrounds the intertextual references, Jameson has been criticised for not considering the critical potential the intertextual character may import into the period piece (Dika, 2003; Sprengler, 2011).

But let's take one step back and proceed level by level. Even without referring to other texts, the period drama may expose a nostalgic narration. Wollen (1991) and Dika (2003) ask how and if the past is "represented as [an] entirely better place[...]" (Wollen, 1991, p. 186) or how the "relationship of the image to the natural real" (Dika, 2003, p. 224) is. In this case the 'gap' would be located between the text and the outside of the text, which is the present living circumstances of the viewers or other (contemporary) texts that surround it in the flow of the television programme. In the case that the "diegetic effect" (Tan, 1996, p. 52) makes the viewers "become immersed in the fictional world" (Bruun Vaage, 2007, p. 190), which in this case is the positively painted past, the triggered nostalgia can be supposed to be 'non-empathetic F nostalgia'.

Later, potential triggers for what has been called 'empathetic F nostalgia' here were investigated in the context of the period drama by author such as Higson (2003),

Cardwell (2002), Holdsworth (2011), or Feyerabend (2009). In this case, the 'gap' between the prelapsarian and the postlapsarian world, which is so essential for nostalgia (Tannock, 1995), may be located inside the text. As Higson describes:

"We are thus presented with both a narrative of loss, charting an imaginary historical trajectory from stability to instability, and at the same time a narrative of recovery, projecting the subject back into a comfortably closed past." (Higson, 2003, p. 83)

Both empathetic and non-empathetic F nostalgia may be supported by every level of the text. In the centre is the period prop, whose positive staging is facilitated by formal and aesthetic devices – or, as Higson (2006, p. 97) calls it in the context of the British heritage film, the special "iconography of the genre". Higson calls that also "a lingering desire to celebrate that past in the loving recreation of the period piece" (Higson, 2003, p. 83). He argues that it is the characteristic "pictorial qualities"[85] of period dramas that make the image seductive and the past desirable (Higson, 2003, p. 80). Thus, "[a]t the level of the image, narrative instability is frequently overwhelmed by the alluring spectacle of iconographic stability, permanence, and grandeur, providing an impression of an unchanging, traditional, and always delightful and desirable England" (Higson, 2003, p. 78). With reference to the literature (Flinn, 1992 cited in Sprengler, 2011; Dyer, 2005; Sprengler, 2011), Chapter 4.4.1 further refers to music or slow motion as supportive for 'F nostalgia'. In each of these cases it has to be considered whether the recreation of the past is based on past media forms or not. With reference to Le Sueur (1977), Sprengler (2011, p. 3) distinguishes between "'deliberate archaism'" – period pieces that "strive to recreate not only the look and feel of the period in question but also the appearance of art from that distant time" (Sprengler, 2011, p. 86) – and the so-called "'surface realism'" which is "produced through the use of period markers" (Sprengler, 2011, p. 85). As proposed by Sprengler (2011), we may assume that in both cases props may import critical potential to the period drama, which provides a further reflexivity or even impedes nostalgia. Apart from that, "textuality, temporality and the relationship of the image to the natural real" (Dika, 2003, p. 224) must be considered in the analysis, which means that the respective temporal context of the period drama must forward the investigation of each example.

'Artefact nostalgia' is not explicitly discussed in the context of the period dramas. However, next to those examples that expose intertextual references to, for example, "art from that distant time" (Sprengler, 2011, p. 86), and that may provoke (nostalgic) associations in the audiences, we may suggest that a concentration on single artefacts, such as props, décor and costumes, may also lead to nostalgia in the case that it is

---

85 Here, Higson names "pictorialist camera style" (Higson, 2003, p. 39) or the frequent inclusion of "set-piece celebratory events" (Higson, 2003, p. 40).

positively put into contrast with the present. According to Tan (1996; 2002), we may expect that twists, incongruences or intensive emotions on the F level may draw the attention to the artefact level. In the context of the heritage films, Higson also highlights that the "heritage spectacle" (Higson, 2003, p. 40) may cause the fact that the "emotional engagement in the drama is displaced by the fascination with the heritage film's loving recreations of the past" (Higson, 2003, p. 40) – thus, it can be argued in the context of aesthetic emotions, with a concern on the single artefact on the side of the viewers. Furthermore, as in the case of the reruns and remakes, it is probably also the sole difference to the contemporary artefacts that may call attention to the level. Here, we may assume that the period drama has again various options to expose its artefacts, certainly not all of which favour nostalgia. Later, also artefacts other than music can be assumed to work as "mnemonic prompt[s]" and, depending on the "retrospective classification", to lead to nostalgia on the side of the single viewer.

Central to the following analysis are the period dramas *Mad Men* (AMC, 2007)[86] and *Borgia* (Sky Italia, 2011), which were broadcasted both on German and Spanish television. The analysis will proceed as follows: In a first step, a sub-chapter on the temporal context will serve the necessary basis in order to reflect the recreations of the past against the backdrop of the "natural real" (Dika, 2003, p. 224) and in the specific German and Spanish context in which the respective audiences supposedly integrate the series. Later, the analysis examines every single level of the texts. The first part focuses on the narration. Leading questions are: In which way is the narration nostalgic? Are there any intertextual references that could lead to a possible 'artefact nostalgia'? Later, the further levels of the series will be investigated. Thereby it shall be considered in which way they support an eventual nostalgia on the level of the narration and in which way possible 'artefact nostalgias' may be conjured up. In the light of the theoretical part on aesthetic emotions it may be supposed that on every level personal associations and/or the viewers' 'own nostalgia' may occur – a fact that cannot be considered before the last section of this work.

6.3.1 Analysis of nostalgia in *Mad Men*

Mad Men is an American period drama created by Matthew Weiner; it was launched in 2007. As of 2012, the series has five seasons. Only "[i]n its first three seasons, *Mad Men* won four Golden Globes, thirteen Emmys, and a prestigious George Foster Peabody Award for excellence in broadcasting" (Edgerton, 2011, p. xxi).

---

86 This analysis mainly focuses on the first season of the series. Detailed observations mainly refer to Season 1, Episode 1.

The pay-TV channel FOX first broadcasted the series on German television in 2009. Since 2010, it could also be watched on ZDFneo. In Spain, the series was launched in 2008 on the pay-TV channel Canal+ (Formula TV, 2011a). Since 2009, *Mad Men* could also be watched on the private channel *Cuatro* and since 2011, on the private channel *Divinity*.[87]

Set in New York of the 1960s, the period drama centres on Don Draper (Jon Hamm), creative director of the fictitious advertising agency *Sterling Cooper,* and a group of 'mad' men and women who work with him in Madison Avenue. Successful, good-looking, married to a beautiful woman, with children, a house in the suburbs, and colleagues who admire him – at first it seems that Don Draper has achieved everything the average 1960s' male could ever have dreamed of. However, in the series nothing is what it seems. It transpires that Draper is hiding a lot of secrets from his past, starting with the false identity he has adopted in order to leave the Korean War. Little by little, his wife, Betty (January Jones), age twenty-something – who is increasingly unsatisfied with her life as a housewife and mother – reveals his secrets, which also leads to the separation of the couple (Season 3) and divorce (Season 4). The relationship to his colleagues – among them Pete Campbell (Vincent Kartheiser), a young, ambitious son of wealthy parents, Peggy Olson (Elisabeth Moss), a secretary who starts 'climbing the career ladder', or Roger Sterling (John Slattery), first boss and later partner of Don – is marked by a mix of appreciation, contempt, envy and intrigue. Apart from that, each of them has their own secrets to hide (see also 6.3.1.2.3).

6.3.1.1 Some contextual notes

The socio-cultural context evoked by *Mad Men* is the North America of the 1960s – a decade which was marked by major social upheavals and events that would shape the society, and not only in the United States: for example the presidency of John F. Kennedy since 1961 and his assassination in 1963, the approval of the Civil Rights Amendment in 1964 and the rise of the Civil Rights Movement, the Vietnam War, which would become a trauma for the whole American nation, the protest movement against the latter, which was further related to the development of the hippie counter-culture, the assassination of Martin Luther King Jr. in 1968, the landing on the moon in 1969 or the Watergate scandal in the early 1970s (Hellmann, 2006, pp. 295 ff.).

Apart from the fact that the citizens of the 1960s Germany and the 1960s Spain learned about American politics through mass media, these incidents left their marks both on Spanish and German 1960s realities and thus cultural memories. Not only that the Vietnam War was one of several proxy wars during the Cold War, Schubert and Klein (2011) also highlight that the movement against it had a major influence

---

87 On Cuatro the first season reached an average audience share of 10.8 per cent (Formula TV, 2011b).

on the German peace and students' movement in the late 1960s and early 1970s (see also 6.1.2.2.1). In Spain, the students' movement left its mark on society under Franco's regime; however, it rather led to even more repression than to liberation (see also 6.1.2.1.1).

Further details on the German society and the Spanish society in the 1960s were outlined in Chapter 6.1.2, where it already became evident that both societies were far from developing parallel to each other or to the United States. They shall not be repeated here – just this: While the 1960s in (West) Germany were marked by economic prosperity (Siegfried, 2003, pp. 25 ff.) and important social upheavals, Francoist Spain was politically and economically still a long way off from the rest of Europe (Boyd, 1999, p. 99).

6.3.1.2 Nostalgia on the single levels of the text

6.3.1.2.1 Narration
Mad Men is set in the New York of the 1960s. It evolves around different plot lines, some of which are spread over various episodes or even seasons. Others are closed within one or two episodes. In doing so, the series provides a mix of "episodic series and the continuing serial" (Shimpach, 2010, p. 36), just as Shimpach, referring to Williams (1994) describes it in the context of the action/melodrama hybrid. The series' main narrative strand centres on Don Draper, the slow revelation of his true identity, past, and character. It spreads over the entire first season. Other strands emphasise the "interpersonal conflict", such as the relationship between Draper and his wife or his various lovers, the relationship between Pete and Peggy, or the relationship between Joan and Roger Sterling. Here is also where the melodramatic elements of the series become most evident (Abercrombie and Longhurst, 2007, p. 222 on melodrama). Apart from that, there are always certain suspense moments insofar as the viewers come to share knowledge with diverse characters – for instance on the false identity of Don Draper – whose revelation in the course of the action can be expected to have a dramatic impact. Weiner himself assumes the soap opera elements of the series due to, as he puts it, its form of "how people change, how they manage the loss of a first love, the abandonment of a child, infidelity, how their eyes are opened slowly, and how they become more transparent" (Weiner, 2011 [o.t.]).[88]

The narration is linear in many parts. However, the series also employs story-telling strategies that differ from the classical principles. In the first season it is mainly the slow revelation of Draper's past that is narrated in flashbacks (see also

---

88 Original quotation: "El aspecto soap opera en *Mad Men* se concentra, más bien, en la manera en que la gente cambia, cómo gestionan la pérdida de un primer amor, el abandono de un niño, la infidelidad, cómo poco a poco se le abren los ojos a un personaje y cómo se hace más lúcido." (Weiner, 2011, p. 19)

6.3.1.2.3). Flash-forwards or dream sequences also break the linearity (see e.g. Season 1, Episode 13, min. 0:43:36). Generally speaking, *Mad Men* is not nostalgic in the sense that the past is presented as a better place, as Wollen (1991, p. 186) had once described it in the context of the heritage films. The series, creating reality effects by including political and social issues of the 1960s up to found footage from the period (see e.g. Season 1, Episode 12), refers to discourses on the discrimination of women[89], unwanted pregnancies, homophobia, or racism[90] (see e.g. Season 1, Episode 1, min. 0:01:33) (see also Yacowar, 2011, p. 86 ff.). In doing so, it reveals the narrowmindedness of its time of reference on the one hand, and, on the other hand, highlights the progressing change of hegemonic power relations. In line with White (2011, p. 153) it can be stated that the real course of history lies like a veil over the narration, with small, obvious frictions appealing to the viewers to bring in their knowledge. In other cases, argues White, *Mad Men* "permeates scenes that seem devised solely to index the difference between then and now" (White, 2011, p. 153). It does so, however, not in a nostalgic, idealising manner, but rather in the contrary way, namely to "serve as conspicuous signs of the era's alluring, disarming, irresponsible, and potentially lethal habits" (White, 2011, p. 154).

Already on this level the series may work as a "mnemonic prompt" in Germany or Spain for the 1960s, too. While the series' reflexivity probably impedes the simple, nostalgic gaze, nostalgia that is based on the synchronisation with the viewers' own or "prosthetic memories" cannot be excluded but can also be expected to appear in a reflexive form. It may be supposed that nostalgia here depends on the subject position and personal background. Since – as has been shown – German recipients who lived through the period are more likely to share similar personal experiences, a 'synchronisation' with personal emotions is more imaginable here, disregarding nostalgias that refer to a possible "prosthetic memory" of the viewers. This has to be seen in the reception study of this work.

Apart from that, *Mad Men*'s narration exposes "horizontal" intertextual references. In line with what Sprengler describes as "'deliberate archaism'" in the context of the period props, many parts of the period *Mad Men* narrates and recreates derive from different art forms of the late 1950s and early 1960s, such as literature, television shows, film or advertising. Most of these references are made explicitly

---

89 As Haralovich shows, the series' "combination of feminine empowerment and sexism engages a subtle critique of patriarchy" (Haralovich, 2011, p. 160) and also highlights sexism in today's society (Haralovich, 2011, p. 164).

90 "*Mad Men* challenges the nostalgic view of previous popular texts [...] that racism was the purview of bad individuals in the south, while the justness of the Civil Rights struggles was apparent to most thoughtful white citizens." (Perlman, 2011, p. 216) For further reading on the topic see Perlman (2011).

either by the series itself or by other discourses, such as the discourse of the producers that surround it.

Here, the narrative references – also explicitly named by Weiner (see Weiner, 2011, p. 20) – to the Hitchcock film *North by Northwest* (Hitchcock, 1959) should be mentioned. With the film, the series shares the setting of the narration in the world of advertising and a plot that focuses on an identity confusion. Later, Weiner refers to period novels by F. Scott Fitzgerald (see e.g. *The Great Gatsby*), John Cheever (see e.g. *The Swimmer*) and J. D. Salinger (see e.g. *The Catcher in the Rye*) (Weiner, 2011, p. 19) – all of which expose issues, such as identity crises and processes of self-discovery that at least could have inspired the narrative strand around Draper. Other direct references, the first of which is a book read by Betty Draper, the latter is also explicitly named by the producer (Weiner, 2011, p. 19), are *The Best of Everything* (Jaffe, 1958, resp. Negulesco, 1959), and *Les Bonnes Femmes* (Chabrol, 1960) – both works that are about a group of women who experience similar discrimination as the female characters of *Mad Men*. Episode titles, such as *Marriage of Figaro* (see Season 1, Episode 3), referring to the Mozart opera, make the viewers correctly anticipate the course of events, which, as the example it employs, deals with a love triangle. In other cases, dialogues refer explicitly to cultural artefacts, such as Wilder's *The Apartment* (1960) (see Season 1, Episode 10, 0:07:36 ff.), a film that offers an ironic look at the humiliating conditions of the workers in an open-plan office, to the television series *The Twilight Zone* (CBS, 1959), or to books by the novelist Ayn Rand (see e.g. Season 1, Episode 8), which also found their way into the narration. In any case, the series explicitly discloses its references, which on the one hand provides the viewers with cues about the course of events and favours 'artefact nostalgia' or the viewers' 'own artefact nostalgia', but which on the other hand opens the text once more and, in importing the socio-critical character of its sources, undermines every possible nostalgia directed towards a better 1960s past.

6.3.1.2.2 Aesthetic and design
The exposition of intertextuality on the level of the narration finds it continuation on the level of aesthetic and design.

Camera, montage and lighting
Camera, montage, and lighting are clearly reminiscent of 1950s/1960s or even 1940s films. The first scene of the series reminds you of Hitchcock's *Notorious* (1946), when an "unchained camera" slowly makes its way through a typical 1950s/1960s bar until it pauses on the back of the protagonist Don Draper (Jon Hamm), who was unknown to the viewers until then. As Gibbs describes it in the context of the Hitchcock film, "[t]his man [due to the lighting mainly shown as 'darkened silhouette'] sits with his back to the camera, at the very edge of the light which falls

on the others" (Gibbs, 2002, p. 6). As the Grant character in Hitchcock's *Notorious* (Gibbs, 2002, p. 6), Draper is here installed as an "onlooker", as an observer of the scene, maybe even as an "onlooker" on his life, drawing, as Gibbs puts it again in the context of *Notorious*, "attention to our own status as members of an audience" (Gibbs, 2002, p. 6).

The first presentation of the characters Peggy Olson, Ken Cosgrove, Harry Krane, and Paul Kinsey (see Season 1, Episode 1, min. 0:06:11 ff.) is a sequence that could have also been taken from the Hitchcock film *North by Northwest* (1959) or Wilder's *The Apartment* (1960).[91] A high-angle long shot of the front of a typical New York skyscraper is followed by the medium close-up of an entrance hall. The camera now travels backwards, showing the panorama of an anonymous mass of workers entering the office building. In the following, the protagonists slowly emerge from this anonymous mass, just as García Monzó and Rubio (2000, p. 15) also describe it in the context of the Hitchcock film *North by Northwest* (1959).

In general, the camera is an autonomous, observing one, which, described in the context of the series' period examples, may be called "unchained", and, in the context of today's television, reflects the "'feature-style cinematography'" (Caldwell, 1995 cited in Shimpach, 2010, p. 131). Depending on the respective narrative focus, it centres more on a character and on his or her perspective. Point of view shots may support the viewer's empathetic understanding of a character (see e.g. Season 1, Episode 1, min. 0:02:49 ff., Season 1, Episode 2, min. 0:14:14 ff.). Furthermore, and typical of the heritage genre, "frequent medium to long shots allow us to gaze at the furnishings as well as the characters" (Cardwell, 2002, p. 146), just as Cardwell (2002) notes in the context of the heritage film *Pride and Prejudice* (Huxley, 1995).

Regarding the vertical level, the camera is predominantly positioned in a slight low-angle, which creates a certain distortion of the image and highlights the constructedness of the text. Here, *Mad Men* also refers to films such as Hitchcock's *The Birds* (1963) or Chabrol's *Les bonnes femmes* (1960), which again was strongly influenced by Hitchcock (see e.g. Monaco, 2002, p. 334). Even regarding the lighting, which varies depending on the dramaturgy and the situation, the series is reminiscent of period examples. As Christoph Manley, one of the *Mad Men* cinematographers, highlights, they tried to keep "'the light clean and white [which] is more reminiscent of the movies of that era when [cinematographers] tried to balance everything all the time'" (Manley cited in Butler, 2011, p. 64). It is a different case regarding the editing. With, according to Butler (2011, pp. 67 f.), "a medium ASL [average shot length] of 5.2 seconds – [it is] up to four times faster than the ASLs of 1960s films and television programmes" and appeals to contemporary audiences.

---

91 Weiner himself asserts the films as reference points of the series (Weiner, 2011, p. 19; Butler, 2011).

Setting

Mad Men is mainly set in interior spaces: the open-plan office of Sterling Cooper, the Draper residence, public bars, hotel rooms or the flats of the main protagonists. The landscape, as it is for instance dominantly exposed in the British heritage film, has little relevance.

The series exposes a clear segregation between men and women[92], between black and white people, upper class and lower class, and between country and city. This is further highlighted by the habitual tendency of *Mad Men* to expose 'transgressive' movements, such as walks through the corridor, train rides or car rides that both connect and separate the different spaces. Conversations explicitly refer to train rides and others (see e.g. Season 1, Episode 1; min. 0:08:23). This spatial distribution stresses the racism and sexism of the 1960s society and supports the critical reflection about it.

Furthermore, the series shows a high degree of intertextuality mainly to 1950s/1960s Hollywood films. Butler (2011) focuses, for instance, on the interior of Sterling Cooper. Beginning with the symmetrical arrangement of the working desks up to the ceiling, an "oppressive grid of fluorescent lights" (Butler, 2011, p. 60), it is clearly reminiscent of Wilder's *The Apartment* (1960). The typical American suburban residential area where the Draper mansion is located, clearly reminds you of similar settings as seen in period melodramas, such as Douglas Sirk's *All That Heaven Allows* (1955) (see also Butler, 2011, p. 60). Apart from the fact that these intertextual references may be described as potential triggers for 'artefact nostalgia' directed towards the respective reference or a viewer's 'own artefact nostalgia', with the socio-critical character of its sources a further reflexive layer is imported to the series.

The fact that *Mad Men*'s locations are 'typical American' with probably less "cultural proximity" to Germany or Spain in the 1960s, probably rather hinders 'internal empathetic artefact nostalgia'. On a general layer, less correspondence to a Spanish or German audience's scenic memory of the 1960s can be assumed, so that a nostalgia situated on this level is rather unlikely. However, it should be considered that *Mad Men*, generally favouring empathy and the contemplative gaze, exposes the sensuous exploration of its settings. An engagement of "the spectator in sensuous playfulness" (Bruun Vaage, 2007, p. 193) is imaginable here. It has to be seen in the reception study if this may lead to nostalgia on the side of the audiences.

---

92 Here, Akass and McCabe also refer to Season 1, Episode 6 with the two-way mirror, showing the "'split between active/male and passive/female'" (Mulvey, 1989 cited in Akass and McCabe, 2011, p. 183).

Décor, props and costumes

Décor, props and costumes are clear signifiers of 'pastness' and directly identifiable as belonging to the late 1950s to early 1960s. With its corded telephones, IBM typewriters, cigarette dispensers, rectangular, minimalistic furniture or period cocktail glasses and a dominant colour spectrum of dark red, yellow ochre, grey, and green, it is clearly reminiscent of the era. Later, *Mad Men* explicitly shows many 1960s brands and products, such as *Coca Cola, Pan Am*, or the *Kodak Carousel*. Since it is about internationally traded commodities, it is probable that the period props work as "mnemonic prompt[s]" for a wide range of audiences.

At first sight, props, décor and costumes support the narration of a better past. Even though *Mad Men* does not refrain from showing the 'dirty' side of its props, such as full ashtrays and dirty dustbins, it expresses a certain appreciation of the artefact – an "alluring spectacle of iconographic stability" which makes the past somehow "delightful and desirable" (Higson, 2003, p. 78), just as Higson describes it regarding the British heritage film. However, simple nostalgia is clearly prevented. Like the perfect characters that inhabit this world, the perfect surface soon becomes scratched. Accordingly, also on the level of props and décor the series reminds you of the constructedness of the past it exposes and questions it systematically.

Firstly, due to its setting in an advertisement agency, *Mad Men* dismantles what Sprengler in the context of the so-called populuxe Fifties had described as the "self-mythologizing efforts" (Sprengler, 2011, p. 47) of an era and circumvents any possible idealisation. Secondly, the fact that the office space contains no period mix regarding the objects it exposes makes it somewhat "artificial and unsettling" as Sprengler also describes it in the context "'surface realism" in general (Sprengler, 2011, p. 85). Thirdly, a further critical layer is imported through the high degree of intertextuality, which also gives *Mad Men* characteristics of "'deliberate archaism'" (Sprengler, 2011, p. 3). In the context of the settings, the references to, for instance, Wilder's *The Apartment* have already been stated. The reference is continued on the level of décor and props. Furthermore, Weiner himself named Chabrol's *Les Bonnes Femmes* (1960) – a story that has its main location in an appliance and furniture store – as one of the main sources of inspiration for *Mad Men* (Weiner, 2011, p. 19). Seen from this perspective, the commodities sold in their store almost appear as if they were absorbed by the series. Apart from the fact that these intertextual references again import a critical component to the level of décor and props – both films are critical examinations of the societies they reflect – the 'artefact nostalgia' that is made possible by them depends on the subject position and the audiences' ability to recognise them.

This similarly applies to the costumes and accessories that are seen throughout the series. The disclosure of the constructedness of the text is more obvious here. Regarding the props and décor, *Mad Men* perfectly recreates the period fashion.

Blouses and knee-length skirts for the office woman, grey flannel and the obligatory tie for the businessman. Also here, the dominant colour spectrum ranges from dark red to a greyish green and green, reflecting the typical late 1950s/early 1960s and the "pronounced change in tonality [...] from paint-box palette to a misty, muted range" (see *Paperpast Yearbook*, 2012). The same applies to the change of hairstyles from the "bouffant coiffure" to a "short boyish haircut" (*Paperpast Yearbook*, 2012a). All in all, a credible recreation of the period which – due to its reliance on internationally traded commodities – is likely to be recognised as such by both Spanish and German audiences, to elicit their own associations and, depending on the subject position, to lead to nostalgia.

However, the costumes in *Mad Men* are not only used as period markers but also reflect the profound changes (American) society went through in the 1960s. As Perlman (2011) highlights, "[t]he costumes accentuate and underline the physical and social differences between men and women" (Perlman, 2011, p. 221); they mark the position of power in a white, masculine-dominated society and distinguish the characters and the changes they went through. Haralovich (2011, pp 166 ff.) refers, for example, to Peggy's change of dress and hairstyles throughout the series, which reflect her self-finding process as a business woman and the process of emancipation she goes through. As on other levels of the text, *Mad Men* favours the reading of costume and accessory as a critical instance by highlighting it explicitly. Various dialogues and events refer to the costumes and accessories and underpin their significance to power relations.[93]

Also, the costumes are characterised by a high degree of intertextuality or "'deliberate archaism'". The characters and their clothes are modelled upon characters taken from films or novels from the 1950s/1960s. Take, for example, Don (Jon Hamm) and Betty Draper (January Jones). While Don's clothes and hairstyle make him resemble 1950s/1960s actors, such as Cary Grant or Gary Cooper, Betty's costume, accessories and hair style are reminiscent of actresses such as Grace Kelly or Eva Marie Saint. As in other cases, these references are explicitly disclosed. In the case of the Betty/Grace Kelly relationship, various dialogues explicitly refer to Betty's resemblance to the actress (see e.g. Season 1, Episode 9). The importance of films such as *North by Northwest* (Hitchcock, 1959), with Cary Grant and Eva Marie Saint as lead actors, was made explicit by Weiner (2011, p. 19). Apart from that, *Mad Men* also refers to Ayn Rand, whose novel *The Fountainhead* was adapted to film (Vidor, 1949) with Gary Cooper as the leading actor.

---

93 Alone in the first episode of the series various examples may be listed that in a way make the costumes and accessory protagonists of the scene. We hear Joan advising Peggy to change her style (see Season 1, Episode 1, min. 0:08:56 ff.), hear Pete commenting on Peggy's clothes (see Season 1, Episode 1, min. 0:16:39) or see Draper changing suits and Sterling commenting on a missing button (see Season 1, Episode 1, min. 0:10:03 ff.).

Music

According to Anderson (2011) *Mad Men*'s music has two functions: it works as period marker and as "critical interlocutor[...] that act[s] as a counterpoint to the on-screen imagery" (Anderson, 2011, pp. 72 f.). The majority of the music, be it diegetic or non-diegetic, is pre-existing music from the late 1950s or early 1960s. It has the narrative function to characterise the temporal frame. Depending on the subject position it is probable to provoke 'artefact nostalgia'. Since "[a] song can function as a mnemonic prompt" (Sprengler, 2011, p. 76), the music is likely to trigger associations in the knowing viewers and personal or "we-group" related nostalgia.

On the one hand, *Mad Men* uses singer-songwriters, such as Bob Dylan, that import the socio-critical character of their music to the series or are used in order to comment it (see also Anderson, 2011). On the other hand, 'self-mythologization' as it also exists in the employed songs is directly contradicted by the other levels of the text. As Anderson (2011) shows, songs are "placed in opposition to the on-screen images to create the disaffection that permeated the period" (Anderson, 2011, p. 76).[94] It can also be stated that the music does not favour a nostalgic narration of a better past – rather the contrary is the case.

6.3.1.2.3 Characters

Mad Men involves an ensemble cast in the general trend of contemporary television (see e.g. Mittell, 2006). Underpinned by the spatial distribution mentioned previously, a clear segregation of different genders, races and social classes can be seen. Apart from that, each character is trapped in a specific social role, reflecting the conditions and grievances, false illusions and upcoming chances of the American society of the early 1960s.

Donald Draper (Jon Hamm), the main character of the series, has a somewhat 'split' personality. His incarnation of the American dream is based on a lie. Behind his white, Anglo-Saxon, Protestant, happily married and successful image as Donald Draper he covers his 'white trash' origins as Dick Whitman and his constant fear to lose everything. Already the opening of *Mad Men* makes the viewers anticipate a further course of events, the dramatic hero's fall – a background that seems to let each career leap and each success increase the extent even more. His wife, Betty (January Jones), a highly educated woman, is on the verge of being destroyed by her monotonous life as a housewife. Also, her counter-models, the women working at Sterling Cooper, have anything but an easy living in their sexist working

---

94 For example, Anderson here refers to the first scene of the series' first episode, which uses Don Cherry's song *Band of Gold*. "Associating the lyrics of 'Band of Gold' with 'Old Gold' and Draper's concentration on cigarettes dislodges the dominant reading of the song from one of a desire for matrimony to a focus on increasing market share." (Anderson, 2011, p. 75)

environment. While, as Akass and McCabe (2011) highlight, Joan (Christina Hendricks), the office manager, falls prey to the illusion that she could gain some sort of domination over her masculine colleagues but finally only reproduces "the sexist culture of *Mad Men*" (Akass and McCabe, 2011, p. 186), Peggy (Elisabeth Moss) climbs the career ladder only at the cost of maltreatment (see also White (2011) on "mad women" in *Mad Men*). Generally speaking, *Mad Men*'s characters do not support the creation of a gap between a positively pictured past and a worse present.

As Tan describes it in the context of empathetic F emotions, inside the narrative "the explication of the meaning of events for the characters enjoy primacy" (Tan, 1996, p. 176). Even though, generally speaking, *Mad Men*'s characters are no nostalgics – each of them has dark spots on his or her memory or 'collects' them throughout the series – the viewers are invited to empathetically share emotional moments, such as first kisses, fights or birthdays with the protagonists, which may support the splitting-off of own (nostalgic) sentiments.

Later, *Mad Men* uses flashbacks. Most of them represent Don Draper's memories and are often triggered by photos (see e.g. Season 1, Episode 12, min. 0:15:25) or situations the character experiences in the series' present and that remind him of analogue situations in the past (see e.g. Season 1, Episode 6, min. 0:1:26 ff.). In general, the device does not reflect the longing of the character. Settled in a distant time before the series' present, the flashbacks represent traumatic experiences the protagonist had in his childhood (see e.g. Season 1, Episode 8) or those he went through as a soldier in the Korean War (see Season 1, Episode 12, min. 0:15:25). In any case, in an understanding of empathy that supposes that "a situation evoked in a character does not necessarily coincide with the empathetic emotion of the viewer" (Tan, 1996, p. 174), various emotions may be adopted that do not have to be congruent with those of the protagonist and may indeed lead to nostalgia directed towards a personal past.

Furthermore, the more we get to know about the character, the more we learn about his fear to lose everything – a phenomenon that creates a growing gap between the present and the recent past of the series and which indeed also supports a possible 'empathetic nostalgia' that is somehow shared with the character. There are various moments in the series with a narrative focus on Don Draper, two in its first season (see Season 1, Episode 3; Season 1, Episode 13), that expose the protagonist's nostalgic look at his own reality. For example, we can refer to the last scenes of the first season (*The Wheel*), in which Draper uses private photos in order to pitch his campaign for a new, circular slide projector. His presentation is embedded in a discourse on the subject of nostalgia. On the one hand, the viewers already have sufficient knowledge about the protagonist in order to make assumptions about his nostalgia for an only recent past, whose happy moments already seem irretrievable to him. On the other hand, they know that the 'past' he is longing for is not as golden as it is presented, something that gives the exposed nostalgia also a reflexive component. Apart from that, the whole situation with the slide projector and family photos is very likely to be recognised by the viewers as something they might have experienced themselves. This further helps the empathetic understanding and may lead to rather personal associations. Point-of-view shots showing the character's gaze at the slides, close-ups from the character's face and a slowed-down rhythm of the music support empathy with Draper.

Finally, on the level of the characters *Mad Men* also exposes a high degree of intertextuality. Next to the clear "period casting", the modelling of the characters is influenced by 1950/1960s films. Donald Draper (Jon Hamm) has clear references to Hitchcock's *North by Northwest* (1995) character Roger Thornhill (Cary Grant). In addition to parallels that have already been observed on the level of the costumes (see 6.3.1.2.2), the actor Jon Hamm has a certain physical resemblance to Cary Grant. Furthermore, the character is obviously modelled on the Hitchcock example: both are in the advertising business and both have a cynical view of the deception of their job. Both find themselves trapped in false identities. Siska (2011, p. 198) further highlights resemblances to period actors such as John Wayne, Gary Cooper, or Clark Gable.

It is a similar case regarding other characters. According to Akass and McCabe (2011, p. 181), "Joan reawakens the 1950s Hollywood pin-up fantasy of a voluptuous female sexuality" and contains references to other 'phallic women', such as Marilyn Monroe (see also Akass and McCabe, 2011, p. 181). Further intertextual references are shown when *Mad Men* makes the characters explicitly contemplate their role models. Thus Joan not only openly admires Marilyn Monroe (see Season 2, Episode 9) but also expresses her desire to step out of her role of a pawn of desire "between Doris Day in '*Pillow Talk*' [(Gordon, 1959)] and '*Midnight Lace*' [(Miller, 1960)]" (see Season 1, Episode 10, min. 0:22:25 ff.) and more into the active role of a 'femme fatale', such as "Kim Novak". The character also compares herself to the *The Apartment* (Wilder, 1960) character Fran Kubelik (Shirley MacLaine) who, too, has influenced much of the character's design. This similarly applies to Betty's (January Jones) physical resemblance to Grace Kelly, which is talked about on various occasions in the series (see e.g. Season 1, Episode 9). In other cases, Paul Kinsey's (Michael Gladis) likeness to Orson Welles is explicitly underlined (see Season 1, Episode 12, min. 0:15:18), not to mention that decisive character traits are modelled here on the basis of the famous actor, director and author as well and that costumes and accessories – the obligatory pipe – are clearly reminiscent.

In conclusion, it can be stated that also on the level of the characters, *Mad Men* builds the ground for a possible 'artefact nostalgia' directed towards the role model or viewers' 'own artefact nostalgia'. 'F nostalgia', however, which highlights the better past against the worse present, is impeded.

6.3.2 Analysis of nostalgia in *Borgia*

The period drama *Borgia* is a French-German-Austrian-Czech co-production launched in 2011. The first season the analysis focusses on is divided into six chapters in the German version and twelve in the Spanish version. In 2011, *Borgia* was broadcasted on the German public channel ZDF. Here, the first episode reached 6.21 million viewers (gol/dpa, 2011). Also in 2011, but under the title *Borgia – Una familia consagrada al vicio*, the series could be watched on the Spanish pay-TV channel Cosmopolitan TV (Formula TV, 2011c). There it reached a total of 1.7 million viewers (Summers, 2011).

Based upon historical facts, the series focuses on the Borgia family, a Spanish aristocratic dynasty that produced various popes during the Middle Ages. It is set in Italy in 1492 – a time when Rodrigo Borgia (played by John Doman) is vice-chancellor under Pope Innocent VIII. Deeply shocked by the news about the death of his first-born, Rodrigo starts to gather his illegitimate children Lucrecia (Isolda Dychauk), Cesare (Mark Ryder), and Juan (Stanley Weber) around him. As soon as his bribery opens the way to the ascent to papacy under the name of Alexander VI, lucrative marriages and posts are arranged for them. However, despite these strategic manoeuvres, peace is not granted for long. Soon, French troops supported by the renegade cardinal Della Rovere (Dejan Cukic) invade the holy city (Episodes 4 and 5). Though an alliance with Spain finally makes Rodrigo Borgia achieve the victory over the invaders, his family falls apart when Cesare finally finds out that Juan was responsible for the murder of their half-brother.

6.3.2.1 Existing gaps – some contextual notes

The series *Borgia* is set during the Renaissance, a time that "stretched from the early fourteenth century to the early seventeenth century and perhaps a bit beyond" (Ruggiero, 2007, p. 5). The period, with its geographical centre in Italy, "opened Europe to contact with other worlds" and brought tremendous changes to its societies, be it regarding political life, private life, religion, art, architecture, literature, music or philosophy (Ruggiero, 2007, p. 5). As its label already suggests, the Renaissance drew its main inspiration from the 'rebirth' of something already existing, that is, from classical antiquity. Since, as Ruggiero puts it, "another world – the past – became a model for the present and its ideologies, culture, and values" (Ruggiero, 2007, p. 5), the period as such could already be described as nostalgic. "Over and over again they chose re-turn (to the good old ways and customs), re-form (to the proven and correct forms), and if necessary re-volt (the violent re-volution at times necessary to overturn new corruptions and regain the golden past)" (Ruggiero, 2007, p. 4). At the same time, as Ruggiero (2007, pp. 1 ff.) highlights, for many thinkers the Renaissance was the dream of an ideal society – and, it could be argued, became itself the object of nostalgic longing. All this, however, does not distract from the "nightmarish sides" (Ruggiero, 2007, p. 10) of the Renaissance, such as the emergence of plagues and disease, the high degree of violence or the increased exclusion of 'others' (Ruggiero, 2007, pp. 6; 18 ff.).

6.3.2.2 Nostalgia on the single levels of the text

6.3.2.2.1 Narration

Borgia has a multiple causal structure with various plot lines. The main narrative strand centres the fate and social position of the Borgia family. It spreads over all six, respectively twelve, episodes and is interwoven with other narrative strands that mainly concentrate on a single character and the interpersonal conflicts between them. Some strands are closed by the end of one episode, others are continued, giving *Borgia* characteristics of the series and the serial. The narration of the series is dominantly linearly structured. It uses flashbacks or flash-forwards only in a few cases (see e.g. Season 1, Episode 1; min. 0:10:17 ff.).

In general, it cannot be stated that *Borgia* is nostalgic insofar as the past is presented as a better place, as Wollen (1991, p. 186) observes in the context of the British heritage film, or that it is narrated from the perspective of a nostalgic character. Instead of narratively foregrounding the achievements of the Renaissance, the development of humanism, growing interest in Greek literature and art, the emergence of innovative and technically most sophisticated artists – also strongly involved with the historical Borgias – or the Renaissance's own nostalgia towards the ancient age, the series focuses on the dark side of the era: violence, wars, power politics, corruption, and intrigue. "We see," Festenberg moans in *Der Spiegel* (2011), "a Renaissance without the grace of renewal, without the spring air of a new time – what a disappointment" (Festenberg, 2011 [o.t.]).[95]

In contrast to *Mad Men*, which rigorously highlights its constructedness and critically reflects its 1960s present, *Borgia* is characterised by a higher degree of narrative closure. Its narration is presented as a true representation of the historical fact. Even though the series stands in the context of other Borgia representations[96],

---

95 Original quotation: "Wir sehen eine Renaissance ohne Aufbruchsanmut, ohne die Frühlingsluft einer neuen Zeit - was für eine Enttäuschung." (Festenberg, 2011)

96 The Borgia family has been subject to various television series, films or novels. See e.g. films and television series such as *The Borgias* (Showtime/Bravo!, 2011; *Die Borgias – Sex. Macht. Mord. Amen* (Pro7, 2011); *Los Borgia* (Cuatro, 2011)), *The Borgia* (BBCtwo,

by pointing to the notes of the chronicler Johannes Burckhard (Fontana cited in Powelz, 2011), the producers of the series foreground the 'true' historical record as the main source of influence. The series not only impedes a possible 'artefact nostalgia' directed towards the intertextual reference, it also undermines the critical reflection of its representation of the past. Here, only the connoisseur is able to determine points of friction with history (see e.g. Müller, 2011; Winkler, 2011). Firstly, this is problematic since it was the Renaissance chroniclers, such as Burckhard, who were largely responsible for the creation of the "Leyenda Negra" of the Borgias (Villarroel González, 2005, p. 319).[97] Secondly, it somehow naturalises the exhibited Renaissance values – such as the hierarchical structure of the society or the distinct separation between men and women – and paints a picture of stability that did not exist in that way[98]. Seen within the flow of contemporary television programmes, it can be stated that *Borgia* "carries the connotation of order within a context of historical disruption and hence serves as a form of denial" (Dika, 2003, p. 203), just as Dika (2003) outlines in the context of reruns and nostalgia. The question whether this indeed may provoke 'fiction nostalgia' directed towards the past remains to be seen in the reception study of this work.

6.3.2.2.2 Aesthetic and design

On the one hand, aesthetic and design of the series correspond to contemporary standards. On the other hand, the level creates intertextual references to the aesthetic of Renaissance art.[99]

Camera, montage and lighting

Concerning camera, montage and lighting, *Borgia* conforms to the "cinematic style" as described by Caldwell (1995, pp. 61 ff.). The expansive studio set enables an 'unchained' camera to freely move and explore the depth of field. Ranging between long shots and close-ups, it is a voyeuristic camera that moves very close to its subject. Point of view shots are exceptional (see e.g. Season 1, Episode 1, min. 0:28:35) but may indicate the respective narrative focus. Generally speaking, the camera and also the continuity-oriented editing are very conventional, ensuring the

---

1981), *Los Borgia* (Hernández, 2011), *The Prince of Foxes* (King, 1949) or novels such as *The Family* by Mario Puzo (2001).

97 Villarroel González also shows this on other Borgia representations in the form of novels. "Many showed them as representations of reality. As if they discovered hidden history." (Villarroel González, 2005, pp. 317 [o.t.])

98 For example, refer to the gender representation of the series (see 6.3.2.2.3).

99 According to Gombrich (1996; 1985), the historical Borgia family was in close contact with artists of the time, such as Pinturicchio (1454-1513) (Gombrich, 1985, p. 108) or Leonardo da Vinci (1452-1519) (Gombrich, 1996, p. 296).

immersion of the viewers. In most cases it is the establishing shot that introduces a sequence (see e.g. Season 1, Episode 1). A decoupage follows, where shot-reverse-shots and close-ups of the human face are dominant, which is rather unusual for the conventional period drama. The first layer is dominantly in sharp focus. This goes hand in hand with *Borgia*'s emphasis on the interpersonal conflict and its tendency towards dramatisation (see e.g. Season 1, Episode 1, 0:09:42 ff.) and lets the series deviate from the "pictorial qualities" (Higson, 2003, p. 80), as they have been described as typical for the heritage film by Higson.

Also, the lighting in *Borgia* is very cinematic, appearing in different shades between low-key and normal-key and always depending on the situation and dramaturgy. Above all, those scenes that are set in interior spaces most truly recreate the period ambience. *Borgia* here uses a dominantly low-key lighting whose direction is often lateral, seemingly from natural sources, such as candles or the small windows of the Renaissance home. It draws sharp and dark shadows and creates chiaroscuro effects. In doing so, the series is most likely to evoke the art forms of the period it is presenting – reminding us of artists such as Leonardo Da Vinci (1452-1519) or later artists such as Rembrandt (1606-1669) or Caravaggio (1573-1610), who utilised light as "sharp and almost glaringly contrasted against the shadows" (Gombrich, 1996, p. 393 [o.t.]).

The series does not expose these intertextual references. However, in case they are recognised by the audiences and respectively classified retrospectively, we can presume that 'artefact nostalgia' is possible.

Settings

Borgia is mainly set in Renaissance Rome. Lavish reconstructions of interiors or whole historical buildings and places, such as the Sistine Chapel or St Peter's Square, reflect the condition of these locations in the 15th/16th centuries (Hirschbiegel, 2011). They play a large part in drawing the historical frame of the series. "Visual correspondence" to a Spanish or German audience's scenic memory can be rather excluded. The same applies to a possible 'internal empathetic artefact nostalgia'. The series indeed favours the empathetic understanding of its characters; however, since *Borgia* puts the focus on the intra- and interpersonal conflict, the settings do not step into the foreground. A sensuous exploration, for instance from the perspective of a protagonist, is also hardly found.

Décor, props and costumes

Décor, props and costumes are decisive period markers in *Borgia*. As the typical Renaissance clothing, the costumes reflect the social rank of its bearer. "[R]ich red robes and wide-brimmed flat hat" (Scott, 2011, p. 65) are reserved to the cardinals. The upper-class women wear "sleeved garment […] that […] [clings] tightly around the upper body and reveal[...][s] a great deal of the shoulders" (Scott, 2011, p. 35). Also décor (see e.g. Winkler, 2011, on the recreation of the Pinturicchio fresco in the Borgia apartment) and furniture (*Encyclopaedia Britannica, 2012)* correspond to the period.

The series indeed displays what Higson calls "set-piece celebratory events" (Higson, 2003, p. 40), such as huge banquets or guesthouse scenes. However, the camera, focusing on the human face instead of on the period detail, does not underpin the creation of a "delightful and desirable" (Higson, 2003, p. 80) past as Higson describes it in the context of British heritage films. It rather supports the dramatic effects and relegates costume, props and décor to a secondary position. In contrast to *Mad Men*, where the diegetic world refers explicitly to the level of décor, props and costumes, it stays undisclosed in *Borgia*. A nostalgia directed at the artefact is possible – at least a clear gap between 'then' and 'now' can be observed – but not favoured by the text. A reflexive layer is not imported.

Music

The level of music and sounds that consists of multiple tracks is very cinematic. The dialogue scenes are normally accompanied by a second, non-diegetic track of instrumental music. This track has a dramatic function, supporting action, suspense or mysticism of a scene. Both the diegetic and the non-diegetic level use musical genres of the Renaissance era, such as polyphonic vocal music and instrumental music with instruments like the medieval lute (see e.g. *Encyclopaedia Britannica*, 2012a; 2012b). In doing this, the audio layer holds its narrative function in the creation of the period atmosphere and can be supposed to produce an "awareness of things past" (Lowenthal, 1986, p. 125) in its viewers or listeners. The generation of a "'nostalgic condition'" is not a function of the music. The medieval music is certainly unlikely to function as a "mnemonic prompt" and may do so only on the basis of a respective "prosthetic memory". In contrast to *Mad Men*, the music has no commentary function. It never steps into the foreground, but rather holds its part in supporting the immersion.

6.3.2.2.3 Characters

According to the trend of contemporary television (see e.g. Mittel, 2006), *Borgia* also has an ensemble cast. Central is the Borgia family, consisting of Rodrigo Borgia (John Doman), Cesare Borgia (Mark Ryder), Juan Borgia (Stanley Weber), Lucrecia Borgia (Isolda Dychauk), Vannozza Catanei (Assumpta Serna), the mother of the illegitimate Borgia children, and Giulia Farnese (Marta Gastini), the mistress of Rodrigo Borgia. In featuring actors from various European countries – some of them well-known in Germany (see Andrea Sawatzki or Isolda Dychauk), some well-known in Spain (see Assumpta Serna, Elisa Mouliáa, Nicolás Belmonte or Nacho

Aldeguer), and again others (see e.g. John Doman) that are widely known, the series appeals to different audiences.

As on the level of narration, also regarding the characters, the series foregrounds the historical record. However, this does not mean that the "relationship of the image to the natural real", as Dika would put it (Dika, 2003, p. 224) reflects historical evidence. Regarding already the narration, it has been stated that *Borgia* rather reproduces the '(dark) legends' around the family (see 6.3.2.2.1). This similarly applies to the characters. Female characters are restricted to be wives, mothers and mistresses. Aspects of Renaissance life, such as the fact that women, as Weaver (2007, p. 189) highlights, "were enclosed in homes and convents", is either disguised – Lucrecia, for instance, is easily able to move between inside and outside – or not further expounded. The female character's main goals are emotionally motivated. In doing so, the series reproduces the Renaissance's misogynist image of women as predominantly passion-controlled, as described by Weaver (2007, p. 190). Other perspectives, separating from the period's own, mostly male-produced records (Weaver, 2007, p. 189), remain impossible to obtain for the viewers of *Borgia*. Regarding the level of narration, here it can be argued that "the connotation of order" (Dika, 2003, p. 203) of the series, contrasted with present upheavals, can indeed be seen as a "form of denial" (Dika, 2003, p. 203) or as a nostalgic longing towards a moment before the break, just as Dika (2003) outlines in the context of reruns and nostalgia. Instead of adopting the critical dialogue, *Borgia* works as "agente historiador" for the era. The question if this indeed may provoke 'fiction nostalgia' directed towards the past role models remains to be seen in the reception study of this work. Since the series does not disclose its references, it somehow naturalises the version of the past it is presenting. The constructedness is not revealed.

The same applies to the design of the single characters. Here the sophistication of the historical examples stays marginal. The series rather puts the emphasis on emotion and conflict. For example, this is illustrated by Rodrigo and Lucrecia Borgia. According to Villarroel González (2005), Rodrigo Borgia was a true Renaissance character who spoke various languages and was very interested in art (Villarroel González, 2005, pp. 99 ff.). These characteristics, however, remain neglected by the series, which emphases the Renaissance man as a godfather-like patriarch, reproducing the legends around the family (see e.g. Villarroel González, 2009, p. 317). Regarding Lucrecia Borgia (Isolda Dychauk), the case is not markedly different. As Gregorovius (2011) highlights, the historical character was widely educated in various languages, music, and arts (Gregorovius, 2011, p. 39) and even assumed the government business at the Vatican in the absence of the pope (Villarroel González, 2005, pp. 317 ff.). The series, however, highlights Lucrecia as a defiant seductress, a preparer of poison and not averse to an incestuous relationship with her brother, which again corresponds to the legends about the family (Villarroel

González, 2005, pp. 317 ff.). Here, *Borgia* holds its part in the mystification of the Renaissance clan. It does so, however, not in order to present a nostalgically pictured past but to stereotype and dramatise the narration.

Apart from that, in the context of *Borgia*, "period casting" can also be observed. At least Isolda Dychauk (Lucrecia) and Marc Ryder (Cesare) were cast because of their physical resemblance to the historical counterparts, as they were portrayed by Renaissance artists, such as Pinturicchio (1454-1513), Giorgione (1478?-1510) or Altobello Melone (1490-1491?). Later, costumes, hairstyle and make-up are also chosen according to the named examples. *Borgia* indeed exhibits intertextual characteristics which, depending on the respective "retrospective classification", may lead to 'artefact nostalgia' or viewers' 'own nostalgia' in case that respective "prosthetic memories" exist. However, here it can neither be stated that this is favoured by the text nor that the intertextual references import some sort of reflexive layer.

6.3.3 First conclusion on period dramas as potential triggers for nostalgia

The previous analyses focused on the period dramas *Mad Men* (AMC, 2007) and *Borgia* (Sky Italia, 2011), two series that were broadcasted both on German and Spanish television. While the first is set in early 1960s America, the latter's period of play is the time of the Renaissance in Rome. Even though potential triggers of 'F nostalgia' could be explained in both texts, a clear dominance could not be observed. In both examples different possible triggers for nostalgia could be detected. The 'modules', which were explained in the theoretical section, proved helpful here. They also turned out to be an applicable and reasonable analysis scheme.

The introductory chapter to this section on period dramas and nostalgia already referred to Cardwell's (2002) work on heritage film. Based on the observation that the genre is "routinely labelled nostalgic" (Cardwell, 2002, p. 142), she proposes to combine the investigation on nostalgia in period dramas with theories on moods. From this, it can be assumed that the period drama as a nostalgia 'genre' creates the expectation of nostalgia – a point that shall be further considered in the subsequent reception study. This conclusion gives an overview of the basic results of the television analysis.

In order to crosscheck the respective period representations with the "natural real", a first section outlined the broad socio-cultural and temporal context of the periods in question. In case the series are seen against the respective temporal background or evoke memories related to it, we may already expect profound differences between German and Spanish recipients and different age groups. In the case of *Mad Men*, set in the 1960s, the 55 to 65-year-old age group disposes of personal memories of the era, while the 25 to 35-year-olds at the utmost have "prosthetic memories". It was also shown that regarding political and socio-cultural aspects, there were tremendous differences between Germany and Spain in the 1960s. While Spain was still under Franco's regime, German society was marked by tremendous social changes, with the student revolution – part of a general cultural and social movement both in Europe and the U.S. – at its centre.

In the case of *Borgia* fewer differences among the "we-groups" can be expected. The Renaissance is clearly outside the lifespan of both age groups. The memory they have about the era is at the most a "prosthetic" one, accessed by popular cultural commodities or history books. The example was chosen in order to crosscheck if nostalgia on this memory basis is at all possible.

Regarding the textual level, the two examples *Mad Men* and *Borgia* differ notably in the way they represent history and in the way they may work as potential triggers for nostalgia. While *Mad Men* is highly self-reflexive and discloses its constructedness, *Borgia*, with its closed form, presents itself as a representative of the historical fact. *Mad Men* favours 'artefact nostalgia' and 'empathetic F nostalgia'. Regarding *Borgia,* which is clearly set outside the personal memory of the viewers, nostalgia seems less probable. Potential triggers mainly encompass triggers for 'artefact nostalgia' and 'F nostalgia'. In both cases, all levels from narration, camera, montage, lighting, setting, décor, props and costumes to music and characters have been analysed.

Mad Men does not show the 1960s with a nostalgic gaze. Whether it's racism, sexism or homophobia, the series does not flinch from showing the negative side of the era. Apart from that the series contains a high degree of disclosed intertextuality to mainly 1950s/1960s films. The disclosure of intertextual references favours 'artefact nostalgia' or viewers' 'own artefact nostalgia' in the case of respective "retrospective classifications" of the references. At the same time, it imports a further critical layer to the series and encourages reflection. Therefore, it can be stated that the series does not favour 'non-empathetic fiction nostalgia'. In cases where a 'synchronisation' with personal experiences of the viewers leads to a personal kind of nostalgia towards the 1960s, the critical perspective of the series is assumed to hold its part in a respective colouring of the viewers' 'own nostalgia'. Due to the "cultural thickenings" between Germany and the U.S. regarding the student movement, such a 'synchronisation' may be supposed to rather arise in the German case. In general, it may be stated that these observations apply to all levels of the series. Simple nostalgia is hindered, intertextual references foregrounded, and a critical perspective favoured.

On the levels of camera, montage and lighting, but also on the levels of settings, décor, props, costumes, music and characters, *Mad Men* shows and discloses widely shared intertextual references to 1950s/1960s films. They can be expected to be recognised both by knowing German and Spanish viewers, and, depending on the subject position, may lead to 'artefact nostalgia' or viewers' 'own artefact nostalgia'. In any case, the functioning of the text and the references are disclosed, highlighting the constructedness of the history it presents and further hindering nostalgia on the fiction- level. Furthermore, décor, props, costumes and music in *Mad Men* are clear signifiers of 'pastness'. The series shows internationally traded consumer products as they were traded in Germany and Spain, too. A concentration on the artefact – which is very likely since the series consciously puts them in the foreground – may lead to 'artefact nostalgia' and/or provoke the viewers' own associations. The "self-mythologizing efforts" of the era are, however, consequently undercut by the text. This past is not presented as desirable.

Finally, *Mad Men* clearly favours the empathetic understanding of its protagonists. It has been shown that some scenes show Draper's nostalgic look at the only recent past. Later, the audience is invited to empathetically share emotional moments. In an understanding of empathy, which supposes that the emotions of the protagonists do not have to be congruent to those of the viewers (Tan, 1996, p. 174), this may support the splitting-off of the viewers' own (nostalgic) sentiments, even though nostalgia is not an issue. Also here the series supports at least a reflexive vision.

It is a very different case with *Borgia*. With its narrative closure, it tends to conceal its intertextual references and undermines critical reflection. Regarding the narration, *Borgia* focuses on the dark side of the Renaissance. The world it presents, however, seems strangely stable, which at least can be described as a potential trigger for 'F nostalgia' from today's perspective. The generation of the viewers' own associations is only possible in cases where they have "prosthetic memories" of the era. Camera, montage, and lighting support the dramatisation of history the series represents. While they may be seen in the trend of contemporary "cinematic style", the latter is also reminiscent of Renaissance painting. However, here the intertextual reference stays concealed behind the closed form. Only in cases where it is recognised by the viewers and/or accordingly retrospectively classified is it likely to provoke 'artefact nostalgia'. Décor, props and costumes contribute to the period recreation and expose a clear gap between 'then' and 'now'. However, due to the low degree of "pictorial qualities", as Higson would call it (Higson, 2003, p. 80), it may be argued that 'artefact nostalgia' is less likely. This similarly applies to the music. It holds its part in creating the period atmosphere but does not favour nostalgia. Apart from that, the characters do support an empathetic understanding. Here, the viewers are invited to empathetically share emotional moments. If we take what Tan says about empathy, namely that "a situation evoked in a character does not necessarily coincide with the empathetic emotion of the viewer" (Tan, 1996, p. 174), as a basis, we may assume that nostalgia is not excluded here, even though it is not explicitly favoured by the text. Nostalgia that 'feels with' a character is not supported. The period casting that makes the characters refer to their respective prototypes as they have been presented by the paintings of the period makes 'artefact nostalgia' possible. Apart from the fact that the references are not explicitly disclosed, we can also assume here that they are not widely shared.

Generally, even though *Mad Men* can be described on many levels as a potential trigger for nostalgia, with its high degree of self-reflexivity, it impedes any simple nostalgia towards the 1960s. *Borgia*, on the other hand, rarely facilitates nostalgia; however, any possible nostalgia – mainly on the level of narration – bares any reflexivity here. While *Mad Men* initiates a dialogue between various versions of the past – the found-footage, the art forms of the period, the nostalgia of its protagonists and the reception of its viewers – *Borgia* claims to present the right one.

6.4 Conclusion on the Television Analysis and Transition to Part III

Nostalgia is an important component of contemporary television fiction. Nevertheless, the subject is only scarcely investigated with regards to the interrelation of textual characteristics and the emotive reaction of nostalgia on the side of (different) audiences. In 2002, Cardwell highlighted this with regards to the British heritage film. In combining textual analysis with theories on mood in the context of film, the scholar accomplished a first step towards closing this lack of research. However, detailed interrelations between text and reception are not yet scrutinised. Even though Cardwell (2002) refers to Tan (1996), his categories of aesthetic emotions are not integrated into the analyses. Reception studies have not been made.

This study begins at this point. Tan's categories are used in order to build the bridge between text and reception. Accordingly, the study falls back on the existing nostalgia discourse and combines it with the categories proposed in the context of studies about aesthetic emotions. The combination of the approaches led to the assumption of different nostalgias, always depending on different objects, namely: 'non-empathetic F nostalgia', 'empathetic F nostalgia', 'artefact nostalgia', and 'internal empathetic artefact nostalgia'. With these categories we had first 'modules' of analysis. They have been re-combined with a view on the respective nostalgia 'genres'. A consideration of the memory discourse allowed first assumptions on possible 'shared' nostalgias.

The general basis of the precedent television analysis was a reception-aesthetic understanding of television. During the analysis it was assumed that nostalgia may be prefigured by different textual aspects. Hereby the radical object-centrism of

Tan's model could indicate the direction of the analysis. Following Tannock (1995), regarding the single potential objects of nostalgia, it was central for the analysis to locate possible 'gaps' between a prelapsarian and a postlapsarian world. According to the premises of television analysis (Mikos, 2008), the levels of narration, aesthetic and design as well as characters were considered. Different memory contexts in Germany and Spain were taken into account to the extent that the respective socio-cultural contexts and programme contexts have been revised and the public discourse in the form of newspaper articles has been integrated into the analysis.

The television analysis focused on a total of six examples of different nostalgia 'genres' as they have been identified in Chapter 5 of this work. More precisely, it was about the categories reruns, remakes, and period dramas that stood in the centre of the analysis. *Knight Rider* (NBC, 1982) and *The Avengers* (ITV, 1961) were chosen as exemplary for the category of the reruns. Their respective remakes *Knight Rider* (NBC, 2008) and *The Avengers* (Chechik, 1998) were analysed as exemplary for the category of the remakes. And *Mad Men* (AMC, 2007) and *Borgia* (Sky Italia, 2011) were chosen as representatives for the period dramas. All six examples were broadcasted both in Germany and in Spain, which is why they were suitable in order to identify first possible similarities and differences between nostalgias in the two countries.

The television analysis had three main purposes: Firstly, it was about to apply the framework of analysis as it was proposed with reference to Tan (1996). Secondly, first hypotheses should be investigated. Here, it was basically assumed that the different 'genres' depend upon different aesthetic structures of media impact with each different relations to the memory of the recipients. Thirdly, the television analysis of potential nostalgia triggers on the level of the text will be the basis for the reception analysis in Part III. Here it will be investigated if these nostalgias are indeed provoked in audiences of different age groups from Germany and Spain.

In general, it can be stated that the 'modules' proved to be applicable. On their basis it was possible to apply and amplify the existing nostalgia discourse systematically in the analysis of different 'genres'. In doing this, it was not only possible to give a differentiated look on the 'genre' examples. It also provided the analysis with a higher degree of comparability. This fact is also important with a view on the following reception study. Especially against the background of an increasing complexity of media landscapes where transcultural approaches are more important than ever before, a best possible systematisation of the analysis also guarantees a better comparability of different receptions.

This chapter shall not repeat all the results. They have already been presented in the respective conclusive chapters of the analysis of the single examples. However, differences and similarities between the 'genres' shall be highlighted. Consequences and further hypotheses with a view on the reception part shall be explained.

On a general level, and with a basis in the academic and non-academic discourse, it was shown that remakes, reruns and period dramas may be called nostalgia 'genres'. Thus, it was first of all assumed that they create the expectation of nostalgia in the viewers, respectively that they may be chosen by the viewers in the course of a nostalgic 'mood-management' (see also Cardwell, 2002, on the British heritage film). This fact could only barely be investigated in the context of the television analysis, but it has to be kept in mind with a view on the reception study.

In any case, in all 'genre' examples, potential nostalgia triggers could be scrutinised. Regarding possible 'shared' nostalgias, first patterns could be identified. The assumption that a clear dominance of 'artefact nostalgia' can be detected in remakes, period dramas dominantly offer 'F nostalgia', and reruns a mix of both, cannot be totally confirmed. Regarding the reruns, the assumption has been verified in the course of the television analysis. Both reruns expose diverse possible triggers of both 'A' and 'F nostalgia'. Regarding the remakes, the assumption has been verified, even though also other forms of possible nostalgia could be highlighted. Regarding the period dramas, the hypothesis must be relativised clearly. Even though potential triggers of 'F nostalgia' could be identified, a clear dominance could not be detected.

In general, all three 'genres' expose a mix of different potential nostalgia triggers. It may be assumed that both reruns and remakes enable 'F nostalgia' on the level of the narration. Thus, seen in the flow of contemporary television, the mystifying good-bad vision that *Knight Rider* (NBC, 1982) presents of the 1980s and the images of masculinity dominant at the time may indeed work as a trigger for 'F nostalgia'. The contemporary present, which is exposed by its remake, is infused with positively painted 1980s ingredients of the premake and equally positively painted traditional role models, which – depending on the subject position –may also enable 'F nostalgia'. This similarly applies to *The Avengers*. While the 1960s television series is critical toward its temporal context and as a rerun rather impedes 'F nostalgia', its remake, with its positively painted traditional gender roles, favours nostalgia.

Furthermore, 'lost' emotions related to the respective first-runs or premakes were assumed to be potential objects of nostalgia. While in the case of *The Avengers* (Chechik, 1998) it is, for instance, the lost fascination with the main characters (F or A emotion) that may trigger the viewers' 'own' nostalgia in those who know and appreciated the premake. In *Knight Rider* (NBC, 2008) a similar loss of fascination (F or A emotion) is presumed to possibly enable nostalgia in the context of the series' main prop.

Regarding the period dramas, it may be stated that *Borgia* (Sky Italia, 2011) with its closed structure and low degree of self-reflexivity, paints a picture of stability that indeed may be called nostalgic and may be seen as a potential trigger for 'F nostalgia'. The highly reflexive *Mad Men* (AMC, 2007), in contrast, does not present a nostalgic vision of the 1960s it exposes. However, it enables 'empathetic F nostalgia'. Above all, especially in the case of *Mad Men* where empathy is favoured and the sensuous exploration of the settings often comes to the fore, 'internal empathetic artefact nostalgia' is expected. The question whether this is true has to be seen in the reception study.

Already these few examples of potential 'F nostalgia' show that the differences between the 'genres' do not lie too much in the nostalgias they favour, but rather in the paths the different 'genres' take towards the past and the different scopes of knowledge against which they may work as potential triggers for nostalgia. In the case of *Knight Rider* (NBC, 1982), the lost fascination with the car (F or A emotion) or, in the case of *The Avengers* (ITV, 1961), the lost or reawakened fascination with Peel's character and costume can only trigger nostalgia towards the 'original' viewing experience in the case that the audiences know the first-run *and* that they indeed enjoyed it. Since both original series were broadcasted in Germany and in Spain, major differences can therefore be expected between the different age groups rather than between the territorial groups. The same applies to the respective remakes *Knight Rider* (NBC, 2008) and *The Avengers* (Chechik, 1998). Here, the reception of the lost provocation with Emma Peel's and Steed's character traits, for example, may also only trigger nostalgia towards the 'original' viewing experience if the audiences know the premake *and* enjoyed it. Other potential triggers for 'F nostalgia' can be presumed to work both in the knowing and the 'not-knowing' audiences. We may here, for instance, refer to possible 'empathetic F nostalgia' in the context of *Mad Men*. Major differences can rather be expected here regarding possible viewers' 'own' nostalgias when the empathetic emotion flows, for instance, into self-reflection. Here, the reception study will reveal further aspects as well.

The difference is more obvious in the case of the possible 'artefact nostalgias'. If we compare the levels on which reruns, remakes and period dramas enable 'A nostalgia', the distribution of possible nostalgias is not too different. However, in each case different knowledge is affordable and different paths towards the past are taken. The period dramas, for example, have the 'connotation of pastness' for every viewer. The 'gaps' between past and present are recognisable for those who do not have personal memories of the concrete props or other elements of the text. However, it can be supposed that major differences between those groups who have personal memories of the time span and those who, at the utmost, have "prosthetic" ones can be observed. The same applies to the reruns. The 'connotation of pastness' is also recognizable here for those audiences who do not know the first-run. This is very similar to what Keightley and Pickering (2006) highlighted in the context of their investigation on popular music and photography – it can be expected that a shift towards the mere "historical representation" (Keightley and Pickering, 2006, p. 152) can be described as well. The reruns become 'icons of their time'. The gap between 'then' and 'now', which is so essential for nostalgia, can also be recognised by the 'not knowing' audiences.

It is a different case when we assume that triggered media memory, which, as O'Sullivan (1991, p. 163) observed, works as a reference point in order to remember, for instance, past and present identity, functions as potential triggers for 'A nostalgia'. In this case the rerun can be assumed to prefigure nostalgia only for the 'knowing audiences'. This also applies to the television remakes *Knight Rider* (NBC, 2008-2009) and *The Avengers* (Chechik, 1998). Here, a possible rhetoric that contrasts a better 'then' with a worse 'now' is in most cases dependent on the knowledge of the premake and its respective valorisation. With regard to the reception analysis, it can be assumed that in this context minor differences between the territorial groups but more obvious differences between the age groups will be observable. In any case, it should be highlighted that both remakes that were analysed update the time frame of the 'originals'. It would be a different case with remakes that maintained the original temporal context. Next to possible 'gaps', an analysis of nostalgia must consequently consider different memory backgrounds of different "we-groups". Apart from that, possible "retrospective classifications" must be considered. The fact that the first-runs, respectively "premakes", of the chosen reruns and remakes fall into the so-called "reminiscence bump" (Eysenck and Keane, 2005, p. 266) and "formative" years of each age group, let us assume first differences in the reception. This must be further investigated in the course of the reception study.

Furthermore, due to the assumption that "retrospective classifications" of the respective first-runs and "premakes" are, above all, relevant regarding possible nostalgias in the context of the reruns and remakes, the public discourse has been taken into consideration. While it didn't allow the study to identify the actual reception, it gave further indicators of possible readings or of possible 'gaps'. Positive retrospective valorisations of both *Knight Rider* and *The Avengers* first-runs and premakes in Germany and Spain support the assumption that a respective 'A nostalgia' directed towards the past television series is possible. Apart from that, the existence of other presumed 'gaps' was supported. Both the German and Spanish public discourse on *Knight Rider* (NBC, 1982), for example, provided evidence that the lost fascination with the once futuristic car may be a source of potential longing. Also the 'gap' on the level of Hasselhoff as a star person(a) was supported by the public discourse. With reference to the discourse, territorial differences can only be assumed in a few cases. In Spain, *El coche fantástico* is, for instance, described as a representative of those years around the *Transición* in "'which not everything was possible, but it seemed that way'" (Garcia Ruipérez, 2011 [o.t.])[100] and is thus

---

100 Original quotation: "Teatro Nuevo Alcalá se embarque en un viaje a los 80, 'aquella época de las primeras veces en que no todo era posible pero, eso sí, lo parecía'." (Garcia Ruipérez, 2011)

installed as possible trigger for nostalgia in the Spanish case. In the German case no such discourse fragments could be found. However, only in a few other cases such differences could be observed. Also here, the reception study will provide further insights.

We may state that, in the course of the analysis, some first patterns of possible receptions among the different territorial groups and age groups could be highlighted. The public discourse in the form of newspaper articles provided first indicators. However, here the television analysis could only take first steps. Only the reception study will be able to identify actual readings and to put potential triggers for nostalgia on the level of the text and its concrete reception into relation.

Lastly, also the degree of self-reflexivity differs among the examples. Both remakes expose a rather uncritical, in parts even reactionary undertone. This similarly applies to the rerun *Knight Rider* (NBC, 1982) and the period drama *Borgia* (Sky Italia, 2011). In contrast to that, the rerun *The Avengers* (ITV, 1961) and the period drama *Mad Men* (AMC, 2007) hold a more reflexive position towards their temporal frame, which in many areas impedes any simple nostalgia.[101] Against this background, we must also ask if this critical disposition one series exposes more clearly than another also has effects on possible nostalgic readings of other levels of the text, respectively the structure of the audiences' 'own nostalgia'.

Similar to what Mikos (2008, pp. 142 ff.) describes in the context of suspense and humour, it can be assumed that the text may contain a disposition of nostalgia; however, this disposition has to be 'accomplished' by the viewers. In order to analyse this matter, this work leads over to the third part, which is the qualitative analysis of the reception. The analysis will be based on the following research questions:

- Do the potential triggers for nostalgia that are offered by the text provoke nostalgia in its audiences?
- Are there any 'necessary' time spans for a potential object of nostalgia?
- Does a reflexive pre-focus of the text have any influence on the characterisation of the viewers' ('own') nostalgias?
- Is nostalgia against the backdrop of "prosthetic memory" or 'transmitted' nostalgia observable?
- Are there any territorial differences regarding the reception of nostalgia?
- Does the reception of nostalgia of the 25 to 35-year-olds differ from the reception of the 55 to 65-year-olds?
- Or in general: How are the examples received by different "we-groups"?

---

101 Certainly this shall not mean that not all of the texts can have "a multiplicity of meanings" (see e.g. Abercrombie and Longhurst, 2007, p. 64 on "closed text").

Part III – Reception

7. The reception of nostalgia

In order to investigate nostalgia in television comprehensively, the study has been divided into three sections. The theoretical section in Part I highlights existing theories of nostalgia. This theory is complemented by further studies about memory and aesthetic emotions. The combination of approaches allows the work to generate 'modules' for the television analysis of three dominant nostalgia 'genres' as it has been conducted in Part II of this study. Based upon a 'reception aesthetic' understanding of television, Part III shall now combine the results from the television analysis with reception studies. This section studies the "systematic interrelations" (see Bartsch et al., 2007a, p. 10 [o.t.]) between the nostalgias the texts offer and nostalgia provoked in its audiences.

Following the premises of triangulation, different methods will also be applied here. The main part of the reception study consists of four focus group discussions. They were supplemented by a standardised questionnaire. Before the method and its suitability for this study will be further outlined, this section takes a short look on previous works in the context.

7.1 EXCURSUS – EMPIRICAL RESEARCH ON NOSTALGIA IN TELEVISION

Part I and Part II already mentioned single empirical studies about nostalgia. They will be taken up and scrutinised here. The aim is not to summarise this research but to highlight those points that will be relevant in the course of the reception study.

As an earlier investigation with empirical purposes, here we can refer to Spigel's (1995) research on the construction of public histories of the role of women through reruns (Spigel, 1995, p. 16), respectively the use of "television reruns and nostalgia programmes as a source for popular memory" (Spigel, 1995, p. 30). Even though nostalgia is not in the centre of that study, by means of oral discussion sessions and written essays conducted in the course of her university seminars, Spigel was able to show that "[b]y imposing a contemporary logic on historical events, nostalgia sitcoms help to do the work of familiarization for their audiences, allowing viewers to remember only those details of the past that seem useful for the present" (Spigel, 1995, p. 25). While regarding the role of women in society, students mainly opposed a positive present against a worse past (Spigel, 1995, p. 27), the study also suggests that the 'whitewashed' rerun realities may provoke "nostalgic longing for the 'good old days' when girls were girls and boys made money" (Spigel, 1995, p. 28). It has to be seen if similar observations can be made in the following reception study.

Further research on television reruns has been done by Furno-Lamude and Anderson (1992). The authors conducted a survey among 1,120 households on the uses and gratifications of the repetitions. Here, nostalgia is not in the centre of the study either but emerges as one mayor aspect. The authors highlight in the discussion of their results the following:

"Three nostalgia items and four recall items were significantly higher for rerun viewing. [...] Nostalgia items involving watching a rerun because it reminds one of their past, liking the program in the past and because it reminds one of watching this program when younger, were significantly higher for rerun viewing. [...] The quality item of watching the program because it is of better quality than other programs was significantly higher for rerun viewing than for first-run viewing." (Furno-Lamude and Anderson, 1992, p. 369)

Against the backdrop of the theoretical part, it must surely be seen as critical that nostalgia is equated with remembrance. It can also be stated that deeper motives of the recipients cannot be brought to light with the questionnaires, just as Tan (1996, p. 17) argued in the context of aesthetic emotions in general – not to mention that the study does not make a textual analysis. However, the authors give useful insights into the reception of reruns that can be attached to in the following study.

Apart from that, we can also refer to the work of Corbalán (2009). As previously mentioned in Chapter 2.2.6.2, Corbalán is one of the few authors who realises what scholars who investigate nostalgia within the spectrum of cultural studies demanded. In the centre of her investigation is the long-running Spanish period drama *Cuéntame cómo pasó* (TVE, 2001), a series that, according to the author, exposes a high degree of "reflexive" nostalgia (Corbalán, 2009, pp. 341 ff. [o.t.]). On the one hand, it is analysed how the series constructs and reconfigures history (Corbalán, 2009, p. 345) and where nostalgia may arise. On the other hand, enquiries among one hundred 25 to 75-year-olds have been made in the form of qualitative questionnaires. Here, cases where recipients mention nostalgia, arise or reflect, as Corbalán (2009, p. 346 [o.t.]) calls it, "emotive responses" as well. Corbalán's study supports that period dramas may provoke the emotion of nostalgia; however, it has to be stated that text and reception are not consequently put into mutual relation. Similar to Furno-Lamude and Anderson's study, it seems that deeper motives cannot be brought to light with the questionnaires (see again Tan, 1996, p. 17). Further research is obviously needed here, respectively: this is where the present study may attach.

Lastly, Davis (1979) also undertook empirical research. His work is in parts about nostalgia provoked by television. Both, however, are not put into mutual interrelation. The seemingly rather informal surveys on associations related to the word nostalgia (Davis, 1979, p. 4) and interviews were made in order to qualitatively grasp the meaning or characteristics of the nostalgia mood (see e.g. Davis, 1979, pp. 12, 14, 16 ff.) as a basis of what has already been highlighted in the theoretical section of this work. Nevertheless, Davis (1979) describes general tendencies of nostalgia, such as its "sociological significance" (Davis, 1979, pp. 12 f.) when relating to life phases, late teens as its frequent object (Davis, 1979, p. 60) or a quantitative dominance of what he calls "Simple Nostalgia" (Davis, 1979, p. 27), as they are also relevant in the context of nostalgia in television and in the context of the present investigation.

Next to these studies, nostalgia is often a 'by-product' of investigations in the spectrum of (media) memory. Here we can point at the research of Dhoest (2007, p. 31). Methodically influenced by oral history studies, the author researches the historical reception of thirteen years of Flemish television fiction among 60-year-olds and older viewers with semi-structured interviews. In the centre are "general memories to detailed questions on specific programs" (Dhoest, 2007, p. 35). Even though textual characteristics of the programmes are not considered in detail and characteristics of the 'genres' of nostalgia are not considered, the text is put in relation to the colouring of the memories. Next to, as Dhoest (2007, p. 39) states, the "nostalgic" argumentation that "'television was better back then'", Dhoest (2007, p. 45) observes here that "[t]o the creation of a cliché image by television corresponds a cliché memory by the viewers". We may at least assume that, in the context of the present study as well, the nostalgic programme may induce a nostalgic look on the context.

Further aspects of nostalgia appear, for example, in the context of the *The Global Media Project* (Volkmer, 2006). Kumar et al. (2006) come to discuss an accumulation of nostalgia among 70 to 75-year-old participants in the course of qualitative focus group discussions made in the Indian context. They suggest, "The more distant and remote in time, and the more pleasurable the event in the imagination, the greater is the nostalgia with which it is recalled." (Kumar et al., 2006, p. 219) This point must at least be considered in the following study. It can only be assumed that in the course of this investigation nostalgia will also be predominantly observable among the 55 to 65-year-olds.

We may state that there is still a lack of empirical research that aspires to study the "interrelation" between the nostalgic text and the nostalgic reception, just as authors from the spectrum of cultural studies bemoaned it. Against this background, the following investigation has in parts an "explorative" character. At the same time, regarding single aspects, there is empirical research on which this study will refer to in the following reception analysis.

7.2 THE PROCESS OF THE INVESTIGATION

In the following, the present approach shall be outlined in more detail. The paragraph will first of all draw on the method of focus group discussions and its suitability for this study. Further sub-chapters focus on the subject of informants and sampling, the concrete proceeding and the applied questioning route.

7.2.1 Focus groups

There are various points that make the qualitative methodology of focus group discussions suitable for this study. Firstly, this work has in parts "explorative" character. Up to now only a few studies have systematically investigated the interrelation between nostalgia on the level of the text and nostalgia on the level of reception. Group discussions, says Lamnek (2005, p. 71), are above all suitable in cases where only limited empirical studies on the subject can be found and where a mere revision of the literature does not grasp a phenomenon sufficiently. Secondly, its "in-depth insights as well as [...] [the] variety of nuances" are, as Volkmer (2006b, p. 13) states, "relevant for internationally comparative research" as it is also done here. Thirdly, the method focuses on the 'why' questions "'instead of 'how many'"" and "'on feelings and attitudes rather than on measurement'" (Levine and Zimmermann, 1997 cited in Lamnek, 2005, p. 80) both on an individual and on a rather 'shared' level. Thus, with Lamnek (2005, p. 84 [o.t.]), we may presume that small-sized groups allow an explanation of "emotional backgrounds". "The confrontation with other opinions in the process of the discussion opens up the chance to additionally identify individual contexts of justification" (Paus-Hpuaase et al., 1999, p. 43 [o.t.]). At the same time, collective views will become apparent (Lamnek, 2005, p. 84 [o.t.]). This will allow this study to explain the individual reception of the potential triggers of nostalgia and the transitions between personal nostalgias and those that are shared among larger "we-groups". All in all, an in-depth articulation and analysis of the different receptions, its motivations, memories and backgrounds will be possible.

Probably, as experienced by Keval et al. (2006) in the context of *The Global Media Project,* it will not always be easy to "distinguish personal verbalizations of memories from personal comments on other's elaborations and from elaborations of elaborations, etc." (Keval et al., 2006, p. 214). However, as it was shown in the theoretical section on memory and as it is also explicitly highlighted by Keval et al. (2006, p. 214), this is one basic characteristic of memory in general where boundaries are difficult to draw. The focus group is able to take these characteristics into account. Apart from that, says Lamnek (2005, p. 87), uneven distributions of verbal contributions may appear. In the course of the discussion this fact was taken into account. Those who remained silent were specifically requested to articulate their opinion. Interrupted or broken-off speech was taken off again, also in order to get a deeper insight into the respective affective reactions. Despite these difficulties, it will be shown in the presentation of the results that different patterns of reception could be explained. At the same time transitions between personal and rather 'collective' elaborations could be shown. Nonetheless, the limits of the methods shall be kept in mind throughout the analysis.

7.2.1.1 Informants and sampling

In order to be able to explain the reception of potential triggers of nostalgia among different "we-groups", a total of four group discussions, two in Germany and two in Spain, with two different age groups each were conducted. In total 29 interviewees (n = 29) participated in the study.

As Lamnek (2005, p. 115 [o.t.]) states, "[s]ince the qualitative methodology necessarily and generally prefers conscious selection techniques (theoretical sampling, a statistically random composition of discussion groups is neither necessary nor helpful". Therefore, the participants were chosen according to their suitability to answer the research questions (see also Keuneke, 2005, p. 263, on theoretical sampling). Most significant was the age and place of residence. Regarding the participants' age, two groups were recruited in both countries: namely one group of 25 to 35-year-olds and one of 55 to 65-year-olds each. In doing this, each one of the analysed reruns and remakes fell into the "formative years", respectively into the so-called "reminiscence bump", of one age group. In both countries the interviewees were recruited in major cities: Berlin (Germany) and Barcelona (Spain). In all groups, gender-equilibrium was desired. In order to gain a higher degree of comparability, a relative consistency of the number of participants among the groups was aspired, just as Lamnek (2005, p. 112) describes it as necessary with reference to Spöhring (1989). Small numbers of participants were chosen. They are, says Lamnek (2005, pp. 110 ff.), especially appropriate when the interviewees are emotionally involved and when an in-depth questioning is necessary. An uneven number was aimed for, to minimise the risk of stalemate in the discussion (see also Lamnek, 2005, p. 110).

The sample was organised in the so-called 'snowball method'. Here, starting from the initial contact with one or more informants, further contacts are generated

(Lamnek, 2005, p. 114).[1] Parents or close relatives of the interviewer were excluded, which according to Hackl (2001, p. 124) could entail a high degree of bias or prevent to address certain topics. Apart from an age and relative gender equilibrium, this also resulted in a relative homogeneity regarding profession and social class, which can be further specified with reference to the questionnaire (see 7.2.2).

All interviewees have an academic degree or higher education and may be associated to a middle-class to upper middle-class spectrum (see appendix 12.1).[2] This is, however, not a problem in the context of this study where a comparison is aspired. Rather the contrary is the case. As Knodel (1993) states:

"'Holding separate sessions with homogenous but contrasting groups is believed to produce information in greater depth than would be the case with heterogeneous groups, because it will be easier for participants sharing similar key characteristics to identify with each other's experiences'." (Knodel, 1993 cited in Lamnek, 2005, p. 116)

As described by Volkmer (2006b, p. 15), a certain trust among the interviewees from similar peer-groups leads to "very subjective and honest responses" and to a freer flow of the discussion and lets them rapidly enter the main part of the discussion. In the context of this study it can be assumed that in doing so a kind of 'nostalgic atmosphere' is supported. In order to avoid so-called in-group/out-group effects (see e.g. Lamnek, 2005, p. 105), the two age groups and territorial groups were interviewed separately.

7.2.1.2 Proceeding

All four interviews were conducted by the author herself and in German and Spanish. The fact that interviewees can debate in their own language, encourages, as Volkmer states, "more elaborate communications than an interview in a second language would allow" (Volkmer, 2006b, p. 15).[3] In order to cope with the media socialisation and cultural background of the Spanish/Catalan participants as well, the German

---

1   In the case of the 55 to 65-year-old Spaniards, the study had to also use members of a local reading circle.

2   All participants of the German groups have been socialized in (political) West Germany. One participant omitted information in the questionnaire.

3   It should be taken into account that next to Spanish, Catalan has official status in Catalonia (see e.g. Vilarós, 1999). Some interviewees from the Spanish groups explicitly highlight their Catalan origin in the questionnaire. Especially in the group of the 55 to 65-year-olds, interviewees sometimes changed into Catalan. Notwithstanding, the fact that the interviews were conducted in Spanish language did not hinder the discussion. The Spanish language competence of both the 25 to 35-year-old and the 55 to 65-year-olds is without doubt on the same level as that of a native speaker.

interviewee who had already lived in the country for three years, had acquired a broad knowledge of country-specific media contents and contexts. Apart from that, in the Spanish case a native language assistant was present during the group discussion, who recorded the order and rough contents of the contributions.

The focus group participants were informed that the discussion was part of a comparative doctoral project on television series and memories in Germany and Spain, that the discussion would take about an hour and a half, and that it would be recorded on tape. The four groups were interviewed in four different evenings in December 2011. Two of them took place in the private flats of two participants. Two others were conducted in specially leased public rooms, which did not hinder the course of the discussion. In the end they had an approximate duration of 120 minutes in Spain and 150 minutes in Germany, including the recordings of any commentaries before, during and after the reception of example media clips and eventual comments before, during and after the filling-in of the questionnaires.

In most cases the discussion developed rapidly and was fluent. A predominantly high disposition to participate and provide also personal memories was observed. Minor differences were noticed regarding the Spanish group of the 55 to 65-year-olds where in parts members of a local reading circle participated in the focus group. Here, the discussion started slower and was a bit more cumbersome, since in the beginning the participants seemed to be rather disposed to judge the (artistic) value of the examples. These first difficulties could be quickly overcome by means of focused questions.

The transcription was finished in February 2012. The complete discussions were transcribed into German and Spanish. The interviewer herself made both the German and one of the Spanish transcripts. In case of uncertainties in the latter case, the respective native speaker's notes were consulted. A native Spanish speaker transcribed the second group discussion. In all cases, GAT, a transcription system implemented by German conversation analysts, was used as a basis. However, a detailed transcription of, for instance, the exact length of pauses has been left out as it is not relevant for the research question. Other details, such as accents on single words or laughter, were considered. [4] The analysis was made on the basis of the original quotations. In the English translation as they are included in the following presentation of results, the rules of transcription were not maintained.

As it is common in reception studies (see e.g. Prommer and Mikos, 2005, p. 195), in each discussion the respective German and Spanish synchronised version of the same media clips were used as a stimulus. On the one hand they were meant to work

---

4   For this publication, also in the original quotations, which are contained in the footnotes, some details such as the marking of short pauses within the flow of words or primary and main accents with capital letters (see teachsam, 2010) have been relinquished in order to enhance the readability.

as memory cues for those who already knew the examples; on the other, they were supposed to enable those who had not seen the examples before to participate in the discussion. According to the design of the research, 2-3 minute clips of those reruns, remakes, and period dramas were used, which were also subject to the television analysis.[5] Those examples which best reflect the presumed potential triggers for nostalgia were chosen. The following excerpts were shown in this order:

Table 1: Examples during the discussion

Remakes	*Knight Rider* (RTL, 2009), resp. *El coche fantástico* (La1, 2008); Episode 9; "Knight Fever" • Opening scene: Michael (Justin Bruening) and KITT chase a truck. At the same time they are attacked by a group of bikers. The car transforms into the 'combat mode' in order to stop the truck. Apparently something strange happens inside the vehicle that KITT is able to detect with its 'infrared sensors'. The team in the hangar home base, which is continuously conversing with Mike, tells him not to enter the truck. However, Mike resists the demands in order to investigate the terrain. What he detects is a glittering electro tension that he's not able to explain. • Intro of the series. *Mit Schirm, Charme und Melone*, resp. *Los Vengadores* (Chechik, 1998) • Opening scene: Steed (Ralph Fiennes) walks through a 'training parlour' where he meets with the typical *Avengers* antagonists. A non-diegetic music that is the 'original' *The Avengers* intro accompanies the scene.

---

5   Remakes: *Knight Rider* (RTL, 2009) and *Mit Schirm, Charme und Melone* (Chechik, 1998) in the German group. *El coche fantástico* (La1, 2008) and *Los Vengadores* (Chechik, 1998) in the Spanish group. Reruns: *Knight Rider* (RTLplus 1985) and *Mit Schirm, Charme und Melone* (ZDF, 1966) in the German group. *El coche fantástico* (TVE, 1985) and *Los Vengadores* (TVE, 1966) in the Spanish group. Period Dramas: *Mad Men* (Fox, 2009) and *Borgia* (ZDF, 2011) in the German group. *Mad Men* (Cuatro, 2009) and *Borgia – Una familia consagrada al Vicio* (Cosmopolitan TV, 2011) in the Spanish group.

	• First meeting between Steed and Peel (Uma Thurman), in which Peel makes her way through a 'bastion of men's privileges' – a men-only sauna club. • Fencing scene between Steed and Peel. Peel easily conquers Steed.
Reruns	*Knight Rider* (RTLplus 1985) resp. *El coche fantástico* (TVE, 1985); Season 1, Episode 5; "Slammin' Sammy's Stunt Show Spectacular" • Intro of the series. • Michael (David Hasselhoff) witnesses an accident of stuntman Sammy during a public stunt session. For the viewer it is already assumed that the accident did not happen by coincidence. • Michael then applies for the job of the show stuntman in order to investigate the case. However, first he has to convince KITT not to show all his skills. *Mit Schirm, Charme und Melone* (ZDF, 1966), resp. *Los Vengadores* (TVE, 1966); intro Season 4; Season 5, Episode 5; "The Bird Who Knew Too Much" • Intro of the fourth season (black and white). • Emma Peel (Diana Rigg) trains her fencing skills in her flat. Steed (Patrick Macnee) appears with the ritual "Mrs Peel – we're needed". • Peel and Steed enter the flat of a friendly agent shortly before he dies. In his last words the dying man informs the agent couple of a secret that is brought out of the country. The murderers escape unrecognised. • One of the murderers fires at Emma Peel from the diving platform of a swimming pool. Peel, however, is able to overpower the man.
Period Dramas	*Borgia* (ZDF, 2011) resp. *Borgia – Una familia consagrada al Vicio* (Cosmopolitan TV, 2011); Season 1, Episode 3 (German version) 6 (Spanish version); "The Bonds of Matrimony/ Legitimacy" • In the circle of his cardinals Rodrigo Borgia (John Doman), Pope Alexander VI, receives the notice that Christopher

Columbus discovered 'the new world'. The news first of all generates mockery from the present cardinals.

- By means of a trick Giovanni (Manuel Rubey) can convince Adriana (Andrea Sawatzki) to leave the room in order to be alone with Lucrecia (Isolda Dychauk). Both start dancing yet their intimate get-together does not last very long. The couple are soon driven apart by the governess.

Mad Men (Fox, 2009), resp. *Mad Men* (Cuatro, 2009); Season 1, Episode 8 ("The Hobo Code") and 13 ("The Wheel")

- The 'mad' men and women of Sterling Cooper hilariously dance the twist in a bar. Peggy (Elisabeth Moss) approaches Pete (Vincent Kartheiser) to ask him for a dance. He, however, rejects her brusquely. The next morning, when the secretary sits at her desk again, he ignores her.
- In a pitch for a new slide projector campaign, Don Draper uses his own family slides in order to develop a discourse on nostalgia and the strong bonds that emotion can generate.

In the course of a pre-test that was made in February 2011 with a group of 25 to 35-year-old Germans – different from the group that is referred to in the analysis – it proved to be necessary not to show all examples in one block but to distribute the clips over the course of the discussion according to the three thematic sections remakes, reruns, and period dramas. In doing so, a more evenly distributed amount of contributions to the examples could be gained. The risk that the focus group members might get confused could be reduced. In order to avoid the creation of an 'artificial memory' in the course of the group discussions, the reruns were shown after the respective remakes.

7.2.1.3 Questioning route

In all four interviews the same questioning route was used. In doing so, a certain degree of standardization could be gained as is necessary in the context of comparative studies (see e.g. Bohnsack, 1997 cited in Lamnek, 2005, p. 67). The questioning route contained pre-formulated questions with a defined order. Flexibility was used in order to accommodate the different situations of the discussions. In general the questioning route contained three main paragraphs (see appendix 12.3), each dedicated to one of the nostalgia 'genres'. Thereby nostalgia was not addressed explicitly until the last phase of the discussion. Regarding the composition and succession of questions, the study mainly followed Lamnek's proposal (2005, pp. 98 ff.) in the general context of group discussions.

An opening question, which focused on television series the participants currently liked watching, was used to 'break the ice'. It was followed by an introductory question where the participants were asked whether they currently watch television series they used to watch earlier in their lives. The question should prompt first memories and lead over to the main part of the group discussion. Structured according to the three blocks of examples mentioned above, each paragraph contained similar questions. Initially it should be spotted if the participants had seen the examples before. In the case of a positive answer they were requested to recall their first experience and to describe it. Later, the participants, whether they already knew the example or not, were asked to recall what had crossed their minds during the reception. In case that it had not already been answered in the course of the respective opening question, more specific questions followed. Participants were now explicitly asked for details that called their attention. Here, especially those aspects which had been worked out as potential nostalgia-triggers in the television analysis were important. Later, at least in the case of remakes and reruns, the participants were asked to make comparisons, be it between premake and remake or be it between contemporary and past television series. Memories of personal living situations in the context of the time frame of the respective examples were investigated. Furthermore, the discussion focussed on possible empathetic sentiments.

In the case that the participants had not already generated the transition to the topic of nostalgia with the *Mad Men* example that explicitly hinted at the subject, a summary question introduced the issue explicitly. The participants were then asked to recall which aspects of the previous discussion had anything to do with nostalgia for them. Following Lamnek (2005, p. 100 [o.t.]), the ending questions consisted of a "final insurance question" where basic aspects of the discussion were repeated by the interviewer in order to avoid any misunderstandings. An "all-things-considered question" (Lamnek, 2005, p. 100 [o.t.]) gave the participants the possibility to come to their own conclusions, or to mention things that had not been brought up in the course of the discussion but that seemed worth mentioning to them. During the whole discussion, the subjects were always changed in case that a "'saturation point'" (see also Morgan, 1997 cited in Lamnek, 2005, p. 118 [o.t.]) had been reached.

7.2.2 Questionnaire

In the aftermath of the discussion, the participants were asked to fill in a standardised questionnaire with both closed and open-ended questions (see appendix 12.2). The questionnaire was basically composed of two parts. A first part contained four open-ended questions on the participants' first television experience, their descriptions of the nostalgic sentiment, their definitions of a 'nostalgic person', and their reflections on nostalgia and causes of possible nostalgia felt in the course of the group discussion. A second part asked for socio-demographic data and information about the current and adolescent television consumption of the participants. While the latter allows a further classification of the composition of the group, the first is meant to further support the in-depth analysis of the group discussions (see 7.2.3). With Tan (1996, p. 17) it can be presumed that the questionnaire does not permit statements on "deeper motives" of the participants. However, it allows for a deeper analysis of possible different connotations and values of nostalgia between and among the age groups, and the further distinction between latent and manifest nostalgias that may further support the qualitative analysis of the focus group discussions (see also 7.2.3.3).

7.2.3 Analysis of the group discussions

"[T]here is no generally preferred or even normative-methodologically prescribed analysis method for group discussions" (Lamnek, 2005, p. 177 [o.t.]). In fact, as argued by Lamnek (2005, p. 177), it depends upon the focus of each investigation and its objectives which method is most suitable. In this study, qualitative content analysis as proposed by Mayring (see e.g. Mayring and Hurst, 2005; Mayring, 2010) shall be applied. Not only is it presented as one possible method of analysing group discussions in general (see e.g. Lamnek, 2005, pp. 195 ff.), next to its explorative character, the verification of hypotheses and theories is also highlighted as one of its functions (see e.g. Mayring, 2010, p. 25). It can be seen as particularly suitable for this study. The analysis firstly serves here as a counter-check for the yet existing hypotheses and the scrutinising of the question to what extent the explained elements of nostalgia are perceived. Secondly, a more detailed survey of the subject matter of nostalgia and television shall be given. Further hypotheses on the reception of nostalgic media texts shall be made. In order to do so, the analysis must aim at making "'statements on the emotional and cognitive background of the communicator's actions'", just as Mayring (2003, cited in Lamnek, 2005, p. 196) highlighted it as one function of the qualitative content analysis in general.

7.2.3.1 Qualitative content analysis

On the one hand, the method of qualitative content analysis developed by Mayring (2010) guarantees the systematisation and verifiability that is also aspired by quantitative analysis, and on the other hand, it makes allowances for the complexity and richness of, in this case, around seven hours of discussion (see Mayring, 2010,

p. 10; see also Lamnek, 2005, p. 195). The three techniques are aggregation, explication, and structuring (Mayring, 2010, p. 65):

"*Aggregation:* The aim of the analysis is to reduce the material in so far that the main contents remain maintained, to create a manageable corpus by abstraction, which still reflects the original material.

Explication: The aim of the analysis is to contribute additional material to single issues of text (words, phrases, ...) that are under question, which enhances the understanding, explains the passage, and interprets it.

Structuring: The aim of the analysis is to filter out certain aspects of the material, to make a cross-section through the material with criteria that have been established before, or to assess the material based upon certain criteria." (Mayring, 2010, p. 65 [o.t.])

As suggested by Mayring (2010, p. 60), the techniques may be combined or exclusively used depending on their suitability for the analysis.

Since, according to Lamnek (2005, p. 236 [o.t.]), from three group discussions with a duration of two hours or more, manual analysis techniques, such as the "cut-and-paste-technique", become unprofitable, the analysis will be supplemented in using the qualitative analysis programme MAXQDA – software that was developed for qualitative text analysis (see Lamnek, 2005, p. 247; Kuckartz, 2010). With this, as Kuckartz (2010, p. 20) argues, the verifiability of the analysis may be improved.

7.2.3.2 Coding of the focus groups

In a first step, following Mayring (2010, p. 95), the complete transcribed material of the four focus group discussions is formally structured in thematic blocks. Here, the main orientation point is the respective structure of the questioning route with its five sections of programme preferences, remakes, reruns, period drama, and the concrete reflection on nostalgia in the context of the group discussion. In a second step, the sections on the nostalgia 'genres' are again divided according to the statements about the single examples. MAXQDA provides the possibility to organise the passages of discussion into document groups. Each document group is then built by the respective excerpts of the four group discussion. Already on this broad level a comparison according to country and age group is therefore possible. Later, the interviewees are also coded, which enables a juxtaposition of single participants or groups of participants.

In the next step, Mayring's (2010) method of aggregation is applied. In order to generate the first inductively gained category system, the respective interview sections of each one of the three nostalgia 'genres' (the rerun *Knight Rider*, the remake *Knight Rider*, and the period drama *Mad Men*) were paraphrased in table form. As proposed by Mayring (2010, p. 113), the memo-function of MAXQDA was used to do so. In the programme, the categories or codes and sub-categories where then assigned to the text. In doing this, main categories could be deduced. Regarding the television remakes, these are as follows:

- Reasons for the reception:
  Here it was coded if the viewers talked about reasons for an eventual earlier reception of the remake.
- Associations with the remake:
  The code ranges from references to other television series up to the contexts of reception. It has later been subdivided into the patterns *(Nostalgic) Context Memories* and *Intertextual References – Roundabout Nostalgia?*.
- Remake versus premake:
  The recipients compare the two versions of the series.
- Past versus present experience:
  How do the recipients describe their experiences with the premake? How do they describe their experiences with the remake? Are these experiences in contrast to each other and if they are, in what way?

In all three cases huge parts of the categories were also concordant in the discussion-sections to the second 'genre' examples, the television rerun *The Avengers*, the film remake *The Avengers* (Chechik, 1998) and the period drama *Borgia*, which is why in the second case the step of making tables of reduction could be relinquished. "Encoding units" of the content analysis (see Mayring, 2010, p. 59 [o.t.]) were single words, for example when interviewees named single objects that attracted their attention (see e.g. DFG25-35: "The Car" (GD25-35_Rerun_Avenger_Deutschland, 119 [o.t.]), up to complete units of meaning or whole text passages if, for example, past and present are put in contrast when taking a nostalgic stance (see e.g. FMS55-65: "When we watch *Los Vengadores*, I remember the past with nostalgia, of course. Because I was twenty years old. (I will be seventy soon). Today I wear glasses and dentures, yes." (GS55-65_Nostalgie Allgemein_Spanien, 11-19 [o.t.])[6])

7.2.3.3 In-depth analysis
The in-depth analysis focuses on the question of whether or not the nostalgias that were explained in the television analysis are indeed decoded by the interviewees. Hereby the presumed triggers of nostalgia, as they are offered by the text, are put into

---

6 Original quotation: "Cuando vemos *Los Vengadores* yo recuerdo tiempos pasados, con nostalgia, claro. Porque tenía 20 años. (Me he vuelto a los 70 pronto). Hoy llevo gafas y dientes postizos, sí." (FMS55-65, GS55-65_Nostalgie Allgemein_Spanien, 11-19)

relation to the patterns of reception. Cases of nostalgia are explained. Here, the analysis proceeds both deductively and inductively. The nostalgic reception is scrutinised with reference to the theoretical section and the television analysis. Influencing parameters for the respective patterns are analysed. The in-depth analysis can also be described as being contextual/explicative. The following points will be considered in detail:

- *Inter-group differences regarding the different patterns*
  On a first and general level, because of its segment matrix MAXQDA allows for the detailed comparison of main and sub-codes. Above all, differences between the territorial groups and age groups can then be explained. The next point is central to this, namely the concrete cases of nostalgia.
- *Concrete cases of nostalgia*
  On the one hand, the analysis searches for the "rhetoric" of nostalgia as described by Tannock (1995).[7] The gradations, as explained by Davis (1979), are also taken into consideration. Following the combination of the approaches, objects of nostalgia are explained in order to cross-check the reception analysis with the presumed triggers of nostalgia on the level of the text. On the other hand, concrete declarations of an emotion as "nostalgia" by the interviewees are coded. Hereby the analysis of the single examples also includes the interview section where they were explicitly asked about nostalgia. Additionally, the respective question in the questionnaire is analysed and contextualised with the (presumed) cases of nostalgia.[8] Eventual contradictions are described and explained by further contextualisation.
- *Are there any context factors that these concrete cases of nostalgia have in common?*
  In a next step, further hypothesis on the necessary conditions of nostalgia are made; something which is only possible in the course of the reception study. The in-depth analysis contrasts the respective cases of nostalgia with those who do not feel nostalgia. Do the interviewees know first-runs or premakes, and how are the texts classified retrospectively? How is the object of appraisal described? Are there intra- and inter-group differences between the connotation of nostalgia, and in which relation does the connotation stand in the development or non-development of the nostalgic longing? Apart from the statements that were made

---

7   That affects may be analysed with reference to spoken language has also been shown by content analysis by Gottschalk and Gleser (Schöfer, 1980).

8   See also Gottschalk and Gleser's work in and as referred to by Schöfer (1980). In their linguistic approach to emotions, the authors explain both "conscious and unconscious affects" (Schöfer, 1980a, p. 12 [o.t.]) by analysing manifest and latent explications of emotions (Gottschalk and Gleser, 1980, p. 15).

in the course of the discussion, the analysis will keep referring to the description of nostalgia in the questionnaire.[9] Regarding the inter-group comparison, the segment matrix function of MAXQDA facilitates the analysis. In order to describe intra-group differences or in general interpersonal differences, the single participants were coded separately.

- *Shared memories*
  To see to what extent the different memories are 'shared', gradations from personal up to "we-group" references are coded in the context of the interviewees' narrations of the past. Hereby, as Liebes and Katz (1990, p. 106) note, "personal and primary references", namely "I" references, can be explained. Later, and whenever it is possible, different 'wes', such as the group, age group, gender, family, friends, or national group, are differentiated (see also Liebes and Katz, 1990, p. 107).

- *Are there any irregularities?*
  For example contradictions between statements of single interviewees fall into this category. Before having seen the rerun examples, two interviewees of the group of the 55 to 65-year-old Spaniards declare that they neither know the first-run or premake, nor the remake of *Knight Rider*, however, they make extensive comparisons between the 'new version' they have already seen and the 'original'. In such cases memos were written that further support the analysis

The in-depth analysis contains some quantitative elements when it comes to the intra- and inter-group comparisons, or when the frequency of single categories is commented upon. Here, the Code-Matrix-Browser of MAXQDA allows for an exact comparison of the frequency of single codes in the four different groups. However, it shall be noted again that the results are neither representative nor desired to be.

Similar to what Smith (2008, p. 26) highlights regarding empathy – namely that there is a difference between empathy that arises in the course of watching a film and empathy that arises in the course of thinking about a film – the material gives evidence that there is a nostalgia the recipients felt in the course of the reception and one they developed in the context of the group discussion or in the process of appropriation. The analysis aspires here, whenever possible, to distinguish between the nostalgias by focusing on the contextualisations ("during the reception", "when we just saw...") made by the interviewees. However, this distinction will not be possible in every case.

---

9 A short excursus preceding the analysis will outline the different connotations in the four age groups.

8. Presentation of results

In order to maintain clarity, the presentation of results follows the basic structure of the television analysis where, for reasons of necessary references of the remake analysis on the rerun or premake background, reruns were followed by remakes and period dramas. This structure does not correspond to the order of the group discussions. When discussing *Knight Rider* (NBC, 2008), the participants had not yet seen the premake, at least not in the course of the focus group.

In each analytical section general tendencies shall be explained in the form of patterns. They shall be exemplified by significant text passages. In each sub-chapter, references to the television analysis of the respective examples are made. The conclusions of the sub-chapters combine the results of the reception analysis with the television analysis. In order to guarantee the anonymity of the interviewees, acronyms such as "JMS25-35" were chosen. The first letter refers to the first name of the respective interviewee (in case of in-group repetitions another letter was randomly chosen), the second letter signifies the sex of the participant ("F" for female and "M" for male), the third letter refers to the country ("S" for Spain and "G" for Germany) and the numbers refer to the respective age group (25 to 35-year-olds or 55 to 65-year-olds). The acronym "M" stands for moderator, which in this case is the investigator herself. In order to maintain the verifiability, each quotation uses the reference of the group of documents (for example *Diskussion Rerun*), the respective discussion group (for example *GS55-65* for Group Spain 55-65), reference series (for example *Rerun Knight Rider*), and the line number it holds in MAXQDA.

Preceding the presentation of results, we shall briefly refer to the different connotations of nostalgia that can be scrutinised with reference to the questionnaires and which will be an important reference point in the course of the analysis. Above all with a view on the question of how to define a 'nostalgic person', clear tendencies can be described. If one structures the answers according to an ordinal scale (see also Mayring, 2010, p.101) from negative to neutral to positive connotation, a clear difference between the groups can be seen (ignoring the intra-group differences). Among the 55 to 65-year-olds negative descriptions are mainly found. Here, the 'nostalgic person' is characterised as "rückwärtsgewandt" [reactionary] (GFG55-65; HFG55-65, DMG55-65) or "altmodisch" [old-fashioned] (HFG55-65). More extensive statements describe the 'nostalgic person' as:

AMS55-65: "A person living in the past and with little desire to live in the present" (Questionnaire_Connotation of nostalgia_55-65-year-old Spaniards, 10 [o.t.]).[1]

PMS55-65: "Someone who is too conscious of past times" (Questionnaire_Connotation of nostalgia_55-65-year-old Spaniards, 12 [o.t.]).[2]

CFPS55-65: "A weak person who enjoys past times" (Questionnaire_Connotation of nostalgia_55-65-year-old Spaniards, 15 [o.t.]).[3]

EFG55-65: "Someone who has the above feelings [sweet and painfully emotional], but hopefully does not always take them seriously" (Questionnaire_Connotation of nostalgia_55-65-year-old Germans, 17 [o.t.]).[4]

It is a different case among the 25 to 35-year-olds. Here predominantly positive and rather neutral descriptions can be found. The 'nostalgic person' is characterised as "[j]emand, der in der Vergangenheit schwelgt" [someone who reminiscences about the past] (FG25-35; Questionnaire_Connotation of nostalgia_25-35-year-old Germans, 14 [o.t.]), "Una persona que recuerda épocas pasadas con agrado y simpatía" [A person who remembers the past with pleasure and sympathy] (JMS25-35, Questionnaire_Connotation of nostalgia_25-35-year-old Spaniards, 14 [o.t.]), "una persona que vive de su pasado porque su presente no es bueno" [a person who lives from his/her past because his/her present is not good] (VMS25-35, Questionnaire_Connotation of nostalgia_25-35-year-old Spaniards, 16 [o.t.]), a person that "lebt in der Vergangenheit, Erinnerung" [lives in the past, memories] (DMG25-35, Questionnaire_Connotation of nostalgia_25-35-year-old Germans, 13 [o.t.]), or "[a]quella que siempre esta recordando el pasado" [the one who always

---

1   Original quotation: "Una persona que vive en el pasado y con pocas ganas de vivir en el presente" (AMS55-65, Questionnaire_Connotation of nostalgia_55-65-year-old Spaniards, 10).

2   Original quotation: "Que vive demasiado pendiente de tiempos pasados" (PMS55-65, Questionnaire_Connotation of nostalgia_55-65-year-old Spaniards, 12).

3   Original quotation: "Una persona apagada y que se recrea en tiempos pasados" (PCFS55-65, Questionnaire_Connotation of nostalgia_55-65-year-old Spaniards, 15).

4   Original quotation: "Jemand, der oben genannte Gefühle [süßlich-schmerzlich-emotional] hat, sie aber hoffentlich nicht immer ernst nimmt" (EFG55-65, Questionnaire_Connotation of nostalgia_55-65-year-old Germans, 17).

remembers the past] (AFS25-35, Questionnaire_Connotation of nostalgia_25-35-year-old Spaniards, 12 [o.t.]).

The negative adjectives, as they dominated the characterisations of the 55 to 65-year-olds, cannot be observed here. Just one 25 to 35-year-old German participant describes the 'nostalgic person' as "verträumt und realitätsfern" [dreamy and escapist] (EMG25-35, Questionnaire_Connotation of nostalgia_25-35-year-old Germans, 16 [o.t.]). However, even here a positive undertone resonates. The (German) lexical meaning of "verträumt" [dreamy] is also "in seinen Träumen, Fantasien lebend" [to live in one's dreams, fantasies] (*Duden*, 2012 [o.t.]). A synonym would be "auf Wolke sieben schweben" [to be on cloud nine] (*Duden*, 2012 [o.t.]). These differences let us draw first assumptions about the different inhibitions regarding the nostalgic emotion or its disclosure. They will be included as one context factor in the following in-depth analysis.

8.1 RECEPTION OF THE RERUNS

8.1.1 The reception of the *Knight Rider* rerun

As assumed in Part II, the results of the analysis can be described in two major blocks. A first part focuses on the *Knight Rider rerun as an artefact as a whole*. It consists of the main pattern *(Nostalgic) contextual memories*, which is divided into further sub-categories. The second block reflects the viewer's concentration on the single levels of the text. It encompasses two main patterns (1) *(Intertextual) references – roundabout nostalgia*, and, (2) *Past versus present experiences*. They shall now be commented on more closely. Since, as Dhoest (2007, p. 36) highlights, "the process of repeated viewing could lead to the revision of former memories and evaluations", an eventual earlier reception of the rerun is considered in the analysis.

8.1.1.1 Reception of the rerun as an artefact as a whole

First of all, as it has been stated previously, on a first level the rerun as a whole, or the rerun as an artefact, is in the centre of the viewer's attention. Each first-run was once integrated into a certain temporal context, programme context, genre context or socio-political context which, so it was assumed, would be remembered in the course of its reception or appropriation. Apart from that, the analytical part refers to O'Sullivan's work on early television memories, against the backdrop of which we may assume that the respective memories also work as reference points that make us remember "aspects of the difference perceived between identity or circumstances 'then' and 'now'" (O'Sullivan, 1991, p. 163).

In the conducted focus group discussions, contextual memories turned out to be one of the major patterns of memory, and, apart from that, also one of the major objects of nostalgia on the side of the participants. They again may be divided into different sub-patterns: (1) *(Nostalgic) childhood memories*, (2) *(Nostalgic) adulthood memories*, (3) *No contextual memories*, and (4) *Memories of other television series*. As assumed, on this general level a clear divide between the two age groups can be observed. Further clear differences appear among those who know the first-run and appraise it positively and those who do not know it or who appraise it negatively.

8.1.1.1.1 (Nostalgic) childhood memories

What is paradigmatic for a decisive group among the 'knowing' 25 to 35-year-olds is the case of DFG25-35. Asked what went through her mind when she watched the *Knight Rider* rerun, she answered:

DFG25-35: "I immediately think of my little brother. And of Sunday afternoons. And we were actually allowed to watch only a little television. And on Sundays we were allowed to watch just after lunchtime or so. By that time my parents had their afternoon nap. And I remember that my brother and I replayed that and that we also hollered, 'I need ya, buddy' and whatever. So somehow I remember this stupid quote. So I haven't watched it for quite a long time. Around 15 years, I guess. But I could, I knew the intro, though I couldn't have repeated it. But I knew exactly what comes next. And my brother somehow had this remote-controlled car. So I was totally influenced by that. I really liked watching it." (GD25-35_Rerun_Knight Rider_ Deutschland, 66 [o.t.])[5]

Not only does the recalled memory consist of aspects of the reception situation related to the series, to a concrete daytime, and to concrete actions in the context of the viewing of *Knight Rider*, the interviewee also undertakes an evaluation of her reception experience and a valorisation of the relevance. The series is characterised here as something special. Later she continues:

---

5   Original quotation: "Also ich muss da sofort an meinen kleinen Bruder denken. Und an Sonntagnachmittag. Und wir durften eigentlich nur eher wenig Fernseh gucken. Und sonntags da durften wir dann halt mal nach dem Essen oder so. Da ham' sich meine Eltern irgendwie hingelegt. Und ich erinner mich halt dran, dass mein Bruder und ich das dann nachgespielt ham' und auch immer so reingesprochen ham'. 'Kumpel hol mich hier raus' und keine Ahnung. Also irgendwie dieser blöde Spruch. Also ich hab' das jetzt schon ganz lang nicht mehr geguckt. Auch bestimmt 15 Jahre nimmer. Aber ich konnte das Intro, ich wusste noch mal, also ich hätt' jetzt nit sofort alles nachsagen können. Aber ich wusste genau, wann was kommt. Und mein Bruder hatte irgendwie dieses ferngesteuerte Auto davon. Also mich hat das total beeinflusst irgendwie. Also ich hab' das total gerne geguckt." (DFG25-35, GD25-35_Rerun_Knight Rider_Deutschland, 66)

DFG25-35: "But with *Knight Rider* I associate, yes, well, childhood and then we always took the sugar bowl and then we ate... sugar and Nutella with a spoon and stuff. Well, my parents. Well, that was rather around the afternoon. Two hours in which we were all alone." (GD25-35_Rerun_Knight Rider_Deutschland, 87 [o.t.])[6]

Knight Rider gained referential character to childhood, for a situation of harmony, a moment of liberty outside parental control but also for family life. In a clear nostalgic stance, this harmony is declared as being lost from today's perspective.

DFG25-35: "Well, if I may speak personally. Regarding *Knight Rider*, I'm partially, I miss this, well my parents are divorced today, my brother lives far away and a lot of things happened over the last twenty-five years. And I somehow associate it with something very personal. Well, a real nostalgia." (GD25-35_Nostalgia_Allgemein_Deutschland, 31, 32 [o.t.].[7]

Not only does the participant explicitly refer to nostalgia, the quotation also closes the circle of what has been described as the rhetoric of nostalgia by Tannock (1995). The interviewee describes (1) her childhood as a source of nostalgia and as free from negative aspects, (2) the 'lapse', be it the divorce of the parents or the brother who moved far away, and, (3) the "postlapsarian world", which lacks all the harmony described above.

DFG25-35 is well aware of the personal "retrospective classification" and that it is this high valorisation of the series' original context which gives *Knight Rider* the importance it has for her.

DFG25-35: "Well, you cannot really consider that by today's standards. [...] For me it has a high value, so to speak. But if I saw it for the first time today [it would] not have such a high value." (GD25-35_Rerun_Knight Rider_Deutschland, 219 [o.t.])[8]

---

6   Original quotation: "Aber mit *Knight Rider* verbind ich ja so Kindheit. Und dann ham' wir uns immer die Zuckerdose noch geholt und dann noch Zucker ge.. und Nutella mit dem Löffel und so. Also meine Eltern. Also das war dann so eher nachmittags so zwei Stunden, in denen wir so alleine war'n." (DFG25-35, GD25-35_Rerun_Knight Rider_Deutschland, 87)

7   Original quotation: "Also wenn ich jetzt mal ganz persönlich werden darf. Also bei *Knight Rider* bin ich teilweise, vermiss ich diese ehm, also meine Eltern sind mittlerweile geschieden, mein Bruder wohnt weit weg und es sind ganz viele Sachen passiert in den letzten fünfundzwanzig zwanzig Jahren. Und ich verbinde damit irgendwie so was ganz Persönliches. So ne wirkliche Nostalgie." (DFG25-35, GD25-35_Nostalgia_ Allgemein_ Deutschland, 31; 32)

8   Original quotation: "Also man kann das gar nit mit heutigen Maßstäben so richtig messen. [...] Für mich hat das halt 'n hohen Wert sozusagen. Aber wenn ich 's jetzt heute zum

This, however, does not mean that the nostalgia in which the memory flows into also has something of this reflexivity. The nostalgic childhood memory rather conforms to what Davis (1979, p. 18 [emphasis in the original]) describes as "simple nostalgia", namely the "largely unexamined belief that THINGS WERE BETTER [...] *THEN THAN NOW*".

Not every interviewee undertakes such an extensive review, however; the memory pattern *(Nostalgic) childhood memories* occurs also throughout the contributions of other interviewees in the age group 25 to 35, both in Germany and in Spain. Also in other cases it leads to nostalgia. Particularly the group of the 25 to 35-year-old Spaniards relate positive childhood memories to the series. Already in the commentaries during the reception, RMS25-35 notes that "I think that it is the memory of when we were children." (GS25-35_Rerun_Knight Rider_Spanien, 9 [o.t.])[9] Other participants agree. VMS25-35: "Yes, it is the memory of childhood" (GS25-35_Rerun_Knight Rider_Spanien, 10 [o.t.])[10], AFS25-35: "La infancia" [childhood] (GS25-35_Rerun_Knight Rider_Spanien, 11 [o.t.]).

Only the 25 to 35-year-old JMS25-35 recalls concrete aspects of the circumstances of reception and the situation where and with whom he watched the series (JMS25-35, GS25-35_Rerun_Knight Rider_Spanien, 14; 262). In other cases, memories are broader. The participants relate the summer months to the series. Accordingly, the childhood memories that relate to the format are wide. The participants remember summer visits to grandfather's pool, childhood games, and time spent in the countryside. In most of the cases, the childhood memory fades into a nostalgic narration that puts the better 'then' in contrast with the worse 'now'.

AFS25-35: "Three months of vacation, no worries, in the village, with the cousins, without worrying about absolutely nothing. To laugh, to play." (GS25-35_Rerun_Knight Rider_ Spanien, 210 [o.t.])[11]

---

ersten Mal sehen würde, keinen so 'n großen Wert." (DFG25-35, GD25-35_Rerun_Knight Rider_Deutschland, 219)

9   Original quotation: "Yo creo que es el recuerdo de cuando éramos niños." (RMS25-35, GS25-35_Rerun_Knight Rider_Spanien, 9)

10 Original quoation: "Sí, es el recuerdo de niño." (VMS25-35, GS25-35_Rerun_Knight Rider_Spanien, 10)

11 Original quotaion: "Tres meses de vacaciones, sin preocupaciones, en el pueblo, con los primos... sin tener que preocuparte absolutamente de nada. De reír, de jugar... ." (AFS25-35, GS25-35_Rerun_Knight Rider_Spanien, 210)

VMS25-35: "To be ten years old is priceless." (GS25-35_Rerun_Knight Rider_Spanien, 227-228 [o.t.])[12]

The childhood is remembered as a time span of harmony without "worries". Not surprisingly, when asked if the examples they saw have something to do with nostalgia, the interviewees explicitly refer to *Knight Rider*.

VMS25-35: "Yes. Surely *El coche fantástico*."
AFS25-35: "Yes. Yes."
JMS25-35: "Nostalgia of a certain age, isn't it? […]."
RMS25-35: "*El coche fantástico*, because I watched it when I was little [...].
AFS25-35: No, me too. *El coche fantástico*. It reminds you of the time when you were small. [...]."
CMS25-35: "Yes, well, I agree with them. Above all *El coche fantástico* because it reminds me of my childhood. When I was little and all that... nostalgia in this sense only... [...]."
OFS25-35: "*El coche fantástico*. Nostalgia. And [regarding] all the others nothing. There was no link to the past." (GS25-35_Nostalgia_ Allgemein_Spanien, 13 ff. [o.t.])[13]

Except for VMS25-35, who refers to the *Knight Rider* music as a "mnemonic prompt" when explaining his nostalgia, these statements are also congruent with the information on the questionnaire. As in the case of the 25-35-German DFG25-35, the positive childhood memory is inevitably related to the television series. It is like a second temporal layer that accompanies it and that makes nostalgia possible. With reference to DFG25-35, we can also describe a transnationally shared nostalgia here. Apart from that, the nostalgia is widely shared among the participants of the Spanish group where "we" references relate more obviously to the age group. Among the 25 to 35-year-old Germans, the "we" rather oscillates between family, friends, and the group.

---

12 Original quotation: "Pero tener diez años tío, eso no tiene precio." (VMS25-35, GS25-35_Rerun_Knight Rider_Spanien, 227-228)
13 Original quotation: VMS25-35: "Sí. *El coche fantástico* seguro". AFS25-35: "Sí. Sí". JMS25-35: "Nostalgia de una edad. ¿No?" [...] RMS25-35: "*El coche fantástico*, porque cuando yo lo veía era pequeño y... [...]". AFS25-35: "No, yo igual eh? *El coche fantástico*. De recordarte la época de cuándo eras pequeño. [...]". CMS25-35: "Sii, bueno, yo coincido con ellos. Más que nada *El coche fantástico* porque me recuerda a mi infancia. Cuando yo eraa pequeño y demás. [...] nostalgia en ese sentido sólo. [...]". OFS25-35: "*El coche fantástico*. Nostalgia y las demás. Nada. No han conectado coon Con tiempos pasados." (GS25-35_Nostalgia_ Allgemein_Spanien, 13 ff.)

Similar to the case of DFG25-35, these nostalgias also take the form of what was described as "simple" by Davis (1979). Only JMS25-35 adopts a more reflexive stance. In the end-discussion of the focus group he states:

JMS25-35: "[...] [T]he older you get, the better does your memory get." (GS25-35_Nostalgia_ Allgemein_Spanien, 124 [o.t.])[14]

Also in earlier moments of the discussion he was the one who more obviously reflected the simple juxtaposition of the better past against the worse present.

JMS25-35: "Everything has good and bad sides because now you can drink wine and then you couldn't. [...] Neither is it very dramatic to live the life we live today." (GS25-35_Rerun_ Knight Rider_Spanien, 221-222, 224 [o.t.])[15]

The participant's appraisal may be subsumed under what has been called "second order" or "reflexive nostalgia" by Davis (1979). Later, the interviewee even goes so far as to name the danger of nostalgic romanticising.

JMS25-35: "[...] what may happen is that it could fool our opinion if we don't filter it as we do it now." (GS25-35_Rerun_KnightRider_Spanien, 445 [o.t.]).[16]

His considerations take the form of Davis' (1979) "third order" or "interpreted nostalgia", a kind of nostalgia that "renders problematic the very reaction itself" (Davis, 1979, p. 24). Among the interviewees JMS25-35 was the only one who had seen the rerun on the morning of the discussion. At least it could be speculated that the positive childhood memory, which is linked to the memory of the series, has already been complemented by a second plane that refers to the more recent reception situation. In contrast to the memories of the other group members, here a "memory anchor" was set at a point of time which is different from the time of the first broadcast, closer to the present and not convenient as an object of nostalgia.

In other cases, nostalgia on the level of the artefact as a whole can be excluded, even though positive childhood memories may be observed. Indeed, EMG25-35 and

---

14 Original quotation: "Y cuantos más años tengas la recordarás mejor." (JMS25-35, GS25-35_Nostalgia_ Allgemein_Spanien, 124)

15 Original quotation: "Todo tiene sus malos y buenos momentos, porque ahora puedes beber vino y entonces nó [...][T]ampoco es tan dramático estar como estamos ahora." (JMS25-35GS25-35_Rerun_Knight Rider_Spanien, 221-222, 224)

16 Original quotation: "[...]que puede daar, (puede engañar a) nuestra opinióon, sino la, sino la matizamos como ahora" (JMS25-35, GS25-35_Rerun_KnightRider_Spanien, 445).

FFG25-35 of the German group of the 25 to 35-year-olds also relate *Knight Rider* to their childhood.

EMG25-35: "It actually just comes to my mind that I was a kid and loved to play and liked watching television. When I was allowed to watch it. I have no other associations." (GD25-35_Rerun_Knight Rider_Deutschland, 31 [o.t.])[17]

FMG25-35: "Well, I've got lots of memories as well. I remember very well how I was sitting there with my brother and watching it. [...]." (GD25-35_Rerun_Knight Rider_Deutschland, 114 [o.t.])[18]

Both later state that they felt nostalgia in the course of the reception. However, in both cases it is rather the positive emotion related to single aspects of the series than the series as a whole, respectively a context memory evoked here that is most relevant to the participants and that becomes the object of the longing. It will be commented in a following section.

8.1.1.1.2 (Nostalgic) adulthood memories
Also in the age group of the 55 to 65-year-olds, contextual memories were related to *Knight Rider*. However, since the first-run fell into different life spans of the interviewees, the memories are distinctly coloured. Similarities to the previously explained childhood nostalgia could only be found in the case of MFS55-65. Apart from the fact that the participant classifies *Knight Rider* positively, she recalls a time of personal freedom with the series.

MFS55-65: "I used to watch it, I didn't have children, I was single and I liked watching *El coche fantástico*. *El coche fantástico* was a trendsetter." (GS55-65_Rerun Rider_Spanien Knight, 60; 62 [o.t.])[19]

Later the participant is more explicit.

---

17 Original quotation: "Fällt mir eigentlich nur ein, dass ich ein Kind war und gerne gespielt hab und gern Fernseh geguckt habe. Wenn ich das gucken durfte. Andere Assoziationen kommen da irgendwie nicht." (EMG25-35, GD25-35_Rerun_Knight Rider_Deutschland, 31)

18 Original quotation: "Also ich hab' auch ganz viele Erinnerungen da. Also ich weiß ganz genau wie ich mit meinem Bruder da saß und das angeguckt habe. [...]." (FFG25-35, GD25-35_Rerun_Knight Rider_Deutschland, 114)

19 Original quotation: "Lo veía. No tenía familia, no tenía hijos, era soltera y me gustaba *El coche fantástico*. Rompía moldes *El coche fantástico*." (MFS55-65, GS55-65_Rerun Knight Rider_Spanien, 60; 62)

MFS55-65: "… then, when I was single, when I didn't have problems, it was a very different time than today. These things are very […] how these times were." (GS55-65_Rerun Knight Rider_Spanien, 90 [o.t.])[20]

In a nostalgic argument, MFS55-65 puts the 'prelapsarian' world, her life as a single woman, and a time span she remembers as having no problems, in contrast with the 'postlapsarian' today. Her statement has a clear stance of 'irretrievability' (see also Cook, 2005, p. 2, on nostalgia in general) and correlates to what Davis (1979) describes as "simple" nostalgia. In contrast to the 25 to 35-year-olds where *Knight Rider* and the childhood memories attached to it exist independent of the socio-political context of the 1980s in general, she explicitly refers to "aquella época" [these times]. Here, it can only be speculated that it is the atmosphere of departure that still surrounded the late years of transition in Spain that is meant here, and that plays a certain role in the longing. The implicit nostalgia that appears during the focus group is, however, not explicitly manifested by the participant, neither during the discussion nor in the questionnaire. In the latter, MFS55-65 indeed describes the experience of nostalgia but refers to *Mad Men*, which was shown at a later point in the group discussion. Compared to the first one, the latter experience is obviously given a higher relevance.

In general, the participant's "retrospective classification" clearly differs from that of others of the same age group. Rather dominant among the 55 to 65-year-olds is a memory pattern that relates *Knight Rider* to viewing experiences in the family circle. A total of four interviewees in the age group of the 55 to 65-year-olds, more mothers than fathers, recall *Knight Rider* in the context of a common reception with their children.

PCFS55-65: "I remember watching it with my children. We said whatever whenever. But when you watch it now, you say, Oh my God! What did we watch?" (GS55-65_Rerun Knight Rider_Spanien, 50 [o.t.])[21]

---

20 Original quotation: "… en la que estaba soltera, en la que no tenía problemas, era una fase muy diferente a la de ahora. Esto son cosas muy (… de decir) como estaba aquella época." (MFS55-65, GS55-65_Rerun Knight Rider_Spanien, 90)

21 Original quotation: "La memoria era cuando la veía con mis hijos decíamos no sé que no sé cuando. Pero ahora lo ves y dices: ¡Madre mía! ¡Que veíamos!" (PCFS55-65, GS55-65_Rerun Knight Rider_Spanien, 50)

BFG55-65: "Somehow I must have seen Knight Rider with our older son. And I think I watched it in order to see what he was watching. I always found it a little silly. I was also not all that interested in it." (GD55-65_Nostalgia_ Allgemein_Deutschland, 31-37 [o.t.])[22]

HFG55-65: "*Knight Rider* and all that nonsense, any series that existed was watched, almost every night, for hours. And of course there are always such communication interfaces, where one watches something like that, where one watches with the child as a parent." (GD55-65_Rerun_Knight Rider_Deutschland, 165 [o.t.])[23]

IMD55-65: "I can only remember my rules. Because I always used to say 'only one show per day', and then the quarrels started." (GD55-65_Rerun_Knight Rider_Deutschland, 221 [o.t.])[24]

In all cases neither a manifest, outspoken nostalgia nor an implicit, nostalgic rhetoric can be observed. Rather the contrary is the case. If the series is not already recalled in a negative context, at least the "retrospective classification" is accordingly. This may be less obvious in the case of the 55 to 65-year-old PCFS55-65 who remembers a situation commenting on *Knight Rider*. However, she also gives the series a low value from today's perspective. Later, the participant says:

PCFS55-65: "Well, I don't know. We watched it together because they [the children] had come home from school, we were there and we watched it, normal. Just like I watch a series now with my grandchildren." (GS55-65_Rerun Knight Rider_Spanien, 58 [o.t.])[25]

Both 'then' and from today's perspective, watching the series was something "normal", something that is not especially relevant to her.

---

22 Original quotation: "*Knight Rider*, das muss ich irgendwie mit unserem älteren Sohn gesehen haben. Und da hab' ich glaub ich eher geguckt, um zu gucken, was der sich da ansieht. … Ich fand das damals immer 'n bisschen blöd. Hat mich auch nicht so interessiert." (BFD55-65, GD55-65_Nostalgia_ Allgemein_Deutschland, 31-37)

23 Original quotation: "*Knight Rider* und eh allen Quatsch, jede Serie, die es überhaupt gab, die wurde geguckt. Beinahe, jeden Abend, Stunden lang. Und eh natürlich gibt's dann immer so 'ne Kommunikationsschnittstellen, wo man dann so was guckt mitguckt als Elternteil." (HFD55-65, GD55-65_Rerun_Knight Rider_Deutschland, 165)

24 Original quotation: "Ich hab' da immer nur mein Reglement im Kopf. Weil ich dann immer sagte, nur eine Sache am Tag gucken, und dann der Streit dann." (IMG55-65, GD55-65_Rerun_Knight Rider_Deutschland, 221)

25 Original quotation: "Bueno. Pues no sé. Lo veíamos juntos, porque habían salido del colegio, estábamos ahí y lo veíamos, normal. Como ahora veo una serie con mis nietas." (PCFS55-65, GS55-65_Rerun Knight Rider_Spanien, 58)

It is a similar case regarding BFG55-65. She also recalls a general irrelevance of the series and furthermore a negative past valorisation ("I always found it a little silly" [o.t.]). The memories that the 55 to 65-year-old HFG55-65 and the 55 to 65-year-old IMG55-65 relate to *Knight Rider* are almost all negative. While IMG55-65 foregrounds the memory of the fights with his daughter that resulted from the TV viewing restrictions he imposed, HFG55-65 recalls that she was really upset about her daughter watching such a 'low-quality' television series. At another moment she says:

HFG55-65: "... What comes to my mind today is that I always thought: What shit is she watching? Why doesn't she watch *Monitor* [a political magazine programme] or something?" (GD55-65_Rerun_Knight Rider_Deutschland, 226 [o.t.])[26]

Above all in this last statement, HFG55-65's argument also adopts reference points to what was subsumed under the label "'ideology of mass culture'" by Ang (1985, p. 94). "In this ideology some cultural forms [...] are *tout court* labelled 'bad mass culture'. 'Mass culture' is a denigrating term, which arouses definitely negative associations." (Ang, 1985, p. 94) In any case, it is the negative connotation that lies upon the series and impedes every nostalgic stance.

8.1.1.1.3 No contextual memories

A decisive group among the interviewees did not relate such contextual memories to the series. On the one hand, unsurprisingly, these are the participants who have never watched *Knight Rider*. Among the 25 to 35-year-olds, this is CFG25-35 who neither knows the first-run nor the rerun, and a larger group, four out of nine in the German group (DFG55-65, FFG55-65, GFG55-65, and CMG55-65) and one out of seven in the Spanish group (FCF55-65) of the 55 to 65-year-olds. On the other hand, a decisive group of interviewees said they had watched the series but did not relate contextual memories to it. BMG25-35 explains this lack as follows.

BMG25-35: "Uh. [I have] no real memories. Didn't really watch that back then. [...] *Knight Rider* is not my thing." (BMG25-35, GD25-35_Rerun_Knight Rider_Deutschland, 147; 149 [o.t.])[27]

---

26 Original quotation: "... Was mir heute so in den Kopf kommt, dass ich immer so dachte, was guckt sie sich denn da für einen Dreck an. Warum guckt sie denn nicht irgendwie Monitor oder so was?" (HFG55-65, GD55-65_Rerun_Knight Rider_Deutschland, 226)

27 Original quotation: "Uh. Gar keine richtigen Erinnerungen. Hab' das damals nicht so verfolgt. [...] Also *Knight Rider* ist auch nicht so meine Sache." (BMG25-35, GD25-35_Rerun_Knight Rider_Deutschland, 147; 149 [o.t.])

This similarly applies to GMG25-35 and AMG25-35.

GMG25-35: "Yes, actually I also don't remember much. [...] Well, I think I also watched it relatively late. I suppose in '95 or so. But then only once in a while. And never really [...]" (GD25-35_Rerun_Knight Rider_Deutschland, 103 [o.t.]).[28]

AMG25-35: "Both then and now, this is something I've watched, and then it was over, and then I didn't waste even one second thinking about it." (GD25-35_Rerun_Knight Rider_Deutschland, 56 [o.t.])[29]

AMG25-35: "... you were just bored and then you watched the series. And that's why I don't have any strong emotions about it." (GD25-35_Nostalgia_Allgemein_Deutschland, 83 [o.t.])[30]

AMG25-35 refers even explicitly to the lack of "strong emotions" in the context of the series. Also ZFS25-35 of the Spanish group, who said earlier she did not remember anything in the context of *Knight Rider* (see ZFS25-35, GS25-35_Rerun_Knight Rider_Spanien, 253-254), highlights the irrelevance that the series had for her.

ZFS25-35: "For me *El coche fantástico* was a series that well ... was at lunchtime and it was what you watched because it was on television, but it wasn't anything that you couldn't miss. That's true in my case." (GS25-35_Rerun_KnightRider_Spanien, 306 [o.t.])[31]

She also says that her childhood was not a time that was worth longing for.

---

28 Original quotation: "Ja ich kann mich eigentlich auch nicht an viel erinnern. Ja ich glaub, ich hab das auch relativ spät erst geguckt. Ich schätz mal so 95 oder so. Aber dann auch nur hin und wieder mal. Und nie wirklich. Ich fand's damals schon wo ich so sechzehn siebzehn war, schon 'n biss(h)chen al(h)bern ((lacht))." (GMG25-35, GD25-35_Rerun_Knight Rider_Deutschland, 103)

29 Original quotation: "[D]amals, wie auch heute, ist das für mich was, was ich angeguckt hab, und dann war 's vorbei, und dann hab' ich nicht mehr eine Sekunde daran gedacht." (AMG25-35, GD25-35_Rerun_Knight Rider_Deutschland, 56)

30 Original quotation: "... man [hat] da halt grad Langeweile gehabt und deswegen hat man dann halt die Serie geschaut. Und deswegen hab' ich keine starken Emotionen da." (AMG25-35, GD25-35_Nostalgia_Allgemein_Deutschland, 83)

31 Original quotation: "Para mí *El coche fantástico* era una serie que eso... que estaba al medio día y que era la que veías porque era la que estaba, pero tampoco era algo que no te podías perder. La verdad. En mi caso."(ZFS25-35, GS25-35_Rerun_KnightRider_Spanien, 306)

ZFS25-35: "Childhood was hard for me. Isn't it? In contrast I remember school as if it was a … lost paradise?" (GS25-35_Nostalgia_ Allgemein_Spanien, 106 [o.t.])[32]

In other cases, the series seems to have left too few impressions that its context could be remembered from a present position. For example the case of PMS55-65. He emphasises:

PMS55-65: "I have tried to remember a chapter. I didn't remember it. I tried to put myself into the situation when I used to watch it because I remember the topic of the chapter and I tried to put myself into that moment. Now, in whatever context I watched it, well, nothing." (GS55-65_Rerun Knight Rider_Spanien, 93 [o.t.])[33]

Reviewing these responses, also in comparison to the previously described cases where the sense of longing emerges, we may highlight that nostalgia on the level of the artefact as a whole is excluded for audiences who do not know the respective television programme. Furthermore, there is an interrelation of high relevance and context memory and high relevance and the viewers' 'own A nostalgia'.

8.1.1.1.5 Television 'then' and 'now'

Apart from memories that refer to the participants' lifeworlds, *Knight Rider* as an artefact is embedded in the context of other specific television series or memories of television 'then' and 'now' in general. In both cases a clear gap between the two age groups can be observed, yet with few territorial differences.

For the 25 to 35-year-old Spaniards *Knight Rider* is integrated into the memory along with other series such as *The A-Team*, *MacGyver* or *V*. When prompted, they start a debate:

CMS25-35: "Well, I don't know …"
VMS25-35: "More than *El coche fantástico*, yes. *El Equipo A [The A-Team]*. [...]"
JMS25-35: "One big competitor at the time … surely … er … *MacGyver*. [...]"
OFS25-35: "And *V*."
AFS25-35: "I liked *MacGyver* a lot. [...]"

---

32 Original quotation: "La infancia, más dura para mí ¿no? Y en cambio luego recuerdo la Escuela como si fuese aquello… El paraíso perdido. ¿noo?" (ZFS25-35, GS25-35_Nostalgia_ Allgemein_Spanien, 106)

33 Original quotation: "He intentado recordar un capítulo. [...] Yo no lo recordaba. Yo intentaba ponerme en la situación de cuando lo veía porque recuerdo el tema de este capítulo y he intentado ponerme en aquel momento. [...] Ahora en que contexto lo veía, pues, tampoco." (PMS55-65, GS55-65_Rerun Knight Rider_Spanien, 93)

ZFS25-35: "[...] I preferred *MacGyver*, for example." (GS25-35_Rerun_Knight Rider_ Spanien, 276-315 [o.t.])[34]

Apart from the fact that the time span of the first-run is decisive here, there is another noticeable point: Only VMS25-35 and ZFS25-35, the first of whom dislikes single aspects of the series, as it will be commented in a later section of this analysis, and the second of whom assigns a general position of irrelevance to *Knight Rider*, explicitly compare the series to others which are given more importance.

This similarly applies to other group discussions. In the group of the 25 to 35-year-old Germans, DFG25-35 (GD25-35_Rerun_Knight Rider_Deutschland, 84; 94) remembers *Knight Rider* spontaneously together with other 1980s programmes, such as *Li-La-Launebär* (RTLplus et al., 1988-1994) or likewise *Das A-Team* (Das Erste, 1987). Both series are not evaluated as being better or more relevant by the interviewee, to whom *Knight Rider* had played an important role in her childhood. BMG25-35 instead puts *Knight Rider* in contrast with Bud Spencer films.

BMG25-35: "[Regarding Bud Spencer,] I have much more vivid memories. Mhm. All these films. They impressed me more." (GD25-35_Rerun_Knight Rider_Deutschland, 348 [o.t.])[35]

Also the 55 to 65-year-old FMS55-65 of the Spanish group says:

FMS55-65: "*El Equipo A [The A-Team]* was more fun. *El Equipo A [The A-Team]* was very funny. This one wasn't funny. I didn't like it so much. The car that speaks." (GS55-65_Rerun Knight Rider_Spanien, 75 [o.t.])[36]

Here the latter two interviewees did not feel nostalgia in the broad context of *Knight Rider* as an artefact. Accordingly, they name other artefacts, which they give more relevance to, and we can assume, which are established as alternative potential nostalgia triggers. In general, an attempt to arrange the media memories in a kind of

---

34 Original quotation: CMS25-35: "Bueno, no lo sé". VMS25-35: "Más que *El coche fantástico* sí. *El Equipo A*. [...]". JMS25-35: "Una gran competencia en la época... seguramente...eh.. *MacGyver*. [...]". OFS25-35: "Y *V*". AFS25-35: "*MacGyver* gustaba mucho. [...]".ZFS25-35: "Pero *MacGyver* me gustaba más, por ejemplo." (GS25-35_Rerun_Knight Rider_Spanien, 276-315)

35 Original quotation: "[Ich hab' bei Bud Spencer] viel lebhaftere Erinnerungen. Ehm. Die ganzen Filme. Die ham' mich schon mehr beeindruckt." (BMG25-35, GD25-35_Rerun_Knight Rider_Deutschland, 348)

36 Original quotation: "*El Equipo A* era más divertido. *El Equipo A* era una serie muy divertida. Esta no era divertida. No me gustaba tanto. El coche que habla." (FMS55-65, GS55-65_Rerun Knight Rider_Spanien, 75)

hierarchy was observed. Only those series that could be given a high value or, as Kompare (2009) says, that underwent a positive "retrospective classification" on the part of the audiences, may work as nostalgia triggers at least on the level of the artefact as a whole. This pattern does not appear among other 55 to 65-year-olds. Obviously, these interviewees see the series less integrated into a programme context and slot. The only interviewee among the 55 to 65-year-olds who remembered the programme context is the 55 to 65-year-old PCFS55-65 who had watched the series together with her children.

It is a different case regarding broader memories, which contrast past and present television. However, here a gap between the age groups can be observed, too. While among the 25 to 35-year-olds statements on television 'then' and 'now' rather support the positive valorisation of the past that already had been made in the context of *(nostalgic) childhood memories*, in the group of the 55 to 65-year-olds an entirely non-nostalgic standpoint can be observed.

Among the 25 to 35-year-old Spaniards, the interviewees came to discuss the few television channels in the 1980s ("... no había otra cosa, claro" [there was no other thing, sure] (OFS25-35, GS25-35_Rerun_Knight Rider_Spanien, 365 [o.t.]), or the low amount of seasons a television series once had (VMS25-35, GS25-35_Rerun_Knight Rider_Spanien, 360-361). Also, the generally "bad" quality of a television that is remembered as being black-and-white[37] is part of the discussion.

AFS25-35: "Of course, it was a bad TV and it was black and white and that, and, yes, I was there remembering when .... That it was summer and yes, it's true, it's true...." (GS25-35_Rerun_Knight Rider_Spanien, 206 [o.t.])[38]

However, even with reference to implicit criteria of quality, this comparison could result in a negative evaluation of past television, together with an invariably positive undertone; in part it is a general fascination and turns into the narration of a better childhood.

It is a similar case among the 25 to 35-year-old Germans. It has been mentioned previously that in the case of DFG25-35, parental television restriction holds its part in the high valorisation of *Knight Rider*. As further support for the special status of the series she says that the family, as she states, "had only four or five channels or so. In general, there were fewer channels. And so it was more valuable anyway."

---

37 Bear in mind, that colour transmission in Spain was already introduced in 1969 (Deacon, 1999, p. 312). However, as Palacio (2012, p. 9) indicates, still in 1977, only 10 out of 100 television sets owned by the Spaniards were colour television sets.

38 Original quotation: "Claro, era una tele mala y era en blanco y negro. Y eso y sí. Que estaba ahí recordando cuando... que era en verano y sí, es cierto, es cierto... ." (AFS25-35, GS25-35_Rerun_Knight Rider_Spanien, 206)

(GD25-35_Rerun_Knight Rider_Deutschland, 219 [o.t.])[39] Also EMG25-35 elevates the series to a scarce commodity ("When I was allowed to watch it") (GD25-35_Rerun_Knight Rider_Deutschland, 31 [o.t.])[40] and in doing this, underpins its particular status.[41]

A different argument can be observed among the 55 to 65-year-olds. They also compare past to present television in the context of *Knight Rider*, yet with different outcomes.

PCFS55-65: "Well, [the series] are much better made. Yes, usually, yes."

FMS55-65: "There are more media."

PMS55-65: "There are more media. Better."

FMS55-65: "Superior technical means ... "

FCFS55-65: "The instruments are more sensitive, more perfect."

MFS55-65: "Movies have advanced, [also] the series and everything."

PCFS55-65: "And furthermore there are good directors who make the series."

AMS55-65: "Martin Scorsese."

PMS55-65: "In *Numb3rs*, you can like it or not, but they are very well done. Or for example the other one... the one by Ridley Scott." (GS55-65_Rerun KnightRider_Spanien, 152-161 [o.t.])[42]

Regardless of whether it concerns the quantity of existing media, the technical possibilities or the quality of television series, the present clearly compares favourably with the past. Also with respect to the quantity of the programme offer, the interviewees are far away from a positive valorisation of the past.

---

39 Original quotation: "wir [die Familie] hatten da irgendwie nur vier oder fünf Sender oder so. Also generell gab's ja viel weniger Programme. Und dann hatte das ja eh schon so 'n andern Wert." (DFG25-35, GD25-35_Rerun_Knight Rider_Deutschland, 219)

40 Original quotation: "Wenn ich das gucken durfte." (EMG25-35, GD25-35_Rerun_Knight Rider_Deutschland, 31)

41 Already this elaboration can be assumed to be a 'romantisation' of the past. According to information he gave in the questionnaire, with an intermediate television-consumption around three to four hours per day in his youth, EMG25-35 clearly was one of the frequent viewers.

42 Original quotation: PCFS55-65: "Es que [las series] están mucho mejor hechas. Sí normalmente sí". FMS55-65: "Hay más medios". PMS55-65: "Hay más medios. Mejor". FMS55-65: "Medios técnicos muy superiores". FCFS55-65: "Las máquinas son más sensibles, más perfectas". MFS55-65: "Ha evolucionado el cine, las series y todo". PCFS55-65: "No además hay directores buenos, que hacen series". AMS55-65: "Martin Scorsese". PMS55-65: "En *Numb3rs* te puede gustar o no, pero está super trabajada. O por ejemplo aquellos ... la de Ridley Scott." (GS55-65_Rerun KnightRider_Spanien, 152-161)

PCFS55-65: "Excuse me, another thing is, as AMS55-65 says, we had two channels. Then we had two channels and now there are ..."

AMS55-65: "The offer was very limited. [...]"

FCFS55-65: "It was either that or nothing." (GS55-65_Rerun Knight Rider_Spanien, 65-71 [o.t.])[43]

Less pronounced is the pattern among the 55 to 65-year-old German group. However, the reduced past programme offer is also discussed here.

GFG55-65: "And very early when we started to watch television."

DMG55-65: "[(yes, there was only)]"

FFG55-65: "Yes, there was only ARD." (GD55-65_Rerun_Knight Rider_Deutschland, 137-140 [o.t.])[44]

It turns into a reflection about the introduction of private television at the time of *Knight Rider*[45] whose implicit negative valorisation serves the necessary explanation for those among the interviewees who never saw the series (see GD55-65_Rerun_Knight Rider_Deutschland, 133).

8.1.1.2 Reception of nostalgia on the single levels of the text

Against the backdrop of the theoretical part and in the course of the television analysis, it has been assumed that nostalgia may be provoked on every single level of the text. This was confirmed in the course of the group discussions. With regard to the single levels of the text, different patterns of reception may be explained, some of which contain concrete examples of nostalgia.

In a first step, however, the single levels have to call the attention of the audiences. It has been proposed that the dislocation of a first-run into a new context as rerun may create frictions that generate attention on single artefacts of the series.

---

43 Original quotation: PCFS55-65: "Perdon, otra cosa es también, como dice [...][AMS55-65], que teníamos dos canales. En aquellos tiempos teníamos dos canales, y ahora hay..". AMS55-65: "La oferta era muy limitada. [...]". FCFS55-65: "Era o esto o nada." (GS55-65_Rerun Knight Rider_Spanien, 65-71)

44 Original quotation: GFG55-65: "Und ganz früher, als wir anfingen zu fernsehn ..". DMG55-65: "[(ja, da gab's ja nur)]..". FFG55-65: "Ja, da gab's ja nur ARD." (GD55-65_Rerun_Knight Rider_Deutschland, 137-140)

45 GMG55-65: "Yes, well, it was in the '80s when private television started." (GMG55-65, GD55-65_Rerun_Knight Rider_Deutschland, 140 [o.t.]) Original quotation: "Jaja also in den 80ern ging's los, was privates Fernsehn anging." (GMG55-65, GD55-65_Rerun_Knight Rider_Deutschland, 140)

As shown in the analytical part, from narration to camera, montage, lighting and props and the characters, this is also the case regarding *Knight Rider*.

The reception study confirms this hypothesis. First and foremost, all of these levels call the attention of the interviewees, independent of age group, gender or country. Participants refer to the simple good-bad dichotomies the series exposes, or highlight the "plumpe Handlung" [crude storyline]. The formal level is also a subject of the discussion. "Allein schon die Schrift!" [Just the font!] emphasises AMG25-35. As PCFS55-65 does, he also refers to the 1980s' colour range.

AMG25-35: "That's such a colour scheme, probably also due to the film material from back then. One can immediately see that this is one of those series of the past." (GD25-35_Rerun_Knight Rider_Deutschland, 75 [o.t.])[46]

Later fashion, props and style are an issue.

AMG25-35: "[When I saw this now, [I thought] about the fashion] Yes, about the fashion. About these pants, the tight tank-tops under there, about the shirts with the collar, well, this retro fashion. Otherwise, I was not interested. The hairstyle ...." (GD55-65_Rerun_Knight Rider_Deutschland, 182 [o.t.])[47]

FCFS55-65: "You see it in the hairstyle, the fashion and by that you can already tell that it is from this era." (GS55-65_Rerun Knight Rider_Spanien, 108 [o.t.])[48]

Also camera and sound attract the attention of the interviewees.

AMS55-65: "Static camera [...]." (GS55-65_Rerun Knight Rider_Spanien, 32 [o.t.])[49]

---

46 Original quotation: "Das ist ja so 'ne Art von Farbgebung wahrscheinlich auch durch das Filmmaterial von damals. Man sieht sofort, dass das von einer dieser Serien von früher ist." (AMG25-35, GD25-35_Rerun_Knight Rider_Deutschland, 75)

47 Original quotation: "[Als ich das jetzt gesehn hab, ich hab an die Mode] Ja, an die Mode. An diese Hose, an den engen Pullunder da drunter, an die Oberhemden mit den Kragen also ne, also das so diese Retro, Mode. Ansonsten hat mich das nicht interessiert. Die Frisur." (GD55-65_Rerun_Knight Rider_Deutschland, 182)

48 Original quotation: "Se ve, se ve por los peinados, por la moda y por eso ya lo ves. Que es de aquella época." (FCFS55-65, GS55-65_Rerun Knight Rider_Spanien, 108)

49 Original quotation: "Cámara fija [...]" (AMS55-65, GS55-65_Rerun Knight Rider_ Spanien, 32).

DMG55-65: "Normal camera position. Just as every series was back then." (GD55-65_Rerun_Knight Rider_Deutschland, 111 [o.t.])[50]

DMG55-65: "Also regarding the sounds. That's all the same. It's just a little different. Basically series were handled like that back then." (GD55-65_Rerun_Knight Rider_Deutschland, 65 [o.t.])[51]

Whether, as it was assumed in the theoretical part, the past is later shown as being worth longing for or not depends upon the text itself but also on factors of context and reception, as will be shown in the following section. Already in the statements quoted here it is evident that the objects of attention are mostly already integrated into a context of references and that they are the subjects of different valorisations.

8.1.1.2.1 (Intertextual) references – roundabout nostalgia

As assumed in the television analysis, the rerun has the 'connotation of pastness', also for those audiences who do not know the first-run. In the group discussions it is shown that *Knight Rider*, on the one hand, stands for the 1980s – be it regarding the props or the aesthetic it exposes – on the other hand, it refers to other, mainly 1980s cultural products.

Independent of whether the interviewees knew the first-run or not, each level leads to respective associations. In parts, this has already been shown regarding the new differential quality of the rerun. Here, the 'don't know' FCFS55-65 highlights, for example, that hairstyles and fashion refer to the 1980s (see FCFS55-65, GS55-65_Rerun Knight Rider_Spanien, 108). The 'don't know' EFG55-65 from the 55 to 65-year-old Germans starts thinking about how her own hairstyle might have looked in the 1980s (GD55-65_Rerun_Knight Rider_Deutschland, 143), again others focus on the typical 1980s' clothes (see e.g. PCFS55-65: "Hombre, los (abrigos) que lleva ves que son de hace años" [Well, the coats he wears, you can see clearly that they are from years ago] (GS55-65_Rerun Knight Rider_Spanien, 107 [o.t.])).

In the television analysis of *Knight Rider* it was assumed that the newly gained reference to its temporal background makes the rerun a potential trigger for 'artefact nostalgia' or viewers' 'own artefact nostalgia', always in case that the "retrospective classification" is accordingly. This is also supported by the group discussion. At least in one case these associations lead to nostalgia on the side of the viewers – a kind of

---

50 Original quotation: "Ganz normale Kamerahaltung. Wie eben auch alle Serien damals waren." (DMG55-65, GD55-65_Rerun_Knight Rider_Deutschland, 111)

51 Original quotation: "Auch von den Geräuschen her. Das ist ja alles dasselbe. Is nur 'n bisschen anders. Im Grunde wurden Serien damals so gehandhabt." (DMG55-65, GD55-65_Rerun_Knight Rider_Deutschland, 65)

'roundabout' nostalgia, as it shall be called. The respective participant, the 25 to 35-year-old CFG25-35, never saw *Knight Rider;* however, she says:

"... one is also somehow transported back into that time when one had a similar hairstyle. Wore similar clothes. A time when all these things were up to date, when one saw it. If you look back, you almost get a little nostalgic ... just regarding the '80s, what ugly clothes you wore. But otherwise ... I relate nothing more to the series. Because I haven't seen it."
M: "But why nostalgic when they [the clothes] were so ugly?"
CFG25-35: "Well, because you were still a child. You were still innocent back then and did not have to work yet." (GD25-35_Rerun_KnightRider_Deutschland, 252 - 254 [o.t.])[52]

CFG25-35 starts thinking about the 1980s and makes a "referential framing"[53] that sets the props of the series in relation to her own lifeworld. Despite the lack of memories related to *Knight Rider*, the hairstyle and clothes the series shows became representatives of an era. The narration of CFG25-35 here takes the form of nostalgia. For the participant the objects are related to a time of childhood harmony that she retrospectively classifies as positive and that she declares as irretrievable from today's perspective. The rhetoric of nostalgia is not concentrated on the artefact as such, so that it could be categorised as 'artefact nostalgia', but on the (personal) context the artefact refers to. As a result, we may talk of viewer's 'own artefact nostalgia'. A reflexive stance cannot be observed.

In the questionnaire, however, this nostalgia is not confirmed. The participant indeed refers to nostalgia here, but talks about "Kindheit" [childhood] and the "Rahmen, in dem Fernsehen konsumiert wurde" [the frame in which television was consumed back then] (CMG25-35, Questionnaire_Connotation of nostalgia_25-35-year-old Germans, 19 [o.t.]). The reason for this change of mind can be found in the

---

52   Original quotation: CFG25-35: "... Man ist natürlich auch irgendwie zurückversetzt in die Zeit, in der man auch 'ne ähnliche Frisur hatte, ähnliche Klamotten anhatte. Und in der das dann damals auch alles zeitgemäß war, in der man das gesehn hat. Wenn man da jetzt zurück blickt dann ist man ja fast so 'n bisschen nostalgisch eben so für die 80er, was man da für hässliche Klamotten anhatte. Aber ich verbinde eben sonst mit der Serie nichts. Weil ich die ja nicht geguckt habe." M: "Aber wieso denn nostalgisch, wenn die so hässlich waren?" C: "Najaaa. Weil man da halt noch 'n Kind war. Da war man noch unschuldig und musste noch nicht arbeiten." (GD25-35_Rerun_KnightRider_Deutschland, 252-254)

53   The term goes back to Liebes und Katz (1990). "These authors distinguish referential from critical framing. If an audience member uses a referential framing in talking about Dallas, it means that she relates the events of the programme to her own life. Critical framings, on the other hand, are used when audiences comment on the acting, sets and locations, narrative structures or themes of the programme" (Abercrombie and Longhurst, 2007, p. 142).

further course of the discussion. In the end-phase of the focus group, the participant talks extensively about the special status early television consumption had in her childhood.[54] As in the context of previously mentioned childhood memories, early television consumption is here described as a scarce commodity of great importance. Retrospectively, this context memory is given more relevance. The earlier description, also explicitly categorised as making her a "little nostalgic", is obviously rivalled by the later prompted memories that became the object of the manifested nostalgia.

Similar observations can be made in the case of CMG55-65. His 'stream of consciousness' is, however, inspired by the reference of *Knight Rider* to other film and television programmes. The participant's memory is jogged by an intertextual film reference on the level of the intro:

CMG55-65: "Well, during the opening credits I immediately had memories of *Easy Rider*. A modern version. This ride through the desert. It came to my mind. And I found it quite pleasant for a moment, because I found that the *Easy Rider* time was a good time. It was not so much this scene. [...] Well, it was '68, I think. Yes, I was sixteen then. [...] Long ago and it was just great to sit in the cinema, yes. *Steppenwolf, Born to be Wild*, etc. [...] Yes, I grew up in cramped conditions. And probably found that great back then. The vastness of the landscape, and then, on the motorbike, which I did not have, and then, yeah, to be able to drive under a wide sky." (GD55-65_Rerun_KnightRider_Deutschland, 31-55 [o.t.])[55]

---

54 CMG25-35 states here: "But I was actually allowed to watch only a little television and due to that I found that always great. I remember that I always looked at the clock and I knew, when it shows that time, it will start. And then I can watch it. For this reason, it was always a highlight. And I actually did not watch series or films out of boredom, but it was always planned, already days before." (CFG25-35, GD25-35_Nostalgia_Allgemein_Deutschland, 95 [o.t.]) Original quotation: "Aber ich durfte auch damals wenig Fernseh gucken und fand das dann immer ganz toll. Ich weiß noch, dass ich dann auf die Uhr geguckt hab und wusste, wenn der große Zeiger da ist, dann fängt das jetzt an. Und dann kann ich das jetzt gucken. Also so war das immer 'n Highlight. Und ich hab' auch eigentlich nich aus Langeweile Serien oder Filme geguckt, sondern das war immer geplant, dann eh, schon Tage vorher." (CFG25-35, GD25-35_Nostalgia_Allgemein_Deutschland, 95)

55 Original quotation: "Also bei diesem Vorspann hatte ich eh sofort die Erinnerung *Easy Rider*. Moderne Auffrischung. Diese Fahrt durch die Wüste. Das fiel mir ein dabei. Und das fand ich 'n Moment lang ganz angenehm, weil ich halt diese *Easy Rider* Zeit gut fand. Das war gar nicht so sehr diese Szene. [...] So sixty eight war das so. Glaub ich. JA, da war ich sechzehn, damals. [...] Lange her halt und es war klasse, da im Kino zu sitzen, ja. Steppenwolf, Born to be Wild, et cetera. [...] Ja, ich bin in beengten Verhältnissen aufgewachsen. Und fand das wahrscheinlich toll damals. Diese Weite der Landschaft und

More concretely, it is an intertextual reference to the mise-en-scène of the 1960s film *Easy Rider* (Hopper, 1969) that works as "mnemonic prompt" for the 1960s film reception and its circumstances. This is very similar to what DFG25-35 had described. It is the positive appraisal of the *"Easy Rider*-time" but also memories of positive emotions in the context of the reception of the film that lead to a positive valorisation of the past experience and which makes this part of the past a potential object of nostalgia.

Further statements of the interviewee suggest an interpretation as nostalgia. The interviewee underlines here, "the stuff from the '60s totally touched me. When I was a teenager." (GD55-65_Rerun_KnightRider_Deutschland, 233 [o.t.])[56] Later he says that "We are confronted with ourselves." (GD55-65_Rerun_KnightRider_Deutschland, 233 [o.t.])[57] It is these two points, the memory of the 1960s time span and the self-confrontation, which make CMG55-65 describe *The Avengers* as an object of nostalgia in the questionnaire. We can only assume that the interviewee also feels nostalgia in the context of *Knight Rider*. However, in this specific example neither a nostalgic rhetoric that explicitly opposes the positively remembered past and the worse present nor an explicit classification of the experience under the label of nostalgia on the side of the interviewee may be observed. Obviously, CMG55-65 also gives another nostalgic experience more relevance, which shall become manifest in his statement in the questionnaire.

In general and apart from this case, it can be stated that the series' single levels are also integrated into a net of references by the interviewees. Not only, but mainly 1980s television series are named. Again, a generational gap can be observed where the original target of the respective series plays a major role. Thus, among the 25 to 35-year olds again *The A-Team* is of relevance.

RMS25-35: "These are the same producers as *El Equipo A [The A-Team]*, it's the same, man. The type of ... it could easily be *El Equipo A!*" (GS25-35_Rerun_Knight Rider_Spanien, 51 [o.t.])[58]

---

dann halt auf 'm Motorrad, was ich nicht hatte, und dann halt, ja so irgendwie unter einem weiten Himmel entlangfahren zu können." (CMG55-65, GD55-65_Rerun_KnightRider_Deutschland, 31-55)

56 Original quotation: "[D]ie Sachen aus den 60s, also da fühl ich mich total berührt. Als ich jugendlich war." (CMG55-65, GD55-65_Rerun_KnightRider_Deutschland, 233)

57 Original quotation: "Wir werden mit uns selbst konfrontiert." (CMG55-65, GD55-65_Rerun_KnightRider_Deutschland, 233)

58 Original quotation: "Son los mismos productores que *El Equipo A*, porque es idéntico tío. El tipo de... ¡Podría ser *El Equipo A* tranquilamente!" (RMS25-35, GS25-35_Rerun_Knight Rider_Spanien, 51)

AMG25-35: "Also *A-Team* or something like that. They also run to some place with a gun, do something and leave again. Here it is the same. He drives to some place with his car. Does something and goes away again." (GD25-35_Rerun_Knight Rider_Deutschland, 64 [o.t.])[59]

It is the aesthetics and the narration that remind the 25 to 35-year-old interviewees of the series. Among both the 55 to 65-year-old Germans and Spaniards, the single levels of *Knight Rider* are rather compared to the spy series *Magnum*, which was broadcasted in both countries in the mid-1980s. Other series named are *Columbo* (ARD, 1969; TVE, 1973), or *Perry Mason* (ARD, 1959; TVE, 1960). In contrast to the group of the 25 to 35-year-olds, these associations are not strictly about television series that were broadcasted in the programme context of *Knight Rider* – *Perry Mason*, for example, was broadcasted in Spain from the 1960s on – but rather series that seem to have prototype character for the interviewees.

Only one series overlapping between the age groups appears, in the case of *Baywatch* (Das Erste, 1990). The series is associated with *Knight Rider*'s mise-en-scène but above all with David Hasselhoff, who was the lead actor in both series. *Baywatch* obviously managed to mediate between the memories of different age groups. In this case, it is between the memories of the female members of the German groups. Apart from that, as assumed in the analytical part, Hasselhoff is further related to when the Berlin Wall came down. CFG25-35 states here:

CFG25-35: "Especially with *Knight Rider* David Hasselhoff matters a lot. Then I think about *Looking for Freedom* and, mhm, there is a whole stream of things related to it. [...] Well, then I see him like, I don't know, dancing when the Wall came down, with his glittering costume, and then I think of *Baywatch.*" (GD25-35_Rerun_Knight Rider_Deutschland, 262 ff. [o.t.])[60]

Nostalgia cannot be observed. In both cases the recalled series are internationally traded programmes. A difference between the territorial groups cannot be observed.

In summary, we can state that, as assumed in the television analysis, the rerun gained a broad referential character, not only to 'the 1980s' but also to other 1980s cultural products, that is recognisable for both those who know and those who do not

---

59 Original quotation: "Auch *A-Team* oder sowas. Die laufen immer irgendwohin mit 'ner Knarre, machen irgendwas und geh'n wieder weg. Das ist hier auch. Der fährt mit seinem Auto irgendwohin. Macht was und fährt wieder weg." (AMG25-35, GD25-35_Rerun_Knight Rider_Deutschland, 64)

60 Original quotation: "Speziell bei *Knight Rider* macht natürlich auch David Hasselhoff viel aus. Da denk ich an *Looking for Freedom* und, ehm, da hängt nochmal 'n Rattenschwanz für mich jetzt dran. [...] Ja, dann seh ich ihn irgendwie, weiß ich nich, beim Fall der Mauer da tanzen mit seinem Glitzerkostüm und dann denk ich auch an, eh, an, eh, *Baywatch*." (CFG25-35, GD25-35_Rerun_Knight Rider_Deutschland, 262 ff.)

know the first-run. In the case of according positive "retrospective classification", nostalgia is possible for both groups. Hereby the associations related to the single levels of the text gain dominance among those who did not know *Knight Rider* or who did not give it a special relevance. These interviewees, as it seems, aspire to integrate the series into a new interpretative context. In other cases, when the first-run is known, interviewees rather refer to context memories related to the first-run or, as it will be shown in the following section, to memories related to the single levels of the programme. They are of greater relevance. For example, we may refer to the case of the 25 to 35-year-old EMG25-35:

EMG25-35: "For me these are two different things, to be honest. First *Knight Rider*, which I think is cool or thought was cool, and then Looking for Freedom and all that came afterwards. Well that's something I don't want to know. What I don't want to associate with it because I somehow, well, when I imagine myself watching *Knight Rider* and think about I'll be Looking for Freedom [original title: I've been Looking for Freedom] playing in the background, then the whole thing is over for me." (GD25-35_Rerun_Knight Rider_Deutschland, 300 ff. [o.t.])[61]

This quotation shall be the transition to the consideration of (the rather direct) nostalgia in the context of the single levels of the text.

8.1.1.2.2 Past and present experiences

The statement of EMG25-35 *"Knight Rider*, which I think is cool or I thought was cool" already hints at one decisive element in the pattern, which is the high relevance and interrelation of past and present reception experiences. The determinants of the present valorisation and finally also the explanation of whether a recipient develops nostalgia regarding a single element of the text or not, can here mainly be found in how and if the interviewees remember past experiences and into which line of argument they integrate their reflection. The following categories have been identified here: (1) *Creating the link to 'common sense', resp. 'acquired' "retrospective classifications"*, (2) *Positive past versus present experiences*, and (3) *A lack of memories of positive past emotions impedes nostalgia.*

---

61 Original quotation: "Bei mir sind's zwei Dinger. Muss ich ehrlich sagen. Also einmal so *Knight Rider*, was ich cool finde oder fand, und dann also so *Looking for Freedom* und das alles was danach kam. Also das ist was, was ich gar nicht wissen will. Was ich gar nicht damit assoziieren will, weil ich irgendwie, also wenn ich mir jetzt vorstelle, ich guck jetzt *Knight Rider* und denke äh an *I'll be Looking for Freedom*, was im Hintergrund läuft, dann wär für mich diese ganze Serie hinüber." (EMG25-35, GD25-35_Rerun_Knight Rider_Deutschland, 300 ff.)

Creating the link to 'common sense', resp. 'acquired'
"retrospective classifications"

That "retrospective classifications" on the macro level favour nostalgia is suggested by Kompare (2005, p. 139) but is probably not always the case. Already Kompare (2005, p. 139) himself makes nostalgia dependent on various factors when he states that "the television nostalgia wave of the 1980s was [...] partially a result of the establishment of the television heritage in the 1970s and partially a pointed appeal to an ageing Baby Boomer audience". Similarly, it can be observed in the context of the group discussions conducted here regarding the single levels of the text. Publicly shared retrospective classifications may also be highlighted here; however, it seems that they are not a sufficient condition for the development of the nostalgia.

In the first example, a clear creation of the 'gap' can be observed where the narration of the (bad) remake becomes part of the valorisation of the rerun. Except from the 55 to 65-year-old Germans, in all other groups and among both the 'knowing' and the 'not knowing' participants, comparisons between the *Knight Rider* (NBC, 2008) remake and the rerun are made. In any case, a negative valorisation of the remake can be observed, which becomes part of the positive valorisation of the rerun. Apart from general statements such as "Esta parece mejor" [this one seems better] (FCFS55-65, GS55-65_Rerun Knight Rider_Spanien, 7 [o.t.]), or "Fantástico. ¡Mucho mejor que la otra!" [Fantastic. Much better than the other one!] (JMS25-35, GS25-35_Rerun_Knight Rider_Spanien, 59 [o.t.]) as they already appear during the reception of the example, these appraisals mainly refer to the single levels of the text. According to the opinion of the participants, the *Knight Rider* rerun is of better quality than the remake. Its protagonists seem "better characterised" to them (see FCFS55-65, GS55-65_Rerun Knight Rider_Spanien, 29-31; FMS55-65, GS55-65_Rerun_Knight Rider_Spanien, 12 [o.t.]), and dialogues are seen as being better tuned:

FFG25-35: "[And you can feel the relationship between the car and KITT ((laughs)) er, between] the car and Michael. [...] And in the case of the other one I didn't feel that. Because it was so ... sterile. Sterile really is the perfect word for it." (GD25-35_Rerun_Knight Rider_Deutschland, 181-184 [o.t.])[62]

Also the rerun music compares positively to the new version.

---

62 Original quotation: "[Und man spürt diese Beziehung zwischen dem Auto und KITT ((lacht)) äh, zwischen] dem Auto und Michael. [...] Ne. Und bei dem andern hab' ich das nicht gespürt. Da war das alles so steril. Steril ist wirklich das perfekte Wort dazu." (FFG25-35, GD25-35_Rerun_Knight Rider_Deutschland, 181-184)

FCFS55-65: "Yes, I liked the music more than in the introduction of the other one. Maybe it reminded me of something, or I once had the TV set switched on and they broadcasted a series on which I focussed mentally, this music is also of the era." (GS55-65_Rerun Knight Rider_Spanien, 133 [o.t.])[63]

Regarding the making, the 'original' one seems less exaggerated to them.

FFG25-35: "That's what makes it so appealing. The bumpiness. And in this remake everything is so smooth. And all like ... ." (GD25-35_Rerun_Knight Rider_Deutschland, 168 [o.t.])[64]

AMG25-35: "Yes, also the opening credits. In the older version, there was no change of images. Or something like that. One actually only sees the car and then again the dashboard." (GD25-35_Rerun_Knight Rider_Deutschland, 169 [o.t.])[65]

AMG25-35: "This whole blinking and something flies in there and then he has another display in his car, which is cut in hologram-like and I don't know what for." (GD25-35_Rerun_Knight Rider_Deutschland, 188 [o.t.])[66]

Similar to the "retrospective classifications" described by Kompare, in doing so, a gap between a positive 'then' and a negative 'now' is constructed. The comparison with the remake leads to a positive "retrospective classification" of the rerun, also on the part of recipients who never saw the rerun or the first-run. Nostalgia, however, cannot be observed. For the participants who have no positive past memories related to the series, the 'common sense', resp. 'acquired' classification, is not sufficient in order to provide the basis for the nostalgic longing. Other factors are relevant, as they shall be commented in the following section.

---

63 Original quotation: "Sí, me gustaba más la música (de ésta) que en la introducción de la otra. A lo mejor me han recordado algo, o alguna vez tenía la tele puesta ahí y hacían unas series en que yo me fijé (en la mente), la música aquella es de la época también." (FCFS55-65, GS55-65_Rerun Knight Rider_Spanien, 133)

64 Original quotation: "Das macht es doch so sympathisch. Dieses Holprige. Und da bei diesem Remake ist alles so glatt und smooth. Und alles so... ." (FFG25-35, GD25-35_Rerun_Knight Rider_Deutschland, 168)

65 Original quotation: "Ja, auch bei dem Vorspann. Bei dem Alten, da gab's einen Bildwechsel. Oder so. Man sieht eigentlich nur das Auto und dann nochmal die Armaturen." (AMG25-35, GD25-35_Rerun_Knight Rider_Deutschland, 169)

66 Original quotation: "Dieses ganze Geblinke und hier fliegt noch irgendwas rein und dann hat er in seinem Auto noch irgendwie ne Anzeige, die so Hologramm-mäßig reingezeichnet wird und weiß ich nich wofür." (AMG25-35, GD25-35_Rerun_Knight Rider_Deutschland, 188)

This similarly applies to other cases where the participants link to the valorising discourses as they were described in the analytical part on *Knight Rider*. Both the 25 to 35-year-old BMG25-35 and the 25 to 35-year-old GMG25-35 had seen the first-run but, as previously mentioned, highlighted the general irrelevance that the series had for them during their childhood. Also regarding the single levels of the series, they only recall dislike:

BMG25-35: "I watched it but not really on a regular basis. I did not find it all that good. Cars and stuff did not impress me very much at the time." (GD25-35_Rerun_Knight Rider_ Deutschland, 153 [o.t.])[67]

GMG25-35: "Well, already back then when I was sixteen or seventeen I thought it was a little bit silly (laughs)." (GD25-35_Rerun_Knight Rider_Deutschland, 103 [o.t.])[68]

Notwithstanding, the evaluation from today's perspective takes a different tone.

BMG25-35: "*Knight Rider* is also a cult series now. Well, alone David Hasselhoff, who said that he has brought us the Fall of the Wall and stuff." (GD25-35_Rerun_Knight Rider_ Deutschland, 228 [o.t.])[69]

GMG25-35: "I think it's kind of stylish to watch it. The whole thing, especially the hairstyle, the clothes, and especially the foolish dialogue." (GD25-35_Rerun_Knight Rider_ Deutschland, 107 [o.t.])[70]

GMG25-35: "But I do not know. Since you asked, the comparison to today is difficult to make on the quality of the series. Because, well, I think, for example, Bud Spencer and Terence Hill or something, that's also such a phenomenon. Actually, it is total trash. Only Bang. Bang. Bang. But nevertheles, it has become an absolute cult. [...] I believe with *Knight Rider* it is similar.

---

67 Original quotation: "Ich hab' sie geschaut, aber, eh, also da nich wirklich regelmäßig. Ich fand' das nicht so gut. Also Autos und so was fand ich damals nicht so beeindruckend." (BMG25-35, GD25-35_Rerun_Knight Rider_Deutschland, 153)

68 Original quotation: "Naja. Ich fand's damals schon, wo ich so sechzehn, siebzehn war, schon 'n bisschen albern ((lacht))." (GMG25-35, GD25-35_Rerun_Knight Rider_ Deutschland, 103)

69 Original quotation: "Und *Knight Rider* ist ja jetzt auch 'ne Kult-Serie. Also alleine mit David Hasselhoff, der irgendwie selber meinte mal, dass er uns den Mauerfall gebracht hat und so." (BMG25-35, GD25-35_Rerun_Knight Rider_Deutschland, 228)

70 Original quotation: "Ich find's auch irgendwie stylisch, sich das anzuschauen. Das Ganze, vor allem die Frisur, die Klamotten und vor allem die albernen Sprüche." (GMG25-35, GD25-35_Rerun_Knight Rider_Deutschland, 107)

[...] With regards to content it has never really beaten the rest. But it's kind of stylish." (GD25-35_Rerun_Knight Rider_Deutschland, 335-345 [o.t.])[71]

From today's perspective the series is described as "cult" and as "stylish", which, when interpreted in accordance with the German lexical connotation of the term, signifies chic or modern (see Duden 2012a). On the one hand, the rerun seemingly gained a kind of 'campiness' for the interviewees. While both interviewees valorised *Knight Rider* rather negatively in the past, from a present position, they "can enjoy [them], instead of be[ing] frustrated by the failure of the attempt" just as Sontag (1964) describes it in the context of camp in general. On the other hand, so it can be argued, both interviewees refer to discourses of "retrospective classifications" of the rerun as a cult as described in the context of the television analysis of the example. In this context, it is surely no coincidence that BMG25-35 refers to *Star Trek*, the example cult series (see e.g. Wilcox 2010), in his re-valorisation of the *Knight Rider* intro.[72] Explicitly articulated nostalgia or a rhetoric that opposed past and present, can also not be observed in the course of the discussion. However, both participants acknowledge nostalgia in the questionnaire. Due to the only vague statements the object of the nostalgias can only hardly be specified.[73] It can only be speculated that the 'common sense', resp. 'acquired' "retrospective classification", of the rerun does not provide the object of the nostalgic longing, but that it works as an indicator for a

---

71 Original quotation: "Aber ich weiß nicht. Weil du gefragt hattest. Der Vergleich zu heute. Ich glaube auch, dass das schwierig ist, das so an der Qualität der Serie festzumachen. Weil, also ich glaube, zum Beispiel bei Bud Spencer und Terence Hill oder so, das ist auch so 'n Phänomen. Ist eigentlich absoluter Trash. Immer nur Bang. Bang. Bang. Aber trotzdem ist es absoluter Kult geworden. [...] Ich glaub' bei *Knight Rider* ist das ähnlich. [...] Das ist irgendwie inhaltlich nie wirklich der Hammer gewesen. Aber das ist irgendwie stylisch." (GMG25-35, GD25-35_Rerun_Knight Rider_Deutschland, 335-345)

72 Original quotation: "Also *Knight Rider* ist auch nicht so meine Sache. Aber ich fand's, das Intro, fand ich schon hübsch gemacht. Also auch mit der Stimme aus dem Off, das ist ja schon sehr an *Star Trek* angelehnt. Also diese kurze Passage. Musst ich nur grade dran denken, weil ich da was gelesen hatte über diese Entwicklung, eh, des *Star Trek* Intros." (BMG25-35, GD25-35_Rerun_Knight Rider_Deutschland, 149)

73 DMG25-35 states here to have felt nostalgia "maybe in parts during *Knight Rider* (only intro)" (DMG25-35, G25-35_Connotation of nostalgia_25-35-year-old Germans, 21 [o.t.]). Original quotation: "vielleicht teilweise bei *Knight Rider* (nur Intro)" (DMG25-35, G25-35_Connotation of nostalgia_25-35-year-old Germans, 21), while BMG25-35 leaves it at a simple "during the *Knight Rider* discussion" (BMG25-35, G25-35_Connotation of nostalgia_25-35-year-old Germans, 25 [o.t.]). Original quotation: "Bei der *Knight Rider* Diskussion" (BMG25-35, G25-35_Connotation of nostalgia_25-35-year-old Germans, 25).

kind of socially desired nostalgia that makes the participants reflect upon the classification of their emotions once again.

Positive past experience versus present experience

Apart from the group of the 55 to 65-year-old Spanish viewers, among which those who gave *Knight Rider* little relevance also recall concrete details of the series, it is predominantly the group of the 25 to 35-year-olds, and here those who stated that they knew and liked *Knight Rider*, where the memory of action, characters, and other details is most relevant. The interviewees recall fragments and courses of action.

EMG25-35: "Yes, well, as I said, twisting backwards out of the truck on a highway. Or speaking into the watch." (GD25-35_Rerun_Knight Rider_Deutschland, 29 [o.t.])[74]

FFG25-35: "I can still remember that this truck was always on a highway, and he [Michael Knight] suddenly came out of nowhere and drove into it. Well, always in the end." (GD25-35_Rerun_Knight Rider_Deutschland, 120 [o.t.])[75]

They remember story lines and episodes:

FFG25-35: "It was always another job to do and always another woman, who was somehow involved with him. Or there was something going on or whatever. [...] She is one of them [pointing at the screen]. But then again she disappeared in the next episode. Then came another one. And I think it is always about father/daughter." (GD25-35_Rerun_Knight Rider_Deutschland, 114 ff. [o.t.])[76]

VMS25-35: "There is one in which he fights against his brother."

---

74 Original quotation: "Ja. Also wie gesagt mit dem Laster und rückwärts herausdrehn. Oder so in die Uhr reinsprechen." (EMG25-35, GD25-35_Rerun_Knight Rider_Deutschland, 29)

75 Original quotation: "Ich kann mich noch erinnern, dass dieser Lastwagen immer auf irgend nem Highway war und er [Michael Knight] dann, wie aus dem Nichts plötzlich kam und dann da reingefahren ist. Also am Ende immer." (FFG25-35, GD25-35_Rerun_Knight Rider_Deutschland, 120)

76 Original quotation: "Das war jedes Mal ein anderer Auftrag und jedes Mal eine andere Frau aber auch, die mit ihm irgendwas am Start hatte. Oder da lief was, oder so. [...] Sie ist eine davon [zeigt auf den Bildschirm]. Die ist aber dann auch wieder verschwunden bei der nächsten Folge. Dann kam wieder eine. Und immer ist es auch, ich glaub', auch Vater/Tochter." (FFG25-35, GD25-35_Rerun_Knight Rider_Deutschland, 114 ff.)

JMS25-35: "Yes, the episode of KITT, the killer." (GS25-35_Rerun_Knight Rider_Spanien, 91, 98-99 [o.t.])[77]

Or they refer to single characters and technical details:

RMS25-35: "But the girls kept on changing, didn't they? Every once in a while she was exchanged, but without any reason."
OFS25-35: "No, there are two, there were two or three."
JMS25-35: "Then there was a smaller girl with a rather childish face." (GS25-35_Rerun_Knight Rider_Spanien, 34 ff. [o.t.])[78]

DFG25-35: "Well, I can still remember the woman in any case and this older man who was always as solid as a rock. And I was always glad that there was someone like him." (GD25-35_Rerun_Knight Rider_Deutschland, 101 [o.t.])[79]

The participants, some more, some less, appear here as 'experts' recalling their knowledge of the series. At the same time their reviews give space to the memories of old fascinations and preferences. Again the comparison between past and present experiences is notable. Among the Spanish 25 to 35-year-olds, a dominant strand of argumentation shows an accordance of positive past and positive present valorisation.

RMS25-35: "But it's strange because I see the car and I keep on liking it."
AFS25-35: "It's so cool."
VMS25-35: "Mmm, it is still handsome." (GS25-35_Rerun_Knight Rider_Spanien, 107 ff. [o.t.])[80]

---

77 Original quotation: VMS25-35: "Hay una que se pelea contra su hermano." JMS25-35: "Sí, en el capítulo de Kitt Asesino." (GS25-35_Rerun_Knight Rider_Spanien, 91, 98-99)

78 Original quotation: RMS25-35: "Pero a las chica las iban cambiando eh? De vez en cuando. Se la cambiaban, pero sin ton ni son." OFS25-35: "No, hay dos, hubo dos o tres ahí." JMS25-35: "Luego hubo una más bajita con cara más de niña." (GS25-35_Rerun_Knight Rider_Spanien, 34 ff.)

79 Original quotation: "Also ich kann mich noch an die Frau erinnern auf jeden Fall und an diesen älteren Mann, der immer so der Fels in der Brandung war. Und ich immer froh war, dass es den irgendwie gab." (DFG25-35, GD25-35_Rerun_Knight Rider_Deutschland, 101)

80 Original quotation: RMS25-35: "Pero es curioso porque yo el coche lo sigo viendo y a mí me sigue molando." AFS25-35: "Es tan chulo." VMS25-35: "Mmm, es que sigue siendo guapo." (GS25-35_Rerun_Knight Rider_Spanien, 107 ff.)

RMS25-35: "I liked the music. It's great. The music is still great!" (GS25-35_Rerun_Knight Rider_Spanien, 13 [o.t.])[81]

VMS25-35: "Umm... I don't know. The music. When I heard the music, I said, 'Awesome!' It's great." (GS25-35_Rerun_Knight Rider_Spanien, 157-158 [o.t.])[82]

VMS25-35: "The music was brilliant. Yes, great." (GS25-35_Rerun_Knight Rider_Spanien, 327-328 [o.t.])[83]

CMS25-35: "I saw it just as I remembered it." (GS25-35_Rerun_Knight Rider_Spanien, 149 [o.t.])[84]

In contrast to the contextual childhood memories that contain the rhetoric of the 'gap' and led to nostalgia on the side of the interviewees, regarding the single levels of the series, no similar lack that could be the basis for nostalgia towards the past emotion can be found. Presumably the positive valorisation of the single levels is one factor that has an effect on the positive memory of the childhood.[85] However, nostalgia, for example towards the lost fascination with the car, can here be excluded since the fascination obviously outlasted the years.

Nevertheless, this cannot always be observed. Thus, in other cases the recapitulation of narrative fragments and aspects of the series is accompanied by a recapitulation of the past emotions as well. Here however, a clear gap between past and present experience may be observed, which is the source of nostalgia in the context of single levels of the text. We can, for example, refer to two cases from the German group. Apart from the memories related to the context of the 'original'

---

81 Original quotation: "A mí me gustaba. ¡La música! Es buenísima. ¡La música sigue siendo buenísima!" (RMS25-35, GS25-35_Rerun_Knight Rider_Spanien, 13)

82 Original quotation: "umm...No sé. La música. ¡Cuando escuchaba la música dije Ostia! Es guay." (VMS25-35, GS25-35_Rerun_Knight Rider_Spanien, 157-158)

83 Original quotation: "La música era genial. Sí. Buenísima." (VMS25-35, GS25-35_Rerun_Knight Rider_Spanien, 327-328)

84 Original quotation: "Lo he visto igual que lo recordaba." (CMS25-35, GS25-35_Rerun_Knight Rider_Spanien, 149)

85 Seemingly in the case of VMS25-35 it is the music that works as a "memory prompt". Thus in the questionnaire he describes his nostalgia in the context of the series as follows: "Solo con la música del *coche fantástico*. Pues me ha recordado a mi infancia, al verano, a la piscina" [Only with the music of *El coche fantástico*. Well, it reminded me of my childhood, of summer, of the pool] (Questionnaire_Nostalgie/GS25-35_Connotation of nostalgia_25-35-year-old Spaniards, 24 [o.t.]). In the discussion, however, this aspect remains unclear.

reception, which seem to adopt a secondary position, it is FFG25-35's reception experience related to the romantic sub-plot of *Knight Rider* that dominates the memories of the 25 to 35-year-old. Besides the above section in which FFG25-35 recalls the recurring of the main character's romantic relationships, in the context of later enquiries about the memories related to the series, she repeatedly comes back to this fact:

M: "And what memories exactly do you have? Well, just those games you played with your brother?"

FFG25-35: "Yes. Yes, yes. But ((laughter)) as I said. I was eight or nine. So I was not that old. Well, I know that, mhm, erm that for me as a child, well, it is also much about the two sexes getting closer to each other. Because he was always the hero in the series but also a womaniser. And I still remember very well that this was what was mainly on my mind." (GD25-35_Rerun_Knight Rider_Deutschland, 123-126)[86]

FFG25-35: "So this fascinated me the most. I believe my brother was rather fascinated with the cars. And then I was always fascinated with the story, when things like that happened." (GD25-35_Rerun_Knight Rider_Deutschland, 134 [o.t.])[87]

The interviewee remembers "fascination" as the basic (F) emotion she had in the context of the *Knight Rider* narration. However, in contrast to other cases as they were commented previously, the constant past perfect she uses leaves no doubt that this emotion is not felt from a present perspective. This lack obviously holds a major part in the nostalgia the interviewee later explicitly describes:

---

86 Original quotation: M: "Und was für Erinnerungen genau kommen da hervor? Also genau diese Spiele eben, die du mit deinem Bruder gemacht hast?" FFG25-35: "Ja. Jaja. Aber auch ((lacht)) doch und wie gesagt. Ich war da acht oder neun. Also ich war da noch nich so alt. Also ich weiß auch, dass ehm dass für mich als Kind, also da geht es ja auch um dieses Annähern von den zwei Geschlechtern. Weil er war ja schon 'n Held in der Serie. Frauenheld aber auch. Und daran kann ich mich noch ganz genau erinnern, dass mich das schon beschäftigt hat." (GD25-35_Rerun_Knight Rider_Deutschland, 123-126)

87 Original quotation: "Also das hat mich am meisten fasziniert. Ich glaub' meinen Bruder [...] ham auch eher die Autos fasziniert. Und mich hat dann immer die Geschichte fasziniert. Wenn das sich so abspielt." (FFG25-35, GD25-35_Rerun_Knight Rider_Deutschland, 134)

FFG25-35: "I really want my children to watch these films that I watched when I was a child. Because I had so many positive emotions at that time. Or now in hindsight. Or this nostalgic feeling." (GD25-35_Nostalgia_ Allgemein_Deutschland, 95 [o.t.])[88]

Not only what *Knight Rider* concerns but also regarding other 1980s children's films that she also presents as potential nostalgia objects, she describes how the original positive emotion related to their reception appears to be nostalgia from today's perspective. Since, at least in the case of *Knight Rider*, the nostalgia has its object in an F emotion, namely a former fascination on the level of the narration, the viewer's 'own F nostalgia' would probably be the right expression for this sort of nostalgia.

It is a similar case with the 25 to 35-year-old EMG25-35. A clear gap between the past and the present reception experience is also constructed here.

M: "And what was it like watching *Knight Rider* back then?"
EMG25-35: "Yes, cool. I looked forward to it, and was certainly curious about what would happen next. And would certainly have been totally excited about the stunt scene we just saw. Because I don't know if he gets the job or not. And today this is different of course." (GD25-35_Rerun_Knight Rider_Deutschland, 36-37 [o.t.])[89]

M: "Hmm. And would you say that it was a better experience back then?"
EMG25-35: "Yes. Definitely. Definitely, yes. So at that time it was. What can I say? Now I just watch it simply for retro reasons. Maybe mainly because of the music. So I found the intro was the best part." (GD25-35_Rerun_Knight Rider_Deutschland, 45-46 [o.t.])[90]

While back then "curiosity", "excitement", and "suspense" accompanied the reception, this is different from today's perspective where "retro reasons", as the

---

88 FFG25-35: Ich möchte unbedingt, dass meine Kinder diese Filme auch sehn, die ich als Kind gesehn habe. Weil ich eben so positive Emotionen da hatte zu der Zeit. Oder jetzt im Nachhinein. Oder dieses nostalgische Empfinden. (GD25-35_Nostalgia_ Allgemein_ Deutschland, 95)

89 Original quotation: M: "Und wie war das damals. *Knight Rider* anzugucken?" EMG25-35: "Ja cool. Also ich hab' mich halt drauf gefreut und war sicher auch gespannt, was gleich passieren würde. Und hätte sicher auch so 'ne Stunt-Szene, so wie wir sie gerade gesehen hatten, total spannend gefunden. Weil ich nich weiß, ob er den Job kriegt oder nicht. Und das ist jetzt heute natürlich anders." (GD25-35_Rerun_Knight Rider_Deutschland, 36-37)

90 Original quotation: M: "Mhm. Und würd'st du sagen, es war damals irgendwie ein besseres Erlebnis." EMG25-35: "Ja. Definitiv. Definitiv Ja. Also damals war 's. Wie soll ich sagen? Jetzt guck ich 's halt einfach so aus so Retro-Gründen heraus. Vielleicht einfach also hauptsächlich wegen der Musik. Also das Intro fand ich noch mit am besten." (GD25-35_Rerun_Knight Rider_Deutschland, 45-46)

interviewee says, are predominant. In a later sequence of the discussion it becomes evident that nostalgia in the context of positive past emotions is actually meant here:

EMG25-35: "I also just wanted to say that with *Knight Rider*, in my case, the nostalgia was most intensive during the intro. Well, I think it also would have worked without the film and only with the music. It almost triggers the feeling of euphoria or 'dumdudum', because it somehow comes like this. [...] Well, it's like that. These are more those signal moments. And then, also a lightweight series is sufficient. Because I identified so much with it as a child, because I replayed it..." (GD25-35_Nostalgia_ Allgemein_Deutschland, 136 ff. [o.t.])[91]

Even though context memories play a role in the narration of the participants, it seems that it is less this memory that is the object of the nostalgia but rather a cocktail of emotions – from joy to fascination – that was related to the 'original' reception.[92] This becomes more explicit in the questionnaire. Here the interviewee describes the nostalgia as follows: "As a child I found the series really exciting, and this feeling is what I remember." (EMG25-35, G25-35_Connotation of nostalgia_25-35-year-old Germans, 24 [o.t.])[93] It seems that the music has a dominant position, seemingly working as a "mnemonic prompt" that helps remember the lost emotions. We may thus talk of the participant's 'own F nostalgia'.

---

91 Original quotation: "Wollt' ich auch grad bei *Knight Rider* sagen. Also bei mir kam die Nostalgie viel stärker beim Intro, also ich glaube, es hätt' auch ohne Film nur mit Musik funktioniert und da kommt bei mir fast so 'n Gefühl der Euphorie oder so weil ich es dumdudum das irgendwie so kommt. Also wenn du jetzt zum Beispiel das Intro nicht gezeigt hättest und nur diese Szene mit dem Stunt oder so, dann hätt's mich wahrscheinlich auch relativ kalt gelassen. Also das ist schon so, das sind eher so diese Signalmomente. Aber dann reicht mir auch 'ne flache Serie. Weil ich mich als Kind so mit dem identifiziert habe, weil ich den ja nachgespielt habe, dass ich eh... ." (EMG25-35, GD25-35_Nostalgia_ Allgemein_Deutschland, 136 ff.)

92 Also in the context of the nostalgia discourse in *Mad Men*, the interviewee (EMG25-35) returns to his nostalgia in relation to *Knight Rider*: "Well, I found he provided an explanation why *Knight Rider* had such a positive echo here. With nostalgia, blah blah blah, I had to think of *Knight Rider*, where we just said, 'Well, that's cool', and we found it super." (EMG25-35, GD25-35_Period Pictures_Mad Men_Deutschland, 170 [o.t.]) Original quotation: "[Also] ich fand der hat ne Erklärung geliefert, warum *Knight Rider* hier so 'n positives Echo hatte. Mit Nostalgie blablabla musst ich sofort an das Beispiel mit *Knight Rider* denken, wo wir grade gesacht ham joah, das ist doch cool, und das fanden wir super." (EMG25-35, GD25-35_Period Pictures_Mad Men_Deutschland, 170)

93 Original quotation: "Ich fand die Serie als Kind total spannend und an dieses Gefühl erinnere ich mich." (EMG25-35, G25-35_Connotation of nostalgia_25-35-year-old Germans, 24)

Lastly, a similar rhetoric of the gap that had also been assumed in the context of the television analysis appears among the 55 to 65-year-old Germans, that is regarding the lost fascination concerning the main prop. Here it is the 55 to 65-year-old IMG55-65 who states:

IMG55-65: "Er, I've always thought of the car. Was thinking that back then the car was something special, something great. And today everybody drives such cars." (GD55-65_Rerun_Knight Rider_Deutschland, 196 [o.t.])[94]

However, it cannot be talked of (F or A) nostalgia in this context. It is more about a distanced comparison. Strong emotions, such as the fascination (F or A emotion) that was recalled by the 25 to 35-year-old EMG25-35 and which are considered to be lost from today's perspective, are not found here.

A lack of memories of positive past emotions impedes nostalgia

Those who neither adopted the valorising discourses that surround *Knight Rider* nor re-valorise the series positively on an individual level perceive the rerun negatively. From today's perspective *Knight Rider* indeed contains differential quality for these participants, therefore props, aesthetics or character traits call their attention, but they do not have a positive differential quality, for example in the form of nostalgia.

"No se vé una modernidad en el coche. Se ve muy anticuada" [You don't see any modernity in this car. It looks very antiquated] (GS55-65_Rerun Knight Rider_Spanien, 32 [o.t.]), as AMS55-65 states, who knows the first-run but does not recall any appreciation of its levels. Besides the main prop, other levels seem anachronistic to him as well:

AMS55-65: "And I don't even talk about the way it was shot. Fixed camera, (a different camera). It looks a bit old. Today, people do not allow that." (GS55-65_Rerun_Knight Rider_Spanien, 32 [o.t.])[95]

This similarly applies to other participants of the German group of the 55 to 65-year-olds, both who did not know the first-run:

---

94 Original quotation: "Eh ich hab' immer an das Auto gedacht. Hab gedacht früher, das Auto, das war was Besonderes, was Tolles. Und heut fährt man selbst so Autos." (IMG55-65, GD55-65_Rerun_Knight Rider_Deutschland, 196)

95 Original quotation: "Ya no hablo digamos de la manera de filmar. Cámara fija, (otra cámara). Se ve un poco antiguo. Esto actualmente la gente no lo permite. [...]." (AMS55-65, GS55-65_Rerun_Knight Rider_Spanien, 32)

DMG55-65: "Well, the trailer [the interviewee refers to the opening credits of the series] was much closer to modern times, as what came afterwards."
GFG55-65: "Yes, then it seems more old-fashioned." (GD55-65_Rerun_Knight Rider_ Deutschland, 80 ff. [o.t.])[96]

Another 'don't know' of the German group of the 25 to 35-year-olds perceives the series as disagreeably slow:

CFG25-35: "[...] If I compare that with any American series of today, I don't know, *CSI Miami*, there is always something inserted. And another screen comes from above. When I watch a slower series like *Knight Rider*, then I realise that I'm distracted faster if there is not a constantly new stimulus." (GD25-35_Rerun_Knight Rider_Deutschland, 242 ff. [o.t.])[97]

In other cases the rather negative "retrospective classification" of the first-run finds its continuation in an equally negative appraisal of the rerun, which also impedes the development of nostalgia regarding single levels of the text. The 55 to 65-year-old HFG55-65, for example, confronts past and present experience in a statement that refers to the protagonist:

HFG55-65: "How awful I found that my daughter watches something like that. David Hasselhoff, whom I rejected as an absolute prole back then and still do." (GD55-65_Rerun_Knight Rider_Deutschland, 169 [o.t.])[98]

---

96 Original quotation: DMG55-65: "Also den Trailer [the interviewee refers here to the opening credits of the series] fand ich viel näher an der heutigen Zeit, als das, was danach kam". GFG55-65: "Ja, danach wirkt es altmodischer." (GD55-65_Rerun_Knight Rider_Deutschland, 80 ff.)

97 Original quotation: "Ja. Also ich hab' ja jetzt *Knight Rider* selber nicht gesehn. Aber ich finde, bei mir selber merk ich, dass ich, mhm, lieber ja schneller, also ich bin irgendwie gewöhnt, dass sich, weiß ich nich, die Einstellung alle fünf Sekunden ändert, und ähm, weiß ich nich, vier verschiedene Ausschnitte auf dem Bildschirm zu sehen sind. [...] Wenn ich das jetzt mit irgendwelchen amerikanischen, weiß ich nich, CSI Miami vergleiche. Da wird ja permanent was reingespielt. Und hier kommt von oben noch 'n Bildschirm. Wenn ich jetzt ne langsamere Serie gucke, die irgendwie, ja wie *Knight Rider*, dann, ja dann merk ich, dass ich da auch schneller abdrifte, wenn da nicht permanent wieder neuer Reiz kommt." (CFG25-35, GD25-35_Rerun_Knight Rider_Deutschland, 242 ff.)

98 Original quotation: "Wie schrecklich ich es fand, dass meine Tochter so was guckt. David Hasselhoff, den ich für mich als absoluten Proleten abgetan habe und abtue. Dass die das guckt. Während heute, wo ich so aus der Distanz heraus denke, och, das war doch gar nicht so schlimm. Es gab bestimmt, oder es gibt bestimmt noch viele schlimmere Dinge inzwischen oder so. Also es war noch recht harmlos. Aber ich fand das eben so, wie soll

The negative appraisal in the context of a negative past reception is also observable among the 25 to 35-year-olds. AMG25-35, who already hinted at the generally lower degree of fascination the television series had for him since he first watched it during his adolescence[99], says the following:

AMG25-35: "Well, no feelings at all. Nothing. Now except maybe that one just realises how ridiculous some of it was. Well, with the stunts. It wasn't actually a great stunt." (GD25-35_Rerun_Knight Rider_Deutschland, 66 [o.t.])[100]

This similarly applies to VMS25-35 and ZFS25-35:

VMS25-35: "The character is nasty, isn't he?"
ZFS25-35: "The character is nasty, in any case."
VMS25-35: "He is nasty if ever there was one. I've found him dislikeable since I was small, and the rest, too."
ZFS25-35: "Me, too." (GS25-35_Rerun_Knight Rider_Spanien, 402 ff. [o.t.])[101]

Here, the interviewees also confront past and present experiences. The negative past reception of the main character is continued in a present depreciation. While the 25 to 35-year-old ZFS25-35 had already highlighted that negative childhood memories impede the development of nostalgia directed towards the context of the 'original'

---

ich sagen, intellektuell so schwach belichtet." (HFG55-65, GD55-65_Rerun_Knight Rider_Deutschland, 169)

99 AMG25-35: "Well, I think for me it was a little bit later. Because I, I don't know, until I was fourteen or fifteen, I actually did not watch any television. That means for me it was more with fifteen or sixteen, and for that reason it was never all that action-loaded for me." (GD25-35_Rerun_Knight Rider_Deutschland, 64 [o.t.]). Original quotation: "Also ich glaub, bei mir war das 'n bisschen später. Weil ich, weiß ich nich, bis ich vierzehn, fünfzehn war, hab' ich eigentlich gar kein Fernsehn geguckt. Das heißt, bei mir war das eher so mit fünfzehn, sechzehn und daaa hab' ich das, deswegen war das für mich auch nie so 'n jetzt super action-reich." (AMG25-35, GD25-35_Rerun_Knight Rider_Deutschland, 64)

100 Original quotation: "Also da keinerlei Gefühle bei. Keine. Gar nichts. Jetzt außer vielleicht mal, dass das jetzt halt, dass man merkt, wie lächerlich doch manches war. Also mit den Stunts. Dass das nicht grade 'n toller Stunt war." (AMG25-35, GD25-35_Rerun_Knight Rider_Deutschland, 66)

101 Original quotation: VMS25-35: "El personaje es odioso eh?" ZFS25-35: "El personaje es odioso o sea, como sea." VMS25-35: "Es odioso dónde los haya tío. A mí ya me caía mal de pequeño y todo también". ZFS25-35: "A mí también." (GS25-35_Rerun_Knight Rider_Spanien, 402 ff.)

reception, the example of the 25 to 35-year-old VMS25-35 shows that nostalgia may indeed work selectively. Triggered by the music, the interviewee develops nostalgia towards the positively valorised childhood context of the first-run, while the negative appraisal, however, impedes the development of the longing emotion towards other single levels of the text.

8.1.1.3 Conclusion on the reception of *Knight Rider*

In the precedent television analysis of *Knight Rider* (NBC, 1982), it was assumed that the rerun may provoke nostalgia on various levels. On a first level, nostalgia may be the emotion audiences expect when they choose to watch the rerun. Later, the artefact as a whole was assumed to be a potential trigger for 'A nostalgia' or the viewers' 'own A nostalgia', be it as a representative of 1980s television, the 1980s programme context, 'the 1980s' or a rather personal context. The single levels of the series were analysed as well. In general, it was assumed here that each level of the text may work as a "mnemonic prompt" for those who knew the first-run. Apart from that, the rerun gained new referential character, be it to 1980s television or to 'the 1980s', which, depending on the respective "retrospective classification", was assumed to be a potential object of nostalgia. On the level of narration and character, potential triggers of 'non-empathetic F nostalgia' were worked out. Other levels are likely to provoke this kind of nostalgia as well, for example the lost fascination (F or A emotion) regarding the main prop of the series as a potential object of nostalgia. Furthermore, 'A nostalgia' was assumed in the context of the anachronistic style the series contains from today's perspective. The "cultural baggage" of single props exposes gaps, which were assumed to work as potential nostalgia offers. Also the level of characters contains various potential triggers of nostalgia. Apart from the character's contrast to dominant trends and its reference to other 1980s series and events, the positively connoted traditional masculinity is offered to be the object of a potential nostalgia, thus to enable 'F nostalgia'. Hasselhoff as a person provides a clear gap between a positive past and worse present, which also, so it can be assumed, may facilitate nostalgia.

Not all of the presumed triggers of nostalgia that the text offers led to nostalgia in the context of the conducted group discussions. However, various cases of nostalgia could be observed. In the analysis two major blocks appeared. A first part was dedicated to the Reception of the *Knight Rider* rerun as an artefact as a whole, where contextual memories were most relevant. The second part, with the main patterns (1) *(Intertextual) references – roundabout nostalgia*, and (2) *Past and present experiences*, concentrated on the reception of potential triggers of nostalgia on the single levels of the text. That nostalgia is the gratification the viewers expect when they watch the rerun could not be deduced from the group discussions. Among the 29 participants, only two 25 to 35-year-olds, namely AMG25-35 and JMS25-35, state that they watched the rerun. For them the "light entertainment" character of the series was most important.[102] Here, surely a deeper investigation would be needed that could not be done in the course of this explorative study.

As assumed in the television analysis, nostalgia may be developed on the level of the artefact as a whole. A necessary condition is first and foremost that the audiences have memories of the series. As the analysis shows, this is the case among recipients from both territorial groups and age groups. However, the memories are differently coloured. Accordingly, the emerging patterns regarding the rerun as an artefact differ clearly. A clear gap between the two age groups, however, less between the different countries, could be observed. In all cases it was the 'original' viewing context that was remembered, even though *Knight Rider* had been re-broadcasted at various times over the years.

In both groups of the 25 to 35-year-olds and solely among those who know the first-run and retrospectively classified its context positively, cases of childhood nostalgia could be identified. Predictably, the socio-political context of the 1980s is not highlighted. Members of the age group were too young at that time to perceive socio-political issues consciously. The nostalgia is rather directed toward a general feeling of childhood insouciance, which is considered to be lost from today's perspective. Members of the same age group describe similar nostalgias.

This contrasts with the group of the 55 to 65-year-olds. Here, only one participant's description contains a clear rhetoric of nostalgia. It is also a positively valorised context here, which is considered to be lost from today's perspective, that is the object of nostalgia. This case suggests, but not sufficiently supports, that the spirit of optimism that dominated Spain during and around the years of transition holds its part in the nostalgic emotion directed towards "aquella época" [this epoch]. Other *Knight Rider*-related memories from within the age group were distinctly coloured, however. The general negative appraisal of the series or the context of

---

102 AMG25-35 says here "Yes. As I said. It's super light entertainment. You must not think about it. It's just there. Entertains a bit. And is gone again within one second." (GD25-35_Rerun_Knight Rider_Deutschland, 56 [o.t]) Original quotation: "Ja. Wie gesagt. Das ist super leicht[e] Unterhaltung. Man muss nicht drüber nachdenken. Das ist einfach da. Unterhält einen 'n bisschen. Und is' in ner Sekunde wieder weg." (AMG25-35, GD25-35_Rerun_Knight Rider_Deutschland, 56) This similarly applies to JMS25-35 who states: "No, but I like it ... because it takes one hour and, well see, you just got up ... you are half stupid, you do not have to think hard and you spend one hour entertained and that's it." (GS25-35_Rerun_Knight Rider_Spanien, 136 [o.t]) Original quotation: "No, pero me gusta porque... dura una hora y, pues mira, te acabas de levantar... estas medio tonto y no tienes ni qué pensar mucho y pasas una hora entretenida y ya está." (JMS25-35, GS25-35_Rerun_Knight Rider_Spanien, 136)

reception does not lead to nostalgia here. In other cases, no memories of a general lifeworld context could be observed.

The patterns *(Nostalgic) childhood memories, (Nostalgic) adulthood memories* and *No contextual memories* are strongly interrelated to Pattern Number Four, *Television 'then' and 'now'*, where the analysis describes memories that focus on television series or past television in general, as it is recalled in the context of *Knight Rider*. Among those (mostly) 25 to 35-year-olds who developed nostalgia towards the context, the pattern becomes part of the "positive classification" of the rerun. The contrary is the case among the 55 to 65-year-olds. In general, interviewees tend to make hierarchies of memories, in which the importance of one memory is sometimes more important than another. Other television memories that are of greater importance and that, it may be argued, are installed as alternative objects of nostalgia, are named.

Regarding the reception of potential triggers of nostalgia on the single levels of the text, the analysis shows that the rerun indeed gained differential quality for a broad audience of 'knowing' and 'not-knowing' audiences. This, however, is surely only a pre- condition for nostalgia as it is shown in the further patterns. As assumed in the theoretical part, the rerun has the 'connotation of pastness' also for those audiences who do not know the first-run. It was assumed that nostalgia on the basis of a respective "retrospective classification" of the reference is possible here. Indeed, *Knight Rider* provokes associations of 1980s' fashion, hairstyles and others which were subsumed under a pattern called *(Intertextual) references – roundabout nostalgia*. This was very apparent in the case of a 25 to 35-year-old who had neither seen the first-run nor the rerun. In contrast to the artefact as a whole, where only those interviewees developed nostalgia who related their own experiences to the rerun, it is the general 'connotation of pastness' that reminds the interviewee of her childhood in the 1980s. In a clear rhetoric of the gap very similar to other cases of childhood memories in the context of the rerun as an artefact, she explains her lost childhood innocence. The nostalgia, however, is not manifested in the questionnaire. Furthermore, the rerun refers to other 1980s' cultural products. Accordingly, in another case of a 'don't know', it is an intertextual reference on the level of the intro that activates a similar stream of consciousness in a 55 to 65-year-old. Nostalgia could not be further specified here.

Further cases of nostalgia were indicated that were developed in the context of positive past emotions related to the single levels of the series. As assumed in the television analysis, they were found exclusively amongin interviewees who know the rerun. In one case the music works as a "mnemonic prompt" for positively classified childhood memories. In two other cases, past emotions, both positively valorised and considered to be lost from today's perspective, became the object of nostalgic longing. With regards to the analysis, the link alone to 'common sense', resp.

'acquired' "retrospective classifications", can be presumed to be insufficient to provide the basis for nostalgia. However, as suggested by the reception study, it may indicate a kind of social desirability, which may lead the recipients to a (retrospective) classification of an emotion as nostalgia. No evidence was found for other forms of nostalgia, as they were assumed in the context of the television analysis.

In summary, it was shown that the text plays an important role in the 'pre-figuration' of nostalgia. The development of the nostalgia, however, always depends on how "we make" the past "contrast", as Davis says (Davis 1977, p. 417). Nostalgia is not the mere narration of a better past – such as a nostalgia that yearns for a specific element from back then that has been classified as being better – it rather showed itself as the yearning for a world of one's own positive past emotions and living contexts, be it on the level of the rerun as an artefact as such or on the single levels of the text. The rerun text is inevitably overlaid with further levels, whether they are memories of the context and reception of the first-run text, memories of context and reception of other texts that are intertextually interrelated to it or memories of the temporal background. They may be provoked by the rerun and, depending on their "retrospective classification", become the object of nostalgia. As the case of the 25 to 35-year-old JMS25-35 shows, it is very likely that a new reception somehow 'overwrites' the past reception and reception context or at least attaches itself to it, which may hinder the "simple" nostalgia. A reception analysis is inevitable if these nuances are to be uncovered. A nostalgia that was developed without positive personal memories and that solely developed on the basis of the nostalgic text could not be found.

8.1.2 The reception of the *The Avengers* rerun

As in the case of the *Knight Rider* rerun, the results of the reception study about *The Avengers* will form two major blocks, the first of which concentrates on the level of the *The Avengers* rerun as an artefact as a whole, and the second of which focuses on its single levels. In both blocks the same main patterns as in the *Knight Rider* discussion emerged. Regarding further sub-patterns, only few differences can be observed.

8.1.2.1 Reception of the rerun as an artefact as a whole

Regarding *The Avengers* rerun as an artefact as a whole, the main pattern consists of *(Nostalgic) contextual memories* as well. It can be divided into further sub-categories which are: (1) *No contextual memories*, (2) *(Nostalgic) adolescence/childhood memories*, and (3) *Television 'then' and 'now'*.

8.1.2.1.1 (Nostalgic) contextual memories

In the first conclusion on reruns as potential triggers of nostalgia, it has already been mentioned that the 'original' broadcast of the 1960s series *The Avengers* (ITV, 1961) is situated outside the life span of the 25 to 35-year-olds. Members of the age group, firstly, at best could have "prosthetic memories" of the 1960s or, secondly, since the series has been shown as a rerun, could remember it in the context of a later broadcast. As shown by the group discussions, neither the first nor the latter is the case. The sub-pattern of *No contextual memories* is dominant among the young ones. It could also be observed among some 55 to 65-year-olds. However, in this respect a clear gap between the age groups could be observed.

No contextual memories

Most of the interviewees from the age group of the 25 to 35-year-olds do not know the series at all. Those who do only vaguely remember fragments of *The Avengers* but neither recall when nor where they saw it last.

CFG25-35: "Well, I knew the series. I knew somehow what is going on there, but I don't recall having seen it." (GD25-35_Rerun_Avengers_Deutschland, 93 [o.t.])[103]

Accordingly, contextual memories of the series that might be the object of nostalgia cannot be observed. This similarly applies to half of the 55 to 65-year-olds of the Spanish group who never saw *Los Vengadores* (TVE, 1966).

(Nostalgic) adolescence/childhood memories

Apart from these few cases, *The Avengers* is clearly a part of the media memory of the older age group. Among the 55 to 65-year-olds, all participants of the German group and half of the Spanish group had watched *Mit Schirm, Charme und Melone* (ZDF, 1966), respectively *Los Vengadores* (TVE, 1966), in their youth. Exclusively in this age group the series is remembered in its 'original' viewing context. It also works as point of reference for memories of individual living circumstances of the recipients, just as it could already be observed among the 25 to 35-year-olds in the *Knight Rider* context.

In contrast to the latter, these memories are, however, clearly coloured by early television, very similar to what O'Sullivan (1991, p. 167) observed in the context of his study about early television memories, too. First and foremost, the participants foreground the (domestic) situation in which the series was seen. They recall with whom, when and where they saw the series. The position of the television set, the

---

103 Original quotation: "Also ich kannte auch die Serie. Ich wusste irgendwie worum es geht, aber ich hab' das nicht so bewusst im Hinterkopf, dass ich das geguckt hab." (CFG25-35, GD25-35_Rerun_Avengers_Deutschland, 93)

kind of chairs and their position, lamps that were switched on, but also rituals related to the series are important memory points:

GFG55-65: "Yes, that was really in the evening, well, I don't know whether we already had dinner or whether it was afterwards that I watched television with my mother. Well, both of us had our chairs. She also loved this series. And at the same time, I studied the vocabulary for school. Either Latin or English or whatever. This could be done at the same time while watching, that was an evening ritual for us [...]." (GD55-65_Rerun_Avengers_Deutschland, 196 [o.t.])[104]

GFG55-65: "Yes, I still know that today. The chair still exists and also the lamp under which I sat." (GD55-65_Rerun_Avengers_Deutschland, 234 [o.t.])[105]

PCFS55-65: "I remember that I watched it at home ... I remember that we watched it because, sure, back then the light was switched off after dinner. ... The small light was switched on. And the four of us, the whole family watched television. ... But, well. We liked it because we had no other option. Because there was nothing else." (GS55-65_Rerun_Avengers_Spanien, 119-124 [o.t.])[106]

The memories clearly show that the series is set in a time that O'Sullivan (1991) describes as the transition from the 'pre-television era' to the 'television era'. This is also very explicit in the description of the two other participants BFG55-65 and FMS55-65 who memorise *Mit Schirm, Charme und Melone* (ZDF, 1966) or *Los Vengadores* (TVE, 1966) in the context of public viewing experiences or in the narration of DMG55-65 who relates *The Avengers* to concrete memories of the television set at his parent's house:

---

104 Original quotation: "Ja, das war wirklich abends, also ich weiß gar nicht, ob es da schon Abendessen gab, oder ob's das danach gab, also, dass ich zusammen mit meiner Mutter ferngesehen habe. Also jeder hatte seinen Sessel. Die liebte diese Serien auch ((lacht)) und ich hab' dabei Vokabeln gelernt. Entweder Latein oder Englisch oder was weiß ich, das konnt man so nebenbei so machen und trotzdem mitgucken, das war so 'n so 'n Abendritual bei uns [...]." (GFG55-65, GD55-65_Rerun_Avengers_Deutschland, 196)

105 Original quotation: "Ja, ich weiß immer noch, also den Sessel gibt's ja heute immer noch und die Lampe, unter der ich gesessen habe." (GFG55-65, GD55-65_Rerun_Avengers_ Deutschland, 234)

106 Original quotation: "Yo recuerdo que la veía en casa ... . Recuerdo que yo la veía la veíamos porque claro entonces en casa se cerraba la luz después de cenar. ... Se poníaba la luz pequeña. Y los cuatro, toda la familia se ponía a la tele. ... Pero bueno. Nos gustaba porque además no teníamos opción. Porque no había otra cosa." (PCFS55-65, GS55-65_Rerun_Avengers_Spanien, 119-124)

DMG55-65: "Yes, I think back then, I think, we did not have a television set yet. Well, that was always something special. (And of course then you looked at it differently)." (GD55-65_Rerun_Avengers_Deutschland, 144 [o.t.])[107]

DMG55-65: "[...] When we got a television set, I memorised where the TV set stood, and then also with the garden behind it and stuff. Well, that did pop up immediately. I directly knew. Emma Peel. I knew it immediately." (GD55-65_Rerun_Avengers_Deutschland, 235 [o.t.])[108]

DMG55-65: ".... In principle you are automatically at home in front of the TV set and watch." (GD55-65_Rerun_Avengers_Deutschland, 265 [o.t.])[109]

As in the descriptions of O'Sullivan (1991) the whole dispositif is part of the context memories. Notwithstanding, the nostalgias that can be observed do not differ from the cases of childhood nostalgia as they were explained in the context of *Knight Rider*.

Also, here the object of nostalgia is again a phase of life, very comparable to the latter. Again the development of the emotion depends upon how the context and the potential trigger are appraised from the present position. Not all of the memories take the form of nostalgia towards the past contexts of reception. Again the development of the emotion depends on how the context is appraised from the present position.

Already in these first quoted sections different appraisals become apparent, which suggest a potential nostalgia of the participants or not. In the statement of PCFS55-65, for instance, it already resonates that she does not consider the series to be all that relevant. In her memory she watched it because there was "no other option". She does not speak explicitly about her general living circumstances but makes clear that nostalgia is not what she felt, clearly differentiating between the mere remembrance and the nostalgic longing.

---

107 Original quotation: "Ja, wir hatten ja damals, glaub ich, noch kein Fernsehn. Das war dann immer was Besonderes. (Und da hat man das natürlich anders gesehn)." (DMG55-65, GD55-65_Rerun_Avengers_Deutschland, 144)

108 Original quotation: "[...] Als wir 'n Fernseher bekamen, das hab' ich mir auch gemerkt, wo der Fernseher stand, und mit dem Garten dann auch dahinter und so. Also das war sofort wieder da. Wusst ich gleich. Emma Peel. Wusst ich sofort." (DMG55-65, GD55-65_Rerun_Avengers_Deutschland, 235 -235)

109 Original quotation: ".... Du bist automatisch im Prinzip ... wieder vorm Fernseher zu Hause und guckst." (DMG55-65, GD55-65_Rerun_Avengers_Deutschland, 265)

PCFS55-65: "Let's see, I remember, but not with nostalgia." (GS55-65_Nostalgie Allgemein_Spanien, 10 [o.t.])[110]

Also in the questionnaire, she states not to have had the experience of nostalgia in the course of the group discussion.

DMG55-65 instead, similar to what has been described regarding the 25 to 35-year-olds in the case of *Knight Rider*, gives the series a special value in rising it to a scarce commodity ("we had no television at that time"). He later allows for the general possibility that he could develop "a kind of nostalgic feeling". Here, however, the object is the broader 1960s context of the series that he retrospectively classified as being better in comparison to the now:

DMG55-65: "[Well, in my case it is, let's say] a kind of nostalgic feelings. Thus if I watched it now, for example, this first episode with Emma Peel, from the old series, unlike today that was an incredibly simple time. Back then there was no climate catastrophe, [...] all that did not exist yet. I'd probably slide into a nostalgic feeling. Well, as I said, everything was still relatively easy." (GD55-65_NostalgieAllgemein_Deutschland, 38 [o.t.])[111]

In the end it seems that the "kind of" nostalgia he claims is indeed only a potential one. At least in the questionnaire the interviewee states to have felt nostalgia, but not in the context of *The Avengers*. It seems that another nostalgia has more relevance here.

Again, it is a different case with GFG55-65, who later specifies the context of the 'original' reception of Mit Schirm, Charme und Melone (ZDF, 1966) as "harmonic" times (GD55-65_Rerun_Avengers_Deutschland, 198 [o.t.]). As she describes it in the questionnaire, she develops nostalgia towards this past world of harmony, towards "evenings in front of the television set with [...][her] mother (Schirm,

---

110 Original quotation: "A ver, yo recuerdo, pero no con nostalgia." (PCFS55-65, GS55-65_NostalgieAllgemein_Spanien, 10)

111 Original quotation: "[Also bei mir ist das so, sagen wir mal] so 'ne Art nostalgische Gefühle. Also wenn ich mir das jetzt angucken würde, da zum Beispiel diese erste Folge mit Emma Peel, da von der alten Serie, ne, also das war doch 'ne unglaublich einfache Zeit im Gegensatz zu heute. Da gab's noch keine Klimakatastrophe [...] gab's alles noch gar nicht, ja. Würd' ich da wahrscheinlich schon in so n' nostalgisches Gefühl so rein gleiten. Ach so. Ne, weil wie gesagt, es war damals noch relativ einfach." (DMG55-65, GD55-65_NostalgieAllgemein_Deutschland, 38)

Charme und Melone) up to the spatial situation and the living room" (GFG55-65, Questionnaire_Connotation of nostalgia_55-65-year-old Germans, 24 [o.t.])[112].

Apart from these three cases, also other participants come to discuss context memories and nostalgia. BFG55-65 at first highlights the general potential of television series to trigger memories of past reception situations.

BFG55-65: "There are indeed these television series or also films where I suddenly see how I used to sit in front of the TV, yes. While I watched them, for example." (GD55-65_Rerun_Avengers_Deutschland, 273 [o.t.])[113]

Asked if this was the case regarding *Mit Schirm, Charme und Melone* (ZDF, 1966), she denies that at first:

BFG55-65: "No, not really. As I said, I know that I watched it but somehow it didn't appeal to me that much." (GD55-65_Rerun_Avengers_Deutschland, 275 [o.t.])[114]

However, in the last section of the discussion she explicitly refers to nostalgia in the context of the rerun:

BFG55-65: "Yes, nostalgia, well, hmm, in the context of some things I really had a reminiscence of how it was at that time. [...] For example. Yes. Indeed this reminiscence about situations or places where I, where I watched it. That this returned. [A]lso, that it suddenly conjures up, that I er, that was the time when I had started my apprenticeship, and at that time I lived in a boarding school and I know, I suddenly remembered that we sat together with several others and watched something. I suddenly saw us sitting there. And one can call that nostalgia, too. But that was not the case regarding all the things we have seen tonight."
M: "Well, especially in the case of *Mit Schirm, Charme und Melone*?"
BFG55-65: "Yes, in that case." (GD55-65_Nostalgie Allgemein_Deutschland, 23-29 [o.t.])[115]

---

112 Original quotation: "Sich erinnern an gemeinsame Fernsehabende mit meiner Mutter (Schirm, Charme und Melone) bis hin zu der räumlichen Situation und Wohnzimmer." (GFG55-65, Questionnaire_Connotation of nostalgia_55-65-year-old Spaniards, 24)

113 Original quotation: "[B]ei mir gibt's manchmal schon so Fernsehserien oder auch Filme, wo ich dann plötzlich mich wiedersehe, wie ich davorsitze, ja, wo ich das gesehen habe, zum Beispiel." (BFG55-65, GD55-65_Rerun_Avengers_Deutschland, 273)

114 Original quotation: "Ne, eigentlich nicht. Wie gesagt, ich weiß, dass ich's gesehn habe, aber das hat irgendwie damals nicht so 'n großen Eindruck gemacht." (BFG55-65, GD55-65_Rerun_Avengers_Deutschland, 275)

115 Original quotation: BFG55-65: "Ja, Nostalgie, ja gut, eh, bei manchen Dingen hatt' ich schon (ne) Erinnerung, wie das zu der Zeit war. [...] Zum Beispiel. Ja. Schon so dieses Zurückerinnern an Situationen oder an Orte, wo ich dann, wo ich das gesehn hab. Dass

Here, the nostalgia also finds its object in a past living condition. However, it is quite clear that it is not about a nostalgia that surged up in the course of the reception but rather one that emerged in the course of the remembering process during the group discussion. The interviewee contradicts herself again in the questionnaire, stating not to have felt nostalgia in the course of the discussion. We can speculate that the negative connotation of nostalgia works as a kind of filter here, too, which hinders the manifestation of the nostalgic emotion. In any case the interviewee describes a process, namely the emergence of contextual memories related to *The Avengers*, just as it already could be observed among others of her age group.

Instead, the reception experience of FMS55-65 is clearly definable as nostalgic. Already in the warm-up phase of the discussion he emphasises that *Los Vengadores* (TVE, 1966) is one of his favourite programmes. Beyond doubt he gives the series a high relevance. The memories he describes as emerging in the course of the reception take clear nostalgic forms:

FMS55-65: "... I watched it the last time five, six years ago when I saw some part of the series. I, of course I watch this series, I remember many things. For example, there is a funny thing, when the series starts in colour, it worsens. [...] It was a series to watch in black and white. [...] We always watched it with three friends, each of us studied at a different site. It was on Tuesdays from four to five when they broadcasted it the first year. And we would meet every Tuesday to watch the series of *Los Vengadores*. [...] Sure, I remember when we watched *Los Vengadores*. It reminded me of these three friends, one of whom we buried last year, [...] but we were always together. And for me *Los Vengadores* brings back many memories. Because it was an era, it was a nice era. I was 18 or 19 years old. The (better) era. [...] Of not doing anything but picking up girls. We had a good time." (GS55-65_Rerun_Avengers_Spanien, 30-33 [o.t.])[116]

das wieder zurückkam. [A]lso, dass ich plötzlich vor mir gesehen habe, dass ich eh. Das war so die Zeit, als ich mit meiner Ausbildung angefangen hatte, und da hab' ich in einem Internat gewohnt und ich weiß, fiel mir plötzlich ein, dass wir da zusammen zu mehreren zusammengesessen haben und ham was geguckt. Das hab' ich dann plötzlich gesehn, also, wie wir da sitzen. Und das kann man auch Nostalgie nennen. Aber das ist nicht bei allen Sachen, die wir heute Abend gesehen haben". M: "Also vor allem bei *Mit Schirm, Charme und Melone?*" BFG55-65: "Ja, da." (GD55-65_Nostalgie Allgemein_ Deutschland, 23-29)

116 Original quotation: "... Yo la vi la última vez hace cinco, seis años que vi alguna cosa de la serie. Yo lo, claro que veo esta serie, me acuerdo de muchas cosas. Por ejemplo hay una cosa curiosa cuando empieza la serie en color baja. [...] Era una serie para verla en blanco y negro. [...] La íbamos a ver siempre con tres amigos que cada uno estudiaba en un sitio diferente. Era un martes de cuatro a cinco que la daban el primer año. Y nos juntamos todo los martes para ver la serie de *Los Vengadores*. Era una serie

Like other interviewees from the age group, FMS55-65 remembers when, where and with whom he used to watch the 'original' series. Even though *Los Vengadores* has been re-broadcasted various times, and even though the participant had seen reruns of the series, the 'original' 1960s reception experience and its context is foregrounded. In a clear nostalgic stance, the better 'then' contrasts with the worse 'now', just as Tannock (1995) describes it as being typical of the rhetoric of nostalgia in general. The notion of the irretrievable and the loss – be it the loss of a friend, the loss of youth or the loss of a general light-heartedness of a time where flirting is remembered to have been his principal preoccupation – is clearly present. Unsurprisingly, the participant later states that he felt nostalgia in the course of the reception, both in the questionnaire and in the course of the discussion:

FMS55-65: "When we watch *Los Vengadores*, I remember the past with nostalgia, of course. Because I was 20 years old. I am 70 soon. Today I wear glasses and dentures, yes." (GS55-65_Nostalgie Allgemein_Spanien, 11-19 [o.t.])[117]

Again, the better in put in contrast with the worse present. Interestingly, in the questionnaire he restricts the trigger of his nostalgia once again to the black and white excerpt (GFG55-65, Questionnaire_Connotation of nostalgia_55-65-year-old Spaniards, 21), which he already had given a higher value in the course of the discussion. The socio-political context, "la época en que estábamos levantando el brazo" [the time when we were lifting our arms] (GS55-65_Rerun_Avengers_Spanien, 54 [o.t.]), as he states in a self-distancing, ironic stance, is brought into the discussion due to the contributions of other interviewees but excluded from this private and personally centred (nostalgic) memory.[118] Also in the other cases, the

---

completamente de culto. Porque esto es completamente diferente. Yo me recordaba claro cuando (hemos visto) *Los Vengadores*. Me he recordado a estos tres amigos que curiosamente uno lo enteramos el año pasado, [...], pero siempre estábamos junto. Y a mi me trae muchos recuerdos *Los Vengadores*. Porque era una época, era una época bonita. Tenía 18, 19 años. La época (mejor). [...] De no hacer (nada que) correr detrás de la chicas. Lo pasábamos bien." (FMS55-65, GS55-65_Rerun_Avengers_Spanien, 30-33)

117 Original quotation: "Cuando vemos *Los Vengadores* yo recuerdo tiempos pasados, con nostalgia, claro. Porque tenía 20 años. (Me he vuelto a los 70 pronto). Hoy llevo gafas y dientes postizos, sí." (FMS55-65, GS55-65_Nostalgie Allgemein_Spanien, 11-19)

118 This is surely similar to what Assmann (2011 [my comments]) explains in the context of ostalgia: "We have here to do with a discrepancy between social and political memory. While East Germany [or in this case Franco's regime] is today officially condemned as having been a criminal state, it continues to live in people's memory as an important phase of their biographies and identities. The abrupt and blanket depreciation of a half or

nostalgia object may rather be located in the private sphere. Socio-political contexts are excluded. An exception was the case of DMG55-65. His (potential) nostalgia indeed concentrates on the "simple time" in general yet does not manifest itself in the questionnaire.

According to Davis, the nostalgia FMS55-65 exposes can be categorised as simple, dominated by the "largely unexamined belief that THINGS WERE BETTER [...] *THEN* THAN *NOW*" (Davis, 1979, p. 18 [emphasis in the original]), just as the other nostalgias and potential nostalgias described in this section. It seems that the general reflexive character of *The Avengers* has, at least on the level of the artefact as a whole, no effect on the colouring of the nostalgias developed in its context.

In other cases context memories are indeed described but they are clearly highlighted as not being worth longing for. For AMS55-65 of the Spanish group *Los Vengadores* (TVE, 1966) is for instance inevitably related to the socio-political background of the Franco-era that is described as "dark" and "sad".

AMS55-65: "*Los Vengadores* [...] what it brings back is the era we lived in, a very dark era, very sad, (that) watches the world through a keyhole. England more or less is like that. [...]." (GS55-65_Rerun_Avengers_Spanien, 72 [o.t.])[119]

In contrast to the case of FMS55-65, it also seems that "the era" is far less separable from the private sphere for him. In the questionnaire he describes his past in general as not being worth longing for. He states here:

"I am not very nostalgic. Well, I think frequently remembering the past leads to nowhere. Mainly in my case, since I didn't have many opportunities to be happy." (AMS55-65, Connotation of nostalgia_55-65-year-old Spaniards, 17 [o.t.])[120]

Comparable to the case of the 25 to 35-year-old ZFS25-35 in the context of the *Knight Rider*-discussion, this negative memory impedes every nostalgic stance. Apart from that, a general negative connotation of nostalgia can be observed, a fact that has been highlighted as being dominant among the age group in general.

---

the whole of a life leads to the resistance in remembrance that we call ostalgie [or nostalgia in this case]."

119 Original quotation: "*Los Vengadores* [...] lo que (me trae) es la época que vivíamos, una época muy oscura, muy triste, (que) ve un poco el mundo por el agujero. Inglaterra más o menos es así. [...]." (AMS55-65, GS55-65_Rerun_Avengers_Spanien, 72)

120 Original quotation: "Yo no soy muy nostálgico pues creo que no conduce a nada el recordar con frecuencia el pasado. Sobre todo, como es mi caso, que no he tenido muchas oportunidades de ser feliz." (AMS55-65, Connotation of nostalgia_55-65-year-old Spaniards, 17)

The same applies to the 55 to 65-year-old FFG55-65 who also highlights her negative context memories:

FFG55-65: "Well, I found the time not nice at all, frankly, the late Sixties. At that time I had my problems with myself, with the world, with everything, but I have noticed that I did not think about *Mit Schirm, Charme und Melone* for forty years." (GD55-65_Nostalgie Allgemein_Deutschland, 40-42 [o.t.])[121]

In the case of MFS55-56 the context memories encompass the parental television restriction due to which she wasn't allowed to watch the series. [122] These memories are not the object of nostalgia.

Television 'then' and 'now'

Only for the 55 to 65-year-olds and only for those who indeed saw the series, *The Avengers* is embedded in memories of the 1960s television programme. Both the 55 to 65-year-old Spaniards and the 55 to 65-year-old Germans dispose of concrete memories of the 'original' programme slot of the series. While the programme context is less an issue among the Germans, only HMG55-65 relates the series to other 1960s British cultural products, such as Edgar Wallace (ZDF, 1969) or television hits, such as the Durbridge crime films, the Spanish group discusses the programme context intensively.[123]

Already in the warm-up phase of the discussion FMS55-65 recalls *Los Vengadores* (TVE, 1966) together with other 1960s series, such as *Los Intocables* (TVE, 1964) [The Untouchables, ABC, 1959], *El Fugitivo* (TVE, 1965) [The Fugitive, ABC, 1963], *Bonanza* (TVE, 1963) [NBC, 1959], or *El Santo* (TVE, 1969)

---

121 Original quotation: "Also ich fand die Zeit überhaupt nicht schön, ehrlich gesagt, Ende der Sechziger. Ich hatte da mit mir meine Probleme, mit der Welt meine Probleme, mit allem Möglichen meine Probleme gehabt, hab aber gemerkt, ich hab' schon seit vierzig Jahren nicht mehr über *Mit Schirm, Charme und Melone* nachgedacht." (FFG55-65, GD55-65_Nostalgie Allgemein_Deutschland, 40-42)

122 In total it seems that the series must have caused a veritable conflict with the parental generation in Spain at that time. Apart from MFS55-65 who refers to the general prohibition to watch the series, also the 55 to 65-year-old PCFS55-65 states that "at home they [the parents] said, 'Not that one!' It was a hoax they didn't like." Original quotation: "En casa decían que esto no. Era una paparruchada que no les gustaba." (GS55-65_Rerun_Avengers_Spanien, 119-124 [o.t.])

123 Here we should mention the fact that the past television consumption of the two groups differs decisively. While the German interviewees watched on average ≤ 1h television per day in their youth, the Spanish group had an average television consumption of > 1h < 3h per day.

[The Saint, ITV, 1967]. Later, other series that are remembered in the programme context of *Los Vengadores* (TVE, 1966) are named. Apart from American productions, such as *Mr. ED* (TVE, 1962[124]) [Syndication/CBS, 1961], decisive memory points are also the Spanish productions of that time. The memory is broader than in the *Knight Rider* context and encompasses not only fictional programme but also shows, show-hosts and other personalities of the era. Here; the interviewees refer to shows such as *Un millón para el mejor* (TVE, 1968), or to the musical programmes *La Gran Parada* (TVE, 1950-1964) or *Los Amigos del Martes* (TVE, 1961-1964). Different to the television memories of the 25 to 35-year-olds, these memories, it may be stated, are rather locally shaped – a fact that also concurs with observations such as those made in the context of *The Global Media Project* (Volkmer, 2006). Only 1960s programmes, i.e. shows from the 'original' time span of broadcasting, are named. However, in contrast to the contributions made in the context of the *Knight Rider* (NBC, 1982) rerun where interviewees indeed name alternative nostalgia triggers and tend towards creating hierarchies among the series they remember, this is not the case in the context of *The Avengers*, which is in no case negatively valorised by those of the age group who know the first-run.

Next to these more specific memories of single television programmes in the context of *The Avengers*, broader memories and reflections of past television are also related to the rerun here. It has been shown that both *Los Vengadores* (TVE, 1966) and *Mit Schirm, Charme und Melone* (ZDF, 1966) stuck out of the programme context of their time. A general rhetoric which poses the better past television against the worse now can therefore not be observed among the 55 to 65-year-olds – rather the contrary is the case. However, for those among the 55 to 65-year-olds who saw the series and liked it, which was everyone without any exception, the accentuation of the bad quality of huge parts of the 1960s programme works in order to highlight the single status of *Los Vengadores* (TVE, 1966) and *Mit Schirm, Charme und Melone* (ZDF, 1966).

IMG55-65: "Now, one also has to state that in the Sixties there was a lot of junk, too. [...]. An original British series, which was good, too, well, that was something special in the '60s." (GD55-65_Rerun_Avengers_Deutschland, 246-251 [o.t.])[125]

---

124   At least this is the date of the first entry I could find about the series in *La Vanguardia* (see *La Vanguardia*, 4.10.1962; p. 32).

125   Original quotation: "Jetzt muss man auch sagen, in den Sechzigern gab's auch viel Schrott. [...]. Jetzt da ne original englische Serie, die auch noch gut war. Also das war schon was Besonderes so in den 60ern." (IMG55-65, GD55-65_Rerun_Avengers_ Deutschland, 246-251)

FMS55-65: "It was an absolute cult series. Because this is totally different." (GS55-65_Rerun_Avengers_Spanien, 30 [o.t.])[126]

In both the German and the Spanish group the series is presented as exceptional in comparison to programme context in general. This contributes to its "retrospective classification" as being "something special" or "cult". Above all, the interviewees from the Spanish group highlight their disappointment with the programme of the 1960s. *The Avengers* was an exception.

Apart from that, it has already been stated that the television memories of the 55 to 65-year-olds can be located in the transition phase from 'pre-television era' to 'television era'. While DMG55-65 indeed highlights that *Mit Schirm, Charme und Melone* (ZDF, 1966) was "something special" due to the mere fact that the family did not have a television set in the beginning (GD55-65_Rerun_Avengers _Deutschland, 144 [o.t.]), the 55 to 65-year-old PCFS55-65 of the Spanish group emphasises that she liked the series but that there was "no other option" anyhow (GS55-65_Rerun_Avengers_Spanien, 119-124 [o.t.]).

It is this argument that leads to a devaluation of the series on the side of the younger age group. VMS25-35 emphasises:

"There was no variety in that time. I think that these series were successful because there was nothing else. [...] And today with all the offers, man! Why should I watch something like that!" (GS25-35_Rerun_Avengers_Spanien, 204-206 [o.t.])[127]

This quotation alone shows that *Los Vengadores* is negatively contrasted with the current programme. In a general comparison of the rerun with today's television the verdict is clear:

JMS25-35: "Well [...], incomparable, for sure [...]"
VMS25-35: "I would never watch it!"
HMS25-35: "Worse."

---

126 Original quotation: "Era una serie completamente culto. Porque esto es completamente diferente." (FMS55-65, GS55-65_Rerun_Avengers_Spanien, 30)

127 Original quotation: "Es que en esa época no había variedad. [...] yo creo que triunfaban esas series porque no había otra cosa que ver. [...]¡Y ahora con todas las que hay tío! ¡Anda que vería yo una cosa así!" (VMS25-35, GS25-35_Rerun_Avengers_Spanien, 204-206)

AFS25-35: "Worse."

VMS25-35: "Worse [...]." (GS25-35_Rerun_Avengers_Spanien, 199-206 [o.t.])[128]

Here, nostalgia is not supported.

8.1.2.2 Reception of nostalgia on the single levels of the text

Later, as in the case of *Knight Rider*, the interviewees focus on the single levels of the rerun. Different patterns of reception may also be highlighted here, (1) *(Intertextual) references – roundabout nostalgia*, and, (2) *Past and present experiences* being the main ones. Again the sub-patterns also coincide on a wide range with those that have been explained in the context of the *Knight Rider* rerun.

No matter whether a single aspect of the rerun provokes nostalgia or not, first of all it has to attract the recipients' attention. Regarding the reruns, it has been assumed that the attention is due to the new "differential quality" the format gains in its new context. It has been shown in the television analysis that the 1960s series *The Avengers* clashes with its context on every imaginable level. Not only the narration, props and costumes but also the camera, montage, lighting, music and characters contrast with today's television.

Unsurprisingly, since the pop genre in general highlights the "surface" (Buxton, 1990, p. 97), the narrative level is less commented by the interviewees[129]. Apart from that, all levels attract their attention. In general, the whole mise-en-scène is discussed.

AFG55-65: "I was mostly interested in the fashion, for example." (GD55-65_Rerun_Avengers_Deutschland, 53-55 [o.t.])[130]

DFG25-35: "The car." (GD25-35_Rerun_Avengers_Deutschland, 119 [o.t.])

---

128 Original quotation: JMS25-35: "Ah [...], nada que ver, claro [...]." VMS25-35: "¡Nunca lo vería!" HMS25-35: "Peor." AFS25-35: "Peor." VMS25-35: "Peor [...]." (GS25-35_Rerun_Avengers_Spanien, 199-206)

129 Only DMG55-65 comes to discuss the absurd contents of one of the scenes of the examples that have been shown: "Alone the scene in which Emma Peel practises stabbing this heart hanging from the door. Today, no one would dare to do such a thing. Are you nuts or what?" (DMG55-65, GD55-65_Rerun_Avengers_Deutschland, 68-71 [o.t.]) Original quotation: "Ich fand allein diese Szene, wo diese Emma Peel an diesem aufgehängten Herz da an der Tür (übt). Das würde doch heute niemand mehr wagen, so was zu machen. Hast du 'ne Meise irgendwie?" (DMG55-65, GD55-65_Rerun_Avengers_Deutschland, 68-71)

130 Original quotation: "Da hat mich zum Beispiel auch die Mode sehr interessiert." (AFG55-65, GD55-65_Rerun_Avengers_Deutschland, 53-55)

EMG25-35: "Above all, the outfit of the woman. The things that are so very much present today, due to the retro trend."

DFG25-35: "The hairstyle."

EMG25-35: "This attracted my attention. There are surely details that are (typical of the) Sixties. This was what I found most striking." (GD25-35_Rerun_Avengers_Deutschland, 116-119 [o.t.])[131]

Action and performance are at issue at various points of the discussions (see also e.g. CFG25-35, FCFS55-65).

AMG25-35: "Well, just regarding the facial expressions and gestures and so on. Not at all excited. Not so pretentious." (GD25-35_Rerun_Avengers_Deutschland, 72-74 [o.t.])[132]

GFG55-65: "You don't really relate to the character. She has such an inner distance or even an outer distance." (GD55-65_Rerun_Avengers_Deutschland, 114 [o.t.])[133]

Apart from that, camera style, music, sounds, and montage attract the attention of the interviewees.

As in the case of the *Knight Rider* rerun, the pattern appears independently of age group, gender or country. However, it should be noted that it is wider spread among the 25 to 35-year-olds. Among the 55 to 65-year-olds, contextual aspects and others, as they will be commented in the following, encompass larger parts of the discussion and gain more relevance. Most of the statements go hand in hand with an integration of the highlighted item into a context of references where it is, for instance, categorised as being "typical for the 60s" or already has a negative or positive connotation. Attention, so it was presumed in the television analysis, is a condition on the basis of which nostalgia may arise. How these aspects, contextualisation and valorisation, are influenced by the factors of how or if the series has been perceived earlier, and if and how nostalgia surges, shall be commented in the following.

---

131 Original quotation: EMG25-35: "Vor allem das Outfit der Frau hat. Also was durch den Retro-Trend jetzt wieder so präsent ist." DFG25-35: "Die Frisur." EMG25-35: "Das ist mir eigentlich hauptsächlich aufgefallen. Da gibt's sicher Details die stimmig sind (typisch) Sechziger. Das fand ich dann auch am auffälligsten." (GD25-35_Rerun_Avengers_Deutschland, 116-119)

132 Original quotation: "Also alleine durch die Mimik und Gestik und so weiter. Überhaupt nicht aufgeregt. Überhaupt nicht so aufgesetzt." (AMG25-35, GD25-35_Rerun_Avengers_Deutschland, 72-74)

133 Original quotation: "Du versinkst nicht in der Rolle, die hat so 'ne innerliche Distanz, oder auch 'ne äußere Distanz da ..." (GFG55-65, GD55-65_Rerun_Avengers_Deutschland, 114)

8.1.2.2.1 (Intertextual) references – roundabout nostalgia

As assumed in the television analysis, both for those who know the first-run and for those who do not, the *The Avengers* rerun has the 'connotation of pastness' from today's perspective. On the one hand it refers to 'the 1960s' in general, and on the other it exposes an indexical relationship to other cultural products from or set in the era.

In the course of the group discussion, the series is commented on as being representative of the 1960s. This pattern is mainly observable among the 25 to 35-year-olds. Here, different aspects, such as props and décor, are seen as being significant of the 1960s. Also "how the films are made" is understood as being typical of the time span. In contrast to the *Knight Rider* discussion, where the general referential character prompted personal, nostalgic memories of the 1980s at least in one case, for the 25 to 35-year-olds it refers to a mediated knowledge of the era at the utmost.

AMG25-35: "[I think] I don't know much about the '60s. Well, actually, not. Well, I'd rather think of a lamp shop in Prenzlauer Berg[134] where they have retro lamps. That's what would come to mind." (GD25-35_Rerun_Avengers_Deutschland, 121 [o.t.])[135]

ZFS25-35: "No, I don't relate it to the past [in Spain]. If at all, I relate it to the television they [the parents] could have watched." (GS25-35_Rerun_Avengers_Spanien, 132 [o.t.] [my comment])[136]

EMG25-35: "Well, I rather associate it with such things, like London in the '60s, with what one knows from images. This is a very strong association. [...] Well it helps me to classify it. If I see it, I naturally look for references in order to be able to say what it IS. Yes, and then this comes to my mind." (GD25-35_Rerun_Avengers_Deutschland, 123-129 [o.t.])[137]

---

134 An urban district in Berlin.

135 Original quotation: "[Ich glaub ich] hab von den 60ern wenig Vorstellungen. Also. Eigentlich nicht. Also ich würd' eher sagen, Prenzlauer Berg und halt irgend 'n Lampenladen. Wo halt die, die Retro-Lampen drinhängen. Würd' ich daran denken." (AMG25-35, GD25-35_Rerun_Avengers_Deutschland, 121)

136 Original quotation: "No, yo tampoco [lo relaciono] de aquí no. Si acaso a la televisión que pudieron haber visto ellos [los padres]." (ZFS25-35, GS25-35_Rerun_ Avengers_Spanien, 132)

137 Original quotation: "Also ich assoziier das dann eher mit so Sachen, mit so London 60s mit dem, was man da von Bildern kennt. Das das ist quasi als Assoziation dann sehr stark bei mir. [...] Also so hilft es mir, das einzuordnen. Wenn ich das sehe, dann such ich halt natürlich nach irgendwelchen Referenzen, dass ich dann sagen kann, was is denn das

The last statement makes it very explicit that by this framing the interviewees are able to make sense of the series. A kind of "prosthetic memory", the presentation of this memory as somehow the interviewees' own memories, which may be the basis for nostalgia, is not found. The distance from their own lives is always obvious. Neither does the rerun inspire a 'whitewashing' narration of the 1960s.

In general, the pattern is less observable among the 55 to 65-year-olds, and when it is there, it is distinctly different. Here, it rather depends on the interviewees' own living reality whether it is put in reference to it or set in contrast. The first is mainly notable in the case of the 55 to 65-year-old EFG55-65. Her associations demonstrate a "referential framing" relating the props of the series to her own life in the 1960s:

EFG55-65: "Well, during the second one I just thought: Is that an Adidas tracksuit? [...] Yes, at that time, they were things that were in. Well, that's when I wondered if it was one or not. That was a totally exciting time. Absolutely wow, that was good." (GD55-65_Rerun_ Avengers_Deutschland, 203, 212 [o.t.])[138]

Despite the positive evaluation of the past ("wow, that was good") she later says:

EFG55-65: "Well, I don't develop feelings of nostalgia. I like to think back because it is part of my history but I'm not nostalgic. Well, you were on the go and that was a pleasant feeling. In your late fifties you're not really on the go. And that's the difference, I think." (GD55-65_Nostalgie Allgemein_Deutschland, 51 [o.t.])[139]

Even though her assessment has the rhetoric of the gap, EFG55-65 claims not to feel nostalgia. One factor that also must be recognised here is the negative connotation of nostalgia of huge parts of the age group. Precisely EFG55-65 is one of those interviewees whose description of a 'nostalgic person' is clearly negative. Regarding

---

eigentlich. Ja, und dann kommt mir halt das so in den Kopf." (EMG25-35, GD25-35_Rerun_Avengers_Deutschland, 123-129)

138 Original quotation: "Also bei dem zweiten hab' ich jetzt gedacht, ist das 'n Adidas Trainingsanzug. [...] Ja, damals, damals waren das so Dinger, ja, die war'n hoch. Da hab' ich gedacht, Mensch war das jetzt einer oder nicht. Das war 'ne absolut spannende Zeit. Absolut eh puhh eh, war gut." (EFG55-65, GD55-65_Rerun_Avengers_ Deutschland, 203; 212)

139 Original quotation: "Also nostalgische Gefühle entwickle ich nicht. Ich denke durchaus gern dran zurück, weil 's ja auch zu meiner Geschichte [gehört] aber ich bin da nicht nostalgisch. Also man war auf dem Sprung und das war 'n angenehmes Gefühl, und das ist man mit Ende fünfzig, ist man nicht mehr so richtig auf dem Sprung. Und das eh ist der Unterschied, denk ich mal." (EFG55-65, GD55-65_Nostalgie Allgemein_ Deutschland, 51)

the latter case, the description of a contrast between the series and one's own living reality, it is referred to an excerpt of the discussion of the 55 to 65-year-old Spaniards. Asked whether they relate the series to the 1960s in Spain, only PCFS55-65 with her intensive private contextual memories says yes. The rest of the interviewees are of the opinion that the contrary is the case:

M: "And does this have anything to do with Spain of the era?"
PCFS55-65: "Yes, yes, sure."
FMS55-65: "The contrary. This was what we didn't have."
PMS55-65: "The contrary."
MFS55-65: "That's right."
FMS55-65: "Because, what were the '60s in Europe compared with what was here, when there was a slight opening, and when the tourists started to come?" (GS55-65_Rerun_Avengers _Spanien, 125-130 [o.t.])[140]

It cannot be said nostalgia comes from associations related to single levels of the series.

At the same time, and comparable to the *Knight Rider* rerun, the *The Avengers* rerun is also integrated in a net of references to cultural products. As in the case of the *Knight Rider* rerun, the pattern may be observed among those who did not know the first-run, here mostly among the 25 to 35-year-olds. They frame the programme and its single levels from protagonists to the mise-en-scène with a wide range of references. First and foremost, cultural texts, such as films and television series, are named. This fact is also explicitly noted by the 25 to 35-year-old interviewees.

CFG25-35: "It mostly reminds me of other films or series from the period." (GD25-35_Rerun_Avengers_Deutschland, 93 [o.t.])[141]

VMS25-35: "I associated it with […] movies, series of these old ones… because I don't like them." (VMS25-35, GS25-35_Rerun_Avengers_Spanien, 157 [o.t.])[142]

---

140 Original quotation: M: "¿Y tiene algo que ver con la España de esa época?" PCFS55-65: "Si, si, claro." FMS55-65: "El contrario. Era lo que aquí no había." PMS55-65: "[El contrario]." MFS55-65: "Eso sí." FMS55-65: "Porque esto [es], lo que fueron los 60 en Europa comparado con lo que (fuera) aquí, cuando hubo un poco la apertura de (fraga), que empezaron a venir turistas." (GS55-65_Rerun_Avengers_Spanien, 125-130)

141 Original quotation: "Mich hat das jetzt eher an andere Filme oder Serien aus der Zeit erinnert." (CFG25-35, GD25-35_Rerun_Avengers_Deutschland, 93)

142 Original quotation: "No. No lo he asociado con nada. O sea, con películas, bueno, con series d'estas antiguas … porque no me gustan … ." (VMS25-35, GS25-35_Rerun_ Avengers_Spanien, 157)

EMG25-35: "I associated it with other, old films, where it's just that I find it totally illogical then regarding the, regarding how it is made." (GD25-35_Rerun_Avengers_Deutschland, 40 [o.t.])[143]

JMS25-35: "I [relate it] to films from the same era. [...]." (GS25-35_Rerun_Avengers_Spanien, 75; 84 [o.t.])[144]

ZFS25-35: "With a television aesthetic, isn't it? Not from here. From what was watched." (GS25-35_Rerun_Avengers_Spanien, 85 [o.t.])[145]

AFS25-35: "[...] other series. The series as such." (GS25-35_Rerun_Avengers_Spanien, 129 [o.t.])[146]

In detail, BMG25-35 associates Steed with *Pan Tau* (ARD, 1970). Two Spanish 25 to 35-year-olds compare Emma Peel to "Sara Montiéel", a Spanish actress who became famous both in Spain and in the United States between the 1950s and the 1970s, or to *Mary Poppins* (Stevenson, 1965). The performance of Diana Rigg reminds CFG25-35 of the German group of Edgar Wallace (ZDF, 1969) actresses.

Apart from that, the 25 to 35-year-old interviewees concentrate on décor and props and the mise-en-scène in general. Here, participants draw references to *James Bond* films, which undeniable were influenced by *The Avengers*, *Batman* (see Martinson, 1966), another pop example or the television series *Mad Men* (Canal+, 2008), which, it was shown previously, is mainly influenced by 1960s films and television series. Aesthetic and style remind some Spanish interviewees of the 1960s-1970s sitcom *La Tribu de los Brady* (TVE, 1972) [The Brady Bunch, ABC, 1969], the 1960s sitcom *Embrujada* (TVE, 1966) [Bewitched, ABC, 1964] or the 1960s science fiction film *Planet of the Apes* (Schaffner, 1968).

Most of these references are indeed 1960s cultural products or are situated in the time span. In contrast to *Knight Rider*, where all groups already situated the series in a time span and partially in a programme context that seemed familiar to them and had more or less a relation to the text as well, it seems that these interviewees who

---

143 Original quotation: "Ich hab' das jetzt assoziiert mit anderen, so alten Filmen, wo's einfach ich find's dann wahnsinnig unlogisch [...] also wie's halt gemacht ist." (EMG25-35, GD25-35_Rerun_Avengers_Deutschland, 40)

144 Original quotation: "Yo [lo relaciono] con las películas de la misma época. [...]." (JMS25-35, GS25-35_Rerun_Avengers_Spanien, 75; 84)

145 Original quotation: "Con una estética de televisión ¿noo? No de aquí. De lo que se ha visto." (ZFS25-35, GS25-35_Rerun_Avengers_Spanien, 85)

146 Original quotation: "Pensaba en otras series. La serie en sí." (AFS25-35, GS25-35_Rerun_Avengers_Spanien, 129)

did not have any direct relation to *The Avengers* nor to the temporal background are only able to integrate the series into their own lifeworld by doing so.[147] Nostalgia could not be observed here. This may be due to the fact that in no case a "referential framing" or the narration of a gap related to the reference can be emphasised. A second point is that in contrast to the *Knight Rider* context the references proved to be less positively connoted.

In general, it may be stated that also in the case of *The Avengers* rerun, it is mainly the associations related to the single levels of the text that gain dominance among those who did not know the series. These interviewees aspire to integrate the series into a new interpretative context. They frame it, be it by focusing on other cultural products or on the knowledge of the 1960s they acquired via cultural texts. In contrast to the *Knight Rider* rerun, however, none of these framings has a relation to the viewers' own or "prosthetic memories". Thus even though *The Avengers* works as an icon of the 1960s and even though the interviewees integrate it into a huge net of references, it does not relate to their own lifeworlds, which is likely to be the basic factor why nostalgia is not an issue.

8.1.2.2.2 Past and present experiences

Also regarding *The Avengers*, a strong interrelation between past and present experiences may be observed, which is articulated in the following sub-patterns (1) *Creating the link to 'common sense', resp. 'acquired', "retrospective classifications"*, (2) *Positive past experience versus present experiences*, and (3) *A lack of memories of positive past emotions impedes nostalgia*.

Creating the link to 'common sense', resp. 'acquired', "retrospective classifications"

As in the case of the *Knight Rider* rerun, the knowledge of the *The Avengers* (Chechik, 1998) remake that has been shown and discussed at an earlier point in the focus group also holds one part in the description and evaluation of the rerun and, as Horton and McDougal (1998) put it, "transforms" (Horton and McDougal, 1998, p. 3) the text. In all groups and among both those who know the first-run or rerun and those who do not know it, comparisons between the *The Avengers* remake and the rerun are made. Among those who don't know the first-run thus a kind of 'artificially created' comparison between a (better) past and (worse) present is made possible.

Above all, among the 55 to 65-year-old Germans a clear gap between remake and premake is constructed. The negative valorisation of the remake becomes part of the positive valorisation of the rerun. Here, a central point is the "self-irony" the interviewees consider to be lacking in the new version of the series:

---

147 The "integration of texts into the horizons of knowledge of a culture" (Mikos, 2008, p. 274 [o.t.]) is named as one basic function of intertextuality by Mikos.

GFG55-65: "Yes, it hasn't got the depth, this self-irony of the actors. They are performing according to different principles. Well, those who perform today embody the role, while the others are out of their roles at the same time." (GD55-65_Rerun_Avengers_Deutschland, 119 [o.t.])[148]

DMG55-65: "Yes, first this self-irony. That [...] is indeed no longer there, I found that quite good." (GD55-65_Rerun_Avengers_Deutschland, 152 [o.t.])[149]

Among the 25 to 35-year-olds it is mainly AMG25-35 who valorises the rerun in the context of the remake. He also comes to discuss the differences between the characters:

AMG25-35: "... even in those few seconds that we just watched, these characters had something ... somehow they had much more character. Also ... the guy himself. And these in the remake ... it bothers me extremely that the actors or the parts they play have no character any more." (GD25-35_Rerun_Avengers_Deutschland, 43-47 [o.t.])[150]

The interviewee is of the opinion that the remake couple are not 'characters' anymore, which interpreted in accordance with the lexical connotation of the term[151] may be understood as a lack of significant qualities. Indeed, a rhetoric of the gap could be observed; however, we cannot speak of a confrontation of a positive lost past versus a negative present, but rather the comparison of two cultural products that are available at the same time, the rerun, thus not the first-run, and the remake. Here, the "retrospective classification" is also not sufficient in order to provide a basis for the nostalgic longing.

---

148 Original quotation: "Ja, es hat diese Tiefe nicht, diese Selbstironie von den Darstellern. Die spielen nach 'nem andern Prinzip, 'ne. Also die, die heute spielen, die verkörpern die Rolle und die sind aus ihrer Rolle gleichzeitig nochmal raus." (GFG55-65, GD55-65_Rerun_Avengers_Deutschland, 119)

149 Original quotation: "Ja, erst mal diese Selbstironie. Das [...] ist ja heute nicht mehr drin, das fand ich ganz gut" (DMG55-65, GD55-65_Rerun_Avengers_Deutschland, 152).

150 Original quotation: "... selbst in diesen paar Sekunden, die wir grad uns angeguckt haben, hatten diese Charaktere, die hatten irgendwie was... irgendwie hatten die viel mehr Charakter... Genauso der Typ selber. Und die jetzt bei dem Remake ... mich stört das extrem, dass einfach die Schauspieler oder die Rollen, die die spielen, gar keinen Charakter haben..." (AMG25-35, GD25-35_Rerun_Avengers_Deutschland, 43-47)

151 Character is "the mental and moral qualities distinctive to an individual" (see Oxford Dictionaries, 2012a).

In other cases, the comparison leads to a further devaluation of the rerun:

CMS25-35: "Dude, after having seen the remake and that ... I'd almost vote for the remake. The newer version. I don't know, I think it's too antiquated for me, but it didn't really attract my attention either." (GS25-35_Rerun_Avengers_Spanien, 170 [o.t.])[152]

FCFS55-65: "If I had to watch it today, I'd pick the modern one. I think there is more quality in regards to the entertainment. Regarding the acting." (GS55-65_Rerun_Avengers_Spanien, 37 [o.t.])[153]

PCFS55-65: "With respect to the direction or the result, I'd watch the modern one." (GS55-65_Rerun_Avengers_Spanien, 39 [o.t.])[154]

Again, this kind of reasoning may be observed among those who did not know the first-run (CMS25-35 and FCFS55-65) or those (PCFS55-65) who at least gave it no special relevance. In any case, questions of cultural capital and habitus (see e.g. Bourdieu, 1984), which cannot be fully recognised in this study, are certainly relevant here. Nostalgia is not observable here.

The link to the valorising discourses as they were described in the analytical part on *Los Vengadores* or *Mit Schirm, Charme und Melone* is less relevant here. Among the interviewees, FMS55-65 indeed discusses the cult status of the series (GS55-65_Rerun_Avengers_Spanien, 30) in his further valorisation yet this has a secondary position. More important, regarding the nostalgia he develops, is the positive classification of the context of reception. In other contributions the cult status or other "retrospective classifications", as they have been described in the context of the series, have no relevance at all.

Among the 25 to 35-year-olds, some interviewees refer to valorising processes that are provided by the culture in the course of 'retro-trends' in general. This applies to props and costumes as they are exposed in the series. AMG25-35 says, for example:

---

152 Original quotation: "Hombre, después de ver el remake y eso... casi me quedo con el remake. La versión más nueva. No sé, creo que es demasiado antiguo para mi gusto, pero tampoco me ha llamado mucho la atención." (CMS25-35, GS25-35_Rerun_Avengers_ Spanien, 170)

153 Original quotation: "[...] Y ahora si la tuviera que ver me iría a la moderna. Dentro del entretenimiento, creo que hay más cualidad. De interpretación." (FCFS55-65, GS55-65_Rerun_Avengers_Spanien, 37)

154 Original quotation: "La dirección o el resultado final, yo veía la moderna." (PCFS55-65, GS55-65_Rerun_Avengers_Spanien, 39)

AMG25-35: "Yes, yes, today this is quite expensive in some retro-shops." (GD25-35_Rerun_Avengers_Deutschland, 98 [o.t.])[155]

Nostalgia, however, is not found here. As in the case of *Knight Rider*, the 'common sense', resp. 'acquired', "retrospective classification" is obviously no sufficient basis of nostalgia.

Positive past experience versus present experience

While in the case of the *Knight Rider* rerun it was the group of the 25 to 35-year-olds whose memories of narrative fragments, characters, and actions were most present and the 55 to 65-year-olds had only few memories, regarding *The Avengers*, it is reverse. Those among the 55 to 65-year-old interviewees who know the first-run and appreciated it have detailed memories of the series. They recall courses of action:

IMG55-65: "When he walked in, he threw his hat on the hat stand." (GD55-65_Rerun_Avengers_Deutschland, 146 [o.t.])[156]

HFG55-65: "And she pschhhhiuuu. Exactly." (GD55-65_Rerun_Avengers_Deutschland, 148 [o.t.])[157]

GFG55-65: "Every time there was some evil to defeat." (GD55-65_Rerun_Avengers_Deutschland, 161 [o.t.])[158]

AFG55-65: "There were always dead people." (GD55-65_Rerun_Avengers_Deutschland, 163 [o.t.])[159]

---

155 Original quotation: "Jaja, das ist jetzt in so 'm Retro-Shop oder so. Also richtig teuer." (AMG25-35, GD25-35_Rerun_Avengers_Deutschland, 98)

156 Original quotation: "Wenn der reinkam, war(f) der (den Hut auf den Hutständer)." (IMG55-65, GD55-65_Rerun_Avengers_Deutschland, 146)

157 Original quotation: "Und sie pschhhhiuuu. Genau." (HFG55-65, GD55-65_Rerun_Avengers_Deutschland, 148)

158 Original quotation: "Jedes Mal galt es irgendwelche Bösen zu besiegen." (GFG55-65, GD55-65_Rerun_Avengers_Deutschland, 161)

159 Original quotation: "Aber Tote gab's da auch immer." (AFG55-65, GD55-65_Rerun_Avengers_Deutschland, 163)

AMS55-65: "... there is this one scene in the new one with Fiennes and Uma Thurman. She enters a private men's club and goes to the sauna where he is naked. This also happened in the other one." (GS55-65_Rerun_Avengers_Spanien, 111 [o.t.])[160]

And refer to often recurring themes that did not appear as such in the stimulus material:

AFG55-65: "East/West. The bad guys were always from the East. Yes."
DMG55-65: "The bad guys were mostly from the East ... well, Russia ... ."
GFG55-65: "And, yes. And always spoke with a specific accent." (GD55-65_Rerun_ Avengers_Deutschland, 252-256 [o.t.])[161]

Differences between those who had recently seen the rerun (BFG55-65, AFG55-65, EFG55-65 among the 55 to 65-year-old Germans and FMS55-65 among the 55 to 65-year-old Spaniards) and those who had not seen it, could not be observed. As in the case of the *Knight Rider* rerun, the review is accompanied by a recalling of how they perceived and evaluated the series in the past and in the present. Mainly among the German group of the 55 to 65-year-olds the discussion again shows a continuity of positive past and positive present receptions. Correspondingly, while others among the Spaniards, such as PMS55-65, FCFS55-65, or MFS55-65, who do not know the series, gave it less relevance in the past (PCFS55-65), or, rather relate negative memories (AMS55-65) to it, are more critical, it is mainly FMS55-65 who evaluates the series positively from a present position. The participants described the performance as having a "wonderful ironical distance" (GFG55-65, GD55-65_Rerun_Avengers_Deutschland, 114). The rerun is perceived as "technically well done", "natural" or less "invasive" as it would have been done today.

However, comparable to the 25 to 35-year-old Spaniards in the context of *Knight Rider*, here no 'gap' between past and present reception can be detected. Rather the contrary is the case. The past reception is continued from a present point of view. In some cases this is explicitly highlighted. On a general level, one interviewee describes here that she used to like the first-run back then and still likes it today:

---

160   Original quotation: "... hay una escena que estaba en esta actual del Fiennes y la Uma Thurman. Entra ella en un club privado de hombres, y iba a la sauna dónde está él desnudo. Esto pasaba también (en la otra creo) ... ." (AMS55-65, GS55-65_Rerun_Avengers_Spanien, 111)

161   Original quotation: AFG55-65 "Ost West. Die Bösen waren immer die aus dem Osten, ne. Ja". DMG55-65: "Die Bösen waren meistens aus dem Osten ... also Russland ..." GFG55-65: "Und, ja. Und sprachen immer mit 'nem bestimmten Akzent." (GD55-65_Rerun_Avengers_Deutschland, 252-256)

HFG55-65: "... I've just seen this clip, and I thought yes. I always liked that, I would like it today. I guess there are patterns in life. What you like and what you don't like. And that also changes little." (GD55-65_Rerun_Avengers_Deutschland, 188-191 [o.t.])[162]

Another interviewee focuses on the humour the series exposes and due to which she did appreciate the first-run:

GFG55-65: "It was so great because it shows an incredible sense of humour." (GD55-65_Rerun_Avengers_Deutschland, 6 [o.t.])[163]

The simple present to which she finally switches already shows that she still perceives the series like that. Also later she describes her present reception experience as follows:

GFG55-65: "... this ... self-irony of the actors ... and this, of course, is the very special and charming thing about it. The reason why they are so amusing, right." (GD55-65_Rerun_ Avengers_Deutschland, 121 [o.t.])[164]

With reference to the "corporeality" of Emma Peel, another interviewee states:

FFG55-65: "Apart from that, I find the movement absolutely beautiful. Well, this is, I remembered, that I already liked it as a teenager. How she moves and the corporeality she has [...] I liked that back then and I still like it." (GD55-65_Rerun_Avengers_Deutschland, 123, 128 [o.t.])[165]

In general, the interviewees tend to describe a continuity of reception impressions in the context of the first-run and rerun.

---

162 Original quotation: "... Ich hab' grade diesen Ausschnitt gesehen, wo ich so dachte, ja. Das hat mir immer gut gefallen, das würde mir heute gefallen. Ich denke mal, es gibt so Muster im Leben, was dir gefällt und was dir nicht gefällt. Und das verändert sich auch wenig. ... ." (HFG55-65, GD55-65_Rerun_Avengers_Deutschland, 188-191)

163 Original quotation: "Das war so klasse, weil das ein unglaublicher Humor ist." (GFG55-65, GD55-65_Rerun_Avengers_Deutschland, 6)

164 Original quotation: "... diese Selbstironie ... von den Darstellern... Und das ist natürlich das ganz Besondere und Reizvolle daran. Deswegen kannst du dich mit denen auch amüsieren, ja." (GFG55-65, GD55-65_Rerun_Avengers_Deutschland, 121)

165 Original quotation: "Außerdem finde ich 'ne absolut schöne Bewegung. Also das hat mir, ich hab' mich erinnert, schon als Jugendliche gefallen. Wie die sich bewegt und was die so für 'ne Körperlichkeit hat. [...] Das hat mir damals gut gefallen und hat mir jetzt auch wieder gut gefallen." (FFG55-65, GD55-65_Rerun_Avengers_Deutschland, 123; 128)

This also applies to those nostalgia triggers that have been explained in the course of the television analysis and that were presumed to depend upon a somehow lost fascination, such as 'F nostalgia' directed towards a past fascination with the 'boundary-breaking' qualities of Emma Peel (Diana Rigg). As shown by a contribution of HFG55-65, Peel and the relationship between Peel and Steed, too, obviously clashed with the predominant gender ratio both in Germany and Spain of the 1960s:

HFG55-65: "For me, Emma Peel was the first liberated woman I'd ever seen on television. That's what I want to say again. That was the first that powerfully prevailed in a men's world. For me as a teenager it was completely new that a woman just does her thing. And that really impressed me as a teenager." (GD55-65_Rerun_Avengers_Deutschland, 77-81 [o.t.])[166]

Also AMS55-65 refers to the clash with predominant images of gender relations in Spain:

AMS55-65: "[...] [A]bove all the relation between the two protagonists ... was unimaginable here." (GS55-65_Rerun_Avengers_Spanien, 72 [o.t.])[167]

While in this latter case the past fascination with the relation of Peel and Steed is linked to the reception of the "cultural gulf that still separated Spain from her European neighbors", as Boyd (1999, p. 100) puts it, and memories of a "dark epoch" that is everything but the object of nostalgia for the interviewee, in the first case no 'gap' between past and present reception is found. The interviewee makes that also clear in a concluding commentary:

HFG55-65: "I realise it does not trigger any nostalgic feelings in me and I somehow found the time great and it is nice and the series is great, but somehow it's over, it's just over. Well, I still find it good and I found it good back then. When I see this extract, I think, yes funny, nice, great, but it's somehow ... ." (GD55-65_Rerun_Avengers_Deutschland, 257-261 [o.t.])[168]

---

166 Original quotation: "Also für mich war Emma Peel die erste emanzipierte Frau, die ich im Fernsehn überhaupt jemals gesehn hab. Das möchte ich nochmal sagen. Das war die erste, die sich in einer Männerwelt schlagkräftig durchgesetzt hat. Für mich war das zum Beispiel als Jugendliche vollkommen neu, dass eine Frau einfach ihr Ding macht. Und das hat mich sehr beeindruckt als Jugendliche." (HFG55-65, GD55-65_Rerun_ Avengers_Deutschland, 77-81)

167 Original quotation: "[...] [S]obre todo la relación que había entre los dos personajes ... era aquí impensable." (AMS55-65, GS55-65_Rerun_Avengers_Spanien, 72)

168 Original quotation: "Ich stelle fest, also es weckt keine nostalgischen Gefühle in mir und irgendwie – ich fand die Zeit toll und es ist schön und die Serie ist klasse, aber irgendwie

Comparable to the group of the 25 to 35-year-old Spaniards in the case of the *Knight Rider* rerun, in most of the cases no 'gap' between past and present experience may be observed. Presumably for this reason nostalgia is less an issue regarding the single levels of the series. At the same time the different connotation of nostalgia in the age group is surely relevant as well and shall be considered in the conclusion to this chapter.

Only in one case, i.e. the case of CMG55-65, nostalgia located on the single levels of *The Avengers* can be observed. The participant first of all describes a strong but at this moment not concretely labelled emotional experience:

"... It's just the atmosphere that touches me very much. Just like I can also totally also with music from the sixties, yes, totally, that's probably the same for all of us, all. Totally, the atmosphere, as if I lived in that time again. For the moment. That's a strange phenomenon. And I enjoy it. [...] As if I lived back then now. [...] As if I was my old self in some ways. Well emotionally." (GD55-65_Rerun_Avengers_Deutschland, 219-224 [o.t.])[169]

Already here it becomes clear that the excerpt somehow transports the recipient back to the past. The emotions he experiences are stated as being equal to those he remembers. This situation corresponds to what Bennett (2003, p. 27) describes with reference to James, namely that emotions are "revivable" when we recall "a situation that produces those sensations". A located gap can thus be excluded here. On enquiry the recipient later describes the experience more detailed:

CMG55-65: "Since I mean the atmosphere, well not so much rational things, I cannot answer your question so well. That's just the atmosphere of that time, I mean the atmosphere that surrounded me. But I cannot say for sure what that specifically means. Certainly it was black and white, this whole grisaille-story when you want to say it like that. Of course the manner in which the film is made. That was something special, but it differs from so many current series or serials. Typical of the time, and so I am somehow in the time. And yes. Yes, for me it is maybe also related to the fact that in '68 I was in England and found it absolutely great there.

---

ist es auch gelaufen, das ist einfach vorbei. Also ich find das auch nach wie vor gut, und es hat mir damals gut gefallen, es gefällt mir heute gut. Wenn ich so diesen Ausschnitt sehe, wo ich so denke, ja, lustig, nett, toll, aber is irgendwie..." (HFG55-65, GD55-65_Rerun_Avengers_Deutschland, 257-261)

169 Original quotation: "... Es ist einfach die Atmosphäre, die mich total, eh, die mich sehr berührt. Also ich kann voll auch durch Musik aus den Sixties, ja vollkommen, das geht den meisten von uns allen sicherlich so, allen. Total, die Atmosphäre, also ob ich, ja, damals lebte. Für den Moment. Das ist auch 'n eigenartiges Phänomen. Und ich genieß das. [...] Als ob ich jetzt damals lebte. Als ob ich der Alte wäre irgendwie. Also rein emotional gemeint." (GD55-65_Rerun_Avengers_Deutschland, 219; 222; 224)

Was in London, also in the Midlands. And the series is from that time, therefore it moves me very much." (GD55-65_Rerun_Avengers_Deutschland, 243-246 [o.t.])[170]

In the questionnaire he explicitly describes the sensation of nostalgia in the course of the *The Avengers* discussion. He states here that he felt nostalgia due to an "[e]ncounter" with himself "in a then pleasant atmosphere (the negative things excluded)" (CMG55-65, Connotation of nostalgia_55-65-year-old Germans, 31 [o.t.]).[171]

As it seems it is here the immersion into the series that makes the F level work as a "mnemonic prompt". It allows the interviewee to kind of re-enact a "comfortable" moment of his past. The re-enactment obviously reminds him of a moment of joy experienced from the perspective of a past 'I' that he states as being worth longing for and irretrievable from a present perspective. It is thus rather a kind of his 'own F nostalgia'.

A lack of memories of positive past emotions impedes nostalgia

Those who neither link to the valorising discourses around the rerun nor could retrospectively valorise the series on the basis of positive memories related to it perceive *The Avengers* negatively. Accordingly, mainly the 25 to 35-year-old Germans and Spaniards, both groups that did not know the series at all or have only diffuse memories of it, reject the rerun. Thereby a clear gap between the perception of those who appreciated the first-run and those who did not can be observed.

The participants perceive the rerun as "antiquarian" (see CFG25-35, GS25-35_Rerun_Avengers_Spanien, 170; RMS25-35, GS25-35_Rerun_Avengers_Spanien, 103; JMS25-35, GS25-35_Rerun_Avengers_Spanien, 134 [o.t.]). While

---

170 Original quotation: "Da ich die Atmosphäre meine, also gar nicht so stark rationale Dinge, kann ich deine Frage gar nicht so genau beantworten. Das ist einfach die Atmosphäre von damals, also die Atmosphäre, die mich umgab, auch. Aber was das so im Einzelnen auch ausmacht, kann ich gar nicht so genau sagen. Sicherlich war's schwarz-weiß, diese ganze Grisaille-Geschichte, wenn man das mal so sagen will. Natürlich die Art, wie der Film gemacht ist. (Das war 'ne Besonderheit, aber es unterscheidet sich ja von ganz vielen Serien oder Reihen des Heutigen) ganz stark. Typisch für damals. Und so bin ich dann irgendwie in der Zeit. Und ja. Ja, es hängt vielleicht auch für mich damit zusammen, dass ich grade '68 in England war und fand das total klasse dort. War in London, in den Midlands auch. Und aus der Zeit stammt ja auch diese Serie, also deswegen ist mir das sehr nah." (CMG55-65, GD55-65_Rerun_Avengers_Deutschland, 243-246)

171 Original quotation: "Begegnung mit mir selbst in mir damals angenehmer Atmosphäre (das Negative ausgeblendet)." (CMG55-65, Connotation of nostalgia_55-65-year-old Germans, 31)

The Avengers is described as being "technically well done", "natural" or less "invasive" by those who appreciated it in the past, they are alienated by many aspects of the series and describe single levels, such as montage or camera, as "annoying", "strange", "bad", "illogical", or "static".

The performance that the German group of the 55 to 65-year-olds described as 'wonderfully ironically distanced', is negatively perceived by these interviewees:

VMS25-35: "Fatal, no?" (GS25-35_Rerun_Avengers_Spanien, 46)

RMS25-35: ".... It looks very phoney... ." (GS25-35_Rerun_Avengers_Spanien, 103 [o.t.])[172]

CFG25-35: "... a bit bolder. [...] A simpler type of performance. Well, you always knew exactly what she is just thinking, or one only saw a short excerpt, but he also performs very minimalistic, you know ... ." (GD25-35_Rerun_Avengers_Deutschland, 93-95 [o.t.])[173]

Equally negative perceptions of the rerun may be observed among a group of 55 to 65-year-old Spaniards. They claim:

FCFS55-65: "This would be impossible today." (GS55-65_Rerun_Avengers_Spanien, 44 [o.t.])[174]

AMS55-65: "[...] very mediocre." (GS55-65_Rerun_Avengers_Spanien, 40 [o.t.]).[175]

MFS55-65: "I would automatically have changed the channel." (GS55-65_Rerun_Avengers_ Spanien, 43 [o.t.])[176]

---

172 Original quotation: "... Se ve muy falso ... ." (RMS25-35, GS25-35_Rerun_Avengers_ Spanien, 103)

173 Original quotation: "... kommt mir so vor 'n bisschen plakativer. ... so 'n bisschen so 'ne einfachere Art der Darstellung... Also man wusste immer genau, was die jetzt grade denkt, oder man hat ja nur 'n kleinen Ausschnitt gesehn, aber auch er, spielt ja sehr minimalistisch, ne, also..." (CFG25-35, GD25-35_Rerun_Avengers_Deutschland, 93-95)

174 Original quotation: "Esto hoy no se puede hacer." (FCFS55-65, GS55-65_Rerun_ Avengers_Spanien, 44)

175 Original quotation: "[...] bastante mediocre." (AMS55-65, GS55-65_Rerun_Avengers _Spanien, 40)

176 Original quotation: "Yo hubiera cambiado automáticamente el canal." (MFS55-65, GS55-65_Rerun_Avengers_Spanien, 43)

FCFS55-65: "... I cannot avoid seeing them [refers here to both *El coche fantástico* and *Los Vengadores*] as old fashioned." (GS55-65_Nostalgie Allgemein_Spanien, 25 [o.t.])[177]

Here, apart from the 55-65-year AMS55-65 who described rather negative memories in the context of *Los Vengadores* (TVE, 1966), it is the 55 to 65-year-old FCFS55-65 and the 55 to 65-year-old MFS55-65, therefore two interviewees who did not know the first-run, who undertake this negative classification. No one among the 55 to 65-year-old Germans who without exception know the first-run and declare to have appreciated it in the past perceives or evaluates the rerun negatively from a present position.

The discussion about the *The Avengers* rerun can be described as a mirror image to the discussion about the *Knight Rider* rerun. Again it is mostly those who neither adopted the valorising discourses that surround the series nor re-valorised it on an individual level that evaluate the rerun negatively. Again the rerun holds a "differential quality" for these audiences but no positive "differential quality", for example in the form of nostalgia (see also Armbruster, 2012a).

8.1.2.3 Conclusion on the reception of *The Avengers*

In the preceding television analysis of *Mit Schirm, Charme und Melone* (ZDF, 1966) or of *Los Vengadores* (TVE, 1966) it has been assumed that the rerun may provoke nostalgia on various levels. First and in general, nostalgia may be the emotive gratification audiences expect when they choose to watch the rerun. Furthermore, the artefact as a whole has been assumed to be a potential trigger for 'artefact nostalgia' or of viewers' 'own artefact nostalgia'. On the narrative level no potential triggers of (F) nostalgia could be detected insofar as the series idealises its temporal background. 'Empathetic F nostalgia' has been excluded as well. Not only is looking back rather negatively connoted in the series but empathy in general is not favoured by the typified characters, who support the emotional distance of the audiences. However, *The Avengers* exposes many intertextual references to film history or earlier episodes of the series which may release 'A nostalgia' or the viewers' 'own A nostalgia'. Further gaps may be located in the context of the first-run reception, which also may facilitate nostalgia, such as nostalgia towards a former fascination (F or A emotion) with Emma Peel's 'boundary-breaking' characteristics that may be lost from a present position. Further 'A nostalgia' or the viewers' 'own A nostalgia' has been assumed in the context of the anachronistic style the series exposes from today's perspective. All levels of the rerun have been assumed to be potential "mnemonic prompt[s]" for those audiences who know the first-run.

---

177 Original quotation: "... no puedo evitar verlas anticuadas... ." (FCFS55-65, GS55-65_Nostalgie Allgemein_Spanien, 25)

The patterns of reception are in huge parts concordant with those that were found in the analysis of the reception of the *Knight Rider* rerun. A first block titled Reception of the rerun as an artefact as a whole encompasses those patterns of reception that focus on the level of the rerun in general. It consists of the main pattern *(Nostalgic) contextual memories* which is further subdivided into the patterns (1) *No contextual memories*, (2) *(Nostalgic) adolescence/childhood memories*, and, (3) *Television 'then' and 'now'*. The second block encompasses the Reception of nostalgia on the single levels of the text with the main patterns (1) *(Intertextual) references – roundabout nostalgia*, and, (2) *Past and present experiences*. As in the case of the *Knight Rider* rerun, not all of the presumed triggers of nostalgia led to nostalgia in the context of the group discussions conducted here. However, cases of nostalgia could be observed inside both blocks. Further explanations for the absence of the nostalgic longing could be deduced.

The assumption that nostalgia is the gratification the viewers expect when they decide to watch the rerun is not supported by the focus groups. Only one interviewee among the 55 to 65-year-old Spaniards and two among the 55 to 65-year-old Germans talk about a rerun reception. Their motivation is not further specified. At this point a deeper survey on the motivations would surely have been necessary, which could not be done in the course of the focus group discussion. However, there is also evidence here that nostalgia played a major part in the reception. Thus, both FMS55-65 (see GS55-65_Rerun_Avengers_Spanien, 30) and GFG55-65 (see GD55-65_Rerun_Avengers_Deutschland, 192) report memories that popped up in the course of the earlier rerun reception. The same memories are later contextualised as nostalgia in the group discussion. For AFG55-65, interest seems to have been the dominant emotion during an earlier rerun reception as well (see GD55-65_Rerun_Avengers_Deutschland, 55).

As assumed in the analytical part, the emerging patterns regarding the rerun as an artefact differ clearly among the two age groups yet less among the different countries. Thus the sub-pattern of No contextual memories is predominant among the age group of the 25 to 35-year-olds. They either do not know the rerun or only have vague memories of it. Nostalgia towards the context cannot be observed here. In contrast to that, for most of the 55 to 65-year-olds, *Mit Schirm, Charme und Melone* (ZDF, 1966) or *Los Vengadores* (TVE, 1966) is part of their media biography. Here, intensive contextual memories could be observed. Without exception they refer to the 'original' time span of broadcasting, namely to the 1960s, even though some of the interviewees watched reruns of the series. Cases of nostalgia could be highlighted both in the German and in the Spanish focus groups. Most decisive is here how the past context is appraised from the present position and, above all, which context exactly is of importance. The most accordance could be found among those Spanish and German interviewees who highlight private memories in the context of the 'original' reception. The interviewees recall with whom and where they watched the series. Their memories are clearly influenced by the transition from 'pre-television era' to 'television era', which has also been highlighted with reference to O'Sullivan's (1991) study about early television memories. In some cases, in a clear nostalgic stance the better 'then' – a time of harmony and carelessness –is put in contrast with the worse 'now', just as Tannock (1995) describes it as being typical of the rhetoric of nostalgia in general. Only in one example, the case of AMS55-65, the socio-political context is clearly foregrounded. Here, the memories are negatively coloured by the era of Franco's regime, which impedes any nostalgia.

Later, only for the 55 to 65-year-olds and only for those who saw the programme, *The Avengers* as an artefact is embedded in memories of the 1960s television programme. Both 55 to 65-year-old Spaniards and 55 to 65-year-old Germans have memories of the 'original' programme context of the series. However, in contrast to what has been assumed in the analytical part, a general confrontation of the 'golden' 1960s television against the current television landscape cannot be observed. In both cases, the pattern rather contrasts *Mit Schirm, Charme und Melone* (ZDF, 1966) or *Los Vengadores* positively with the rest of the 1960s programme and in doing so supports its status as something special and relevant. A general confrontation of the better television past against the worse television present could not be observed. Also the low amount of television channels is in parts described as supporting the special status. Alternative nostalgia triggers are not mentioned in either case. As in the case of the *Knight Rider* rerun, it is the positive "retrospective classification" of the reception situation on a personal level that determines the nostalgia. Furthermore, a transnationally shared nostalgia could be observed.

This similarly applies to the single levels of the text. Also here it is the "retrospective classification" on a personal level which is decisive for the development of nostalgia. As assumed in the analytical part, the rerun gained new differential quality due to its contrast to today's dominant aesthetic and styles. Not surprisingly, the pattern appears independent of age group, gender or country even though it is wider spread among the 25 to 35-year-olds. It could be shown that the rerun indeed wears the 'connotation of pastness' also for those audiences who do not know the first-run. It triggers associations of 1960s fashion, hairstyles and other aspects. References to mostly 1960s film and television programmes and those that may be located in the era may be observed. The pattern is dominant among those who did not know the series, thus mostly among the 25 to 35-year-olds. These interviewees seem to be able to relate the series to their lifeworlds only by this framing. However, nostalgia is not developed by these participants. The memory is in any case described as mediated and has no relation to their personal memories. Apart from that, no explicit positive "retrospective classification" of the objects could be observed.

It is a different case regarding the 55 to 65-year-olds. Here, rather "referential framing" may be observed. However, nostalgia is also not the case since the present is not perceived as contrasting negatively with the positively evaluated past. The intertextual references named by the interviewees do not coincide with those that have been scrutinised in the television analysis. Here it should be considered what Chapter 4.4.1 highlights with reference to Mikos (2008), namely that intertextuality may never be analysed conclusively since it is determined by all texts with which viewers approach a current text (Mikos, 2008, p. 273).

Summarised under the label *A lack of memories of positive past emotions impedes nostalgia*, it can be stated that what has been said regarding the context applies to the single levels. The positive valorisation of the memory points is central. One interviewee reduces this phenomenon to a common denominator:

DMG55-65: "... it does not work without the link to back then. It wouldn't even exist any longer. You would say, 'What kind of a strange film is that?'. If the link didn't exist, with all this, in principle you're automatically ... you're sitting right in front of the television set at home again, watching TV." (GD55-65_Rerun_Avengers_Deutschland, 263-266 [o.t.])[178]

Those who did not know or who disliked the first-run make a negative classification. Also the link to 'common sense', resp. 'acquired', "retrospective classifications" turns out to be insufficient for the development of nostalgia. Here, the pattern that takes a look on *Positive past experience versus present experience* is also decisive. Comparable to the 25 to 35-year-old Spaniards in the context of *Knight Rider*, the discussion among the 55 to 65-year-olds reflects continuity between positive past and positive present reception. Here no 'gap' between past and present reception can be detected. Rather the contrary is the case. The past reception is continued from a present point of view. Consequently 'F or A nostalgia' directed towards 'F or A emotions' that are lost from today's perspective could not be observed. Yet nostalgia is also an issue in so far that the single levels of the text may work as "mnemonic prompt[s]". In the case of one participant, the viewer's 'own F nostalgia' in the context of an immersion into the rerun could be highlighted. It allows him to kind of re-enact a past reception experience, reminding him of a moment of joy and positive aspects of his past identity that are worth longing for from today's perspective.

Potential triggers of nostalgia that do not rely on reference points outside the text and that may lead to 'empathetic F nostalgia' or 'F nostalgia' have been excluded in

---

178 Original quotation: "... es geht gar nicht ohne die Verknüpfung nach damals. Da würd' so was gar nicht bestehn. Da würdste sagen, was ist das denn für 'n komischer Film. Wenn 's die Verknüpfung nicht gäbe, mit diesem ganzen, du bist automatisch im Prinzip ... sofort biste wieder vorm Fernseher zu Hause und guckst." (DMG55-65, GD55-65_Rerun_Avengers_Deutschland, 263-266)

the course of the analysis. A respective nostalgia could not be observed. Even though *The Avengers* exposes a high degree of reflexivity, nostalgias that were developed in its context without exception take the form of what Davis (1979) labels "simple" nostalgia.

In summary, it may be stated that for those who know the first-run, the text is inevitably overlaid with their own past experiences. As O'Sullivan (1991) describes it in the context of early television memories in general, the confrontation with the rerun here becomes a confrontation between past and present and one's past and present identity. Depending on the relevance, the "retrospective classification" and whether the memory is considered to be lost or not from today's perspective nostalgia is possible.

8.1.3 Conclusion on reruns as potential triggers of nostalgia

This part of the reception study focused on reruns of the 1980s television series *Knight Rider* (NBC, 1982; TVE, 1985, RTLplus, 1985) and the 1960s television series *The Avengers* (ITV, 1961; TVE, 1966; ZDF, 1966). The series were broadcasted both as first-runs and as reruns in Germany and Spain.

Since in the academic and the non-academic discourse, reruns and nostalgia are named in one course, on a first and general level the television analysis assumed that the rerun as a nostalgia 'genre' also creates the expectation of nostalgia. Experimental studies made by Furno-Lamude and Anderson (1992) already showed that nostalgia is one of other gratifications audiences relate to rerun viewing. Later, the 'modules' as they have been highlighted in the theoretical part have been applied in a television analysis in order to scrutinise possible nostalgias on the textual levels. Both triggers of 'A and F nostalgia' have been highlighted. This section shall now take a comparative look at the actual reception of both reruns. The reflection of similarities and differences will allow for conclusions and further hypotheses regarding the reception of reruns as nostalgia contents.

Huge parts of the patterns of reception of *The Avengers* can be described as a mirror image of the reception of *Knight Rider* and vice versa. While in the latter nostalgia was predominantly observable among the 25 to 35-year-olds, namely those who grew up with the series, in the case of *The Avengers*, nostalgia can be found in the group of the 55 to 65-year-olds. As assumed in the analytical part, the emerging patterns regarding the rerun as an artefact differ clearly between the two age groups yet less among the different countries. A transnationally shared media memory can be observed, inside which mainly the "formative" series become the starting point for an age-group specific nostalgia.

First of all, the major patterns of reception are concordant in both examples. In both cases the results build two major blocks, one that reflects the concentration of the audiences on the reruns as an artefact as a whole and one that shows a focus on the reception of single levels of the text. Block I refers to (nostalgic) context memories of the audiences with the patterns (1) *(Nostalgic) childhood/ adolescence memories*, (2) *(Nostalgic) adulthood memories* (only in the context of *Knight Rider*), (3) *No contextual memories*, and (4) *Television 'then' and 'now'*. Block II contains the patterns (1) *(Intertextual) references – roundabout nostalgia*, and (2) *Past and present experiences* with the sub-patterns (2.1) *A lack of memories of positive past emotions impedes nostalgia*, (2.2) *Creating the link to 'common sense', resp., 'acquired' "retrospective classifications"*, and (2.3) *Positive past versus present experiences*. Concrete cases of nostalgia could be detected in both analyses (see Table 2). In some cases, contradictions between discussion and questionnaires appeared – here marked with a question mark. Also this fact shall be shortly reflected in this section.

Table 2: Cases of nostalgia in the course of the rerun reception.

	Cases of nostalgia
Knight Rider	• Viewers' 'own A nostalgia' on the level of the artefact as a whole (DFG25-35; AFS25-35, JMS25-35, RMS25-35, CMS25-35, OFS25-35, MFS55-65 (?), DMG25-35 (?)) • Viewers' 'own A nostalgia' on the level of the music (VMS25-35, AMG25-35 (?)) • Viewer's 'own A nostalgia' on the level of the props (CFG25-35) (?) • Viewers' 'own F nostalgia' towards past F emotions (FFG25-35, EMG 25-35)
The Avengers	• Viewers' 'own A nostalgia' on the level of the artefact as a whole (GFG55-65, BFG55-65 (?), FMS55-65) • Viewers' 'own F nostalgia' coming from an immersion into the fictional world (CMG55-65)

For the 'knowing' audiences, those who have seen the first-run, the rerun is inevitably accompanied by memories of the earlier reception. As O'Sullivan (1991) describes it in the context of his study, "comparison between senses of the past and the present state of television and of the past and present situations and qualities of life of the interviewee, were inevitable and important" (O'Sullivan, 1991, p. 170). Major differences between the sub-patterns of *(Nostalgic) contextual memories* arise mainly from the fact that the two series fall into different life-spans of the age groups. The first-run of *The Avengers* (*Mit Schirm, Charme und Melone* (ZDF, 1966); *Los*

Vengadores (TVE, 1966)) lies outside the personal memory of the 25 to 35-year-olds.

Correspondingly, the pattern of *No contextual memories* is more dominant regarding the reception of *The Avengers* and mainly contains statements of the group of 25 to 35-year-olds. In the case of *Knight Rider*, the pattern could also be observed among those who know the first-run but gave the series little relevance. This group does not exist in the *The Avengers* discussion, a fact that may surely be ascribed to the changing television landscapes, too. While both in Germany and Spain of the 1960s one saw a programme or not, and *The Avengers* definitely was one of the 'must-sees' in that era, in the light of the increasing multiplications of channels, single programmes were no longer able to reach such large audiences.

In both examples the pattern *(Nostalgic) adolescence/childhood and/or adulthood memories* is most dominant. Here, the reruns serve as memory anchors to remember the context of reception (when, where, with whom). Just as Furno-Lamude and Anderson observed in the context of their study about rerun viewing, "[f]or the rerun viewer who has extensive history with a program, the viewing experience may extend beyond the program itself to the era it represents or aspects of one's own life experiences" (Furno-Lamude and Anderson 1992, p. 365). In both groups it is without exception the time span of the 'original' broadcast that is remembered. In contrast to the memories of the 25 to 35-year-olds in the context of *Knight Rider*, the context memories of *The Avengers* the 55 to 65-year-olds are clearly characterised by 'early TV experiences'. The analytical chapter refers to O'Sullivan's (1991) research on early television memories. Observations made are congruent to what O'Sullivan observed: "Early viewing in these instances appears to be remembered as a more deliberate, self-conscious activity, often requiring a move into a separate room from those who were allowed to watch." (O'Sullivan, 1991, p. 167) However, as it seems, it is not the dispositif that is the object of nostalgia. Regarding both reruns, it is the context of the adolescence or childhood memories where concrete examples of the viewers' 'own A nostalgia' may be observed, thus in the case of *Knight Rider* among the 25 to 35-year-olds and in the case of *The Avengers* among the 55 to 65-year-olds. Each age group, we can state, has its own set of potential nostalgia triggers.

Nostalgia based upon "prosthetic memory" did not occur. Here, the positive "retrospective classification" of the memory, the fact that it is considered to be lost from today's perspective, and a strong relevance of the respective trigger, in this case the artefact as a whole, is inevitable for the development of nostalgia. This is also shown by those cases where nostalgia may be excluded. Two similar cases from the discussion on *Knight Rider* and *The Avengers* show that negative childhood memories (see the case of ZFS25-35 on *Knight Rider*) or negative memories regarding the era a series was broadcasted in (see the case of AMS55-65 on *The*

Avengers) impede nostalgia. The latter case, the case of AMS55-65, is also one of the few cases where the socio-political context is broached at all. Here it is *The Avengers* that triggers a memory of the "dark" era of Franco's regime that impedes nostalgia. Another interviewee, the 55 to 65-year-old FMS55-65, indeed talks about this context, though in a distanced, ironical manner. His own nostalgic memory is focused on the positive reception experiences in the circle of his friends. The analysis here refers to what Assmann (2011) in the context of *ostalgia* called "resistance in remembrance". In other cases, the socio-political context is not broached at all by the interviewees. The memories and nostalgias exclusively focus on the viewers' private sphere.

In general, concerning both discussions it can be stated that when nostalgia appears, it is mostly in the form of what Davis (1979) calls "simple nostalgia". Only in one case, namely that of the 25 to 35-year-old JMS25-35, a "reflexive" shape of the nostalgic longing or even what Davis (1979) calls "interpreted nostalgia" can be observed. The interviewee was the only one who had seen the rerun on the morning of the discussion. Thus, we can argue, on the one hand, the contrast to present times that according to Davis (1977, 1979) and Lowenthal (1986, 1989) is so necessary for nostalgia, does exist. If it didn't, the recipient would not have developed nostalgia. On the other hand, it has at least been relativised by the only recent reception of the rerun or, as the reception analysis assumes, the memory of the early reception experience has already been accompanied by a recent memory that is less appropriate as an object of nostalgia. It seems that it is the awareness or pure existence of a second memory anchor, so to say, that leads to an awareness of the different possible views of the past that enable the recipients to question nostalgia or, as Davis (1979, p. 21) puts it in the context of "reflexive nostalgia", to pose "certain empirically oriented questions".

Despite a quantitative difference of cases of nostalgia in the context of the *Knight Rider* discussion and the context of the *The Avengers* discussion, a more difficult handling of nostalgia could be observed mostly among the 55 to 65-year-old Germans. Indeed here the rhetoric of the pre- and postlapsarian could also be highlighted; however, the interviewees in part contradict themselves in their statements on nostalgia. Nostalgia (see e.g. BFG55-65), which is expressed in the course of the discussion, is not manifested by the statement in the questionnaire. We can only suppose that the negative connotation of nostalgia in the age group works as a barrier here. In others cases, participants obviously balance between different nostalgias that have been felt in the context of different examples throughout the group discussion, whereby only that experience which is given most relevance finds its manifestation in the questionnaire. In other cases, mostly observable among the 25 to 35-year-olds, vague statements in the discussion are retrospectively classified as nostalgia in the questionnaire. Nostalgia here seems to be more 'aspired' to. This is also concordant with the rather positive connotation of nostalgia in that age group.

Later, regarding both reruns, the reception pattern *Television 'then' and 'now'* can be detected. In both groups, the rerun is integrated into memories of the 'original' programme context for those who saw the first-run. While those among the 25 to 35-year-olds that disliked *Knight Rider* measure the series against other programmes they consider to be more significant, a similar 'hierarchisation' of memories cannot be found among the 55 to 65-year-olds. Also we can here refer to the different television landscapes in the 1960s and 1980s. In the 1960s, one saw a programme or did not. Accordingly, the participants of the older age group also create fewer hierarchies among different possible nostalgia triggers. In addition, regarding broader television memories, the discussion on *The Avengers* can in part be described as a mirror image of the discussion on *Knight Rider*. Thus, while in the context of *The Avengers*, the pattern *Television 'then' and 'now'* among the 55 to 65-year-olds is part of the positive evaluation of the first-run, among the 25 to 35-year-olds the contrary is the case. Regarding *Knight Rider*, it is vice versa. Hereby a clear nostalgic re-classification of the past can be observed. While the description of television as a scarce commodity serves to increase the value of *Knight Rider* for the 25 to 35-year-olds, the same argument, used in the context of *The Avengers*, explains the fact that the 'bad' series had audiences at all.

Congruent to what Rusch and Volkmer (2006, p. 92) describe in the context of their investigation, namely that "[e]ach generation had a distinctive media memory", regarding this media-memory-related kind of nostalgia, a clear generational gap can be observed as well. Thus *The Avengers* mediate between the countries but not between the age groups. This is less extreme in the case of *Knight Rider*. But here a clear generational gap can be found as well.

This, namely that huge parts are concordant or the mirror image of each other, similarly applies to Block II, the reception of potential triggers of nostalgia on the single levels of the text. In both the context of *The Avengers* and the context of *Knight Rider* the discussions reflect how, as assumed in the television analysis, the first-run in a new context causes frictions that draw the attention of both the 'knowing' and the 'not knowing' audiences to the single levels of the text. Attention was assumed to be the first step towards any possible nostalgia. If nostalgia indeed developed, this was analysed in the further patterns.

Here the pattern *(Intertextual) references – roundabout nostalgia* is dedicated to the reception of the referential character of the reruns. Both examples gained referential character to their respective temporal context. *Knight Rider* thus stands for the 1980s and *The Avengers* stands for the 1960s. A rhetoric of nostalgia could here only be observed in the case of a "referential framing" of a 25 to 35-year-old in the context of *Knight Rider* – however, the description is later relativised in the questionnaire later. In the context of the 1960s series *The Avengers*, no such framing is possible for the 25 to 35-year-olds; the memories they have of the era are always considered to be transmitted. "Referential framings" are not made. The existence of a "prosthetic memory" cannot be observed. There is no nostalgia here.

Furthermore, both examples expose intertextual references to other cultural products and are integrated into such a net by the audiences. The television analysis assumed that nostalgia is also possible on this level. While regarding *Knight Rider*, the pattern arises among both those who knew the first-run and those who did not, in the case of *The Avengers* it can be mainly observed among those who did not know the first-run, thus predominantly among the 25 to 35-year-olds. By doing that, the audiences are able to understand the example and to "integrate" it into their repertory of knowledge, just as it is described as one function of intertextuality in the literature (see Mikos, 2008, p. 274). Nostalgia, however, cannot be found. Against the backdrop of the other cases of nostalgia, it may be assumed that this is due to the fact that a "referential framing" is not made in these cases and due to a general negative appraisal of the 'source' series. For the 55 to 65-year-olds, most of whom knew the first-run, other aspects are given more relevance.

Later, a major pattern contrasts past and present experiences and reflects the high interrelation of both. The memory of a past positive emotion in the context of the first-run influences the reception of the rerun decisively. To that effect, as it has been shown in a pattern with the same title, *a lack of memories of positive past emotions impedes nostalgia.* 'Common sense' resp. 'aquired' "retrospective classifications", as they may be observed on few examples in the context of *Knight Rider* and *The Avengers*, indeed lead to a positive valorisation of the rerun; nostalgia, however, is not possible on this basis. It can be presumed that the retrospective valorisations on the macro level, as described in the television analyses, indeed reflect a 'climate' that indicates whether a series is available as a potential trigger of nostalgia or not. As two cases from the *Knight Rider* discussion show, it further seems that they favour the categorisation of vague emotions as nostalgia. Nevertheless, the link to the valorising discourses alone is surely no sufficient basis for nostalgia. It is similar regarding the contrast of rerun and remake. As Horton and McDougal (1998) state: "In the strictest use of the term *remake*, a new text (the hypertext) transforms a hypotext." (Horton and McDougal, 1998, p. 3 [italic emphasis in the original]) Already against this backdrop it was therefore assumable that the remake will influences the rerun and how it is perceived by the audiences. This was also the case in the group discussions. It could even be argued that due to the fact that the remake was part of the stimulus material that had been shown before the rerun, a kind of 'artificial' narration of the gap was made possible in the course of the discussion. However, it was shown that the 'acquired' valorisation is not sufficient for the development of nostalgia.

Instead, the pattern *Positive past versus present experiences* is most decisive. Concrete cases of nostalgia could be found here as well. Again the *The Avengers* discussion turns out to be the mirror image of the *Knight Rider* discussion. In all cases a continuity of positive past and positive present appraisal can be observed. Two concrete cases in the context of *Knight Rider* show that nostalgia on the single levels of the rerun may arise in case that a specific positive past emotion is declared as being irretrievably lost from today's perspective. In this case we may talk of the viewers' 'own F nostalgia'. In one case in the *The Avengers* context, a viewer's 'own F nostalgia' could be observed that developed in the course of a kind of re-enactment of past F emotions. In another case in the *Knight Rider* context, it was the music that worked as a "mnemonic prompt". Apart from that, no narrations of the gap could be observed. Nostalgia was not found here.

In summary, it may be stated that reruns work as nostalgia contents. Due to their general referential character, this does not only apply to those audiences who know the first-run but also to those who do not know the first-run. In any case, the "referential framing" is an inevitable basis for the development of nostalgia both regarding the reruns as an artefact as a whole and regarding the single levels of the reruns. The viewers have to give the object of nostalgic longing a high degree of relevance, an observation that is also congruent to descriptions made by Tan (1996) in the context of aesthetic emotions in general[179], 'retrospectively classify' it positively, and declare that it is irretrievably lost from today's perspective. The nostalgias that arose in the course of the group discussion on the reruns was above all viewers' 'own A nostalgia' on the level of the rerun as an artefact as a whole. Hereby only private memories, not a narration of a better era or better past television, were the object of nostalgia. To that extent the nostalgias are partly shared not solely because a "we-group", in this case the age group, shares the memory of a series but because memories of similar phases of life have attached themselves to this memory. We may also talk here of a transnationally shared nostalgia. Apart from that, the 25 to 35-year-old Spaniards expose a somewhat stronger "we" of the age group. A more private "we" of family and siblings may be observed among the 25 to 35-year-old Germans in this context. Regarding the single levels, as assumed in the television analysis, a viewer's 'own A nostalgia' in the context of the newly gained referential character of the 1980s series *Knight Rider* could be observed. Later audiences' 'own F nostalgia' towards past emotions in the context of *Knight Rider* was highlighted. Before this background it can be assumed that all emotions in the context of a first-run can be the object of nostalgia in a later rerun reception as long as they are retrospectively classified positively and considered to be irretrievably lost from a present point of view. Hereby nostalgia proves to be selective. None of the

---

179 The author states that "the emotional system is geared toward establishing the relevance of certain situations for the concerns" (Tan, 1996, p. 44).

interviewees develops nostalgia on various levels of the text. There is evidence that it is the object that is given the highest relevance in whose context nostalgia may develop. A kind of hierarchy of the memories could also be observed here. With regards to the mere quantity of nostalgia directed towards the context and the single levels, the concern for the context seems to be more important than the concern for details of the text. This is also in accordance with Marc (1984), as referred to by Furno-Lamude and Anderson (1992, p. 371), who observed that "cultural concerns override the concern for plot and character development in rerun viewing".

8.2 RECEPTION OF THE REMAKES

8.2.1 Reception of the *Knight Rider* remake

The television analysis of *Knight Rider* (NBC, 2008) shows that the remake is clearly contextualised within the frame of the premake. From the title, which evokes the predecessor, to the discourses of producers, television channels or newspaper articles that surround it, one can clearly state that both in Germany and in Spain all these factors appeal to the memory of *Knight Rider* (NBC, 1982). Indeed, some aspects that could potentially provoke nostalgia for those viewers who do not see the relation to the premake, too, have been highlighted. However, the remake has been mainly assumed to be a nostalgia offer in this context.

Except for those viewers who do not know the premake (CFG25-35, FFG55-65, DMG55-65, GFG55-65, CMG55-65, FCS55-65), namely predominantly members of the age group of the 55 to 65-year-olds, the remake is clearly related to the premake for the participants of the focus groups as well. Most of the patterns of reception are inevitably related to the premake. Hereby the following could be highlighted: (1) *Reasons for the reception – a reencounter with the past*, (2) *Creating the gap – remake versus premake*, (3) *Present experience versus past experience*, and, (4) *(Nostalgic) contextual memories*. Only one pattern with the title (5) *Intertextual references – roundabout nostalgia?* reflects a different focus of the recipients that is distant from the premake. The patterns shall now be looked at more closely.

8.2.1.1 Reasons for the reception – a reencounter with the past

Following Cardwell's (2002) study about period dramas, it has been assumed that remakes as nostalgia 'genres' also go hand in hand with the expectation of nostalgia on the side of the audiences. In the focus group discussion, mainly the 25 to 35-year-olds, both Germans and Spaniards, discuss the reasons for their remake reception. Among the 55 to 65-year-olds, only PMS55-65 had seen the remake and briefly discusses this experience.

None of the interviewees say they have expected nostalgia; however, in some cases, and always on the condition that they knew the premake, the expectations with which the participants approached the *Knight Rider* (NBC, 2008) remake are connected to earlier experiences with the 'original' series. While PMS55-65 simply states:

PMS55-65: "I intended to watch it because I liked the other one. But I saw some chapters and it seemed to me that it was very poorly made." (GS55-65_Remakes_ Knight Rider_Spanien, 37 [o.t.])[180]

AFS25-35 says that her motivation was curiosity in the context of the premake:

AFS25-35: "Once I watched a single episode, one of those they broadcasted again, because I was curious what it was like. But, sure, I am already very old and I stick to the old one! I liked it better." (GS25-35_Remakes_Knight Rider_Spanien, 308 [o.t.])[181]

Other interviewees are more explicit. For AMG25-35, the step back into the past was decisive for his reception decision:

AMG25-35: "I thought I would watch it because it somehow transfers you into the past. But it is really bad. I didn't watch it till the end, either." (GD25-35_Remakes_Knight Rider_ Deutschland, 25 [o.t.])[182]

EMG25-35 states:

EMG25-35: "Well, I think when you watch *Knight Rider*, then you also do it because of this retro feeling. Maybe one remembers how it was when you watched it, I don't know, with

---

180 Original quotation: "Yo intenté seguirla porque la otra me gustó. Pero vi un par de capítulos y me pareció muy mal trabajado." (PMS55-65, GS55-65_Remakes_ Knight Rider_Spanien, 37)

181 Original quotation: "Alguna vez he visto un episodio así suelto que la volvían a poner y aquello por la curiosidad de saber còmo era. Pero claro, yo es que soy muy antigua y ¡Me quedo con la antigua! Me gustaba más." (AFS25-35, GS25-35_Remakes_Knight Rider_Spanien, 308)

182 Original quotation: "[I]ch dachte ich guck mir den mal an, weil es halt so 'n bisschen in die Vergangenheit zurückversetzt. Aber der is ja. Is ja superschlecht. Also ich hab' den auch nicht zu Ende geguckt." (AMG25-35, GD25-35_ Remakes_Knight Rider_Deutschland, 25)

excitement at the age of fourteen or fifteen. And this would eventually come again if ... [...]." (GD25-35_ Remakes_Knight Rider_Deutschland, 159 [o.t.])[183]

In the context of the *Knight Rider* rerun, it has already been shown that retro feelings and nostalgia are used as equivalent by the interviewee. In any case, it becomes clear that the remake did not meet the expectations of the viewers. A certain deception can already be noticed here that will also pervade the majority of other patterns of reception.

Thus, independent of age group or territorial group, according to the opinion of most of the recipient, the remake is of a bad quality. The spontaneous comments during the viewing are already unambiguous, such as:

PMS55-65: "Oh, lousy." (GS55-65_Remakes_ Knight Rider_Spanien, 5 [o.t.])[184]

RMS25-35: "A total flop!" (GS25-35_Remakes_Knight Rider_Spanien, 5 [o.t.])[185]

BMG25-35: "Wow, that's really bad." (GD25-35_Remakes_Knight Rider_Deutschland, 4 [o.t.])[186]

The same applies to the later discussion. Among others, the remake is perceived as "demasiado exagerada" [too exaggerated], "muy mal trabajado" [very badly done], "laut" [loud], "langweilig" [boring], or "einfach nur Stress" [just stress]. The interviewees who, in comparison to the premake, will later highlight positive aspects in the remake, are rather reserved here (see VMS25-35, ZFS25-35, AMS55-65, MFS55-65). Despite the cases where the interviewees do not know the premake, independent of age group and territorial group, these contributions are interrelated to the comparison of premake and remake and a valorisation of both in this context. As assumed in the television analysis, the remake is clearly contextualised within the frame of the premake.

---

183 Original quotation: "Also ich glaub, wenn man *Knight Rider* guckt, dann macht man 's ja auch wegen diesem Retro-Gefühl. Vielleicht dass man sich eben dran erinnert, wie man dann da mit 14/15, was weiß ich, da so mitgefiebert hat. Und was man da gespürt hat. Und das würde jetzt eventuell wiederkommen, wenn er eben in seine Uhr sprechen würde. [...]." (EMG25-35, GD25-35_ Remakes_Knight Rider_Deutschland, 159)

184 Original quotation: "Uh. Malísimo." (PMS55-65, GS55-65_Remakes_ Knight Rider_ Spanien, 5)

185 Original quotation: "¡Fracaso total!" (RMS25-35, GS25-35_Remakes_Knight Rider_ Spanien, 5)

186 Original quotation: "Boah. Das ist aber richtig schlecht." (BMG25-35, GD25-35_Remakes_Knight Rider_Deutschland, 4)

8.2.1.2 Creating the gap – remake versus premake

First of all and even though the premake was shown after the remake in the group discussion, on a general level the participants – predominantly the 25 to 35-year-olds – simply compare the two versions. As assumed in the television analysis, the remake here contains a differential quality for the 'knowing audiences' where it exposes similarities and where it exposes differences to the premake. The participants recapitulate patterns of action of the premake *Knight Rider* (NBC, 1982) and search for them inside the remake. They compare aesthetic and characters and other aspects, including the remake music and main prop.

That this comparison is essential in their reception of the remake is also explicitly commented by the participants:

CMS25-35: "I couldn't help comparing it: The car, the characters, the protagonist ... I don't know, it was unavoidable." (GS25-35_Remakes_Knight Rider_Spanien, 100 [o.t.])[187]

VMS25-35: "Well. Nothing. I wanted to see the same characters, to see how they were. It's ridiculous. When you see it and you compare it, you say, damn, what a shame, man, just because it's not the same." (GS25-35_Remakes_Knight Rider_Spanien, 160 [o.t.])[188]

GMG25-35: "Yes. Well, I did. Well, at first I listened to the soundtrack, of course. And then you start comparing them at once, of course." (GD25-35_Remakes_Knight Rider_ Deutschland, 126 [o.t.])[189]

MFS55-65: "We compare them all the time." (GS55-65_Remakes_Knight Rider_Spanien, 47 [o.t.])[190]

As assumed in the television analysis, the mere comparison becomes part of the creation of a gap between premake and remake. Here two main sub-patterns can be observed: One in which the (bad) premake is set against the (good) remake, and one

---

187 Original quotation: "[N]o pude evitarlo, compararlo: el coche, el personaje, el prota... no sé, no pude evitarlo." (CMS25-35, GS25-35_Remakes_Knight Rider_Spanien, 100)

188 Original quotation: "Pues nada. Buscaba a ver los mismos personajes, a ver cómo eran. Es igual... Es ridículo, cuando los ves y buscas la comparación dices, joder, qué pena tío, porque igual no e[s] ¿cómo se llamaba el abuelo?" (VMS25-35, GS25-35_Remakes_ Knight Rider_Spanien, 160)

189 Original quotation: "Ja. Ich hab' schon. Also erst mal natürlich den Soundtrack gehört. Und dann vergleicht man natürlich sofort." (GMG25-35, GD25-35_Remakes_Knight Rider_Deutschland, 126)

190 Original quotation: "[...] estamos comparando [...]" (MFS55-65, GS55-65_Remakes_ Knight Rider_Spanien, 47).

in which it is done vice versa. It can be said that in both cases the respective experience with the premake and its "retrospective classification" by the viewers is decisive.

8.2.1.2.1 (Bad) premake versus (good) remake

Only a relatively small group of interviewees are of the opinion that the remake or aspects of it are better than the premake. For instance, the 25 to 35-year-old VMS25-35 states concerning the remake's aesthetic:

VMS25-35: "At least aesthetically it seems much better. But I don't think that I'd watch it. [...] I also wouldn't watch *El coche fantástico* today. Because it's too shabby. There are other series that are not, which are old but you still perceive them as nice, but this one ... not." (GS25-35_Remakes_Knight Rider_Spanien, 120 [o.t.])[191]

The remake car seems "más guapo" [more handsome] (VMS25-35, GS25-35_Remakes_Knight Rider_Spanien, 69 [o.t.]) to him. Also the 25 to 35-year-old ZFS25-35 prefers the remake's protagonist to the premake's Michael. "¡Es más guapo este!" [This one is more handsome] (ZFS25-35, GS25-35_Remakes_Knight Rider_Spanien, 40 [o.t.]) she states. This similarly applies to AMS55-65 and MFS55-65 of the Spanish group of the 55 to 65-year-olds. Both refer to the technical quality of the remake:

AMS55-65: "Regarding the technical aspect of the product, this is a clearly modernised thing. Because if not, although there are nostalgic people that like the other one better, I think the contemporary things have to be done as it is done today. [...] It has to be an advanced car because otherwise it would be an anachronism." (GS55-65_Remakes_ Knight Rider_Spanien, 50-52 [o.t.])[192]

---

191 Original quotation: "[A]l menos estéticamente me parece mucho mejor (pero [...] no creo que la vea ((risas)). [...] tampoco vería ahora *El coche fantástico*. [..] porque es demasiado cutre. Hay otras series que no, que son antiguas y las sigues viendo guapas, pero esta... no." (VMS25-35, GS25-35_Remakes_Knight Rider_Spanien, 120)

192 Original quotation: "[...] el aspecto técnico del producto evidentemente aquí hay una cosa modernizada, porque si no, aunque hay nostálgicos que les gusta mucho más el otro, me parece que si hay una cosa actualmente se debe hacer como se hace ahora. [...] Tiene que ser un coche adelantado porque si no sería un anacronismo." (AMS55-65, GS55-65_Remakes_ Knight Rider_Spanien, 50-52)

MFS55-65: "There are things that look enhanced. Let's see, the car was very ordinary." (GS55-65_Remakes_ Knight Rider_Spanien, 57 [o.t.])[193]

In these cases, a totally un-nostalgic stance can be observed. Not surprisingly, except from MFS55-65 who had described the premake as innovative and emphasised her appreciation (see GS55-65_Rerun Knight Rider_Spanien, 86), these statements stand in the context of a negative "retrospective classification" of the premake, respectively aspects of it, by the respective viewer. In the case of VMS25-35, this already becomes apparent in the section quoted above. Here he describes the premake, respectively rerun, as "demasiado cutre" [too shabby] (GS25-35_Remakes_Knight Rider_ Spanien, 120 [o.t.]). Instead he assigns a higher value to other reruns, such as *The A-Team*. ZFS25-35 highlights her dislike of the premake character whom she rejects as "machista" [chauvinistic] (GS25-35_Remakes_Knight Rider_Spanien, 392 [o.t.]) in the context of the further remake discussion. And in the case of AMS55-65, in the context of the rerun discussion it becomes clear that he classifies the rerun/premake car as "mera copia de Hal de 2001" [a mere copy of Hal from [Kubrick's] 2001] (see GS55-65_Rerun Knight Rider_Spanien, 80 [o.t.]). Presumably, it is the negative "retrospective classification" of the premake that undermines the narration of the better past, at least on these levels. Nostalgia is not favoured here. It is a different case among those viewers for whom the bad remake more clearly contrasts with the good premake, as it shall be explained in the following section.

8.2.1.2.2 (Bad) remake versus (good) premake

Already the analysis of the rerun reception highlights that the remake becomes part of the valorisation process of the premake. With reference to the public discourse, discourse of producers, and discourse of the channels in the television analysis of the remake as well, this fact has been highlighted. Mostly in the context of the public discourse in the form of newspaper articles, the premake is clearly installed as a potential object of nostalgia. The same applies to the focus group discussions and here mainly to those among the 25 to 35-year-olds who know the premake.

A clear gap between the (good) premake and (bad) remake is constructed here as well. On a first level, this applies to the premake and remake as a whole. Just as it has been described by Oltmann (2008) in the context of remakes and premakes in general, the discourse about the remake declares the premake to be the "original".[194]

---

193 Original quotation: "Hay cosas que se ve mejorado. A ver, el coche era muy básica también. [...]." (MFS55-65, GS55-65_Remakes_ Knight Rider_Spanien, 57)

194 This applies not only to the knowing audiences (see e.g. HFG55-65, IMG55-65, AFG55-65, GMG25-35, RMS25-35, OFS25-35); those, who stated that they had never seen the premake, naturally make this classification (see e.g. FFG55-65, FFG55-65, GFG55-65,

By doing that, the premake gains a higher status than its predecessor. Later, single aspects of the remake and premake are compared, which also leads to a clearly positive "retrospective classification" of the premake.

While the remake is perceived as "demasiado exagerada" [too exaggerated], "zu glatt" [too clean], or "zu perfekt" [too smooth], the premake is remembered as being "más humilde" [more moderate], "[m]ás inocentona" [more innocent] or "más sencillo" [simpler]. This applies to almost every level. Patterns of action are highlighted against the simpler premake version (AMG25-35, GD25-35_ Remakes_Knight Rider_Deutschland, 103; 333). Décor and characters are put in contrast with the more moderate premake.

AMG25-35: "Well, they didn't have those hundreds of people standing around. And a thousand screens and I don't know what else..." (GD25-35_ Remakes_Knight Rider_Deutschland, 61 [o.t.])[195]

RMS25-35: "The team he has behind him didn't exist in the original. There were only two or three, I think. And here there are some chicks. It's too exaggerated." (GS25-35_Remakes_ Knight Rider_Spanien, 366 [o.t.])[196]

JMS25-35: "He [Michael] was very solitary. He worked alone, and that is his image and his facade of the hard guy." (GS25-35_Remakes_Knight Rider_Spanien, 399 [o.t.])[197]

Mainly the characters are clearly held against the positively classified past predecessor. They are, so AMG25-35, "keine Charaktere mehr" [no characters any more], which can be interpreted as a lack of peculiar qualities of the 'original' characters. The 'new' Michael looks to him as if he was cut out of a fashion catalogue (see AMG25-35, GD25-35_Remakes_Knight Rider_Deutschland, 35). He is put in contrast with the premake Michael who is described as being "nicht so clean" [not that clean] (AMG25-35, GD25-35_Remakes_Knight Rider_Deutschland, 45 [o.t.]).

CMG25-35). Here, the remake term seems to automatically imply a lack of originality for these participants.

195 Original quotation: "[Also die waren nicht mit] diesen hundert Leuten, die da noch rumstanden. Und tausend Screens und weiß ich nicht noch... ." (AMG25-35, GD25-35_ Remakes_Knight Rider_Deutschland, 61)

196 Original quotation: "El equipo que tiene (detrás) en la original no estaba, eran sólo dos ó tres, me parece. Y aquí unas tías ahí. Demasiado exagerado." (RMS25-35, GS25-35_Remakes_Knight Rider_Spanien, 366)

197 Original quotation: "Era muy solitario. Trabajaba sólo y es su imagen y su fachada dura de tío." (JMS25-35, GS25-35_Remakes_Knight Rider_Spanien, 399)

Also the actor Hasselhoff comes into play when the character status of the premake Michael is supported by the description of the person(a):

AMG25-35: "Just the hairstyle and all that. His chest hair and all that is unbelievable. He really is a character. In some way, yes. And also because… that he just fucked it up so many times." (GD25-35_ Remakes_Knight Rider_Deutschland, 41-43 [o.t.])[198]

Two other participants of the Spanish group remind the premake character as "mucho más espabilado" [more clever] or "más chulo" [more cute]. In the case of the 25 to 35-year-old DFG25-35, it is a certain stylisation of the premake character that disturbs her:

DFG25-35: "Well, there are his mannerisms or the characteristics that you know from the past, but here they are stylised." (GD2535_ Remakes_Knight Rider_Deutschland, 115 [o.t.])[199]

Obviously Hasselhoff as Michael Knight is a "*charactor*, a character that is particularly resistant to abstraction from a given actor" (Black, 2004, p. 106 [italic emphasis in the original]) just as Black had described it in the context of Diana Rigg and Emma Peel. At least for both German and Spanish audiences (see EMG25-35, VMS25-35) Hasselhoff is inevitably related to *Knight Rider*. The fact that the main actor has been substituted is perceived as negative.

Later the participants continue with the remake car, which is "schwer zu akzeptieren" [hard to accept] for EMG25-35 and "demasiado exagerada" [too exaggerated] for RMS25-35. In the case of EMG25-35, it is mainly the voice of the premake car that is disturbing. The interviewee contrasts "dieses Knistern, was KITT früher hatte" [that crackling sound KITT had back then] with "dieses Navigationssystem-Sprech" [that GPS voice] of the remake car (EMG25-35, GD25-35_Remakes_Knight Rider_Deutschland, 50 [o.t.]). The narration is also perceived as being too exaggerated in contrast to the premake:

---

198 Original quotation: "Allein schon die Matte und so. Die Brustbehaarung und das Ganze ist doch schon unglaublich. Das ist halt 'n Charakter. Also in irgendeiner Form schon. Und auch dadurch… dass er einfach so viel Scheiße gebaut hat […]." (AMG25-35, GD25-35_Remakes_Knight Rider_Deutschland, 41-43)

199 Original quotation: "Also es ist schon seine Eigenheiten oder die Charakteristika, die man von damals kennt, die sind hier halt stilisiert […]." (DFG, 25-35, GD2535_Remakes_ Knight Rider_Deutschland, 115)

JMS25-35: "It is based on a similar script, but it's too fanciful." (GS25-35_Remakes_Knight Rider_Spanien, 93 [o.t.])[200]

CMS25-35: "Too much fantasy, very exaggerated, everything. Well, the other one was fanciful, too, but it could be true, it could become true. In this one you see that this is not the case. It's all science fiction." (GS25-35_Remakes_Knight Rider_Spanien, 107 [o.t.])[201]

As assumed in the television analysis, a clear gap between the positively painted 'then' and the negative 'now' is created. Here it is not about two versions that are available at the same time but most of the statements related to the premake clearly refer to the past. However, we cannot speak of a general confrontation of better past and worse present television as it has been assumed in the television analysis. The assessments quoted above indeed implicitly highlight the "zero-degree" style of the premake against the modern remake. Also the contrast of the ensemble cast to the "lone crusader" protagonist somehow points to a trend in today's television. However, they are always very 'near' to the remake. Generalisations are not really found. Back then, *Knight Rider* was better, simpler, more impressive.

Normally, the positive "retrospective classification" is concordant with statements as made in the rerun-context. In a few cases, negative statements that were made in the rerun context clearly contrast with positive appraisals made in the remake context. The relative distance to the premake in the remake context seems to stimulate the creation of a contrast and leaves enough space for nostalgic romanticising of the past.[202] In any event, *Knight Rider* (RTLplus, 1985) or *El coche*

---

200 Original quotation: "Se basaba en un guión parecido, pero demasiado fantasiosa." (JMS25-35, GS25-35_Remakes_Knight Rider_Spanien, 93)

201 Original quotation: "Demasiado... fantasía, muy exagerado, todo. Bueno... el otro también era fantasía, pero dentro de lo malo podía ser verdad, podía llegar a ser verdad. Esto ya se ve que no... es todo... ciencia ficción." (CMS25-35, GS25-35_Remakes_Knight Rider_Spanien, 107)

202 While GMG25-35 (GD25-35_Remakes_Knight Rider_Deutschland, 122 [o.t]) remembers in the remake context to have found the "original" "sehr cool" [very cool], in the context of the rerun, the past is suddenly far less golden. The participant (GMG25-35, GD25-35_Reruns_Knight Rider_Deutschland, 103 [o.t]) states that already back then he found the premake "ein bisschen albern" [a little silly]. This similarly applies to AMG25-35. Apart from his clearly positive "retrospective classification" of single layers of the premake as compared to the remake, he also idealizes the premake in the remake context as being something special. "Back then," says AMG25-35, "watching TV was still something that was kind of rare. Well, I wasn't allowed to watch that much. And to that effect it [Knight Rider] was something completely different." (GD25-35_Remakes_Knight Rider_Deutschland, 31 [o.t.]) Original quotation: "Damals war

fantástico (TVE, 1985), is installed as an ideal object for nostalgic longing. The statements made in the context show a clearly nostalgic stance. However, against the assumptions made in the television analysis, 'A nostalgia' doesn't seem to be the case. Not one of the participants explicitly refers to nostalgic longing developed towards the past product as such, neither in the group discussions nor in the questionnaire. An explanation for that, mainly in the case of the 25 to 35-year-olds, might be that the interviewees did not find the fulfilment of their expectations, be it the "retro-feeling" or the mere step back into the past, as it has been mentioned previously. They thus aspire to explain the absence of the expected emotions in focusing on lacks on the artefact level of the text. In the context of the negative appraisal of the potential nostalgic trigger, no positive emotion, such as nostalgia, seems to be possible. Apart from that, the object that is longed for is also accessible in the present, namely in the form of the rerun. Similarly, this seems to apply to another strand of argument that contrasts past with present experiences and that will be commented in the next section. Since all assessments regard the artefact level of the text in a kind of "critical framing", an immersion, which, for instance, leads to an 'empathetic F nostalgia', as it has been presumed as being possible in the television analysis, cannot be observed.

The 55 to 65-year-olds make the same comparison; however, here the contrast is mainly less distinct. Mostly the 55 to 65-year-old Germans remember the formal level of the premake as simply being less "eklig" [nasty] (BFG55-65, GD55-65_Remakes_Knight Rider_Deutschland, 73 [o.t.]), less loud, less fast (AFG55-65, GD55-65_Remakes_Knight Rider_Deutschland, 68; DMG55-65, GD55-65_Remakes_Knight Rider_Deutschland, 71 [o.t.]). "Back then," states HFG55-65, "it still had something. Well, I always found it a bit absurd with that car and stuff. However, back then there was something normal about it, while now it is totally artificial" (GD55-65_Remakes_Knight Rider_Deutschland, 157 [o.t.]).[203] Here, a gap between the better 'then' and worse 'now' is also constructed: the past, however,

---

Fernsehen noch ne Sache, die nicht so oft da war. Also ich hab' nicht sehr viel gucken dürfen und können. Und, eh, dementsprechend war das natürlich was ganz anderes." (GD25-35_Remakes_Knight Rider_Deutschland, 31)] In the context of the rerun, the case is reverse. Here, AMG25-35 stated that he didn't watch television until the age of fourteen or fifteen, which is why *Knight Rider* was never "so was super Spezielles" [something very special] to him (GD25-35_Reruns_Knight Rider_Deutschland, 64 [o.t.]).

203 Original quotation: "[F]rüher hatte das noch so was, also ich fand das schon immer vollkommen absurd mit diesem Auto oder so. Aber da hatte es noch so was Normales, während inzwischen ist das so vollkommen künstlich geworden." (HFG55-65, GD55-65_Remakes_Knight Rider_Deutschland, 157)

is far less golden than in the description of the younger age group. The premake is the lesser of two evils. Nostalgic longing can be excluded.

8.2.1.3 Past versus present experience

Next to the past and present product, the participants also oppose past and present experiences. Aspects of the remake that previously were described as lacking in comparison with the premake are in parts related to past emotions that are described as being lost from today's perspective. The pattern may be observed among both territorial and age groups. However, similar to the pattern (bad) remake versus (good) premake, it is mainly found among the 25 to 35-year-olds. While rather factual comparisons or the confrontation of bad against worse experiences may be observed among the 55 to 65-year-olds[204], it is among the younger age group, and here among those who describe positive experiences in the context of the premake, that a clear gap between a positive past and a worse present can be outlined.

In a general manner, this is also explicitly highlighted by some interviewees from the age group of the 25 to 35-year-olds. For instance, FFG25-35 states:

FFG25-35: "I think we are comparing things all the time and the emotions we had in those days. Well, I can still remember how I watched it back then. [...] And there was also this sexual tension. That's what I remember. That there was always a kidnapped woman..." (GD25-35_ Remakes_Knight Rider_Deutschland, 148; 152 [o.t.])[205]

As the interviewee stresses, it is not only premake and remake that the "we-group", in this case her age group, compares, but also the emotions related to it. At another point of the discussion she states that it is "nicht mehr so spannend" [not as exciting] (GD25-35_Remakes_Knight Rider_Deutschland, 106 [o.t.]) and that it does not inspire imagination any more:

---

204 The 55 to 65-year-old HFG55-65 states, for instance, that she feels "nich so gestört" [less disturbed] (HFG55-65, GD55-65_Remakes_Knight Rider_Deutschland, 161 [o.t.]). FMS55-65 (GS55-65_Remakes_ Knight Rider_Spanien, 53-55), another participant of the Spanish group of the 55 to 65-year-olds, highlights the loss of a sensation of novelty not from a personal but from a rather distanced position.

205 Original quotation: "[W]ir vergleichen ja ständig, und die Emotionen, die wir damals hatten. Also ich also kann mich noch dran erinnern, als ich das angeguckt hab. [...]Und da gab's doch auch immer so sexuelle Spannungen. Kann ich mich erinnern, dass da immer 'ne Frau entführt worden ist. [...] Ja, für mich war das spannend als Kind." (FFG25-35, GD25-35_ Remakes_Knight Rider_Deutschland, 148; 152)

FFG25-35: "[W]hen I see this flickering something, I cannot imagine... anything... this simply didn't exist twenty, thirty years ago. They didn't show any flickering viruses back then." (GD25-35_Remakes_Knight Rider_Deutschland, 108 [o.t.])[206]

The 25 to 35-year-old DFG25-35 who had criticised the remake protagonist as being too stylised in comparison to the premake situates the loss of excitement on this level:

DFG25-35: "[...]...what it makes less exciting is that in the past you were somehow discovering the character of Michael Knight. And here many things are very stylised, and they also show that he does things on his own account. And that is just a little bit too explicit." (GD25-35_Remakes_Knight Rider_Deutschland, 113 [o.t.])[207]

Among the 25 to 35-year-old Spaniards it is a certain reality effect, respectively a sensation of reality, that is described as being lost from today's perspective:

CMS25-35: "I liked it more. Because it could be – it was more likely, I don't know, to become real. This one is too exaggerated." (GS25-35_Remakes_Knight Rider_Spanien, 109 [o.t.])[208]

JMS25-35: "Yes. It was more recognisable. They were driving a truck and... When you were on the highway and you saw a truck, it could be ...
AFS25-35: Yes, sure. You said, 'I don't believe it, they are really here!'" (GS25-35_Remakes_Knight Rider_Spanien, 370 [o.t.])[209]

---

206 Original quotation: "[W]enn ich so 'n flimmerndes Irgendwas sehe, da kann ich mir überhaupt nichts damit vor–, das ist ... das gab 's vor zwanzig, dreißig Jahren nicht. Da gab 's kein flimmerndes Virus, wo man da irgendwie gezeigt hat oder so" (FFG25-35, GD25-35_Remakes_Knight Rider_Deutschland, 108).

207 Original quotation: "[...] was das auch so 'n bisschen unspannend macht, ist, dass man damals so den Charakter von Michael Knight so 'n bisschen entdeckt hat. Und hier sind die Sachen teilweise schon so stilisiert dargestellt, und es wird schon gezeigt, dass er auch auf eigene Faust die Sachen trotzdem macht. Und es ist eben ein bisschen zu deutlich. [...]." (DFG25-35, GD25-35_ Remakes_Knight Rider_Deutschland, 113)

208 Original quotation: "A mí me gustaba más. Por eso porque podía ser... era más factible, no sé, podía llegar a ser real... esta... es, demasiado exagerada." (CMS25-35, GS25-35_Remakes_Knight Rider_Spanien, 109)

209 Original quotation: JMS25-35: "Sí [...] conocías más a todo el mundo. Iban en un camión... y... Ibas por la autopista, veías un camión y podías pasar que... ." AFS25-35: "Claro, sí, decías: ¡No puede ser que estén ahí!" (GS25-35_Remakes_Knight Rider_Spanien, 369-370)

Thus back in the 1980s, excitement, surprise, imagination, and the reality effect were part of the viewing experiences they describe. These elements are lacking from today's perspective.

Before the backdrop of the pattern (good) premake versus (bad) remake and already in part in the previously quoted sections it becomes clear that it is mostly the text that is made responsible for this lack. This is very obvious in a statement made by EMG25-35:

EMG25-35: "Maybe I could be satisfied with a remake as long as it is in the '80s, where he speaks into his watch and the car looks the same and the whole set of problems is dealt with again. Not so futuristic. With glittering viruses." (GD25-35_Remakes_Knight Rider_ Deutschland, 156 [o.t.])[210]

Again in this case, "satisfied" means the attainment of "retro-feeling", as he explains shortly thereafter (see GD25-35_ Remakes_Knight Rider_Deutschland, 159 [o.t.]).

EMG25-35: "[The retro-feeling] would maybe come back now if he spoke into his watch and didn't have that plug in his ear. Because it takes all those elements away that fascinated me and that I, well, re-enacted as a child." (GD25-35_ Remakes_Knight Rider_Deutschland, 159 [o.t.])[211]

Also among the 25 to 35-year-old Spaniard the lost emotions are clearly related to deficiencies of the text:

JMS25-35: "I guess what we liked back then ... when we like a way of doing things, usually ... when it is too exaggerated, we see it as unreal or false. I liked it better the way it was the first time." (GS25-35_Remakes_Knight Rider_Spanien, 73 [o.t.])[212]

---

210 Original quotation: "[E]ventuell wär' ich mit 'nem Remake zufrieden, das eben in den '80ern is, wo er so in seine Uhr reinspricht und dann das Auto noch wenigstens so aussieht und die ganze Problematik dann auch noch mal aufgerollt wird. Und nicht so futuristisch. Mit glitzernden Viren." (EMG25-35, GD25-35_ Remakes_Knight Rider_Deutschland, 156)

211 Original quotation: "[D]as [Retro-Gefühl] würde jetzt eventuell wiederkommen, wenn er eben in seine Uhr sprechen würde. Und nicht jetzt 'n Stöpsel im Ohr hat. Weil das nimmt ja alle Elemente raus, die mich dann damals fasziniert haben und die ich als Kind, ja, ich sag mal, nachgespielt hab [...]." (GD25-35_ Remakes_Knight Rider_Deutschland, 159)

212 Original quotation: "Supongo que lo que nos ha gustado... cuando nos gusta una manera de hacer las cosas, normalmente... cuando es demasiado exagerada, pues lo vemos como irreal o falso, yo qué se. A mí me gustaba más como era la primera vez." (JMS25-35, GS25-35_Remakes_Knight Rider_Spanien, 73)

AFS25-35: "Well, back then I really believed that maybe the car could talk, that there was a car that opened the door by itself. But of course, this one is already so fanciful that I know that it won't happen, isn't it? And in the innocence of back then, yes, indeed you believed that, you believed in the existence of *Baywatch*, you believed that Chanquete[213] really died..." (GS25-35_Remakes_Knight Rider_Spanien, 310 [o.t.])[214]

Apart from the stance that is somehow more reflexive in comparison to the 25 to 35-year-old Germans, there is a certain implicit childhood nostalgia here that is also observable in further context memories as commented in a subsequent sub-chapter. "At that time, when we were eight years old," states JMS25-35 from the same group, "nothing seemed unreal – and now, with thirty, well, damn!" (GS25-35_Remakes_Knight Rider_Spanien, 82 [o.t.]).[215] A certain nostalgia towards the lost childhood can be observed here.

In general it can be stated that in this pattern most of the contributions also have a clear nostalgic rhetoric that puts a prelapsarian world in contrast with a postlapsarian world. The re-enactment to which the remake obviously inspires the interviewees makes this gap even larger. The interviewees long for the "restoration" (Böhn, 2007, p. 150) of emotions once felt in the context of the remake, similar to how Böhn (2007) had supposed it in the context of quotations. However, it seems that 'F or A nostalgia' directed towards these emotions is actually not at stake. None of the interviewees explicitly refers to nostalgia in the context of the single levels of the remake, neither in the course of the discussion nor in the questionnaire. The contrary is the case. EMG25-35 hints at the absence of the "retro-feeling". Indeed, the narration of the gap may be observed. Also a high relevance of the potential object of nostalgia is given. However, it may be assumed, there is no irretrievability either of aspects of the rerun or of emotions felt in its context since the participants locate the lack in an insufficiently realised remake.

---

213 Chanquete is one of the main characters of *Verano Azul* (TVE, 1981), the, as Palacio (2012, p. 410) puts it, "referente mítico de la españolidad televisiva" [the mythical referent of television Spanish-ness] (for further reading see Palacio, 2012, pp. 401 ff. [o.t]).

214 Original quotation: "Pues que en aquella época sí que me creía que quizás el coche pudiera hablar, que hubiera un coche que abriera la puerta sólo. Pero claro, esto ya es tan fantástico que ya sé que no pasaría ¿no? Y en la inocencia de aquella etapa sí que te creías esto, te creías el vigilante de la playa, te creías que Chanquete realmente había muerto." (AFS25-35, GS25-35_Remakes_Knight Rider_Spanien, 310)

215 Original quotation: "Cuando en esa época teníamos ocho años nada parecía irreal y ahora con treinta, pues ¡coño!" (JMS25-35, GS25-35_Remakes_Knight Rider_Spanien, 82)

8.2.1.4 (Nostalgic) context memories

Lastly, the *Knight Rider* (NBC, 2008) remake triggers context memories. As assumed in the television analysis, it is the reference to the premake that functions as "mnemonic prompt" for those interviewees who know the premake. The premake hereby always takes an intermediate position for any further reminiscences. Without exception these memories concern the time span of the 'original' broadcast. However, they remain a passing remark in comparison to the rerun reception where context memories encompassed one major part.

This applies to the 55 to 65-year-olds. Their references to context experiences with the premake, such as watching it with children, serve as an explanation for their knowledge of the premake (see IMG55-65, GD55-65_Remakes_Knight Rider_Deutschland, 21; AFG55-65, GD55-65_Remakes_Knight Rider_Deutschland, 31; PCFS55-65, GS55-65_Remakes_Knight Rider_Spanien, 35) but does not lead to nostalgia. The context memories have more significance among the 25 to 35-year-olds. In the German group, FFG25-35 and EMG25-35 discuss childhood memories in the context of the premake:

FFG25-35: "I mean I watched it with my brother, and we were twelve or ten or something." (GD25-35_Remakes_Knight Rider_Deutschland, 148 [o.t.])[216]

FFG25-35: "I can remember the Matchbox cars very well. And my brother had them. But I can't remember if I also played with them. Or if I was just watching." (GD25-35_Remakes_KnightRider_Deutschland, 171-173 [o.t.])[217]

EMG25-35: "Well, we built sandcastles and streets, and then we drove along them and with the cars we gradually ... the sandcastles in order to feel like in a movie scene. Well, the bad guys were living there, and we just drove around. [...] We identified with it. That's what I wanted to say." (GD25-35_Remakes_Knight Rider_Deutschland, 163-164 [o.t.])[218]

---

216 Original quotation: "[...] Ich meine, ich hab das mit meinem Bruder gesehn. Und da war'n wir zwölf, zehn oder so." (FFG25-35, GD25-35_Remakes_Knight Rider_Deutschland, 148)

217 Original quotation: "Aber ich [...] kann mich an die Matchbox-Autos auch noch ganz genau erinnern. [...] Und mein Bruder hatte das, aber ich weiß nicht, ich kann mich nicht mehr dran erinnern, ob ich mitgespielt hab oder ob ich das nur beobachtet hab." (FFG25-35, GD25-35_Remakes_KnightRider_Deutschland, 171-173)

218 Original quotation: "Na ja. Also wir ham halt Sandburgen gebaut und dann Straßen und sind da lang gefahren und ham dann sukzessive mit den Autos die Sandburgen [zerstört], um dann also so 'ne Filmhandlung nachzuempfinden. Also da ham dann die Bösen gewohnt, und wir sind da so rumgefahrn [...]. Aber wir haben uns da halt mit identifiziert.

The reference mainly serves to support the narration of the fascination with the premake. Interestingly, FFG25-35 here refers to a kind of "prosthetic memory". At least it is difficult for her to decide whether the memories she describes derive from her own experiences or from observing her brother. In no case, however, a gap between the lost, golden now and a darker then is constructed. Nostalgia cannot be observed in this context.

This is slightly different among the 25 to 35-year-old Spaniards. Here it is VMS25-35 who contributes the childhood context of the 'original' reception to the discussion. The premake memory that is triggered by the remake leads him directly to childhood experiences; more precisely, he remembers visits to his grandfather's pool in the summer:

VMS25-35: "I remember the pool. Because it was like they broadcasted *El coche fantástico* and I went swimming." (GS25-35_Remakes_Knight Rider_Spanien, 269 [o.t.])[219]

His contribution inspires other interviewees to reminiscence about their better childhood:

OFS25-35: "When we were ten years old, this was on television and you came home and watched it. There was nothing else. And everybody watched it."
M: "And how did it feel? How was that time?"
OFS25-35: "Great."
AFS25-35: "Carefree. Much better than today!"
OFS25-35: "We had nothing else to do but to come home from school, to watch television for a while and to play with friends." (GS25-35_Remakes_Knight Rider_Spanien, 276-282 [o.t.])[220]

These statements are surrounded by a clear nostalgic stance. Contrasting the golden then with the worse now. Here, the 'golden' past is indeed irretrievably lost. In the light of the recipients' declaration that they felt nostalgia in the context of *Knight*

Das wollt' ich damit sagen." (EMG25-35, GD25-35_Remakes_Knight Rider_ Deutschland, 163-164)

219 Original quotation: "Yo es que me acuerdo por lo de la piscina porque era de … ponían *El coche fantástico* y me iba a la piscina." (VMS25-35, GS25-35_Remakes_Knight Rider_Spanien, 269)

220 Original quotation: OFS25-35: "Cuando teníamos diez años y es lo que había por la tele y llegabas a casa y lo veías no había otra cosa y lo seguía todo el mundo". M: "¿Y cómo era? Este tiempo". OFS25-35: "Geniál". AFS25-35: "Sin preocupaciones. ¡Mejor que ahora!" OFS25-35: "No tenías otra cosa qué hacer: llegar del cole ver un rato la tele jugar con los amigos." (GS25-35_Remakes_Knight Rider_Spanien, 276-282)

Rider it can only be assumed that this is also the case in this discussion. However, again no interviewee refers explicitly to nostalgia.

In contrast to the rerun, where already the spontaneous comments during the viewing reflect the inspiration of context memories, these assessments clearly arise in the course of the discussion and not in the context of the reception.

8.2.1.5 Intertextual reference – roundabout nostalgia?

This last pattern is predominantly observable among those audiences who do not know the premake (CFG25-35, FFG55-65, DMG55-65, GFG55-65, CMG55-65, FCS55-65). To them, *Knight Rider* (NBC, 2008) exists independently of the premake. In some statements this is also explicitly highlighted. Thus, argues CFG25-35, "[d]as ist für mich eigentlich so 'ne unabhängige Sache" [[f]or me it actually is an independent thing] (GD25-35_ Remakes_Knight Rider_Deutschland, 94 [o.t.]). GFG55-65 also states, "Yes, I don't know either the original or the remake. I can only..." (GD55-65_Remakes_Knight Rider_Deutschland, 173 [o.t.])[221] And FFG55-65 highlights, "I neither know the original nor the remake and it simply reminded me of a car commercial." (GD55-65_Remakes_Knight Rider_Deutschland, 171 [o.t.])[222] Accordingly, these interviewees frame the remake with references to film and television. Apart from FFG55-65's reference to a commercial, aesthetic and characters remind CFG25-35 of the television series *Smallville* (The WB, 2001). DMG55-65 and GFG55-65 compare the plot of the excerpt with the Spielberg TV-movie *Duel* (1971). The pattern is comparable to the rerun reception where mostly those who did not know the first-run approached the text via other intertextual references. However, in contrast to the latter, no ('roundabout') 'A nostalgia' is found here. None of the references is explicitly positively classified or related to positive context memories, as it was, for instance, the case in the rerun discussion. This is probably due to the fact that a negative appraisal is predominant.

Other intertextual references, such as to the 1980s animation series *The Transformers* (Sky one, 1984), as they were highlighted in the course of the television analysis, are indeed mentioned by GMG25-35 and VMS25-35, who also know the premake. However, they also neither lead to 'A nostalgia' nor to any further associations in general.

---

221 Original quotation: "Ja, ich kenn auch weder Original noch Remake. Kann's also sozusagen nur...." (GFG55-65, GD55-65_Remakes_Knight Rider_Deutschland, 173)

222 Original quotation: "Ich kenne weder das Original noch das Remake und ich fand's einfach wie Autowerbung. Ja, wie zwischen zwei Sachen auf RTL." (GD55-65_Remakes_Knight Rider_Deutschland, 171)

8.2.1.6 Conclusion on the reception of the *Knight Rider* remake

The television analysis assumed *Knight Rider* (NBC, 2008), a remake, which updates the time frame of its 1980s predecessor, to work on various levels as a potential trigger for nostalgia. The remake as a nostalgia 'genre' has been supposed to make the viewers expect nostalgia, respectively to choose it in a nostalgic mood. Later, the single levels of the remake were investigated. On a first and general level, the intertextual relation to the premake *Knight Rider* (NBC, 1982) was supposed to be the main trigger of nostalgia. Alone the title and discourses that surround the remake clearly refer to the reference and in part also install it as potential object of a possible feeling of longing. Later the level of narration integrates narrative fragments of the premake. As has been supposed, the "awareness of things past", as Lowenthal (1986, p. 125) put it, comes from the comparison with the premake, be it because of differences or similarities that can only be recognised by the 'knowing' audiences. Next to the position the remake adopts towards the premake, it is the "retrospective classifications" of the 'original' that make the remake a potential trigger for nostalgia both in the German and Spanish case. It has been supposed that in those who recognise the reference, the remake may elicit television memories, which, with O'Sullivan (1991, p. 163), may work as reference points and thus lead to a personal kind of nostalgia. Mainly the music, the settings, the car as the main prop and Michael Knight as the leading character refer to the premake. A critical stance or dialogue with the premake could not be observed. Furthermore, few potential nostalgia triggers for 'F nostalgia' or 'empathetic F nostalgia' in the context of narration and characters or 'A nostalgia' in the context of intertextual references on the level of the narration that can be supposed to work without the knowledge of the premake have been emphasised.

The fact that the assumed triggers for nostalgia indeed provoked nostalgia is hardly supported by the reception study. The supposed gaps were also generated by the audiences; however, distinct cases of nostalgia could not be found. In general, the following five patterns of reception could be observed: (1) *Reasons for the reception – a reencounter with the past* (2) *Creating the gap – remake versus premake*, (3) *Past versus present experience*, (4) *(Nostalgic) context memories*, and (5) *Intertextual reference – roundabout nostalgia?*.

That nostalgia is the gratification audiences expect when they choose to watch the remake is in part supported by the discussion. At least the majority of statements that refer to the viewing motivation suggest an intended *Reencounter with the past* among those audiences who know the premake. One recipient, EMG25-35, here refers explicitly to a "retro-feeling" that he expected. In the course of the rerun discussion, it was shown that he refers to nostalgia. The fact that the remake meets the expectations of the viewers is not supported by the discourse; rather the contrary is the case.

As assumed in the television analysis, the main gap the remake exposes and that makes it a potential trigger for nostalgia is its reference to the premake. Without exception and independent of the age group or the territorial group, all interviewees who know the premake create this relation. As assumed in the television analysis, both differences and similarities to the premake call the attention of the 'knowing' audiences. In most cases the mere comparison inevitably leads to the valorisation of one or the other. It is mainly those audiences who valorise the premake or aspects of it negatively, where the comparison is favourable for the remake. In the majority of cases a clear valorisation of the premake on the expense of a devalorisation of the remake can be observed. Mainly among the younger age group, a distinct gap between a golden 'then' and a worse 'now' is created. Here, it may be argued that this provides the basis for or supports nostalgic longing in the context of the premake yet this is probably not already nostalgia. It is rather assumed that the recipients mostly concentrate on the artefact level of the text because they do not find the fulfilment of their expected gratification, be it the "retro-feeling", respectively nostalgia, or the mere step back into the past.

It is, so to say, in the lack of the remake where a further gap comes into play that is subsumed under the label *Past versus present experience*. Those among the interviewees who know and enjoyed the premake put their positive experiences with the premake in contrast with the negative and deficient ones with the remake. Again, at least among the 25 to 35-year-olds, a clear gap between the positive past and an unsatisfactory present could be highlighted. However, nostalgia is not observed here, either. The cause of the loss is found in the bad remake that makes the lost emotion potentially retrievable in a better version or in the rerun, as the analysis assumes.

Later, as in the context of the rerun, also in the context of the *Knight Rider* remake, contextual memories are mentioned. They are, however, less important than in the rerun context and encompass a smaller range. Here, each context memory takes the detour of the premake. Only in the case of the 25 to 35-year-old Spaniards these memories take a clear nostalgic stance where the better childhood is put in contrast with the worse present. At least with reference to the final discussion, where the Spanish interviewees explicitly refer to nostalgic childhood memories in the context of *Knight Rider*, it can be supposed that this also accounts for the remake.

Lastly, the remake is framed by intertextual references that are distinct from the premake. This applies mainly to those recipients who do not know the premake. The references, however, neither lead to the viewers' own associations nor to the viewers' own nostalgia. In contrast to the 'roundabout' nostalgia in the rerun context, neither a "referential framing" nor a positive "retrospective classification" of the reference could be observed.

Concluding, it may be stated that for those who know the premake – the majority of the interviewees – the remake text is inevitably accompanied by the premake and the experiences connected to it. However, in contrast to the reruns, where the confrontation with the text becomes a confrontation between past and present and also past and present identity, the contributions of the interviewees are far more related to the text. Clear gaps are constructed, but it seems that the mere narration of the lack is not sufficient for the appearance of nostalgia in the course of the remake reception. In contrast to the reruns, where the past pleasure, fascination, etcetera, is thought to be irretrievably lost, the irretrievability is probably not given here since the lost emotion is thought to be reencountered in the premake. It seems that only if the appropriation of the remake in the course of the discussion leads to a kind of re-enactment of the past reception, the remake can trigger the emotion of nostalgia. In any case and as assumed, the territorial differences have less relevance here. A clear gap between the age groups could be observed instead.

8.2.2 Reception of *The Avengers* remake

As already assumed in Part II and similar to the reception of the *Knight Rider* remake, also in the context of the group discussion on *The Avengers* (Chechik, 1998), the main patterns of reception turn out to be related to the premake. A total of four main patterns could be highlighted. These are: (1) *Creating the gap – remake versus premake*, (2) *Past versus present experience*, (3) *(Nostalgic) context memories*, and (4) *Intertextual references – roundabout nostalgia?*. A pattern such as *Reasons for the reception – a reencounter with the past,* as it has been explained in the context of the reception of the *Knight Rider* remake could not be observed. None of the interviewees discuss explicitly expected gratifications regarding *The Avengers* (Chechik, 1998), neither in the context of the group discussions nor of earlier reception experiences. While no interviewee among the 25 to 35-year-old and the 55 to 65-year-old Germans had seen the remake before the group discussion, the participants OFS25-35 and AFS25-35 of the 25 to 35-year-old Spaniards state to have watched the remake accidentally on television. They do not know the premake. VMS25-35 saw the remake in the cinema. He restricts his comments to highlighting his deception. It may be deduced from the fact that he does not know the premake that nostalgia was probably not what he expected. This does not apply to FMS55-65, a declared fan of the premake. He does not discuss his motivation to watch the movie. It can only be speculated that it was an aspired re-encounter with the past. He left the cinema after the first thirty minutes (see FMS55-65, GS55-65_Remakes_ The Avengers_Spanien, 8). The sole difference to the premake led to his deception (GS55-65_Remakes_ The Avengers_Spanien, 12).

It can be stated that already on a general level an altogether different course of discussion may be observed among the 25 to 35-year-olds and the 55 to 65-year-olds. Among the first group, of which only BMG25-35 knows the premake and two remember the title vaguely, a ponderous and less enthusiastic discussion with an altogether smaller amount of contributions arises. It is a different case among the 55 to 65-year-olds, above all among the 55 to 65-year-old Germans, of whom everybody knows the premake without exception.

As in the case of the *Knight Rider* remake, a predominantly negative appraisal of the remake may be observed. This again applies mainly to the 55 to 65-year-old Germans, of whom everybody knows the premake. The remake is here described as being "total platt" [totally banal], "langweilig" [boring], "aufdringlich" [obtrusive], "Konglomerat-artig" [conglomerate like], "[a]rtifiziell[es]" [artificial] or simply "schlecht" [bad]. Some aspects are indeed positively valorised – thus GFG55-65, for instance, emphasises the technical and dramaturgical quality positively (see GD55-65_Remakes_The Avengers_Deutschland, 101; 103; 154) – however, it will be shown that these contributions are relativised in comparison with the premake.

This similarly applies to the 55 to 65-year-old Spaniards. Here it is first and foremost FMS55-65, the declared premake fan, who highlights that the remake "no es original, no es fresco, no es nada" [is not original, is not fresh, is nothing] (FMS55-65, GS55-65_Remakes_The Avengers_Spanien, 14 [o.t.]). In general, he describes the remake as "[u]n insulto a los fans" [an insult to the fans] (FMS55-65, GS55-65_Remakes_The Avengers_Spanien, 5 [o.t.]). The rest of the group is rather reluctant with the general appraisal. PCFS55-65 feels indeed positive about the actors (see PCFS55-65, GS55-65_Remakes_The Avengers_Spanien, 81), however, she will later relativise the positive assessments as well.

Among the 25 to 35-year-olds it is mostly the 'don't know' VMS25-35, who had seen the remake and who makes a similar negative appraisal. He describes the remake as "ridícula" [ridiculous] (GS25-35_Remakes_The Avengers_Spanien, 74 [o.t.]). It is a different case among the rest of his age group. In the group of the 25 to 35-year-old Germans no such appraisals can be observed. On the contrary, the 'don't know' EMG25-35 declares explicitly to have liked the example (see GD25-35_Remakes_The Avengers_Deutschland, 6). Also JMS25-35 of the Spanish group states that "[le] ha hecho gracia" [it amused him] (JMS25-35, GS25-35_Remakes_The Avengers_Spanien, 33 [o.t.]). As in the case of *Knight Rider* (NBC, 2008), these contributions are usually interrelated to the comparison of premake and remake and a valorisation of both in this context. As assumed in the television analysis, the remake is thus contextualised within the frame of the premake. At the same time, among those who do not know and those who know the premake, a different framing may be observed where other intertextual references of the remake gain more relevance.

8.2.2.1 Creating the gap – remake versus premake

For those audiences who know the premake, the remake is inevitably related to it. Again, on a general level and even though the premake was shown after the remake in the course of the discussion, the interviewees, this time predominantly the 55 to 65-year-olds, simply compare the two versions. Intertextual references on the level of the narration are highlighted. Later, the music – as shown in the television analysis, it is clearly reminiscent of the premake – has recognition value for the 'knowing' audiences. Both continuities and discontinuity on the level of the characters are highlighted. This similarly applies to the reminiscences regarding the props of the 'original' series. Above all, the continuities regarding the bowler hat and umbrella have recognition value here:

GFG55-65: "Yes, of course. That you look for the bowler hat, what he is doing with his stick, there are different symbols of recognition (GD55-65_Remakes_The Avengers_Deutschland, 106 [o.t.])[223]

Against the assumptions made in the television analysis, none of the highlighted aspects works directly as a "mnemonic prompt" that leads to a viewer's 'own nostalgia'. First and foremost the interviewees are reminded of the premake. In every case, the premake takes an intermediate position for any further reminiscences. As in the context of the *Knight Rider* remake, the premake becomes part of the creation of a gap when these statements turn into a valorising comparison of remake and premake. Again two main sub-patterns can be observed: One in which the bad premake is set against the good remake and vice versa.

8.2.2.1.1 (Bad) premake versus (good) remake

In contrast to the *Knight Rider* remake where some interviewees, predominantly those who negatively evaluated the premake or aspects of it, undertake a comparison that is in favour of the remake, in the context of *The Avengers* remake, only a few positive appraisals of the remake in the context of the premake can be observed. Presumably also since most of the 25 to 35-year-olds do not know the premake, the pattern may in general be mainly observed among the 55 to 65-year-olds. AMS55-65, for instance, emphasises that:

---

223 Original quotation: "Ja, natürlich, dass man guckt, wo ist die Melone, wie geht er mit seinem Stock um, es gibt ja so verschiedene Erkennungszeichen." (GD55-65_Remakes_ The Avengers_Deutschland, 106)

AMS55-65: "There is a lot of spectacle. But the same opera, the same songs. Visually it is completely different. There was an evolution here." (GS55-65_Remakes_The Avengers_ Spanien, 70 [o.t.])[224]

Also IMG55-65 (GD55-65_Remakes_The Avengers_Deutschland, 165) and GMG55-65 (GD55-65_Remakes_The Avengers_Deutschland, 103) of the German group describe the remake as technically better realised. HFG55-65 states:

HFG55-65: "Yes. It is well made, it is better made than the original but something is missing." (GD55-65_Remakes_TheAvengers_Deutschland, 196 [o.t.])[225]

In the end, however, the positive appraisal is only about single aspects of the remake. The final assessment is always in favour of the premake. One explanation for the difference to the reception of the *Knight Rider* remake is surely that, without exception, everyone of the interviewees who knows the premake appraises it positively. "Irgendwas" [something], as it is stated by HFG55-65, is missing.

8.2.2.1.2 Bad premake versus good remake
Already in the context of the television analysis on *The Avengers* (Chechik, 1998) it has been shown that the discourses that surround the remake become part of the "retrospective classification" of *The Avengers* (ITV, 1961). The same applies to the group discussions about the remake. Here, too, it is first of all the contrast between the 'original' and the copy that leads to the devalorisation of the remake. Among the 25 to 35-year-olds this line of argument can only be observed in the contributions of BMG25-35 (see GD25-35_Remakes_The Avengers_Deutschland, 73), the only interviewee in that age group who stated to have concrete memories of the premake. Apart from that, it is mainly observable among the 55 to 65-year-olds (see HFG55-65, CMG55-65, GFG55-65, IMG55-65, FFG55-65, BFG55-65, FMS55-65, PCFS55-65, MFS55-65, PMS55-65[226]). In most cases, the comparison is

---

224 Original quotation: "[...] hay mucho espectáculo. (misma opera, mismas canciones) Visualmente es completamente diferente. Ahí ha habido una evolución." (AMS55-65, GS55-65_Remakes_ The Avengers_Spanien, 70)

225 Original quotation: "Ja, das ist gut gemacht, das ist viel besser gemacht, als das Original, aber irgendwas fehlt mir." (HFG55-65, GD55-65_Remakes_TheAvengers_Deutschland, 196)

226 Hereby the statements of MFS55-65 and PMS55-65 have to be handled with caution. Both participate in the comparison and contrast 'original' with remake yet they do not actually know the premake. In the case of MFS55-65 this can be explained by the fact that she uses generalisations and puts her statements in context with those that have been made by other group members. The statements made by PMS55-65, however, could

accompanied by further devaluating arguments regarding the remake. For instance, HFG55-65 states:

HFG55-65: "That's when I thought, oh my God! How awful, how awfully this is! Well, that's one of those remakes that totally went wrong. I'd rather watch the original ten times over than watch a series like this one even once." (GD55-65_Remakes_The Avengers_Deutschland, 56 [o.t.])[227]

FMS55-65 can be quoted with these words:

FMS55-65: "Gee! I think the original is a great series, *Los Vengadores*. [...] It was an entirely innovative series in its time, which was completely different from anything what was made. For me, a new version doesn't make any sense." (GS55-65_Remakes_ The Avengers_Spanien, 16 [o.t.])[228]

The devaluing comparisons apply the remake in general, including single aspects of it. Above all, the characters are described as being mere copies of the 'original'. PCFS55-65 describes the acting of Thurman as "copia de como actuaba ella [Diana Rigg]" [copy of how Diana Rigg performed] (GS55-65_Remakes_The Avengers_Spanien, 86 [o.t.]). According to FMS55-65, Fiennes "imitaba al otro, puramente" [purely imitated the other one] (GS55-65_Remakes_The Avengers_ Spanien, 58 [o.t.]).

The comparison of 'original' versus 'copy' or remake versus premake in general is accompanied by more detailed assessments that focus upon the single levels of the remake. The new version is described as being "platter" [more banal], "langweiliger"

---

easily be misleading when they are not framed respectively. Probably it is the negative connotation that adheres to the term 'remake', which leads the interviewee to the premature assessment. Apart from that, it has to be considered that the interviewee is also a member of a local reading circle and has been recruited in this context. Before this background it could at least be speculated that he is somehow 'trained' to 'pretend to know'.

227 Original quotation: "Da hab' ich gedacht: Gott, wie schlecht! Wie schlecht ist es denn gemacht! Also das ist so 'n Remake, was vollkommen in die Hose gegangen ist. Also da würd' ich mir zehn Mal das Original angucken, bevor ich mir ein einziges Mal so 'ne Serie von denen angucke." (HFG55-65, GD55-65_Remakes_The Avengers_Deutsch- land , 56)

228 Original quotation: "Hombre, yo creo que el original es una gran serie *Los Vengadores*. [...] [E]s una serie completamente innovadora en su tiempo que era completamente diferente a todo lo que se hacia. [...] Una nueva versión no tiene, para mi no tienen ningún sentido. [....]." (FMS55-65, GS55-65_Remakes_ The Avengers_Spanien, 16)

[more boring] or "schlechter" [worse]. Particularly premake and remake characters are put in contrast with each other:

HFG55-65: "I found them kind of cool, [...] while now I found it rather sterile and I kind of disliked it. It was rather like one of these cartoon series." (GD55-65_Remakes_The Avengers_Deutschland, 36 [o.t.])[229]

BMG25-35: "Yes, I mean the protagonist looks like the old one. With the bowler hat, the umbrella and all that. Whereupon the old one did have a little bit more gravitas." (GD25-35_ Remakes_The Avengers_Deutschland, 37 [o.t.])[230]

FMS55-65: "It's not the same character as Emma Peel. She doesn't have that [...] chutzpa." (GS55-65_Remakes_ The Avengers_Spanien, 90-92 [o.t.])[231]

Concordant with what Black (2004, p. 106) describes, namely that Emma Peel is a "charactor, a character that is particularly resistant to abstraction from a given actor", for the two participants FMS55-65 (GS55-65_Remakes_ The Avengers_Spanien, 12) and HFG55-65 (GD55-65_Remakes_The Avengers_Deutschland, 14), Diana Rigg is inevitably related to the series and perceived as missing from today's perspective.

Next to the characters, the mise-en-scène is compared as well. In general, you could say that the interviewees bemoan the loss of "charm" in comparison to the premake:

GFG55-65: "It doesn't really have that kind of charm today." (GD55-65_Remakes_The Avengers_Deutschland, 77 [o.t.])[232]

---

229 Original quotation: "[D]ie fand ich irgendwie ganz cool, die waren trotzdem noch normal. Das waren Menschen. Die ham sich – Emma Peel hat sich dann diesen schwarzen Anzug angezogen, dann hat sie gekämpft gegen das Unrecht der Welt, während jetzt, fand ich das so irgendwie steril, also mir hat das nicht gefallen. Das war wie so 'ne Zeichentrickserie ... ." (HFG55-65, GD55-65_Remakes_The Avengers_Deutschland, 36)

230 Original quotation: "Ja, ich meine die, der [...] Protagonist sieht ja schon so aus wie der Alte. Also mit der Melone, mit dem Schirm und so. Wobei der Alte irgendwo so 'n bisschen mehr Gravitas hatte. [...]." (BMG25-35, GD25-35_Remakes_The Avengers_Deutschland, 37)

231 Original quotation: "[N]o es el mismo personaje que la Emma Peel. No tiene aquella, [...] chispa." (FMS55-65, GS55-65_Remakes_ The Avengers_Spanien, 90-92)

232 Original quotation: "Es hat nicht mehr ganz den Charme heute." (GFG55-65, GD55-65_Remakes_The Avengers_Deutschland, 77)

HFG55-65: "It lacks the elegance (the naturalness)." (GD55-65_Remakes_The Avengers_ Deutschland, 159 [o.t.])[233]

CMG55-65: "Well. It is quite some time ago since I've seen the original. It was much smoother." (GD55-65_Remakes_The Avengers_Deutschland, 58 [o.t.])[234]

PMS55-65: "From series to series, there is what he said about special effects, a tendency to add many special effects at the expense of script, and less subtlety, so to speak." (GS55-65_ Remakes_The Avengers_Spanien, 27 [o.t.])[235]

Participants bemoan the loss of a certain imperfectness the premake had. As mentioned previously, the interviewees are indeed aware of the fact that the remake is technically superior and also reflect about that yet something is always lacking.

IMG55-65: "[…] Well, I think that it is technically perfect and really fast, (but) you somehow long for the old stuff. That something is built up slowly and small movements are sufficient. I mean, it was really well done. A different world." (GD55-65_Remakes_The Avengers_ Deutschland, 165 [o.t.])[236]

GMG55-65: "Yeah, this is really suspenseful. It's all very well regarding the editing and the dramaturgy. But this one isn't, it's much cleaner." (GD55-65_Remakes_The Avengers_ Deutschland, 103 [o.t.])[237]

In summary, it can be stated that here the comparison also contributes to the "retrospective classification" of the premake. A general confrontation of past and

---

233 Original quotation: "[Es fehlt so die Eleganz (das Selbstverständliche)]." (HFG55-65, GD55-65_Remakes_The Avengers_Deutschland, 159)

234 Original quotation: "Na ja. Also es ist lange her, als ich das Original gesehn hab. Das war viel geschmeidiger [...]." (CMG55-65, GD55-65_Remakes_The Avengers_ Deutschland, 58)

235 Original quotation: "De serie a serie, lo que ha dicho (sobre) los efectos especiales es una tendencia de añadir mucho efecto especial a costa de menos guión, y menos sutileza por decirlo de alguna manera." (PMS55-65, GS55-65_Remakes_ The Avengers_Spanien, 27)

236 Original quotation: "Also ich fand's technisch perfekt gemacht und ganz schnell und so, (aber) man sehnt sich nach dem Alten irgendwie. [...]." (IMG55-65, GD55-65_Remakes_The Avengers_Deutschland, 165)

237 Original quotation: "Ja, das hat schon 'ne totale Spannung. Das ist einfach schnitttechnisch und dramaturgisch total gut gemacht. Aber es ist eben nicht, es ist viel glatter." (GMG55-65, GD55-65_Remakes_The Avengers_Deutschland, 103)

present television cannot be observed. Instead, as in the case of the *Knight Rider* remake, a clear gap between the prelapsarian and the postlapsarian world is constructed that makes the premake a potential trigger for nostalgia. IMG55-65 even explicitly refers to a certain longing for the 'original' here, however, in the context of the negatively appraised remake, nostalgia again seems to be impossible. Here, we may also assume that the object the participants long for is available in the present which is why nostalgia is not developed. A participant explicitly emphasises the retrievability of the premake:

FMS55-65: "Well, this is something where they play the fool, but from my perspective it makes no sense to watch this today. It is much more interesting to watch old episodes of the series." (GS55-65_Remakes_The Avengers_Spanien, 12 [o.t.])[238]

8.2.2.2 Past versus present experience

As in the case of the *Knight Rider* remake, the comparison between the premake and the remake, or the comparison between a (good) premake versus a (bad) remake, turns into a similar comparison between past versus present experiences. Again the remake is described as lacking in this context. The contributions, however, encompass a more reduced scale than in the case of the *Knight Rider* remake. This can probably be explained by the quantitatively less cases of participants who state that they know the premake and with the predominantly larger temporal distance to the last reception.

Even though the interviewees do not explicitly point out this fact, alone their contributions, which oppose the (good) premake versus the (bad) remake, suggest that the premake was related to other emotions. Particularly the assessments of HFG55-65 reflect that:

HFG55-65: "[...] They were humans. Like... Emma Peel put on this black suit and fought against the evil in this world, while now I found it rather sterile [...]." (GD55-65_Remakes_The Avengers_Deutschland, 36 [o.t.])[239]

---

238 Original quotation: "Para mí, eh *Los Vengadores*, Steed es Patrick Macnee y la señora Peel es la Diana Rigg. No puede otra Señora Peel. Y punto. Entonces esto es una dónde hacen el indio pero no tiene, para mi no tiene ningún interés ver hoy esto, es mucho más interesante ver viejos episodios de la serie." (FMS55-65, GS55-65_Remakes_ The Avengers_Spanien, 12)

239 Original quotation: "[D]ie fand ich irgendwie ganz cool, die war'n trotzdem noch normal. Das waren Menschen. Die ham sich – Emma Peel hat sich dann diesen schwarzen Anzug angezogen, dann hat sie gekämpft gegen das Unrecht der Welt, während jetzt, fand ich das so irgendwie steril, also mir hat das nicht gefallen. Das war wie so 'ne

It seems that while the 'original' character inspired her imagination on a real existing emancipation, the remake Emma does not represent the visionary character of the predecessor to the interviewee. It is rather clearly perceived as being fictitious. In other cases, such as the case of FMS55-65, the interviewees refer more explicitly to a loss from today's perspective:

FMS55-65: "There is also this very important thing. Diana Rigg was one of the first women who wore a mini skirt. Back then all of us were watching her legs. Now we've seen legs for forty years – today, it's very different." (GS55-65_Remakes_The Avengers_Spanien, 64-65 [o.t.])[240]

In this case it is the lost fascination with the 'boundary-breaking' characteristics of the premake character, as it also has been supposed to be a potential trigger for nostalgia in the context of the television analysis, which is in the centre of attention. Other recipients, such as the 55 to 65-year-old PCFS55-65, make simpler assessments:

PCFS55-65: "I liked the first one much better. Although I don't put it down as much as FMS55-65 does." (GS55-65_Remakes_The Avengers_Spanien, 79 [o.t.])[241]

Indeed, in all these cases a distinct narration of the gap may be observed, which puts the positive past in contrast with a rather negative present experience; however, nostalgia cannot be manifested. Also it can only be supposed that this is due to the general negative appraisal of the potential source of nostalgia in the context of which a positive emotion such as nostalgia does not arise. Furthermore, the gap can be found in a 'bad' version, the deficits of which can be made responsible for the absence of pleasure.

Apart from that, a decisive degree of reflexivity may be observed among the 55 to 65-year-old Germans when they discuss the fact that the 'original' has this high status due to their earlier experiences with it. For example, HFG55-65 states:

Zeichentrickserie ...." (HFG55-65, GD55-65_Remakes_The Avengers_Deutschland, 36)

240 Original quotation: "Además hay una cosa muy importante. Diana Rigg era una de las primeras que corrían en minifalda. Entonces todos miramos las piernas. Y es que hace cuarenta años que vemos piernas, ya, es muy diferente." (FMS55-65, GS55-65_Remakes_ The Avengers_Spanien, 64-65)

241 Original quotation: "Me gustó, sí, me gustaba mucho más la primera que está. [...] Aunque no la denuesto tanto como [...][FMS55-65] ((laughs)) Pero. Me gustaba más la primera." (PCFS55-65, GS55-65_Remakes_ The Avengers_Spanien, 79)

HFG55-65: "Well, generally I always prefer the original over the remake. Well, it's like this somehow. No matter how good the remake is, the original is the original. This is what you know. What you appreciate or what you like and what you are used to, well, what accompanied you, whatever. There is something what stays with you. Something normal." (GD55-65_Remakes_The Avengers_Deutschland, 189 [o.t.])[242]

HFG55-65: "Well, there is always the story in your head and what you actually see." (GD55-65_Remakes_The Avengers_Deutschland, 201 [o.t.])[243]

HFG55-65: "And that's why I think all of this has a different significance today. For us, nowadays, everything relates a bit to history. We would never approach a series like that totally unbiased." (GD55-65_Remakes_The Avengers_Deutschland, 240-242 [o.t.])[244]

This similarly applies to EFG55-65 who states:

EFG55-65: "I believe this has a lot to do with age and different viewing habits of old people and adolescents. And I'm not sure if I had found the original, which I find nicer right now, simply because I know it from the past, more appealing, I'm more used to it, if I had found that better than this colourful thing. I'm not sure about that." (GD55-65_Remakes_The Avengers_ Deutschland, 210-212 [o.t.])[245]

---

242 Original quotation: "Also ich hab' grundsätzlich dieses Ding, dass ich das Original lieber mag als das Remake. Also des is so irgendwie. Egal wie gut das Remake ist, das Original ist einfach das Original. Des ist das, was man kennt. Was man schätzen, geschätzt hat, oder was man mag oder womit man vertraut ist, also was einen so begleitet hat, also wie auch immer. Da ist so irgendwas, was bei dir ist. Was so normal ist." (HFG55-65, GD55-65_Remakes_The Avengers_Deutschland, 189)

243 Original quotation: "Also das ist immer die Kopfgeschichte und das, was du siehst." (HFG55-65, GD55-65_Remakes_The Avengers_Deutschland, 201)

244 Original quotation: "[...] Und deswegen finde ich hat das heute alles 'n anderen Stellenwert. Und für uns ist heute alles so 'n bisschen vergangenheitsbesetzt. So gar nicht unvoreingenommen würden wir [...] an so 'ne Serie rangehen [...]." (HFG55-65, GD55-65_Remakes_The Avengers_Deutschland, 240-242)

245 Original quotation: "[...] Ich glaube, das hat ziemlich viel mit Alter und anderen Sehgewohnheiten zwischen Alten und Jugendlichen zu tun. Und ich bin mir nicht sicher, ob ich dann damals das Original, was ich jetzt heute schöner finde, einfach weil ich's von früher kenne, angenehmer finde, is mir vertrauter, ob ich das dann damals besser gefunden hätte als dieses bunte Teil. Da wär' ich mir nicht sicher." (EFG55-65, GD55-65_Remakes_The Avengers_Deutschland, 210-212)

The interviewees certainly put a large part of the functioning of the pattern into a nutshell here. That is, the negative appraisal of the remake does not result solely from an 'objective' comparison but is rather influence by the memory of positive past emotions. At the same time, the positive appraisal of the premake is relativised, which makes nostalgia in the remake context difficult once again.

8.2.2.3 (Nostalgic) context memories

Also in the discussion on the *The Avengers* remake, (nostalgic) context memories are one pattern of reception. Again the premake takes an intermediate position. Thus the arousal of these memories is restricted to those who saw the premake, predominantly among the age group of the 55 to 65-year-olds. As in the case of *The Avengers* (ITV, 1961) contextual reminiscences concentrate on early adulthood memories in relation to the 'original' series. Even though the premake was broadcasted in various reruns, they concentrate on the 'original' broadcast of the 1960s.

The context memories that may be observed in two cases, that of the 55 to 65-year-old FMS55-65 and the 55 to 65-year-old GFG55-65, are concordant with those that are also discussed in the rerun context. It is above all the reception situation that is in the focus. GFG55-65 highlights how watching *Mit Schirm, Charme und Melone* (ZDF, 1966) belonged to the evening ritual at home in her childhood:

GFG55-65: "Well, I watched it at home when I still lived at home; I still went to school back then." (GD55-65_Remakes_The Avengers_Deutschland, 95-97 [o.t.])[246]

GFG55-65: "And of course it was kind of a ritual back then. I know it very well, all these series. *Bezaubernde Jeannie [I Dream of Jeannie]*, and then there was a Wild West series and they were broadcasted around 6:30 pm or so, and I learned vocabularies for school in the meantime. Yes. But I actually still watched the series, somehow I could do both, but that was rather daily routine. It was part of that. Like supper or whatever." (GD55-65_Remakes_The Avengers_ Deutschland, 226-230 [o.t.])[247]

---

246 Original quotation: "Also ich hab' das zu Hause noch gesehn, da hab' ich noch zu Hause gewohnt, da hab ich eh, da bin ich noch zur Schule gegangen [...]." (GFG55-65, GD55-65_Remakes_The Avengers_Deutschland, 95-97)

247 Original quotation: "Und es hatte natürlich auch so 'n Ritual damals. Ich kenne des ganz stark, auch diese ganzen Serien, [...] [Be]zaubernde Jeannie, dann gab's irgend so 'ne Wildwest-Serie und und und die liefen irgendwie 18:30 Uhr oder irgendwie so, und ich hab' dabei Vokabeln gelernt, ja, aber trotzdem Serie geguckt, das war irgendwie beides möglich, aber das war irgendwie Tagesablauf. Das gehörte irgendwie dazu. So wie's Abendbrot-Essen, oder ich weiß nicht." (GFG55-65, GD55-65_Remakes_The Avengers_Deutschland, 226-230)

GFG55-65: "But watching television was also different back then. I remember that we always went to the neighbour's. Well, I was about eight years old and we didn't have a TV set and always went to our neighbour's house or to granny's and grandpa's, and of course having a TV set in your own place was something very special." (GD55-65_Remakes_The Avengers_ Deutschland, 234; 237-239 [o.t.])[248]

Also in the context of the remake, FMS55-65 remembers watching it with his university friends:

FMS55-65: "I know that we met with a lot of people in the bars, because it was a time when not everyone had a television set at home. [...] It was the time when I was at the university. We left class and went to a bar to watch *Los Vengadores.*" (GS55-65_Remakes_The Avengers_Spanien, 16 [o.t.])[249]

In both cases, as in the context of the rerun, the reception experience is stylised into something special by making television a scarce commodity. Memories are coloured by the early television era. The context memories, however, remain a passing remark in comparison to the rerun reception. A clear rhetoric of the gap that contrasts the better past with a worse or lacking present or cases of nostalgic longing as they distinctly appeared in the rerun context cannot be observed.

8.2.2.4 Intertextual references – roundabout nostalgia?

In contrast to the *Knight Rider* remake, where a decisive group among the interviewees knew the premake, regarding *The Avengers*, the contrary is the case. Not only among the 25 to 35-year-olds (see FFG25-35, DFG25-35, EMG25-35, CFG25-35, AMG25-35, GMG25-35 among the 25 to 35-year-old Germans and JMS25-35, OFS25-35, AFS25-35, VMS25-35, RMS25-35, ZFS25-35 among the 25

---

248 Original quotation: "Aber Fernsehn war ja auch früher was anderes. Ich erinner' mich, dass wir immer zum Nachbarn gegangen sind. [...] Also ich war acht oder so, und wir hatten keinen Fernseher und wir gingen immer noch zum Nachbarn oder zu Oma und Opa, und da war dann natürlich der Fernseher, der dann im eigenen Haus war, was ganz Besonderes." (GFG55-65, GD55-65_Remakes_The Avengers_Deutschland, 234; 237-239)

249 Original quotation: "[...] Yo sé que nos reuníamos un montón de gente en los bares, porque era una época dónde no todo el mundo tenía televisión en casa. Salíamos de clase y entonces... . Era la época cuando iba a la universidad. Salíamos de clase y nos íbamos a un bar a ver *Los vengadores.* [...]." (FMS55-65, GS55-65_Remakes_ The Avengers_Spanien, 16)

to 35-year-old Spaniards)[250] but also among the 55 to 65-year-old Spaniards, some interviewees have no knowledge of the earlier version. Mostly these audiences frame the remake differently. For the 'knowing' audiences, the comparison serves the purpose to highlight the negatively valorised differences to the premake once again.

In both age groups it is above all *The Avengers'* (Chechik, 1998) reference to James Bond films, which has already been explained in the course of the television analysis that is highlighted by the interviewees.

MFS55-65: "*Los Vengadores* is a James Bond-mix." (GS55-65_Remakes_The Avengers_ Spanien, 21 [o.t.])[251]

AFS25-35: "It's like, it was like action, wasn't it? Like 007 or something like that." (GS25-35_Remakes_The Avengers_Spanien, 34 [o.t.])[252]

FCFS55-65: "Like 007 or *Mission Impossible*, or..." (GS55-65_Remakes_The Avengers_ Spanien, 50 [o.t.])[253]

The remake Steed is compared to James Bond (see FMG55-65, GD55-65_Remakes_The Avengers_Deutschland, 81; FMS55-65, GS55-65_Remakes_The Avengers_Spanien, 14). Uma Thurman is related to *Kill Bill* (Tarantino, 2003 and 2004).

MFS55-65: "And the girl, Uma Thurman, reminded me of *Kill Bill*. Well, it made me mix up some movies." (GS55-65_Remakes_ The Avengers_Spanien, 87 [o.t.])[254]

---

250 Among the 25 to 35-year-olds only BMG25-35 has concrete memories of the premake. For CFG25-35, CMS25-35 and RMS25-35 the series seems somehow familiar; however, they do not have any concrete memories of the series nor do they relate the remake to the premake in the course of the discussion.

251 Original quotation: "*Los Vengadores* es una mezcla de James Bond." (MFS55-65, GS55-65_Remakes_ The Avengers_Spanien, 21)

252 Original quotation: "Es como de...Era como de acción y no?? Algo como el 007, algo así... ." (AFS25-35, GS25-35_Remakes_The Avengers_Spanien, 34)

253 Original quotation: "Tipo 007, o *Misión Imposible*, o..." (FCFS55-65, GS55-65_Remakes_The Avengers_Spanien, 50)

254 Original quotation: "La chica, la Uma Thurman, me ha recordado a *Kill Bill*. Bueno me ha mezclado películas." (MFS55-65, GS55-65_Remakes_ The Avengers_Spanien, 87)

FMS55-65: "Here, Uma Thurman acts a bit like in *Kill Bill.*" (GS55-65_Remakes_ The Avengers_Spanien, 90 [o.t.])[255]

RMS25-35: "When Uma Thurman appeared, I was thinking of *Kill Bill.*"
AFS25-35: "Me, too!" (GS25-35_Remakes_The Avengers_Spanien, 75-76 [o.t.])[256]

In contrast to the rerun context, where intertextual references indeed led to further positive associations and a case of (roundabout) nostalgia could be supposed, the contributions of the interviewees in the context of the *The Avengers* remake stay concentrated on the mere explication of the reference. Neither their positive classification nor further context memories, as it was, for instance, observable in the discussion about the *Knight Rider* rerun, could be highlighted. Examples of nostalgia could not be found in any of these cases.

8.2.2.5 Conclusion on the reception of *The Avengers* remake

With a view on the television analysis, various aspects of *The Avengers* (Chechik, 1998) were presumed to work as potential triggers of nostalgia. First and in general, it has been assumed that the remake as a nostalgia 'genre' creates the expectation of nostalgia, respectively makes it likely that audiences choose to watch the remake when they are in a nostalgic mood. Later, as in the case of *Knight Rider* (NBC, 2008), the television analysis of *The Avengers* (Chechik, 1998) shows that the remake is clearly contextualised within the frame of the 1960s premake. The title already evokes the predecessor here, too. The discourses of producers, television channels or newspaper articles that surround the remake clearly appeal to the memory of *The Avengers* (ITV, 1961) and establish it as a nostalgia offer. Later, the single levels of the remake have been analysed. The remake actualises its time frame. The 'connotation of pastness' comes with the knowledge of the premake. On nearly every level of the text, the remake exposes intertextual references to the premake which, favoured by the position the remake adopts towards its predecessor and depending on the respective "retrospective classification", are assumed to work as potential triggers of 'artefact nostalgia' or the viewers' 'own artefact nostalgia'. Furthermore, 'A and F nostalgia' that stands in the context of the premake such as a presumed 'A or F nostalgia' towards a lost fascination with the 'boundary-breaking' characteristics of the premake Emma Peel, has been supposed in this study. Moreover, other potential nostalgia offers have been presumed to work without the knowledge of the

---

255 Original quotation: "Aquí la Uma Thurman hace un poco como en *Kill Bill.*" (FMS55-65, GS55-65_Remakes_ The Avengers_Spanien, 90)

256 Original quotation: RMS25-35: "Yo estaba... Cuando ha salido la Uma Thurman estaba pensando en *Kill Bill.* [...]." AFS25-35: "Yo también." (GS25-35_Remakes_The Avengers_Spanien, 75-76)

premake. With various other intertextual references, the remake appeals, for instance, to the memory of the 'not knowing' audiences, which, depending on the respective "retrospective classification" of the reference, may lead to 'A nostalgia' or the viewers' 'own A nostalgia' in this way. On the level of the characters, this study assumed that the remake works as a potential trigger for 'F nostalgia' due to the positive presentation of the past role models it exposes.

The assumption that the assumed nostalgia offers indeed lead to nostalgia on the side of the audiences is only hardly supported by the group discussions. As in the case of *Knight Rider*, supposed 'gaps' were created without leading to nostalgia. The reception analysis provides initial explanations why this is the case. All in all, four different patterns of reception could be highlighted: (1) *Creating the gap – remake versus premake*, (2) *Past versus present experience*, (3) *(Nostalgic) context memories,* and (4) *Intertextual references – roundabout nostalgia?*. A pattern that reflects the expectation of 'past' emotions as it was observable in the context of the reception of the *Knight Rider* remake could not be highlighted. Most of the patterns of reception stand in the context of the premake and could predominantly be observed among those who know the premake. In this case, these were mostly members of the age group of the 55 to 65-year-olds. Again, a clear generational gap could be observed while differences between the territorial groups are of minor importance.

As assumed in the television analysis, the main gap the remake exposes is its reference to the premake. Mainly those who do not know the premake frame the remake with references different from the premake. Nostalgia, however, is not found here. Participants restrict their contributions to mere indications of the references. Further associations, which, depending on a respective "retrospective classification", may have led to nostalgia, cannot be found. This may be explained by the general negative classification of the remake. In the context of the negative appraisal, no positive emotions, such as nostalgia, seem to be possible.

More dominant, as previously mentioned, are those patterns that put the remake in relation to the 1960s predecessor. As assumed in the television analysis, here is also where the main gap may be located. As in the case of *Knight Rider*, first of all participants simply make comparisons between the two products. Here, mainly the 55 to 65-year-olds and mostly those who know the premake highlight intertextual references to the premake. They refer to continuities on the level of narration, music, characters or props as they were highlighted in the television analysis of *The Avengers* (Chechik, 1998), too. In most cases the comparison is accompanied by a clear valorization of the remake against the premake or vice versa. Effectively, in only a few cases the (good) remake is held against the (bad) premake. In contrast to the *Knight Rider* remake, where it was the group of those interviewees who know the premake and valorised it negatively, the 55 to 65-year-old interviewees only appraise aspects of the remake as being technically better realised. The cinematographic 'now' is here contrasted positively with the 'then'. However, no one appraises the premake in general negatively. This may be due to the fact that no one states that he or she disliked the premake.

The pattern rather arises vice versa, that is, as *(Bad) remake versus (good) premake*. The interviewees here clearly valorise the premake against the backdrop of the remake in integrating it into the opposition of 'original' versus 'copy' or 'second version'. Later on in the study, single levels of the premake and remake are always compared in favour of the premake. Undeniably, these comparisons hold their part in the "retrospective classification" of the premake and valorise it as a potential trigger for nostalgia. A clear narration of the gap can be observed. However, concrete cases of nostalgia could not be identified.

This similarly applies to the pattern *Past versus present experience*. As in the case of the *Knight Rider* remake, it is, so to say, in the lack of the remake where a further gap comes into play that refers to the loss of zestfulness, fascination or other positive emotions as they were experienced in the context of the premake. Again the pattern is solely observable among the 55 to 65-year-olds and only among those who knew and liked the premake. However, even though a clear rhetoric of the gap is observable in this pattern as well, nostalgia is not the case.

Lastly, also regarding *The Avengers*, one pattern of reception reflects the existence of *(Nostalgic) contextual memories*. At least two cases are observable here. As in the case of the *Knight Rider* remake, the premake takes an intermediate position here. The context memories are about early adulthood memories in the context of the 'original' broadcast. They remain a passing remark, though. Nostalgia cannot be observed in this context.

All in all, it can be stated that despite the assumptions made in the television analysis, the *The Avengers* remake does not provoke nostalgia. Among the presumed nostalgia offers that were assumed to work without the relation to the premake, none was perceived as such. The analysis can only assume that this is due to the general negative appraisal of the remake, in whose context positive emotions, such as nostalgia, can rather be excluded. However, the presumed triggers for nostalgia that work in the context of a gap between remake and premake and the positive valorisation of the latter could not be confirmed in the reception study either. Distinct narrations of the gap could be observed but nostalgia does not arise. As in the case of *Knight Rider*, it seems that instead of being irretrievable, the loss is thought to be possibly compensated by a better remake version or a renewed reception of the 'original' series.

8.2.3 Conclusion on remakes as potential triggers for nostalgia

In the light of the fact that remakes are included in the broad category of nostalgia film and nostalgia television on the side of the academic discourse and that in the non-academic discourse nostalgia and remakes are also frequently mentioned together, it has been assumed that remakes are able to provoke the emotion of nostalgia in their audiences. In order to investigate this on the textual level, the 'modules' as defined in the theoretical part of the work have been applied to a television analysis. First, it was assumed that remakes as nostalgia 'genre' make the audiences expect nostalgia. Later, on the level of the text, a possible 'nostalgic' relation of the remake to the premake has been assumed to be the main focus of nostalgia on the side of the audiences.

With *Knight Rider* (NBC, 2008) and *The Avengers* (Chechik, 1998), two remakes that "update the time frame" (Black, 2004, p. 101) of their premakes have been chosen. While the first remake is based on the 1980s television series *Knight Rider* (NBC, 1982; TVE, 1985, RTLplus, 1985), the second one refers to the 1960s television series *The Avengers* (ITV, 1961; TVE, 1966; ZDF, 1966). Both were broadcasted as remakes and as premakes in Germany and Spain. While *The Avengers* falls into the "reminiscence bump", respectively the "formative years" of the 55 to 65-year-olds and is outside the lifespan of the 25 to 35-year-olds, *Knight Rider* falls into the "reminiscence bump" or "formative years" of the 25 to 35-year-olds but may also be remembered by the older age group. Regarding possible nostalgias evoked in the recipients, the television analysis assumes strong differences between the age groups. Territorial differences are thought to have less relevance in this case.

The assumption that the two remakes indeed provoke nostalgia in their audiences is only hardly supported by the group discussions (see Table 3). If at all, cases of the viewers' 'own A nostalgia' on the level of the artefacts as a whole could be presumed, which however, could not be fully confirmed with reference to the discussion. Notwithstanding, this does not mean that the reception study was purposeless. Only by doing so, important knowledge about the functioning of nostalgia and the functioning nostalgia and remakes could be highlighted. The formulation of further hypotheses is possible.

Table 3: Cases of nostalgia in the course of the remake reception.

	Cases of nostalgia in the remake context
Knight Rider	• Viewers' 'own A nostalgia' on the level of the artefacts as a whole (?) (VMS25-35, AFS25-35, OFS25-35)
The Avengers	—

The fact that nostalgia is the gratification viewers expect when they chose to watch a remake is in part supported by the group discussions. Above all, in the case of *Knight Rider* (NBC, 2008) it becomes very clear that the motivation to watch the series was an intended reencounter with the past. One interviewee here refers explicitly to an expected "retro-feeling" that in the context of the discussion turns out to be equivalent to nostalgia. The assumption is less supported by the discussion on *The Avengers* (Chechik, 1998). Here a deeper questioning would have been necessary. The interviewees do not explicitly discuss their expected gratifications in the context of the series. In one case among the 55 to 65-year-olds, it turns out that it is the unfulfilled expectation of a re-encounter with a premake-equivalent that led to the interviewee's disappointment. In the context of both discussions it becomes obvious that expectations are not fulfilled by the respective remake.

Perhaps due to that reason the interviewees in both cases mostly focus on the artefact level of the remakes. In both groups and among those who know the premake and remember to have liked it, a dominant negative appraisal of the remake that focuses on the deficiencies in comparison with the premake is found. Those who know the premakes clearly contextualise the remakes within this frame. Hereby the patterns of reception that could be observed are concordant regarding both examples: (1) *Creating the gap – remake versus premake*, (2) *Past versus present experience*, (3) *(Nostalgic) context memories*, and (4) *Intertextual references – roundabout nostalgia?*. This conclusion shall now focus on differences and similarities between the discussions about the two remakes, and explanations for the non-existence of nostalgia shall be deduced.

First of all, the assessments of the 'knowing' audiences inevitably contain a comparison between premake and remake. The main reference to the past is the reference to the premake. In both discussions the participants simply compare the two versions. Here, the main difference can be found between the age groups. Thus, while in the context of *The Avengers* (Chechik, 1998) it is the group of the 55 to 65-year-olds that predominantly makes this comparison, in the context of *Knight Rider* (NBC, 2008) it can be mainly observed among the 25 to 35-year-olds. Despite the assumptions in the television analysis, none of the aspects that refer to the premake directly work as a "mnemonic prompt". In each case it is the premake that is remembered first. Normally, the premake and the experiences related to it are the final point of the viewers' associations.

In both cases, the comparison inevitably turns into the valorisation of the premake in the light of the remake or vice versa. A comparison that highlights the *(Bad) premake versus the (good) remake* is infrequent. In the case of *Knight Rider* (NBC, 2008), it is observable among a few audiences and mainly among those whose "retrospective classification" of the premake or aspects of it is negative. In the case of *The Avengers* (Chechik, 1998), the contrast is less strong and only aspects of the remake are valorised as being better, while the general appraisal is always in favour of the premake. This may be explained by the fact that none of the 'knowing audiences' retrospectively classifies the premake negatively.

Regarding both *Knight Rider* (NBC, 2008) and *The Avengers* (Chechik, 1998), the comparison in favour of the premake is prevalent. As Horton and McDougal (1998, p. 3) state in the context of remakes in general, the remake "transforms" the "hypotext". Here, the remake becomes part of the valorisation of the premake. As assumed, a distinct gap between the higher-valued premake and the lower-valued remake is constructed. In both cases, on a broader level the remake serves to give the premake the status of the 'original', just as Oltmann (2008, p. 27) describes it in the context of her investigation on remakes in general. Later, regarding both examples, single levels of the remake are devaluated against the backdrop of the premake. The strongest contrast is always observable among those who retrospectively classified the premake positively, which again are the 55 to 65-year-olds in the case of *The Avengers* (Chechik, 1998) and the 25 to 35-year-olds regarding *Knight Rider* (NBC, 2008). Both *The Avengers* (Chechik, 1998) and *Knight Rider* (NBC, 2008) are perceived as being too "clean", characters are described as being insufficient since they lack decisive aspects of the premake characters. In both cases the term "sterile" is used. One can only assume that a lack of emotional attachment is part of its connotation. In the context of *The Avengers* (Chechik, 1998), two interviewees from the age group of the 55 to 65-year-olds state explicitly that "irgendwas fehlt" [something is missing] (HFG55-65, GD55-65_Remakes_TheAvengers_Deutschland, 196 [o.t.]). "[M]an sehnt sich nach dem Alten" [you long for the old] (IMG55-65, GD55-65_Remakes_The Avengers_Deutschland, 165 [o.t.]), as IMG55-65 says.

The pattern that contrasts the (bad) remake with the (good) premake finds its continuation in a comparison of past versus present experiences. Both in the case of *The Avengers* and in the case of *Knight Rider*, textual aspects that have been described as lacking something correlate with a respective lack of positive emotions as remembered in the context of the premake. Again, the differences concern the territorial groups less than the age groups, and again a division between those who retrospectively classify the premake positively and those who retrospectively classify it negatively can be noticed. Some audiences of the group of the 55 to 65-year-olds explicitly reflect on the influence of past experiences on their present appraisal. Against the backdrop of observations that have been made by Furno-Lamude and Anderson (1992) we may also assume that certain nostalgia comes into play here. "Nostalgia for a program," the authors state, "could explain why viewers perceive their favorite rerun as having better quality than newer programs" (Furno-Lamude and Anderson, 1992, p. 371). However, no participant classifies his/her emotion as nostalgia.

In both cases, a clear narration of the gap that contrasts a prelapsarian with a postlapsarian world can be observed. The interviewees are inspired to reminisce about the better past programme or better past emotions. The remake text as such, however, provokes mainly negative emotions, such as deception. Despite the existence of a 'gap' and the distinct mentioning of "sehnsucht" [yearning], the experience is not classified as being nostalgic by the audiences. We may not talk of 'artefact nostalgia' directed towards the premake nor of 'A or F nostalgia' directed toward the past emotions. In order to explain that, it certainly makes sense to return to the definition of nostalgia as it has been quoted in the very beginning of this work. Following Cook (2005, p. 2), nostalgia is a "state of longing for something that is known to be irretrievable". In the light of this we may thus emphasise that despite the clear narration of the gap it is the irretrievability that cannot be observed in the explications of the audiences. "Irgendwas" [something], as HFG55-65 states, is indeed described as being missing. However, this 'something' is not classified as irretrievable from the perspective of the audiences, but is thought to be available in the premake or in a 'better' remake version. Since the remake is negatively appraised, it is the text that is made responsible for the lack.

It is a slightly different case regarding the *(Nostalgic) context memories*. As in the case of the reruns, also the remake discussions reflect the existence of a context memory. Again, in both cases the respective premakes are triggers of the viewers' memories and have an intermediate position. Their memories exclusively refer to the time span of the 'original' broadcast of the series, even though both premakes were broadcasted as reruns within the course of time. Presumably the first broadcast left the strongest impression on the audiences, which is why they predominantly remember this moment. This would also be concordant with observations that have been made by Hoffmann and Kutscha (2010) in the context of memories of motion pictures. The pattern again clearly supports the narration of the better premake. In general and in comparison with the reruns, however, the context memories rather remain a passing remark. A distinct nostalgic rhetoric – both simple and reflexive – can only be observed in the context of the *Knight Rider* (NBC, 2008) discussion and here only among the 25 to 35-year-old Spaniards. They clearly contrast the better childhood past with the present. The interviewees do not explicitly refer to nostalgia in this context. Only in the light of their later statements that they developed childhood nostalgia in the context of *Knight Rider* can it at least be assumed that they also refer to the discussion about the remake. In any case it seems that the viewers' 'own artefact nostalgia' did not arise in the course of the reception but is an emotion that developed in the context of 're-enactment' in the course of the discussion.

Finally, both *The Avengers* (Chechik, 1998) and *Knight Rider* (NBC, 2008) are approached with intertextual references that differ from the premake. In both cases mainly those audiences who do not know the premake undertake this framing. Again, in contrast to the reruns, no cases of (roundabout) nostalgia may be observed. Here, the reception analysis assumes that this is due to the general negative appraisal of the remake that does not give way to positive emotions in the context of the text.

In summary, it can be stated that for those who know the premake, both remakes are inevitably related to reception experiences and emotions from the context of the premake. The remakes appeal to the memory of a "we" that is in this case neither a gendered "we" nor a national "we" but a "we" of the age group. In both cases it seems that the remake reception supports a possible nostalgia in the context of the premake, respectively the rerun, but it does not provoke nostalgic longing by itself. This conclusive chapter could highlight probable explanations for this specific fact. However, this does not apply to remakes and nostalgia in general. Surely not every remake is appraised negatively. The "critical framing" does not dominate every remake reception.

8.3 RECEPTION OF THE PERIOD DRAMAS

The period drama was the last nostalgia 'genre' that was discussed in the focus groups. While, as shall be stated preceding the analysis, in the context of *Mad Men* livelier discussions could be observed, *Borgia* did not provoke as many contributions from the participants.

8.3.1 The reception of the period drama *Mad Men*

The television analysis of *Mad Men* (AMC, 2007; Fox, 2009; Cuatro, 2009) showed that the self-reflexive period drama exposes a mix of different potential triggers of 'A nostalgia', 'F nostalgia' and 'empathetic F nostalgia'. This is also reflected in the reception study. Hereby, the discussion is somehow divided into two sections. In the first part a clearer gap between different "we-groups" could be observed. The second part, more focused on the nostalgia scene of the stimulus material, rather mediates between the two age groups and gives more space to the development of empathetic emotions. In order to maintain the clarity, the reception of this second section shall be commented separately in this presentation of results. Apart from this focus on an empathetic understanding in the second section, the reception of *Mad Men* can be divided into two major patterns: (1) *Reception of the references to the "natural real"*, which mainly focuses on the level of narration, and, (2) *(Inter-) textual references – (roundabout) nostalgia* that refers to the reception of potential triggers of nostalgia on other levels of the text. They shall be commented on as follows.

A pattern of reception that reflects an expectation of nostalgia on the part of the participants could not be identified. In the group of the 25 to 35-year old Spaniards and the group of the 55 to 65-year-old Germans, no one saw the series before and could report about corresponding expectations. In the group of the 25 to 35-year old Germans, FFG25-35 watched the first three seasons of the series and BMG25-35 saw a few episodes. Also, in the Spanish group FCFS55-65 knows the series and AMS55-65 saw "a part". However, in this general context no participant mentions nostalgia. Earlier experiences are reported only vaguely. Only FCFG55-65 and FFG25-35 highlight their general appreciation of the series.

8.3.1.1 Reception of the references to the "natural real"

Starting on the level of the narration, the television analysis shows that the drama series *Mad Men* does not favour 'F nostalgia' directed towards an idealised 1960s time of reference but rather reflects the era critically. It has been assumed that this perspective will also shape the reception of the participants or contribute to a possible transfer to a German or Spanish 1960s reality. Above all, and with a view on the 55 to 65-year-old Spaniards and the 25 to 35-year-old Germans, where in each case one of the participants has a more extensive knowledge of the episodes, this has been verified by the group discussions. Already a re-telling of the main-plot on the side of FFG25-35 clearly reflects the non-nostalgic perspective on the era that is induced by the series:

FFG25-35: "Well, it's an agency in the '60s. An advertising agency. [...] It's all about Don Draper. This is the main part. He somehow slipped into the agency and, well, has a dubious past. You do not know it very well. You learn about his past bit by bit. He is married to a beautiful young woman. [...] And he has a lot of affairs. They are constantly smoking and drinking, drinking whiskey in the agency, and you get an impression of the '60s." (GD25-35_Period Pictures_Mad Men_Deutschland, 9 [o.t.])[257]

AFG25-35: "Well, the men are back in the executive office, and in the front the women have the secretary jobs."
FFG25-35: "Yes. The women are secretaries. There were none. Peggy is the only one, the one with the ponytail, who looks a little bit unspectacular. Who [throws] herself at the other one, well, and she is – she becomes pregnant by the [...]. And has an abortion, and it's all under the,

---

257 Original quotation: "Also das ist ne Agentur in den 60er Jahren. Ne Werbeagentur. [...] Es geht um Don Draper. Das ist die Hauptrolle. Der ist da irgendwie reingerutscht in die Agentur und, joa, hat ne zwielichtige Vergangenheit. Man weiß nich so. Man erfährt erst so stückchenweise von seiner Vergangenheit. Und er ist mit 'ner jungen, schönen Frau verheiratet. [...] Und er hat ganz viele Affären. Die, äh, sind da ständig am Rauchen und am Trinken, Whisky trinken in der Agentur und man is – man kriegt so 'n Eindruck von den 60er Jahren." (FFG25-35, GD25-35_Period Pictures_Mad Men_Deutschland, 9)

well, no one really notices." (GD25-35_Period Pictures_Mad Men_Deutschland, 82-87 [o.t.])[258]

The "impression of the '60s" reflects a time span of moral bigotry, unwanted pregnancies and gender inequality. Also in the following discussion the participants highlight gender relations as they are exposed and 'imposed' on the agenda by the series. In both groups this leads into a critical reflection of gender roles during the 1960s. Mostly the 55 to 65-year-old Spanish women relate the observations to their own 1960s' lifeworld.

FCFS55-65: "There's also a mentality here. He [Don Draper] doesn't let his wife work ... Because he is a boss, earns a lot ... Well, at the same time, he's with everyone he wants to be apart from his wife. This was also at the time you also saw that. Here." (GS55-65_Period Pictures_Mad Men_Spanien, 54-56 [o.t.])[259]

PCFS55-65: "... there were sites of responsibility, especially in small villages, where for example the director of the bank could not, his wife could not work. It was regarded with disapproval because since he represented the bank, he had to be, he was perfectly able to sustain the family. No, not once did they think that his wife wanted to work, because it fulfilled them, they liked it, because she was a doctor, because she was I don't know what. ... It was only about economic aspects." (GS55-65_Period Pictures_Mad Men_Spanien, 57-61 [o.t.])[260]

---

258 Original quotation: AFG25-35: "Also die Männer sind hinten in dem, dem Chef-Zimmer und die Frauen machen vorne den Sekretärinnen-Job." FFG25-35: "[Ja. Die Frauen sind Sekretärinnen] Es gab keine. Die, die, die Peggy ist die – die, also die eine mit dem Zopf, die 'n bisschen unspeh – unspektakulärer aussieht, die sich an diesen, an diesen andern, na und sie ist ja, und sie wird auch schwanger von dem. [...] Und sie treibt aber das Kind ab, und es ist alles halt schön unter, also es kriegt eigentlich fast niemand mit." (GD25-35_Period Pictures_Mad Men_Deutschland, 82-87)

259 Original quotation: "Aquí también hay una mentalidad. Él [Don Draper] no deja trabajar a su mujer... Porque él es jefe, gana mucho ... Ara después el va con quien quiere aparte de su mujer. Eso también era en la época también se veía. Aquí." (FCFS55-65, GS55-65_Period Pictures_Mad Men_Spanien, 54-56)

260 Original quotation: "... habían sitios de responsabilidad, sobre todo en pueblos pequeños, que por ejemplo el director de la caja [...] no podía, su mujer no podría trabajar. Estaba mal visto porque ya como representaba la caixa, pues tenía que ser, podía mantener perfectamente a la familia. No, no pensaban ni en un momento, que su mujer quería trabajar, porque les realizaba, les gustaba, porque era médico, porque era yo qué sé. ... Era solo el (aspecto) económico." (PCFS55-65, GS55-65_Period Pictures_Mad Men_Spanien, 57-61)

FCFS55-65: "Those of us who started to work at that time, well, we had no facilities, childcare facility, of any kind, nothing." (GS55-65_Period Pictures_Mad Men_Spanien, 63 [o.t.])[261]

In general, the comments reflect the moral standards and the marginal position of females under Franco's strictly Catholic regime. The "referential framing" does not serve the object of nostalgia but, favoured by the television series, is rather part of a negative "retrospective classification" of the 1960s.

This similarly applies to the 25 to 35-year-old Germans. Mainly with a view on gender issues, the participants explicitly highlight the era as not being worth longing for.

CFG25-35: "Well, I would not have liked to live there. Let's say it this way." (GD25-35_Period Pictures_Mad Men_Deutschland, 130 [o.t.])[262]

FFG25-35: "Well, I find the costumes great. And I like the women and I like female bodies, but ... but I would not want to swap my present life." (GD25-35_Period Pictures_Mad Men_Deutschland, 142 [o.t.])[263]

GMG25-35: "Well, at that time, like it is reflected here, I would not have wanted to live, ... Answered not from a male, but from a female perspective ..... ." (GD25-35_Period Pictures_ Mad Men_Deutschland, 144; 154 [o.t.])[264]

EMG25-35: "... well, this is, for me it is very clearly from this conservative time. And because of that I would definitely deny that I would like to live there." (GD25-35_Period Pictures_Mad Men_Deutschland, 134 [o.t.])[265]

---

261 Original quotation: "Las que empezábamos a trabajar en aquella época, pues, de facilidades ninguna, [...] de guarderías, de ningún tipo de facilidad, nada." (FCFS55-65, GS55-65_Period Pictures_Mad Men_Spanien, 63)

262 Original quotation: "Also ich hätte da nicht gern gelebt. Sagen wir's mal so." (CFG25-35, GD25-35_Period Pictures_Mad Men_Deutschland, 130)

263 Original quotation: "Also, ich find halt die Kostüme großartig. Und mir gefallen die Frauen und ich mag weibliche Körper, aber ... so meine Rolle jetzt in der heutigen Zeit will ich nicht tauschen." (FFG25-35, GD25-35_Period Pictures_Mad Men_Deutschland, 142)

264 Original quotation: "Na, zu der Zeit, wie das da rüber kommt, hätte ich nicht leben wolln,... Nicht aus männlicher, sondern aus weiblicher Sicht beantwortet..." (GMG25-35, GD25-35_Period Pictures_Mad Men_Deutschland, 144; 154)

265 Original quotation: "... das ist ja, find ich jetzt für mich ziemlich deutlich, aus dieser biederen Zeit. Und aufgrund dessen würd' ich das deutlich verneinen, dass ich da gern gelebt hätte." (EMG25-35, GD25-35_Period Pictures_Mad Men_Deutschland, 134)

Here, the participants also make a "referential framing". Their point of reference is their present living reality that is put into positive contrast with the 1960s past as reflected by *Mad Men*. Furthermore, nostalgia is clearly hindered here.[266] Apart from that, a positive "prosthetic memory" of the era on the basis of which nostalgia would have been possible can be excluded. At various points of the discussion, the 25 to 35-year-old participants highlight the mediated nature of their knowledge of the 1960s by explicitly referring to history books, photos, press reports and others.

In other cases, the "scenes that seem devised solely to index the difference between then and now", as White (2011, p. 153) says, are highlighted both among the 25 to 35-year-old Germans and Spaniards. FFG25-35 and JMS25-35 state:

FFG25-35: "... later she is pregnant, and then she is constantly smoking and drinking alcohol. And when you look at that, you think, alas, oh my God, but they did not know it back then. Well, this is just one example." (GD25-35_Period Pictures_Mad Men_Deutschland, 12 [o.t.])[267]

JMS25-35: "I saw a man smoking next to a child on a swing. I think, err, well, that would be impossible nowadays." (GS25-35_Period Pictures_Mad Men_Spanien, 202 [o.t.])[268]

As White (2011) presumed on a theoretical level, these scenes "serve as conspicuous signs of the era's alluring, disarming, irresponsible, and potentially lethal habits" (White, 2011, p. 154) and also impede nostalgia.

Apart from this comment of JMS25-35, in those groups, namely the group of the 25 to 35-year-old Spaniards and the 55 to 65-year-old Germans, where none of the participants had ever seen a complete episode of the series and no *aficionado* describes complete plot-lines and influences the 'agenda setting' within the discussion, the plot of the series is not further discussed. In these groups, other levels of the text become more important, as will be commented in the following context.

---

266   At this point it shall at least be hinted at the fact that in this last quotation by EMG25-35 it also becomes apparent that the 1960s as such are not excluded as potential object of nostalgic longing by the participant. *Mad Men* seems to depict that part of the 1960s which seems less worth longing for to the participant. Here it may only be assumed that EMG25-35 points at common clichés of the swinging Sixties as a counter example.

267   Original quotation: "... sie is ja dann schwanger und sie ist ständig am Rauchen und am Alkohol trinken. Und wenn du dir das dann anguckst, denkst du, hach, oh Gott, aber das wussten die ja damals alles noch nicht. Also das ist jetzt nur ein Beispiel..." (FFG25-35, GD25-35_Period Pictures_Mad Men_Deutschland, 12)

268   Original quotation: "Yo ahí he visto un señor fumando al lado de un niño en un columpio... me ha parecido, ahmm... que ahora mismo sería imposible, vamos." (JMS25-35, GS25-35_Period Pictures_Mad Men_Spanien, 202)

8.3.1.2 Nostalgia on other levels of the text

With a view on the television analysis we may state that *Mad Men* exposes a high degree of disclosed intertextuality to other cultural products. The "'deliberate archaism'" imports a further critical layer into the series and highlights the constructedness of the text. Depending on respective "retrospective classifications" of the references, it may also lead to nostalgia. At the same time *Mad Men* distinctly refers to 'the 1960s'. Consumer products it exposes may, it can be assumed, work as "mnemonic prompt" for those who have their own or "prosthetic memories" of the era.

As the reception analysis shows, these references are indeed perceived as such. Hereby, however, the foci of attention differ clearly among the groups – as it seems, always depending on where "proximity" to one's the own lifeworld is most likely to be generated. Accordingly, differently distributed are the nostalgias that may be observed. We can roughly distinguish two sub-patterns here: (1) *Intertextual references – (roundabout) nostalgia* and (2) *Reference to the 1960s*.

8.3.1.2.1 Intertextual references – (roundabout) nostalgia

In a major pattern, mainly observable among the 25 to 35-year-old Spaniards, the interviewees make sense of the series by integrating it into a net of intertextual references. They predominantly name other period pictures that are set in an era around the 1950s and 1960s. Above all, the aesthetic and music of *Mad Men* remind the 25 to 35-year-olds of other films:

JMS25-35: "I saw it in [the context of] other American series, dancing twist." (GS25-35_Period Pictures_Mad Men_Spanien, 64 [o.t.])[269]

VMS25-35: "Yeah, the aesthetic I saw in the other scene reminded me of this movie or this series of the prom, these ones where they are all coming in order to dance twist, where they are all worried because they will stop seeing each other." (GS25-35_Period Pictures_Mad Men_Spanien, 102 [o.t.])[270]

---

269 Original quotation: "Yo la he visto, en [el contexto de] otras series americanas, bailando twist." (JMS25-35, GS25-35_Period Pictures_Mad Men_Spanien, 64)

270 Original quotation: "Síi, la estética que he visto en la otra escena me ha recordado a esta película o a estas series de baile de graduación ese que van todos ahí bailando twist ahí, de, que se apenan porque van a dejar de verse." (VMS25-35, GS25-35_Period Pictures_Mad Men_Spanien, 102)

CMS25-35: "Yes, I totally agree with him. It reminds me of the aesthetic of this, of the old movies and apart from that..." (GS25-35_Period Pictures_Mad Men_Spanien, 108 [o.t.])[271]

As a concrete example, *Dirty Dancing* (Ardolino, 1987), a period drama that is set in the early 1960s, is named by the two female participants AFS25-35 and OFS25-35. Other examples that regard both female and male members as memory community are the science fiction trilogy *Back to the Future* (Zemeckis, 1985, 1989, 1990), which among other centuries also 'returns' to the late 1950s, or *Grease* (Kleiser, 1978), a period musical set in the late 1950s (see e.g. VMS25-35, GS25-35_Period Pictures_Mad Men_Spanien, 142; ZFS25-35, GS25-35_Period Pictures_Mad Men_Spanien, 65).

It is the latter reference, *Grease*, which in the case of ZFS25-35 leads to 'artefact nostalgia', respectively the viewer's 'own artefact nostalgia':

ZFS25-35: "I must say that – that with the dances and the entire series of *Mad Men* and the one, I don't know the title ... For me, this refers to *Grease* and all that, this kind of dance, these films which bring me a lot of nostalgia or, be it, they touch me, for example; [A nostalgia] of having watched them at a time when I did not have any concerns. I don't know." (GS25-35_Nostalgia_ Allgemein_Spanien, 32 [o.t.])[272]

In line with this elaboration, later in the questionnaire, the participant describes nostalgia at the moment of "recordar las series antiguos, al volver a un pasado sin preocupaciones" [reminding old series, going back to a past without sorrows] (ZFS25-35, S25-35_Connotation of nostalgia_25-35-year-old Spaniards, 19 [o.t.]). Similar to the case of CFG25-35 in the context of the *Knight Rider* rerun, it is not the series *Mad Men* as such that provokes nostalgia, but rather a kind of 'roundabout' nostalgia that is provoked by an intertextual reference of the text. Furthermore, the respective positive "retrospective classification" of the object of nostalgia that she calls "un pasado sin preocupaciones" [a past without sorrows] is essential. It can only be assumed that ZFS25-35 here refers to a period in life, more precisely to her

---

271 Original quotation: "Sí. Yo coincido perfectamente con él. Me recuerda la estética de esto, de películas antiguas y demáas [...]." (CMS25-35, GS25-35_Period Pictures_Mad Men_Spanien, 108)

272 Original quotation: "Y yo debo decir que eso, que lo de los bailes y toda la serie esta de *Mad Men* y esaa... que no sé como se llama. Eso que me remite a *Grease* y todo eso, ese tipo de baile, esas películas también me dan mucha nostalgia o sea que, me tocan la sensibilidad, por ejemplo. [Una nostalgia] [d]e haberlo visto yo, en una época en la que yo no tenía preocupacionees. No sé. Mmm." (ZFS25-35, GS25-35_Nostalgia_ Allgemein_Spanien, 16; 18; 32)

schooldays, that she also describes as "el paraíso perdido" [the lost paradise] (GS25-35_Nostalgia_ Allgemein_Spanien, 106 [o.t.]) at another point in the discussion.

In correspondence to the intertextual references, the series is perceived as being 'typical American' by these 25 to 35-year-olds:

VMS25-35: "It has nothing to do with Spain, because things like that weren't done. But nothing." (GS25-35_Period Pictures_Mad Men_Spanien, 191 [o.t.])[273]

CMS25-35: "I think it's rather American." (GS25-35_Period Pictures_Mad Men_Spanien, 115 [o.t.])[274]

JMS25-35: "Here, the Sixties were perhaps rather paso doble [a Spanish dance] than anything else." (GS25-35_Period Pictures_Mad Men_Spanien, 117 [o.t.])[275]

A relation to the Spanish context of the 1960s is clearly denied. In their further explication of the differences, the participants refer explicitly to Franco's regime.

VMS25-35: "No. Here we are in another world. In this time in Spain. We were 50 years behind."
JMS25-35: "The dictatorial involution."
VMS25-35: "Yes. respectively Franco ... here we were..."
HMS25-35: "Paquito."
VMS25-35: "Paquito."
JMS25-35: "Don Paquito."
VMS25-35: "Respectively, we didn't have any progress simultaneously with the Americans. We were stagnating, totally."
M: "But the fashion, for example?"
VMS25-35: "The fashion, well, a bit, but..."
RMS25-35: "Later. Here it arrived later."
VMS25-35: "Later and, apart from that, not that uninhibited. Because, sure, Don Franco didn't allow too much either." (GS25-35_Period Pictures_MadMen_Spanien, 119-134 [o.t.])[276]

---

273 Original quotation: "[...] Nada que ver con España porque nunca se ha hecho nada así. Pero nada." (VMS25-35, GS25-35_Period Pictures_Mad Men_Spanien, 191)

274 Original quotation: "[...] Creo que es más americano." (CMS25-35, GS25-35_Period Pictures_Mad Men_Spanien, 115)

275 Original quotation: "Los sesenta de aquí, quizás son más pasodoble que otra cosa." (JMS25-35, GS25-35_Period Pictures_Mad Men_Spanien, 117)

276 Original quotation: VMS25-35: "No, aquí estamos en otro mundo. En esa época. En España. Estábamos, cincuenta años atrás [...]." JMS25-35: "La involución dictatorial." VMS25-35: "Sí. O sea Franco y... aquí estábamos que iban." HMS25-35: "Paquito."

The mention of Franco's regime makes a new "we" appear, namely a national "we" in contrast to the "they", the former Franco leadership. No nostalgia can be observed in this context. Not to mention the clear non-existence of positive "prosthetic" memories from the era. The elaborations of the 25 to 35-year-old Spaniards differ distinctly from the ones of their older compatriots, as it will be outlined in the following section on *References to the 1960s*.

Later, also in the group of the 55 to 65-year-olds, the "deliberate archaism" of *Mad Men* is highly relevant. More than in the group of the 25 to 35-year-old Spaniards, "they comment on how [the text] is constructed and performed", just as Chandler and Munday (2011, p. 161) describe Liebes and Katz's (1990) term of the "critical framing". Except for the case of EFG55-65, who relates the *Mad Men* protagonists to Rock Hudson and Doris Day (EFG55-65, GD55-65_Period Pictures_ Mad Men_Deutschland, 52), the elaborations concern the accentuation of the series' formal level in general. *Mad Men*'s clear emphasis of the constructedness of the text is respectively perceived:

DMG55-65: "But I also found it was like a decal. The room was never illuminated like that, and also the things that they were wearing. That never existed like that, yes. [...] it's not real." (GD55-65_Period pictures_ Mad Men_Deutschland, 81-85 [o.t.])[277]

DMG55-65: "I immediately thought that someone was trying to represent the '60s. The carousel, for example, existed only in the '60s. Today, they don't have something like that." (GD55-65_Period pictures_ Mad Men_Deutschland, 169 [o.t.])[278]

VMS25-35: "Paquito." JMS25-35: "Don Paquito." VMS25-35: "O sea, que no habíamos avanzado een paralelo los americanos y nosotros, estábamos estancados, totalmente." M: "¿Pero la moda por ejemplo?" VMS25-35: "La moda ye-ye, un poco, pero..." RMS25-35: "Más tarde, aquí llegó más tarde." VMS25-35: "Más tarde y además no tan desatada, porque estaba Don Franco, claro, que tampoco permitían demasiado... jmmm." (GS25-35_Period Pictures_MadMen_Spanien, 119-134)

277 Original quotation: "Aber das fand ich wie so'n Abziehbild. Der Raum war nie so ausgeleuchtet, und auch die Sachen, die die anhatten. Das hat 's so nie gegeben, ja. [...] gar nicht echt." (DMG55-65, GD55-65_Period Pictures_ Mad Men_Deutschland, 81- 85)

278 Original quotation: "[A]lso ich dachte sofort, da versucht jemand, die Sechziger darzustellen. Das Karussell gab 's auch nur in den 60er Jahren. Das gibt's heut nicht mehr." (DMG55-65, GD55-65_Period Pictures_ Mad Men_Deutschland, 169)

GFG55-65: "It is clichéd. [...] You recognise some things but it's still like a, like DMG55-65 said, a decal. That I distance myself from it at the same time." (GD55-65_Period Pictures_ Mad Men_Deutschland, 147 [o.t.])[279]

BFG55-65: "[...] I had to smile in between because I found it so artificial." (GD55-65_Period Pictures_ Mad Men_Deutschland, 163 [o.t.])[280]

These interviewees indeed recognise past objects, such as clothes, the carousel, "so 'n paar Sachen" [things like that] that they also know from the 1960s Germany; the contrast to their own living reality, however, is always highlighted. The "critical framing" creates an emotional distance that puts the interviewees in the position of observers. Besides GFG55-65, DMG55-65 highlights this experience as well:

DMG55-65: "I stepped out of it. Didn't want to stay. Rather like to stay outside." (GD55-65_Period Pictures_ Mad Men_Deutschland, 89-91 [o.t.])[281]

Nostalgia is not developed. On the F level it is impeded by the emotional distance, and on the A level a possibly positive "retrospective classification" of the reference the way it was found among the 25 to 35-year-old Spaniards is not the case.

8.3.1.2.2 References to the 1960s

Among the Spanish 55 to 65-year-olds and a smaller group of 55 to 65-year-olds of the German group, the focus of attention is obviously on the level of décor, props, costumes, and music, and the referential character of the latter to 'the 1960s'. Among these participants clear "referential framings" that draw the relation to their own lifeworld. The interviewees, above all the 55 to 65-year-old Spaniards, recognise a whole list of objects, from electric typewriters to clothing to hair style and music, and relate them to their 1960s reality (see e.g. FCFS55-65, GS55-65_Period Pictures_Mad Men_Spanien, 16; IFG55-65, GD55-65_Period Pictures_ Mad Men_Deutschland, 7; PCFS55-65, GS55-65_Period Pictures_Mad Men_Spanien,

---

279 Original quotation: GFG55-65: "[...] das so klischeehaft war, [...] man erkennt so 'n paar Sachen irgendwie wieder, aber es ist trotzdem wie 'n, wie DMG55-65 sagte, so 'n Abziehbild, das ich gleichzeitig auch gleich wieder in so 'ne Distanz gehe." (GFG55-65, GD55-65_Period Pictures_ Mad Men_Deutschland, 147)

280 Original quotation: "Also ich weiß, dass ich zwischendurch mal schmunzeln musste, weil mir das alles so aufgesetzt vorkam, so." (BFG55-65, GD55-65_Period Pictures_ Mad Men_Deutschland, 163)

281 Original quotation: "Ich hab' mich rausgezogen. (Wollte da [...] nicht) Bleib ich doch lieber draußen." (DMG55-65, GD55-65_Period Pictures_ Mad Men_Deutschland, 89-91)

42; FMS55-65, GS55-65_Period Pictures_Mad Men_Spanien, 98; PCFS55-65, GS55-65_Period Pictures_Mad Men_Spanien, 44; FCFS55-65, GS55-65_Period Pictures_Mad Men_Spanien, 45). The objects and sounds are part of their memories of the era and work as "mnemonic prompt[s]" in order to reminiscence about it:

PCFS55-65: "For example, at the very beginning, when the girl appears in this petticoat with that hem line of about fifteen centimetres below the knees. Back then these skirts existed. They danced twist in these skirts."

FCFS55-65: "Sure, we all wore them, all of us." (GS55-65_Period Pictures_Mad Men_ Spanien, 82-87 [o.t.])[282]

FCF55-65: "You went to work like that, with the shirt-collar put up. Afterwards, you did what you could or what they could. But there were some manners, there was a... Well, I don't know, I liked it because of that." (GS55-65_Period Pictures_Mad Men_Spanien, 93 [o.t.])[283]

MFS55-65: "I remember that my cousin, for example, dressed her hair like this. With the hair boosted like that. She made her own clothes and such. And the moment she went out I had to accompany her." (GS55-65_Period Pictures_Mad Men_Spanien, 109 [o.t.])[284]

The exposed skirts are related to going dancing in the 1960s. The high-collar blouses and the offices remind them of their own working experiences. Hair and dresses are related to families and neighbours in the era. The same applies to the twist, which the participants also relate to their own 1960s life-styles. MFS55-65 continues her elaboration as follows:

MFS55-65: "And then, of course, the music reminds me of dancing the twist. Dancing? Well, sure, I was younger back then. I can picture myself in the backyard of our house. We lived next

---

282 Original quotation: PCFS55-65 "Por ejemplo al principio dónde viene la chica con esta falda a taulas estaba cocida hasta mas o menos hasta un poco unos quince centímetros antes de la rodilla. [...] Entonces las taulas si había. Esto (se bailaba twist) con esto." FCFS55-65: "Claro, y todas lo llevábamos, todas." (GS55-65_Period Pictures_Mad Men_Spanien, 82-87)

283 Original quotation: "... ibas a trabajar con (cuello camisero que daba) hasta aquí. ¿No? Después hacías lo que podías o lo que podían. Pero habían unas formas había un. Bueno yo no sé esta me gusta por esto." (FCFS55-65, GS55-65_Period Pictures_Mad Men_ Spanien, 93)

284 Original quotation: "Yo recuerdo que por ejemplo mi prima se peinaban así con este pelo levantado, se hacía la ropa y tal. (Y en el momento de salir) tuve que acompañarla." (MFS55-65, GS55-65_Period Pictures_Mad Men_Spanien, 109)

door to each other. And that was where we were putting make-up on each others' faces, where they sewed their clothes at home, they sewed my clothes." (GS55-65_Period Pictures_Mad Men_Spanien, 109 [o.t.])[285]

As already shown, other exposed objects as well as the music remind the participant of her childhood in Barcelona in the 1960s. Also in the case of AMS55-65, the music works as a "mnemonic prompt". His statement, while up to this point rather factual and impersonal, adopts a more emotional tone here:

AMS55-65: "At that time, music was the liberation. It was the moment of getting rid of everything and of showing how you really were. Dancing gave you the chance to socialise with girls or with friends. It was a different formal level. Music acted like a change of chip." (GS55-65_Period Pictures_Mad Men_Spanien, 110 [o.t.])[286]

In the cases of AFG55-65 and IMG55-65, the twist music encourages memories about their youth in the Germany of the 1960s':

AFG55-65: "I thought of IMG55-65. He used to be the king of the twist." (GD55-65_Period Pictures_ Mad Men_Deutschland, 72-74 [o.t.])[287]

AFG55-65: "Yes, I thought. Exactly. Yes, that means something to me or it opens up my heart. I like dancing." (GD55-65_Period Pictures_ Mad Men_Deutschland, 80 [o.t.])[288]

---

285 Original quotation: "(Y luego bueno claro toda la música me suena a bailar el twist. Bailar venga claro que era más pequeño) estoy imaginándome en el patio de casa, vivíamos todos (en los alrededores en casas y donde la una pintaba a la otra no sé que [...] el vestido lo hacía en casa, a mí me lo hacían)." (MFS55-65, GS55-65_Period Pictures_Mad Men_Spanien, 109)

286 Original quotation: "En aquella época, la altra [otra] música era la liberación. (Era el momento de deshacerse) de todo y mostrarte como eras. A través del baile te daba opción a relacionarte con chicas. O o o los amigos. Era un plano totalmente diferente del plano formal. La música actuaba como un cambio de chip." (AMS55-65, GS55-65_Period Pictures_Mad Men_Spanien, 110)

287 Original quotation: "Da hab' ich an [...] IMG55-65 gedacht. Der war mal Twist-König." (AFG55-65, GD55-65_Period Pictures_ Mad Men_Deutschland, 72-74)

288 Original quotation: "Doch, da hab' ich. Genau. Ja, da kann ich was mit anfangen, oder da, ehm, geht mein Herz gleich hoch, ich tanz gerne." (AFG55-65, GD55-65_Period Pictures_ Mad Men_Deutschland, 80)

IMG55-65: "That was completely spacey. [...] Yes, my memories are similar to those AFG55-65 has." (GD55-65_Period Pictures_ Mad Men_Deutschland, 104 154 [o.t.])[289]

That the objects clearly work as "mnemonic prompt[s]" for reminiscences about the time span is not only evident in the quotations mentioned above but is also explicitly highlighted by the interviewees:

FCFS55-65: "Yes. The whole era comes to mind."
PCFS55-65: "Yes, sure."
PMS55-65: "It's because it's more 'costumbrista'."
FCFS55-65: "Everything comes to your memory suddenly. Because it transports you back to the moment."
PMS55-65: "This one is more the ordinary life. You associate it more with what you saw." (GS55-65_Period Pictures_Mad Men_Spanien, 68-76 [o.t.])[290]

FCFS55-65 addresses this function of the text at diverse other points in the discussion:

FCFS55-65: "This is, for me, this is very well done, with much attention to the detail. All that is decoration, furniture, costumes, truly represents the era. I put myself back into that era." (GS55-65_Period Pictures_Mad Men_Spanien, 27 [o.t.])[291]

FCFS55-65: "It's not that they wear this because it's the era, but in this one it's a time travel. You go straight there. You're there in the office. I see it and perfectly live it." (GS55-65_Period Pictures_Mad Men_Spanien, 81 [o.t.])[292]

---

289 Original quotation: "Das war ganz ausgeflippt. […] Ja, mir ging's ähnlich wie AFG55-65." (IMG55-65, GD55-65_Period Pictures_ Mad Men_Deutschland, 104; 154)

290 Original quotation: FCFS55-65: "Sí. Pues me viene toda la época a la memoria, sí." PCFS55-65: "[Sí, sí, sí, sí, claro]." PMS55-65: "Es que es más costumbrista, entonces." FCFS55-65: "Todo te viene a la memoria de golpe porque te transporta en aquel momento." PMS55-65: "Estas son más de la vida cotidiana. Lo asocias más a lo que has visto." (GS55-65_Period Pictures_Mad Men_Spanien, 68-76)

291 Original quotation: "Una, es una para mí esta muy bien hecha. Mmmm. Muy cuidado en detalles. Todo lo que es decoración, mobiliario, vestuario, (porque ha contado todo) reproduce muy fiel a la época. Yo me transporto. En la época." (FCFS55-65, GS55-65_Period Pictures_Mad Men_Spanien, 27)

292 Original quotation: "No es que van vestidos porque era la época pero es que en esta es un viaje en el tiempo. Te metes directamente, estás ahí en la oficina. Yo lo veo y lo vivo perfectamente." (FCFS55-65, GS55-65_Period Pictures_Mad Men_Spanien, 81)

In contrast to those among the 55 to 65-year-old Germans who, due to their focus on the formal level, frame the exposed objects as "artificial", these interviewees actually perceive them as being realistic. While the first group explicitly describes the distance to the series, among the latter, references to experiences of immersion can be observed and participants are indeed emotionally involved.

Hereby, even though in the elaborations during the main discussion no rhetoric of the gap could be outlined, nostalgia is commented by the 55 to 65-year-old Spaniards. In the final discussion, FCFS55-65, AMS55-65, and MFS55-65 refer to nostalgia in the context of *Mad Men*:

FCFS55: "Well, the adolescence, the excerpt with the dance, in this case it is."
AMS55-65: "In this case it might be."
MFS55-65: "Ah yes. There is much nostalgia."
FCFS55-65: "In this case it is." (GS55-65_NostalgieAllgemein_Spanien, 4-7 [o.t.])[293]

With a view on their further statements, the objects of nostalgia can be further outlined. Particularly FCFS55-65 expresses this nostalgia more comprehensively:

FCFS55-65: "What gives me the most nostalgic feelings is the modern one, this *Mad Men*. When I started working, how were the offices, the manners, the music and the dancing? How was it? What did the boys wear? What did the girls wear? Yes." (GS55-65_Nostalgie Allgemein_Spanien, 25; 29 [o.t.])[294]

The emotion is specified in the questionnaire. The participant states that she felt nostalgia in the context of *Mad Men* because it was a series which "inevitably transports" her back to the times of her youth (FCFS55-65, Questionnaire_ Connotation of nostalgia_55-65-year-old Spaniards, 20 [o.t.]).[295] The description is concordant with her other elaborations cited previously. Based on that, it can be assumed that it is the "visual correspondence" of her memories of the 1960s with the described aspects of the series that allow her to kind of re-enact a moment of her

---

293 Original quotation: FCFS55-65: "Bueno, la juventud, el trozo esto con el baile, eso sí." AMS55-65: "[Esto sí, esto quizás sí]." MFS55-65: "[Ah sí, hay mucha nostalgia]." FCFS55-65: "Eso sí." (GS55-65_NostalgieAllgemein_Spanien, 4-7)

294 Original quotation: "[A mi que me inspira] más nostalgia es la moderna esta de *Mad Men*. Cuando empecé a trabajar como eran las oficinas, la relación esta, los (cassettes) con la música y el baile, como eran, como iban los chicos, como iban las chicas, sí." (FCFS55-65, GS55-65_Nostalgie Allgemein_Spanien, 25; 29)

295 Original quotation: "[d]urante el pase de los fragmentos de *Mad Men* porque es una serie que me transporta inevitablemente a los tiempos de mi juventud." (FCFS55-65, Questionnaire_Connotation of nostalgia_55-65-year-old Spaniards, 20)

youth. The apparently high degree of "visual correspondence" allows a 'synchronisation' with her own memories. The interviewee is, so to say, inside the text in her own past world. Instead of 'artefact nostalgia' it is rather a kind of the viewer's 'own F nostalgia'. The rhetoric of nostalgia is not found here. It can only be assumed that it is the passage of adolescence and positive memories related to it that can be shortly re-enacted but that are gone from today's perspective, which causes this nostalgia. In contrast to her elaborations in the context of the narration of the series, her nostalgia does not seem to contain a reflexive layer and can rather be classified as what Davis called "simple nostalgia".

While AMS55-65 later denies to have felt nostalgia – as he states "It's reflecting about the situation. But not necessarily nostalgia" (GS55-65_Period Pictures_Mad Men_Spanien, 160 [o.t.])[296] – MFS55-65's elaborations also allow a further description of the case. In the questionnaire the participant confirms the previously mentioned nostalgia and comments on the object of her longing as follows:

MFS55-65: "[...] I remember how it was when I was a teenager, and the whole family was more united than we're now. I think these times were ignorant and happy." (MFS55-65, Connotation of nostalgia_55-65-year-old Spaniards, 18 [o.t.])[297]

Her contribution contains a clear rhetoric of nostalgia. She describes a phase of felicity and familiar harmony in her distant past that is lost from today's perspective. Against the backdrop of her further statements – where it is the description of twist music and typical hairstyles and less the immersion in the text that seem to lead to the narration of her domestic family situation – it can be assumed that the elements worked as "mnemonic prompt[s]" and lead to the viewer's 'own A nostalgia'. A final explanation cannot be made at this point. Also, the nostalgia appears in its non-reflexive, "simple" form here.

Apart from these three participants, PMS55-65 states as well that he felt nostalgia "[e]n las series más costumbristas" [in the series that are more 'costumbrista'] (PMS55-65, Questionnaire_Connotation of nostalgia_55-65-year-old Spaniards, 19 [o.t.]). However, it can only be presumed that he is referring to *Mad Men*. Due to the fact that his elaborations in the course of the discussion only have an agreeing character, a further specification of the object of his nostalgia is not possible either.

Other interviewees exclude nostalgia in the context of *Mad Man*. PCFS55-65, for example, highlights that it is about "recordar" [remembering] – a kind of

---

296 Original quotation: "Es reflejar la situación. Pero no necesariamente nostalgia." (GS55-65_Period Pictures_Mad Men_Spanien, 160 [o.t.])

297 Original quotation: "[...] [M]e recuerdo una situación familiar muy parecida a la vida de adolescente i toda la familia estaba más unida que ahora. Creo que en aquella época era ignorante i feliz." (MFS55-65, Connotation of nostalgia_55-65-year-old Spaniards, 18)

synchronisation with her memories can be assumed here – but not nostalgia (see PCFS55-65, GS55-65_Period Pictures_Mad Men_Spanien, 161 [o.t.]). This similarly applies to AFG55-65 of the German group. "The feeling," she states, "was not all that deep" (GD55-65_NostalgieAllgemein_Deutschland, 17 [o.t.])[298].

8.3.1.3 Nostalgia across generations – the slide projector scene

In contrast to this clear distribution of different foci of attention in the first section of the discussion, in the second part, as has been mentioned previously, the discussion takes a different form.

8.3.1.3.1 Intertextual references – (roundabout) nostalgia

While the majority of props, décor, costumes and music basically inspire the memories of the 55 to 65-year-olds, the technical apparatus, i.e. the slide projector, appeals to the memory of a broader group of participants. It kind of mediates between the different age groups and territorial groups. Depending on the "retrospective classifications" of the memorised context, nostalgia becomes apparent here, too.

Among the 55 to 65-year-olds this applies to DMG55-65. While his focus of attention in the remaining discussion lies upon the constructedness of the text, which also leads to an emotional distance triggered by the slide projector scene, the recipient recalls situations from his private life. He adopts the term "Zeitmaschine" [time machine] that is use by the series' protagonist in order to describe the effect:

DMG55-65: "Basically, it's like that. Only in my mind, of course. For me it's like a time machine in my head. In my head I can switch back and forth. But I'm still here." (GD55-65_Period Pictures_Mad Men_Deutschland, 35 [o.t.])[299]

Later he elaborates on the association in more detail:

DMG55-65: "To watch slide shows. That is a very special experience. And I still think that today. But unfortunately they're not available anymore." (GD55-65_Period Pictures_ Mad Men_Deutschland, 59 [o.t.])[300]

---

298 Original quotation: "So tief war das Gefühl jetzt nicht." (AFG55-65, GD55-65_Nostalgie Allgemein_Deutschland, 17)

299 Original quotation: "[Es ist im Grunde so. Das ist natürlich nur im Kopf.] Das ist für mich 'ne Zeitmaschine im Kopf. Ich kann im Kopf hin- und herspringen. Bin ja immer noch hier." (DMG55-65, GD55-65_Period Pictures_ Mad Men_Deutschland, 35)

300 Original quotation: "Ja, aber des sofort, dieses Dias-gucken von früher. Das ist ja 'ne ganz spezielle Erfahrung, Dias zu gucken. Das find ich ja heute noch. Nur leider gibt es die nicht mehr." (DMG55-65, GD55-65_Period Pictures_ Mad Men_Deutschland, 59)

DMG55-65: "An incredibly beautiful experience. Although I can still remember it since I have such a big family, six brothers and sisters, and then during these family gatherings up to five, six, seven or eight years ago we would still look at slides from back then. Or from some journeys someone made. And that was actually always really nice." (GD55-65_Period Pictures_ Mad Men_Deutschland, 63 [o.t.])[301]

In both contributions a clear rhetoric of the 'gap' can be observed. While the first viewer focuses on the technical dispositive of the slide projector, which "unfortunately" does not exist anymore, the second one refers to slide shows in the family circle as they existed in the past but no longer exist in the present. In the questionnaire, the participant describes his reaction as nostalgia, stating that he felt it when "[m]emorizing family slide-shows during the film clips about the time machine" (DMG55-65, Questionnaire_Connotation of nostalgia_55-65-year-old Germans, 29 [o.t.]).[302] In the light of the fact that DMG55-65 has periodically explained that he did not 'enter' the diegetic world and also in the context of the slide projector scene highlights that he 'stayed outside' the story (GD55-65_PeriodPictures_Mad Men_Deutschland, 193), we may assume that it is rather the viewer's 'own artefact nostalgia' that is described here. The slide projector scene works as a "mnemonic prompt" for the recipient's positive own experiences that become the object of "simple" nostalgic longing.

The elaborations made by DMG55-65 are similarly echoed in other groups. Regarding other participants, the apparatus inspires memories of comparable situations as well. CFG25-35 says, for example:

CFG25-35: "Well, my father always used to set up slide shows in the evening." (GD25-35_PeriodPictures_Mad Men_Deutschland, 180 [o.t.])[303]

CFG25-35: "That was nice. Hmm, it is not so long ago when my father still watched slide shows from the '80s when, well, I don't know, my brother and I were infants. And I always

---

301 Original quotation: "Ne unheimlich schöne Erfahrung. Wobei ich kann mich auch erinnern, weil ich hab' ja so 'ne große Familie, also sechs Geschwister, und dann auf diesen Familientreffen wurde bis vor fünf, sechs, sieben acht Jahren so, da ham wir immer Dias von früher anguckt oder so. Oder von irgendwelchen Reisen (die einer gemacht hat), und das war eigentlich immer unheimlich schön." (DMG55-65, GD55-65_Period Pictures_ Mad Men_Deutschland, 63)

302 Original quotation: "Beim Filmausschnitt über die Zeitmaschine eigene Erinnerungen an Familiendiashows." (DMG55-65, Questionnaire_Connotation of nostalgia_55-65-year-old Germans, 29)

303 Original quotation: "Ja, also mein Vater hat ständig Dia-Abende gemacht." (CFG25-35, GD25-35_PeriodPictures_Mad Men_Deutschland, 180)

liked that. Also the medium, the projector." (GD25-35_Period Pictures_Mad Men_Deutschland, 202 [o.t.])[304]

Similar to DMG55-65, the interviewee describes a positive experience in the family context; however, in contrast to the first case, no rhetoric of nostalgia can be observed here. Unlike the case of DMG55-65, the experience is not clearly part of the past but, as CFG25-35 explicitly states, also part of her only recent reality. Nostalgia does not arise here.

In other cases it is a neutral or negative "retrospective classification" that obviously impedes nostalgia. FCFS55-65 (GS55-65_Period Pictures_Mad Men_ Spanien, 122) for example, also recalls her own experiences in the family circle; however, her comments are far less emotional than those made in the context of the other period props. A positive valorisation of the experience cannot be observed. It can only be assumed that the memory is given less relevance than the previously mentioned ones that inspired her nostalgia. Almost all the memories of DFG25-35 (GD25-35_Period Pictures_Mad Men_Deutschland, 181 ff.) and AMG25-35 (GD25-35_Period Pictures_Mad Men_Deutschland, 183 ff.) are negative. The slide projector scene prompts memories of school and university experiences that are clearly negatively classified. DFG25-35 also explicitly explains the lack of emotional involvement with the scene with these negative associations:

DFG25-35: "Well, normally I let myself be captivated very fast and also have to cry in talk shows, but in this one I didn't really because, like I said, slide projector and all that you [refers here to CFG25-35]... I did not have such an experience, means, I don't relate something positive or something nostalgic to it. I just had – it didn't touch me that much." (GD25-35_Period Pictures_Mad Men_Deutschland, 249 [o.t.])[305]

Nostalgia is not the case. The interviewee rather dislikes this part of the past. Also in other cases, neutral to negative associations impede a possible nostalgia felt in the

---

304 Original quotation: "War schön. Mhm, mein Vater hat da auch jetzt noch vor verhältnismäßig kurzer Zeit dann, äh, so Dia-Filme angeguckt aus den Achtzigern, als, weiß ich nicht, mein Bruder und ich irgendwie Kleinkinder warn. Und ich fand das immer schön. Also auch so dieses Medium, äh, Dia-Projektor." (CFG25-35, GD25-35_Period Pictures_Mad Men_Deutschland, 202)

305 Original quotation: "Also normalerweise lass ich mich total schnell einlullen und muss auch schon bei Talk Shows heulen oder so, aber da fand ich 's jetzt nit soo, weil, wie gesacht, Dia-Projektor oder so, also was du [refers here to CFG25-35] jetzt so 'ne Erfahrung hatte ich jetzt, also damit verbind ich jetzt nix so Positives oder so oder so was Nostalgisches. Also hab grad – fand des jetzt nit so berührend irgendwie." (DFG25-65, GD25-35_Period Pictures_Mad Men_Deutschland, 249).

context of the slide projector scene (see EMG25-35, GD25-35_Period Pictures_Mad Men_Deutschland, 255-257; FFG25-35, GD25-35_Period Pictures_Mad Men_ Deutschland, 207; JMS25-35, GS25-35_Period Pictures_Mad Men_Spanien, 257; GMG25-35, GD25-35_Period Pictures_Mad Men_Deutschland, 215).

Apart from that, a few members of the group of the 25 to 35-year-olds frame the programme with intertextual references to films.[306] Nostalgia is not found here either.

8.3.1.3.2 Empathetic understanding

In the television analysis it was presumed that empathy may also lead to nostalgia. The reception of the slide projector scene with its relative closure reflects this, even though unambiguous cases of nostalgia could not be identified here. Apart from those who, due to reflections on personal experiences with the slide projector, leave the fictional world and others whose focus of attention is on the intertextual references the series exposes[307], two basic types of relation to the Draper character can be identified: one that valorises Draper's comportment negatively and leads to a distanciation from the scene, and one where a positive valorisation results in a high degree of understanding for the character.

The negative valorisation of Draper's presentation by the interviewees is mainly owed to an appraisal as 'pure advertisement'. Here, participants highlight that he "intenta como vender un producto" [tries to sell a product] (CMS25-35, GS25-35_Period Pictures_Mad Men_Spanien, 224 [o.t.]), "ist berechnend" [is calculating] (DFG25-35, GD25-35_Period Pictures_Mad Men_Deutschland, 238 [o.t.]) or that it's just about "marketing, de un ejecutivo" [managers' marketing] (OFS25-35,

---

306 "I was thinking of one of these typical scenes of the business man who risks everything and who sells a product like that. A film like this one, right now I can't remember anyone, but, yes, I do remember scenes likes this." (JMS25-35, GS25-35_Period Pictures_Mad Men_Spanien, 210 [o.t.]) Original quotation: "Yo pensaba en la típica escena del típico hombre de negocios arriesgado que vende un producto así. Una película d'estas de, no tengo ninguna en mente ahora mismo, pero sí que tengo escenas como esas en varios sitioos ubicadas aquí." (JMS25-35, GS25-35_Period Pictures_Mad Men_Spanien, 210) "It also reminded me of this series, *Aquellos maravillosos años* [*The Wonder years*]." (VMS25-35, GS25-35_Period Pictures_Mad Men_Spanien, 238 [o.t.]) Original quotation: "(Pero) a mí también me ha recordado a la serie esa de (Aquellos maravil, aquellos maravillosos años)." (VMS25-35, GS25-35_Period Pictures_Mad Men_ Spanien, 238)

307 A third group of interviewees was rather confused by the excerpt which likewise undermined any emotional involvement (see FFG55-65, GD55-65_Nostalgie Allgemein_Deutschland, 61; 63; AFG55-65, GD55-65_Period Pictures_ Mad Men_ Deutschland, 67; 70; IMG55-65, GD55-65_Period Pictures_ Mad Men_Deutschland, 154; BFG55-65, GD55-65_Period Pictures_ Mad Men_Deutschland, 163).

GS25-35_Period Pictures_Mad Men_Spanien, 296 [o.t.]).[308] Especially members of the group of the 55 to 65-year-olds explicitly describe how they 'step out' of the fictional world due to this appraisal:

GFG55-65: "I stepped out the moment I understood that it is an advertising show. When he said – shortly before he used the term 'carousel' himself. I thought that basically everything is about that, everything he's saying." (GD55-65_Period Pictures_ Mad Men_Deutschland, 126 [o.t.])[309]

DMG55-65: "Yes, that was obvious from the very beginning. I didn't get into the story that much. Since I didn't believe him that this is his own wife or that these are his own children. He does that for advertising purposes." (GD55-65_Period Pictures_ Mad Men_Deutschland, 127; 193 [o.t.])[310]

CMG55-65: "I stayed out of it." (GD55-65_Period Pictures_ Mad Men_Deutschland, 195 [o.t.])[311]

Nostalgia is not the case here. Apparently the negative valorisation creates similar effects of emotional distance than the focus on the constructedness of the text – an interpretation that is also congruent with works on immersion or empathy. In the context of computer games, Mikos (2008, p. 184), for example, supposes that immersion depends upon both empathy and sympathy. As we already learned from the theoretical section, sympathy can again foster empathy (Brinckmann, 2005, p. 339; Eder, 2005, pp. 236 f.).

On the other side, "[i]mmersed viewers", according to Visch et al. (2010, p. 1443), feel "[...] closer to events as a witness in the fictional world and experience

---

308 Original quotation: "Yo creo que eso es marketing, de un ejecutivo." (OFS25-35, GS25-35_Period Pictures_Mad Men_Spanien, 296)

309 Original quotation: "Ich bin ausgestiegen in dem Moment, wo ich erkannt hab, das ist jetzt die, das ist jetzt 'ne Werbeveranstaltung. Also in dem er sagte, kurz bevor er den Begriff Karussell selber verwendet hatte, hab' ich gedacht, es ging eigentlich nur darum – das alles, was er jetzt erzählt." (GFG55-65, GD55-65_Period Pictures_ Mad Men_Deutschland, 126)

310 Original quotation: "Ja, das war von Anfang an schon klar. [Soweit bin ich in die] Geschichte gar nicht eingestiegen. Weil ich hab' dem ja gar nicht abgenommen, dass das seine eigene, seine eigene Frau oder Kinder sind. Das macht der aus Werbungsgründen." (DMG55-65, GD55-65_Period Pictures_ Mad Men_Deutschland, 127; 193)

311 Original quotation: "[Ich war auch mehr draußen]." (CMG55-65, GD55-65_Period Pictures_ Mad Men_Deutschland, 195)

stronger emotions towards these events than less immersed viewers". Correspond-ingly the contributions of those interviewees who do not make the negative valorisation and take a less distant position towards the text are characterised by a higher degree of emotionality. This is very obvious in the case of HFG55-65. In contrast to other interviewees who take a distant position due to their valorisation of the scene as 'pure advertisement', HFG55-65 describes the sentiments of the protagonist as follows:

HFG55-65: "I thought he was terribly sad. He really suffered for what he had lost. What he hasn't got anymore. What he started at some point and what he lost on the way. For whatever reason." (GD55-65_PeriodPictures_Mad Men_Deutschland, 186 [o.t.])[312]

Obviously the participant is deeper involved in the scene and the perspective of the protagonist. When later questioned on whether the scene evoked similar sentiments in her, she distinctly affirms that (GD55-65_Period Pictures_ Mad Men_Deutschland, 187-188). Notwithstanding that, it is probably not about nostalgia. What the interviewee describes here and what she obviously feels herself is more likely to be one of those spin-offs of nostalgia in whose context Frijda (1986, p. 76) argues that "if impotence with respect to desire is added, it turns into belated painful suffering". We can only assume that HFG55-65 synchronises her own sentiments with the scene.

Furthermore, in other cases the interviewees are clearly immersed in the fictional world (see e.g. EMG, GD25-35_Period Pictures_Mad Men_Deutschland, 251) and also report an empathetic understanding of the protagonist (see EMG25-35, GD25-35_Period Pictures_Mad Men_Deutschland, 276; FFG25-35, GD25-35_Period Pictures_Mad Men_Deutschland, 223). Yet the rhetoric of nostalgia or any concrete mentioning of nostalgia is not observed here either.

This applies to ZFS25-35 of the Spanish group of the 25 to 35-year-olds only to a certain degree. The participant makes a clearer "referential framing". The emotions she describes are more likely to be nostalgia. In this case it is not the slide projector but the exposed style of the slides that remind the participant of her childhood:

---

312 Original quotation: "Ich finde, er war furchtbar traurig. Er hat echt gelitten, um das, was er verloren hat. Das, was er nicht mehr hat. Was er eben mal begonnen hat, und was er verloren hat unterwegs. Wie auch immer, aus welchen Gründen." (HFG55-65, GD55-65_PeriodPictures_Mad Men_Deutschland, 186)

ZFS25-35: "The type of photos reminded me of my childh– Maybe of my brother, pictures of our childhood, these types of photos? Yes, they were, they weren't distanced, they weren't American, I'd say." (GS25-35_Period Pictures_Mad Men_Spanien, 263 [o.t.])[313]

ZFS25-35 affirms explicitly that she somehow shares similar emotions to nostalgia with the protagonist (GS25-35_Period Pictures_Mad Men_Spanien, 302). Despite her 'common sense' understanding of empathy she stresses that:

ZFS25-35: "No. I didn't feel empathy for him, rather for the type of photos." (GS25-35_Period Pictures_Mad Men_Spanien, 309 [o.t.])[314]

Here, we can probably talk of the viewer's 'own empathetic F nostalgia'. In contrast to those interviewees who, due to their own associations with the slide projector, left the diegesis, the interviewee seems to synchronise her own emotions with those of the protagonist. Nostalgia probably emerges from a splitting-off of her own emotions. In the questionnaire, ZFS25-35 indeed describes a feeling of nostalgia that she had in the course of the group discussion, referring to another experience though. Compared to the first one, the latter experience is obviously given a higher relevance.

8.3.1.4 Conclusion on the reception of *Mad Men*

In the television analysis it has been assumed that *Mad Men* may provoke nostalgia on various levels. Since the series is part of the 'nostalgia genre' of the period dramas, following Cardwell (2002), it has been assumed that nostalgia may be the gratification audiences expect when they choose to watch the series, respectively the mood in which they choose it. Later, on the single levels of the text, potential triggers of nostalgia have been identified. On the F level *Mad Men* does not favour nostalgia towards the 1960s it exposes. Rather the contrary is the case. Yet a high degree of disclosed intertextual references could be observed here already, which, on the one hand, import a further critical layer into the text and, on the other hand, depending on respective "retrospective classifications", may be potential triggers of 'A nostalgia' or the viewers' 'own A nostalgia'. This similarly applies to nearly all other levels of the text. The constructedness of the exposed past is always present. Additionally, the series employs many 1960s consumer products and typical music

---

313 Original quotation: "El tipo de fotos si que a mí me recordaba la infanc.. a lo mejor fotos de mis herman... de mi hermano, fotos de infancia, ese tipo de fotos si, por ejemplo ¿no?... Sí que eraaan... no eran distantes, no eran americanas, diría." (ZFS25-35, GS25-35_Period Pictures_Mad Men_Spanien, 263)

314 Original quotation: "Noo. Yo no, por ejemplo, yo no he sentido empatía con el tipoo, sino poor, por el tipo de fotos ¿no?" (ZFS25-35, GS25-35_Period Pictures_Mad Men_Spanien, 309)

that may work as a "mnemonic prompt" for those audiences who have their own or "prosthetic" memories of it. Empathy as well as 'empathetic nostalgia' is favoured by the text.

Some of these potential triggers on the level of the text have indeed been decoded as such by the audiences. The reception analysis can name various examples of nostalgia. Further factors for the absence of nostalgic longing could be deduced. Depending on the respective focus of the interviewee's contributions, the following patterns of reception have been identified. On a first level the (1) *Reception of references to the "natural real"* can be outlined. Further patterns focus on other single levels of the text. Here, mainly the referential character of the series is of relevance. It is subsumed under the sub-patterns *Intertextual references – (roundabout) nostalgia* and *References to the 1960s*. Since in contrast to others, the discussion of *Mad Men* is somehow split into two parts whereby the latter, the slide projector scene, more clearly mediates between the different age groups, the presentation of results was also done in two sections. Next to a pattern that again reflects the focus on the *Intertextual references*, a second pattern encompasses those elaborations that are marked by a certain degree of empathy. The question whether nostalgia is the gratification viewers expect when they decide to watch *Mad Men* is not further supported by the group discussion. In general, it can be stated that there is not one way of reception that is dominant. Even though clear intra- and inter-group congruencies can be described, the foci of attention are diverse; different 'hierarchies of relevance' can be identified that again influence the observed nostalgias.

As assumed in the television analysis, the critical perspective of *Mad Men* impedes a nostalgic lecture of the temporal context but rather inspires the critical perspective. The pattern *Reception of references to the "natural real"* is mainly found among those groups where at least one of the recipients could retell complete plot lines of the series. The existence of a "prosthetic memory" cannot be observed here. Nostalgia can be excluded.

In the television analysis it has been shown that each level of *Mad Men* contains a high degree of intertextuality. As already in the context of the reruns and subsumed under the pattern *Intertextual references – (roundabout) nostalgia*, these references are predominantly in the focus of attention of those who are not able to generate "proximity" to their own lifeworlds on other levels of the text.[315] It seems that mostly the 25 to 35-year-old Spaniards, those don't have their own memories of the 1960s, are only able to make sense of the series if they integrate the text into a net of

---

315 In general, the intertextual references that are named by the recipients differ from those that have been identified in the television analysis. This is not surprising, nor does it undermine the analysis. Already in Chapter 4.4.1 with reference to Mikos (2008, pp. 272 ff.) it has been indicated that such an analysis may never be done conclusively since the intertextuality of a text is defined by all texts in which viewers integrate a current text.

intertextual references. As assumed, the case of ZFS25-35 shows that intertextual references may indeed trigger 'artefact nostalgia' or the viewers' 'own artefact nostalgia', always depending on a respective positive "retrospective classification" of the memory point and its declaration as lost from today's perspective. Also among a group of 55-65-Germans, the focus of attention lies upon the referential character of *Mad Men* to other cultural products. Here, however, it is rather about the artificiality the text itself exposes. The "critical framing" impedes nostalgia.

While these recipients deny that the series has any reality effect, the contrary is the case among those participants where the referential character to the 1960s is central to the reception. The pattern *References to the 1960s* appears exclusively among the 55 to 65-year-olds and here mostly among the Spanish recipients. A respective nostalgia based upon "prosthetic memories" could thus not be observed. First of all, a gross contrast to the 25 to 35-year-old Spaniards can be highlighted here. While the younger age-group completely denies any relation of the series to 1960s' Spain, the 55 to 65-year-olds emphasise the reality effect of the series against the specific Spanish background. The realism they describe stands in contrast to the 'American-ness' that is highlighted by the younger Spanish participants. The correspondence with their own memories of the era seemingly allows for a 'synchronisation' of the series with their own experiences, which in one distinct case also leads to a viewer's 'own F nostalgia'. In another example, the case of MFS55-65, the 1960s artefacts work as a "mnemonic prompt" and triggers the viewer's 'own A nostalgia' towards a positively classified past that is declared as being lost from today's perspective.

It cannot be conclusively clarified which knowledge the 25 to 35-year-olds base their elaborations of 1960s' Spain on – be it a knowledge taught to them, a knowledge transmitted by the media or a knowledge acquired in the family circle. Clearly, however, while in the case of the 25 to 35-year-old Spaniards the intertextual references dominate the reception, in the case of the 55 to 65-year-olds few parallels are enough in order to generate the synchronisation with their own memories from that era. The still huge distance between Spain and the other European countries, which Boyd (1999, p. 100) described with a view on the 1960s, fades into the background here.

Apart from that, the different elaborations seem to reflect different concepts of realism. While those among the 25 to 35-year-old Spaniards, but also 55 to 65-year-old Germans with their focus on the constructedness of the text, focus on what Ang (1985, p. 36) calls "'empiricist realism'", namely "[t]he definition of realism, in which a comparison of the realities 'in' and 'outside' a text is central", for the second group, the group of the 55 to 65-year-old Spaniards, it is rather realistic since they highlight the emotional correspondence of the exposed past and the past they remember. In Ang's (1985, p. 45) words, we can speak of an "'emotional realism'".

In any case the observations are concordant with Assmann (2006). According to the author (2006, p. 27 [o.t.]), each generation has its "own approach to history", which may be independent of the "perspective" of "precedent generations".

Again it is shown that nostalgia works selectively, for example, in the case of the 55 to 65-year-old FCS55-65. While she, inspired by the narrative of the series, reflects her position as a working woman in Franco's Spain of the 1960s critically, the synchronisation with her own experiences in the course of the immersion into the diegetic world obviously guides her to positive memories that she classifies as being worth longing for. This corresponds with what Tannock states regarding the nostalgic emotion, namely that "[t]he 'positively evaluated' past [...] need not be thought of as a time of general happiness, peacefulness, stability, or freedom" (Tannock, 1995, p. 454). The fact that a reflexive layer of her nostalgia cannot be observed here conflicts with our assumption that the reflexive stance of the series will influence the colouring of possible nostalgia developed in its context.

In contrast to this clearer distribution of different foci of attention in the first section of the *Mad Men* discussion, the second section, which was dedicated to the reception of the slide projector scene, shows rather overarching patterns with regards to the age groups and territorial groups. On the one hand, reflected in the pattern *Intertextual references – (roundabout) nostalgia*, here it is the apparatus of the slide projector, respectively the whole 'dispositif', that works as a "mnemonic prompt" for the groups. On the other hand, subsumed under the pattern *Empathetic understanding*, empathy as a possible trigger for nostalgia mediates between them. In both patterns cases of nostalgia appear again. Thus in the first case the slide projector works as a "mnemonic prompt" and leads to a viewer's 'own artefact nostalgia'. It also becomes apparent here that the positive "retrospective classification" of the object of memory and its declaration as being irretrievable lost from today's perspective is essential for the development of nostalgic longing. In a second case, it is presumably the splitting-off of a viewer's own experiences in the context of an empathetic understanding that leads to the recipient's 'own empathetic F nostalgia'.

In summary, we may state that diverse aspects of the series that were presumed as potential triggers of nostalgia also led to one or more cases of nostalgia. Hereby, it is not the case that one participant or group of participants decode all potential triggers of nostalgia, but a kind of 'hierarchy of memories' can be observed here as well. The participants seem to search for relevance, or as Tan suggests in the context of aesthetic emotions in general, the "emotional system is geared toward establishing the relevance of certain situations for the concerns of the individual" (Tan, 1996, p. 44). Similar to the nostalgia discourse, the reception is dominated by different foci on different aspects of the text. Correspondingly, the sensation of nostalgia or not differs throughout the reception and among the groups. While the 55 to 65-year-old

Spaniards, for example, generate "proximity" via the text as such, the 25 to 35-year-olds, who have no memories of the 1960s, take the 'detour' via the intertextual references.

As it seems, the foci of attention may also change in the course of the reception. In one moment a "critical framing" may lead to emotional distance and impede 'F nostalgia'; in another moment, a viewer's 'own A nostalgia' can be observed when an emotional relevant object appears. Apart from that, participants seem to create hierarchies of relevance between different nostalgias. Only the one that is given most relevance manifests itself in the questionnaire.

Even though in general the different patterns are, so to say, 'closer' to the text here than in the case of the reruns, at least nostalgia in the context of the period drama does not depend on a previous reception; nostalgia is in no case the mere narration of a better past here either, such as nostalgia towards a better past product or nostalgia 'shared' with a protagonist. The observed nostalgia is rather always imbued with personal experiences of the recipients and finds its object on this level.

As shown, the reflexive character of *Mad Men* indeed influenced a similar reflexive perspective on the 1960s from the participants. The observed nostalgias, however, appeared in its "simple" form, reflecting the "unexamined belief that THINGS WERE BETTER [...] *THEN* THAN *NOW*", as Davis (1979, p. 18 [emphasis in the original]) puts it in the context of nostalgia in general. Nostalgia, which is based upon "prosthetic memories", could not be identified.

8.3.2 Reception of the period drama *Borgia*

The period drama *Borgia*, set in the time of the Renaissance, is most clearly outside the interviewees' life-span and also outside their family memory. It has mainly been used as a 'counter-check' to discover if nostalgia on a purely media-transmitted, "prosthetic" memory is possible. As in the case of *Mad Men*, on a first and more general level a pattern of reception that concentrates on the (1) *References to the "natural real"* could be identified. A second main pattern specified as (2) *Intertextual references – (roundabout) nostalgia* rather focuses on potential triggers of nostalgia on other levels of the text. A pattern of reception that reflects the expectation of nostalgia on the part of the audiences could not be observed. Only AFG55-65, GFG55-65, CFG25-35, and EMG25-35 of the German groups have seen whole episodes or parts of the series. None of them came to discuss expected gratifications in the course of this earlier reception. The same applies to the excerpt that has been shown in the course of the group discussions.

8.3.2.1 References to the "natural real"

Only the two interviewees AFG55-65 and EMG25-35 watched a whole episode of the series. To that effect, only few re-narrations can be highlighted. Here however, the perspective as it is induced by the period drama already becomes apparent. EMG25-35 explains:

EMG25-35: "Well, it starts as follows. The guy who is the Pope isn't the Pope from the very beginning. And he's just trying to take over somehow, that's just, well, you see the corruption in Rome." (GD25-35_Period Pictures_Borgia_Deutschland, 28 [o.t.])[316]

The short statement with its emphasis on the "corruption" in ancient Rome already reflects a rather 'pessimistic' view on the era. A similar perspective on the Renaissance becomes apparent among those interviewees who based their elaborations only on the excerpt shown in the discussion. They discuss the "harte Zeit" [hard times] (FFG55-65, GD55-65_Period Pictures_Borgia_Deutschland, 61 [o.t.]) when the church "lo manejaban todo" [controlled everything] (CMS25-35, GS25-35_Period Pictures_Borgia_Spanien, 153 [o.t.]), a time which was "buena para los de arriba" [good for the upper class] (VMS55-65, GS25-35_Period Pictures_Borgia_Spanien, 143 [o.t.]) but "para los de abajo, no" [not for the lower class] (ZFS25-35, GS25-35_Period Pictures_Borgia_Spanien, 145 [o.t.]). Others criticise the dramatisation, which makes the series depart from the 'real' historical fact:

DMG55-65: "There's this pattern, it doesn't actually deal much with the history but instead with topics such as forbidden love, for example. Such things are briefly brought up. Because that's always exciting. Whether that's actually historical or not, well, that's not really interesting." (GD55-65_Period Pictures_Borgia_Deutschland, 37; 39 [o.t.])317

HFG55-65: "Borgias. Well, they were all just playing around and whatever, and I think to myself that whoever is interested in something like that can watch it. But actually it's about

---

316 Original quotation: "Also eigentlich fängt das Ganze so an, der Typ, der dann Papst ist, der ist am Anfang noch gar nicht Papst. Und der versucht halt irgendwie, an die Macht zu kommen, das ist halt, man sieht halt so dieses korrupte Rom, da." (EMG25-35, GD25-35_Period Pictures_Borgia_Deutschland, 28)

317 Original quotation: "...ist so dieses Muster, also das hat mit der Historie eigentlich gar nichts zu tun, sondern nur damit, mit so Themen, also verbotene Liebe zum Beispiel. Also solche Sachen werden damit kurz [...] hochgeholt. Weil das ja immer spannend ist. Ob das nun historisch, also das ist ja eigentlich uninteressant." (DMG55-65, GD55-65_Period Pictures_Borgia_Deutschland, 37; 39)

something else. Perhaps there is something else you want to know and not just this silly stuff." (GD55-65_Period Pictures_Borgia_Deutschland, 75 [o.t.])[318]

EMG25-35: "What I found was also an apparent sexual component. Actually around about every ten minutes you see how they suddenly go to the bedroom together. Well, I don't think that the perception of women was like that in the Middle Ages. Well, every female is exceptionally attractive there." (GD25-35_Period Pictures_Borgia_ Deutschland, 81-82 [o.t.])[319]

In any case, this past is not installed as a potential object of nostalgia. A positive "prosthetic memory" of the era on the basis of which nostalgia would be imaginable can be excluded. Participants associate the series with historical persons or events, such as Christopher Columbus (RMS25-35, GS25-35_Period Pictures_Borgia _Spanien, 123; CFG25-35, GD25-35_Period Pictures_Borgia_Deutschland, 42) or the Discovery of America in general (DFG25-35, GD25-35_Period Pictures_ Borgia_Deutschland, 64) up to the Catholic monarchs of Spain (JMS25-35, GS25-35_Period Pictures_Borgia_Spanien, 20) or refer to respective reports in the media (GFG55-65, GD55-65_Period Pictures_Borgia_Deutschland, 22). Hereby, it is always clear that the knowledge they base these elaborations on is mediated through history books or other media.

Indeed, in one case a "referential framing" can be observed. JMS25-35 states here that *Borgia* reminded him of his own history lessons at school (see JMS25-35, GS25-35_Period Pictures_Borgia_Spanien, 30). In the final discussion the participant even explicitly classifies the experience as nostalgia. At other points, the experience is, however, ironically appraised as "una época mala de mi vida" [a bad time of my life] (JMS25-35, GS25-35_Period Pictures_Borgia_Spanien, 27 [o.t.]). In the questionnaire the association is not mentioned by the participant. Against the backdrop of these ambiguous elaborations the case cannot be clarified conclusively. Nostalgia is unlikely here.

---

318 Original quotation: "[Borgias. So alle ham durcheinander] gevögelt und was weiß ich und wo ich so denke, also wen so was interessiert, der möchte sich so was bestimmt gerne angucken. Aber es geht ja um was anderes. Vielleicht ist es doch was anderes, was man gerne wissen würde und nicht nur so platte Sachen." (HFG55-65, GD55-65_Period Pictures_Borgia_Deutschland, 75)

319 Original quotation: "Was ich an der Serie. Ich fand' da gibt's auch 'ne augenscheinliche sexuelle Komponente. Man sieht eigentlich alle zehn Minuten, wie die dann plötzlich im Bett miteinander landen. Da also. Ich kann mir nicht vorstellen, dass im Mittelalter dieses Frauenbild war. Also die Frauen sind da alle ausnehmend attraktiv." (EMG25-35, GD25-35_Period Pictures_Borgia_Deutschland, 81-82)

8.3.2.2 Nostalgia on other levels of the text?

It has been assumed in the television analysis that the 'gap' between then and now *Borgia* exposes on the level of props, décor and costumes has the 'connotation of pastness' and may first of all call attention to the artefact. This was verified by the group discussion. Independent of age group, gender or country, participants all mainly focused on costumes, scenery, paintings or lighting. Some of them only mention this. In other cases the objects of attention are integrated into a broader frame of references, as it will be shown in the following sections.

8.3.2.2.1 (Intertextual) references – (roundabout) nostalgia?

Independent of age group or territorial group, *Borgia* is framed by other cultural products. Here, the participants name mostly period dramas located in similar or related eras. Interviewees refer to *Los Tudors* (BBCtwo et al., 2007) (AMS55-65, GS55-65_Period Pictures_Borgia_Spanien, 9; AFS 25-35; AFS25-35, GS25-35_Period Pictures_Borgia_Spanien, 173) or are reminded of other BBC period drama productions (AMS55-65, GS55-65_Period Pictures_Borgia_Spanien, 7). Further period films, such as *Braveheart* (Gibson, 1995), set in the thirteenth century (see VMS25-35, GS25-35_Period Pictures_Borgia_Spanien, 68), or the German period telenovela *Sophie - Braut wider Willen* (Das Erste, 2005), set in the nineteenth century, are named. Intertextual references to Renaissance paintings are highlighted as well. DFG25-35- states:

DFG25-35: "I was able to locate it quite well somehow. Well, that you thought, you already know it from like, Renaissance paintings with this gaudy velvet or something like that." (GD25-35_Period Pictures_Borgia_Deutschland, 64 [o.t.])[320]

Neither the mentioning of emotions nor a "referential framing" can be observed. The references, as DFG25-35 explicitly states, rather serve to locate *Borgia* historically and have a rather analytical character. No cases of nostalgia can be found.

8.3.2.2.2 Reference to the Renaissance

Regarding props and décor, some interviewees are of the opinion that the series truly reflects history:

---

320 Original quotation: "Also ich konnt 's jetzt irgendwie ganz gut verorten oder so. Also dass man so dachte, das kennt man von so, äh, na ja, fast Renaissance-Gemälden, also mit diesen, äh, prunkhaften Samt, eh, Sachen oder so." (DFG25-35, GD25-35_Period Pictures_Borgia_Deutschland, 64)

JMS25-35: "Yes, it seems to be true for the time. Sure!" (GS25-35_Period Pictures_Borgia_ Spanien, 109 [o.t.])[321]

(?)MS25-35: "Yes, I think the ambience has been captured very well. The costumes and all that." (GS25-35_Period Pictures_Borgia_Spanien, 126 [o.t.])[322]

Other participants focus on the question if the casting correctly reflects their image of the era (see FFG25-35, GD25-35_Period Pictures_Borgia_Deutschland, 94; EMG25-35, GD25-35_Period Pictures_Borgia_Deutschland, 86). In the television analysis of *Borgia*, it has already been shown that the period drama does not expose its props as desirable, which makes nostalgia on this level rather improbable. It has been assumed that they could work as "mnemonic prompt[s]" only on the basis of a "prosthetic memory". As the group discussion shows, neither the first nor the latter is the case. A positive classification of the era cannot be observed. The relation to a personal experience is not generated. No type of nostalgia, neither 'A nostalgia' nor the viewers' 'own A nostalgia', could be identified.

8.3.2.3 Conclusion on the reception of *Borgia*

The period drama *Borgia*, set in the time of the Renaissance, is most clearly set outside the interviewee's life-span. It has, above all, been used as 'counter-check' to see if nostalgia on a purely media-transmitted, "prosthetic memory" is possible. In general, the television analysis assumes only few levels of *Borgia* as potential triggers of nostalgia. First of all, with reference to Cardwell (2002), as an example of the nostalgia 'genre' of the period drama, *Borgia* was assumed to provoke expectations of nostalgia among the audiences. Later, single levels of the text have been investigated in the television analysis. Nostalgia is not inherent to the structure of the series, the era is also not represented as a golden vanishing point; however, the representation of the era has the "connotation of order" and stability that indeed could make it the subject of nostalgic longing. The viewers' 'own nostalgia' located on this level would only be possible on the basis of a respective "prosthetic memory". On the level of aesthetic and design, *Borgia* exposes intertextual references to Renaissance paintings, which, depending on respective "retrospective classifications", could lead to 'A nostalgia' or the viewers' 'own nostalgia' in case that respective "prosthetic memories" exist. This similarly applies to the music, which clearly has the 'connotation of pastness'. However, only if that respective "prosthetic memories" existed, it can be supposed to work as a "mnemonic prompt".

---

321 Original quotation: "Sí, que parezca real para ser de la época que es. ¡Claro!" (JMS25-35, GS25-35_Period Pictures_Borgia_Spanien, 109)

322 Original quotation: "Sí, la ambientación yo creo que está muy bien lograda. El vestuario y todo esooo." ((?)MS25-35, GS25-35_Period Pictures_Borgia_Spanien, 126)

Lastly, on the level of the characters, *Borgia* also explores a "connotation of order" regarding its gender relations which, depending on the subject position, makes the past somehow desirable. Here, intertextual references to Renaissance paintings may also lead to 'artefact nostalgia' or the viewers' 'own artefact nostalgia' in case that a respective positive "retrospective classification" of a "prosthetic memory" exists.

Depending on the focus of the interviewee's statements, the following patterns have been identified: (1) *Reception of references to the "natural real"*, (2) *Intertextual references – (roundabout) nostalgia?* and (3) *Reference to the Renaissance* have been outlined. None of the examples led to nostalgia on the side of the interviewees nor was there any evidence that the audiences expected nostalgia when they chose to watch the series. As assumed in the television analysis, the interviewees' statements reflect a critical, pessimistic look at the era, which already impedes nostalgia. The 'connotation of stability' that has been assumed to be a potential trigger for nostalgia on the F level is not mentioned, respectively perceived as such. The question whether the series reflects historical facts or not divides the participants. However, all cases clearly show that the knowledge they base their statements on is transmitted by the media. The existence of a "prosthetic memory" of the era could not be observed.

Later, it has been shown that the 'connotation of pastness' *Borgia* exposes on the levels of props, décor and costumes indeed draws the participants' attention though nostalgia is not the case here either. On the one hand, the series is framed by film and television series. These references are predominantly positively evaluated but do not lead to nostalgia either. On the other hand, the interviewees think that the décor props and costumes indeed stand for the Renaissance era, but that does not lead to nostalgia. The existence of a "prosthetic memory" on whose basis the objects could have worked as "mnemonic prompt[s]" could not be observed.

In principle, the section supports that nostalgia without any "referential framing" can be excluded. In the end phase of the discussion, one participant also discusses this aspect when he justifies the fact that he did not feel nostalgic in the context of *Borgia* as follows:

AMG25-35: "Well. I didn't live back then. I was never involved with the Pope ..." (GD25-35_Nostalgia_Allgemein_Deutschland, 116 [o.t.])[323]

---

323 Original quotation: "Na ja. Ich hab' da ja nicht gelebt. Ich hab auch mit dem Papst nichts gehabt, also das ist alles so... ." (AMG25-35, GD25-35_Nostalgia_Allgemein_Deutschland, 116)

8.3.3 Conclusion on period dramas as potential triggers of nostalgia

Period dramas are named most often when it comes to nostalgia in the academic discourse. From this, and with reference to Cardwell (2002), it has been assumed that the period drama as a nostalgia 'genre' creates the expectation of nostalgia or is chosen by the audiences in the course of a 'nostalgia mood management'. Later, on the background of the theoretical part, the single levels of the period dramas were expected to provoke nostalgia.

The subject has been investigated in a television analysis. Two examples have been chosen, one of which, the period drama *Borgia* (F/D/A/CZ, 2011) (*Borgia* (ZDF, 2011); *Borgia – Una familia consagrada al vicio* (Cosmopolitan TV, 2011)), is most clearly outside the interviewees' life-span. The second, the period drama *Mad Men* (AMC, 2007) (ZDFneo, 2010; Cuatro, 2009), is set in the 1960s and thus outside the life-span of the 25 to 35-year-olds and inside the so-called "reminiscence bump" or "formative years" of the 55 to 65-year-olds. Both series were broadcasted on Spanish and German television between 2009 and 2011. Potential triggers of nostalgia were analysed.

The reception study served to see if these potential triggers of nostalgia are indeed perceived as such by the audiences. Further characteristics of nostalgia in the context of period dramas should be explained. The assumption that the period dramas create the expectation of nostalgia was not supported by the reception study. Here a further, deeper interrogation would have been necessary, which could not be done in the course of the focus group discussion. Apart from that, the patterns of reception that were identified are in many parts concordant regarding the two examples. On a first level, a focus on the *Reception of the references to the "natural real"* has been described. Further patterns focus on other single levels of the text. Here above all, the referential character of the series was relevant. It is subsumed under the sub-patterns *Intertextual references – (roundabout) nostalgia* and *References to the 1960s* respectively, in the case of *Borgia*, *Reference to Renaissance*. A kind of bisection of the discussion could be observed regarding the reception of the slide projector scene of the *Mad Men* stimulus, which is why the results have been presented separately. Here an additional pattern that reflects the *Empathetic understanding* on the part of the recipients was identified in the analysis. As expected in the context of *Mad Men*, various cases of nostalgia could be detected. In the context of *Borgia* no case of nostalgia has been identified (see Table 4).

Table 4: Cases of nostalgia in the course of the period drama reception.

	Cases of nostalgia in the context of the period dramas
Mad Men	• Viewers' 'own A nostalgia' on the level of the intertextual references (ZFS25-35) • Viewers' 'own F nostalgia' coming from an immersion into the fictional world (FCFS55-65, PMS55-65 (?)) • Viewers' 'own F nostalgia' on the level of the music (?) (MFS55-65) • Viewers' 'own A nostalgia' on the level of the props (DMG55-65) • Viewers' 'own A nostalgia' on the level of the props (DMG55-65) • Viewers' 'own empathetic F nostalgia' (?) (ZFG25-35)
Borgia	−

In general, it can be stated that while, in the case of *Mad Men*, different foci of attention can be observed that also influence the fact that nostalgia is provoked on different levels of the text, in regards to *Borgia*, patterns arise in all groups. That is maybe least evident regarding the pattern *Reception of the references to the "natural real"*. Even though clear "referential framings" in the case of *Mad Men* can already be observed here, while regarding *Borgia*, there is always a clear gap to the lifeworld of the recipients', both cases show a rather critical perspective on the respective era that impedes nostalgia.

The difference becomes more evident regarding other patterns of reception. As assumed in the television analysis, in both series costumes, décor, and props draw the attention of the audiences due to their sole contrast to the contemporary artefacts. It is not before a second step, namely in the sub-patterns *Intertextual references – (roundabout) nostalgia (?)* and *References to the 1960s* respectively *Reference to Renaissance*, that cases of nostalgia could be observed. Here, indeed in both examples, the referential character of the period drama to its respective era, be it 'the Renaissance', be it 'the 1960s', is perceived as such by the audiences. Also both series are framed by a net of intertextual references, mostly other period dramas set in the same era as the period example. However, while in the case of *Borgia* both the 25 to 35-year-olds and the 55 to 65-year-olds approach the series equally with references to other cultural products or to their historical knowledge of the era in order to make sense of the text that is distant from their own lifeworlds, in the case of *Mad Men* clear differences between the age groups can be observed. Depending on the age group, different 'hierarchies' of relevance could be identified. The fact that *Mad Men* is approached via a net of intertextual references is mainly seen among the 25 to 35-year-old Spaniards who have no memories of their own of the 1960s. Here one case of (roundabout) nostalgia appears. In contrast to the *Borgia* context where the references have a rather factual character in order to intellectually grasp the series, the references mentioned here are remembered with a higher degree of emotional involvement and are subject to a positive "retrospective classification". Also, the nostalgia does not concern the reference as such but the retrospective positively classified context of its reception.

This similarly applies to the references to 'the 1960s' *Mad Men* exposes on the level of props and others. They are only relevant among the 55 to 65-year-olds. An exception, it has been shown in the analysis, is the slide projector scene. The apparatus somehow mediates between the memories of different "we-groups". In both cases nostalgia could be observed. Later, a case of a viewer's 'own empathetic F nostalgia' provoked by *Mad Men* could be found. In all cases it is a "referential framing" on the basis of which nostalgia develops and which was not possible for the audiences in the context of *Borgia*.

In summary it may be stated that period dramas work as triggers for nostalgia. Contrary to assumptions made in the television analysis, the provoked nostalgias are not directed toward the "connotation of order" in the representation of a past era or towards the period prop that is exposed as desirable. Observed nostalgias are always related to the participants' own experiences. 'Empathetic nostalgia' could be highlighted. Here it is also based on a 'synchronisation' with a viewer's own lifeworld. Therefore we may say that a "referential framing" turned out to be an inevitable basis for the development of nostalgia, just as the positive "retrospective classification" of the object. Apart from that, participants seem to deliberate about the importance of an object. Only the most relevant one becomes part of the nostalgia that is manifested in the questionnaire.

Mainly in the context of *Mad Men* it could be shown that patterns of reception clearly differ among the age groups. Only for the 55 to 65-year-olds from both territorial groups the reference to 'the 1960s' turned out to be a potential trigger for nostalgia. Due to the few cases of nostalgia, you can hardly talk about 'shared' nostalgias. At the same time *Borgia* is somehow too 'distant' from the participants' own liveworld to provoke nostalgia. However, it should not be assumed that this is due to the fact that the series is set in the Renaissance, a time span which is most clearly outside the participants's personal or family memories. Via intertextual references that are again part of a recipient's personal experience, "proximity" might possibly be generated, which was, however, not the case regarding *Borgia*. At this point there is further need of research.

9. Discussion of the results of the reception study

The preceding analysis focused on the reception of six examples from different nostalgia 'genres', more precisely on the reception of the reruns *Knight Rider* (NBC 1982) and *The Avengers* (ITV, 1961) and their respective remakes, and the reception of the period dramas *Mad Men* (AMC, 2007) and *Borgia* (Sky Italia, 2011). In a first step, all six examples were subjected to an in-depth television analysis, where it was identified in which way the examples "prefigure" possible nostalgic readings. The reception analysis scrutinised in which way the presumed offers of nostalgia on the level of the text are decoded as such by 25 to 35-year-olds and 55 to 65-year-olds from Germany and Spain. A further characterisation of the phenomenon of nostalgia and its reception was possible.

The conclusive chapters about the reception of the single nostalgia 'genres' gave a detailed overview of the interrelations between potential triggers of nostalgia on the level of the text and cases of nostalgia as they could be observed in the focus group discussions. This discussion of results shall identify general tendencies. It shall reflect the results in the light of the working hypotheses and focus on remaining open questions. Preceding this, it can be stated that the broad conception of the study makes detailed observations possible. Findings partly arise precisely from the comparison of the different nostalgia 'genres' and their nostalgic or explicitly non-nostalgic reception. At the same time limitations arise. They shall be reflected upon in the last paragraph of this section, which also highlights the further need for research. Due to the small sample, the results cannot be generalised regarding the reception of nostalgia as a whole. However, further hypothesis on the functioning of nostalgia can be drawn and an in-depth articulation and analysis of the reception of nostalgia in particular examples can be made.

9.1 THE CASES OF NOSTALGIA

With a view to the conclusions of the sub-chapters, we may state that diverse cases of nostalgia could be identified in the course of the reception study. This chapter will take a concrete look at these cases and first of all examine their commonalities, which let us draw further conclusions about the characteristics of nostalgia in the course of the television reception. In the beginning, inter- and intra-group differences will be set aside. They shall be commented on at a later point in this discussion of the results.

9.1.1 General characteristics of the objects of nostalgia

In general, around 25 cases of nostalgia could be observed in the course of the reception study. As presumed, these nostalgias are provoked on different levels of the texts, but, as Carroll (1999, p. 27) states in the context of aesthetic emotions in general, "in order to be an appropriate object of the emotion in question, the relevant object must meet certain necessary conditions". On the basis of these cases, we may state that the respective object of nostalgia was appraised according to the following essential components:

Table 5: Components of nostalgia

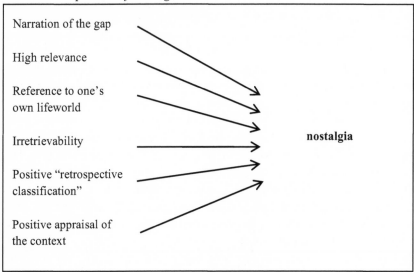

- It is the representative of a better, positive past inside the 'narration of the gap'.
- It is of high relevance to the audiences.
- It contains a reference to their lifeworlds.

- It is considered as being irretrievable.
- It is retrospectively positively classified.
- It arises in a context that is also positively appraised.

Most of these components were mentioned earlier in the literature on nostalgia or on aesthetic emotions; however, not in this combination and not with an exclusive view on the appraisal process in the context of the reception of nostalgia in television. The narration of the gap is part of the rhetoric of nostalgia that has been described by Tannock (1995, pp. 456 f.). The same applies to the positive "retrospective classification" (see Kompare, 2005, p. 105). On a macro level, this subject has been investigated by Kompare (2005). With a view on Davis (1977; 1979), it may also be applied on the micro level. Both aspects were part of the pre-assumptions of the analysis that could be confirmed and further specified here. Other components, such as the high relevance, reference to one's own lifeworld, and the importance of irretrievability, resulted from the analysis, however, they are also concordant with the literature on nostalgia, aesthetic emotions or memory. Thus Cook's (2005, p. 2) general definition highlights 'irretrievability' as a major element of nostalgia. The fact that the nostalgia object needs to have some relation to the recipients' lifeworlds is also concordant with what has been written on nostalgia's dependence on (personal) memory or "prosthetic memory". Further it may be explained by the strong interrelation between nostalgia and memory in general. As Teer-Tomaselli (2006, p. 235) highlights in the context of *The Global Media Project*, an "important influence on what is remembered is that of cultural proximity". The relation to personal "lifeworlds" is explained as another important factor (Teer-Tomaselli, 2006, pp. 240 ff.). Finally, in the context of aesthetic emotions in general, appraisal theory (see e.g. Tan, 1999, p. 44; Mangold et al., 2001, p. 171) names "relevance" as a major aspect in the development of certain emotions.[1]

The reception analysis provides evidence to the fact that it is precisely an appraisal of an object as containing all these components which leads to nostalgia. Firstly, apart from those contributions, in the context of which the identification of the single components could not be achieved, in more elaborated statements the components could be identified. Secondly, this is also evident when we compare the different examples and cases of nostalgia and non-nostalgia.

Apart from a few exceptions, such as PMS55-65, who simply states to have felt nostalgia but neither says why nor in which context, in nearly all cases a clear gap could be located, be it in a rhetoric of nostalgia or in the fact that the object of nostalgia may be ascribed to a phase in the recipient's life that is clearly separable

---

1 As Winter (2010, p. 144 [o.t.]) highlights on the example of Fiske's (1988) research, the factor "relevance" has more importance in the "analysis of media communication" than the factor "preference".

from the present. The importance of "relevance" can, above all, be deduced from the comparison of the cases of nostalgia with those cases where nostalgia does not appear. Without exception, the object of nostalgia or the object in whose context nostalgia appears is given a high relevance. We may here, for instance, remember the context of the *Knight Rider* rerun. Those audiences who appraise, for example, the *Knight Rider* first-run as having had little relevance in their past, have less memories and also do not develop nostalgia in its context and vice versa. Shades of relevance, as this case shows, may be observed on the macro-levels, thus regarding the reruns, remakes, period dramas as an artefact as a whole, but also inside the single formats, when formal elements is given more relevance than contextual ones or vice versa, and only in this context nostalgia may be detected. It also seems that between different indications of nostalgia in the course of the discussion, only the emotion that finally is given most relevance becomes manifest in the questionnaire.

Relevance is then again strongly interrelated to the question how far a format has something to do with the recipient's lifeworld. Is it interrelated to important moments in life? Did it once cause intensive emotions that are still remembered today? Accordingly, and without exception, all cases of nostalgia contain a "referential framing". Even in the case of 'empathetic F nostalgia' where it could at least have been assumed that a nostalgia that is only 'shared' with a protagonist is possible, nostalgia arises only on the basis of a relation to the lifeworld of the nostalgic subject. In the course of the end discussion, one participant explicitly highlights the necessity of a relation to "persönlichen Erfahrungen und Lebenssituationen" [personal experiences and life situations] (DFG25-35, GD25-35_Nostalgia_Allgemein _Deutschland, 9 [o.t.]) in the development of nostalgia.

Apart from the fact that no participant developed nostalgia towards a retrievable object, the comparison between rerun and remake reception, especially in the case of the rerun and remake of *Knight Rider*, could show that when the component of 'irretrievability' is missing, nostalgia is not developed. In both contexts the rhetoric of nostalgia could be detected; however, since the remake is negatively appraised, the 'missing' element is thought to be available in the premake or in a 'better' remake version. Nostalgia is not developed. The same becomes apparent when we compare statements that have been made in the context of the period drama *Mad Men*. Here a clear rhetoric of nostalgia in the context of the slide projector scene could be observed in two cases, yet only in one case the respective memory point – viewing sessions in the family circle – was appraised as being irretrievable by the participant and nostalgia was indeed developed. Furthermore, one participant highlights this component of the nostalgic appraisal explicitly in the final discussion. As BMG25-35 states:

BMG25-35: "You just have to have both, you have to find it nice but you also have to be aware that it is bygone and that it will never come back." (GD25-35_Nostalgia_Allgemein _Deutschland, 49 [o.t.])[2]

In no case was nostalgia developed towards an object that has been retrospectively classified as negative nor was it triggered on the basis of negatively appraised contents. Clear cases of nostalgia that were solely based on the 'common sense', resp. 'acquired' "retrospective classifications", could not be observed. Yet it has to be emphasised that the "retrospective classifications" indicate a kind of 'social desirability' in whose context nostalgia can be presumed to be favoured.

9.1.2 The 'genres' of nostalgia

In both the academic and the non-academic discourse, reruns and nostalgia, remakes and nostalgia, and period dramas and nostalgia are frequently mentioned together. The television analysis has assumed that all three categories may be described as nostalgia 'genres' that also create the expectation of nostalgia on the side of the recipients, respectively that are chosen in a kind of nostalgia mood-management. The reception study does not support that assumption in regards to all cases. However, it can be stated that further evidence has indeed been found.

In general, only a few participants of the focus groups saw the reruns, remakes and period pictures some time before the discussion and could actually report any expectations and experiences in the course of this reception. Only in the discussion about the *Knight Rider* remake do the elaborations of single participants support the assumption that nostalgia is the gratification audiences expected when they choose to watch the remake. At least the majority of statements that refer to the viewing motivation suggest a *Reencounter with the past* intended by those participants who know the premake. One recipient here refers explicitly to a "retro-feeling" he expected. Regarding other examples, no such elaborations could be highlighted. Here, a deeper survey of the motivations would have been necessary, as it could not be done in the course of the focus group discussions.

Notwithstanding this, you may indeed talk of a certain nostalgia mood that was prevalent in the focus groups. Firstly, in all 'genres' cases of nostalgia could be observed, which gives us reason to believe that the participants were 'disposed' to nostalgia. Later, participants also tended to have hierarchies of memories. Often alternative nostalgia triggers from within the same 'genre' are mentioned, which are given more relevance, are better remembered and somehow have more "proximity"

---

2   Original quotation: "Du musst halt beides drin haben, du musst es schön finden, aber du musst dir auch dessen bewusst sein, dass es vergangen ist. Und dass es nie wieder zurückkommt." (BMG25-35, GD25-35_Nostalgia_Allgemein_Deutschland, 49)

to the recipients' lifeworlds. If nostalgia was not the case in one example, some alternative nostalgia triggers were named that show that other, more relevant 'genre' examples may indeed trigger the feeling of nostalgia or are at least approached with such an expectation.

This may be observed in the context of the reruns where the quantitatively largest amount of nostalgia cases could be identified. Mainly *Knight Rider* recipients who have no nostalgic feelings in the context of the artefact as such or in the context of single aspects of the artefact name more relevant television series or film reruns that would 'work' as nostalgia contents in their case. Among the 25 to 35-year-old Germans this can also be observed in the final discussion of the focus group. Especially the two participants AMG25-35 and GMG25-35 who, in the course of the main discussion, displayed a cumbersome dealing with *Knight Rider* as nostalgia content referred to other rerun films to which they clearly ascribe the potential to provoke nostalgia in their case (AMG25-35, GD25-35_Nostalgia_Allgemein_ Deutschland, 103; 106; 112; GMG25-35, GD25-35_Nostalgia_Allgemein_ Deutschland, 109). The higher degree of relevance is again justified here with the higher degree of "proximity" to the viewer's own lifeworlds (see AMG25-35, GD25-35_Nostalgia_Allgemein_Deutschland, 114).

This similarly applies to the remake context. Apart from the fact that in the context of the 'failed' *Knight Rider* remake some recipients explicitly discuss a reencounter with the past that was at least expected and expectations of nostalgia, alternative nostalgia triggers from the same 'genre' that are thought to 'work' better (AMG25-35; GMG25-35, GD25-35_Remake_Knight Rider_Deutschland, 227-229) or that were also approached with expectations of nostalgia are mentioned here as well (see e.g. AFS25-35, GS25-35_Rerun_Knight Rider_Spanien, 371).[3]

In the context of the period pictures, alternative nostalgia triggers from the same 'genre' were not mentioned. Here, however, at least cases of nostalgia in the *Mad Men*-context are indicative for a certain prevalence of the nostalgic mood, too. In any case there is a need for further research here.

---

3 Against this backdrop we may assume that even if in the case of the two remake examples hardly any cases of nostalgia appeared, this does not mean that nostalgia in the context of remakes is not possible in general. Both examples, *Knight Rider* (NBC, 2008) and *The Avengers* (Chechik, 1998), are mainly appraised negatively by the recipients. Both examples almost invite the audiences to consider their 'lacks' as an explanation for the absence of positive emotions, such as nostalgia. Therefore both examples are surely only one of other possible and presumable cases. All assessments of remakes and nostalgia this study makes have to be seen in this context. It is up to further studies to investigate the possible development of nostalgia in the context of positively appraised remakes.

9.1.3 Triggers of nostalgia

The question was in which way potential triggers of nostalgia, as they were explored on the level of the text, were decoded as such by the participants. The respective conclusive chapters on the reception of the single 'genres' already described these interrelations. First of all, we may state that the assumed forms 'F nostalgia', 'empathetic F nostalgia' and 'A nostalgia' and the object-centrism central here served as applicable categories in the course of the analysis. Apart from 'internal empathetic artefact nostalgia', both cases of 'F nostalgia' and 'A nostalgia' could be detected. Also the assumption that intertextual references may lead to 'A nostalgia' could be verified.

However, in all cases we are dealing with the 'personal' shape of these aesthetic emotions. For example, 'F nostalgia' appears as the viewers' 'own F nostalgia' when F emotions as they are remembered in the context of a first-run become the object of nostalgia. 'Empathetic F nostalgia' appears as the viewers' 'own empathetic F nostalgia' if the sensation of empathy leads to the splitting-off of a person's own experiences that are the object of the nostalgic longing. 'A nostalgia' takes the form of the viewers' 'own A nostalgia' in the context of memories that are attached to a rerun as an artefact as a whole or A emotions as they are remembered in the context of an earlier reception. In the final discussion, one participant reflects on this phenomenon. She distinguishes here between a "persönlichen Nostalgie" [personal nostalgia] and the "Nostalgie der Gesellschaft" [nostalgia of society] (DFG25-35, GD25-35_Nostalgia_Allgemein_Deutschland, 5 [o.t.]), whereby the "personal nostalgia" is again strongly related to "persönlichen Erfahrungen und Lebenssituationen" [personal experiences and life situations] (DFG25-35, GD25-35_Nostalgia_Allgemein_Deutschland, 9 [o.t.]).

If we now take one step back and consider general tendencies in comparison to the examples, dominances within the 'genres' are observable, as they were already assumed in the context of the television analysis, but as they turned out to be less distinct on the level of the text. These dominances are again related to the previously described hierarchies of relevance or, as you might also say, to a certain aspiration of "proximity" on the side of the audiences.[4] In the context of the television reruns, nostalgia is mainly related to the first-run experience. The rerun as an artefact as such, or single aspects of it, work here as "mnemonic prompt[s]" to recall events that 'attached themselves' to the media memory and lead to the viewers' 'own A nostalgia'. The viewers' 'own F nostalgia' is developed in the context of strong, positive past emotions as they are remembered in the context of the first-run.

---

4   At this place we may again create the link to what Teer-Tomaselli (2006) highlights in the context of the The Global Media Project. The "triggers" that functioned here in order to recall (media) events are likewise explained by "the concept of relevance and proximity" (Teer-Tomaselli, 2006, p. 242).

Intertextual references or the general referential character of the rerun may lead to the viewers' 'own A nostalgia'. In addition, we may state that the nostalgias are clearly arranged in a kind of hierarchy. In accordance with Marce (1984), as referred to by Furno-Lamude and Anderson (1992), "cultural concerns override the concern for plot and character development in rerun viewing" (Furno-Lamude and Anderson, 1992, p. 371), respectively, as should be added, in the context of rerun nostalgia. Only if the personal link to the text is not given, will viewers focus on intertextual references or the general referential character of the rerun.

Regarding the remake viewing, the 'gap' between remake and premake is most important. The artefact level of the text is central here and overrides any other concern. One interviewee described this fact explicitly:

AFS25-35: "Well, when I watch the remake, sure, when you watch the remake, you remember the old one. And now, when I saw this one [the rerun], well, I intended to remember the summers. [....]." (AFS25-35, GS25-35_Rerun_Knight Rider_Spanien, 202 [o.t.])[5]

Still, and despite the assumptions made in the television analysis, no cases of nostalgia surging from this gap between remake and premake could be observed. The F level of the text has no importance at all in the course of the reception. Only in one case a viewer's 'own A nostalgia' on the level of the artefact as a whole may indeed be observed. The nostalgia, which in this case could hardly be further specified, did not develop during the reception but in the context of reminiscences about a lost childhood harmony in the course of the discussion. As mentioned earlier, we must here consider that both remakes are negatively appraised which influences this concentration on the artefact and has further effects on the factor of 'irretrievability' and a nostalgia that is possible here. Both examples are special cases whose reception obviously differs from other potential nostalgia remakes. Within the constellation of the selected examples, the gap between past and present identity becomes rather apparent in the context of the reruns. Here, the text may not be made responsible for the loss since it did not undergo any changes.

Concerning the period dramas, mostly in regards to *Mad Men*, the nostalgias are distributed more widely. As assumed, for those who grew up in the era period, artefacts may work as "mnemonic prompt[s]". The slide projector as a technical apparatus, which has been applied throughout the decades, mediates here between the age groups. On the F level, "visual correspondence" to the audiences' own experiences may lead to the viewers' 'own F nostalgia'. Furthermore, a case of a participant's 'own empathetic nostalgia' and a viewer's 'own A nostalgia' triggered

---

5   Original quotation: "Ah, pues yo cuando veo el remake, claro, cuando ves el remake, te acuerdas de la antigua. Y ahora que he visto esta [the rerun]. Pues sí que estaba intentando ahí recordar los veranos. [...]." (AFS25-35, GS25-35_Rerun_Knight Rider_Spanien, 202)

on the level of the intertextual reference of the series can be detected. Again, different hierarchies of relevance can be identified. Only the aspects that reached the highest relevance and that, apart from that, were appraised according to the above-mentioned criteria, led to nostalgia. Intertextual references are only relevant when no other "referential framing" is possible. Thus, in the case of *Mad Men*, it can mainly be observed among the 25 to 35-year-olds. In the case of *Borgia*, a respective framing is generally impossible for both 25 to 35-year-olds and 55 to 65-year-olds. Only in one case, where the Renaissance-series triggers autobiographical memories of school lessons, nostalgia is indicated but cannot be further substantiated due to an ironic framing provided by the participant.

Recipients developed nostalgia on the basis of single aspects of the texts and related to single objects that were appraised according to the previously mentioned categories. Respective focuses may change in the course of the reception. Thus, while at one moment emerging emotions are classified as nostalgia, nostalgia may not be observed regarding other aspects. Nostalgia in the context of television reception can also be described as being episodic, just as authors highlight it in regards to emotions and aesthetic emotions (see e.g. Zillmann, 2004; Eder, 2005; Bruun Vaage, 2007; 2008) in general.

9.1.4 Reception and appropriation

In a general context, media and communication studies (see e.g. Mikos, 2001a; Hepp, 2005) distinguish between reception and appropriation. While the first refers to the "duration of the concrete interaction with the text in the reception situation" (Mikos, 2001a, p. 62 [o.t.]), the latter describes, among other aspects, the "follow-up communication" (Mikos, 2001a, 67 [o.t.]) after the reception. In the context of aesthetic emotions, Smith (2008, p. 26 [o.t.]) refers to empathy that arises in the course of the film reception and empathy that arises afterwards "when we think about the experience". This distinction can also be made regarding nostalgia.

Independent of the nostalgia 'genre', here we may also distinguish nostalgia that arises in the course of the reception and nostalgia that arises in the course of the appropriation of the television series in the group discussions. Both cannot always be clearly distinguished. As Mikos (2001a) states in a general context, reception and appropriation can hardly be separated, "since appropriation already takes place during the reception" (Mikos, 2001a, 63 [o.t.]). The same applies to this study. However, some cases at least suggest the interpretation that nostalgia did not arise before the discussion of the respective stimulus material.

The reception analysis referred to, for example, the viewers' 'own A nostalgia' that some of the 25 to 35-year-old Spaniards developed in the context of the *El coche fantástico* (La1, 2008) discussion. It is a similar case with *Mit Schirm, Charme und*

Melone (ZDF, 1966). Statements of participants indicate here that nostalgia was not experienced in the course of the reception but rather in the course of the remembrance process during the group discussion. The analysis of the questionnaire allows some further concretisation. While most of the participants relate to the concrete stimulus excerpt in their description of nostalgia, one participant indicates explicitly to have felt nostalgia during the *Knight Rider* discussion (BMG25-35, Questionnaire_ Connotation of nostalgia_25-35-year-old Spaniards, 25).

The topic of appropriation and nostalgia cannot and will not be explored in depth here; however, with a view on these cases, at least two points can be highlighted that should also be considered in further studies on nostalgia and television. First, against the backdrop that already in the group discussions memories were triggered that became the basis of nostalgia, we may assume that mostly regarding television, a medium that in contrast to film encourages television talk (Abercrombie and Longhurst, 2007, p. 344), appropriation is especially relevant in the development of nostalgia. Secondly, this is further supported when we consider that audiences "use" television talk in order to "relate television to their own lives and thus help them to make sense of both" (Abercrombie and Longhurst, 2007, p. 344). A "referential framing", it has been shown previously, is again one important component of appraisal in the reception of nostalgia. We may thus assume that it may also be 'added' in the course of the appropriation and lead to nostalgia this way.

9.1.5 Necessary time spans of nostalgia

The reception analysis only allows a few statements on the necessary time spans of nostalgia. In order to investigate this issue more closely, it would have been necessary to use a broader range of examples that encompass various decades, yet this would have exceeded the scope of this study. However, some points emerge that allow us to characterise the 'longing' emotion more closely.

First of all, the study supports the assumption that there is no general minimum time span of nostalgia. The previously mentioned components of nostalgia show that the importance of the creation of a 'gap', respectively a contrast to present times, as has already been highlighted in the literature on nostalgia in general (Davis, 1977; 1979; Lowenthal, 1986; 1989; Tannock, 1996), has been confirmed. These observations are supported by explicit reflections of participants during the final discussion of the study. DFG25-35 emphasises, for example, that she developed nostalgia only in the past years of her life:

DFG25-35: "[...] When does it actually begin? Well, I think it's also interesting that you suddenly developed it just a few years ago. Because first some time must indeed go by." (GD25-35_Nostalgia_Allgemein_Deutschland, 159 [o.t.])[6]

A comparable reflection is made by CFG25-35, who says her first media memory is an example of nostalgia:

CFG25-35: "With the *Dschungelbuch* [The Jungle Book] I already felt nostalgic at a very young age. [...] Yes, I watched it for the first time when I was eight, I was already nostalgic when I was fifteen, when the film was repeated. [...] was just my first feature film." (GD25-35_Nostalgia_Allgemein_Deutschland, 165, 167, 170 [o.t.])[7]

The indications of the age show that the experience, which is the subject of nostalgia, falls into another lifespan, namely into the lifespan of childhood, which clearly contrasts with adolescence from the perspective of the time she developed the nostalgic feeling. When these conditions are given, nostalgia may be developed already within a few years.

With a view on the reception study regarding the maximum time span of nostalgia, it can be stated that no participant developed nostalgia in the context of an object that was outside his/her own experienced time. Nostalgia based upon "prosthetic memories" cannot be found either. The same applies to presumed 'adopted nostalgia'. We may, however, not exclude that that type of nostalgia is possible. Even though it was not any basis of nostalgia, indeed one case of "prosthetic memory" could be identified in the course of the group discussions. Apart from that, also without "prosthetic memories", that does not mean that a period picture or rerun which is obviously outside the lifespan of a recipient cannot become the object of nostalgia. The question is not from which era, for example, a period picture comes or in which era it is plays but rather at what point memory may enter the text. Indeed, regarding *Borgia*, the example that was most clearly outside the lifespan of the participants, nostalgia could not be observed. However, the case of JMS25-35 suggests that also a television series that is clearly outside the viewer's lifespan may lead to nostalgia when a "referential framing" generates the relation to his/her own

---

6   Original quotation: "[...] Ab wann beginnt das eigentlich? Weil ich find's auch interessant, dass man das plötzlich so entwickelt seit 'n paar Jahren erst. Weil es muss ja auch erst Mal was vergehn." (DFG25-35, GD25-35_Nostalgia_Allgemein_Deutschland, 159)

7   Original quotation: "[Ich war zum Beispiel für Dschungelbuch] ganz früh nostalgisch, schon. [...] Ja, das hab' ich zum ersten Mal gesehn, da war ich acht, da war ich schon nostalgisch, als ich fünfzehn war, wenn [...] der Film wiederholt wurde. [...] war halt mein erster Kinofilm." (CFG25-35, GD25-35_Nostalgia_Allgemein_Deutschland, 165; 167; 170)

lifeworld. Similarly, this was demonstrated in the *Mad Men* context. Participants who have no memories of their own of the 1960s are able to generate "proximity" through the detour of the intertextual references. Always in case that "proximity" is generated, the development of nostalgia is also possible regarding texts whose time of reference is clearly outside the lifespan of the recipients.

9.1.6 Relevance of the reflexive pre-focus of the text

It can be said that some of the six examples that have been examined in the television analysis particularly encourage the reflexive view on their time of reference. Among the period dramas it is *Mad Men* that dismantles the "self-mythologizing efforts" of the 1960s. In the group of the reruns, *The Avengers* (ITV, 1961) may be described as being reflexive regarding its temporal context. *Knight Rider* (NBC, 1982) presents at least an ambiguous gaze on its 1980s present, even though from today's perspective it can also be described as an idealising "agente historiador". In the light of this it has been assumed that the different foci of the examples will influence the quality of nostalgias developed in their context. This hypothesis could not be verified by the reception study.

The observed nostalgias can predominantly be classified as "simple" according to Davis' (1979, p. 18) definition. In that aspect the reception study is also congruent with Davis' research, in the context of which the author likewise observed that "Simple nostalgia is experienced more frequently than Reflexive, and Reflexive, in turn, more than Interpreted" (Davis, 1979, p. 27). Therefore in the research conducted here, most of the participants do not question the correctness of their nostalgia either. Instead they "harbor [...] the largely unexamined belief that THINGS WERE BETTER [...] *THEN* THAN *NOW*", as Davis (1979, p. 18 [emphasis in the original]) puts it in the context of nostalgia in general. The reception study indeed shows that, for example, the narration of *Mad Men* encourages a critical look at the 1960s. This perspective of the text, however, does not prevent the participants from developing "simple" nostalgia regarding other levels of the text. The same applies to the other examples. When it comes to nostalgia, it is always in its "simple" form.

There is only one case where clear "reflexive", even "interpreted nostalgia" can be observed. However, here the analysis provides evidence that the different colouring was not provoked by the reflexive character of the nostalgia trigger – in this case *El coche fantástico* (TVE, 1985). It is rather a memory of a recent rerun reception that conflicts with the earlier *Knight Rider* experience. That case indicates a point which in the context of this study can only be touched upon and which has been described by Assmann (2006) in the context of memory in general. As Assmann highlights, "in the course of life structures of relevance and patterns of appraisal change insofar that once important things gradually become unimportant and once unimportant things become important in retrospect" (Assmann, 2006, p. 25 [o.t.]). Dhost (2007, p. 36), as has been mentioned previously, emphasises that "repeated viewing" may have an impact on "former memories and evaluations". Both, it can be assumed, also decisively influence the development of nostalgia. In the case mentioned previously it is a reflexive layer that is added to the nostalgic view. Against the backdrop of the components of the nostalgia appraisal where "relevance" is one major factor, we may assume that whatever triggers nostalgia at one moment in time can be supposed to trigger very different emotions at another point in time and vice versa.

In the context of this study that subject could not be investigated conclusively. The statements made are still hypothetical. In order to further investigate this issue, a study would be necessary that focuses on the development of nostalgia in the context of television series over various decades or at least years – something that would have exceeded the limits of this project. Once more, however, the observations underline the ephemeral character of nostalgia and its dependence on multiple factors. Nostalgia is a fleeting emotion.

9.1.7 Inter-group differences

Against the backdrop of the nostalgia discourse and theories on memory, it has been assumed that nostalgias differ depending on the different groups of recipients. The conclusion to the reception analysis poses one main question, namely: How are the examples received from within the frames of different 'we groups'? This study has mainly referred to a territorial "we" of German or Spanish audiences and a "we" of different age groups, in this case the group of the 25 to 35-year-olds and the group of the 55 to 65-year-olds. The reception study was organised correspondingly. Altogether, four different focus group discussions with one age group each from each country were conducted.

Differences have not only been assumed due to the different memories of the groups. Against the backdrop of Krotz, according to whom "feeling depends [...] on cultural, social and personality-related determinants" (Krotz, 1993, p. 98 [o.t.]), also with a view on the emotive aspects of nostalgia, differences between Spain and Germany have been expected. Findings on this subject shall be summarised in this conclusive sub-chapter.

Altogether, cases of nostalgia could be observed among all groups, the groups of the 25 to 35-year-old Germans and Spaniards and the groups of the 55 to 65-year-old Germans and Spaniards (see Table 6).

Table 6: Cases of nostalgia in the course of the reception study.

	Cases of nostalgia
Reruns	
Knight Rider	• Viewers' 'own A nostalgia' on the level of the artefact as a whole (DFG25-35; AFS25-35, JMS25-35, RMS25-35, CMS25-35, OFS25-35, MFS55-65 (?), DMG25-35 (?)) • Viewers' 'own A nostalgia' on the level of the music (VMS25-35, AMG25-35 (? questionnaire)) • Viewers' 'own A nostalgia' on the level of the props (?) (CFG25-35) • Viewers' 'own F nostalgia' towards past F emotions (FFG25-35, EMG 25-35)
The Avengers	• Viewers' 'own A nostalgia' on the level of the artefact as a whole (GFG55-65, BFG55-65 (?), FMS55-65) • Viewers' 'own F nostalgia' coming from an immersion into the fictional world (CMG55-65)
Remakes	
Knight Rider	• Viewers' 'own A nostalgia' on the level of the artefacts as a whole (?) (VMS25-35, AFS25-35, OFS25-35)
The Avengers	–
Period dramas	
Mad Men	• Viewers' 'own A nostalgia' on the level of the intertextual references (ZFS25-35) • Viewers' 'own F nostalgia' coming from an immersion into the fictional world (FCFS55-65, PMS55-65 (?)) • Viewers' 'own F nostalgia' on the level of the music (?) (MFS55-65) • Viewers' 'own A nostalgia' on the level of the props (DMG55-65) • Viewers' 'own empathetic F nostalgia' (?) (ZFG25-35)
Borgia	–

As a first look at the table shows, decodings mainly relate to the age groups and less to the territorial groups. As a general tendency it can be observed that the *The Avengers* is not able to provoke nostalgia among the 25 to 35-year-olds, while *Knight Rider* rather prohibits the development of the 'longing' emotion in the 55 to 65-year-olds. More convergence between the age groups can be observed in the case of *Mad Men*.

In regards to the single types of nostalgia, a comparison is not always possible. Indeed, around 25 cases could be identified; however, the table already shows that there are only few 'accumulations'. Nostalgia, as has been mentioned previously, is a fleeting, almost intangible emotion. However, tendencies can be found, and further hypothesis can be outlined.

9.1.7.1 Comparison between the countries

With a view on the reception analysis, we may state that in general nationality does not correlate with specific nostalgias. The national "we", even though it appears on a few occasions during the discussions, is unimportant when it comes to the nostalgias detected. *Mit Schirm, Charme und Melone* (ZDF, 1966), respectively *Los Vengadores* (TVE, 1966) and *Knight Rider* (RTLplus, 1985), respectively *El coche fantástico* (TVE, 1985), are part of a transnational German/Spanish media memory against the backdrop of which the remakes can be decoded for both groups, too. As Hepp (2009) suggested, the "deterritorial cultural thickening" here appears on the basis of internationally traded cultural products.

A certain degree of transnationally 'shared' nostalgia was mostly seen regarding the reruns as artefacts as a whole. Here, the general socio-political contexts were mainly excluded in the nostalgia narration of the recipients. Instead, influenced by developmental stages, such as childhood or early adulthood, and seemingly equal sections of life phases, very similar experiences attached themselves to the media memories across the countries, which again became the objects of nostalgia. In this point, the investigation is also congruent with what has been observed by Davis (1979). The author highlights that:

"nostalgia acquires considerable sociological significance – is often of a highly conventional cast, e.g., marriage, children, job success, a home of one's own. These are institutional staples which we are socialized to contemplate from an early age and which, indeed, we are required to anticipate if there is to be cultural continuity between generations." (Davis, 1979, pp. 12 f.)

The presumed difference between Germany and Spain, if the general socio-political context of the 1980s is of relevance, is only suggested by one case of adulthood nostalgia in the context of the *Knight Rider* rerun in the Spanish group of the 55 to 65-year-olds. However, here the analysis could only make first assumptions. Considering the broad range of the interviewees' comments and since due to the few cases a comparison was impossible, further evidence in support of the assumption could not be given.

While the period drama *Borgia* neither provoked nostalgia among Germans nor Spaniards, in the case of *Mad Men* similar statements in both territorial groups could be highlighted. Furthermore, cases of nostalgia could be observed both among the

German and Spanish participants. While further comparisons could not be made due to the broad distribution of the single cases, it can also be stated that internationally traded consumer goods or cultural products such as twist music mediate between the territories. Again, very similar memories of life phases or developmental stages – in this case early adulthood memories – attached themselves, which makes overlaps between German and Spanish memories observable.

The reception study suggests that nostalgia is not only equally defined both in Germany and Spain but that this equality also corresponds to the cognitive and emotive aspects of nostalgia. In both territorial groups cases of 'F nostalgia' and 'A nostalgia' could be observed. The components of the nostalgic appraisal are congruent throughout the countries.

9.1.7.2 Age groups

It is a different case when we look at the two age groups. Regarding the reruns and remakes, we can observe a clear gap between the 25 to 35-year-old Germans and Spaniards on the one hand and the 55 to 65-year-old Germans and Spaniards on the other. Regarding *Mad Men*, nostalgia can be exemplified among both yet here differences between the age groups appear as well.

The clear gap regarding the reruns and remakes can be related to the fact that media memories are in the centre of the provoked nostalgias. Each age group has different media memories – here, the study is congruent with observations that have been made by Rusch and Volkmer (2006, p. 92) – respectively gives different media memories different relevance on the basis of which nostalgia may arise. This is especially the case with the series that fall into the respective "formative years" of the age group. Corresponding to the "set of important events", as it is also described by Rusch and Volkmer (2006, p. 92), it is here where each age group finds its own set of potential triggers of nostalgia. Here it can also not be distinguished between 'experts' and 'non-experts', but, as assumed in 4.4, everybody who was a child of his/her time can be a *connaisseur*.[8]

Thus, on the one hand both the 25 to 35-year-olds and the 55 to 65-year-olds have memories of *Knight Rider*, but these memories are differently coloured. Predominantly, the 25 to 35-year-olds give *Knight Rider* a high value in the context of which nostalgia may develop. The rerun works as a "mnemonic prompt", for example for the lost lightheartedness of childhood in general, which makes it a starting point for an age-group specific, 'shared' nostalgia that is partly transnational. On the other hand, while most of the 25 to 35-year-olds have no memories of the *The*

---

8 Here it can be pointed at the work of Ian Chamber (1986), as referred to in Winter (2010, p. 94), who in the 1980s had highlighted the dissolution of the concept of 'expert' and 'layperson' in the context of metropolitan popular culture.

Avengers first-run that is set outside their lifespans, the 55 to 65-year-olds remember it intensively. In part nostalgia is developed in the context of the series.

The different colouring of the media memories of the 25 to 35-year-olds and 55 to 65-year-olds is also reflected in other areas in the context of which nostalgia not necessarily appears. The analysis shows, for example, that the memories of the 55 to 65-year-olds are clearly marked by early television similar to how it had been described by O'Sullivan (1991) in a more general context of television memories. Apart from that, while the 25 to 35-year-olds in the context of *Knight Rider* tend to name alternative nostalgia triggers if the first-run has less relevance for them, among the 55 to 65-year-olds no such 'hierarchisations' can be observed. In the 1960s, one saw a programme or one didn't. Other differences that appeared in the course of the group discussions shall not be investigated in this conclusive chapter, which focuses exclusively on the findings in the context of nostalgia.

Overlaps between the different age groups can be observed regarding the period drama *Mad Men*. However, while the 55 to 65-year-olds are able to generate "proximity" due to a "correspondence" to their own memories of the 1960s, such an 'easy' "referential framing" cannot be observed among the 25 to 35-year-olds. Here, nostalgia has to take the 'detour' of intertextual references, for example. It is only different in regards to the prop slide projector, which mediates between the age groups and territorial groups. Other forms, such as 'empathetic F nostalgia', are not age group specific. Indeed, only in one case of a 25 to 35-year-old Spaniard nostalgia could be presumed here as well. Empathetic emotions, however, also appear independent of age group or territorial group.

Finally, differences between the age groups concern the handlings of nostalgia. In Chapter 7.1 it has been indicated that during their focus group discussions in the context of *The Global Media Project*, Kumar et al. (2006, p. 219) observed an accumulation of nostalgia among older Indian participants. The authors explain that with the relatively larger temporal distance of the remembered events (Kumar et al., 2006, p. 219). Against this backdrop, it could be assumed that in the course of this investigation nostalgia could also have been prepredominantly observed among the 55 to 65-year-olds. However, the contrary is the case. Apart from a quantitative accumulation of cases of nostalgia among the 25 to 35-year-olds, different connotations of nostalgia among the two age groups that influence the participants' 'disposition' for the emotion can be observed as well. Already the analysis of the descriptions of "a nostalgic person" in the questionnaires reflects a negative connotation of nostalgia among the 55 to 65-year-olds, while among the 25 to 35-year-olds rather neutral or positive descriptions can be found. Among the 55 to 65-year-olds cases of nostalgia are suggested in the course of the discussion but are not manifested as nostalgia in the questionnaire. Among the 25 to 35-year-olds the opposite is the case. There are various occasions where notions of nostalgia don't appear in the course of the group discussion, in the questionnaire the respective recipient, however, states that he/she felt nostalgic. For the 25 to 35-year-olds, nostalgia seems to be a socially desirable emotion while it is rather problematic for the 55 to 65-year-olds. While the young age group strives for nostalgia, among the 55 to 65-year-olds its negative connotation inserts itself successfully between the nostalgic offer and its recipient.[9]

9.1.8 Intra-group differences

Next to aspects such as the connotation of nostalgia, which work on an inter-subjective level, here we shall at least refer to other factors since they can be presumed to be important with regards to a rather intra-subjective level. The theory of aesthetic emotions highlights that different individuals may have different 'dispositions' for certain emotions or emotions in general. Mangold et al. (2001, p. 165 [o.t.]) discuss "[i]nterindividuell unterschiedliche affektive Reagibilität" [different intra-individual affective responsiveness]. The authors here refer both to isolated "individual conditions" during the respective reception and general character dispositions" (Mangold et al., 2001, p. 165 [o.t.]).

In addition, in the course of the reception study aspects came to the surface that certainly have to be seen in this context as well. For example, we can refer to the case of DFG25-35 who describes herself as being a very empathetic person (GD25-35_Period Pictures_Mad Men_Deutschland, 249). Other interviewees have preferences for fashion (see e.g. FFG25-35, AFG55-65) or aversion against historical media contents (see e.g. AMG25-35), which also influences their elaborations.

These aspects should be acknowledged, but, as Morley says, in the context of this study they surely "do not erase the patterns of consistency and similarity of perspectives within groups" (Morley, 1980, p. 138). Following Mikos:

"Despite all the uniqueness of the experiences, there exists no purely individual film or video reception, because since all spectators go through similar developmental psychological stages – and this normally in the frame of a specific society and a specific cultural context – and, apart from that pass institutions of socialisation such as parental home, school etc., all reception experiences which are singular for the individual are socially mediated." (Mikos, 2001, p. 255 [o.t.])

---

9 Here it can only be speculated that the history of fascism had a certain influence on the connotation of nostalgia among the 55 to 65-year-olds. In the course of the discussion, other 'filters', such as what Ang (1985, p. 94) describes as "'ideology of mass culture'", have been suggested, which could not be further investigated in the course of the study.

Apart from that – here we may again draw the line to Chapter 3 on memory, "[p]rivate memory cannot [...] be [...] unscrambled from the effects of dominant historical discourses" (Popular Memory Group, 1982, p. 211).

9.2 OUTLOOK

It could be shown that the reception of nostalgia is a complex phenomenon that depends on diverse factors. It depends on textual and contextual factors, is memory-related, depends on a complex process of appraisal and diverse 'filters' that may enter the space between text and audiences. The use of different methods of data collection, as it has been argued for in the context of the *Babelsberg Approach* or other approaches of triangulation, has been proved to be productive in the investigation of the phenomenon. Due to possible comparisons of cases of nostalgia and non-nostalgia and the in-depth articulation of the recipients, aspects of reception could be identified that would not have been grasped by the mere application of a questionnaire. At the same time, the questionnaire enriched the qualitative analysis of the focus group discussion.

The categories of analysis deduced from a combination of approaches on aesthetic emotions, memory, and nostalgia have been proved to be applicable in the process of the reception study. In large parts the reception study supports the viability of the categories to the extent that it confirms its "predictive validity" (Krippendorf, 1980 cited in Lamnek, 2005, p. 222 [o.t.]). Regarding the concrete appraisal process as it has been explained as being decisive for the development of nostalgia, the components, even though not in this combination, contain "correlative validity" (Krippendorf, 1980 cited in Lamnek, 2005, p. 222 [o.t.]) to categories as they are highlighted in the theory of aesthetic emotions, nostalgia or memory. Few relations to previous investigations could be made. However, wherever overlaps existed, correlations could also be observed and differences could be explained.

The study could exemplify major factors of the interrelation of nostalgic texts and nostalgic reception. However, this is surely only a beginning. With reference to Kuckartz (2010, p. 172), we may state that the inductively gained categories can only claim hypothetical character. They have to be verified in further studies. Later, the investigation had a partly "explorative" character. Its conceptualisation was accordingly wide regarding the different 'genres' and types of nostalgia. At the same time, the group discussions were limited with regards to the number of sessions and participants. In this conclusive chapter some open questions have already been outlined. Major limitations shall be highlighted in this outlook on the reception study.

With the stimulus excerpts and examples, a selection had to be made, and an order had to be installed, which may have influenced the reception. Confusions could be prevented due to the separated distribution of the stimulus examples in the course of the discussion. However, since different 'genres' have been discussed within one focus group, it cannot be excluded that nostalgias, which were developed in the context of single examples and 'genres', did not 'compete' or retreat against each other. At this point further research is needed that exposes a more selective design, focusing upon the single 'genres'. Later, given the small sample, only a relatively few cases of nostalgia appeared, which in part hindered extensive comparisons of the same sub-type of nostalgia in different groups. With the sample of interviewees, a selection with regard to age group and social group had to be made, which limits the generalizability of the observations. Here, further research is needed.

This study is conscious of its limitations. It therefore aspired to disclose any possible sources of error, not only in this outlook but also in the course of the work. Apart from that, it has striven for the highest possible traceability. Here, the study was led by general criteria of quality of qualitative study (see e.g. Lamnek, 2006). Lamnek (2006) states in this context:

"Regarding its acceptance, the focus group as an explicit qualitative method will live – and this is not meant ironically – less of elaborated approaches of reliability and validity but rather of plausibility and the persuasiveness of the results. The main condition should always be the disclosure of data collection and analysis and the chance of traceability." (Lamnek, 2006, p. 223 [o.t.])

Following this advice, any reader of this study is given the possibility to trace the single steps of analysis and possible shortcomings, which, especially in the course of an "explorative" study, cannot be excluded.

10. Afterword

What is nostalgia in television? And how can the phenomenon be grasped theoretically? These were the main questions of this study. Further sub-questions were: What are the 'genres' of nostalgia? What textual characteristics does it have? To what extent do potential triggers for nostalgia provoke nostalgic emotions? And finally: How are the nostalgic texts received from within the frames of different "we-groups" and against the backdrop of different lifeworlds? In order to approach these questions, the investigation combined studies from the spectrum of the nostalgia discourse, memory studies, and theories on aesthetic emotions in a first step. In a second step, textual analysis and reception studies were made with two examples each from the nostalgia 'genres' reruns, remake and period drama. Thus, a comparison between different countries has been chosen. Only by doing that can characteristics of contemporary nostalgia be grasped broadly.

It has been stated that if we want to analyse nostalgia adequately we must analyse the textual characteristics, must ask if these characteristics indeed provoke nostalgia, and must ask if there are any differences between different audiences with different (memory) contexts. As shown in Part I, with a view on the discourse, characteristics of nostalgia could be explained. However, an approach that could be used in order to analyse the interrelation of nostalgia offered by the text and nostalgia provoked in the audiences is not provided. Due to that reason the present work made use of theories on aesthetic emotions and memory as they exist within film, television and media studies. Suspecting that there must be certain similar mechanisms as in the case of suspense, for example, as a central point of combination, Tan's model (1996) has been chosen. A combination of the discourse of nostalgia with the theory of aesthetic emotions and memory provided a first step in the investigation of the "systematic interrelation" of text and reception in nostalgia and television. The application of Tan's model was successful insofar as it allowed an 'ordering', combination and amplification of the existing theoretical works. Studies that mainly centre on textual aspects of nostalgia could be made fertile for the investigation of the interrelation between text and reception. In the textual analysis it provided the study with analysis categories in the context of which the existing discourse could be better applied and amplified. First suggestions on possible nostalgic readings were made possible, which, due to their systematic mapping in Tan's model, could be brought together easier with observations made in the reception study. Mainly in the context of transnational comparative studies the systematisation focused and facilitated the analysis. This afterword shall not further comment on the results of the analysis. They have already been summarised in the earlier discussions of results. Here it shall rather be reflected beyond the limits of this study and further possibilities of research.

Due to its partly "explorative" character this study could only give a first view on the subject. The limited ability to generalise the results was hinted at in the conclusion to the reception study. Open questions were highlighted. Among them: Is nostalgia in the context of a positively appraised remake more likely? How far does the reception of nostalgia formats change relevance structures? And can the nostalgia reception be repeated? With a view on the whole work, we may state that further studies are now needed that focus on the single forms of nostalgia, such as 'non-empathetic F nostalgia', 'A nostalgia' or 'empathetic F nostalgia' and their reception. Apart from that, broader comparisons among countries should be considered. This study is only a beginning. The definition of nostalgia does not differ between Germany and Spain. Due to similar lifeworld memories and connotations of nostalgia there were rather differences between the two age groups than between the countries that were perceived. The observed nostalgias extended the territorial borders. It has to be seen if this is different when we apply broader comparisons between countries. In this context, what would also be interesting is what, subsequent to Kompare's (2005, p. 208 [italic emphasis in the original]) "*acquisitive repetition*", could be called 'acquisitive nostalgia' – those potential triggers of nostalgia namely, which in the form of internet and DVD compilations are always and easily accessible even across national borders. Apart from that, the focus of this study was set on international series broadcasted both in Germany and Spain. Here, audiences, as was shown, generate a variety of links to their own lifeworlds and memories against the backdrop of which nostalgia arises. Further studies should include domestic reruns, remake, and period dramas in order to see if further nuances of nostalgia and its reception are observable. Lastly, this study has only barely considered relations of power as they are underlying the observed nostalgias. Similarly to memory studies in general (Bommes and Wright, p. 258), it could be asked which nostalgias are, for instance, "excluded, suppressed and socially devalued". There is further need of research here as well. In summary, we may state that a first framework for the investigation of the "systematic interrelation" of text and reception in nostalgia and television could be developed in this study. First empirical studies could be made. Now further steps will have to follow in the future.

11. Bibliography

ABC, 1967. Progamas de Televisión. *ABC*, 17 September, p. 106b.

ABC, 1967a. Programas de Televisión. *ABC*, 27 August, p. 78b.

ABC, 1967b. Programas de Televisión. *ABC*, 8 October, p. 110a.

ABC, 1967c. Programas de Televisión. *ABC*, 11 April, p. 78c.

ABC, 1987. A Beneficio de la Asociación Española de lucha contra la poliomelitis. *ABC*, 8 July, p. 27.

ABC, 2004. Coche fantástico "made in Madrid". *ABC*, 17 July, p. 107c.

ABC, 2004a. Rehabilitación para David Hasselhoff. *ABC*, 31 October, p. 105b.

ABC, 2008. Las nuevas aventuras de "El coche fantástico" llega a España. *ABC*, 7 April, p. 109a.

ABC, 2009. David Hasselhoff, salvado de la muerte por su hija. *ABC*, 27 September, p. 90a.

Abercrombie, N. and Longhurst, B., 2007. *Dictionary of Media Studies*. London: Penguin Books.

Akass, K. and McCabe, J., 2011. The Best of Everything: The Limits of Being a Working Girl in *Mad Men*. In: Edgerton, G.R., ed. *Mad Men*. London/New York: Tauris, 177-192.

Alcojar, A. et al., 2006. *1960. Spain is different. Llega la fiebra del turismo*. Madrid: Pradillo.

Allan, S., 2006. Ostalgie, fantasy and the normalization of east-west relations in post-unification comedy. In: Clarke, D., ed. *German Cinema since unification*. London: Continuum, 105-126.

Amat Noguera, N., 1998. *Nostalgia de los libros perdidos*. Santa Cruz de Tenerife: Servicio de Publicaciones de la Universidad de La Laguna.

Amezaga Aresti, V., 1993. *Nostalgia. La cultura del exilio vasco*. Donostia: J.A. Ascunce.

Anderson, S., 2001. History TV and Popular Memory. In: Edgerton, G.R. and Rollins, P.C., eds. *Television Histories. Shaping Collective Memory in the Media Age*. Kentucky: The University Press of Kentucky, 19-36.

Anderson, S., 2010. Modern Viewers, Feudal Television Archives: How to Study German Fernsehspiele of the 1960s form a National Perspective. *Critical Studies in Television*, 5 (2), 91-104.

Anderson, T., 2011. Uneasy Listening: Music, Sound, and Criticizing Camelot in Mad Men. *In:* Edgerton, G.R., ed. *Mad Men.* London/New York: Tauris, 72-85.

Anfang, G. and Schorb, B., 1998. Was machen "Airwolf" und "Knight Rider" mit ihren jugendlichen Zuschauern? Eine Untersuchung zweier Fernsehserien und ihrer Beurteilung durch Jugendliche. *Medien + Erziehung*, 33 (3), 132-143.

Ang, I., 1985. *Watching Dallas. Soap Opera and the melodramatic imagination.* London/New York: Methuen.

Ang, I., 1986. *Das Gefühl Dallas. Zur Produktion des Trivialen.* Bielefeld: Daedalus.

Aniorte, C., 2008. La televisión se viste de nostalgia. *ABC (Televisión y Radio),* 23 November, p. 120.

Antena 3, 2012. Video Archive. [online] Available at: http://www.antena3.com /videos/ [Accessed 23 September 2012].

apl, 2007. Ohne Charme auch kein Schirm. *Frankfurter Allgemeine Zeitung,* 20 February, p. 35.

Armbruster, S. and Mikos, L., 2009. *Innovation im Fernsehen.* Konstanz: UVK.

Armbruster, S., 2012. Watching Nostalgia – Past and its Affective Re-Enactment in Contemporary Television. In: Discourse, Communication, Conversation Conference. Loughborough University, United Kingdom 21-23 March 2012 (unpublished conference paper).

Armbruster, S., 2012a. Re-interpreting the Past – Nostalgia and Reruns of Popular Television Series. In: Pursuing the Trivial, Vienna, Austria 1-2 June 2012 (unpublished conference paper).

Armbruster, S., 2012b. Nostalgia transnational: television reruns in Germany and Spain. In: 4th European Communication Conference, Bilgi University Istanbul, Turkey 24-27 October 2012 (unpublished conference paper).

Armbruster, S., 2014. Transnational Nostalgia in Europe. Television Reruns in the Reception of two Generations in Germany and Spain. *In:* Eichner, S. and Prommer, E., eds. *Fernsehen: Europäische Perspektiven. Festschrift Prof. Dr. Lothar Mikos.* Konstanz/München: UVK, 121-135.

ARTE, 2011. *Mit Schirm, Charme und Melone – Zum 50. Geburtstag* [online]. Available at: http://www.arte.tv/de/film/Mit-Schirm-Charme-und-Melone/355 3048,Cm C=35531 32.html [Accessed 22 September 2011].

Assmann, A., 2006. *Der lange Schatten der Vergangenheit. Erinnerungskultur und Geschichtspolitik.* München: C.H. Beck.

Assmann, A., 2006a. *Erinnerungsräume. Formen und Wandlung des kulturellen Gedächtnisses.* 3rd ed. München: C.H. Beck.

Assmann, A., 2011. *What exactly does remembrance mean? – Interview with Aleida Assmann* by Roland Detsch [online]. Goethe-Institut. Available at: http://www.goethe.de/ges/pok/pan/en7000483.html [Accessed 4 July 2012].

A.Z., 1974. U.S.A. Nostalgia, más nostalgia. *La Vanguardia*, 17 April, p. 26b.

Baacke, D., 1976. Nostalgie. Ein Phänomen ohne Theorie. *Merkur. Deutsche Zeitschrift für europäisches Denken*, 30 (5), 442-452.

Bäumer, P., 2003. Mit dem Turbo über die Dächer. *Berliner Zeitung*, 28 April.

Balló, J. et al., 1999. *Món TV la cultura de la televisió*. Barcelona: CCCB.

Barlett, C.P. and Gentile, D. A., 2011. Affective and emotional consequences of the mass media. *In:* Döveling, K. et al., eds. *The Routledge Handbook of Emotions and Mass Media*. London: Routledge, 60-78.

Bartetzko, D., 1998. Die Lady in Leder. *Frankfurter Allgemeine Zeitung*, 20 July.

Bartsch, A., 2007. Meta-Emotion and Genre Preference: What makes horror films and tear-jerkers enjoyable? *In:* Anderson, J.D. and Anderson Fisher, B., eds. *Narration and spectatorship in moving images*. Newcastle: Cambridge Scholar Publishing, 124-135.

Bartsch, A. et al., eds., 2007. *Audiovisuelle Emotionen. Emotionsdarstellungen und Emotionsvermittlung durch audiovisuelle Medienangebote*. Köln: Halem.

Bartsch, A. et al., 2007a. Einleitung: Emotionsdarstellung und Emotionsvermittlung durch audioviduelle Medien. *In*: Bartsch, A. et al., eds. *Audiovisuelle Emotionen. Emotionsdarstellungen und Emotionsvermittlung durch audiovisuelle Medienangebote*. Köln: Halem, 8-38.

Battle Caminal, J., 1999. El bombón y el bombín. *La Vanguardia*, 19 December, p. 45.

Baumgart, L., 2002. *Das Konzept Emma Peel. Der unerwartete Charme der Emanzipation: "The Avengers" und das Publikum*. Kiel: Ludwig.

Belinchón, G., 2011. David Hasselhoff participará en 'Fuga de cerebro 2'. *El País*. [online] 1 July. Available at: http://blogs.elpais.com/version-muy-original/2011/07/davidhas.html [Accessed 1 July 2011].

Belmonte, R., 2006. Temas a la medida de la autora. *ABC*, 8 August.

Benjamin, W., 1936. The Work of Art in the Age of its Technological Reproducibility. Translated 2008. *In*: Jennigs, William et al., eds., 2008. *The work of art in the age of its technological reproducibility, and other writings on media*. Cambridge: Harvard University Press.

Bennett, J., 2003. The Aesthetics of sense-memory. Theorising trauma through the visual arts. *In:* Radstone, S. and Hodgkin, K., eds. *Regimes of Memory*. London/New York: Routledge, 26-39.

Bennett, T. and Woollacott, J., 1987. *Bond and Beyond. The Political Career of a Popular Hero*. New York: Methuen.

Berciano, R., 1990. Televisón Española repone la serie 'Los Vengadores'. *El País*, 11 November.

Bernal, F., 2012. Este Verano, Curro (Jiménez) para todos. *Què!*, 13 June, p. 4a.

Berthold, A. et al., 2010. The ARD and ZDF Mediathek portals. *CATCH-UP RADIO & TV*, [online] 12 March. Avilable at: http://tech.ebu.ch/docs/techreview/trev_2010-Q1_Mediathek.pdf [Accessed 19 August 2010].

Black, D.A., 2004. Character; or, The Strange Case of Uma Peel. *In:* Gwenllian-Jones, S. and Pearson, R.E., eds. *Cult Television.* Minneapolis/London: University of Minnesota Press, 99-114.

Blanco, A., 1999. *Televisión de Culto. 100 Series Miticas.* Barcelona: Glénat.

Bleicher, J.K., 2007. The old in the new: Forms and Functions of archive material in the presentation of history on television. *In:* Nöth, W. and Bishara, N., eds. *Self-reference in media.* Berlin: Mouton de Gruyter, 183-193.

Blum, M., 2000. Remaking the East German Past: Ostalgie, Identity, and Material Culture. *Journal of Popular Culture,* 34 (3), 229-253.

Böhn, A., 2007. Nostalgia of the media/in the media. *In:* Nöth, W. and Bishara, N., eds. *Self-reference in media.* Berlin: Mouton de Gruyter, 143-154.

Boie, J., 2009. Hasselhoff und die Elektronen. *Süddeutsche Zeitung (Bayern),* 16 July, p. 9.

Boie, J., 2009a. No title. *Süddeutsche Zeitung (Bayern),* 1 October, p. 30.

Bommes, M. and Wright, P., 1982. 'Charms of residence': public and the past. *In:* Johnson, R., et al., eds. *Making Histories. Studies in history-writing and politics.* London: Hutchinson, 205-251.

Bordwell, D., 1985. *Narration in the Fiction Film.* Madison: Methuen & Co.

Bordwell, D., 1989. *Making Meaning. Inference and Rhetoric in the Interpretation of Cinema.* Cambridge: Harvard University Press.

Bosch, O., 2011. El duro peso de la fama. *La Vanguardia (TV Manía),* 14 May, p. 12a.

Bourdieu, P., 1984. *Distinction: A Social Critique of the Judgement of Taste.* London: Routledge and Kegan Paul.

Boyd, C., 1999. History, politics, and culture, 1936-1975. *In:* Gies, D.T., ed. *The Cambridge Companion to Modern Spanish Culture,* Cambridge: Cambridge University Press, 86-103.

Boym, S., 2001. *The future of nostalgia.* New York: Basic Book.

Bracero, F., 2011. El retorn de JR i els àngels. *La Vanguardia,* 6 June.

Brand, J.B., Pauli, H., 2012, Wer hat an der Uhr gedreht? *Focus,* 8, 83-85.

Braudy, L., 1998. Afterword: Rethinking Remakes. *In:* Horton, A. and McDougal, S.Y., eds. *Play it again, Sam. Retakes on Remakes.* Berkeley/Los Angeles/London: University of California Press, 327-334.

Brinckmann, C.N., 2005. Die Rolle der Empathie oder Furcht und Schrecken im Dokumentarfilm. *In:* Brütsch, M. et al., eds. *Kinogefühle. Emotionalität und Film.* Marburg: Schüren, 333-360.

Broc, O., 2009. En Portada. *La Vanguardia (TV Manía),* 18 July, p. 6a.

Brockhaus, 1931. *Handbuch des Wissens in 20 Bänden.* Vol. 8, Leipzig/Mannheim: Bockhaus.

Brockhaus, 1991. *Enzyklopädie in 24 Bänden.* Vol. 16, Leipzig/Mannheim: Brockhaus.

Brockmann, T., 2005. Slow E-Motion. Gefühlswelten in Zeitlupe. *In:* Brütsch, M. et al., eds. *Kinogefühle. Emotionalität und Film.* Marburg: Schüren, 153-167.

Bruun Vaage, M., 2007. Empathy and the Episodic Structure of Engagement in Fiction Film. *In:* Anderson, J.D. and Anderson Fisher, B., eds. *Narration and spectatorship in moving images.* Newcastle: Cambridge Scholar Publishing, 186-201.

Bruun Vaage, M., 2008. Empathie. Zur episodischen Struktur der Teilhabe am Spielfilm. *In:* Ebbrecht, T. and Schick, T., eds. *Emotion – Empathie – Figur. Spielformen der Filmwahrnehmung.* Berlin: Vistas, 29-48.

Butler, J.G., 2011. 'Smoke gets in your Eyes': Historicizing Visual Style in Mad Men. *In:* Edgerton, G. R., ed. *Mad Men.* London/New York: Tauris, 55-71.

Buxton, D., 1990. *From the Avengers to Miami Vice. Form and ideology in television series.* Manchester/New York: Manchester University Press.

Caldwell, J.T., 1995. *Televisuality. Style, Crisis, and Authority in American Television.* New Brunswick: Rutger University Press.

Calle de la, P., 1994. Teledeporte inicia mañana sus emisiones. *El Mundo*, 11 February.

Capilla, A. and Solé, J., 1999. *Telemanía. Las 500 mejores series de TV de neustra vida.* Spain: Salvat.

Cardwell, S., 2002. *Adaptation revisited. Television and the classic novel.* Manchester/New York: Manchester University Press.

Carol, M., 2009. El final de una leyenda. *La Vanguardia*, 4 May, p. 20.

Carroll, N., 1999. Film, Emotion, and Genre. *In:* Plantinga, C. and Smith, G.M., eds. *Passionate Views. Film, Cognition, and Emotion.* Baltimore/London: John Hopkins University Press, 21-47.

Català, J.M., 2009. *Pasión y conocimiento. El nuevo realismo melodramático.* Madrid: Cátedra.

Cavestany, J., 1998. Hollywood se inspira en las teleseries más famosas para realizar sus grandes producciones. *El País*, 17 August.

Çelik Norman, S., 2009. Nostalgia versus Feminism in British Costume Drama. *Ilitisim.* 10, 53-69.

cepes, 2002. No title. *Süddeutsche Zeitung (Freising)*, 6 August, p. R2.

Chandler, D. and Munday, R., 2011. *Oxford Dictionary of Media and Communication.* Oxford/New York: Oxford University Press.

Chase, M. and Shaw, C., 1989. The dimensions of nostalgia. *In:* Chase, M. and Shaw, C., eds. *The Imagined Past. History and Nostalgia.* Manchester University Press: Manchester, 1-17.

Chase, M. and Shaw, C., eds., 1989a. *The Imagined Past. History and Nostalgia.* Manchester University Press: Manchester.

Christiansen, B., 1909. *Philosophie der Kunst.* Hanau: Clauss & Feddersen.

Clarasó, N., 1956. El Estiolo "¡Oh!". *La Vanguardia Española*, 17 January, p. 5c.

Club de fans, 2011. *Knight Rider fan-club Spain* [online]. Available at: http://www.clubdefans.info/el-coche-fantastico/noticias [Accessed 2 September 2011].

Collector's Homepage (2011). *Mit Schirm, Charme und Melone* [online]. Available at: http://cyranos.ch/aveng-d.html [Accessed 28 September 2011].

Contreras, J.M. and Palacio, M., 2003. *La programación de televisión.* Madrid: Sintesis.

Cook, P., 2005. *Screening the past. Memory and nostalgia in cinema.* London: Routledge.

Cooke, P., 2003. Performing 'Ostalgie'. Leander Haussmann's Sonnenallee. *German Life and Letters*, 56 (2), 156-167.

Corbalán, A., 2009. Reconstrucción del pasado histórico. Nostalgia reflexiva en Cuéntame Cómo Pasó. *Journal of Spanish Cultural Studies*, 10 (3), 341-357.

Cornejo, A., 2008. Viva la vida. *El Mundo*, 23 July, p. 12j.

Corominas, J., 1981. *Diccionario Crítico Etimológico Castellano e Hispánico.* Madrid: Gredos.

Creeber, G., 2008. 24. *In:* Creeber, G., ed. *The television genre book.* 2nd edition. London: BFI Publishing, 27-28.

Croft, A., 1989. Forward to the 1930s. The literary politics of amnesia. *In:* Chase, M. and Shaw, C., eds. *The Imagined Past. History and Nostalgia.* Manchester University Press: Manchester, 147-169.

Cuartango, P., 2008. Vidas Paralelas/Ernest Benach/Michael Knight; Coches fantásticos. *El Mundo*, 25 October, p. 2b.

Cuatro, 2006. *Manuel Velasco vuelve a los fines de semana de Cuatrosfera* [online]. Available at: http://www.cuatro.com/mas-de-cuatro/Manuela-Velasco-vuelve-semana-Cuatrosfera_0_257374262.html [Accessed 22 July 2011].

Cuervo, J., 2004. El conductor fantástico. *La Vanguardia (Magazine)*, 27 June 2004, p. 77b.

Cuna, F., 1999. David Hasselhoff abandona "Los vigilantes de la playa" El actor realizará otras series, un musical y un disco. *El Mundo*, 23 September.

Das Vierte, 2007. *Pressemitteilung.* Press release [online]. 30 May. Available at: http://www.nbc-universal.de/nbc/data/cache/pdf/PM_283_das_vierte.pdf [Accessed 2 September 2011].

Davis, F., 1977. Nostalgia, Identity and the Current Nostalgia Wave. *Journal of Popular Culture*, 11 (2), 414-424.

Davis, F., 1979. *Yearning for Yesterday: A Sociology of Nostalgia.* New York/London: The Free Press.

Deacon, P., 1999. The media in modern Spanish culture. *In:* Gies, T.D., ed. *The Cambridge Companion to Modern Spanish Culture.* Cambridge: Cambridge University Press, 309-317.

Denk, 2009. Michael Knight. *tageszeitung*, 5 October.

D'Heil, S., 2011. Mit Schirm, Charme und Melone (Fanpage) [online]. Available at: http://www.steffi-line.de/archiv_text/nost_serie/k_schirm.htm [Accessed 28 September 2011].

Dhoest, A., 2007. Nostalgic memories: Qualitative reception analysis of Flemish TV fiction, 1953-1989. *Communications: The European Journal of Communication Research*, 32 (1), 31-50.

Die größten TV Hits aller Zeiten – die besten Kultserien. 2004. [CD] Universal.

Dika, V., 2003. Recycled Culture in Centemporary Art and Film: the Uses of Nostalgia. Cambridge: Cambridge University Press.

Dinauer, M., 1999. No title. *Süddeutsche Zeitung (Dachau)*, 18 March, p. 10.

Döveling, K., 2005. *Emotionen – Medien – Gemeinschaft. Eine kommunikations-soziologische Analyse.* Wiesbaden: Verlag für Sozialwissenschaften.

Döveling, K. et al., eds., 2011. *The Routledge Handbook of Emotions and Mass Media.* London: Routledge.

Duden, 2012. Duden Online. Search for "verträumt" [online]. Available at: http://www.duden.de/rechtschreibung/vertraeumt [Accessed 2 October 2012].

Duden, 2012a. Duden Online. Search for "stylisch" [online]. Available at: http://www.duden.de/rechtschreibung/stylish [Accessed 13 June 2012].

Dyer, R., 2005. Film, Musik und Gefühl – Ironische Anbindung. Translated from English by P. Brunner. *In*: Brütsch, M. et al., eds. *Kinogefühle. Emotionalität und Film.* Marburg: Schüren, 121-135.

Ebbrecht, T., 2008. Gefühlte Erinnerung. Überlegungen zum emotionalen Erleben von Geschichte im Spielfilm. *In:* Ebbrecht, T. and Schick, T., eds. *Emotion – Empathie – Figur. Spielformen der Filmwahrnehmung.* Berlin: Vistas, 85-106.

Eberwein, A., 1998. Remakes and Cultural Studies. *In*: Horton, A. and McDougal, S.Y., eds. *Play it again, Sam. Retakes on Remakes.* Berkeley/Los Angeles/London: University of California Press, 15-33.

Eder, J., 2002. Aufmerksamkeit ist keine Selbstverständlichkeit. Eine Diskurskritik und Klärungsvorschlag. *In:* Hickethier, K. and Bleicher, J.K., eds. Aufmerksamkeit, Medien und Ökonomie. *In*: Hickethier, K., ed. *Beiträge zur Medienästhetik und Mediengeschichte*, Vol. 13, Hamburg: LIT, 15-47.

Eder, J., 2005. Die Wege der Gefühle. Ein integratives Modell der Anteilnahme an Filmfiguren. *In:* Brütsch, M. et al., eds. *Kinogefühle. Emotionalität und Film.* Marburg: Schüren, 225-242.

Edgerton, G.R., 2011. Introduction. When Our Parents became us. *In*: Edgerton, G.R., ed. *Mad Men.* London/New York: Tauris, xxi-xxxvi.

Edmondson, R., 1997. *AV Archiving: changes, choices and challenges* [online]. Screening the Past. Available at: http://www.latrobe.edu.au/screeningthepast/firstrelease/firjul/ray.html [Accessed on 16 April 2011].

EFE, 2009. Fallece Valerio Lazarov, un 'revolucionario' de la televisión. *El País.* [online] 11 August. Available at:http://www.elpais.com/articulo/cultura/Fallece/

Valerio/Lazarov/revolucionario/television/elpepucul/20090811elpepucu
l_1/Tes [Accessed 28 April 2011].

El Coche Fantástico: Temporada 1. 2008. [DVD] Universal Studios.

Elcochefantastico.net, 2011. *Knight Rider discussion forum Spain* [online]. Available at: http://www.elcochefantastico.net/ [Accessed 2 September 2011].

El Doblaje, 2010. *Ficha Doblaje. Los Vengadores (4x08).* Synchronization of John Steed (Patrick Macnee) in Spain [online]. Available at: http://www.eldoblaje. com/datos/FichaPelicula.asp?id=19578 [Accessed 1 November 2011].

El Doblaje, 2011. *Ficha Doblaje. Los Vengadores (1998).* Synchronization of John Steed (Ralph Fiennes) in Spain [online]. Available at: http://www.eldoblaje. com/datos/FichaPelicula.asp?id=3963 [Accessed 15 November 2011].

El Mundo, 2010. Album. *El Mundo,* 3 August, p. 6d.

El País, 1997. TV Programme. *El País,* 4 November.

El País, 2007. La lucha de David Hasselhoff contra el alcohol. *El País,* 5 May, p. 59b.

El País, 2009a. No title. *El País,* 16 July.

Elsaesser, T., 2005. "Zu spät zu früh". Körper, Zeit und Aktionsraum in der Kinoerfahrung. *In:* Brütsch, M. et al., eds. *Kinogefühle. Emotionalität und Film.* Marburg: Schüren, 415-439.

Enciclopedia Universal Ilustrada, 1958. *Etimologías Sánscrito, Hebreo, Griego, etc. Tomo XXXVIII.* Madrid: Espasa-Calpe.

Encyclopaedia Britannica, 2012. *Encyclopaedia Britannica Online.* Search for "Renaissance furniture" [online]. Available at: http://www.britannica.com/ EBchecked/topic/222627/furniture [Accessed 14 February 2012].

Encyclopaedia Britannica, 2012a. *Encyclopaedia Britannica Online.* Search for "Renaissance musical performance" [online]. Available at: http://www.britannica.com/EBchecked/topic/399251/musical-performance/644 86/The-Renaissance [Accessed 16 September 2012].

Encyclopaedia Britannica, 2012b. *Encyclopaedia Britannica Online.* Search for "lute" [online]. Available at: http://www.britannica.com/EBchecked/topic/ 351873/lute [Accessed 16 September 2012].

Engell, L. and Kissel, W., 1994. Das allmähliche Verschwinden der Aufklärer. *Frankfurter Allgemeine Zeitung (Bilder und Zeiten),* 22 October, p.1.

Enns, A., 2007. The politics of Ostalgie: post-socialist nostalgia in recent German film. *Screen,* 48 (4), 475-491.

Ernst, W., 2007. *Das Gesetz des Gedächtnisses. Medien und Archive am Ende (des 20. Jahrhunderts).* Berlin: Kadmos.

EvaSF, 2005. *Los canales de TVE en digital* [online]. Vayatele. Available at: http://www.vayatele.com/tve-1/los-canales-de-tve-en-digital [Accessed 3 July 2011].

Eysenck, M.W. and Keane, M.T., 2005. *Cognitive Psychology. A student's handbook.* 5th edition. Hove/New York: Psychology Press.

Feldmer, S., 2006. Wo geht's hier nach Hollywood? *Süddeutsche Zeitung*, 6 March.

Felluga, D., 2011. Modules on Jameson: On Postmodernity. Introductory Guide to Critical Theory [online]. 31 January. Available at: http://www.purdue.edu/ guidetotheory/postmodernism/modules /jamesonpostmodernity.html [Accessed 28 September 2012].

Fernández-Quijada, D. and Fortino, M., 2009. Servicio público de televisión y patrimonio audiovisual: el proyecto VideoActive. *El profesional de la información*, 18 (5), 545-551.

Festenberg von, N., 2011. ZDF-Historienserie "Borgia": Der Papst das Ferkel. *Der Spiegel*, [online] 17 October 2011. Available at: http://www.spiegel.de/ kultur/tv/0,1518,792158,00.html [Accessed 8 February 2012].

Feyerabend, B., 2009. *Seems like old times. Postmodern nostalgia in Woody Allen's Work*. Heidelberg: Universitätsverlag.

Filmoteca Valencia, 1989. *Nostalgia de la aventura*. Valencia: Conselleria de Cultura, Educació i Ciència, Vol. 1.

Fischer, F., 2009. *"Mrs. Peel, wir werden gebraucht!". Mit Schirm, Charme und Melone – Das Buch zur Serie*. Bertz: Berlin.

Fischer, V., 1980. *Nostalgie. Geschichte und Kultur als Trödelmarkt*. Luzern/Frankfurt: Verlag C. J. Bucher.

Fiske, J., 1987. *Television Culture*. London: Methuen & Co.

Formula TV, 2009. *La secuela de 'El coche fantástico' aterriza en el prime time del jueves* [online]. Formula TV, 5 July. Available at: http://www.formulatv.com/ 1,20090705,11986,1.html [Accessed 25 October 2011].

Formulat TV, 2011. Ratings of El coche fantástico (2008) in Spain [online]. Formula TV. Available at: http://www.formulatv.com/series/280/el-coche-fantastico/ audiencias/capitulos/, [Accessed 2 October 2011].

Formula TV, 2011a. Canal+ Dos programa un marathon de la cuarta temporada de 'Mad men' [online]. Formula TV, 3 June. Available at: http://www.formulatv.com/noticias/19947/canal-plus-dos-programa-maraton-cuarta-temporada-mad-men/ [Accessed 29 November 2011].

Formula TV, 2011b. *Ratings of Mad Men* [online]. Formula TV. Available at: http://www.formulatv.com/series/204/mad-men/audiencias/capitulos/ [Accessed 29 November 2011].

Formula TV, 2011c. *Cosmopolitan estrena en exclusica 'Borgia' el próximo domingo 23*. [online] Formula TV. 18 October. Available at: http://www.formulatv.com/noticias/21719/cosmopolitan-estrena-exclusiva-borg ias-domingo-23/ [Accessed 8 February 2012].

Forn, M., 2008. Nueva vida para series viejas. *La Vanguardia (Vivir)*, 1 November, p. 13a.

Frankfurter Allgemeine Sonntagszeitung, 1995. Heute sehenswert. *Frankfurter Allgemeine Sonntagszeitung*, 6 August, p. 32.

Frankfurter Allgemeine Sonntagszeitung, 1996. Knight Rider/The Highwayman Zwei amerikanische Actionserien. *Frankfurter Allgemeine Sonntagszeitung*, 16 June, p. 32.

Frijda, N.H., 1986. *The Emotions*. Cambridge: University Press.

Fromme, C., 2010. Looking for Stadl. *Süddeutsche Zeitung (Bayern)*, 24 April, p. 13.

Frutkin, A., 2008. Back to the Past. *Mediaweek*, 18 (37), p. 6.

Furno-Lamude, D. and Anderson, J., 1992. The Uses and Gratifications of rerun viewings. *Journalism Quarterly*, 69 (2), 362-372.

Gabbard, K., 2008. Hombres de Película. *In:* Carabí, À. And Armengols, J.A., eds. *Masculinidad al Debate*. Barcelona: Icaria, 47-64.

Gärtner, S., 1998. 60er-Jahre-Kult auf großer Leinwand. *Berliner Zeitung*, [online] 24 August. Available at: http://www.berliner-zeitung.de/archiv/neuauflage-der-fernsehserie--mit-schirm--charme-und-melone-kommt-am-donnerstag-in-die-kinos-60er-jahre-kult-auf-grosser-leinwand,10810590,9469358.html [Accessed 7 December 2012].

García de Castro, M., 2002. *La ficción televisiva popular. Una evolución de las series de televisión en España*. Barcelona: gidesa.

García Monzó, J.M. and Marco Rubio, S., 2000. *Con la Muerte en los talones*. Valencia: Octaedro.

García-Muñoz et al., 2012. The occupational roles of television fiction characters in Spain: distinguishing traits in gender representation. *Comunicación y Sociedad*, XXV (1), 349-366.

Garcia Ruipérez, G., 2011. Madrileños, Naranjito ha vuelto. *El Mundo*, 4 May, p. 6e.

Gehlen, A., 1976. Das entflohene Glück. Eine Deutung der Nostalgie. *Merkur. Deutsche Zeitschrift für europäisches Denken*, 30 (5), 432-442.

Georgescu, V., 1998. Superrechner mit der Lizenz zum Fahren. *Süddeutsche Zeitung*, 1 December.

Gibbs, J., 2002. *Mise-en-scène. Film Style and Interpretation*. London/New York: Wallflower.

gol/dpa, 2011. Borgia bei Pro7 schwächer als im ZDF. *Der Spiegel,* [online] 10 November. Available at: http://www.spiegel.de/kultur/tv/0,1518,796953,00.html [Accessed 8 February 2012].

Goldbeck, K., 2004. *Gute Unterhaltung, schlechte Unterhaltung. Die Fernsehkritik und das Populäre*. Bielefeld: transcript.

Golz, H.-G., 2003. Editorial. *In:* Bundeszentrale für Politische Bildung, ed. *Aus Politik und Zeitgeschichte. Beilage zur Wochenzeitschrift Das Parlament*, 45, 3 November, p. 2.

Gombrich, E. H., 1985. *Das symbolische Bild. Zur Kunst der Renaissance II*. Stuttgart: Klett.

Gombrich, E.H., 1996. *Die Geschichte der Kunst*. 16th edition. Frankfurt a.M.: S. Fischer.

Gómez, L., 1997. 'Los Vengadores', contra Sean Connery. *El País,* [online] 17 July. Available at: http://elpais.com/diario/1997/07/17/ultima/869090401_850215. html [Accessed 12 December 2012].

Gómez, L., 1997a. Soy la quintaesencia del 'gentleman'. *El País,* [online] 24 August. Available at: http://elpais.com/diario/1997/08/24/cultura/872373608_850215. html [Accessed 12 December 2012].

González-Fierro Santos, J.M. and Mena, J.L., 2008. *Las mejores series de la historia de televisión.* Madrid: Cacitel.

Gottschalk, L.A. and Gleser, G.C., 1980. Spezifische Aspekte unseres sprachinhaltsanalytischen Ansatzes. *In:* Schöfer, G., ed. *Gottschalk-Gleser-Sprachinhaltsanalyse. Theorie und Technik. Studien zur Messung ängstlicher und aggressiver Affekte.* Weinheim/Basel: Beltz Verlag, 15-41.

Graham, A., 1984. History, Nostalgia, and the Criminality of Popular Culture. *Georgia Review,* 38 (2), 348-364.

Grainge, P., 2002. *Monochrome Memories: Nostalgia and Style in Retro America.* Westport/London: Praeger.

Gregorovius, F., 2011. *Lucrezia Borgia.* Hamburg: tredition/Projekt Gutenberg.

Groys, B., 2004. *Über das Neue. Versuch einer Kulturökonomie.* Frankfurt a.M.: Fischer.

Güntzel, K., 2000. "Automania" - die Jagd nach Emma Peels weißem Lotus. *Süddeutsche Zeitung,* 5 June.

Gutiérrez Gili, J., 1936. Sentido de lo natural. *La Vanguardia,* 31 May, p. 5c.

Hackl, C., 2001. *Fernsehen im Lebenslauf. Eine medienbiografische Studie.* Konstanz: UVK.

Haderer, C. and Bachschwöll, W., 1996. *Kultserien im Fernsehen.* München: Heyne.

Haible, E., 2003. *Narrative Strukturen und Spannungserleben im Film.* Diploma Thesis. HFF "Konrad Wolf".

Hall, S., 1973. Encoding, Decoding in Television Discourse. *In:* During, S. ed, 2000. *The Cultural Studies Reader.* 2nd edition. London/New York: Routledge, 507-517.

Hall, S., 1992. Cultural Studies and its Theoretical Legacies. *In:* Grossberg, L. et al. eds. *Cultural Studies.* London/New York: Routledge, 277-286.

Hart, J., 1973. Toward a phenomenology of nostalgia. *Man and World,* 6, (4), 397-420.

Haralovich, M.B., 2011. Women on the Verge of the second Wave. *In:* Edgerton, G.R., ed. *Mad Men.* London/New York: Tauris, 159-176.

Hediger, V. (2002): Des einen Fetisch ist des andern Cue. Kognitive und psychoanalytische Filmtheorie. Lehren aus einem verpassten Rendez-vous. *In:* Wulff, H.-J. and Sellmer, J., eds. *Film und Psychologie nach der kognitiven Phase? Schriftenreihe der Gesellschaft für Medienwissenschaft GFM,* Marburg: Schüren, 41-58.

Heidemann, G., 2002. Entwicklung der DDR bis Ende der 80er Jahre. *Informationenen zur Politischen Bildung,* [online] 270, 4 April. Available at: http://www.bpb.de/publikationen/0447933752483194102048249444688,0,0,E ntwicklung_der_DDR_bis_Ende_der_80er_Jahre.html [Accessed 7 August 2011].

Hellmann, J., 2006. Vietnam and the 1960s. *In:* Bigsby, C., ed. *The Cambridge Companion to Modern American Culture.* Cambridge: Cambridge University Press, 295-313.

Helwig, G., 1997. Entwicklung der Neuen Frauenbewegung, *Informationen zur Politischen Bildung,* [online] 254. Available at: http://www.bpb.de/ publikationen/D6SSWQ,2,0,Frau_und_Gesellschaft.html#art2 [Accessed 6 September 2011].

Helwig, G., 1997a. Einleitung, *Informationen zur Politischen Bildung,* [online] 254. Available at: http://www.bpb.de/publikationen/D6SSWQ,0,0,Frau_und_Gesell schaft.html#art0, [Accessed 1 October 2011].

Helwig, G., 1997b. Gleichberechtigung als Grundrecht. Offizielle Leitbilder der 50er und 60er Jahre, *Informationen zur Politischen Bildung,* [online] 254. Available at: http://www.bpb.de/publikationen/2FD0S4,0,0,Gleichberechtigung_als_ Grundrecht.html, [Accessed 1 October 2011].

Hepp, A., 2005. Kommunikative Aneignung. *In:* Mikos, L. and Wegener, C., eds. *Qualitative Medienforschung. Ein Handbuch.* Konstanz: UVK, 67-79.

Hepp, A., 2009. Transculturality as a Perspective: Researching Media Cultures Comparatively. *Qualitative Research Net,* [online] Forum: Qualitative Social Research (FQS), 10 (1), Art. 26. Available at: http://www.qualitative-research.net/index.php/fqs/article/view/1221/2657 [Accessed 1 April 2012].

her, 2003. Diana-Rigg-Hommage. Mit Emmas Charme. *Süddeutsche Zeitung (SZ-Extra),* 17 July, p. 5.

Hermanski, 1998. Die neuen Kleider der Emma Peel. *Süddeutsche Zeitung (SZ-Extra),* 27 August, p. 3.

Herms, B. J.M., 1998. Hasselhoff, doble sesión. *La Vanguardia (Vivir),* 13 July, p. 8a.

Herms, B.J.M., 1990. Vuelven "Los Vengadores". *La Vanguardia (Revista),* 11 November, p. 7a.

Herrera-De La Muela, T., 2009. Nostalgia y mitos transicionales de sobremesa en Verano Azul. In: López, F. et al., eds. *Historias de la pequeña pantalla: representaciones históricas en la televisión de la España democrática.* Frankfurt a.M./Madrid: Vervuert/Iberoabermicana, 157-172.

Hickethier, K., 1991. Die Zugewinngemeinschaft. Zum Verhältnis von Film und Fernsehen in den sechziger und siebziger Jahren. *In:* Hoffmann, H. and Schobert, W., eds. *Abschied vom Gestern. Bundesdeutscher Film der sechziger und siebziger Jahre.* Frankfurt a.M.: Deutsches Filmmuseum, 190-211.

Hickethier, K., 1998. *Geschichte des Deutschen Fernsehens.* Stuttgart/Weimar: J.B. Metzler Verlag.

Hickethier, K., 2001. *Film- und Fernsehanalyse.* Stuttgart/Weimar: J.B. Metzler Verlag.

Higson, A., 1993. Re-presenting the National past: Nostalgia and Pastiche in the Heritage film. *In*: Friedman, L., ed. *Fires Were Started: British Cinema and Thatcherism.* 1st edition. Minneapolis: University of Minesota Press, 109-129.

Higson, A., 2003. *English Heritage, English Cinema. Costume Drama since 1980.* New York: Oxford University Press.

Higson, A., 2006. Re-presenting the National past: Nostalgia and Pastiche in the Heritage film. *In*: Friedman, L., ed. *Fires Were Started: British Cinema and Thatcherism.* 2nd edition. London: Wallflower Press, 91-109.

Hirsch, M., 2001. Surviving Images. Holocaust Photographs and the Work of Postmemory. *The Yale Yournal of Criticism*, 14 (1), 5-37.

Hirsch, M. and Spitzer, L., 2002. We would never have come without you. Generations of Nostalgia. *American Imago*, 59 (3), 253-276.

Hirschbiegel, O., 2011. *Interview in TV-Digital* Interviewed by Mike Powelz, [online] TV-Digital, 30 August 2011. Available at: http://www.tvdigital.de/magazin/interviews/regisseur-oliver-hirschbiegel-im-interview [Accessed 13 February 2012].

Hodgson, G., 2006. The American century. *In*: Bigsby, C., ed. *The Cambridge Companion to Modern American Culture.* Cambridge: Cambridge University Press, 33-52.

Hoffmann, D. and Kutscha, A., 2010. Medienbiografien. Konsequenzen medialen Handelns, ästhetischer Präferenz und Erfahrungen. *In*: Hoffmann, D. and Mikos, L., eds. *Mediensozialisationstheorien. Neue Modelle und Ansätze in der Diskussion.* 2nd edition. Wiesbaden: VS Verlag, 221-244.

Holak, S. and Havlena, W., 1998. Feelings, Fantasies, and Memories. An Examination of the Emotional Components of Nostalgia. *Journal of Business Research*, 42, 217-226.

Holdsworth, A., 2011. *Television, Memory and Nostalgia.* London: Palgrave Macmillan.

Horton, A. and McDougal, S.Y., 1998. Introduction. *In*: Horton, A. and McDougal, S.Y., eds. *Play it again, Sam. Retakes on Remakes.* Berkeley/Los Angeles/London: University of California Press, 1-11.

Hoskins, A., 2004. Television and the Collapse of Memory. *Time & Society*, 13 (1), 109-127.

Hutcheon, L., 1984. *A Poetics of Postmodernism: History, Theory, Fiction.* London: Routledge.

Hutcheon, L., 2000. Irony, nostalgia, and the postmodern. *In*: Vervliet, R. and Fischer, A., eds. *Methods of the Study of Literature as Cultural Memory.* Amsterdam: Rodopi, 189-207.

I.G., 2009. Adiós al 'rey del zoom'. *El País*, [online] 12 August. Available at: http://www.elpais.com/articulo/Pantallas/Adios/rey/zoom/elpepirtv/20090812el pepirtv_2/Tes [Accessed 28 April 2011].

Imfernsehen, 2011. *Dates of broadcasting of Knight Rider* [online]. Imfernsehen. Available at: http://www.fernsehserien.de/index.php?serie=352&seite=8 [Accessed 7 August 2011].

Imfernsehen, 2011a. *Dates of broadcasting of Mit Schirm, Charme und Melone* [online]. Imfernsehen. Available at: http://www.fernsehserien.de/index.php?serie=836&sender=&seite=6&start=100 [Accessed 11 August 2011].

Imfernsehen, 2011b. *Dates of broadcasting of Mit Schirm, Charme und Melone* in Germany [online]. Imfernsehen. Available at: http://wunschliste.de/2373/tv [Accessed 5 September 2011].

Innis, H., 1972. *Empire & Communications.* Toronto/Buffalo: University of Toronto Press.

Jameson, F., 1991. *Postmodernism, or, the cultural logic of late capitalism.* Duke University Press: Durham.

Jameson, F., 1998. Postmodernism and Consumer Society. In: Jameson, F., ed. *The Cultural Turn. Selected Writings on the Postmodern. 1983-1998.* London/New York: Verso, 1-20.

Jimenez, B., 1987. David Hasselhoff, un actor popular que quiere ser cantante. *La Vanguardia (Clasificados)*, 19 July, p. 31a.

Jimenez, E., 1996. Asuntos Exteriores. *El Mundo*, 14 November, p. 61b.

Johnson, M.K. and Multhaup K. S., 1992. Emotion and MEM. *In*: Christianson, S-Å., ed. *The handbook of emotion and memory.* Hilsdale: Lawrence Erlbaum Associates, 33-66.

Jordan, B. and Morgan-Tamosunas, R., 2000. Introduction. *In*: Jordan, B. and Morgan-Tamosunas, R., eds. *Contemporary Spanish cultural studies.* New York: Oxford University Press, 1-12.

Jose, J. and Moreno M. 2003. Bombín, paraguas y cuero: agentes para la eternidad. *El País (ciberpaís)*, [online] 17 April. Available from: http://elpais.com/diario/2003/04/17/ciberpais/1050544947_850215.html [Accessed 12 December 2012].

Juliá, S., 1999. History, politics, and culture, 1975-1996. *In*: Gies, T.D., ed. *The Cambridge Companion to Modern Spanish Culture.* Cambridge: Cambridge University, 104-120.

Kappelhoff, H., 2005. Tränenseligkeit. Das sentimentale Geniessen und das melodramatische Kino. *In*: Brütsch, M. et al., eds. *Kinogefühle. Emotionalität und Film.* Marburg: Schüren, 33-49.

Keightley, E. and Pickering, M., 2006. For the record. Popular music and photography as technologies of memory. *European Journal of Cultural Studies*, 9 (2), 149-165.

Keightley, E and Pickering, M., 2012. The mnemonic imagination. Remembering as creative practice. London: Palgrave Macmillan.

Keller, H., 1998. *Kultserien und ihre Stars.* Berlin: Bertz+Fischer.

Keuneke, S., 2005. Qualitatives Intverview. *In*: Mikos, L. and Wegener, C., eds. *Qualitative Medienforschung. Ein Handbuch.* Konstanz: UVK, 254-267.

Kilb, A., 2002. Träumen Geparden von Studiomikrofonen?. *Frankfurter Allgemeine Zeitung*, 14 December, p. 40b.

Kirchenwitz, L., 2003. 1968 im Osten – Was ging uns die Bundesrepublik an?. *In*: Bundeszentrale für Politische Bildung, ed. *Aus Politik und Zeitgeschichte. Beilage zur Wochenzeitschrift Das Parlament*, 45, 3 November, pp. 6-8.

Kirchhoff, S., et al., 2010. Der Fragebogen. 5th edition. Wiesbaden: VS Verlag.

Klippel, H., 1997. *Gedächtnis und Kino.* Frankfurt a. M.: Stroemfeld Verlag.

Klippel, H. and Winkler, H., 1994. 'Gesund ist, was sich wiederholt'. Zur Rolle der Redundanz im Fernsehen. *In*: Hickethier, K., ed. *Aspekte der Fernsehanalyse. Methoden und Modelle.* Münster/Hamburg: Lit, 121-136.

Kompare, D., 2005. *Rerun Nation. How Repeats Invented American Television.* New York/London: Routledge.

Krei, A., 2009. *RTL: "Knight Rider" verliert auf hohem Niveau* [online]. Quotenmeter, 25 October 2009. Available at: http://www.quotenmeter.de/cms/?p1=n&p2=38048&p3= [Accessed 26 March 2012].

Krei, A., 2009a. *Ratings Knight Rider in Germany* [online]. Quotenmeter, 18 October 2009. Available at: http://www.quotenmeter.de/cms/?p1=n&p2=37903&p3= [Accessed 25 March 2012].

Kremkau, S., 2003. *Vergangenheit, Erinnerung und Nostalgie im englischen Roman nach 1945.* Göttingen: Cuvillier.

Krotz, F., 1993. Emotionale Aspekte der Fernsehnutzung. Konzeptionelle Überlegungen zu einem vernachlässigten Thema. *In*: Hügel, H.-O. and Müller, E., eds. *Fernsehshows. Form- und Rezeptionsanalyse. Dokumentation einer Arbeitstagung an der Universität Hildesheim.* Hildesheim: Institut für Theater und Medienwissenschaften, 91-119.

Kucinski, S., 2012. Mit Schirm, Charme und Melone [online]. Available at: http://www.sk96.de/sk_av.htm [Accessed 30 July 2012].

Kuckartz, U., 2010. *Einführung in die computergestützte Analyse qualitativer Daten.* 3rd edition. Wiesbaden: VS Verlag.

Kumar, K. et al., 2006. Construction of Memory. *In*: Volkmer, I. ed. *News in public memory. An international study of media memories across generations.* New York: Peter Lang, 211-224.

Laffond Rueda, J.C. and Gómez Guerra, A., 2009. Televisión y nostalgia. The Wonder Years y Cuéntame cómo pasó, *Revista Latina de Comunicación Social*, [online] 64, pp. 396-409. Available at: http://www.ull.es/publicaciones/latina/09/art/32_831_55_Complutense/Rueda_y_Guerra.html [Accessed 29.11.2011].

Lamnek, S., 2005. *Gruppendiskussion.* 2nd edition. Weinheim: Beltz.

Landsberg, A., 1995. Prosthetic Memory. Total Recall and Blade Runner. *In:* Featherstone, M. and Burrows, R., eds. *Cyberspace/Cyberbodies/Cyberpunk. Cultures of Technological Embodiment.* 4th edition. London/Thousand Oaks/New Delhi: Sage, 175-189.

Landsberg, A., 1997. America, the Holocaust, and the Mass Culture of Memory: Toward a Radical Politics of Empathy. *New German Critique*, Spring-Summer (71), 63-86.

Lasch, C., 1984. The Politics of Nostalgia. Losing History and Mists of Ideology. *Haper's*, 269 (1614), 65-70.

La Vanguardia Española, 1970. Programas de Radio. *La Vanguardia Española*, 15 March, p. 44b.

La Vanguardia Española, 1974. La Decadencia de la Pareja Comica. *La Vanguardia Española*, 11 March, p. 56b.

La Vanguardia, 1985. TVE estrena hoy "El coche fantástico", serie de ciencia-ficción y aventuras en la sobremesa. *La Vanguardia*, 1 August, p. 44.

La Vanguardia, 1990. Antena 3 TV compra un importante lote de series. *La Vanguardia (Revista)*, 1 September 1990, p. 7.

La Vanguardia, 1990a. "Los Vengadores" vuelve a TVE1 el 4 de noviembre. *La Vanguadia (Revista)*, 18 October, p. 5a.

La Vanguardia, 1991. Televisión. *La Vanguardia (Revista)*, 18 July, p. 6.

La Vanguardia, 1991a. Televisión. *La Vanguardia (Revista)*, 1 August, p. 8.

La Vanguardia, 1997. TV Programme. *La Vanguarida (Vivir en Girona)*, 24 November, p. 7.

La Vanguardia, 1999. Canal+ dedica hoy casi trece horas a la TV como medio. *La Vanguardia (Vivir)*, 10 March, p. 11a.

La Vanguardia, 2000. Sin pareja y con 'vengadora'. *La Vanguardia*, 8 February, p. 20.

La Vanguardia, 2006. Td8 estrena esta noche la serie de acción 'Los vigilantes de la noche'. *La Vanguardia (Vivir)*, 10 September, p. 13b.

La Vanguardia, 2009. El coche que se reinventa. *La Vanguardia (Edición sabado)*, 28 March, p. 29a.

La Vanguardia, 2009a. Para destacar. *La Vanguardia (Vivir)*, 9 July, p. 13.

La Vanguardia, 2009b. Para destacar. *La Vanguardia (Vivir)*, 15 July, p. 13.

La Vanguardia, 2011. *La Hemeroteca de la Vanguardia desde 1881.* Search for Nostalgia [online]. La Vanguardia. Available at: http://hemeroteca.lavanguardia. es/search.html?fromISO=true&q=nostalgia&aux=nostalgia&bd=01&bm=02&b y=1881&ed=01&em=12&ey=2011&x=0&y=0 [Accessed 1 March 2011].

La Vanguardia, 2011a. TV Programme. *La Vanguardia (TVMania)*, 12 November, p. 16.

La Vanguardia, 2012: La Hemeroteca de la Vanguardia desde 1881. Search for Twist. [online]. La Vanguardia. Available at: http://hemeroteca.lavanguardia.

com/search.html?q=%22twist%22&bd=01&bm=01&by=1950&ed=31&em=12 &ey=1971&keywords=&__checkbox_home=true&edition=&exclude=&x=53& y=11&excludeAds=true&sortBy=&order= [Accessed 21 August 2012].

Legg, S., 2004. Review Essay. Memory and Nostalgia. *Cultural Geographies*, 11, 99-107.

Leitch, T., 1990. Twice-Told Tales: The Rhetoric of the Remake. *Literature/Film Quarterly*, 18 (3), 138-149.

Leitch, T., 2003. Twelve Fallacies in Contemporary Adaptation Theory. *Criticism*, 45 (2), 149-171.

Lersch, E., 2008. *Richesses et complexités de la mémoire audiovisuelle en Allemagne* [online]. Institut National du Patrimoine. Available at: http://mediatheque-numerique.inp.fr/index.php/actes_de_colloque/archimages/cinema_et_audiovis uel_quelles_memoires_numeriques_pour_l_europe/richesses_et_complexites_d e_la_memoire_audiovisuelle_en_allemagne [Accessed 13 April 2011].

L.G., 1997. Tres estrellas para el salto a la gran pantalla. *El País*, 24 August.

Liebes, T. and Katz, E., 1990. *The Export of Meaning. Cross-Cultural Readings of Dallas.* New York/Oxford: Oxford University Press.

Linke, N., 1987. Die Rezeption der Programme von ARD und ZDF in der DDR als Gegenstand der SED Kommunikationspolitik. *Publizistik*, 32, 45-68.

Lipsitz, G., 1994. *Time Passages. Collective memory and American popular culture.* 3rd edition. Minneapolis: University of Minnesota Press.

Listri, M., 2009. La última batalla de Pontiac. *El País (Motor)*, 6 June.

Livestream (2012): Nostalgic. Un canal para recorder [online]. Available from: www.livestream.com/nostalgic [Accessed 15 September 2012].

Llopart, S., 2010. Dinvinas de la Muerte. *La Vanguardia*, 19 August, p. 21b.

Llopart, S., 1998. 'Los Vengadores' preparan el camino al 'Tango' de Saura. *La Vanguardia*, 24 September, p. 55a.

Löbert, A., 2006. Ein hoffnungsloser Fall. *tageszeitung*, [online] 13 October. Available at: http://www.taz.de/1/archiv/print-archiv/printressorts/digi-artikel/?ressort=tz&dig= 2006 %2F10%2F13%2Fa0192&cHash=6e68567892 [Accessed 7.12.2012].

López, F., et al., eds., 2009. Historias de la pequeña pantalla: representaciones históricas en la televisión de la España democrática. Frankfurt a.M./Madrid: Vervuert/Iberoabermicana.

Loschke, I., 2005. *Reclams Mode- und Kostümlexikon.* Stuttgart: Reclam.

Lowenthal, D., 1989. Nostalgia tells it like it wasn't. *In*: Chase, M. and Shaw, C., eds. *The Imagined Past. History and Nostalgia.* Manchester University Press: Manchester, 18-32.

Lowenthal, D., 1986. *The Past is a Foreign Country.* 2nd edition (reprint). Cambridge: Cambridge University Press.

Ludewig, A., 2006. 'Ostalgie' und 'Westalgie' als Ausdruck von Heimatsehnsüchten. Eine Reise in die Traumfabriken deutscher Filme. *In*:

Gebhard, Gunter et al., eds. Heimat. Konturen und Konjunkturen eines umstrittenen Konzepts. Bielefeld: Transcript, 141-160.

Ludewig, A., 2011. *Screening Nostalgia. 100 Years of German Heimat Film.* Bielefeld: transcript.

malt, 1998. Nicht nur mit Schirm, Charme und Melone. *Süddeutsche Zeitung (SZ-Extra)*, 8 October, p. 5.

malt, 2008. Für immer Emma: Diana Rigg. *Frankfurter Allgemeine Zeitung*, 19 July, p. 35b.

Maldonado, L., 1975. *Religiosidad popular. Nostalgia de lo mágico.* Madrid: Cristiandad.

Mangold, R., et al., 2001. Zur Erklärung emotionaler Medienwirkungen. Fortentwicklung theoretischer Ansätze. *In*: Rössler, P. et al., eds. *Theoretische Perspektiven der Rezeptionsforschung.* München: R. Fischer, 164-180.

Manuls, 2007. *Ficción Internacional. Vuelve el Coche Fantástico* [online]. Vayatele. Available at: http://www.vayatele.com/ficcion-internacional/vuelve-el-coche-fantastico [Accessed 19 July 2011].

Martenstein, H., 1998. Wenn der Charme fehlt. Die Kultserie "Mit Schirm, Charme und Melone" im Kino. *Der Tagesspiegel*, 26 August.

Martínez, C., 2010. Are you ready for TV? [online]. Museum d'Art Contemporani de Barcelona (MACBA). Available at: http://www.macba.cat/en/exhibition-ready-for-tv [Accessed 8 April 2011].

Martínez, C., 2010a. Television Atmosphere. *In*: Martínez, C., et al., eds. *Are you ready for* TV. Barcelona: Museu d'Art Contemporani de Barcelona, 4-9.

Mateos, P.P. and Campelo, S., 2009. Operación bikini en TV. *ABC*, 1 July, p. 91a.

Mayring, P., 2010. *Qualitative Inhaltsanalyse. Grundlagen und Techniken.* 11th edition. Weinheim/Basel: Beltz.

Mayring, P. and Hurst, A., 2005. Qualitative Inhaltsanalyse. *In*: Mikos, L. and Wegener, C., eds. *Qualitative Medienforschung. Ein Handbuch.* Konstanz: UVK, 436-444.

Meyer, M., 2010. Die ARD in der DDR. *In*: Bundeszentrale für Politische Bildung, ed. *Aus Politik und Zeitgeschichte. Beilage zur Wochenzeitschrift Das Parlament*, 20, 17 May, pp. 28-34.

Mikos, L., 1996. The Experience of Suspense. Between Fear and Pleasure. *In*: Vorderer, P., et al., eds. *Suspense. Conceptualizations, Theoretical Analyses, and Empirical Explorations.* Mahwah: Lawrence Erlbaum Associates, 37-49.

Mikos, L., 2001. *Fern-Sehen. Bausteine einer Rezeptionsästhetik des Fernsehens.* Berlin: Vistas.

Mikos, L., 2001a. Rezeption und Aneignung. *In*: Rössler, P., et al. eds. *Theoretische Perspektiven der Rezeptionsforschung.* München: R. Fischer, 59-71.

Mikos, L. and Prommer, E., 2005. Das Babelsberger Modell. *In*: Mikos, L. and Wegener, C., eds. *Qualitative Medienforschung. Ein Handbuch.* Konstanz: UVK, 162-169.

Mikos, L. and Prommer, E., 2007. The Babelsberg Approach: Critical Audience Research. Conference Paper. International Communication Association 2007 Annual Meeting, Abstract only [online]. Available through: UAB library http://www.uab.cat/servlet/Satellite?c=Page&cid=1100266971243&pagename= BibUAB%2FPage%2FTemplatePageBib2UAB [Accessed 4 December 2012].

Mikos, L., 2008. Film- und Fernsehanalyse. 2nd revised ed. Konstanz: UVK.

Miller, T., 1997. The Avengers. London: British Film Institute.

Miller, T., 2001. The Action Series. In: Creeber, G., ed. The television genre book. 1st edition. London: BFI Publishing, 17-19.

Miller, T., 2004. Trainspotting the Avengers. In: Gwenllian-Jones, S. and Pearson, R. E., eds. Cult Television. Minneapolis/London: University of Minnesota Press, 187-197.

Miller, T., 2008. The Action Series. In: Creeber, G., ed. The television genre book. 2nd edition. London: BFI Publishing, 24-29.

Ministerio de Educación y Ciencia, 2007. Media Televisión [online]. Available at: http://recursos.cnice.mec.es/media/television/index.html [Accessed 6 July 2011].

Ministerio de la Presidencia, 2006. Boletín Oficial del Estado (BOE) número 134. [pdf] Madrid: Spanish Government. Available at: http://www.boe.es/boe/ dias/2006/06/06/pdfs/A21207-21218.pdf [Accessed 7 April 2011].

Mittell, J., 2006. Narrative complexity in contemporary American television. The Velvet Light Trap, 58 (Fall), 29-40.

Monaco, J., 2002. Film Verstehen. Reinbek: Rohwolt.

Montsant de, O., 1946. Franco si, comunismo no, se grita al atracar el crucero 'Galicia'. La Vanguardia Española, 4 June, p. 4a.

Moody, N., 2001. 'A lone crusader in the dangerous world'. Heroics of science and technology in Knight Rider. In: Osgerby, B. and Gough-Yates, A., eds. Action TV. Tough Guys, Smooth Operators and Foxy Chicks. New York/London: Routledge, 69-80.

Moorstedt, M., 2009. Mein elektronisches Herz blinkt, blinkt, blinkt. Süddeutsche Zeitung, 8 October, p. 15.

Moragas de, M. and Prado, E., 2000. La televisió pública a l'era digital. Barcelona: Pòrtic.

Moran, A., 2009. Global franchising, local customizing: The cultural economy of TV program formats. Continuum, 23 (2), 115-125.

Moran, A., 2010. TV Formats Worldwide. Localizing Global Programs. Bristol/Chicago: Intellect Books.

Morari, C. E., 2007. Forms Mirroring Feelings. Iconicity and Empathy in visual metaphors and non-narrative structures. In: Anderson, J.D. and Anderson Fisher, B., eds. Narration and spectatorship in moving images. Newcastle: Cambridge Scholar Publishing, 92-104.

Morgan-Tamosunas, R., 2000. Screening the past: History and nostalgia in contemporary Spanish cinema. In: Jordan, B. and Morgan-Tamosunas, R., eds.

Contemporary Spanish cultural studies. New York: Oxford University Press, 111-122.

Morley, D., 1980. *The 'Nationwide' Audience.* London: British Film Institute.

Müller von, A., 2011. Politik ohne Unterleib. *Zeit,* [online] 17 October. Available at: http://www.zeit.de/2011/42/Fernsehserie-Borgia/komplettansicht [Accessed 13 February 2012].

Neely, S., 2005. Scotland, heritage and devolving British cinema. *Screen,* 46 (2), 241-245.

Neill, A., 1996. Empathy and (Film) Fiction. *In:* Bordwell, D. and Carroll, N., eds. *Post-Theory. Reconstructing Film Studies.* Madison/London: University of Wisconsin Press, 175-194.

Nelson, R. and Cooke, L., 2010. Editorial. Television Archives: Accessing TV History. *Critical Studies in Television,* 5 (2), xvii-xix.

Nelson, R., 2008. Costume Drama. *In:* Creeber, G., ed. *The television genre book.* 2nd edition. London: BFI Publishing, 49-52.

Neox, 2011. *El coche fantástico* [online]. Neox. Available at: http://www.neox8.com/PortalNeox/El-coche-fantastico/P_9734269 [Accessed 22 July 2011].

Niggemeier, S. and Reufsteck, M. 2005. *Das Fernsehlexikon. alles über 7000 Sendungen von Ally McBeal bis zur ZDF-Hitparade.* Wilhelm Goldmann Verlag: München.

Niggemeier, S., 2006. Bilder für uns alle. *Frankfurter Allgemein Sonntagzeitung,* 28 May, p. 31a.

Nuys-Henkelmann de, C., 1987. Happening ist überall. *In:* Hoffmann, H. and Klotz, H., eds. *Die Sechziger.* Düsseldorf: Econ, p. 46.

O'Day, Marc, 2001. Of Leather Suits and Kinky Boots. The Avengers, style and Popular Culture. *In:* Osgerby, B. and Gough-Yates, A., eds. *Action TV. Tough Guys, Smooth Operators and Foxy Chicks.* New York/London: Routledge, 221-235.

Oliver, M.B. and Woolley, J., 2011. Tragic and poignant entertainment. The gratifications of meaningfulness as emotional response. *In:* Döveling, K., et al., ed. *The Routledge Handbook of Emotions and Mass Media.* London: Routledge, 132-147.

Oltmann, K., 2008. *Remake – Premake. Hollywoods romantische Komödie und ihre Gender-Diskurse, 1930-1960.* transcript: Bielefeld.

Orbanz, E., 2007. To have... and to have not! Legal Deposit in Germany today. *Journal of Film Preservation,* 74/75, 83-84.

O'Sullivan, T., 1991. Television Memories and Cultures of Viewing, 1950-65. *In:* Corner, J., ed. *Popular Television in Britain. Studies in Cultural History.* London: BFI, 150-181.

ots, 2006. *Topwerte mit Kampfstern Galactica und Knight Rider: DAS VIERTE mit 1,4 Prozent in der Prime Time und bis zu einer halben Mio. Zuschauer bei Knight*

Rider [online]. Presseportal. 24 June. Available at: http://www.presseportal.de /pm/59618/790380/topwerte-mit-kampfstern-galactica-und-knight-rider-das-vierte-mit-1-4-prozent-in-der-prime-time-und [Accessed 2 September 2011].

Oxford Dictionaries, 2012. *"Remake"* [online]. Available at: http://oxford dictionaries.com/definition/english/remake?q=remake [Accessed 6 October 2012].

Oxford Dictionaries, 2012a. *"Character"* [online]. Available at: http://oxford dictionaries.com/definition/english/character?q=character [Accessed 4 October 2012].

Palacio, M., 2001. *Historia de la televisión en España.* 1st edition. Barcelona: Gedisa.

Palacio, M., 2008. *Historia de la televisión en España.* 3rd edition. Barcelona: Gidesa.

Palacio, M., 2011. Transición und demokratische Konsolidierung in Spanien 1974-1977: Die Rolle des spanischen Fernsehens (TVE). *In:* Türschmann, J. and Wagner, B., eds. *TV global. Erfolgreiche Fernseh-Formate im internationalen Vergleich.* Bielefeld: transcript, 201-216.

Palacio, M., 2012. *La televisión durante la Transición española.* Madrid: Ediciones Cátedra.

Paperpast Yearbook, 2012. *Fashion 1959* [online]. Available at: http://www.paper past.com/html/1959_fashion.html [Accessed 1 February 2012].

Paperpast Yearbook, 2012a. Fashion 1960 [online]. Available at: http://www.paper past.com/html/1960_fashion.html [Accessed 1 February 2012].

Parkin, A., 1993. *Gedächtnis. Ein einführendes Lehrbuch.* Weinheim: Beltz.

Parrondo, J., 1998. El cine fantástico, líder entre los nuevos grandes estrenos en EE.UU. *La Vanguardia,* 1 March.

Parrondo, J., 1998a. La ironía de la película 'Los Vengadores' se impone a las críticas negativas. *La Vanguardia,* 20 August, p. 63a.

Paus-Haase, I., et al., 1999. *Talkshows im Alltag von Jugendlichen. Der tägliche Balanceakt zwischen Orientierung, Amüsement und Ablehnung.* Opladen: Leske + Budrich.

Pavlovic, M., 2007. Erhöhte Dosis. *Süddeutsche Zeitung (Bayern),* 9 June, p.21.

Pérez, X., 1998. *El universo de Los Vengadores.* Barcelona: Glénat.

Pérez, X., 2010. No title. *La Vanguardia (Cultura|s),* 23 June, p. 3.

Perlman, A., 2011. The Strange Career of Mad Men: Race, Paratexts and Civil Rights Memory. *In:* Edgerton, G.R., ed. *Mad Men.* London/New York: Tauris, 209-225.

Pfannkuche, K.J., 1978. *Johannes Hofers Dissertation 'De Nostalgia' (1678) und die zeitgenössische Medizin.* Marburg: Dissertation Universität Marburg.

Pickering, M. and Keightley, E., 2006. The Modalities of Nostalgia. *Current Sociology,* 54 (6), 919-941.

Plutchik, R., 1991. *The Emotions.* Revised ed. Lanham/Maryland: University Press of America.

Pollmer, C., 2011. Light Rider. *Süddeutsche Zeitung*, 14 February, p. 9a.

Popular memory Group, 1982. Popular memory. Theory, politics, method. *In*: Johnson, R., et al., eds. *Making Histories. Studies in history-writing and politics.* London: Hutchinson, 253-371.

Powelz, M., 2011. *"Borgia"* – *Wie viel Wahrheit steckt in der Serie?* [online]. TV-Digital, 17 October 2011. Available at: http://www.tvdigital.de/magazin/specials/tvserien/borgia-wie-viel-wahrheit-steckt-in-der-serie [Accessed 13 February 2012].

Powrie, P., 1997. *French cinema in the 1980s. Nostalgia and the crisis of masculinity.* New York: Oxford University Press.

Prado, E. and Delgado, M., 2010. La televisión generalista en la era digital. Tendencias internacionales de programación. *Telos,* [e-journal] 84, Fundación Telefónica, 52-64. Available at: http://sociedadinformacion.fundacion.telefonica.com/seccion=1266&idioma=es_ES&id=2010083011290001&activo=6.do# [Accessed 28 November 2011].

Prado, E., 1999. Traficantes de emociones. *Diálogos de la Comunicación*, 55, 9-17.

Prat, P., 2005. El coche fantástico. *La Vanguardia (Nuevo Motor)*, 30 January, p. 8.

Prado, E., 2010. Contenidos y servicios para la televisión digital. *Telos* [e-journal] 84, Fundación Telefónica. Available at: http://sociedadinformacion.fundacion.telefonica.com/DYC/TELOS/REVISTA/Dossier/DetalleArtculoTELOS_84TELOS_DOSSIER0/seccion=1266&idioma=es_ES&id=2010083009560001&activo=6.do# [Accessed 3 July 2011].

Prommer, E., et al., 2003. Pre-Teens und Erwachsene lachen anders. *TelevIZIon*, 16 (1), 58-67.

Prommer, E. and Mikos, L., 2005. Rezeptionsforschung. *In*: Mikos, L. and Wegener, C., eds. *Qualitative Medienforschung. Ein Handbuch.* Konstanz: UVK, 193-199.

Pulzer, P., 1999. The citizen and the State in modern Germany. *In*: Kolinsky, E. and Will Van der, W. eds. *The Cambridge Companion to Modern German Culture.* Cambridge University Press. Cambridge Collections Online. Cambridge University Press, 20-43.

Pumphrey, M., 2001. The Games we play. TV Westerns, memory and 'masculinity'. *In*: Osgerby, B. and Gough-Yates, A., eds. *Action TV. Tough Guys, Smooth Operators and Foxy Chicks.* New York/London: Routledge, 145-158.

Quilez, R., 2008. "Nadie dijo que mirar al pasado fuese fácil"; José Corbacho vuelve a la mítica década de los 80 con 'Peta Zeta'. *El Mundo*, 6 January, p. 53d.

Radstone, S. and Hodgkin, K., 2003. Regimes of Memory: an introduction. *In:* Radstone, S. and Hodgkin, K., eds. *Regimes of Memory.* London/New York: Routledge, 1-22.

Ramoneda, J., 1999. Television Culture (Prologue to the CCCB's catalogue) [online]. Centre de Cultura Contemporània de Barcelona (CCCB). In: http://www.cccb.org/rcs_gene/22-MonTV-trad-ang.pdf [Accessed 21 July 2011].

Ramos, R., 1995. El orgullo de las estrellas masculinas frena la adaptación al cine de 'Los Vengadores'. *La Vanguardia*, 19 December, p. 45a.

Ramos, R., 1998. "Fedra" convierte a Diana Rigg en una gran trágica del teatro británico. *La Vanguardia*, 19 October, p. 40a.

Ramos, R., 1996. Diana Rigg, el éxito a los 60. *La Vanguardia*, 29 December, p. 45a.

Rathgeb, E., 1999. Ein Aufwachsen in Serie. *Franfurter Allgemeine Zeitung*, 1 December, p. 50.

Raulff, U., 2002. Augenblickszertrümmerer. *Süddeutsche Zeitung*, 24 December, p. 13.

Rehfeld, N., 2011. Schlappe TV-Serien-Remakes. Geh in Rente, J.R.!. *Spiegel Online*, [online] 1 September. Available at: http://www.spiegel.de/kultur/tv/0,1518,782693,00.html [Accessed 8 August 2012].

Reyes, J., 2006. El rey del pecho palomo. *El País*, 28 September, p. 56.

Robinson, J., 1992. Autobiographical Memory. *In*: Gruneberg, M. and Morris, P., 1992. *Aspects of Memory. Volume 1: The Practical Aspects.* 2nd edition. London/New York: Routledge, 223-251.

Rogers, E.M., 2003. *Diffusion of Innvoation.* 5th edition. New York: Free Press.

RTL, 2011. *Knight Rider* [online]. RTL. Available at: http://www.rtl.de/cms/sendungen/serie/knight-rider-uebersicht.html [Accessed 25 October 2011].

RTVE, 2011. *El coche fantástico* [online]. Corporación de Radio y Televisión Española (RTVE). Available at: http://www.rtve.es/television/coche-fantastico/ [Accessed 22 July 2011].

RTVE, 2011a. Making-off of El coche fantástico [online]. Corporación de Radio y Televisión Española (RTVE). Available at: http://www.rtve.es/alacarta/videos/television/making-off-coche-fantastico/549452/, [Accessed 27 October 2011].

RTVE a la carta, 2011. *Cuéntame cómo pasó* [online]. Corporación de Radio y Televisión Española (RTVE). Available at: www.rtve.es/alacarta/videos/cuentame-como-paso/ [Accessed 12 April 2011].

RTVE a la carta, 2011a. *Telediario* [online]. Corporación de Radio y Televisión Española (RTVE). Available at: www. Rtve.es/alacarta/videos/telediario/ [Accessed 12 April 2011].

RTVE a la carta, 2011b. *RTVE Archive* [online]. Corporación de Radio y Televisión Española (RTVE). Available at: http://www.rtve.es/archivo/ [Accessed 12 April 2011].

Ruggiero, G., 2007. Introduction. Renaissance Dreaming: In Search of a Paradigm. *In*: Ruggiero, G., ed. *A Companion to the Worlds of the Renaissance.* Malden/Oxford/Victoria: Blackwell Publishing, 1-20.

Rusch, G. and Volkmer, I., 2006. Germany. *In*: Volkmer, I., ed. *News in public memory. An international study of media memories across generation.* New York: Peter Lang, 69-93.

Salleras, J., 2010. Hasselhoff, Fulminante. *La Vanguardia (TV Manía)*, 18 December, p. 8a.

Sanchéz, C.A., 2010. *Canal Nostalgic. Las emisiones del extinto Canal Nostalgia estarán disponibles en internet* [online]. Adslzone. Available at: In: http://www.adslzone.tv/2010/04/13/canal-nostalgic-las-emisiones-del-extinto-ca nal-nostalgia-estaran-disponibles-en-internet/ [Accessed 3 July 2011].

Sauerbrey, A., 2009. Der gedrosselte Ritter. *Der Tagesspiegel,* [online] 8 October. Available at: http://www.tagesspiegel.de/medien/schlaues-auto-der-gedrosselte-ritter/1611918.html [Accessed 7 December 2012].

Schader, P., 2006. Mach's gut MTV. *tageszeitung,* [online] 3 August. Available at: http://www.taz.de/1/archiv/print-archiv/printressorts/digi-artikel/?ressort=fl&di g=2006%2F08%2F03%2Fa0192&cHash=92305076f8d5718ec20d2e3c11ec8ee d [Accessed 7.12.2012].

Schäffer, B., 2005. Gruppendiskussion. *In:* Mikos, L. and Wegener, C., eds. *Qualitative Medienforschung. Ein Handbuch.* Konstanz: UVK, 304-314.

Schiele, S. ed., 1999. Die sechziger Jahre in der Bundesrepublik Deutschland. In: Politik und Unterricht. Zeitschrift zur Gestaltung des politischen Unterrichts, 25 (3), Stuttgart: Landeszentrale für politische Bildung.

Schildt, A., 2002. Die innere Entwicklung der Bundesrepublik bis 1989, *Informationen zur Politischen Bildung,* [online] 270. Bundeszentrale für Politische Bildung (BPB), 4 April. Available at: http://www.bpb.de/publi kationen/0112043587598650332934144193983,0,0,Innere_Entwicklung_der_ Bundesrepublik_bis_1989.html [Accessed on 8 August 2011].

Schinhofen, P., 2009. Die Leichtigkeit der Lotus-Blüten. *Frankfurter Allgemeine Sonntagszeitung (Technik und Motor),* 24 May, p. 8.

Schivelbusch, W., 1973. Das Nostalgische Syndrom. Überlegungen zu einem neuen antiquarischen Gefühl. *Frankfurter Hefte,* 270-276.

Schlipphacke, H., 2010. *Nostalgia After Nazism: History and Affect in German and Austrian Literature and Film.* Lewisburg, PA: Bucknell University Press.

Schmidt, S., 1991. Gedächtnisforschung. Positionen, Probleme, Perspektiven. *In:* Schmidt, S., ed. *Gedächtnis. Probleme und Perspektiven der interdisziplinären Gedächtnisforschung.* Frankfurt a.M.: Suhrkamp, 9-55.

Schmidbauer, M. and Löhr, P., 1992. *Fernsehkinder. Neue Sozialisationstypen.* München: Stiftung Prix Jeuness.

Schneider, A., 2005. "Ein folkloristisches Strassentheater, das unbeabsichtigt einen Brecht oder Godard gibt". Zur Kodierung von Emotionen im zeitgenössischen Hindi-Mainstream-Film. *In:* Brütsch, M., et al., eds. *Kinogefühle. Emotionalität und Film.* Marburg: Schüren, 137-152.

Schöfer, G., ed., 1980. *Gottschalk-Gleser-Sprachinhaltsanalyse. Theorie und Technik. Studien zur Messung ängstlicher und aggressiver Affekte.* Weinheim/Basel: Beltz Verlag.

Schöfer, G., 1980a. Einleitung. *In:* Schöfer, G., ed. *Gottschalk-Gleser-Sprachinhaltsanalyse. Theorie und Technik. Studien zur Messung ängstlicher und aggressiver Affekte.* Weinheim/Basel: Beltz Verlag, 12-14.

Schubert, K. and Klein, M., 2011. Vietnamkrieg [online]. Bundeszentrale für Politische Bildung (BPB). Available at: http://www.bpb.de/nachschlagen/lexika/politiklexikon/18426/vietnamkrieg [Accessed 7 December 2012].

Schulte, E.A., 2009. *Das Knight Rider Buch – Das große Buch eines Fans über die 80er Jahre TV-Serie und das Comeback in 2008. Mit allem, was ein Fan wissen muss.* Norderstedt: Books on Demand.

Schulte, E.A., 2011. *Knight Rider – Fan-& Infoseite* [online]. Available at: http://www.knight-online.info/ [Accessed 1 September 2011].

Schümchen, A., 2006. *Fernsehprogrammplanung in Deutschland. Eine Untersuchung zu ökonomischen und programmkulturellen Aspekten des Wettbewerbs der Vollprogramme im deutschen Fernsehmarkt im Spannungsverhältnis zwischen öffentlich-rechtlichem und kommerziellem System* [online]. Ph.D. dissertation, HFF "Konrad Wolf". Available at: http://opus.kobv.de/hff/volltexte/2007/43/pdf/SchuemchenDiss.pdf [Accessed 1 December 2010].

Schweinitz, J., 2006. *Film und Stereotyp. Eine Herausforderung für das Kino und die Filmtheorie. Zur Geschichte eines Mediendiskurse.* Berlin: Akademie Verlag.

Scott, M., 2011. *Fashion in the middle ages.* Los Angeles: Getty Publications.

Sedikides, C., et al., 2004. Nostalgia: Conceptual issues and existential functions. *In*: Greenberg, J., et al., eds. *Handbook of Experimental Existential Psychology.* New York: Guilford Press, 200-213.

Seidel, H.-D., 1998. Mrs. Peel, wir würden gebraucht: "The Avengers" im Kino. *Frankfurter Allgemeine Zeitung*, 31 August, p. 46.

Semler, C., 2003. Essay. 1968 im Westen – Was ging uns die DDR an? *Aus Politik und Zeitgeschichte. Beilage zur Wochenzeitschrift Das Parlament*, B/45/2003, 3-5.

Sevillano, E., 2009. El coche fantástico. *El País (Extra)*, 3 March, p. 4-5.

Shimpach, S., 2010. *Television in Transition.* Oxford: Wiley-Blackwell.

Siegfried, D., 2003. "Trau' keinem über 30"? Konsens und Konflikt der Generationen in der Bundesrepublik der langen sechziger Jahre. *In*: Bundeszentrale für Politische Bildung, ed. *Aus Politik und Zeitgeschichte. Beilage zur Wochenzeitschrift Das Parlament*, 45, 3 November, pp. 25-32.

Siska, W., 2011. Men Behaving as Boys: The Culture of Mad Men. *In*: Edgerton, G.R., ed. *Mad Men.* London/New York: Tauris, 195-208.

Sky, 2011. *Channel overview* [online]. Sky Deutschland Fernsehen GmbH & Co. KG. Available at: www.sky.de/web/cms/de/abonnieren-senderinfos.jsp [Accessed 4 July 2011].

Smith, M., 2005. Wer hat Angst for Charles Darwin? Die Filmkunst im Zeitalter der Evolution. Translated from English by N. Böhler. *In*: Brütsch, M., et al., eds. *Kinogefühle. Emotionalität und Film.* Marburg: Schüren, 289-312.

Smith, M., 2008. Empathie und das erweiterte Denken. *In*: Ebbrecht, T. and Schick, T., eds. *Emotion – Empathie – Figur. Spielformen der Filmwahrnehmung*. Berlin: Vistas, 13-28.

Smith, P.J., 2006. *Television in Spain. From Franco to Almodóvar*. Cornwall: MPG Books.

Smith, P.J., 2009. Una telenovela transnacional: Amar en tiempos revueltos. *In*: López, F., et al., eds. *Historias de la pequeña pantalla. Representaciones históricas en la televisión de la España democrática*. Frankfurt a.M.: Vervuert, 121-135.

Smith, P. J., 2009a. Media migration and cultural proximity. Television fiction in Spain. *Studies in Hispanic Cinemas*, 5 (1&2), 73-84.

Sontag, S., 1964. "Notes" on camp [online]. Georgetown University. Available at: http://www9.georgetown.edu/faculty/irvinem/theory/sontag-notesoncamp-1964 .html [Accessed 1 August 2011].

Sotelo de, E., 2006. *Feminist Theory and Feminist Movement in Spain* [online]. FU Berlin, gender...politi...online. Available at: http://web.fu-berlin.de/gpo/pdf/ tagungen/feminist_de_sotelo.pdf [Accessed 1 October 2011].

Spigel, L., 1995. From the dark ages to the golden age: women's memories and television reruns. *Screen*, 36 (Spring), 16-33.

Spillmann, K., 2011. *Serien im Deutschen Fernsehen* [online]. Available at: http://www.tvder 60er.de/tvserien/tvser011.htm [Accessed 28 September 2011].

Sprengler, C., 2011. *Screening Nostalgia. Populuxe props and Technicolor aesthetics in contemporary American film*. 1st paperback edition. New York/Oxford: Berghahn.

Stafford, W., 1989. 'This once happy country': nostalgia for pre-modern society. *In*: Chase, C. and Shaw, M., eds. *The imagined past. History and nostalgia*. Manchester/New York: Manchester University Press, 33-46.

Stauth, G. and Turner, B.S., 1988. Nostalgia, Postmodernism and the Critique of Mass Culture. *Theory, Culture & Society*, 5 (2–3), 509-526.

Stearns, P. N., 2008. The History of Emotions. Issues of Change and Impact. *In*: Lewis, M., et al., eds. *The Handbook of Emotions*. New York: The Guilford Press, 17-31.

Steinberg, B., 2010. Book 'em, Danno: Why nostalgia may win over novelty this fall. *Advertising Age*, 81 (29), p. 8.

Sterneborg, A., 2008. Seine Frau für alle Fälle. *Süddeutsche Zeitung*, 19 July, p. 14.

Stiftung Deutsche Kinemathek, 2005. *Jahresbericht (Annual Report) 2005* [online]. Stiftung Deutsche Kinemathek. Available at: http://osiris22.pi-cunsult.de/ userdata/l_7/p_72/library/data/jahresber_2005_inhalt.pdf [Accessed 22 Septem ber 2011].

Stiftung Deutsche Kinemathek, 2012. *History of Deutsche Kinemathek* [online]. Stiftung Deutsche Kinemathek Available at: http://www.deutsche-kinema thek.de/en/deutsche-kinemathek/history [Accessed 5 December 2012].

Storey, J., 2001. The Sixties in the Nineties. Pastiche or hyperconsciousness? *In:* Osgerby, B. and Gough-Yates, A., eds. *Action TV. Tough Guys, Smooth Operators and Foxy Chicks.* New York/London: Routledge, 236-250.

Straubhaar, J.G., 1991. Beyond Media Imperialism: Asymmetrical Interdepence and Cultural Proximity. *Critical Studies in Mass Communication,* 8 (1991), 39-59.

Striedter, J., 1989. *Literary Structure, Evolution, and Value.* Cambridge/London: Harvard University Press.

Süddeutsche Zeitung, 1999. No title. *Süddeutsche Zeitung,* 9 August, p. 12.

Süddeutsche Zeitung, 2009. Vip-Klick. David Hasselhoff. *Süddeutsche Zeitung,* 22 September.

Sullivan, E., 2010. Historical Keyword. Nostalgia. *The Lancet,* 376 (2010), 585.

Summers, S. 2011. *"Borgia" éxito international* [online]. Audiencias. Available at http://www.audiencias.info/2011/10/11/borgia-exito-internacional/ [Accessed 8 February 2012].

Sutton, J., 2010. *Memory* [online]. *The Stanford Encyclopedia of Philosophy,* Edward N. Zalta (ed.). Available at: http://plato.stanford.edu/archives/sum2010/entries/memory/ [Accessed 7 December 2012].

Talen, J., 2002. *"24"- Split-screen's big come back* [online]. Salon Media Group. Available at: http://dir.salon.com/story/ent/tv/feature/2002/05/14/24_split/index3.html [Accessed 28 July 2011].

Tan, E., 1996. *Emotion and the Structure of Narrative Film. Film as an Emotion Machine.* Mahwah: Lawrence Erlbaum Associates.

Tan, E., 2002. Interest as Global Affect Motivation in Film. A Reply to Carl Plantinga. *The Journal of Moving Image Studies,* 4 (1), 30-40.

Tan, E., 2005. Gesichtsausdruck und Emotionen im Comic und Film. Translated from Dutch by D. Ahrend. *In:* Brütsch, M., et al., eds. *Kinogefühle. Emotionalität und Film.* Marburg: Schüren, 265-287.

Tannock, S., 1995. Nostalgia Critique. *Cultural Studies,* 9 (3), 453-464.

Tashiro, C.S., 1998. *Pretty Pictures. Production Design and The Historiy of Film.* Austin: University of Texas Press.

Teachsam, 2010. *Basistranskript des Gesprächsanalytischen Transkriptionssystems (GAT) GAT transcription rules* [online]. Teachsam. Available at: http://www.teachsam.de/deutsch/d_lingu/gespraechsanalyse/gespraech_9_4_4.html [Accessed 12 December 2011].

Teer-Tomaselli, R., 2006. Memory and Markers. Collective Memory and Newsworthiness. *In:* Volkmer, I., ed. *News in public memory. An international study of media memories across generations.* New York: Peter Lang, 225-249.

Telecinco, 2012. Mitele. TV Achive Mediaset España [online]. Telecinco. Available at: http://www.mitele.es/#/portada [Accessed 23 September 2012].

Tele Digital, 2010. *Canal Nostalgia regresa a nuestra pantalla ... del ordenador* [online]. Tele Digital, 14 April. Available at: http://www.sateliteinfos.com/

actu/tp.asp/tp/19127/canal-nostalgia-regresa-a-nuestras-pantallas-del-orddenad or.html [Accessed 3 July 2011].

TheAvengers.TV, 2008. *Los Vengadores. Amar a todos* [online]. TheAvengers.TV. Available at: http://losvengadores.theavengers.tv/amar.html [Accessed 22 September 2011].

Thumin, J., 1986. 'Miss Hepburn Is Humanized': The Star Persona of Katharine Hepburn. *Feminist Review,* 24 (Autumn), 71-102.

Tröhler, M. and Hediger, V., 2005. Ohne Gefühl ist das Auge der Vernunft blind. Eine Einleitung. *In*: Brütsch, M., et al., eds. *Kinogefühle. Emotionalität und Film.* Marburg: Schüren, 7-20.

Vilarós, T.M, 1999. A cultural mapping of Catalonia. *In:* Gies, D.T., ed. *The Cambridge Companion to Modern Spanish Culture,* Cambridge: Cambridge University Press, 37-53.

Vilches, L., et al., 2009. España. *In*: Vilches, L., et al., ed. *Mercados globales. Historias nacionales.* Barcelona: Gedisa, 93-122.

Vilches, L., et al., 2009a. España. Las adaptaciones como recurso industrial. *In*: Vilches, L., et al., ed. *Mercados globales. Historias nacionales.* Barcelona: Gedisa, 193-196.

Villarroel González, Ó., 2005. *Los Borgia. Iglesia y poder entre los siglos XV y XVI.* Madrid: Sílex.

Visch, V., et al., 2010. The Emotional and Cognitive Effect of Immersion in Film Viewing. *Cognition & Emotion,* 24 (8), 1439-1445.

Voigts-Virchow, E., 2007. Heritage and literature on screen: Heimat and heritage. *In*: Cartmell, D. and Whelehan, I., eds. *The Cambridge Companion to Literature on Screen.* Cambridge University Press, 2007, 123-137.

Volkmer, I., 2005. Kulturvergleichende Studien. *In*: Mikos, L. and Wegener, C., eds. *Qualitative Medienforschung. Ein Handbuch.* Konstanz: UVK, 232-239.

Volkmer, I., ed., 2006. *News in public memory. An international study of media memories across generations.* New York: Peter Lang.

Volkmer, I., 2006a. Preface. *In*: Volkmer, I., ed. *News in public memory. An international study of media memories across generations.* New York: Peter Lang, 1-9.

Volkmer, I., 2006b. Introduction. *In*: Volkmer, I., ed. *News in public memory. An international study of media memories across generations.* New York: Peter Lang, 13-18.

Volkmer, I., 2006c. Globalization, generational entelechies, and the global public space. *In*: Volkmer, I., ed. *News in public memory. An international study of media memories across generations.* New York: Peter Lang, 252-268.

Warner Brothers, 2011. The Avengers [online]. Warner Brothers. Available at: http://www.warnerbros.com/#/page=movies&pid=f-d02ed1e/THE_AVENGER S&asset=057061/Avengers_The_-_Trailer&type=video/ [Accessed 8 November 2011].

Weaver, E.B., 2007. Gender. *In*: Ruggiero, G., ed. *A Companion to the Worlds of the Renaissance*. Malden/Oxford/Victoria: Blackwell Publishing, 188-207.

Weichert, S.A., 2002. Knight Rider. *Der Tagesspiegel*, [online] 19 July. Available at: http://www.tagesspiegel.de/medien/knight-rider/330776.html [Accessed 7 December 2012].

Weiner, M., 2011. Interview in Cahier de Cinema España by Chauvin, Jean-Sébastien/Tessé, Jean-Philippe. Cahier de Cinema España, No. 47, July-August 2011, 18-21.

Weis, M., 2009. Primetime-Check: Dienstag, 17. Februar 2009 [online]. Quotenmeter, 18 February. Available at: http://www.quotenmeter.de/cms/ ?p1=n&p2=33210&p3=, [Accessed 7 November 2011].

Werber, N., 1998. *Zweierlei Aufmerksamkeit in Medien, Kunst und Politik* [online]. Telepolis. Available at: http://www.heise.de/tp/r4/artikel/6/6310/1.html [Accessed 15 September 2012].

White, M., 2011. Mad Women. *In*: Edgerton, G.R., ed. *Mad Men*. London/New York: Tauris, 147-158.

Wilcox, R.V., 2010. The *Star Trek* Franchise. *In*: Lavery, D., ed. *The Essential cult TV reader*. Lexington: University Press of Kentucky, 244-259.

Williams, P., 1994. Feeding off the past. The Evolution of the Television Rerun. *Journal of Popular Film and Television*, 21 (4), 162-175.

Wilson, J. L., 1999. Remember When. A Consideration of the Concept of Nostalgia. *ETC.*, [online]. 56 (3), pp. 296-304. Available at: http://www.thefreelibrary.com/ %22REMEMBER+WHEN...%22+A+Consideration+of+the+Concept+of+Nost algia.-a058056070 [Accessed 2 March 2011].

Winter, R., 2010. *Der produktive Zuschauer. Medienaneignung als kultureller und ästhetischer Prozess*. 2nd revised ed. Köln: Herbert von Harlem Verlag.

Winkler, W., 2011. Heuchelnd und hurend in Kardinalspurpur. *Süddeutsche Zeitung* [online] 17 October. Available at: http://www.sueddeutsche.de/medien/tv-serie-borgia-heuchelnd-und-hurend-in-kardinalspurpur-1.1166230 [Accessed 13 February 2012].

Wirth, U., 2005. Archiv. *In*: Roesler, A. and Stiegler, B., eds. *Grundbegriffe der Medientheorie*. Paderborn: Fink, 17-27.

Wollen, T., 1991. Over our shoulders. Nostalgic screen fiction for the 1980s. *In*: Corner, J. and Harvey, S., eds. *Enterprise and Heritage. Crosscurrents of national culture*. New York/London: Routledge, 178-193.

Wuss, P., 2005. Konflikt und Emotion im Filmerleben. *In*: Brütsch, M., et al., eds. *Kinogefühle. Emotionalität und Film*. Marburg: Schüren, 205-222.

Yacowar, M., 2011. Suggestive Silence in Season One. *In*: Edgerton, G.R., ed. *Mad Men*. London/New York: Tauris, 86-98.

Zillmann, D., 1988. Mood management. Using entertainment to full advantage. *In*: Donohew, L., et al., eds. *Communication, social cognition, and affect*. Hillsdale/New Jersey: Lawrence Erlbaum Associates, 147-171.

Zillmann, D., 2004. Emotionspsychologische Grundlagen. Translated from English by T. Fischer. *In*: Vorderer, P., et al., eds. *Lehrbuch der Medienpsychologie*. Göttingen/Bern/Toronto/Seattle: Hogrefe, 101-128.

Zirnstein, M., 2011. Ein Held, der sich gefällt. *Süddeutsche Zeitung (Extra)*, 17 February, p. 8.

Zylka, J., 1998. Komisches Wasserwerk bedroht U.K. *Die Tageszeitung*, 27 August.

11.1 EXAMPLES FOR THE ANALYSIS

Borgia (2011) (AT/ CZ/DE/FR/IT, Sky Italia, Season 1)

Knight Rider (1982) (USA, NBC, Season 1)

Knight Rider (2008) (USA, NBC, Season 1)

Mad Men (2007) (USA, AMC, Season 1)

The Avengers (1961) (GB, ITV, Season 5)

The Avengers (1998) (USA, R: Chechik, J.S.)

12. Appendix

12.1 THE COMPOSITION OF THE SAMPLES

Age group/Country	Women (15n)	Men (14n)
55 to 65-year-old Germans (9n)	Doctor (2n), Language secretary Administrative assistant Teacher/journalist Physiotherapist	Artist/University professor Teacher (retired) Advocate
55 to 65-year-old Spaniards (6n)	Clerk (2n) Director's secretary	Economist (retired) Chemist Corporate leader (retired)
25 to 35-year-old Spaniards (7n)	Doctoral student (Philosophy and Classical Philology) Nurse Treasury officer	Engineer Engineer/Information technician Higher technician Clerk
25 to 35-year-old Germans (7n)	Fashion assistant Art historian Doctor	Student Research assistant (engineer) Architect Teacher

12.2 QUESTIONNAIRES

12.2.1 Questionnaire Germany

BEFRAGUNG – zum Thema Nostalgie

A) Fragekomplex: Nostalgie

1. Erinnern Sie sich an Ihr erstes Fernseh-Erlebnis? Wenn ja, bitte beschreiben Sie es? Welche Rolle spielt dieses Erlebnis heute für Sie?

2. Wie würden Sie das Gefühl der Nostalgie ganz allgemein beschreiben?

3. Wie würden Sie eine „nostalgische Person" beschreiben?

4. Wenn Sie einmal zurückdenken, wann haben Sie während der Gruppendiskussion Nostalgie empfunden? Wie würden Sie das erklären?

B) Fragekomplex: Soziodemographische Daten

5. Geschlecht:

weiblich	
männlich	

6. Alter:

25 bis 29 Jahre	
30 bis 35 Jahre	
55 bis 59 Jahre	
60 bis 65 Jahre	

7. Nationalität (Mehrfachnennungen erforderlich!):

deutsch	
in Ostdeutschl. geboren und aufgewachsen	
in Westdeutschl. geboren und aufgewachsen	
im Ausland geboren und aufgewachsen	
sonstige Nationalität (bitte nennen)	

....

8. Beruf/Ausbildung (bitte nennen):

....

9. Schulabschluss (bitte nennen):

....

10. Täglicher Fernsehkonsum an einem gewöhnlichen Werktag (aktuell):

≤ 1 Stunde/Tag	
> 1 Stunde bis < 3 Stunden/Tag	
≥ 3 Stunden bis < 4 Stunden/Tag	
≥ 4 Stunden/Tag	

11. Täglicher Fernsehkonsum an einem gewöhnlichen Werktag in ihrer Jugend:

≤ 1 Stunde/Tag	
> 1 Stunde bis < 3 Stunden/Tag	
≥ 3 Stunden bis < 4 Stunden/Tag	
≥ 4 Stunden/Tag	

Raum für Anmerkungen und Kommentar Nutzen Sie diesen Raum, um anzumerken, falls Ihnen etwas in der Diskussion oder an diesem Fragebogen gefehlt hat oder falls Sie etwas gestört oder verärgert hat.

Nochmals herzlichen Dank für Ihre Kooperation!

* Regarding the final request for commentary see Kirchhoff et al., 2010, p. 130.

12.2.2 Questionnaire Spain

ENCUESTA - sobre el tema de la nostalgia

A) Parte I: La nostalgia

1. ¿Recuerda usted su primera experiencia televisiva? En caso que sí, por favor descríbala. ¿Qué rol tiene esta experiencia para usted hoy en día?

   _____

   _____

   _____

   _____

2. ¿Cómo describiría usted el sentimiento de la nostalgia?

   _____

   _____

   _____

3. ¿Cómo define usted una "persona nostálgica"?

   _____

   _____

   _____

   _____

4. Si recapacitan, ¿en qué situación de la discusión ha sentido nostalgia? ¿Cómo lo explicaría?

   _____

   _____

   _____

   _____

B) Parte II: Datos sociodemográficos

5. Sexo:

Hombre	
Mujer	

6. Edad:

25 – 29 años	
30 – 35 años	
55 – 59 años	
60 – 65 años	

7. Nacionalidad (por favor indíquela):

   ....

8. Ha nacido y crecido en ....

9. Profesión/Formación (por favor indíquela):

   ....

10. Nivel de Educación (por favor indíquelo):

    ....

11. Consumo de televisión en un día laboral normal (hoy en día):

≤ 1 hora/día	
> 1 hora < 3 horas/día	
≥ 3 horas < 4 horas/día	
≥ 4 horas/día	

12. Consumo de televisión en un día laboral normal en su joventud:

≤ 1 hora/día	
> 1 hora < 3 horas/día	
≥ 3 horas < 4 horas/día	
≥ 4 horas/día	

Espacio para notas y comentarios - Utilice este espacio para nombrar, si le ha faltado algo en el debate o en el cuestionario o si le ha molestado algo.

¡Muchas gracias por su cooperación!

12.3 Questioning route

12.3.1 Questioning route Germany (25 to 35-year-olds)

Opening Question
Bitte sagt uns euren Namen und die Fernsehserien, die ihr euch gerne im Fernsehen anschaut!

Introduction
Guckt ihr euch Serien an, die ihr auch schon früher, zum Beispiel in der Kindheit oder Jugend, gesehen habt? Was gefällt euch daran?

Transition
Fangen wir mit *Knight Rider* an. Hat einer von euch die neue Version der Serie bereits vorher gesehen?
* JA: Welchen Eindruck hattet ihr da von der Serie? NEIN: weiter

Bsp. 1 – *Knight Rider* (NBC, 2008)

Key
Remakes
Was ist Euch durch den Kopf gegangen, als wir das *Knight Rider* Remake gesehen haben?
* Welche Aspekte sind euch besonders aufgefallen?
* Gibt es Aspekte des Remakes, die euch an das 'Original' erinnern? Welche Erinnerungen werden da wach?
* Vergleicht bitte die beiden Sendungen (die Neue und die Alte), was fällt euch auf?

Bsp. 2 – *Mit Schirm, Charme und Melone* (Chechik, 1998)

Hat einer von euch das Remake von *Mit Schirm, Charme und Melone* bereits vorher gesehen?
* JA: Welchen Eindruck hattet ihr damals von dem Film? NEIN: weiter
* Was ist euch durch den Kopf gegangen, als ihr das Remake von *Mit Schirm, Charme und Melone* gesehen habt?
* Welche Aspekte sind euch besonders aufgefallen?
* Gibt es Aspekte des Remakes, die euch an das `Original´ erinnern?
* Welche Erinnerungen werden da wach? (Lebenssituation)
* Vergleicht bitte die beiden Sendungen (die neue und die alte), was fällt euch auf?

Reruns

Was ich euch jetzt zeige sind die beiden Serien *Knight Rider* und *Mit Schirm, Charme und Melone*. *Knight Rider* wurde in Deutschland erstmals 1985 ausgestrahlt. 2009 wurde die Serie beispielsweise bei Das Vierte gesendet.

Bsp. 3 – *Knight Rider* (NBC, 1982)
Bei *Mit Schirm, Charme und Melone* handelt es sich um eine Serie, die zwischen 1966 und 1970 erstmals im Deutschen Fernsehen ausgestrahlt wurde. Zwischen 2009 und 2011 wurde die Serie erneut von dem Kultursender ARTE gezeigt.
Bsp. 4 - *Mit Schirm, Charme und Melone* (ITV, 1961)

Fangen wir mit *Knight Rider* an, könnt ihr euch erinnern, wann ihr diese Serie, abgesehen von heute, das letzte Mal gesehen habt?
* Wenn ihr euch mal zurückerinnert, was ist euch durch den Kopf gegangen, als wir *Knight Rider* gesehen haben?
* Wenn wir mal mehr ins Detail gehen, ist euch etwas Spezielles aufgefallen?
* *Knight Rider* ist eine Serie aus den Mitte/Ende-80ern. Ihr wart damals im Alter von 5 bis 15. Musstet ihr an das Deutschland der 80er Jahre denken?
* Was geht euch durch den Kopf, wenn wir *Knight Rider* mit dem vergleichen, was man heute hauptsächlich im TV sehen kann?

Und wie sieht es mit *Mit Schirm, Charme und Melone* aus, könnt ihr euch erinnern, wann ihr diese Serie, abgesehen von heute, das letzte Mal gesehen habt?
* Wenn ihr euch mal zurückerinnert, was ist euch durch den Kopf gegangen, als wir *Mit Schirm, Charme und Melone* gesehen haben?
* Ist euch etwas Besonderes aufgefallen?
* *Mit Schirm, Charme und Melone* ist eine Serie aus den 60ern. Eine Zeit, die vor eurer Geburt liegt. Entspricht diese Serie euren Vorstellungen des Deutschlands der 60er Jahre?
* Was war das für eine Zeit?
* Was geht euch durch den Kopf, wenn wir *Mit Schirm, Charme und Melone* mit dem vergleichen, was heute hauptsächlich im TV läuft?

Period Picture
Die letzten Beispiele, die ich euch zeige, sind *Mad Men* und *Borgia*. Beide Serien werden zurzeit im Fernsehen ausgestrahlt. *Mad Men* auf ZDFneo und *Borgia* bei ZDF.
Bsp. 5 – *Mad Men*
Bsp. 6 – *Borgia*

Auch hier zunächst die Frage: Habt ihr *Mad Men* bereits vorher im Fernsehen gesehen?
* Wenn ja, welchen Eindruck hattet ihr von der Serie?
* Wenn ihr euch mal zurückerinnert. Was ist euch durch den Kopf gegangen, als wir *Mad Men* gesehen haben?
* Welche Aspekte der Serie sind euch besonders aufgefallen?
* Die Serie spielt in den USA der 60er Jahre. Eine Zeit, die vor eurer Geburt liegt. Entsprichtdiese Serie euren Vorstellungen der 60er Jahre?
* Was für eine Zeit war das, zu der die Serie spielt?
* Wenn ihr mal zurückdenkt, was ging euch bei der Dia-Szene durch den Kopf?
* Was genau hat euch diesen Eindruck vermittelt?
* Wie würdet ihr die Gefühle des Protagonisten beschreiben?
* Könnt ihr diese Gefühle nachvollziehen?

Wenn ihr euch zurückerinnert. Was ist ihnen durch den Kopf gegangen, als wir *Borgia* gesehen haben?
* Welche Aspekte der Serie sind euch besonders aufgefallen?
* Würdet ihr sagen, dass *Borgia* ein historisch richtiges Bild zeigt?

Summary
Hat all das eurer Meinung nach etwas mit Nostalgie zu tun?
Also verstehe ich es richtig, dass ... .

All-things-Considered/Final Question
Was, würdet ihr sagen, ist zusätzlich wichtig? Musstet ihr im Laufe dieses Gesprächs an etwas denken, wovon ihr meint, dass es noch erwähnt werden sollte?

Vielen Dank!

12.3.2 Questioning route Germany (55 to 65-year-olds)

Opening Question
Bitte sagt uns euren Namen und die Fernsehserien, die ihr euch gerne im Fernsehen anschaut.

Introduction
Guckt ihr euch Serien an, die ihr auch schon früher, zum Beispiel in der Kindheit oder Jugend, gesehen habt? Was gefällt euch daran?

Transition

Ich zeige euch jetzt zwei Beispiel-Episoden. Bei der ersten handelt es sich um ein Remake der 80er Jahre Serie *Knight Rider*, die 2010 bei RTL ausgestrahlt wurde.

Bsp. 1 – *Knight Rider* (NBC, 2008)

Das zweite, was ich euch zeige ist der Film *Mit Schirm, Charme und Melone* (1998, Chechik), ein Remake der 60er Jahre Fernsehserie *Mit Schirm, Charme und Melone*, das bereits mehrmals auch im Fernsehen ausgestrahlt wurde und wird. Das nächste Mal Ende Dezember bei kabel eins.

Bsp. 2 – *Mit Schirm, Charme und Melone* (Chechik, 1998)

Fangen wir mit *Knight Rider* an. Hat einer von euch die neue Version der Serie bereits vorher gesehen?
* JA: Welchen Eindruck hattet ihr da von der Serie? NEIN: weiter

Key
Remake
Was ist Euch durch den Kopf gegangen, als wir das *Knight Rider* Remake gesehen haben?
* Welche Aspekte sind euch besonders aufgefallen?
* Gibt es Aspekte des Remakes, die euch an das `Original´ erinnern? Welche Erinnerungen werden da wach?
* Vergleicht bitte die beiden Sendungen (die neue und die alte), was fällt euch auf?

Hat einer von euch das Remake von *Mit Schirm, Charme und Melone* bereits vorher gesehen?
* JA: Welchen Eindruck hattet ihr damals von dem Film? NEIN: weiter
* Was ist euch durch den Kopf gegangen, als ihr das Remake von *Mit Schirm, Charme und Melone* gesehen habt?
* Welche Aspekte sind euch besonders aufgefallen?
* Gibt es Aspekte des Remakes, die euch an das 'Original' erinnern?
* Welche Erinnerungen werden da wach?
* Vergleicht bitte die beiden Sendungen (die neue und die alte), was fällt euch auf?

Reruns

Was ich euch jetzt zeige sind die beiden Serien *Knight Rider* und *Mit Schirm, Charme und Melone*. *Knight Rider* wurde in Deutschland erstmals 1985 ausgestrahlt. In 2009 wurde die Serie beispielsweise bei Das Vierte gesendet.

Bsp. 3 – *Knight Rider* (NBC, 1982)

Bei *Mit Schirm, Charme und Melone* handelt es sich um eine Serie, die zwischen 1966 und 1970 erstmals im Deutschen Fernsehen ausgestrahlt wurde. Zwischen 2009 und 2011 wurde die Serie erneut von dem Kultursender ARTE gezeigt.

Bsp. 4 - *Mit Schirm, Charme und Melone* (ITV, 1961)

Fangen wir mit *Knight Rider* an. Könnt ihr euch erinnern, wann ihr diese Serie, abgesehen von heute, das letzte Mal gesehen habt?
* Wenn ihr euch mal zurückerinnert: Was ist euch durch den Kopf gegangen, als wir *Knight Rider* gesehen haben?
* Wenn wir mal mehr ins Detail gehen, ist euch etwas Spezielles aufgefallen?
* *Knight Rider* ist eine Serie aus den Mitte/Ende-80ern. Ihr wart damals im Alter von 30 bis 40. Musstet ihr an das Deutschland der 80er Jahre denken?
* Was geht euch durch den Kopf wenn wir *Knight Rider* mit dem vergleichen, was man heute hauptsächlich im TV sehen kann?

Und wie ist es bei *Mit Schirm, Charme und Melone*? Könnt ihr euch erinnern, wann ihr diese Serie, abgesehen von heute, das letzte Mal gesehen habt?
* Wenn ihr euch mal zurückerinnert, was ist euch durch den Kopf gegangen, als wir *Mit Schirm,Charme und Melone* gesehen haben?
* Ist euch etwas Besonderes aufgefallen?
* *Mit Schirm, Charme und Melone* ist eine Serie aus den 60ern. Ihr wart damals im Alter von 10 bis 20. Musstet ihr an das Deutschland der 60er Jahre denken?
* Was war das für eine Zeit?
* Was geht euch durch den Kopf wenn wir *Mit Schirm, Charme und Melone* mit dem vergleichen, was heute hauptsächlich im TV läuft?
Period Picture

Die letzten Beispiele, die ich euch zeige sind *Mad Men* und *Borgia*. Beide Serien werden zurzeit im Fernsehen ausgestrahlt. *Mad Men* (USA, 2007) auf ZDFneo und *Borgia* (F/D/A/CZ 2011) bei ZDF.

Bsp. 5 – *Mad Men*
Bsp. 6 – *Borgia*

Auch hier zunächst die Frage: Habt ihr *Mad Men* bereits vorher im Fernsehen gesehen?
* Wenn ja, welchen Eindruck hattet ihr von der Serie?
* Wenn ihr euch mal zurückerinnert. Was ist euch durch den Kopf gegangen, als wir *Mad Men* gesehen haben?
* Welche Aspekte der Serie sind euch besonders aufgefallen?
* Die Serie spielt in den USA der 60er Jahre. Eine Zeit, die vor eurer Geburt liegt. Ihr wart damals zwischen 10 und 20 Jahre alt. Musstet ihr an das Deutschlands der 60er Jahre denken?
* Was für eine Zeit war das, zu der die Serie spielt?
* Wenn ihr mal zurückdenkt, was ging euch bei der Dia-Szene durch den Kopf?
* Was genau hat euch diesen Eindruck vermittelt?
* Wie würdet ihr die Gefühle des Protagonisten beschreiben?
* Könnt ihr diese Gefühle nachvollziehen?

Wenn ihr euch zurückerinnert. Was ist ihnen durch den Kopf gegangen, als wir *Borgia* gesehen haben?
* Welche Aspekte der Serie sind euch besonders aufgefallen?
* Würdet ihr sagen, dass *Borgia* ein historisch richtiges Bild zeigt?

Summary
Hat all das eurer Meinung nach etwas mit Nostalgie zu tun?
Also verstehe ich es richtig, dass ... .

All-things-Considered/Final Question
Was, würdet ihr sagen, ist zusätzlich wichtig? Musstet ihr im Laufe dieses Gesprächs an etwas denken, wovon ihr meint, dass es noch erwähnt werden sollte?

Vielen Dank!

12.3.3 Questioning route Spain (25 to 35-year-olds)

Opening Question
Por favor, dígannos sus nombres y cuáles son los programas que le gustan ver en la televisión.

Introduction
¿Ven ustedes series que habían visto en su infancia?

Transition
Les voy a mostrar dos extractos de remakes de series televisivas. El primer extracto es del remake de *El Coche Fantástico* que se emitió en 2009 en TVE.

Bsp. 1 – *Knight Rider* (NBC, 2008)
El segundo extracto es el remake de *Los Vengadores*, una película de Jeremiah Chechik de 1998, que también se emitió más recientemente en la televisión.
Bsp. 2 – *Mit Schirm, Charme und Melone* (Chechik, 1998)

Empezamos con *El Coche fantástico*. ¿Habían visto esta emisión antes?
* Sí: ¿Cómo les pareció? No: Next question.

Key
Remake
¿Qué les pasó por la cabeza cuando vimos el remake de *El Coche Fantástico*?
* ¿Hay alguna cosa que ha llamado su atención?
* ¿Hay aspectos en la nueva versión que les recuerdan al 'original'?
* Si comparamos las dos versiones (la nueva y la antigua), ¿que les gusta, que les parece mal?

Seguimos con *Los Vengadores*. ¿Habían visto esta emisión antes?
* Sí: ¿Cómo les pareció? No: Next question.
* ¿Qué les pasó por la cabeza cuando vimos el remake de *Los Vengadores*?
* ¿Hay alguna cosa que ha llamado su atención?
* ¿Hay aspectos en la nueva versión, que les recuerdan al 'original'?
* ¿Qué memorias surgen en usted?
* ¿Si comparamos las dos versiones (la nueva y la antigua), qué les gusta, qué les gusta menos?

Rerun
Ahora les voy a mostrar algunos extractos de las series *El Coche Fantástico* y *Los Vengadores*. *El Coche Fantástico* se emitió por primera vez en 1985 en TVE. Recientemente, la han mostrado en el canal Cuatro (hasta 2009) y en el canal Antena Neox (2010).

Bsp. 3 – *Knight Rider* (NBC, 1982).

Los Vengadores es una serie se emitió a partir de 1966 y recientemente en Calle 13.

Bsp. 4 – *Los Vengadores* (ITV, 1961).

Empezamos con *El Coche Fantástico*. ¿Recuerdan cuando vimos esta emisión la última vez?
* Si recapacitan, ¿qué les pasó por la cabeza cuando vimos la serie?
* ¿Hay alguna cosa especial que ha llamado su atención?
* *El Coche Fantástico* es una serie de los años 80 cuando ustedes tenían entre 5 a 15 años. ¿Los extractos les ha hecho pensar en la España de los años 80?
* Si comparamos *El Coche Fantástico* con lo que vemos mayormente en la televisión de hoy en día, ¿Qué destaca?

¿Y *Los Vengadores*? ¿Recuerdan cuando vimos esta emisión la última vez?
* Si recapacitan, ¿qué les pasó por la cabeza cuando vimos la serie?
* ¿Hay alguna cosa especial que ha llamado su atención?
* *Los Vengadores* es una serie de los años 60, un tiempo en el que ustedes todavía no habían nacido. ¿Corresponde esta serie con su imaginación de la España de los años 60?
* Si comparamos *Los Vengadores* con lo que vemos mayormente en la televisión de hoy en día, ¿Qué destaca?

Period Picture
Los dos últimos ejemplos que os voy a mostrar son *Mad Men* (USA 2007), una serie ambientada en los años 60, emitida por ejemplo en canal Cuatro, y luego *Borgia – Una familia consagrada al vicio*, ambientada en el Renacimiento y que está en emisión en el canal Cosmopolitan.

Bsp. 5 – *Mad Men*
Bsp. 6 – *Borgia*

Empezamos con *Mad Men*. También aquí la misma pregunta: ¿Habían visto esta serie antes de hoy?
* Sí: ¿cómo les pareció la serie? No: Next question.
* Si recapacitan, ¿qué les pasó por la cabeza cuando vimos *Mad Men*?
* ¿Hay alguna cosa que ha llamado su atención?
* La serie está ambientada en los EE.UU. de los años 60, un tiempo antes de su nacimiento. ¿Corresponde esta serie con su imaginario de esa época?
* ¿Qué les pasó por la cabeza cuando vimos la escena con los dispositivos?
* ¿Qué les ha hecho pensar así?

* ¿Como describirían los sentimientos del protagonista en esta escena?
* ¿Pueden entender estos sentimientos?

Si se acuerdan. ¿Qué les pasó por la cabeza cuando vimos *Borgia*?
* ¿Hay alguna cosa que ha llamado su atención?
* ¿Dirían ustedes que la serie muestra una imagen históricamente correcta?

Summary/Ending questions
¿Tiene todo esto algo que ver con nostalgia para ustedes?
¿Si entiendo bien ...?

All-things-Considered/Final Question
¿Hay alguna cosa más que les parece importante; Los extractos les han hecho pensar en alguna otra cosa?

¡Muchas gracias!

12.3.4 Questioning route Spain (55 to 65-year-olds)

Opening Question
Por favor, díganos sus nombres y cuáles son los programas que les gusta ver en la televisión.

Introduction
¿Ven ustedes series que habían visto en su infancia?

Transition
Les voy a mostrar dos extractos de remakes de series televisivas. El primer extracto es del remake de *El Coche Fantástico* que se emitió en 2009 en TVE.

Bsp. 1 – *Knight Rider* (NBC, 2008)
El segundo extracto es el remake de *Los Vengadores*, una película de Jeremiah Chechik de 1998, que también se emitió más recientemente en la televisión.
Bsp. 2 – *Mit Schirm, Charme und Melone* (Chechik, 1998)

Empezamos con *El Coche fantástico*. ¿Habían visto esta emisión antes?
* Sí: ¿Cómo les pareció? No: Next question.

Key
Remakes

¿Qué les pasó por la cabeza cuando vimos el remake de *El Coche Fantástico*?

* ¿Hay alguna cosa que ha llamado su atención?

* ¿Hay aspectos de la nueva versión que les recuerdan al 'original'?

* Si comparamos las dos versiones (la nueva y la antigua), ¿que les gusta, qué les parece mal?

Seguimos con *Los Vengadores*. ¿Han visto esta emisión antes?

* Sí: ¿Cómo les pareció? No: Next question.

* ¿Qué les pasó por la cabeza cuando vimos el remake de *Los Vengadores*?

* ¿Hay alguna cosa que ha llamado su atención?

* ¿Hay aspectos de la nueva versión, que les recuerdan al 'original'?

* ¿Qué memorias surgen en ustedes?

* ¿Si comparamos las dos versiones (la nueva y la antigua), qué les gusta, qué les gusta menos?

Reruns

Ahora les voy a mostrar algunos extractos de las series *El Coche Fantástico* y *Los Vengadores*. *El Coche Fantástico* se emitió por primera vez en 1985 en TVE. Recientemente, la han mostrado el canal Cuatro (hasta 2009) y en el canal Antena Neox (2010).

Bsp. 3 – *Knight Rider* (NBC, 1982).

Los Vengadores es una serie que se emitió a partir de 1966 y recientemente en Calle 13.

Bsp. 4 – *Los Vengadores* (ITV, 1961).

Empezamos con *El Coche Fantástico*. ¿Recuerda cuando vieron esta emisión la última vez?

* Si recapacitan, ¿qué les pasó por la cabeza cuando vimos la serie?

* ¿Hay alguna cosa especial que ha llamado su atención?

* *El Coche Fantástico* es una serie de los años 80. Cuando ustedes tenían entre 25 a 35 años. ¿Dirían ustedes que la serie tiene algo que ver con la España de los años 80?

* Si comparamos *El Coche Fantástico* con lo que vemos mayormente en la televisión de hoy en día. ¿Qué destaca?

¿Y *Los Vengadores*? ¿Recuerdan cuando vieron esta emisión la última vez?

* Si recapacitan, ¿qué les pasó por la cabeza cuando vimos la serie?

* ¿Hay algo especial que ha llamado su atención?

* *Los Vengadores* es una serie de los años 60. Cuando tenían ustedes entre 10 a 20 años. ¿Dirían ustedes que la serie tiene algo que ver con la España de los años 60?

* Si comparamos *Los Vengadores* con lo que vemos mayormente en la televisión de hoy en día, ¿Qué destaca?

Los dos últimos ejemplos que voy a mostrar son *Mad Men*, una serie ambientada en los 60s emitida por ejemplo en canal Cuatro, y luego *Borgia – Una familia consagrada al vicio*, ambientada en el Renacimiento y que está en emisión en el canal Cosmopolitan.

Bsp. 5 – *Mad Men*

Bsp. 6 – *Borgia.*

Empezamos con *Mad Men*. También aquí la pregunta: ¿Habían visto esta serie antes de hoy?

* Sí: ¿Cómo les pareció la serie? No: Next question.

* Si recapacitan, ¿Qué les pasó por la cabeza cuando vimos *Mad Men*?

* ¿Hay alguna cosa que ha llamado su atención?

* La serie está ambientada en los EE.UU. de los años 60. Ustedes tenían entre 10 a 20 años. ¿Dirían ustedes que la serie tiene algo que ver con sus recuerdos de esa época?

* ¿Qué les pasó por la cabeza cuando vimos la escena con los dipositivos?

* ¿Qué les hizo pensar así?

* ¿Cómo describirían los sentimientos del protagonista en esta escena?

* ¿Pueden entender estos sentimientos?

Si se acuerdan. ¿qué les pasó por la cabeza cuando vimos *Borgia*?

* ¿Hay alguna cosa que ha llamado su atención?

* ¿Dirían ustedes que la serie muestra una imagen historicamente correcta?

Summary/Ending questions

¿Tiene todo esto algo que ver con nostalgia para ustedes?

¿Si entiendo bien …?

All-things-Considered/Final Question

¿ Hay alguna cosa más que les parece importante? Los extractos les han hecho pensar en alguna otra cosa?

¡Muchas gracias!